WITHDRAWN

The Irish in America

Patrick J. Blessing

The Irish in America

A Guide to the Literature and
the Manuscript Collections

The Catholic University of America Press
Washington, D.C.

Publication of this book has been supported in part by a grant from the National Endowment for the Humanities, an independent federal agency.

Copyright © 1992
The Catholic University of America Press
All rights reserved
Printed in the United States of America

The paper used in this publication meets the minimum requirements of American National Standards for Information Science-Permanence of Paper for Printed Library materials, ANSI z39.48-1984.
∞

LIBRARY OF CONGRESS CATALOGING-IN-PUBLICATION DATA
Blessing, Patrick J.
    The Irish in America : a guide to the literature and the manuscript collections / by Patrick J. Blessing.
      p. cm.
    1. Irish Americans—History. 2. Irish Americans—History—Sources—Bibliography. I. Title.
z1361.17b54   1991
[e184.16]
016.973′049162—dc20   90-1667
ISBN 0-8132-0731-2 (alk. paper)

To mo seanathair, Proinsias
O'Maoilbheannachta; do bhi fhios aige
ar an cealg dòn croidh

Contents

Introduction / ix

Section I: Bibliography

1. Bibliographies, Biographical Dictionaries, and General Guides / 3
2. Sources of Statistics and Data / 11
3. Origins: Ireland / 22
4. Social Adjustment, Ethnicity, General / 30
5. Politics / 56
6. Religion / 73
7. Labor / 96
8. Nationalism / 102
9. War and the Military / 109
10. Biographies, Autobiographies, Reminiscences / 114
11. Women / 122
12. Writers, Literature, Criticism / 135
13. Scotch-Irish / 160
14. Irish in Places, by Regions and States / 168

Section II: Manuscript Collections

Alabama
Alaska
Arizona
California
Colorado
Connecticut
Delaware
District of Columbia
Florida
Georgia
Hawaii
Illinois
Indiana
Iowa
Kansas
Kentucky
Louisiana
Maine
Maryland
Massachusetts
Michigan
Minnesota
Mississippi
Missouri
Montana
Nebraska
Nevada
New Jersey
New Mexico
New York
North Carolina
North Dakota
Ohio
Oklahoma
Oregon
Pennsylvania
Rhode Island
South Carolina
South Dakota
Tennessee
Texas
Utah
Vermont
Virginia
Washington
West Virginia
Wisconsin
Wyoming

viii   Contents

Section III: Government Manuscripts and Publications

Government Manuscript Record Groups (RG): / 259

RG 10: National Commission on Law Observance and Enforcement
RG 11: General Records of the United States Government
RG 15: Veterans' Administration
RG 16: Office of the Secretary of Agriculture
RG 20: Office of the Special Advisor to the President on Foreign Trade
RG 21: District Courts of the United States
RG 24: Bureau of Naval Personnel
RG 26: United States Coast Guard
RG 29: Bureau of the Census
RG 32: United States Shipping Board
RG 36: Bureau of Customs
RG 38: Office of the Chief of Naval Operations
RG 42: Office of Public Buildings and Grounds
RG 45: Naval Records Collection of the Office of Naval Records and Library
RG 46: United States Senate
RG 48: Office of the Secretary of the Interior
RG 49: Bureau of Land Management
RG 50: Treasurer of the United States
RG 56: General Records of the Department of the Treasury
RG 59: General Records of the Department of State
RG 60: General Records of the Department of Justice
RG 63: Committee on Public Information
RG 66: Commission of Fine Arts
RG 69: Work Projects Administration (WPA)
RG 75: Bureau of Indian Affairs
RG 79: National Park Service
RG 80: General Records of the Department of the Navy
RG 84: Foreign Service Posts of the Department of State
RG 85: Immigration and Naturalization Service
RG 90: Public Health Service
RG 93: War Department Collection of Revolutionary War Records
RG 94: Adjutant General's Office, 1780s–1917
RG 95: Forest Service
RG 98: United States Army Commands, 1784–1821
RG 107: Office of the Secretary of War
RG 109: War Department Collection of Confederate Records
RG 110: Provost Marshal General's Bureau (Civil War)
RG 111: Office of the Chief Signal Officer
RG 120: American Expeditionary Forces, 1917–23
RG 125: Office of the Judge Advocate General (Navy)
RG 127: United States Marine Corps
RG 129: Bureau of Prisons
RG 130: White House Office
RG 153: Office of the Judge Advocate General (Army)
RG 163: Selective Service System (World War I)
RG 165: War Department General and Special Staffs
RG 166: Foreign Agricultural Service
RG 188: Office of Price Administration
RG 204: Office of Pardon Attorney
RG 206: Solicitor of the Treasury
RG 208: Office of War Information
RG 241: Patent Office
RG 257: Bureau of Labor Statistics
RG 391: United States Regular Army Mobile Units, 1821–1942
RG 393: United States Army Continental Commands, 1821–1920

Published Government Documents

Section IV: Statistical Overview

List of Tables / 287   Sources of Tables / 333

Index / 337

Introduction

For the rest of his life he remembered the silence of his fellow passengers as the vessel pulled away from the pier in Cobh Harbor, County Cork, bound for New York. Only the muffled throb of the ship's engines and the shouts of seamen preparing for the long voyage broke the early morning stillness. As the ship slid down the narrow bay in the grey dawn he envied the tiny figures hurrying to work along the coast road: they had jobs, they could stay at home. Why did he have to be the first in his family to travel more than ten miles from home? Long after the coastline disappeared he stood at the rail, straining for a last glimpse of Ireland. Many of the passengers lined the rail until dark.

Two days earlier on a wet April morning in 1899 Francis Blessing had left his wife and young children on a farm in County Leitrim and walked ten miles to the narrow-gauge railroad in Mohill to begin his journey to America. The isolation of the region and the poverty of the soil that had kept his family on the farm—albeit for almost the last century as tenants of the notorious Lord Leitrim—while other Catholics were dispossessed by the Penal Laws eventually created the poverty that brought about his decision to depart his native land at a time when farms in other parts of Ireland were experiencing unprecedented prosperity. A strong quiet man, well over six feet tall, Francis travelled alone for weeks across ocean, plains, and mountains before arriving at the job he had arranged with the Northern Pacific Railroad in Bozeman, Montana. There he became one of a vast army of Irishmen who provided the strong backs to build America during its period of greatest expansion. But unlike millions of Irish men and women who never again saw their homeland after making the grand crossing, six years of hard labor and Spartan living in one of the most inhospitable regions in the United States allowed Francis Blessing to save enough money to return home and buy the materials to build a magnificent stone house for his family. As he proudly put the finishing touches to the new abode he developed pneumonia. Two days later he died. Francis Blessing lies today in the family graveyard in Aughavas, County Leitrim—his American odyssey forgotten by his descendents who remain in Ireland. In addition to the fine farm house he built, presently occupied by his grandchildren and great grandchildren, Francis Blessing left another monument to his life hidden in faraway America: a pile of papers generated by government agencies, the Catholic Church, railroad agents, and others who recorded his travels, his religious commitment, and his labor. My search for those papers inspired the present volume: some of my grandfather's records I found in the National Archives, some in church archives throughout Montana, and others I am still trying to locate.

Despite my interest in seeking out sources for the study of the experience of one immigrant from Ireland, it did not occur to me to extend that search to include as many Irish as possible until I began writing a survey of the Irish in America for the *Harvard Encyclopedia of American Ethnic Groups* (Cambridge: Harvard University Press, 1981). The writing of the encyclopedia piece resulted in a cardfile of almost 10,000 bibliographical items. Alas, at that stage ambition took over: Why not supplement the bibliography with information on manuscript collections, government documents, and statistical sources and thus produce a comprehensive guide to the background and experiences of the third largest ethnic group in the United States, those twenty-eight million Americans who claimed Irish birth or ancestry on the U.S. Census for 1980? Shortly thereafter I began the search in earnest. The dream provided little evidence of the difficulty of the undertaking.

At the outset it was necessary to agree on definitions and limits. "Irish" was defined as the Irish-born and their descendents. Migration was defined as a process involving experiences in the area of origin, on the journey, and at the destination. In deciding on items to include I have concentrated on books and manuscripts that deal largely with the Irish or that provide important coverage on the origin and the adjustment of the group: works or manuscripts that cover the Irish only in passing were avoided. The volume is subdivided into four sections: bibliography; manuscript collections; government manuscripts and publications; and a statistical overview. The index covers manuscript collections, and government documents and publications.

In addition to published works, the bibliographic section lists theses and dissertations completed in American universities. For all bibliographical items, information on publisher and place of publication is included where available, but a small number of items are incomplete. It should be kept in mind that the chapter on Ireland was developed with the intention of identifying published works on Irish history only insofar as background conditions influenced departures: the chapter was not intended to serve as a complete bibliography to the Irish past. The Irish-American literature chapter attempts to catalogue references to works by authors who identify with Irish America. A particular effort was made to survey the largely forgotten "literature of accommodation"—works with Irish characters or themes written by Irish Americans and others and read throughout the larger society—which began appearing in the mid-nineteenth century. Finally, a great deal of time and effort was spent attempting to arrive at the best organization for the bibliographic items. A sincere effort was made to prevent duplicate entries: over ninety-five percent of items are listed in only one chapter. But a diligent researcher should peruse more than one chapter in a search for useful items.

To generate the entries in the manuscript section an inquiry was mailed to every research library listed in the National Historical Publications and Records Commission, *Directory of Archives and Manuscript Repositories in the United States* (Washington, D.C.: National Archives and Records Service, 1978) and to every archdiocesan center and Catholic church depository listed in the annual *Official Catholic Directory* (New York: P. J. Kennedy & Sons, 1980). Approximately fifty percent of those surveyed responded almost immediately; others replied after several letters and perhaps a phone call or two; some did not provide any information until a personal visit was undertaken. Altogether about 2,000 letters, hundreds of phone calls, and numerous personal visits were required to produce the information in the manuscript section. The procedures involved in generating information in the government documents section are described therein.

After almost a year wrestling with the data on the Irish in America it was decided to limit the statistical section to the provision of a basic set of tables that researchers could use with appropriate caution, perhaps after reading many of the articles listed in chapter 2 dealing with the accuracy of data. It is hoped at a later stage to produce a full volume providing data on the Irish in America.

As the process of collecting information progressed, the importance of generating now a guide such as this became increasingly obvious. Irish immigrants are aging and dying at an increasingly rapid rate. Moreover, significant changes have taken place in the composition of the Irish immigrant tide since the 1965 U. S. immigration laws. Irish newcomers are obviously arriving in far smaller numbers than in earlier days and it is doubtful that they will ever regain a prominent position in the overall American immigrant stream. Soon all that will be left to give testimony to the late nineteenth- and early twentieth-century movement of the largest proportion of any European population ever to come to America will be manuscripts and memories. It is important therefore that the process of identifying published and archival sources for the study of the Irish in America begin in this generation: it will be much more difficult in the future.

One year ago it looked as if the process of gathering information would continue indefinitely if a time limit was not placed on the project. Accordingly, it was decided to wind up the effort in the spring of 1989. The guide therefore is not presented as definitive; indeed, no guide of this kind could ever be viewed as definitive. I would be most appreciative of information on errors and omissions.

This work therefore is as detailed and accurate as I could make it in eight years of labor with the assistance of an army of undergraduate and graduate students at the University of Tulsa. Outstanding among this group was fellow Irish immigrant John McNamee, who aided in the data collection. I am grateful also to Pattipey Harjo, Christine E. Supernaw, and Donna Godwin; to Steve Nobles—a true professional—for his assistance in searching government depositories and publications; to Dean of Graduate Studies Al Soltow and the University of Tulsa for essential financial assistance; and to my department chairman when the project started, Thomas Buckley, for his unfailing professional support and his appreciation of the complexity and variety of American academic life. Credit for any clarity in the presentation of this work belongs to Susan Needham and the professional staff of the Catholic University of America Press.

I dedicate this work to Francis Blessing, who would have understood the need of his immigrant grandson to further the remembrance of the contribution of millions of sons and daughters of Ireland to a land that allowed them to undertake the often precarious task of making their own future.

Firhouse, Co. Dublin
August 1989

Section I
Bibliography

1. Bibliographies, Biographical Dictionaries, and General Guides

Akenson, D. H. *Being Had: Historians, Evidence and the Irish in North America*. Toronto: P. D. Meany, 1985.

American Committee for Irish Studies. *A Guide to Irish Studies in the United States*. 3d ed. Hempstead, New York: Hofstra University, American Committee for Irish Studies, 1987.

American Committee for Irish Studies. *Report on Research in Progress*. Hampstead, New York: Hofstra University, American Committee for Irish Studies. Annually since 1976.

Andrews, J. H. *A Paper Landscape: The Ordnance Survey in Nineteenth Century Ireland*. Oxford: At the Clarendon Press, 1980.

———. *Plantation Acres: An Historical Study of the Irish Land Surveyor and His Maps*. Belfast: Ulster Historical Foundation, 1985.

Annual Bibliography of British and Irish History: Publications. Atlantic Highlands, New Jersey: Humanities Press. Annually since 1975.

Armour, William C. *Scotch-Irish Bibliography of Pennsylvania*. Nashville, Tennessee, 1897.

Atlantic and Pacific Railroad Company, *A Guide to Irish Settlements in Southwest Missouri*. St. Louis: n.p., 1875. Copy in Yale Western Americana Collection, Yale University.

Ballou, Patricia K., comp. *Women: A Bibliography of Bibliographies*. Boston: G. K. Hall, 1980.

Begley, Donal F. *Handbook on Irish Genealogy*. 6th ed. Dublin: Genealogy Bookshop, 1984.

Begley, Donal F., ed. *Irish Genealogy: A Record Finder*. Dublin: Genealogy Bookshop, 1981.

Best, Richard I. *Bibliography of Irish Philology and Manuscript Publications, 1913–41*. Dublin: Institute for Advanced Studies, 1942. Reprinted 1969.

———. *Bibliography of Irish Philology and of Printed Irish Literature*. New York: Johnson Reprints, 1970. First published 1913.

A Bibliographical Congressional Directory, 1774–1911. Washington, D.C.: Government Printing Office, 1913.

Bibliographical Directory of the American Congress, 1774–1971. Washington, D.C.: Government Printing Office, 1972.

Bibliographical Encyclopedia of the Dead and Living Men of the Nineteenth Century. Cincinnati: J. M. Armstrong, 1878.

Billington, Ray Allen. "Tentative Bibliography of Anti-Catholic Propaganda in the United States, 1800–60." *Catholic Historical Review* 18 (January 1933): 492–513.

Biographical Directory of the United States Congress, 1774–1989. Bicentennial edition. Washington, D.C.: Superintendent of Documents 1989.

Blessing, Patrick J. "The Irish." In *Harvard Encyclopedia of American Ethnic Groups*, edited by Stephan Thernstrom. Cambridge, Massachusetts: Harvard University Press, 1980.

———. "The Irish in America, 1800–

3

4 Bibliography

1920." In *The Irish in America: Emigration, Assimilation, and Impact*, edited by P. J. Drudy. Irish Studies No. 4. Cambridge: Cambridge University Press, 1985.

———. "Paddy: The Image and Reality of Irish Immigrants in the American Community: A Review Essay." *Journal of American Ethnic History* 9 (Fall 1989): 112–19.

Bradley, John. *A Bibliography of Irish Archaelogy, 1980–1982*. Belfast: Ulster Archaeological Society, 1983.

Breffny, Brian de, ed. *Bibliography of Irish Family History and Genealogy*. Cork: Golden Eagle Books, 1974.

———. *Ireland: A Cultural Encyclopedia*. New York: Facts on File, 1983.

Brown, Stephen J. *Ireland in Fiction: A Guide to Irish Novels, Tales, Romances, and Folklore*. New York: Barnes & Noble, 1969.

———. *A Survey of Catholic Literature*. Milwaukee: Bruce Publishing Co., 1945.

Brye, D. L., ed. *European Immigration and Ethnicity in the United States and Canada: A Historical Bibliography*. Santa Barbara: Clio Press, 1983 ("The Irish," 50–57).

Buenker, John D., Nicholes C. Burcher, and J. Rudolf. *Immigration and Ethnicity: A Guide to Information Sources*. Detroit: Gale Research Company, 1977.

Burchell, Robert. "The Historiography of the American Irish," *Immigrants and Minorities* 1 (1982).

Burke's Irish Family Records. London: Burke's Peerage, 1976.

Burr, Nelson R. "A Critical Bibliography in Religion." In *Religion in American Life*, vol. 4, edited by J. Ward Smith and A. Leland Jamison. Princeton: Princeton University Press, 1965.

Cadden, John Paul. *The Historiography of the American Catholic Church: 1785–1943*. John T. Zubal, 1944.

Calkin, Homer L. "The United States Government and the Irish." *Irish Historical Studies* 19 (March 1954): 28–54.

Callahan, Bob, ed. *The Big Book of American Irish Culture*. New York: Viking Press, 1988.

Canning, Bernard J. *Bishops of Ireland, 1870–1987*. Ballyshannon: Donegal Democrat, 1988.

Casey, Daniel J., Robert K. Raymond, and Robert E. Rhodes. "Bibliography." In *Irish-American Fiction: Essays in Criticism*, edited by Daniel J. Casey and Robert K. Rhodes, 173–343. New York: AMS, 1979.

"A Checklist of Irish Titles." *Eire-Ireland* 1 (Summer 1966), 56–62.

"A Checklist of Irish Titles: II." *Eire-Ireland* 3 (Summer 1968), 48–56.

Chen, Joseph Ti Ti, "A Survey of Catholic Americana and Catholic Book Publishing in the United States, 1871–1895." Master's thesis, The Catholic University of America, 1956.

Chubb, Basil, ed. *A Source Book of Irish Government*. Dublin: Institute of Public Administration, 1964.

Chubb, Basil. *The Republic of Ireland: Its Government and Politics*. London: University of London Press, 1970.

Church of Ireland Directory. Dublin: Irish Church Publications. Annually since 1967. A continuation of the *Irish Church Directory*.

Clark, Mary Ann. *Great American Catholics*. Notre Dame, Indiana: Ave Maria Press, 1976.

Clarke, Richard A. *Lives of the Deceased Bishops of the Catholic Church in the United States,* 3 vols. New York: Clarke, 1888.

Cleeve, Brian. *Dictionary of Irish Writers. First Series: Fiction, Novelists, Playwrights, Short Story Writers in English*. Cork: Mercier Press, 1967.

———. *Dictionary of Irish Writers. Second Series: Non-Fiction*. Cork: Mercier Press, 1969.

———. *Dictionary of Irish Writers. Third Series: Writers in the Irish Language*. Cork: Mercier Press, 1971.

Code, Joseph. *Dictionary of the American Hierarchy*. New York: Longmans, Green, 1940.

Cohan, Al. *The Irish Political Elite*. Dublin: Gill and Macmillan, 1972.

Colket, Meredith B., Jr., and Frank E. Bridges. *Guide to Genealogical Records in the National Archives*. Washington, D.C. The National Archives and Records Service, 1964.

Collins, Timothy. *Floreat Hibernia: A Bio-Bibliography of Robert Lloyd Praeger*. Dublin: Royal Dublin Society, 1985.

Condon, P. "Irish in the United States." *Catholic Encyclopedia*. Vol. 1:132–45.

Council on National Defense, Committee on Women's Defense Work. *Women in the War: A Bibliography*. Prepared by Marion R. Nims. Washington, D.C., 1918.

Crimmins, John D. *Irish-American Historical Miscellany*. New York: The Author, 1905.

Crown, James Tracy. *The Kennedy Literature: A Bibliographical Essay on John F. Kennedy*. New York: New York University Press, 1975.

Cullen, Clara, ed. *Writings on Irish History, 1985*. Compiled by Clara Cullen and Monica Henchy. Dublin: The Irish Committee of Historical Sciences, 1987.

Curran, Thomas J. "From Paddy to the Presidency: The Irish in America." In *The Immigrant Experience in America*, edited by Frank J. Coppa and Thomas J. Curran. Boston: Twayne Publishers, 1976.

Dawson, Aveline. "A Survey of Catholic Americana and Catholic Book Publishing in the United States, 1881–1885." Master's thesis. The Catholic University of America, 1951.

Department of the Interior. *Signers of the Constitution*. Washington, D.C.: National Park Service, 1976.

Department of the Interior. *Signers of the Declaration of Independence*. Washington, D.C.: National Park Service, 1975.

Deutsch, Richard R. *Northern Ireland 1921–74: A Select Bibliography*. Garland Reference Library of Social Science. Vol. 2. London: Garland, 1975.

Dinneen, Rev. Patrick S., ed. and comp. *Irish-English Dictionary*. Dublin: Educational Company of Ireland, 1927.

Directory of Data Sources on Racial and Ethnic Minorities. Washington, D.C.: Government Printing Office, n.d. circa 1980. (Stock no. 029–001–01777–4)

Donnelly, Brian. "Archives Report: Irish Manuscripts Commission Survey of Business Records." *Irish Economic and Social History* 11 (1984): 122–24.

———. "Irish Manuscripts Commission Survey of Business Records (Archives Report)." *Irish Economic and Social History* 12 (1985): 117–19.

Doyle, David Noel. "The Irish in North America, 1776–1845." In *A New History of Ireland*. Vol. 5, edited by T. W. Moody, F. X. Martin, and F. J. Byrne. New York: Oxford University Press, 1990.

———. "The Regional Bibliography of Irish America, 1800–1930." *Irish Historical Studies* 23, no. 91 (1983): 254–83.

Duff, John B. *The Irish in the United States*. Belmont, California: Wadsworth Publishing Co., 1971.

Duffy, Robert. *Who Said This: A Book of Irish Lists*. Dublin: Poolbeg, 1987.

Dunleavy, Gareth, and Janet E. Dunleavy. "The Irish Abroad: Evidence from the O'Connor Papers." *Ethnicity* 2, no. 3 (1975): 258–70.

Dunleavy, Janet E., and Gareth W. Dunleavy, eds. *Hibernia-Irlande-Eire: Images of Ireland: A Bibliography of Old and Rare Books about Ireland in the American Geographical Society Collection*. Compiled by John Gleeson. Milwaukee: Golda Meir Library, University of Wisconsin, 1983.

Eager, Alan R. *A Guide to Irish Bibliographic Materials: A Bibliography of Irish Bibliographies and Sources of Information*. 2d ed., rev. and enl. London: Library Association,1964. Reprint. Westport, Connecticut: Greenwood Press, 1980.

Edwards, Ruth Dudley. *An Atlas of Irish History*. New York: Barnes and Noble, 1974. 2d ed. 1981.

Ekloff, Tony. *Irish Stationery Office Reports, 1973–1986*. Dublin: Library, University College, 1988.

Ellis, Eilish. *Emigrants from Ireland, 1847–1852: State-Aided Emigration Schemes from Crown Estates in Ireland*. Baltimore: Genealogical Publishing Co., 1983.

Ellis, Eilish, and P. Beryl Eustace., eds. *Registry of Deeds (Dublin). Abstracts of Wills*. Vol. 3: 1785–1832. Dublin: Stationery Office for the Irish Manuscripts Commission, 1984.

Ellis, John Tracy. *A Select Bibliography of the History of the Catholic Church in the*

United States. New York: Macmillan, 1947.

Ellis, John Tracy, and Robert Trisco. *Guide to American Catholic History*. 2d ed. Santa Barbara: ABC-Clio, 1982.

Fahey, Margaret Ann. "A Survey of Catholic Americana and Catholic Book Publishing in the United States, 1876–1880." Master's thesis. The Catholic University of America, 1954.

Falley, Margaret Dickson. *Irish and Scotch-Irish Ancestral Research, A Guide to the Genealogical Records, Methods and Sources in Ireland*. Vol. 1: *Repositories and Records*; Vol. 2: *Bibliography and Family Index*. Evanston, Illinois: Privately printed, 1961.

Fallows, M. R. *Irish Americans: Identity and Assimilation*. Englewood Cliffs: Prentice-Hall, 1979.

Feitin, Patricia. "A Survey of Catholic Americana and Catholic Book Publishing in the United States, 1896–1900." Master's thesis. The Catholic University of America, 1958.

Fink, Gary M., ed. *Biographical Dictionary of American Labor Leaders*. Westport, Connecticut: Greenwood Press, 1974.

Finn, Brendan A. *Twenty-Four American Cardinals*. Boston: Humphries, 1948.

Fishbein, Meyer H., ed. *The National Archives and Statistical Research*. Athens, Ohio: Ohio University Press, 1973.

Flackes, W. D. *Northern Ireland: A Political Directory, 1968–79*. New York: St. Martin's Press, 1980.

Ford, P., and G. Ford. *A Select List of Reports of Inquiries of the Irish Dail and Senate, 1922–72*. Shannon: Irish University Press, 1974.

Foster, R. "The Problems of Writing Irish History." *History Today* 34 (1984): 27–30.

French, Charles, ed. *Biographical History of the American Irish in Chicago*. Chicago and New York: American Biographical Publishing Company, 1897.

Funchion, Michael F., ed. *Irish American Voluntary Organizations*. Westport, Connecticut: Greenwood Press, 1983.

General Alphabetical Index to the Townlands and Towns, Parishes and Baronies of Ireland. Census of Ireland 1851. Reprinted. Baltimore: Genealogical Publishing Co., 1986.

General Services Administration. *Guide to the National Archives of the United States*. Washington, D.C.: Government Printing Office, 1974.

General Services Administration. *National Archives and Records Service, Directory of Archives and Manuscript Repositories in the United States*. Washington, D.C.: Government Printing Office, 1978.

Gilbert, V. F. "Current Bibliography of Immigrants and Minorities: Monographs, Periodical Articles, and Theses, 1981. Minority Groups, Irish." *Immigrants and Minorities* 3 (1985).

Glaizer, Ira A., and Michael H. Tepper, eds. *The Famine Immigrants: Lists of Irish Immigrants Arriving at The Port of New York, 1846–1851*. Vols. 1–4. Baltimore: Genealogical Publishing Co., 1983–84.

Glass, D. V., and P. A. M. Taylor. *Population and Emigration: Commentaries on British Parliamentary Papers*. Dublin: Irish Academic Press, 1976.

Gleason, Philip. "Coming to Terms with American Catholic History." *Societas* 3 (1973): 283–313.

Gowney Literary Society. "Catholic Authors in Modern Literature, 1880–1930." In *The Mariale* 6 (1930). Loretto, Pennsylvania: St. Francis Seminary Press, 1930.

Greenwood, Val D. *The Researchers Guide to American Genealogy*. Baltimore: Genealogical Publishing Co., 1988.

Gribben, Arthur, and Marsha Maguire, comps. *Irish Cultural Directory for Southern California*. Los Angeles: University of California Mythology Center, 1985.

Griffin, William D., ed. and comp. *The Irish in America, 550–1972*. Dobbs Ferry, New York: Oceana Publications, 1973.

A Guide to Catholic Literature. Detroit: Walter Romig, 1948.

Guide to Research Collections of Former Members of the United States House of Representatives, 1789–1987. Cynthia Pease Miller, editor-in-chief. Washington, D.C.: Historical Office, House of Representatives, 1988.

Guide to Research Collections of Former

United States Senators, 1789–1982. Kathryn Allamons Jacob, editor-in-chief. United States Senate Bicentennial Publication, no. 1, Washington, D.C.: Historical Office, United States Senate, 1983. See also Supplement, April 1985.

Guide to the Records of the United States Senate at the National Archives, 1789–1989. Bicentennial Edition. Washington, D.C.: National Archives and Records Administration, 1989.

Guptill, F. F. "A Popular Bibliography of the Fenian Movement." *Eire/Ireland* 4 (1969): 18–25.

Hacket, James Dominick. *Bishops of the United States of Irish Birth or Descent.* New York: American-Irish Historical Society, 1936.

Harmon, Maurice. *Select Bibliography for the Study of Anglo-Irish Literature and Its Backgrounds.* Atlantic Highlands, New Jersey: Humanities Press, 1977.

Harrison, Cynthia. *Women in American History: A Bibliography.* Santa Barbara: ABC-Clio Press, 1979.

Hassard, J. R. G. "Catholic Literature and the Catholic Public." *Catholic World* 7 (1870): 399–407.

Hayes, Richard J., ed. *Manuscript Sources for the History of Irish Civilization.* Vols. 1–9 and supplements. Boston: Hall, 1966.

———. *Sources for the Study of Irish Civilization: Articles in Periodicals.* Vols. 1–9. Boston: Hall, 1970.

Heferty, Seamus, and Raymond Refausse. *Directory of Irish Archives.* Dublin: Irish Academic Press, 1988.

Hennesey, James, S.J. *American Catholic Bibliography 1970–82.* South Bend, Indiana: University of Notre Dame, Center for the Study of American Catholicism. Working Paper series 12, number 1, Fall 1982.

Hennessey, M. E. "Men of the Irish Blood Who Have Attained Distinction in American Journalism." *Journal of the American-Irish Historical Society* 3:62–77.

Hickey, D. J., and J. E. Doherty. *A Dictionary of Irish History Since 1800.* New Jersey: Littlefield, Adams, 1980.

Hickman, Mary J., ed. *The History of the Irish in Great Britain: A Bibliography.* Compiled by Maureen Hartigan. London: Irish in Britain History Center, 1986.

Hill, Jacqueline R., ed. *Writings on Irish History 1979–1983.* Compiled by Clara Cullen and Monica Henchy. Dublin: Irish Committee of Historical Sciences, 1983 (microfiche edition).

———. *Writings on Irish History, 1984. Incorporating Addenda from 1973–1982.* Compiled by Clara Cullen and Monica Henchy. Dublin: Irish Commitee of Historical Sciences, 1986.

Historical Materials in the John F. Kennedy Library. Boston: John F. Kennedy Library, 1986.

Hogan, Robert., ed. *Dictionary of Irish Literature.* Westport, Connecticut: Greenwood Press, 1979.

Hoglund, A. William. *Immigrants and Their Children in the United States: A Bibliography of Doctoral Dissertations, 1885–1982.* New York: Garland Publishing, 1987.

Hudson, Winthrop. *Religion in America: An Historical Account of the Development of American Religious Life.* 3d ed. New York: Scribners, 1981.

Ireland, Government Libraries Group of the Library Association of Ireland. *A Directory of Government Libraries in the Republic of Ireland.* Dublin: Government Libraries Group, 1987.

Irish Feminist Information. *Missing Pieces—Women in Irish History. Volume 1, Since the Famine.* Dublin: Irish Feminist Information Center, 1983.

Irish Manuscripts Commission. *Catalogue of Publications, 1928–66.* Dublin: Stationery Office, 1966.

James, Edward T., ed. *Notable American Women.* Cambridge: Harvard University Press, 1971.

Janeway, W. R. *Bibliography of Immigration, 1900–1930.* 1934.

Johnston, Edith May. *Irish History: A Select Bibliography.* Helps for Students of History, 73. London: Historical Association, 1972.

Keating, Carla, and Graeme Kirkham. "Select Bibliography of Writings on Irish Economic and Social History Published in 1983." *Irish Economic and Social History* 11 (1984): 129–41. Annually since 1972.

8 Bibliography

King, Joseph A. "Genealogy, History, and Irish Immigration." *Canadian Journal of Irish Studies* 10 (1984): 41–50.

Kirwan, Frank, and J. McGilvray. *Irish Economic Statistics*. Dublin: Institute of Public Administration, 1983. A guide to sources of economic statistics.

Kolmer, Elizabeth. *Sources for Studying Catholic Women. American Quarterly*. Special edition, 1978.

Lee, Joseph, ed. *Irish Historiography 1970–1979*. Cork, 1981.

Lester, Dee Gee. *Irish Research: A Guide to Collections in North America, Ireland, and Great Britain*. Westport, Connecticut: Greenwood Press, 1987.

Library Association (Northern Ireland Branch). *Northern Ireland Newspapers 1737–1987*. Cultra: Ulster Folk and Transport Museum, 1988.

"List of Publications on the Economic and Social History of Great Britain and Ireland published in 1983." *Economic History Review* 37 (1984): 563–608.

MacDonagh, Oliver. "Irish Emigration to the United States of America and the British Colonies During the Famine." In *The Great Famine*, edited by Robert Dudley and T. Desmond Williams. Dublin: Browne and Nolan, 1956.

———. "The Irish Famine Emigration to the United States." *Perspectives in American History* 10 (1976): 379–82.

MacLysaght, Edward. *Bibliography of Irish Family History*. 2d ed. Dublin: Irish Academic Press, 1982.

———. *Irish Families: Their Names, Arms, and Origins*. 3d rev. ed. Dublin: Hodges Figgis, 1972.

———. *The Surnames of Ireland*. Shannon: Irish University Press, 1969.

Madden, Richard R. *History of Irish Periodical Literature from the End of the Seventeenth Century to the Middle of the Nineteenth Century*. New York: Johnson Reprints, 1969 edition. First published 1867.

Mageen, Deidre M. "Nineteenth-Century Irish Emigration: A Case Study Using Passenger Lists." In *The Irish in America: Emigration, Assimilation and Impact*, edited by P. J. Drudy. Irish Studies No. 4. Cambridge: Cambridge University Press, 1985.

Mallagh, Thomas. "Friends Historical Library, 6 Eustace St., Dublin 2: Sources for Genealogy." *Ulster Genealogical & Historical Guild* 9 (1983): 294–96.

Maltby, Arthur. *The Government of Northern Ireland, 1922–72: A Catalogue and Breviate of Parliamentary Papers*. Dublin: Irish University Press, 1974.

Mangalam, J. J., and Cornelia Morgan. *Human Migration: A Guide to Migration Literature in English, 1955–1962*. Lexington: University of Kentucky Press, 1968.

McCaffrey, Lawrence. "Irish-America." *The Wilson Quarterly* (Spring 1985), 78–93.

McCann, James H. "Towers of Silence Speak." *American-Irish Historical Society Journal* 30 (1932): 134–63.

McFetridge, L. "The Northern Ireland Local Studies List." *Local Studies Librarian* 2 (1983): 7–11.

McGillivary, Charles A. "Irish-born Recipients of the U.S. Congressional Medal of Honor." *Irish Sword* 13 (Winter 1975): 149–51.

McGuire, Constantine E., et al., eds. *Catholic Builders of the Nation*. New York: Catholic Book Company, 1935.

McKee, Eamonn, and Vivienne Pollock, eds. "Select Bibliography of Writings on Irish Economic and Social History Published in 1984." *Irish Economic and Social History* 12 (1985): 125–38.

Meally, Victor, ed. *Encyclopedia of Ireland*. Dublin: Figgis, 1968.

Meehan, Thomas F. *Catholic Builders of the Nation*. New York: 1923.

Metress, Seamus P. *The Irish-American Experience: A Guide to the Literature*. Washington, D.C.: University Press of America, 1981.

Mikhail, E. H., ed. *A Bibliography of Modern Irish Drama 1899–1970*. London: Macmillan, 1972.

———. *Dissertations on Anglo-Irish Drama: A Bibliography of Studies, 1870–1970*. London: Macmillan, 1973.

Miller, W. C. "Irish-Americans." In *A Comprehensive Bibliography for the Study of American Minorities*, by Wayne Charles

Miller, et al., 1: 381–422. 2 vols. New York: New York University Press, 1975.

Mitchell, Arthur, and Padraig O Snodaigh, eds. *Irish Political Documents, 1916–49*. Dublin: Irish Academic Press, 1985.

Moody, T. W., ed. *Irish Historiography 1936–70*. Dublin: Irish Committee of Historical Sciences, 1971.

Moody, T. W., F. X. Martin, and F. J. Byrne, eds. *A Chronology of Irish History to 1976: A Companion to Irish History, I*. Vol. 8. *A New History of Ireland*. Oxford: At the Clarendon Press, 1982.

———. *Illustrations, Statistics, Bibliography, Documents: A Companion to Irish History, III*. Vol. 10. *A New History of Ireland*. Oxford: At the Clarendon Press, 1986.

———. *Maps, Genealogies, Lists: A Companion to Irish History, II*. Vol. 9. *A New History of Ireland*. Oxford: At the Clarendon Press, 1984.

Morgan, Raine. "Annual List and Brief Review of Articles on Agrarian History, 1982." *Agricultural Historical Review* 32 (1984): 75–85.

Mulligan, Patrick. "Catholic Parish Registers in Clogher Diocese." *Clogher Record* 12 (1985): 13–17.

Murphy, Maureen. *A Guide to Irish Studies in the United States*. Hempstead, New York: Hofstra University, American Committee for Irish Studies, 1979.

Neill, Kathleen. "How to Trace Family History in Northern Ireland." Part 3. *Irish Family Links* 2, no. 1 (1984): 4–7; Part 4. *Irish Family Links* 2, no. 2 (1984): 21–25.

New Catholic Encyclopedia. New York: McGraw-Hill, 1967.

Newcomb, J. L. *John F. Kennedy: An Annotated Bibliography*. New Jersey: Scarecrow Press, 1977.

Nims, Marion R. *Women in the War: A Bibliography*. Washington, D.C.: U.S. Council of National Defense, Committee on Women's Defense Work, Government Printing Office, 1918.

Nolan, William. *Tracing the Past: Sources for Local Studies in the Republic of Ireland*. Templeogue, Dublin: Geography Publications, 1982.

O'Brien, James. *Irish Celts: A Cyclopedia of Race History*. Detroit: Kilroy, 1884.

O'Donnell, E. E. *The Annals of Dublin-Fair City: A Chronology from Earliest Times*. Dublin: Wolfhound Press, 1988.

O'Donnell, John H. *The Catholic Hierarchy of the United States: 1790–1922*. Washington, D.C.: AMS, 1922.

O'Donnell, Sean. "Irish American Scientists," *Eire-Ireland* 14, no. 2 (1979): 106–9.

O'Hanlon, Rev. John Canon. *Irish-American History of the United States*. 2 vols. Riverside, New Jersey: Benziger, Bruce, and Glencoe, 1903.

O'Higgins, Paul. *A Bibliography of Irish Trials and Other Legal Proceedings*. Dublin: Professional Books, NPG, Trinity College, 1988. A guide to printed materials: books, pamphlets, and broadsides covering litigation, both civil and criminal.

O'Reilly, Edward. A *Chronological Account of Nearly Four Hundred Irish Writers with a Descriptive Catalogue of Their Works*. Introduction by Gearoid S. Mac Eoin. Reprint. Shannon: Irish University Press, 1970. First published in 1820.

O'Suilleabhain, Sean. *A Handbook of Irish Folklore*. Hatboro, Pennsylvania: Folklore Associates, 1963.

O'Toole, James M. *Guide to the Archdiocese of Boston*. Boston: Archdiocese of Boston, 1982.

Official Catholic Directory, The. New York: P. J. Kennedy & Sons. Annually since 1817.

Parsons, Wilfrid. *Early Catholic Americana*. New York: Macmillian, 1939.

Phadraig, Maire Nic Ghiolla. "Bibliography of the Social Sciences in Ireland," *Social Studies* 2 (1973): 75–90.

———. "Bibliography of the Sociology of Education in Ireland." *Social Studies* 1 (1972): 350–66.

———. "Bibliography of the Sociology of Religion in Ireland." *Social Studies* 1 (1972): 246–62.

———. "Select Bibliography of Social Problems and Social Services in Ireland." *Social Studies: Irish Journal of Sociology*. Vol. 1 (1972).

Prochaska, Alice. *Irish History from 1700: A Guide to Sources in the Public Record Office*. British Records Association. Archives and the User, no. 8. London: British Records Association, 1985.

Raimo, John W., ed. *A Guide to Manuscripts Relating to America in Great Britain and Ireland*. British Association of American Studies. Westport, Connecticut: Meckler Books, 1979. Rev. ed. of 1961 guide ed.

"Register of Current Research in Labor History." *Saothar* (Ireland), 10 (1984): 119–22.

"Research on Irish History in Irish Universities." *Irish Historical Studies* 24 (1984): 373–74.

Romig, Walter. *Guide to Catholic Literature*. Detroit: Romig, 1940.

Rose, Walter R. *A Bibliography of the Irish in the United States*. Afton, New York: Tristram Shandy, 1969 (mimeo).

Rouchek, Joseph S., comp. *The Immigrant in Fiction and Bibliography*. New York: Bureau for Intercultural Education, 1945.

Ruskin, Mary Patricia. "A Survey of Catholic Americana and Catholic Book Publishing in the United States, 1886–1890." Master's thesis. The Catholic University of America, 1952.

Ryan, James G. *A Guide to Tracing Your Dublin Ancestors*. Glenageary, Co. Dublin: Flyleaf Press, 1988.

——. *Irish Records: Sources for Family and Local History*. Salt Lake City, Utah: Ancestry Publishing, 1988.

A Select List of Books on Ireland. Dublin: Stationary Office for the National Library of Ireland, 1978.

Shannon, Michael Owen. *Modern Ireland: A Bibliography of Politics, Planning, and Development*. Westport, Connecticut: Greenwood Press, 1981.

Smyth, Daragh. *A Guide to Irish Mythology*. Dublin: Irish Academic Press, 1988.

Smyth, William J. "Social Geography of Rural Ireland: Inventory and Prospect." *Irish Geography* (1984), 204–36.

"Some Early Catholic Newspapers." *American Catholic Historical Researches* 19 (Oct. 1902), 18 (1911).

Sullivan, Daniel., ed. *Ireland: A Directory and Yearbook*. Dublin: Institute of Public Administration. Annually since 1976.

Sullivan, Michael F. "Extracts from American-Irish History and Biographies." *American Irish Historical Society Journal* 9 (1910): 196–205.

Thom, A. *Thom's Irish Almanac and Official Directory*. Dublin: A. Thom. Annually since 1841.

Tollmar, Edward R. *The Catholic Church in America: An Historical Bibliography*. Metuchen, New Jersey: Scarecrow, 1963.

Vaughn, W. E., and A. J. Fitzgerald, eds. *Irish Historical Statistics, Population, 1821–1971*. Dublin: Royal Irish Academy, 1978.

Weaver, Jack W., and Dee Gee Lester, comps. *Immigrants from Great Britain and Ireland: A Guide to Archival and Manuscript Sources in North America*. Westport, Connecticut: Greenwood Press, 1986.

Webb, Alfred John. *A Compendium of Irish Biography*. New York: Lemma, 1970. First published in 1878.

Weinberg, Daniel E. "Viewing the Immigrant Experience in America Through Fiction and Autobiography: With a Select Bibliography." *History Teacher* 9, no. 3 (1976): 109–32.

Who's Who, What's What and Where in Ireland. Dublin: Chapman, 1973. Published in association with the *Irish Times*.

Willging, Eugene, and Herta Hatzfeld. *Catholic Serials of the Nineteenth Century*. 15 vols. Washington, D.C., 1959–68.

Willigan, W. L. "A Bibliography of the Irish American Press, 1691–1835." Ph.D. dissertation, Fordham University, 1934. Published, Brooklyn: n.p., 1934.

Woods, C. J. "Research on Irish History in Irish Universities, 1984." *Irish Historical Studies* 24 (1984): 528–29.

Writings on Irish History. Annually, 1936–79, in the autumn issue of *Irish Historical Studies*.

Yetman, Norman R. "The Irish Experience in America." In *Irish History and Culture*, edited by H. Orel. Manhattan, Kansas: University of Kansas Press, 1976.

2. Sources of Statistics and Data

Abrams, Elliot, and Franklin S. Abrams. "Immigration Policy—Who Gets in and Why." *The Public Interest* 38 (August 1975): 16.

Akenson, D. H. "'Data': What Is Known about the Irish in North America?" In *Ireland and Irish-Australia*, edited by Oliver MacDonagh and W. F. Mandle. London and Sydney: 1986.

"Alleged Increase of Heart Disease among Irish Immigrants." *Catholic World* 121 (April 1925): 119–22.

American Council of Learned Societies. *Report of Committee on Linguistic and National Stocks in the Population of the United States*. Annual Report of the American Historical Association for 1931.

Annual Report of the Secretary of Labor. Washington, D. C.: Government Printing Office. Annually 1933–1940.

Annual Report of the Commissioner General of Immigration to the Secretary of Labor. Washington, D.C.: Government Printing Office. Annually 1911–32 (Annual Immigration Report).

Annual Report of the Attorney General. Washington, D.C.: Government Printing Office, 1941 (Annual Immigration Report).

Barron, T. J. "Emigration from Co. Cavan in the Nineteenth Century." *Heart of Breifne* 2 (1983): 90–100.

Barry, Ursula. *Lifting the Lid: Handbook of Facts and Information on Ireland*. Dublin: Attic Press, 1986.

Baxter, Jedediah H. *Statistics, Medical and Anthropological, of the Provost Marshal General's Bureau*, 2 vols. Washington, D.C.: Government Printing Office, 1875.

Bere, May. *A Comparative Study of the Mental Capacity of Children of Foreign Parentage*. New York: Teachers College, Columbia University, 1924.

Bernard, Richard M. "Intermarriage Patterns among Immigrants and Natives in Wisconsin, 1850–1920." Ph.D. dissertation, University of Wisconsin, 1976.

———, *The Melting Pot and the Altar: Marital Assimilation in Early Twentieth-Century Wisconsin*. Minneapolis: University of Minnesota Press, 1980.

Boies, Henry M. *Prisoners and Paupers: A Study of the Abnormal Increase of Criminals, and the Public Burden of Pauperism in the United States*. New York: Putnam, 1893.

Bourke, P. M. Austin. "The Agricultural Statistics of the 1841 Census of Ireland: A Critical Review." *Economic History Review*, 2d ser., vol. 18, no. 2 (August 1965): 376–91.

———. "The Extent of the Potato Crop in Ireland at the Time of the Famine." *Statistical Society of Ireland Journal* 20, pt.3 (1959–60): 72–96.

Bouvier, Leon F., and S. L. N. Rao. *Socio-Religious Factors in Fertility Decline*. Cambridge, Massachusetts: Ballinger Publishing Co., 1975.

Boyle, P. O and Cormac O'Grada. "Fertility Trends, Excess Mortality, and the Great Irish Famine." *Demography*. 23(1986): 542–62.

Breen, Richard. "Population Trends in Late Nineteenth and Early Twentieth Century Ireland: A Local Study." *Economic and Social Review* 15 (1984): 95–108.

Brunner, Edmund. *Immigrant Farmers and Their Children*. Garden City, New York: Doubleday, 1929.

Bureau of the Census. Census of Population: 1970. Final Report PD (2)–1A: *National*

12 Bibliography

Origins and Language. Washington, D.C.: U. S. Government Printing Office, 1973.

Campton, Paul A., et al. *Northern Ireland: A Census Atlas.* Atlantic Highlands, New Jersey: Humanities Press, 1977.

Carney, F. J. "Pre-Famine Irish Population: The Evidence from the Trinity College Estates." *Irish Economic and Social History* 2 (1975): 35–45.

Carpenter, Niles. *Immigrants and Their Children.* New York: Arno Press and the New York Times, 1969.

Carrier, N. H., and J. R. Jeffrey. *External Migration: A Study of the Available Statistics, 1815–1950.* London: Her Majesty's Stationery Office, 1953.

Carter, Hugh, and Paul G. Glick. *Marriage and Divorce: A Social and Economic Study.* Cambridge: Harvard University Press, 1970.

Caulfield, B., and A. Bhat. "The Irish in Britain: Intermarriage and Fertility Levels, 1970–76." *New Community* (1981): 73–83.

Census of Population, Reports. Dublin: Stationery Office. 1926, 1936, 1946, 1951, 1961, 1971, 1981, and 1986.

Central Statistics Office. "Agricultural Statistics, 1934–1956." Dublin: Central Statistics Offfice, 1960.

Central Statistics Office. *Report on Vital Statistics.* Dublin: Stationery Office, Periodically, latest issue September 1985.

Cestello, B. D. "Catholics in American Commerce and Industry." *American Catholic Social Review* 17: 219–33.

Cho, Lee-Jay, Wilson H. Grabill, and Donald J. Bogue. *Differential Current Fertility in the United States.* Chicago: University of Chicago, Community and Family Study Center, 1970.

Clarkson, L. A. "Population Change and Urbanization, 1821–1911." In *An Economic History of Ulster*, edited by Liam Kennedy and Philip Ollerenshaw. Manchester: Manchester University Press, 1985.

Cohn, Raymond L. "Mortality on Immigrant Voyages to New York, 1836–53." *Journal of Economic History* 44 (1984): 289–300.

Commission on Emigration and Other Population Problems. Reports, 1948–1954. Dublin: Stationery Office, 1954.

Connell, K. H. *The Population of Ireland, 1750–1845.* Oxford: Oxford University Press, 1950.

Connolly, Sean J. "Marriage in Pre-Famine Ireland." In *Marriage in Ireland*, edited by Art Cosgrove. Dublin: College Press, 1985.

Cousens, S. H. "Regional Death Rates in Ireland During the Great Irish Famine, 1846–1851." *Population Studies* 14 (July 1960): 55–74.

———. "The Regional Pattern of Emigration during the Great Famine, 1846–1851." *Transactions and Papers of the Institute of British Geographies* 28 (1960).

———. "The Regional Variation in Emigration From Ireland Between 1821–1841." *Institute of British Geographers Transactions* 37 (December 1965).

———. "The Regional Variations in Population Changes in Ireland, 1861–1881," *Economic History Review*, 2d series, 17 (1964).

———. "The Restrictions of Population Growth in Pre-Famine Ireland." *Proceedings of the Royal Irish Academy* 64 (November 4, 1966).

———. "Population Trends in Ireland at the Beginning of the Twentieth Century." *Irish Geography*, 5, (1968).

Crawford, E. M. "Death, Diet and Disease in Ireland, 1850: A Case Study of Nutritional Deficiencey." *Medical History* 28 (1984).

Crotty, Raymond D. *Irish Agricultural Production: Its Volume and Structure.* Cork: Cork University Press, 1966.

Current Population Reports. Population Characteristics. "Ancestry and Language in the United States: November 1979." Series P–23, no. 116. Washington, D.C.: Bureau of the Census, Department of Commerce, March, 1982.

Current Population Reports. Population Characteristics. "Characteristics of the Population by Ethnic Origin: March 1972 and 1971." Series P–20, no. 249. Washington, D.C.: Bureau of the Census, Department of Commerce, April 1973.

Current Population Reports. Population Characteristics. "Fertility Variations by Ethnic Origin: November 1969." Series P–20, no. 226. Washington, D.C.: Bureau of the Census, Department of Commerce, November 1971.

Cutsumbis, Michael N. "The National Archives and Immigration Research," *The International Migration Review* 6 (Spring 1970): 90–99.

Department of Commerce, *Historical Statistics of the United States* 2 vols., Washington, D.C.: Government Printing Office, 1976.

Department of Industry and Commerce. "Agricultural Statistics, 1847–1926: Reports and Tables." Dublin, 1928 also later volumes.

Department of Justice. Immigration and Naturalization Service. *Annual Report of the Immigration and Naturalization Service*. Washington, D.C.: Government Printing Office. Annually 1943–77.

Department of Justice. Immigration and Naturalization Service. *Statistical Yearbook of Immigration and Naturalization Service*. Washington, D.C.: Government Printing Office. Annually 1978–85.

Dillingham Commission, see below under United States, *Reports of the Immigration Commission*, Washington, D.C. 1911.

Drachsler, Julius. *Intermarriage in New York City*. New York: Columbia University, 1921.

Drudy, P. J. "Irish Population Change and Emigration since Independence." In *The Irish in America: Emigration, Assimilation and Impact*, edited by P. J. Drudy. Irish Studies No. 4. Cambridge: Cambridge University Press, 1985.

Dublin, L. I. "The Mortality of Foreign Race Stocks in Pennsylvania and New York, 1910." *Quarterly Publications of the American Statistical Association* 17 (1920): 13–44.

Dunlevy, J. A., and H. A. Gemery. "British-Irish Settlement Patterns in the U. S. : The Role of Family and Friends." *Scottish Journal of Political Economy* 24, no. 3 (November 1977): 257–63.

Dunn, Edward. "Mixed Marriages in 1947." *The American Ecclesiastical Review* 120 (1949).

Eblen, Jack E. "An Analysis of Nineteenth Century Frontier Populations." *Demography* 2 (1965).

Edwards, Ruth Dudley. *An Atlas of Irish History*. London: Methuen and Co., 1973. 2d ed. 1981.

Facts about Ireland. Dublin: Department of Foreign Affairs, 1985.

Fairchild, H. P. "The Distribution of Immigrants." *Yale Review* 16: 296–310.

———. "Some Immigration Differences." *Yale Review* 19: 79–97.

"Famine Series." Shannon: Irish University Press, 1968. 8 Volumes. A selection of the most important Blue Books covering famine relief policy in Ireland.

Ferenczi, Imre, and W. F. Willcox. *International Migrations*. Vol. 1, *Statistics*. Vol. 2; *Interpretations*. New York: National Bureau of Economic Research for the International Labor Office, 1929.

Fishbein, Meyer H., ed. *The National Archives and Statistical Research*. Athens, Ohio: Ohio University Press, 1973.

Fitzpatrick, David. "Irish Farming Families before the First World War." *Comparative Studies in Society and History* 25 (1983): 339–74.

Fitzpatrick, Franklin E. "Irish Immigration into New York from 1865 to 1880." Master's thesis. The Catholic University of America, 1948.

Gailey, Alan. "Local Life in Ulster, 1843–1881: The Statistical Surveys of Maurice Collis." *Ulster Local Studies* 9 (1985): 120–27.

Gallaway, Lowell E., and Richard K. Vedder. "The Increasing Urbanization Thesis—Did 'New Immigrants' to the United States Have a Particular Fondness for Urban Life." *Explorations in Economic History* 8 (Spring 1971).

Gallaway, Lowell E., Richard V. Vedder, and Vishwa Shukla. "The Distribution of the Immigrant Population in the United States: An Economic Analysis." *Explorations in Economic History,* 2, no. 3 (Spring 1974): 213–26.

Gibbon, P., and C. Curtin. "Irish Farm Families: Facts and Fantasies." *Comparative Studies in Society and History* 25 (1983): 375–80.

Gibson, C. "The Contribution of Immigration to U. S. Population Growth." *International Migration Review* 9 (1975): 157–77.

Glick, Paul C. "Intermarriage Among Ethnic Groups in the United States." *Social Biology* 17 (December 1970).

Goodrich, Carter L. *Migration and Economic Opportunity*. Philadelphia: University of Pennsylvania, 1936.

Gould, Benjamin Apthorp. *Investigations in the Military and Anthropological Statistics of American Soldiers*. New York: n. p., 1869.

Gould, J. D. "European Inter-Continental Emigration: Patterns and Causes." *Journal of European Economic History* 8, no. 3 (Winter 1979): 513–679 [Essays 1 and 2].

———. "European Inter-Continental Emigration The Road Home: Return Migration to the U. S. A." *Journal of European Economic History* 9, no. 1 (Spring, 1980): 41–112 [Essays 3 and 4].

Gould, J. D. "European Inter-Continental Emigration: The Role of 'Diffusion' and 'Feedback'." *Journal of European Economic History* 9 no. 2 (Fall 1980): 267–315 [Essay 5].

Great Britain, Parliamentary Papers, Irish University Press Series of following eight volumes on famine in Ireland:

Volume 1: Copies or extracts of correspondence relating to the state of the union workhouses in Ireland, first, second, and third series, 1847.

Volume 2: Papers relating to the relief of distress and the state of unions and workhouses in Ireland, fourth and fifth series, 1847–48.

Volume 3: Papers relating to the relief of distress and the state of unions and workhouses in Ireland, sixth series, 1847–48.

Volume 4: Papers relating to the relief of distress and the state of unions and workhouses in Ireland, seventh and eighth series, 1847–49.

Volume 5: Correspondence on measures adopted by the government for relief of distress arising from the failure of the potato crop and the commissariat series (part 1) with index, 1846–47.

Volume 6: Correspondence on relief measures, board of works series, July 1846 to January 1847, with index, 1847.

Volume 7: Correspondence on relief measures, board of works series, January to March 1847, with indices, 1847.

Volume 8: Reports from the relief, Board of Works and Health Commissioners, with other reports and papers, 1846–53.

Great Britain, Parliamentary Papers, Irish University Press Series of the twenty-eight volumes on British Emigration. While they vary in their usefulness to students of Irish cross-Atlantic migration, all of the volumes provide some information on Irish departures, and as an overall group they are invaluable. The series is divided into three separate but complementary subsets within which volumes are arranged in chronological order. The first subset (volumes 1–9) provides select committee reports on emigration and colonization from the United Kingdom. The second subset (volumes 10–18) comprises the reports of the Colonial Land and Emigration Commissioners, which include detailed statistics on movement from Ireland. Subset three (volumes 29–28) includes the remaining general reports, correspondence, and statistics relating to emigration.

Volume 1: Report from the select committee on emigration from the United Kingdom, with minutes of evidence, appendix and index, 1826.

Volume 2: First, second and third reports from the select committee on emigration from the United Kingdom, with minutes of evidence, appendix and index, 1826–27.

Volume 3: First and second reports from the select committee on emigration , Scotland, with minutes, appendices and index, 1841.

Volume 4: Report from the select committee of the House of Lords on colonization from Ireland, with minutes of evidence, appendix and index, 1847.

Volume 5: First, second and third reports from the select committee of the House of Lords on colonization from Ireland, with minutes of evidence, appendix and index, 1847–49.

Volume 6: Report from the select committee on the passenger act with proceedings, minutes of evidence, appendix and index, 1851.

Volume 7: First, second reports from the select commiteee on emigrant ships with proceedings, minutes of evidence, appendix and index, 1854.

Volume 8: Reports from the select committees on emigration and immigration (foreigners) with proceedings, minutes of evidence, appendices and indices, 1888–89.

Volume 9: Reports from select committees on colonization from congested districts with minutes of evidence, appendices and indices, 1889–91.

Volume 10: General reports of the colonial land and emigration commissioners with appendices, 1842–48.

Volume 11: *General reports of the colonial land and emigration commissioners with appendices,* 1849–52.

Volume 12: *General report of the colonial land and emigration commissioners with appendices,* 1852–55.

Volume 13: *General report of the colonial land and emigration commissioners with appendices,* 1856–58.

Volume 14: *General report of the colonial land and emigration commissioners with appendices,* 1859–61.

Volume 15: *General report of the colonial land and emigration commissioners with appendices,* 1862–64

Volume 16: *General report of the colonial land and emigration commissioners with appendices,* 1865–66

Volume 17: *Twenty-seventh, twenty-eighth, twenty-ninth and thirtieth general reports of the colonial land and emigration commissioners with appendices,* 1867–70

Volume 18: *Thirty-first, thirty-second and thirty-third general reports of the colonial land and emigration commissioners with appendices,* 1871–73.

Volume 19: *Reports, returns and correspondence relating to emigration,* 1828–38.

Volume 20: *Reports, returns and correspondence relating to emigration,* 1839–42.

Volume 21: *Report, returns and correspondence relating to emigration, with appendix,* 1842–43.

Volume 22: *Reports, returns and correspondence relating to emigration,* 1843–53.

Volume 23: *Reports, returns and correspondence relating to emigration,* 1854–59.

Volume 24: *Reports, returns and correspondence relating to emigration,* 1860–71.

Volume 25: *Report, returns and correspondence relating to emigration,* 1872–81.

Volume 26: *Reports, returns and correspondence and other papers relating to emigration,* 1882–87.

Volume 27: *Reports, returns and correspondence relating to emigration,* 1888–94.

Volume 28: *Reports, returns and correspondence relating to emigration,* 1894–99.

Great Britain. *Emigration Statistics of Ireland for the year 1876.* [C1700], H. C. 1877, lxxxv, 643.

Emigration Statistics of Ireland for the year 1877. [C 2066], H. C. 1878, lxxvii, 631.

Emigration Statistics of Ireland for the year 1878. [C 2221], H. C. 1878–79, lxxv, 703.

Emigration Statistics of Ireland for the year 1879. [C 2501], H. C. 1880, lxxvi, 985.

Emigration Statistics of Ireland for the year 1880. [C 2828], H. C. 1881, xciv, 703.

Emigration Statistics of Ireland for the year 1881. [C 3170], H. C. 1882, lxxiv, 273.

Emigration Statistics of Ireland for the year 1882. [C 3489], H. C. 1883, lxxvi, 979.

Emigration Statistics of Ireland for the year 1883. [C 3899], H. C. 1884, lxxxv, 493.

Emigration Statistics of Ireland for the year 1884. [C 4303], H. C. 1884–85, lxxxv, 193.

Emigration Statistics of Ireland for the year 1885. [C 4660], H. C. 1886, lxxi, 191.

Emigration Statistics of Ireland for the year 1886. [C 4967], H. C. 1887, lxxxix, 239.

Emigration Statistics of Ireland for the year 1887. [C 5307], H. C. 1888, cvii, 75.

Emigration Statistics of Ireland for the year 1888. [C 5647], H. C. 1889, lxxxiv, 83.

Emigration Statistics of Ireland for the year 1889. [C 6010], H. C. 1890, lxxix, 755.

Emigration Statistics of Ireland for the year 1890. [C 6295], H. C. 1890–91, xcii, 57.

Emigration Statistics of Ireland for the year 1891. [C 6679], H. C. 1892, lxxxviii, 663.

Emigration Statistics of Ireland for the year 1892. [C 6977], H. C.1893–94, cii, 55.

Emigration Statistics of Ireland for the year 1893. [C 7288], H. C.1893–94, cii, 71.

Emigration Statistics of Ireland for the year 1894. [C 7647], H. C. 1895, cvii, 57.

Emigration Statistics of Ireland for the year 1895. [C 7959], H. C. 1896, xciii, 61.

Emigration Statistics of Ireland for the year 1896. [C 8366], H. C. 1897, xcix, 63.

Emigration Statistics of Ireland for the year 1897. [C 8740], H. C. 1898, ciii, 63.

Emigration Statistics of Ireland for the year 1898. [C 9193], H. C. 1899, cvii, 69.

Emigration Statistics of Ireland for the year 1899. [Cd III], H. C. 1900, cii, 69.

Emigration Statistics of Ireland for the year 1900. [Cd 531], H. C. 1901, lxxxviii, 673.

Emigration Statistics of Ireland for the year 1901. [Cd 976], H. C. 1902, cxvi, pt ii, 71.

Emigration Statistics of Ireland for the year 1902. [Cd 1489], H. C. 1903, lxxxii, 813.

Emigration Statistics of Ireland for the year 1903. [Cd 2030], H. C. 1904, cvi, 79.

Emigration Statistics of Ireland for the year 1904. [Cd 2467], H. C. 1905, xcviii, 79.

Emigration Statistics of Ireland for the year 1905. [Cd 2868], H. C. 1906, cxxxiv, 267.

Emigration Statistics of Ireland for the year 1906. [Cd 3376], H. C. 1907, xcvii, 429.

Emigration Statistics of Ireland for the year 1907. [Cd 3987], H. C. 1908, cxxii, 239.

Emigration Statistics of Ireland for the year 1908. [Cd 4550], H. C. 1909, ciii, 169.

Emigration Statistics of Ireland for the year 1909. [Cd 5088], H. C. 1910, cix, 479.

Emigration Statistics of Ireland for the year 1910. [Cd 5607], H. C. 1911, lx, 699.

Emigration Statistics of Ireland for the year 1911. [Cd 6131], H. C. 1912–1913, cv, 595.

Emigration Statistics of Ireland for the year 1912. [Cd 6727], H. C. 1913, lv, 933.

Emigration Statistics of Ireland for the year 1913. [Cd 7313], H. C. 1914, lxix, 1001.

Emigration Statistics of Ireland for the year 1914. [Cd 7883], H. C. 1914–1916, lxxx, 319.

Emigration Statistics of Ireland for the year 1915. [Cd 8230], H. C. 1916, xxxii, 915.

Emigration Statistics of Ireland for the year 1916. [Cd 8520], H. C. 1917–1918, xxxvii, 269.

Emigration Statistics of Ireland for the year 1917. [Cd 9013], H. C. 1918, xxv, 17.

Emigration Statistics of Ireland for the year 1918. [Cmd 77], H. C. 1919, li, 401.

Emigration Statistics of Ireland for the year 1919. [Cmd 721], H. C. 1920, l, 439.

Emigration Statistics of Ireland for the year 1920. [Cd 1414], H. C. 1921, xli, 401.

Green, Evarts B., and Virginia D. Harrington. *American Population before the Federal Census of 1790.* Gloucester, Massachusetts: Peter Smith, 1966.

Grimshaw, Thomas W. *Facts and Figures about Ireland.* Dublin: 1893.

———. "A Statistical Survey of Ireland, from 1840 to 1888." *Journal of the Statistical and Social Inquiry Society of Ireland* 9, pt. 68 (November 1888): 321–61. Attached tables.

Hacker, Andrew, ed. *U/S: A Statistical Portrait of the American People.* New York: Viking Press, 1983.

Hackett, James Dominick. "Passenger Lists Published in the *Shamrock* or *Irish Chronicle.*" *American-Irish Historical Society Journal* 28 (1930).

Haller, John S. "Civil War Anthropometry: The Making of a Racial Ideology." *Civil War History* 16 (December 1970): 309–24.

Hancock, Dr. "On the Remittances from North America by Irish Immigrants." *Journal of the Statistical and Social Inquiry Society of Ireland* 6 (January 1871): 280–90.

Harevan, Tamara K., and Maris A. Vinoskis. "Marital Fertility, Ethnicity, and Occupation in Urban Families: An Analysis of South Boston and the South End in 1880." *Journal of Social History* (Spring 1975).

Harkness, D. A. E. "Irish Emigration." In *International Migrations,* edited by Walter F. Willcox and Imre Ferenczi. Part 2, chap. 10. London: Ayer, 1931.

Heer, David M. "The Marital Status of Second-Generation Americans." *American Sociological Review* 26, no. 2 (1961): 233–41.

Hershberg, Theodore, et al. "Occupation and Ethnicity in Five Nineteenth-Century Cities: A Collaborative Inquiry." *Historical Methods Newsletter* 7, no. 3 (June 1974): 174–216.

Higgs, R. "Race, Skill, and Earnings: American Immigration in 1909." *Journal of Economic History* 31 (June 1971).

Hill, Joseph A. "Comparative Fecundity of Women of Native and Foreign Parentage of the United States." *Quarterly Publications of the American Statistical Association* 8, no. 104 (1913): 583–604.

House Judiciary Comm. Subcomm. No. 1. "The Effect of the Act of October 3, 1965, on Immigration from Ireland and Northern Europe." *Hearings: July 3 and September 18, 1968* Washington, D.C. U.S. Government Printing Office, 1968.

Hughes, J. G., and B. M. Walsh. "Migration Flows between Ireland, the United Kingdom, and the Rest of the World, 1966–71." *European Demographic Information Bulletin* 7, no. 4 (1976): 125–49.

Hutchinson, Edward P. *Immigrants and Their Children, 1850–1950.* New York: Russell & Russell, 1956.

———. "Notes on Immigration Statistics of the United States." *American Statistical Association Journal.* (December 1958): 961–1025.

Immigration Commission, Reports of the (Dillingham Commission). Listed below under United States, Reports of the Immigration Commission, Washington, D.C. 1911.

Insane and Feebleminded in Hospitals and

Institutions, 1904. Washington, D.C.: Bureau of the Census, 1906.

"International Migration and Naturalization." *Historical Statistics of the United States*. 97–118. Washington, D.C.: 1976.

Ireland, *Statistical Abstract*. Dublin: Stationery Office. The basic source of official statistics on modern Ireland. Fifty volumes published since initial issue appeared in 1926.

"Irish Immigration Adversely Affected by Immigration and Nationality Act of 1965." *Congressional Record—House* 113, pt. 10: 13166–8.

Irwin, Richard. "Changing Patterns of American Immigration." *International Migration Review* 6, no. 1(Spring 1972): 19–31.

Jackson, Pauline. "Women in Nineteenth Century Irish Emigration." *International Migration Review* 18: 4 (Winter 1984).

Jupp, Peter. *British and Irish Elections, 1784–1831*. New York: Barnes and Noble, 1973.

Kahn, E. J., Jr. *The American People*. Baltimore: Penguin, 1974.

Kapp, Fredrich. *European Emigration to the U.S.* New York: Nation Press, 1869.

———. "Immigration." *Journal of Social Science*, no. 2 (1870): 1–30.

———. *Immigration and the Commissioners of Emigration of the State of New York*. New York: Douglass Taylor, 1870.

Keep, George Rex Crowley. "The Irish Migration to North America in the Second Half of the nineteenth Century." Ph.D. dissertation, Trinity College, Dublin, 1951.

Kennedy, Robert E., Jr. *The Irish: Emigration, Marriage, and Fertility*. Berkeley: University of California Press, 1973.

Kennedy, Ruby Jo Reeves. "Single or Triple Melting-Pot?: Intermarriage Trends in New Haven, 1870–1940." *American Journal of Sociology* 49 (1944): 333.

Kennedy, Stanislaus, ed. *One Million Poor? The Challenge of Irish Inequality*. Dublin: Turoe Press, 1981.

Kirwan, Frank, and J. McGilvary. *Irish Economic Statistics*. Dublin: Institute of Public Administration, 1983. A guide to sources of economic statistics.

Kiser, Clyde V., Wilson H. Grabill, and Arthur A. Campbell. *Trends and Variations in Fertility in the United States*. Cambridge: Harvard University Press, 1968.

Kitagawa, Evelyn M., and Philip M. Hauser. *Differential Mortality in the United States*. Cambridge: Harvard University Press, 1973.

Lee, Joseph. "Introduction." In *The Population of Ireland Before the Nineteenth Century*. (Farnborough, 1973).

Linguistic and National Stocks in the Population of the U.S., Committee on. "Report of the Committee on Linguistic and National Stocks in the Population of the U.S." *Annual Report of the American Historical Society, 1931*.

"List of Publications on the Economic and Social History of Great Britain and Ireland published in 1983." *Economic History Review* 37 (1984): 563–608. Annually.

MacDonagh, Oliver. "The Irish Famine Emigration to the United States." *Perspectives in American History* 10 (1976): 357–446.

MacDonnell, Randal W. "Statistics of Irish Prosperity." *Journal of the Statistical and Social Inquiry Society of Ireland* 3, pt. 18 (January 1861) to pt. 25 (December 1863).

Malzberg, Benjamin. "Mental Disease among Irish-born and Native Whites of Irish Parentage in New York State, 1949–1951." *Mental Hygiene* 47 (1963): 13ff.

Massachusetts, Bureau of Statistics of Labor. *Eleventh Annual Report of the Bureau of Statistics of Labor of Massachusetts, January, 1880*. Boston: Wright & Potter Printing Co., State Printers, 1880.

Massachusetts, Bureau of Statistics of Labor. *Fifteenth Annual Report of the Bureau of Statistics of Labor, July, 1884*. Boston: Wright & Potter Printing Co., State Printers, 1884.

Massachusetts, Bureau of Statistics of Labor. *Ninth Annual Report of the Bureau of Statistics of Labor of Massachusetts, 1878*. Boston: Wright & Potter Printing Co., State Printers, 1878.

McDonald, Forrest, and Ellen S. McDonald. "The Ethnic Origins of the American People, 1790." *William and Mary Quarterly* 37 (1980): 179–99.

McDonald, F., and G. McWhiney. "The

Celtic South." *History Today*, 30 (1980), 11–15.

McGilvary, James. *Irish Economic Statistics*. Dublin: Institute of Public Administration, 1968.

Meehan, Thomas F. "Army Statistics of the Civil War." *United States Catholic Historical Society Records and Studies* 13 (1919): 129–39.

Meenen, J. "Some Features of Irish Emigration." *International Labour Review* 69 (February 1954): 126–39.

Meghen, P. J. *Statistics in Ireland*. 2d rev. ed. Dublin: Institute of Public Administration, 1970.

Mitchell, B. R. *European Historical Statistics, 1750–1970*. New York: Columbia University Press, 1976.

Moekyr, Joel. *Why Ireland Starved: A Quantitative and Analytical History of the Irish Economy, 1800–1845*. London: Allen and Unwin, 1983.

Moekyr, Joel, and Cormac O'Grada. "New Developments in Irish Population History, 1799–1850." *Economic History Review* 37 (1984): 473–88.

Morgan, V., and W. Macafee. "Irish Population in the Pre-Famine Period: Evidence from County Antrim." *Economic History Review* 37 (1984): 182–96.

Morrissey, Patrick J. *Working Conditions in Ireland and Their Effect on Irish Emigration: An Industrial Relations Study*. New York: P. J. Morrissey, 1958.

Mott, Frank L. "Portrait of an American Mill Town: Demographic Response to Mid-Nineteenth Century Warren, Rhode Island." *Population Studies* 26 (March 1972).

Mulvaney, Bernard, C.S.V. "How Catholics and Non-Catholics Differ in Fertility." *The American Sociological Review* 7 (1946): 124–27.

Munroe, Day. *Chicago Families: A Study of Unpublished Census Data*. Chicago: Chicago University Press, 1932.

National Center for Health Statistics. "Comparability of Marital Status, Race, Nativity, and Country of Origin on the Death Certificate and Matching Census Record, U.S., May–August, 1960." *Vital and Health Statistics* series 2, no. 34. Washington, D.C.: U.S. Department of Health, Education, and Welfare, 1969.

Neal, Larry, and Paul Uselding. "Immigration, A Neglected Source of American Economic Growth: 1790–1912." *Oxford Economic Papers*, series 2, 24 (1972): 68–88.

O'Brien, Michael J. *An Alleged First Census of the American People*. New York, 1930.

———. "Births, Marriages, and Burials and Other Records of the Irish in America in and about the Eighteenth Century." *American Irish Historical Society Journal* 12 (1913): 129–75.

———. "Immigration, Land, Probate, Administration, Baptismal, Marriage, Burial, Trade, Military, and Other Records of the Irish in America in the 17th and 18th Centuries." *American Irish Historical Society Journal* 14 (1915): 163–268.

———. ed. *The Irish in America*. Baltimore: Genealogical Society, 1965.

———. "Shipping Statistics of the Philadelphia Custom House, 1733 to 1774, Refute the Scotch-Irish Theory." *American Irish Historical Society Journal* 22 (1923): 132–41.

———. "Some Interesting Statistics of the Eighteenth Century." *American Irish Historical Society Journal* 13 (1914): 191–201.

O'Donoghue, D. J. *Geographical Distribution of Irish Ability*. New York: Benziger, 1906.

O'Grada, Cormac. *Catholic Families Weren't Always Bigger: Religion, Wealth, and Fertility in Rural Ulster before 1911*. Dublin: Center for Economic Research, University College, Dublin, 1984.

———. "A Note on Nineteenth-Century Irish Immigration Statistics." *Population Studies* 29 (March 1975): 143–49.

———. "Some Aspects of Nineteenth-Century Irish Emigration." In *Comparative Aspects of Scottish and Irish Economic and Social History, 1600–1900*, edited by L. M. Cullen and T. C. Smout. Edinburgh: John Donald (circa 1980).

O'Hanlon, Rev. John Canon. *Irish-American History of the United States*. 2 vols. Riverside, New Jersey: Benziger, Bruce and Glencoe, 1903.

O'Leary, Cornelius. *Irish Elections 1918–1977: Parties, Voters, and Proportional Representation.* New York: St. Martin's Press, 1980.

O'Malley, Austin. "Irish Vital Statistics in America." *Studies.* (December 1918): 623–32.

Oldham, C. H. "The Interpretation of Irish Statistics." *Statistical Society of Ireland Journal,* 15 pt. 100 (1924): 16–33.

Opler, M. K. and Singer, J. L. "Ethnic Differences in Behavior and Psycho-Pathology: Italian and Irish." *International Journal of Social Psychiatry* 2 (1956): 11–22.

Page, Thomas Walker. "The Distribution of Immigrants in the United States before 1870." *Journal of Political Economy* 20 (1912): 676–94.

———. "Some Economic Aspects of Immigration Before 1870, II," *Journal of Political Economy* 21 (January 1913): 34–55.

Pim, Joseph Todhunter. "A Review of the Economic and Social Condition of Ireland." *Journal of the Statistical and Social Inquiry Society of Ireland* 10, pt. 79 (August 1899): 453–93.

"Population. Special Report on Foreign-Born White Families by Country of Birth of Head." Special Report. *Fifteenth Census of the Untied States: 1930.* Washington, D.C.: Government Printing Office, 1933.

Poulson, Barry W., and James Holyfield, Jr. "A Note on European Migration to the United States: A Cross Spectral Analysis." *Explorations in Economic History* 2, no. 3 (Spring 1974): 299–309.

Price, C. A., and J. Zubrzycki. "The Use of Intermarriage Statistics as an Index of Assimilation." *Population Studies* 16 (1962).

Price, Charles A. "Methods of Estimating the Size Groups." In *Harvard Encyclopedia of American Ethnic Groups*, edited by Stephan Thernstrom, 1033–44. Cambridge: Harvard University Press, 1980.

"Progress of the Nation." *Report on the Population of the United States at the Eleventh Census, 1890.* Part I. Washington, D.C.: Government Printing Office, 1890.

Purvis, Thomas L. "The European Ancestry of the United States population, 1790." *William & Mary Quarterly* 41 (1984): 84–135.

Rabkin, Judith G. and Elmer J. Struening. *Ethnicity, Social Class, and Mental Illness.* New York: Institute on Pluralism and Group Identity, 1976.

Raymond, Raymond James. "A Reinterpretation of Irish Economic History (1930–1950)." *Journal of European Economic History* 2 (1982): 651–64.

Reilly, D. "Irishmen in American Science." *Ave Maria* 74 (1951): 167–70.

"Remarks on the Statistics of Foreign Parentage." *Statistics of the Population of the United States at the Tenth Census, June 1, 1880.* Washington, D.C.: Government Printing Office, 1883.

Reports of the Immigration Commission (Dillingham Commission), 42 Volumes, Washington, D.C., 1911.

Volumes 1 and 2. *Abstracts of Reports of the Immigration Commission, with Conclusions and Recommendatons and Views of the Minority.*

Volume 3. *Statistical Review of Immigration, 1819–1910—Distribution of Immigrants, 1830–1920.*

Volume 4. *Emigration Conditions in Europe.*

Volume 5. *Dictionary of Races and Peoples.*

Volumes 6 and 7. *Immigrants in Industries: Pt. 1, Bituminous Coal Mining.*

Volumes 8 and 9. *Immigrants in Industries: Pt. 2, Iron and Steel Manufacturing.*

Volume 10. *Immigrants in Industries: Pt. 3, Cotton Goods Manufacturing in the North Atlantic State—Pt. 4, Woolen and Worsted Goods Manufacturing.*

Volume 11. *Immigrants in Industries: Pt. 5, Silk Goods Manufacturing and Dyeing—Pt. 6, Clothing Manufacturing—Pt. 7, Collar, Cuff, and Shirt Manufacturing.*

Volume 12. *Immigrants in Industries: Pt. 8, Leather Manufacturing—Pt. 9, Boot and Shoe Manufacturing—Pt. 10, Glove Manufacturing.*

Volume 13. *Immigrants in Industries: Pt. 11, Slaughtering and Meat Packing.*

Volume 14. *Immigrants in Industries: Pt. 12, Glass Manufacturing—Pt. 13, Agricultural Implement and Vehicle Manufacturing.*

Volume 15. *Immigrants in Industries: Pt. 14, Cigar and Tobacco Manufacturing—Pt. 15, Furniture Manufacturing—Pt. 16, Sugar Refining.*

Volume 16. *Immigrants in Industries: Pt. 17, Copper Mining and Smelting—Pt. 18, Iron Ore Mining—Pt. 19, Anthracite Coal Mining—Pt. 20, Oil Refining.*

Volume 17. *Immigrants in Industries: Pt. 21, Diversified Industries, Vol. I.*

Volume 18. *Immigrants in Industries: Pt. 21, Diversified Industries, Vol. II—Pt. 22, The Floating Immigrant Labor Supply.*

Volumes 19 and 20. *Immigrants in Industries: Pt. 23, Summary Report on Immigration in Manufacturing and Mining.*

Volumes 21 and 22. *Immigrants in Industries: Pt. 24, Recent Immingrants in Agriculture.*

Volumes 23–25. *Immigrants in Industries: Pt. 25, Japanese and Other Immigrant Races in the Pacific Coast and Rocky Mountain States.*

Volumes 26 and 27. *Immigrants in Cities.*

Volume 28. *Occupations of the First and Second Generations of Immigrants in the United States— Fecundity of Immigrant Women.*

Volumes 29–33. *The Children of Immigrants in Schools.*

Volumes 34 and 35. *Immigrants as Charity Seekers.*

Volume 36. *Immigrants and Crime.*

Volume 37. *Steerage Conditions—Importation and Harboring Women for Immoral Purposes—Immigrant Homes and Aid Societies—Immigrant Banks.*

Volume 38. *Changes in Bodily Form of Descendants of Immigrants.*

Volume 39. *Federal Immigration Legislation— Digest of Immigration Decisions—Steerage Legislation, 1819–1908—State Immigrant and Alien Laws.*

Volume 40. *The Immigration Situation in Other Countries: Canada-Australia-New Zealand-Argentina-Brazil.*

Volume 41. *Statements and Recommendations Submitted By Societies and Organizations Interested in the Subject of Immigration.*

Volume 42. *Index of Reports of the Immigration Commission.*

Room, Robin. "Cultural Contingencies of Alcoholism: Variations between the Nineteenth-Century Urban Ethnic groups in Alcohol-Related Deaths." *Journal of Health and Human Social Behavior* (1968): 99–113.

Rosenkrantz, Barbara. *Public Health and the State.* Cambridge: Harvard University Press, 1972.

Sandalls, K. F. "An Investigation of the Differential Fertility Patterns of Irish and Italian Americans." Master's thesis. Georgetown University, 1970.

Saver, Herbert J. "Epidemiology of Cardiovascular Mortality— Geographic and Ethnic." *The American Journal of Public Health* 52 (1962): 102.

Smith, Richmond Mayo. *Emigration and Immigration.* New York: Charles Scribner's Sons, 1890.

Solar, Peter. "The Reconstruction of Irish External Trade Statistics for the Nineteenth-Century (Documents and Sources)." *Irish Economic and Social History* 12 (1985): 63–78.

Sowell, Thomas. "Irish Americans." In *Essays and Data on American Ethnic Groups*, edited by Thomas Sowell. Washington, D.C.: Urban Institute Press, 1978.

Staehle, Hans, Dr. "Statistical Notes on the Economic History of Irish Agriculture, 1847–1913." *Journal of the Statistical and Social Inquiry Society of Ireland* 18 (1950–51): 411–71.

Stare, Frederick J. "Epidemiologic Factors relating to Heart Disease." *World Review of Nutrition and Dietetics* 12 (1970): 142.

Taeuber, Irene B., and Conrad Taeuber. *People of the United States in the Twentieth Century.* Washington, D.C.: United States Dept. of Commerce Bureau of the Census, 1970.

Thistlewaite, Frank. "Migration from Europe Overseas in the Nineteenth and Twentieth Centuries." *Rapports Du Xieme Congres International Des Sciences Historique Stockholm.* Stockholm, 1960.

Thomas, Brinley. *Migration and Economic Growth.* New York: Cambridge University Press, 2d ed., 1973.

Thompson, Warren S. *Ratio of Children to Women, 1920.* Washington, D.C.: Government Printing Office, 1931.

Thompson, William J. "The Development of the Irish Census, and Its National Importance." *Statistical Society of Ireland Journal* 12, pt. 91 (1911): 474–88.

Tsushima, William T. "Responses of Irish and Italians of Two Social Classes on the Marlow-Crowne Social Desirability Scale." *Journal of Social Psychology* 77 (April 1969): 225–29.

Tucker, G. S. L. "Irish Fertility Ratios before the Famine." *Economic History Review.* 2d series, 23, no. 2 (Aug 1970): 267–84.

Varley, Anthony. "The Stem Family in Ireland Reconsidered." *Comparative Studies in Society and History* (1983): 381–92.

Vaughn, W. E., and A. J. Fitzpatrick, *Irish*

Historical Statistics: Population 1821–1971. Dublin: Royal Irish Academy, 1978.

Vaughn, William E. *Landlords and Tenants in Ireland, 1848–1904*. Studies in Irish Economic and Social History, 2. Dublin: Economic and Social History Society of Ireland, 1984.

Vedder, Richard K., and Lowell E. Gallaway. "The Geographical Distribution of British and Irish Emigrants to the United States after 1800." *Scottish Journal of Political Economy* 19 (Feb. 1972).

"Vital Statistics. Part I. Analysis and Ratio Tables." *Census Reports, Volume III. Twelfth Census of the United States, Taken in the Year 1900*. Washington, D.C.: Government Printing Office, 1902.

"Vital Statistics. Part II. Statistics of Deaths." *Census Reports, Volume IV. Twelfth Census of the United States, Taken in the Year 1900*. Washington, D.C.: Government Printing Office, 1902.

Walsh, B. M. *Migration to the United Kingdom from Ireland, 1961–66*. Dublin: Economic and Social Research Institute, Memorandum Series, no. 70, 1970.

Walsh, Brendan. "An Empirical Study of the Age-Structure of the Irish Population." *Economic and Social Review* 1, no. 2 (January 1970): 259–80.

War Department. *Defects Found in Drafted Men. Statistical Information Compiled from the Draft Records*. Washington, D.C.: Government Printing Office, 1920.

Warner, Robert M., and Francis X. Blouin, Jr. "Documenting the Great Migrations and a Century of Ethnicity in America." *The American Archivist* 39, no. 3 (July 1976).

Weber, Adna Ferrin. *The Growth of Cities in the Nineteenth Century*. Ithaca, New York: Cornell University Press, 1967.

Wells, Robert V. *The Population of the British Colonies in America*. Princeton: Princeton University Press, 1975.

Who Owns Ireland: Who Owns You? Dublin: Attic Press, 1985.

Willcox, Walter F. "The Distribution of Immigrants in the United States." *Quarterly Journal of Economics* 20 (1905): 523–46.

Williamson, Jeffrey G. "Migration to the New World: Long Term Influences and Impact." *Explorations in Economic History* 2, no. 4 (Summer 1974): 357–89.

Wilson, James Q. "Generational and Ethnic Differences among Career Police Officers." *American Journal of Sociology* 69 (March 1964): 522–28.

Young, Edward. *Special Report on Immigration*. Washington, D.C.: Government Printing Office, 1872.

Young, Kimball. *Mental Differences in Certain Immigrant Groups*. Eugene: University of Oregon Press, 1923.

3. Origins: Ireland

Aalen, F. H. A., and H. Brody. *Gola: The Life and Last Days of an Island Community*. Cork: Mercier Press, 1969.

Adams, William F. *Ireland and Irish Emigration to the New World*. New Haven: Yale University Press, 1932.

Akenson, Donald H. *Between Two Revolutions: Islandmagee, County Antrim 1798–1920*. Hamden, Connecticut: Achron Books, 1979.

———. *The Irish Education Experiment: The National System of Education in the Nineteenth Century*. Toronto: University of Toronto Press, 1970.

Almquist, Eric Lucien. "Mayo and Beyond: Land, Domestic Industry, and Rural Transformation in the Irish West." Ph.D. dissertation, Boston University, 1977.

———. "Pre-Famine Ireland and the Theory of European Proto-industrialization: Evidence from the 1841 Census." *Journal of Economic History* 39 (1979).

Arensberg, Conrad. *The Irish Countryman*. New York: Natural History Press, reissued 1968. Original edition 1937.

Arensberg, Conrad M., and Solon T. Kimball. *Family and Community in Ireland*. 2d ed. Cambridge: Harvard University Press, 1967.

Atkinson, A. *Ireland in the Nineteenth Century*. n.p., n.d., 1833.

Bales, Robert E. "Attitudes Toward Drinking in Irish Culture," In *Society, Culture, and Drinking Patterns*, edited by David J. Pittman and Charles R. Snyder. New York: John Wiley & Sons, 1962.

Barrow, Lennox. "The Use of Money in Mid-Nineteenth Century Ireland." *Studies* 59 (1970).

Becker, Bernard Henry. *Disturbed Ireland: Being the Letters Written during the Winter of 1880–81*. London: Macmillan & Co., 1881.

Bell, J. Bowyer. *The Secret Army: A History of the I.R.A., 1916–1970*. New York: John Day, 1971.

Black, R. D. Collision. *Economic Thought and the Irish Question, 1817–1870*. New York: Cambridge University Press, 1962.

Bourke, P. M. A. "The Use of the Potato Crop in Pre-Famine Ireland." *Journal of the Statistical and Social Inquiry Society of Ireland* 12 (1968): 72–96.

Brannick, T. O. "A Study of Returned Immigrants in an Irish Rural Parish." Master's thesis, University College, Dublin, 1978.

Bretherton, George Cornelius, III. "The Irish Temperance Movement: 1829–1847." Ph.D. dissertation, Columbia University, 1978.

Brody, Hugh. *Inishkillane: Change and Decline in the West of Ireland*. New York: Schocken Books, 1974.

Brookfield, H. C. "Ireland and the Atlantic Ferry: A Study in Changing Geographical Values." *Irish Geography* 3, no. 2 (1955): 69–78.

Buchanan, Ronald H. "The Rural Change in an Irish Townland." *Advancement of Science* 2 (1958): 291–300.

———. "Tradition and Change in Rural Ulster." *Folklife* 3 (1965): 39–45.

Burnett, Nicholas Richard. "Emigration and Modern Ireland." Ph.D. dissertation, Johns Hopkins University, 1976.

"Bye-bye, Ireland (Economic Mismanagement Spurs Emigration)." *The Economist* 305 (Oct. 3, 1987).

Callaghan, W. Sydney. "Ireland's Agonizing Clash of Cultures." *The Christian Century* 98 (Aug. 12, 1981).

Canny, Nicholas. "Early Modern Ireland: An

Appraisal Appraised." *Irish Economic and Social History* 4 (1977): 63ff.

Cant-Wall, Edward. *Ireland under the Land Act: Letters Contributed to the "Standard" Newspaper.* London: Chatto & Windus, 1882.

Carey, M. *Vindicae Hibernicae or Ireland Vindicated.* Philadelphia: M. Carey and Son, 1819.

Carroll, J. P., and John A. Murphy, eds. *De Valera and His Times.* Cork: Cork University Press, 1983.

Casey, Daniel J., and Robert E. Rhodes. eds. *Views of the Irish Peasantry, 1800–1916.* Connecticut: Archon Books, 1977.

Christianson, Gale Edward. *Rural Ireland, 1800–1830: An Economic History of a Backward Society.* Ph.D. dissertation. Carnegie-Mellon University, 1971.

Clancy, Patrick., et. al. *Ireland: A Sociological Profile.* Dublin: Institute for Public Administration in association with the Sociological Association of Ireland, 1986.

Clark, Samuel, and James S. Donnelly, Jr., eds. *Irish Peasants: Violence and Political Unrest, 1780–1914.* Manchester: Manchester University Press, 1983.

Cobden, Richard. *England, Ireland & America.* London: P. Brown, 1836.

Connell, Kenneth Hugh. *Irish Peasant Society.* London: Oxford, Clarendon Press, 1968.

———. "Peasant Marriage in Ireland: Its Structure and Development since the Famine." *Economic History Review.* 2d series, 14 (1962): 502–23.

———. "Peasant Marriages in Ireland after the Great Famine." *Past and Present* 12 (November 1957): 16–91.

———. *The Population of Ireland, 1750–1845.* Oxford: Clarendon Press, 1950.

Connolly, S. J. *Priests and People in Pre-Famine Ireland, 1780–1845.* Dublin: Gill and Macmillan, 1982.

Connolly, Sean. *Religion and Society in Nineteenth Century Ireland.* Studies in Irish Economic and Social History, 3. Dundalk: Dundalgan Press, 1985.

Coote, Sir Charles. *Statistical Survey of the County of Armagh, with Observations on the Means of Improvement.* Dublin: Craisberry and Campbell, 1804.

Corish, Patrick J. *The Origins of Catholic Nationalism.* Vol. 3, pt. 8, *History of Irish Catholicism.* Dublin: Gill and Macmillan, 1967–72.

Corkery, Daniel. *The Hidden Ireland.* Dublin: Gill and Macmillan, 1970.

Coulter, Henry. *The West of Ireland: Its Existing Condition and Prospects.* Dublin and London: Hodges & Smith, 1862.

Cousens, S. H. "Population Trends in Ireland at the Beginning of the Twentieth Century." *Irish Geography* 5, no. 5 (1968).

———. "Regional Death Rates in Ireland During the Great Irish Famine, 1846–1851." *Population Studies* 14 (July 1960): 55–74.

———. "The Regional Pattern of Emigration During the Great Famine, 1846–1851." *Transactions and Papers of the Institute of British Geographies* 28 (1960).

———. "The Regional Variation in Emigration From Ireland Between 1821–1841." *Institute of British Geographers Transactions* 37 (December 1965).

———. "The Regional Variations in Population Changes in Ireland, 1861–1881." *Economic History Review.* 2d series, 17 (1964).

———. "The Restrictions of Population Growth in Pre-Famine Ireland." *Proceedings of the Royal Irish Academy* 64 (November 4, 1966).

Cresswell, Robert. *Une communaute rurale de l'irlande.* Paris: Institut D'Ethnologie, 1968.

Cronin, Sean. *The McGarrity Papers: Revelations of the Irish Revolutionary Movement in Ireland and America, 1900–1940.* Tralee: Anvil Books, 1972.

Crotty, Raymond D. *Irish Agricultural Production: Its Volume and Structure.* Cork: Cork University Press, 1966.

Cullen, L. M. *An Economic History of Ireland Since 1660.* London: B.T. Batsford, 1972.

———. "The Hidden Ireland: Re-Assessment of a Concept." *Studia Hibernica* 9 (1969).

———. "Irish Economic History: Fact and Myth." In *The Formation of the Irish Economy*, edited by L. M. Cullen. Cork: Mercier Press, 1969.

24 Bibliography

———. "Irish History without the Potato." *Past and Present* 40 (1968).

———. *Life In Ireland*. London: B.T. Battsford, 1968.

———. *Six Generations: Life and Work in Ireland from 1790*. Cork: Mercier Press, 1970.

———, ed. *The Formation of the Irish Economy*. Cork: The Mercier Press, 1968.

Cunningham, Terence P., et al. *The Church since Emancipation*. Vol. 5, pts. 7, 8, 9, and 10. *History of Irish Catholicism*. Dublin: Gill and Macmillan, 1967–72.

Daly, Mary E. *Social and Economic History of Ireland since 1800*. Dublin: The Educational Company, 1981.

———. "Women in the Irish Workforce from Pre-Industrial to Modern Times." *Soathar: Journal of the Irish Labor History Society*, no. 7, Dublin: 1981.

Davitt, Michael. *The Fall of Feudalism in Ireland, Or the Story of the Land League Revolution*. London: Harper & Brothers, 1904.

Devoy, John. *Recollections of an Irish Rebel*. Shannon: Irish University Press, 1969. First edition, New York, 1929.

Donnelly, James S., Jr. *The Land and the People of Nineteenth-Century Cork: The Rural Economy and the Land Question*. London and Boston: Routledge and Kegan Paul, 1975.

Douglas, J. N. H. "Emigration and Irish Peasant Life." *Ulster Folklife* 9 (1962).

Drake, Michael. "Marriage and Population Growth in Ireland, 1750–1845." *Economic History Review* 2d series, 16 (1963).

Drudy, P. J., ed. *Ireland: Land, Politics and People*. Irish Studies 2. Cambridge: Cambridge University Press, 1982.

———. *The Irish in America:: Emigration, Assimilation, and Impact*. Irish Studies 4. Cambridge: Cambridge University Press, 1985.

Dufferin, Lord. *Irish Emigration and the Tenure of Land in Ireland*. Dublin: John Falconer, 1870.

Duffy, Brian, and Robin Knight. "A Fresh Irish Wave Laps U.S. Shores: 200,000 Illegals?" *U.S. News and World Report* 102 (March 2, 1987).

Duncan, Dr. of Liverpool. *Observations of the Habits of the Labouring Classes in Ireland*. Dublin: Milliken and Son, 1836.

Edwards, Ruth Dudley. *An Atlas of Irish History*. New York: Barnes and Noble, 1974. 2d ed. 1981.

Evans, E. Estyn. "Introduction to Lord George Hill." In *Facts From Gweedore*. Belfast: Institute of Irish Studies, 1971.

———. *Irish Folkways*. London: Routledge and Kegan Paul. 1957.

———. *Irish Heritage*. Dundalk, Ireland: Dundalgan Press, 1942.

———. *Mourne County*. Dundalk: Dundalgan Press, 1967.

———. *The Personality of Ireland: Habitat, Heritage, and History*. New York: Cambridge University Press, 1973.

Fanning, Connell M. "An Analysis of Aggregate Employment Policy in Ireland, 1954–1974." Ph.D. dissertation, 1980.

Fennel, Desmond. *The State of the Nation: Ireland Since the Sixties*. Swords, Co. Dublin: Ward River Press, 1983.

Fitzgerald, Garrett. "Estimates for Baronies of Minimum Level of Irish-Speaking amongst Successive Decenial Cohorts: 1771–1781 to 1861–1871." In *Proceedings of the Royal Irish Academy* 84, C, no. 3, 117–55.

Fitzpatrick, D. *Irish Emigration, 1801–1921*. Studies in Irish Economic and Social History, 1 Dundalk: Dundalgan Press, 1984.

Ford, James J. "Some Records of the Irish Language in the Greater Boston Area." *Bulletin: The Eire Society of Boston* 32 (1973).

Flatley, Patrick J. *Ireland The Land League: Key to the Irish Question*. Boston: D. O'Laughlin, 1881.

Fogarty, Michael, Liam Ryan, and Joseph Lee. *Irish Values and Attitudes: The Irish Report of the European Values Systems Study*. Dublin: Dominican Publications, 1984.

Foster, Thomas Campbell. *Letters on the Condition of the People of Ireland*. London: Chapman and Hall, 1846.

Fox, J. R. *Reports on the Condition of the Peasantry of the County of Mayo, During the Famine Crisis of 1880.* Dublin: Browne & Nolan, 1880.

Fox, J. R. "Tory Island." *Problems of Smaller Territories.* London: Athlone Press, 1967.

———. "The Vanishing Gael." *New Society* 1, no. 2 (1969): 17–19.

Freeman, Thomas Walter. *Pre-Famine Ireland: A Study in Historical Geography.* Manchester: Manchester University Press, 1957.

Gailey, R. Alan. "Aspects of Change in a Rural Community." *Ulster Folklife* 5 (1959): 27–34.

———. "Settlement and Population in the Aran Islands." *Irish Geography*, 4 (1959):65–78.

Gailey, Alan. *Scotland, Ireland and America: Migrant Culture in the Seventeenth and Eighteenth Centuries.* Working Papers in Irish Studies. Boston: Northeastern University, 1984.

Glad, Donald D. "Attitudes and Experiences of American-Jewish and American-Irish Male Youth as related to Differences in Adult Roles of Inebriety." *Quarterly Journal of Studies on Alcohol* 8 (1948): 406–72.

"Going, Going: The Expensively Educated Young Emigrate." *The Economist* 306 (January 16, 1988).

Grimshaw, Thomas W. "A Statistical Survey of Ireland, from 1840–1888." *Journal of the Statistical and Social Inquiry Society of Ireland* 9 (November 1888).

Gwynn, Aubrey. "Cromwell's Policy of Transportation." Part 1, 2. *Studies*, (December 1930, June 1931): 291–305, 607–23.

———. "Documents Relating to the Irish in the West Indies." *Analecta Hibernica* (October 1932): 139–286.

———. "Early Irish Emigration to the West Indies, 1612–1643."*Studies*(September 1929): 377–93.

———. "Indentured Servants and Negro Slaves in Barbados, 1642–1650." *Studies* (June 1930): 279–94.

Halpern, Jeffrey. "Working in the Factory: Resistance to Industrialization in Rural Ireland." Ph.D. dissertation. University of Pittsburgh, 1978.

Hannan, Damian. "Kinship, Neighborhood, and Social Change in Irish Rural Communities." *The Economic and Social Review* 3 (1972): 163–88.

Harris, Ruth-Ann Mellish. "The Nearest Place That Wasn't Ireland: A Study of Pre-Famine Irish Circular Migration to Britain." Ph.D. dissertation, Tufts University, 1980.

Hitchins, Fred H. *The Colonial Land and Emigration Commission.* Philadelphia: University of Pennsylvania Press, 1931.

Hoppen, K. Theodore. "Landlords, Society and Electoral Politics in Mid-Nineteenth Century Ireland." *Past and Present* 75 (May 1977): 62–93.

Horner, A. A. "The Pre-Famine Population of Some Kildare Towns." *Journal of the County Kildare Archeological Society.*

Hughes, T. Jones. "Society and Settlement in Nineteenth Century Ireland." *Irish Geography* 5, no. 2 (1965): 79–96.

Humphreys, Alexander J. "The Family in Ireland." In *Comparative Family Systems.* Boston: Houghton Mifflin, 1965.

Hunter, J. A. "Population Changes in the Lower Roe Valley, 1831–1861." *Ulster Folklife* 17 (1971).

Hutchinson, Bertram. "On the Study of Non-Economic Factors in Irish Economic Development." *The Economic and Social Review* 1 (1970).

Inglis, Henry David. *Ireland in 1834.* London: Whittaker, 1834.

Inquiry into Condition of the Poorer Classes in Ireland. Dublin: Milliken and Sons, 1835.

"Ireland: The Kennedy Cult." *Look* 28 (November 17, 1964): 66–72.

Johnson, James H. "Harvest Migration from Nineteenth Century Ireland." *Transactions of the Institute of British Geographers* 41 (1967): 97–112.

———. "Marriage and Fertility in Nineteenth Century Londonderry." *Journal of the Statistical and Social Inquiry Society of Ireland* 20, pt. 1 (1958).

———. "Partnership and Clachans in Mid-Nineteenth Century Londonderry." *Ulster Folklife* 9 (1963).

———. "The Population of Londonderry during the Great Irish Famine." *The Eco-*

nomic History Review, 2d series (1957–58).

———. "Population Movement in County Derry during a Pre-Famine Year." *Proceedings of the Royal Irish Academy* 60, C., no. 3 (1959).

———. "Rural Population Changes in Nineteenth Century Londonderry." *Studies in Folklore Presented to Emry Estyn Evans*. Belfast: Ulster Folk Museum, 1970.

———. "Studies of Irish Rural Settlements." *Geographical Review* 48 (1958): 544–66.

———. "The Two 'Irelands' at the Beginning of the Nineteenth Century." In *Irish Geographical Studies in Honor of E. Estyn Evans*. Belfast: Queen's University of Belfast, 1970.

Jordan, Donald Elmer, Jr. "Land and Politics in the West of Ireland: County Mayo: 1846–82." Ph.D. dissertation, University of California, Davis, 1982.

Kane, Eileen. "Man Kin in Donegal: A Study of Kinship Functions in a Rural Irish and an Irish American Community." *Ethnology* 7, no. 3 (1968): 245–58.

———. "Rural Poverty." *Social Studies* L (1972): 413–26.

Kennedy, David. "Education and the People." In *Social Life in Ireland*. Dublin: At the Sign of the Three Candles, 1957.

Kennedy, Robert E., Jr. *The Irish: Emigration, Marriage, and Fertility*. Berkeley: University of California Press, 1973.

Kerr, Barbara M. "Irish Seasonal Migration to Great Britain, 1800–1823." *Irish Historical Studies* 3 (1943).

Kierse, Sean. *The Famine Years in the Parish of Killaloe, 1845–1851*. Killaloe, Co. Clare: Boru Books, 1984.

Kohl, J. G. *Travels in Ireland*. London: Bruce and Wyld, 1844.

Lane, Ralph. "Change and Organization in Rural Ireland." *Human Organization* 14, no. 2 (1955): 4–8.

Large, David. "The Wealth of the Greater Irish Landowners, 1750–1815." *Irish Historical Studies* 15 (March 1966): 21–45.

Larkin, Emmet. "Church and State in Ireland in the Nineteenth Century." *Church History* 31 (September 1962).

———. "Church and State, and Nation in Modern Ireland." *American Historical Review* 80, no. 5 (December 1975): 1244–76.

———. *The Consolidation of the Roman Catholic Church in Ireland, 1860–1870*. Chapel Hill: University of North Carolina Press, 1987.

———. "The Devotional Revolution In Ireland, 1850–75." *American Historical Review* 77 (1972): 623–52.

———. "Economic Growth, Capital Investment, and the Roman Catholic Church in Nineteenth-Century Ireland." *American Historical Review* 21 (1968).

———. *The Historical Dimensions of Irish Catholicism*. New York: Arno Press, 1976.

———. *The Making of the Roman Catholic Church in Ireland, 1850–1860*. Chapel Hill: University of North Carolina Press.

———. *The Roman Catholic Church and the Creation of the Modern Irish State, 1878–1886*. Philadelphia: American Philosophical Society, 1975.

———. *The Roman Catholic Church in Ireland and the Fall of Parnell, 1888–1891*. Chapel Hill: University of North Carolina Press.

Lee, Joseph. "The Dual Economy In Ireland, 1800–50." *Historical Studies: Papers Read before the Irish Conference of Historians* 8, n.d.

———. "Irish Agriculture." *Agricultural History Review* 17, pt. 1, 1969.

———. "Marriage and Population in Pre-Famine Ireland," *Economic History Review* 21 (1968).

———. *The Modernization of Irish Society, 1848–1918*. Dublin: Gill & Macmillan, 1973.

———. "Railroads in the Irish Economy." In *The Formation of the Irish Economy*. Cork: Mercier Press, 1969.

———. "Women and the Church since the Famine." In *Women in Irish Society: The Historical Dimension*, edited by O. MacCurtain and D. O. Corrain. Dublin: Arlen House, 1978.

Le Fanu, William Richard. *Seventy Years of Irish Life*. New York and London: Edward Arnold, 1893.

Loughnane, Mary Fionula. "Through Irish Eyes: A Mainly Women's Perspective on the Influence of Women and Men in Irish Families." Ph.D. dissertation, University of Michigan, 1983.

Lynch, Patrick, and John Vaizey. *Guiness's Brewery in the Irish Economy*. Cambridge: Cambridge University Press, 1960.

Lyons, Francis Stewart Leland. *Ireland since the Famine*. New York: Charles Scribner's Sons, 1971.

MacDonagh, Oliver. "The Irish Clergy and Emigration during the Great Famine." *Irish Historical Studies* 5 (1947): 287–302.

———. "Irish Emigration During the Great Famine, 1845–1852." Master's thesis, University College Dublin, 1946.

———. "Irish Emigration to the United States of America and the British Colonies during the Famine." In *The Great Famine: Studies in Irish History, 1845–1852*, edited by R. D. Edwards and T. D. Williams. New York: New York University Press, 1957.

———. "The Irish Famine Emigration to the United States." *Perspectives in American History*, vol. 7. Cambridge, Massachusetts: Harvard University Press, 1972, 357–446.

———. *A Pattern of Government Growth, 1800–1860*. London: MacGibbon and Kee, 1961.

MacIntyre, Angus. *The Liberator: Daniel O'Connell and the Irish Party, 1830–1847*. New York: Macmillan, 1965.

Madden, Richard Robert. *The Life and Times of Robert Emmet; With Numerous Notes and Additions*. New York: Haverty, Kennedy, 1856.

Maguire, W. A. *The Downshire Estates in Ireland, 1801–1845*. New York: Oxford University Press, 1972.

Manasian, David, Carol Reed, and Carole Craig. "The Exodus of the Elite (the European Brain Drain)." *International Management* 43 (Feb. 1988): 54–57.

Mansergh, Nicholas. *Ireland in the Age of Reform and Revolution*. London: G. Allen and Unwin, 1940.

Mathewson, William. "Irish Brain Drain." *The Wall Street Journal*, Sept. 28, 1989.

McCourt, Desmond. "Infield and Out Field in Ireland." *Economic History Review*. 2d series, 7 (1955): 369–76.

———. "The Rundale System in Donegal: Its Distribution and Decline." *Donegal Annual* 3 (1955): 47–60.

McCourt, Desmond, and Alan Gailey, eds. *Studies in Folklife Presented to Emyr Estyn Evans*. Ulster: Ulster Folk Museum, 1970.

McDevitt, James J., Jr. "Social Conflict in the Irish Peasant Subculture." Master's thesis. Ohio State University, 1972.

McDowell, Robert Brendan. *The Irish Convention, 1917–1918*. London: Routledge and Kegan Paul, 1970.

———, ed. *Social Life in Ireland, 1800–1845*. Dublin: At the Sign of Three Candles, 1957.

Meena, J. F. "Eire." In *Economics of International Migration*. London: Macmillan, 1958.

Messenger, John C. "The Influence of the Irish in Montserrat." *Caribbean Quarterly* 13 (1967): 3–26.

———. *Inis Beag: Isle of Ireland*. New York: Holt, Rinehart and Winston, 1969.

———. "Man of Aran Revisited: An Anthropological Critique." *Irish University Review* 3 (1966): 15–47.

———. "Sex and Repression in an Irish Folk Community." In *Human Sexual Behavior*. New York: Basic Books, 1971.

Miller, David W. "Irish Catholicism and the Great Famine." *Journal of Social History* 9, no. 1 (Fall 1975): 80–90.

Miller, Hugh. *An Autobiography. My Schools and Schoolmasters: Or the Story of My Education*. Boston: Gould and Lincoln, 1854.

Miller, Kerby A. *Emigrants and Exiles: Ireland and the Irish Exodus to North America*. New York: Oxford University Press, 1985.

———. "Emigrants and Exiles: Irish Cultures and Irish Emigration to North America 1790–1922." *Irish Historical Studies* 22 (1980): 97–125.

Mitchel, John. *Jail Journal*. First published in Ireland by M. H. Gill and Son, 1913. Paperback ed. London: Sphere Books, 1983.

Mokyr, Joel. *Why Ireland Starved: A Quantitative and Analytical History of the Irish Economy, 1800–1850*. London: Allen and Unwin, 1983.

Newman, Jeremiah, ed. *The Limerick Rural Survey*. Tipperary: Muintir Na Rire Rural Publications, 1964.

O'Brien, George. *The Economic History of Ireland from the Union to the Famine*. London: Longmans, Green and Co., 1921.

O'Brien, William, and Desmond Ryan. *Devoy's Post Bag, 1871–1928*. Dublin: D. J. Fallon, 1948.

O'Connell, Maurice R. "The American Revolution and Ireland." *Eire-Ireland*, 1976.

O'Crohan, Tomas. *The Islandman*. Oxford: Clarendon Press, 1969.

O'Cuiv, Brian, ed. *A View of the Irish Language*. Dublin: Stationery Office, 1969.

O'Flaherty, R. *A Choreographic Description of the West or H-iar Connaught*. Dublin: Irish Archaeological Society, 1846.

O Grada, Cormac. *The Great Irish Famine*. Dublin: Gill and Macmillan, Ltd., 1989.

———. *Ireland Before and After the Famine: Explorations in Economic History 1800–1930*. Manchester: Manchester University Press, 1988.

O'Kane, Daniel Finbar. "The Myth of Irish Identity." Ph.D. dissertation. Drew University, 1982.

O'Neill, Conor. "The Social Function of Physical Violence in an Irish Urban Area." *The Economic and Social Review* 2 (1971): 11–22.

O'Neill, Kevin. *Family and Farm in Prefamine Ireland: The Parish of Killashandra*. Madison: University of Wisconsin Press, 1984.

———. "'Man Overboard': Change and Stability in Post-Famine Ireland." In *From Paddy to Studs: Irish American Communities at the Turn of the Century Era, 1880 to 1920*, edited by Timothy J. Meager. New York: Greenwood Press, 1986.

O'Neill, Thomas P. "From Famine to Near Famine, 1845–1879." *Studia Hibernica* 1 (1961).

O'Reilly, Kevin Richards. "Population Dynamics and Family Planning In Dublin, Ireland." Ph.D. dissertation, University of Connecticut, 1981.

Orme, A. R. *Ireland*. Chicago: Aldine Publishing Co., 1970.

O'Tuathaigh, Gearoid. *Ireland before the Famine, 1798–1848*. Dublin: Gill and Macmillan, 1972.

"Packed and Gone (Recent Irish Emigration)." *The Economist* 312 (Sept 9, 1989).

Paor, Liam de. *The Peoples of Ireland*. Notre Dame: University of Notre Dame Press, 1986.

Paul-Dubois, L. *Contemporary Ireland*. London: T. Fisher Unwin, 1908.

Perceval-Maxwell, M. *The Scottish Migration to Ulster in the Reign of James I*. New York: Humanities Press, 1973.

Pollard, Hugh Bertie Campbell. *The Secret Societies of Ireland*. London: Philip Allan Co., 1922.

Pomfret, John E. *The Struggle for Land in Ireland, 1800–1923*. New York: Russell and Russell, 1930.

Poor Inquiry Commission. *Selection of Parochial Examinations Relative to the Destitute Classes In Ireland, From the Evidence Received by His Majesty's Commissioner for Inquiry into the Condition of the Poorer Classes in Ireland*. Dublin: Milliken and Sons, 1835.

Proudfoot, V. Bruce. "Changes in Settlement and Population in Northern Ireland, 1835–1860." *Ulster Folklife* 5 (1959).

Quigley, Michael. "Farmers, Merchants and Priests: The Rise of the Agrarian Petty-Bourgeoisie in Ireland, 1850–85." Ph.D. dissertation. McMaster University, 1980.

Quinn, David Beers. *The Elizabethans and the Irish*. New York: Cornell University Press, 1966.

Raymond, Raymond James. "The Economic of Neutrality: The United States, Great Britain, and Ireland's War Economy: 1937–1945." Ph.D. dissertation, University of Kansas, 1980.

Salaman, Redcliffe N. *The History and Social Influence of the Potato*. New York: Cambridge University Press, 1949.

Scheper-Hughes, Nancy. *Saints, Scholars and Schizophrenics: Mental Illness in Rural Ireland*. Berkeley: University of California Press, 1979.

Schrier, Arnold. *Ireland and the American*

Emigration, 1850–1900. Minnesota: University of Minnesota Press, 1958.

Senior, Nassau William. *Journals, Conversations, and Essays Relating to Ireland*. 2 vols. London: Longmans, Green and Company, 1868.

Spenser, Edmund. *A View of the Present State of Ireland*. New York: Oxford University Press, 1970.

Stapels, Hugh B., ed. *The Ireland of Sir Jonah Barrington*. Seattle: University of Washington Press, 1967.

Staski, Edward. "Alcohol Comsumption among Irish-Americans and Jewish Americans: Contributions from Archaeology." Ph.D. dissertation, University of Arizona, 1983.

Tobin, Fergal. *The Best of Decades: Ireland in the 1960s*. Dublin: Gill and Macmillan, 1984.

Trench, William Steuart. *The Realities of Irish Life*. London: Longmans, Green and Co., 1868.

Tucker, G. S. L. "Irish Fertility Ratios before the Famine." *Economic History Review* 23, no. 2 (August 1970): 267–84.

Tuke, James H. *Irish Distress and its Remedies: The Land Question*. London: W. Ridgeway, 1880.

———. *A Visit to Connaught in the Autumn of 1847*. London: Charles Gilfin, 1848.

Two Irelands: Or, Loyalty Versus Treason. London: P. S. King & Son, 1884.

Vaughan, W. E. *Landlords and Tenants in Ireland, 1848–1904*. Studies in Irish Economic and Social History 2. Dundalk: Dundalgan Press, 1984.

Wakefield, Edward. *An Account of Ireland: Statistical and Political*. London: Longmans, Hurst, Rels, Orme, and Browne, 1812.

Walford, Thomas. *The Scientific Tourist Through Ireland . . . By an Irish Gentleman*. London: 1818.

Wall, Maureen. "Catholics in Economic Life." In *The Formation of the Irish Economy*. Cork: Mercier Press, 1969.

———. "The Decline of the Irish Language." In *A View of the Irish Language*. Dublin: The Stationery Office, 1969.

Walsh, Brendan M. "Marriage Rates and Population Pressure: Ireland, 1871 and 1911." *Economic History Review* 23, no. 1 (April 1970): 148–62.

Walsh, E. J. "Language Problem of Irish Immigrants at the Time of the Famine." In *St. Meinrad's Essays* 12 (1959–60).

Walshe, John. "Survey Finds Rising Graduation Emigration." *Times Educational Supplement*, Dec. 23, 1988.

Weld, Isaac. *Statistical Survey of the County of Roscommon*. Dublin: R. Graisberry, 1832.

Whyte, John H. *Political Problems, 1850–60* 3, pt. 3. *History of Irish Catholicism*. Dublin: Gill and Macmillan, 1967–72.

4. Social Adjustment, Ethnicity, General

Abbott, Edith. *The Tenaments of Chicago: 1908–1935.* Chicago: University of Chicago Press, 1936.

Abbott, Edith and Sophonisba Breckinridge. *Truancy and Non-Attendance in the Chicago Schools.* Chicago: University of Chicago Press, 1917.

Abrams, Elliot and Franklin S. Abrams. "Immigration Policy—Who Gets In and Why." *The Public Interest* 38 (August 1975): 16.

Abramson, Harold J. "On the Sociology of Ethnicity and Social Change: A Model of Rootedness and Rootlessness." *Economic and Social Review* 8, no. 1 (October 1976): 43–59.

Adams, William F. *Ireland and Irish Emigration to the New World.* New Haven: Yale University Press, 1932.

Akenson, D. H. "An Agnostic View of the Historiography of the Irish-Americans." *Labor/La Travail*, 14 (Fall 1984), 123–159.

———. *Being Had: Historians, Evidence and the Irish in North America.* Toronto: P. D. Meany, 1985.

———. "Books and Authors: The Irish in North America." *Eire-Ireland* 21, no. 1 (Spring 1986): 122–29.

———. " 'Data': What Is Known about the Irish in North America?" In *Ireland and Irish-Australia*, edited by Oliver MacDonagh and W. F. Mandle. London and Sydney, 1986.

———. "Why the Accepted Estimates of the Ethnicity of the American People, 1790, are Unacceptable." *William and Mary Quarterly* 41 (January 1984): 102–19 and 125–29.

Alba, R. D. "Assimilation among American Catholics." Ph.D. dissertation, Columbia University, 1974.

———. "Social Assimilation among American Catholic National Origin Groups." *American Sociological Review* 41: 1030–46.

Alcorn, Alfred J. "The Irish in America: An Interview with Daniel Patrick Moynihan." *The Irish Times*, Friday, June 11, 1971.

Alfred, W. "Pride and Poverty: An Irish Integrity." In *The Immigrant Experience*, edited by T. C. Wheeler. Baltimore: Pelican Books, 1971.

American Council of Learned Societies. *Report of Committee on Linguistics and National Stocks in the Population of the United States. Annual Report of the American Historical Association.* Volume 1, Proceedings. Washington, D.C.: Government Printing Office, 1932.

"American Irish: A Long Way From the Auld Sod," *Senior Scholastic* 95:8–11 (November 10, 1969).

American Irish Historical Society. *The Story of the American Irish Historical Society.* New York: American Irish Historical Society, 1938.

Ancient Order of Hibernians. *Official Register . . . Ancient Order of Hibernians and Ladies Auxillary in America.* Scranton: The Secretary, n.d.

Appel, John J. "The New England Origins of the American Irish Historical Society." *The New England Quarterly* 33 (1960): 462–75.

———. "From Shanties to Lace Curtains: The Irish Image in Puck, 1876–1910." *Comparative Studies in Society and History* 13 (October 1971): 365–75.

Aronson, Virginia. "The Luck of the Irish (Heart Disease)." *Runner's World* 20 (July 1985).

Asbury, Herbert. *The Barbary Coast: An Informal History of the San Francisco Underworld.* New York: Knopf, 1933.

———. *The Gangs of New York.* New York: A. A. Knopf, 1928.

Averback, Alvin. "San Francisco's South of Market District, 1850–1950: The Emergence of a Skid Row." *California Historical Quarterly* 53 (Fall 1973): 199–200.

Bagenal, Philip H. "Uncle Pat's Cabin." *Nineteenth Century* 12 (1882): 925–38.

Bailey, Harry A., Jr., and Ellis Katz. *Ethnic Group Politics.* Columbus, Ohio: Charles E. Merrill, 1969.

Baldwin, F. S. "What Ireland Has Done for America." *New England Magazine* 24 (March 1901): 68–85.

Banning, M.C. "There is Still Hope for the Irish." *Jubilee* 1 (January 1954): 7–11.

Barrett, J. P. "The Life and Death of an Irish Neighorhood." *Philadelphia Magazine* 61, no. 3 (1970): 85–87.

Barrett, Patricia. *Religious Liberty and the American Presidency.* New York: Herder & Herder, 1963.

Barron, Milton L. "Intermediacy: Conceptualization of Irish Status in America." *Social Forces* 27 (1948–1949): 163–256.

———. *The Blending American: Patterns of Intermarriage.* Chicago: Quadrangle Books, 1972.

Barry, M. J. *Irish Emigration Considered.* Cork: n.p., 1863.

Bayor, Ronald H. *Neighbors in Conflict: The Irish, Germans, Jews, and Italians of New York City, 1929–1941.* Baltimore: Johns Hopkins University Press, 1978.

Beadles, J. A. "The Syracuse Irish 1812–1928: Immigration, Catholics, Socioeconomic Status, Politics and Irish Nationalism." Ph.D. dissertation, Syracuse University, 1974.

Beamish, North Ludlow. *The Discovery of America by the Northmen, in the Tenth Century, With Notices of the Early Settlements of the Irish in the Western Hemisphere.* London: Boone, 1841.

Bean, William G. "Puritan Versus Celt, 1850–1860." *New England Quarterly* 7 (March 1934): 70–89.

Beer, Thomas. *The Mauve Decade.* New York: Alfred A. Knopf, 1926.

Bell, Daniel, ed. *The Radical Right.* Garden City, New York: Doubleday, 1964.

Bercovice, Konrad. *Around the World in New York.* New York: Appleton, 1938.

Bere, May. *A Comparative Study of the Mental Capacity of Children of Foreign Parentage.* New York: Teachers College, Columbia University, 1924.

Berger, M. "Irish Emigrant and American Nativism as Seen by British Visitors, 1836–1860." *Dublin Review* 219 (October 1946): 174–86.

Bernard, Richard M. "Intermarriage Patterns among Immigrants and Natives in Wisconsin, 1850–1920." Ph.D. dissertation, University of Wisconsin, 1976.

———, *The Melting Pot and the Altar: Marital Assimilation in Early Twentieth-Century Wisconsin.* Minneapolis: University of Minnesota Press, 1980.

Bernhard, Virginia. "Poverty and the Social Order in Seventeenth-Century Virginia." *Virginia Magazine of Historical Biography* 85 (April 1977): 141–55.

Berrol, Selma Cantor. "The Schools of New York in Transition, 1898–1914." *Urban Review* 1 (December 1966): 15–20.

———. "Immigrants at School: New York City, 1898–1914." Ph.D. dissertation, City University of New York, 1967.

Berthoff, Rowland T. *British Immigrants in Industrial America, 1790–1950.* Cambridge: Harvard University Press, 1953.

———. "The Social Order of the Anthracite Region, 1825–1902." *Pennsylvania Magazine* 89 (July 1965).

Betts, J. R. "The Negro and the New England Conscience in the Days of John Boyle O'Reilly." *Journal of Negro History* 51, no. 4: 246–61.

Biddle, E. H. "The American Catholic Irish Family." In *Ethnic Families in America*, edited by C. M. Mindel and R. Habenstein, 89–123. New York: Elsevier.

Biever, Bruce Francis. *Religion, Culture, and Values: Native Irish and American Irish Catholicism.* New York: Arno Press, 1976.

Billington, Ray Allen. *The Origins of Nativism in the United States, 1800–1844*. New York: 1974.

Birmington, Stephan. "From the Banks of the Shannon to the Banks of Wall Street." *U. S. Catholic* 39: 30–35.

———. *Real Lace: America's Irish Rich*. New York: Harper and Row, 1973.

Blake, J. "The Americanization of Catholic Reproductive Ideals." *Population Studies* 20, no. 1 (1966): 27–43.

Blake, John W. "Transportation from Ireland to America, 1653–60." *Irish Historical Society* 3, no. 11 (March 1943): 268–80.

Bland, J. *Hibernian Crusade: The Story of the Catholic Total Abstinence Union of America*. Washington, D.C: The Catholic University Press of America, 1951.

Blessing, Patrick. "The Irish." In *Harvard Encyclopedia of American Ethnic Groups*, edited by Stephan Thernstrom. Cambridge: Harvard University Press, 1980.

———. "The Irish in America, 1800–1920." In *Irish Studies*, edited by P. J. Drudy. Cambridge: Cambridge University Press, 1985.

Bliven, Bruce. "What Have the Irish Done?" *New Republic* 30 (May 10, 1922): 307–9. (May 24, 1922): 367–69.

———. "The Blooding Boss and the Musical Mayor." *American Heritage* 11 (December 1959): 8–11, 100–104.

Bocock, J. P. "The Irish Conquest of Our Cities." *Forum* 17: 186–95.

Bodnar, John. *Immigration and Industrialization: Ethnicity in an American Mill Town, 1870–1940*. Pittsburgh: University of Pittsburgh Press, 1977.

Bouvier, Leon F., and S. L. N. Rao. *Socio-Religious Factors in Fertility Decline*. Cambridge, Massachusetts: Ballinger Publishing Co., 1975.

Bradshaw, Benjamin S. "Ethnic Congregation-Segration, Assimilation, and Stratification." *Social Forces* 42–43: 482–18.

Brayley, Arthur Wellington. *The Complete History of the Boston Fire Department*. Boston, 1889.

Breen, G. *An Immigrant's Shenanigans: Thirty-Three Jobs in Twenty Years*. New York: Exposition, 1951.

Brinley, Thomas. *Migration and Economic Growth*. 2d ed. Cambridge: Cambridge University Press, 1973.

Brooks, Van Wyck. *The Confident Years, 1885–1915*. New York: n.p. 1952.

Brown, Francis J., and Joseph S. Roucek, eds. *One America*. Englewood Cliffs, New Jersey: Prentice-Hall, 1946.

Brown, R. H. *I Am of Ireland*. New York: Harper and Row, 1974.

Brown, Richard Maxwell. *Strain of Violence*. New York: Oxford University Press, 1975.

Brown, Thomas N. *Social Discrimination against the Irish in the United States*. American Jewish Committee, November 1968.

———. "The Irish Layman." In *A History of Irish Catholicism: The United States of America*, edited by Patrick J. Cornish. Dublin: Gill and Macmillan, 1970.

Brunner, Edmund. *Immigrant Farmers and Their Children*. Garden City, New York: Doubleday, 1929.

Bullough, William A. *Cities and Schools in the Gilded Age: The Evolution of an Urban Institution*. New York: Kennikat, 1974.

Burchell, Robert. "The Historiography of the American Irish." *Immigrants and Minorities* 1 (1982).

Bureau of Education. *Education of the Immigrant*. Bulletin no. 51. Washington, D.C.: Government Printing Office, 1913.

Burke, Nicholas R. "Some Observations on the Migration of Laborers from the South of Ireland to Newfoundland in Pre-Famine Times." *Journal of the Cork Historical and Archealogical Society* 76 (1971).

Burrows, F. W. "Our National Debt to Ireland." *New England Magazine* 47 (August 1912): 255–56.

Busey, Samuel C. *Immigration: Its Evil and Consequences*. New York, 1866.

Byrne, S. *Irish Emigration to the United States: What It Has Been, and What It Is*. New York: Catholic Publishing Society, 1873.

Cammann, Henry. *The Charities of New York, Brooklyn, and Staten Island*. New York: Hurd and Houghton, 1868.

Campbell, John H., ed. *History of the Friendly Sons of St. Patrick and of the Hibernian Society for the Relief of Emigrants from Ireland*. Philadelphia: Hibernian Society, 1892.

Carey, Mathew. *Miscellaneous Essays*. Philadelphia: Carey and Hart, 1830.

———. *Reflections on the Subject of Emigration from Europe with a View to Settlement in the United States*. 2d. ed. Liverpool: E. Smith, 1827.

———. *Vindiciae Hibernicae; or Ireland Vindicated: An Attempt to Develop and Expose a Few of the Multifarious Errors and Misrepresentations Respecting Ireland*. Philadelphia: M. Carey and Son, 1819.

Carter, Carole J. "Ireland: America's Neutral Ally, 1939–1941." *Eire-Ireland* 12(Summer 1977): 5–13.

Carter, Edward C. "Naturalization in Philadelphia, 1789–1806." *Pennsylvania Magazine of Historical Biography* 94 (1970): 331.

Casey, G. W. "Vanishing Irish-American." *Information* 71 (March 1957): 39–41.

Casson, H. N. "Irish in America." *Mensey* 35 (April 1906): 86–104.

Castellini, Joseph J. *America's Debt to the Irish*. Cincinnati: Macey-Hall, 1924.

Cestello, B. D. "Catholics in American Commerce and Industry." *American Catholic Social Review* 17: 219–33.

Chudacoff, Howard P. *Mobile Americans*. New York: Oxford University Press, 1972.

Cinel, Dean. "Ethnicity: A Neglected Dimension of American History." *International Migration Review* 3 (Summer 1969): 58–63.

Clark, D. "Muted Heritage: Gaelic in an American City." *Eire-Ireland* 6, no. 1 (1971): 3–7.

Clark, Dennis. *Hibernia America: The Irish and Regional Cultures*. Westport, Connecticut: Greenwood Press, 1986.

———. "Urban Violence: Past Riots of Irish Immigrants." *America* 118 (June 1, 1968): 728–30.

Coblentz, Stanton A. *Villains and Vigilantes*. New York: Wilson-Erickson, 1936.

Cochran, Alice Lida. *The Saga of an Irish Immigrant Family: The Descendants of John Mullanphy*. New York: Arno Press, 1976.

Cockburn, Claud. "Proper Thoughts on Ireland." *Esquire* 83 (January 1975): 71–75.

Cohler, B. J., and M. A. Lieberman. "Personality Change across the Second Half of Life: Findings from a Study of Irish, Italian and Polish American Men and Women." In *Ethnicity and Aging*, edited by D. E. Gelfand and A. J. Kutjk. New York: Springer, 1979.

Coleman, Terry. *Going to America*. New York: Pantheon, 1972.

Commons, John R. *Race and Immigrants in America*. New York: 1908.

Condon, E. "Irish Immigration to the United States since 1790." *American Irish Historical Society Journal* 4 (1904): 80–94.

Condon, Edward O'Meagher. *The Irish Race in America*. New York: Ford, 1887.

Condon, P. "Irish in the United States." *Catholic Encyclopedia*, Vol. I: 132–45.

Congress. House. "Emigration to U.S." *Special Consular Report*, Vol. 30: 160–62.

Congress. House. *Hearings before Subcommittee no. 1, Committee on the Judiciary, House of Representatives, Ninetieth Congress, Second Session: The Effect of the Act of October 3, 1965 on Immigration from Ireland and Northern Europe*. Washington, D.C.: Government Printing Office, 1968.

Congress. *Statutes of the United States of America passed at the First Session of the Sixty-Eighth Congress, 1923–1924, part 1 Public Acts and Resolutions*. Washington, D.C.: Government Printing Office, 1924.

Congress. *United States Statutes at Large, Containing the Laws and Concurrent Resolutions Enacted during the First Session of the Eighty-Ninth Congress of the United States, 1965*. Washington, D.C.: Government Printing Office, 1966.

Considine, Robert B. *It's the Irish*. Garden City, New York: Doubleday, 1961.

Cook, Adrian. *The Armies of the Streets*. The University Press of Kentucky, 1974.

Cormier, R. "Yesterday's Negro." *Sign* 47 (July 1968): 5–7.

34   Bibliography

Corry, John. *Golden Clan*. New York: Houghton Mifflin, 1977.

Costello, Augustine E. *Our Firemen: A History of the New York Fire Departments*. New York, 1887.

———. *Our Police Protectors: History of the New York Police*. New York, 1884.

Coughlin, Rev. Charles E. *Eight Lectures on Labor, Capital, and Justice*. Royal Oak, Michigan: Radio League of the Little Flower, 1934.

Coyle, John G. "American Irish Governors of Pennsylvania." *American Irish Historical Society Journal* 14 (1915): 145–61.

Crimmins, John D. *Irish-American Historical Miscellany*. New York: The Author, 1905.

Cronin, Joseph M. *The Control of Urban Schools: Perspective on the Power of Educational Reformers*. New York: Free Press, 1973.

Cross, R. D. "American Irish." *Commonwealth* 75 (March 6, 1964): 695–96.

———. "The Changing Image of the City among American Catholics." *Catholic Historical Review* 48 (1962): 33–52.

———. "The Irish." In *Ethnic Leadership in America*, edited by John Higham. Baltimore: Johns Hopkins University Press, 1978.

Crozier, Dorothy. "Kinship and Occupational Succession." *Sociological Review*. Series 13 (1954).

Cubberley, Ellwood P. "The School Situation in San Franicsco." *Educational Review* 21 (April 1901): 364–81.

Cuddy, E. "Are the Bolsheviks Any Worse Than the Irish? Ethno-Religious Conflict in America during the 1920s." *Eire-Ireland* 11, no. 3: 13–32.

Cullen, John H. *Young Ireland in Exile*. Dublin: 1928.

Curran, T. J. "The Irish Family in Nineteenth Century Urban America: The Role of the Catholic Church." *Working Papers*. Series 6, no. 2. Notre Dame, Indiana: Center for Studies in American Catholicism, Notre Dame University, 1979.

Curran, Thomas J. "From Paddy to the Presidency: The Irish in America." In *The Immigrant Experience in America*, edited by Frank J. Coopa and Thomas J. Curran. Boston: Twayne Publishers, 1976.

Curtain, Mary Alice. *Pilgrims All*. Milwaukee: Bruce, 1943.

Curtis, L. Perry, Jr. *Apes and Angels: The Irishman in Victorian Caricature*. Washington, D.C.: Smithsonian Institution Press, 1971.

Cusack, Mary Frances. *Advice to Irish Girls in America*. New York: Pustet, 1886.

Cushing, Archbishop Richard J. "The Irish in New England in the Seventeenth Century." *The Recorder* 14 (1952).

Daniels, John. *America Via the Neighborhood*. New York: Harper and Brothers, 1920.

Davie, Maurice R. *World Immigration with Special Reference to the United States*. 1936.

Davin, Nicholas F. *Irishmen in Canada*. London: S. Low, Marston and Co., 1877.

DeFord, Miriam Allen. *They Were San Franciscans*. Caldwell, Idaho: Caxton, 1941.

DeForest, R. W. and L. Veiller, eds. *Tenement House Problem*. New York: Macmillan, 1903.

Deming, Angus. "The American Connection." *Newsweek* 86 (December 2, 1976): 52.

Desmond, Humphrey Joseph. *The A.P.A Movement*. Washington, D.C.: New Century. 1912.

———. "Century of Irish Immigration." *American Monthly Review of Reviews* 22 (August 1900): 227–28.

———. "Century of Irish Immigration." *Catholic Quarterly* 25 (July 1900): 518–30.

Devine, E. T. "Ourselves and the Irish." *Survey* (May 7, 1921): 167–68.

Dickens, Charles. *American Notes*. London: MacGibbon and Kee, 1842.

Dilnot, F. "America and Ireland." *Lifing Age* 303 (October 11, 1919): 70–72.

Dinnerstein, Leonard, and Frederic C. Jaher, eds. *The Aliens: A History of Ethnic Minorities in America*. New York: Appleton Century-Crofts, 1970.

———, eds. *Uncertain Americans: Read-*

ings in Ethnic History. New York: Oxford University Press, 1977.

Dobie, Charles Caldwell. *San Francisco's Chinatown.* New York: D. Appleton-Century, 1936.

Dobkowski, Michael N. "American Anti-Semitism: A Reinterpretation." *American Quarterly* 29 (Summer 1977): 166–81.

Doerflinger, W. M. *Shantymen and Shantyboys.* New York: Macmillan, 1951.

Donohoe, J. "Gaelic Benevolence: An Interpretation." *American Catholic Hist. Society Records* 74 (June 1963): 67–69.

Donovan, H. D. A. "The Continuity of the Irish Idea." *American Irish Historical Society Journal* 28 (1930): 112–18.

Donovan, Kathleen. "Good Old Pat: An Irish-American Stereotype in Decline." In *Eire-Ireland* 15, no. 3 (1980): 6–14.

Douglass, J. N. H. "Emigration and Irish Peasant Life." *Ulster Folklife* 9 (1963).

Downing, F. "So They Tell Me." *Commonweal* 53 (April 6, 1951): 643–44.

Doyle, David Noel. *Irish American, Native Rights, and National Empires.* New York: Arno Press, 1976.

———. "The Irish in North America, 1776–1845." In *A New History of Ireland*, vol. 5, edited by T. W. Moody, F. X. Martin, and F. J. Byrne. New York: Oxford University Press, 1990.

Doyle, David Noel, and D. O. Edwards. *America and Ireland, 1776–1976.* Westport, Connecticut: Greenwood Press, 1980.

Doyle, L. F. "Irish Cavalcade." *Catholic World* 166 (March 1948): 522–29.

Doyle, T. F. "Negro in the Irish Empire." *Catholic World* 154 (February 1942): 536–44.

Dubnoff, Steven Jan. "The Family and Absence from Work: Irish Workers in a Lowell, Massachusetts Cotton Mill, 1860." Ph.D. dissertation, Brandeis University, 1976.

Duff, John B. *The Irish in the United States.* Belmont, California: Wadsworth Publishing Co., 1971.

Duffy, Brian, and Robin Knight. "A Fresh Irish Wave Laps U.S. Shores: 200,000 Illegals?" *U. S. News and World Report* (March 2, 1987).

Duffy, Sr. Vincent Marie. "Catholic Attitudes toward the Great Depression in America, 1929–1933." Master's thesis, University of Notre Dame, 1958.

Duis, P. "The Saloon and the City." Ph.D. dissertation, University of Chicago, 1975.

Duncan, Hannibal G. *Immigration and Assimilation.* Boston: D. C. Heath, 1933.

Duncan, Kenneth. "Irish Famine Immigration and the Social Structure of Canada West." *Canadian Review of Sociology and Anthropolohy* 2 (February 1965).

Dunleavy, G. W., and J. E. Dunleavy. "The Irish Abroad: Evidence from the O'Connor Papers." *Ethnicity* 2:3: 258–70.

Dunn, Edward S., S. J. "Mixed Marriages in 1947." *The American Ecclesiastical Review* 120 (1949).

Dunn, Joseph. "The Brendan Problem." *Catholic Historical Review* 6 (January 1921): 395–477.

Dwyer, Joseph J. "The Liberating of San Francisco: A Review of the Battle." *Cosmopolitan Magazine* 43 (August 1907): 442–44.

Early, Charles Montague. "Passenger Lists." *American Irish Historical Society Journal* 29 (1930–1931): 183–205.

"Early Irish Emigrants to America, 1803–1806." *Recorder* 3, no. 5 (June 1926): 19–23.

Eblen, Jack E. "An Analysis of Nineteenth Century Frontier Populations." *Demography* 2 (1965).

Edwards, Owen Dudley. "The American Image of Ireland: A Study of its Early Phases." In *Perspectives in American History* 4 (1970): 214–41.

———. "They Never Came Back." *America* 110 (March 14, 1964): 336–40.

Edwards, Ruth Dudley. *An Atlas of Irish History.* 2d ed. New York: Barnes and Noble, 1979.

Elazar, Daniel, and Murray Friedman. *Moving Up: Ethnic Succession in America: With a Case History from the Philadelphia School System.* New York: Institute on Pluralism and Group Identity, 1976.

Ellington, George. *The Women of New York.* New York: Vanguard Press, 1940.

Elliot, A. R. D. "Great Irish Conspiracy." *Edinburgh Review* 177: 257–81.

Emmet, Thomas Addis. *Irish Emigration during the Seventeenth and Eighteenth Centuries.* New York, 1899.

"English Taxation in America" (Money sent home by Irish). *North American Review* 145: 563–67.

Erickson, Charlotte. *American Industry and the European Immigrant, 1860–1885.* Cambridge: Harvard University Press, 1957.

Ethridge, Winter, III. "Flim Flamming Travellers Come Home for Winter Gambling Time." (Irish Tinkers in America) *Los Angeles Times.* November 16, 1973.

Fairchild, H. P. "The Distribution of Immigrants." *Yale Review* 16: 296–310.

Fairchild, Henry Pratt. *The Melting Pot Mistake.* Boston: Little, Brown, 1926.

Fairclough, Joseph W. *An Address Delivered before the Hibernian Society of Alexandria, D.C.* Alexandria, D.C., 1825.

Fallows, M. R. *Irish Americans: Identity and Assimilation.* Englewood Cliffs: Prentice-Hall, 1979.

Fanning, Charles. *Finley Peter Dunne and Mr. Dooley: The Chicago Years.* Lexington: University Press of Kentucky, 1978.

Farrand, Max. "Immigrant in the Light of History." *New Republic* 9 (December 23 and 29, 1916).

Farrell, James. *Give Us Your Poor.* Rulton-Hall, 1975.

Fell, S. Marie Lenore. *The Foundations of Nativism in American Textbooks, 1783–1860.* Washington, D.C.: The Catholic University of America Press, 1941.

"Fenian Society." *New International Encyclopedia,* Vol. 7.

Finney, P. B. "Real Lace." *Business Week* 10 (December 1, 1973).

Fisher, D. "Exporting Death to Ireland: Arms Purchased with American Donations." *Commonweal* 104 (June 10, 1977): 356–58.

Fitzgerald, James. "The Causes That Led to Irish Emigration." *American Irish Historical Society Journal* 10 (1911): 114–23.

Fleischer, Nat. *The Heavyweight Championship.* New York: Putnam and Sons, 1961.

Fleming, Donald, and Bernerd Bailyn, eds. "Dislocation and Emigration." *Perspectives in American History* 7, no. 4 (1973).

Fleming, Thomas J. "The Irish of '76." *Catholic Digest* 26 (March 1962): 57–62.

———. "The Policeman's Lot." *American Heritage* 21, no. 2 (February 1970): 4–9.

Flood, Chevalier, and W. H. Grattan. "Irish Emigration to the American Colonies, 1723 to 1773." *American Irish Historical Society Journal* 22 (1923): 204–6.

Florcken, Herbert G. "The Law and Order View of the San Francisco Committee of 1856." *California Historical Society Quarterly* (December 1935).

Foner, Eric. "Radicalism in the Gilded Age: The Land League and Irish-America." *Marxist Perspectives* (Summer 1978): 6–55.

Forbes, Allan. *Towns of New England and Old England, Ireland and Scotland: Connecting Links between Cities and Towns of New England and Those of the Same Name in England, Ireland, and Scotland: Containing Narratives, Descriptions, and Many Views, Some Done from Old Prints: Also Much Matter pertaining to the Founders and Settlers of New England and to Their Memorials on Both Sides of the Atlantic . . .* New York: Tudor, 1936.

Forbes, Henry A., and Henry Lee. *Massachusetts Help to Ireland during the Great Famine.* Salem, Massachusetts: Museum of the American China Trade, 1967.

Francis, John W. *Old New York or, Reminiscences of the Past Sixty Years.* New York, 1958.

Franklin (pseud.). *Know Nothingism; or, The American Party.* Boston, 1855.

Fried, Marc. *The World of the Urban Working Class.* Cambridge: Harvard University Press, 1973.

Friedman, D. J. *White Militancy in Boston.* Lexington, Massachusetts: Lexington Books, 1973.

"Friends of the I.R.A." *New Republic* 173 (October 18, 1975): 3–5.

Frisch, Michael H. *Town into City.* Cambridge: Harvard University Press, 1972.

Froude, J. A. "Romanism and the Irish Race in the United States." Parts 1, 2. *North American Review* 129, no. 277: 519–36, 130, no. 278: 31–50.

Fry, George T. "The Decline of Bigotry in America." *Current History* 27 (June 1928): 396–402.

Fry, James B. *New York and the Conscription of 1863*. New York: n. p., 1885.

Gallaway, Lowell E., and Richard K. Vedder. "The Increasing Urbanization Thesis—Did 'New Immigrants' to the United States Have a Particular Fondness for Urban Life." *Explorations in Economic History* 8 (Spring 1971).

Gallaway, Lowell E., Richard K. Vedder, and Vishwa Shukla. "Distribution of the Immigrant Population in the United States: An Economic Analysis." *Explorations in Economic History* 2, no. 3 (Spring 1974): 213–26.

"Galway Catholics as Settlers on Land of Washington's." *American Catholic Historical Researchers* 19 (1902): 128–31.

Gans, Herbert J. "Symbolic Ethnicity: The Future of Ethnic Groups and Cultures in America." In *On the Making of Americans: Essays in Honor of David Riesman*, edited by Herbert J. Gans, et al. Philadelphia: University of Pennsylvania Press, 1979.

Garraty, John A. *The New Commonwealth, 1877–1890*. New York: Harper and Row, 1968.

Gates, Paul W. *The Farmer's Age*. New York: Harper Torchbooks, 1960.

Gavin, J. "Irish Myth." *Forum* 87 (June 1932): 320–33.

Gayley, C. M. "Irish Influence on Civilization." *California University Chronicle* 11: 204–15.

George, Henry, Jr. *The Life of Henry George*. New York: Doubleday and McClure, 1900.

George, Henry. *Progress and Poverty*. New York: W. J. Black, 1942.

Gersman, Elinor M. "Progressive Reform of the St. Louis School Board, 1897." *History of Education Quarterly* 10 (Spring 1970): 3–21.

Ginsberg, Stephen. "The Police and Fire Protection in New York City, 1800–1850." *New York History* 52 (April 1971).

Gladden, W. "The Anti-Catholic Crusade." *Century Magazine* 47: 789–95.

Glanz, Rudolf. *Jew and Irish: Historic Group Relations and Immigration*. New York: Waldon Press, 1966.

Glazer, Nathan, and Daniel Patrick Moynihan. *Beyond the Melting Pot*. Cambridge: Massachusetts Institute of Technology Press, 1964.

———, eds. *Ethnicity*. Cambridge: Harvard University Press, 1974.

Gleason, P. "Thanks to the Irish." *America* 114 (May 14, 1966): 696–98.

Godfrey, Aaron W. "Irish Catholic Was Beautiful." *America* 123 (December 5, 1970): 493.

Godkin, E. L. "Irish-American Suspects." *Nation* 34: 264.

———. "Irish-Americans and England." *Nation* 36: 268.

Good, P. K. "Irish Adjustment to American Society: Integration or Separation? A Portrait of an Irish Catholic Parish, 1863–1886." *Records of American Catholic History Society*, Philadelphia, 1975.

Goodrich, Carter L. *Migration and Economic Opportunity*. Philadelphia: University of Pennsylvania, 1936.

Gordon, Milton M. *Assimilation in American Life: The Role of Race, Religion, and National Origins*. New York: Oxford University Press, 1964.

Gottlieb, David, and Virginia Sibbison. "Ethnicity and Religiousity: Some Selective Explorations among College Seniors." *The International Migration Review* 8 (Spring 1974): 43–57.

Gould, Benjamin Apthorp. *Investigations in the Military and Anthropological Statistics of American Soldiers*. New York: n. p., 1869.

Government of Ireland. *Commemorating Ireland's Participation in the World's Fair, New York, 1939*. Dublin: Browne and Nolan, 1940.

Government. "Irish Distress and Emigration." *U.S. Consular Reports* 9, no. 30 (April 1883): 627–41.

Government. "Irish Emigration Statistics for 1904." *U.S. Monthly Consumer and Trade Report*. No. 298 (July 1905): 97–98.

Grace, William R. *The Irish in America: A Lecture*. Chicago: McDonnell Brothers, 1886.

Graham, James M. "Irish Loyalty to American Institutions." *American Irish Historical Society Journal* 21 (1922): 164–71.

Grant, T. B. "Irish-Americans: Do They Hate England?" *American Monthly Civics* 7: 516.

———. "A New Ireland: A Reply to Lord Salisbury." *American Journal of Politics* 5: 30–55.

Grattan, E. A. "Irish in the United States." *North American Review* 51: 191.

Gray, David M. "The Protestant Ethic and Equal Opportunity for Working Class Whites: A Research Note." *Ethnicity* 2, no. 2 (June 1975): 225–28.

Gredel, Stephen. *Pioneers of Buffalo: Its Growth and Development*. Buffalo: Commission on Human Relations, Buffalo, 1966.

Greeley, Andrew M. "American Sociology and the Study of Ethnic Immigrant Groups." *International Migration Digest* 1, no. 2 (Fall 1964): 107–13.

———. *America's White Ethnic Groups*. New York: E. P. Dutton, 1975.

———. "Editoral." *Ethnicity* 2, no. 3 (September 1975): 229.

———. "The Ethnic and Relogous Origins of Young American Scientists and Engineers: A Research Note." *International Migration Review* 6 (1972): 282–89.

———. *Ethnicity, Denomination, and Inequality*. Beverly Hills, California: Sage Publications, 1976.

———. "Ethnicity as an Influence on Behavior." In *Ethnic Groups in the City: Culture, Institutions and Power*, edited by Otto Feinstein. (Lexington, Massachusetts: D. C. Heath, 1971).

———. "The Importance of a Neighborhood." *The Recorder: Irish-American Historical Society* 36 (1975): 80–87.

———. "Last of the American Irish Fade Away." *New York Times Magazine* (March 14, 1971): 32–34.

———. "Making It in America: Ethnic Groups and Social Status." *Social Policy* 4 (1973): 21–29.

———. *That Most Distressful Nation*. Chicago: Quadrangle Books, 1972.

———. *Neighborhoods*. Somers, Connecticut: Seabury Press, 1978.

———. "Occupational Choice among the American Irish." *Eire-Ireland* 7, no. 1 (1972): 3–9.

———. "Political Attitudes among White Ethnics." *Public Opinion Quarterly* 36 (1972): 213–20.

———. "The Success and Assimilation of Irish Protestants and Irish Catholics in the United States." *Sociology and Social Research: An International Journal* 72 (July 1988): 229–37.

———. *Why Can't They Be Like Us?* New York: E. P. Dutton, 1971.

Greeley, Andrew M., and Peter Rossi. *The Education of Catholic Americans*. Chicago: Aldine, 1966.

Greeley, Andrew M., and William C. McCready. "An Ethnic Group Which Vanished: The Strange Case of the American Irish." *Irish Journal of Social Studies* 1, no. 1 (January 1972): 39–50.

———. "Does Ethnicity Matter?" *Ethnicity* 1, no. 1 (1974): 91–108.

———. *Ethnicity in the United States*. New York: John Wiley and Sons, 1974.

———. "A Preliminary Reconnaissance Into the Persistence and Explanation of Ethnic Subcultural Drinking Patterns." *Medical Anthropology* 2, no. 4: 31–52.

———. "The Transmission of Cultural Heritages: The Case of the Irish and Italians." In *Ethnicity*, edited by Nathan Glazer and Daniel P. Moynihan, 209–35. Cambridge: Harvard University Press, 1975.

Green, James Jeremiah. "First Impact of the Henry George Agitation on Catholics in the United States." Master's thesis, University of Notre Dame, 1948.

Greene, Robert W. "Lost Identity." Review of *That Most Distressful Nation*, by Andrew M. Greeley. *Commentary* 55 (April 1973).

Greer, Colin, ed. *Divided Society: The Ethnic Experience in America*. New York: Basic Books, 1974.

Greer, Edward. "Toward a Structural Theory of Contemporary Working Class Culture." *Ethnicity* 3 no. 1 (March 1976): 4–18.

Greer, Scott, and Ann Lennarson Greer, eds.

Neighborhood and Ghetto. New York: Basic Books, 1974.

Gregory, A. "Coming of the Irish Players." *Collier's* 48:15.

Grinnell, C. E. "Warning to the Irish-American Lawyers." *American Law Review* 16:540.

Griscom, John. *The Sanitary Condition of the Laboring Population of New York.* New York: Harper, 1845.

Gross, H. B. *Aliens or Americans.* New York: Eaton, 1906.

Guillet, Edwin C. *Great Migration: Atlantic Crossing by Sailing Ship since 1770.* Toronto: University of Toronto Press, 1963.

Guinther, J. "Has Anybody Here Seen Paddy?" *Philadelphia Magazine* 63, no. 3 (1972): 150–63.

Gusfield, Joseph. *Symbolic Crusade: Status Politics and the American Temperance Movement.* Urbana, Illinios: University of Illinois Press, 1966.

Hackett, James Dominick. *How to Trace Your Irish Relatives and Ancestors.* New York: American Irish Historical Society, n.d.

Hackett, James Dominick, and Charles Montague Early. *Passenger Lists from Ireland.* Baltimore: Genealogical Society, 1965.

Hackett, F. "Irish in America." *Nation* 98 (April 5, 1958): 662–63.

Hale, E. E. *Letters on Irish Emigration.* Boston: Phillips, 1852.

Hall, P. F. *Immigration.* New York: Holt, 1907.

Haller, John S. "Civil War Anthropometry: The Making of a Racial Ideology." *Civil War History* 16 (December 1970): 309–24.

Halliday, G. "St. Patrick's Folk in America." *Catholic World* 110: 787–95.

Halliday, Samuel B. *The Little Street Sweeper or Life among the Poor.* New York: Phinney, Blakeman & Mason, 1861.

Hancock, Dr. "On the Remittances from North America by Irish Emigrants." *Journal of the Statistical and Social Inquiry Society of Ireland* 6 (January 1871): 280–90.

Handlin, Oscar. *Boston's Immigrants: 1790–1865: A Study in Acculturation.* Cambridge: The Belknap Press of Harvard University Press, 1941. Rev. and enl. ed.

———. *Boston's Immigrants: 1790–1880: A Study in Acculturation.* Cambridge: The Belknap Press of Harvard University Press, 1959.

———. "Immigrant in American Politics." In *Foreign Influences in American Life,* edited by David F. Bowers, 84–98. Princeton: Princeton University Press, 1944.

———. "The Immigrant Contribution." In *Problems in American History,* edited by R. W. Leopold and A. W. Link, 643–90. Englewood Cliffs, New Jersey: Prentice Hall, 1952.

———. "The New History and Ethnic Factor in American Life." *Perspectives in American History* 4 (1970).

———. *Race and Nationality in American Life.* Boston: Little, Brown, 1957.

———. *The Uprooted: The Epic Story of the Great Migrations that Made the American People.* Boston: Little, Brown, 1951. 2d ed., enl. Boston: Little, Brown, 1973.

———, ed. *Children of the Uprooted.* New York: G. Braziller, 1966.

———, ed. *Immigration as a Factor in American History.* Englewood Cliffs, New Jersey: Prentice-Hall, 1959. Extended version of "The Immigrant Contribution," above.

"Hands Off to Irish-Americans." *Literary Digest* 69, no. 18 (June 25, 1921).

Hansen, Marcus Lee. *The Atlantic Migration, 1607–1860.* Cambridge: Harvard University Press, 1940.

———. *The Immigrant in American History.* Cambridge: Harvard University Press, 1940.

Hareven, Tamara K., ed. *Anonymous Americans.* Englewood Cliffs, New Jersey: Prentice-Hall, 1971.

———. *Family and Kin in Urban Communities, 1700–1930.* New York: New Viewpoints, 1977.

Hareven, Tamara K., and Maris A. Vinovskis. "Marital Fertility, Ethnicity, and Occupation in Urban Families: An Analysis of South Boston and the South End in

1880." *Journal of Social History* (Spring 1975).

Harper, J., and C. Hudson. "Irish Traveler Chant in Its Social Setting." (Irish Tinkers). *Southern Folklore Quarterly* 37 (June 1973): 101–14.

Harrison, Leonard Vance. *Police Administration in Boston*. Cambridge, Massachusetts, 1934.

Hart, A. B., ed. *The Commonwealth History of Massachusetts*. New York, 1930.

Hartt, R. L. "More Irish than Ireland, New York." *Independent and Weekly Review* 106 (August 20, 1921): 68–69.

Harvey, E. "Emigration from Ireland in 1902 and 1903." *U.S. Consular Reports*, no. 290 (November 1904): 136.

Haskin, Frederic J. *The Immigrant, an Asset and a Liability?* New York: Revell, 1913.

Hattman, Edward G. *Movement to Americanize the Immigrant*. 1948.

Hatton, J. "Irish Questions in America." *Day in America* 1 (1882).

Headley, Joel Tyler. *The Great Riots of New York, 1712–1873*. New York: Bobbs-Merrill Co., 1970.

Healy, T. F. "No More Irish Will Apply." *Saturday Evening Post* 210, no. 25 (January 1, 1938).

Hearst, William R. *Selections from the Writings and Speeches of William R. Hearst*. San Francisco: Hearst, 1948.

Hedges, James B. *Building the Canadian West: The Land and Colonization Policies of the Canadian Pacific Railway*. New York: Macmillan, 1939.

Heer, David M. "The Marital Status of Second-Generation Americans." *American Sociological Review* 26, no. 2 (1961): 233–41.

Hellwig, D. J. "Black Attitudes towards Irish Immigrants." *Mid-America* 59, no. 1:39–49.

Hencken, Hugh O'Neill. "What Are Pattee's Caves? Are They the Remains of a Medieval Irish Monastery in New Hampshire As Is Claimed?" *Scientific American* 163 (1940): 258–59.

Herberg, Will. *Protestant-Catholic-Jew*. New York: Doubleday, 1960.

Herlihy, Reverend Cornelius J. *The Celt above the Saxon, or a Comparative Sketch of the Irish and English People in War, in Peace, and in Their Character*. Boston: Angel Guardian Press, 1904.

Hernon, Joseph M., Jr. *Celts, Catholics and Copperheads*. Ohio State University Press, 1968.

Hershberg, Theodore. "Occupation and Ethnicity in Five Nineteenth-Century Cities: A Collaborative Inquiry." *Historical Methods Newsletter* 7 (June 1974).

"Hibernians on History." *Time* 30: 68 (September 6, 1937).

Hibernicus. *What Brings So Many Irish to America!* New York: The Author, 1845.

Higgins, P., and F. V. Connolly. *The Irish in America*. London: John Ouseley, 1909.

Higham, John. *From Boundlessness to Consolidation: The Transformation of American Culture, 1848–1860*. Ann Arbor, Michigan: William L. Clements Library, 1969.

———. *Strangers in the Land*. New York: Atheneum, 1969.

Hirsch, Arnold. "Race and Housing: Violence and Communal Protest in Chicago, 1940–1960." In *The Ethnic Frontier*, edited by Melvin G. Holli and Peter d'A. Jones. Grand Rapids, Michigan: Eerdmans, 1977.

Hitchman, Robert, and William Jones Wassrich. "Names and Places." *Western Folklore* 8 (October 1949): 366–70.

Hofstadter, Richard. *The Age of Reform*. New York: Vintage Books, Random House, 1955.

Hofstadter, Richard, and Michael Wallace. *American Violence*. New York: Vintage Books, 1971.

Hogan, James Francis. *The Irish in America*. London, 1887.

Hogan, Peter E. *The Catholic University of America, 1896–1903: The Rectorship of Thomas J. Conaty*. Washington, D.C.: The Catholic University of America Press, 1949.

Holiday, Carl. "St. Patrick's Folk in America." *Catholic World* 10 (March 1920): 787–95.

Holli, Melvin G., and Peter d'A. Jones., eds. *The Ethnic Frontier*. Grand Rapids, Michigan: Eerdmans, 1977.

Social Adjustment, Ethnicity, General 41

Hotten, J. C., ed. *Original Lists of Persons of Quality, Emigrants. . . and Others Who Went from Great Britain to the American Plantations, 1600–1700*. London: Chatto, 1874.

Howe, Frederic C. *The City*. New York: Scribner's, 1914.

Howe, Walter Henry. *Irish Wit and Humor*. Philadelphia: Jacobs and Co., 1898.

Hueston, Robert Francis. "The Catholic Press and Nativism, 1840–1860." Ph.D. dissertation, University of Notre Dame, 1972.

Hull, J. "Irish in America." *Chaut* 8 (1887): 31–33.

Hunt, George W. "Of Many Things (Irish America)." *America* 153 (November 15, 1985).

Hunt, Henry M. *The Crime of the Century or the Assassination of Dr. Patrick Henry Cronin*. Chicago: Kochersperger, 1899.

Hunter, Robert J. "Dublin to Boston, 1719." *Eire-Ireland* 6, no. 2:18–24.

Hurley, Doran. "Irish Persecutions in America." *American History* 47 (May 1939): 49–55.

Hutchinson, E. *Young Sam: Or, Native American's Own Book*. New York, 1855.

Hyman, Harold M., and Leonard W. Levy, eds. *Freedom and Reform*. New York: Harper and Row, 1967.

Ibson, John Duffy. "Will the World Break Your Heart? A Historical Analysis of the Dimensions and Consequences of Irish American Assimilation." Ph.D. dissertation, Brandeis University, 1976.

"From Ireland to Castle Garden." In *Irish American Almanac for 1881*. New York: Lynch, Cole and Meehan, 1880.

"Irish-American or Just Americans." *World's Work* 38 (August 1919): 249–50.

"Irish-Americans: Their Position and Influence." *Westminster Review* 133 (March 1890): 290–91.

"Irish in America." *Life* 50 (March 17, 1961): 88–96; (March 24, 1961): 114–23.

"Irish in American History." *Mentor* 9 (April 1921): 31.

"The Irish Element in Our Population." *World's Work* 39 (October 1919): 576.

"Irish Emigrant Societies." *Nile's Register* 14: 211–15.

"Irish in Our Public Life." *Nation* 98 (March 26, 1914): 320–21.

Jackson, J. A. "Migration, Editorial Introduction." In *Migration*, edited by J. A. Jackson. New York: Cambridge University Press, 1969.

Jackson, Kenneth R. *The Ku Klux Klan in the City*. New York: Oxford University Press, 1967.

Jenkins, Thomas J. *Six Seasons in Our Prairies and Six Weeks in Our Rockies*. Louisville, Kentucky: C. A. Rogers, 1884.

Jenks, Albert E. "Types of Important Racial Information Which Teachers of Americanization Should Possess—Abstracts." *NEA Addresses and Proceedings* 62d Annual Meeting. Washington, D.C., 1924.

Jitodai, Ted T. "Migrant Status and Church Attendence." *Social Forces* 43 (December 1964): 241–48.

Johnson, James E. *The Irish in America*. Minneapolis: Lerner, 1966.

Johnson, Stanely C. *A History of Emigration from the United Kingdom to North America, 1763–1912*. London: Rutledge, 1912.

Johnston, H. M. J. *British Emigration Policy, 1815–1830*. Oxford: Clarendon Press, 1972.

Jolly, Ellen Ryan. "The Irish Element in America." *American Irish Historical Society Journal* 10 (1911): 215–32.

Jones, Maldwyn Allen. *American Immigration*. Chicago: University of Chicago Press, 1960.

Jones, Howard Mumford. *O Strange New World*. New York: Viking Press, 1968.

Jones, Maldwyn Allen. *Destination America*. New York: Holt, Rinehart and Winston, 1976.

Jones, Thomas Jesse. *The Sociology of a New York City Block*. New York: Columbia University Press, 1904.

Joyce, William Leonard. "Editors and Ethnicity: A History of the Irish-American Press, 1848–1883." Ph.D. dissertation, University of Michigan, 1974.

Judson, E.Z.C. *Mysteries and Miseries of New York*. New York: Berford, 1848.

Kaestle, Carl F. "The Origins of an Urban School System: New York City, 1750–1850." Ph.D. dissertation, Harvard University, 1970.

Kahn, E. J., Jr. *The Merry Partners: The Age and Stage of Harrigan and Hart*. New York: Random House, 1955.

Kapp, Friedrich. *European Emigration to the U.S.* New York: Nation Press, 1869.

Kapp, Freidrich. "Immigration." *Journal of Social Science*, no. 2 (1870): 1–30.

Katz, Michael B. *The Irony of Early School Reform*. Boston: Beacon Press, 1968.

———. "The People of a Canadian City, 1851–52." *Canadian Historical Review* 53 (1972).

———. *The People of Hamilton, Canada West*. Cambridge: Harvard University Press, 1975.

Keenan, C. "A Challenge to Irish-Americans: Civil Rights for Negroes." *Interracial Review* 37 (May 1964): 102.

Keenan, C. "On Being Irish in America." *America* 94 (March 17, 1956): 658–60.

Keehan, M. J. "The Irish Catholic Beneficial Societies Founded between 1818 and 1869." Ph.D. dissertation, The Catholic University of America, 1953.

Kelleher, John V. "Communication." *New Republic* 110 (April 10, 1974): 501–2.

———. "Irishness in America." *Atlantic* 208 (1961): 38–40.

———. "A Long Way from Tipperary." *Reporter* 22 (May 12, 1960): 44–46.

Keller, Morton. *The Art and Politics of Thomas Nast*. London: Oxford University Press, 1968.

Kelly, J. *The History of the Early Irish Settlers in America*. New York: P. J. Kenedy, 1884.

Kelly, R. J. "The First Irishman in America." *American Irish Historical Society Journal* 29 (1930–31): 35–48.

Kelton, Jane Gladden. "New York City's St. Patrick's Day Parade: Invention of Contention and Consensus." *The Drama Review* 29 (Fall 1985): 93–107.

Kennedy, R. E., Jr. "Selective Migration and the Acculturation of Immigrants: The Overseas Irish Family." *Working Paper*. Series 4:1. Center for the Study of American Catholicism, Notre Dame University, 1978.

Kennedy, Robert E. *The Irish*. Berkeley: University of California Press, 1973.

Kennedy, Ruby Jo Reeves. "Single or Triple Melting-Pot?: Intermarriage Trends in New Haven, 1870–1940." *American Journal of Sociology* 49 (1944): 333.

Kennett, Lee. *The French Forces in America, 1780–1783*. Westport: Greenwood Press, 1977.

Kerhan, J. Frank. *Reminiscences of the Old Fire Laddies and Volunteer Fire Departments of New York and Brooklyn*. New York: 1885.

Keyes, Charles F. "Towards a New Formulation of the Concept of Ethnic Group." *Ethnicity* 3, no. 3 (September, 1976): 202–13.

Kiefer, Michael. "Games from the Old Sod; Gaelic Football and Hurling Have a Fond Following in Chicago." *Sports Illustrated* 67 (August 24, 1987): 82–85.

Kiley, Danile Urban. "Staging History's Greatest Trial." *The Recorder: Irish-American Historical Society* 36 (1975): 95–115.

Killen, J. B. *The Irish Question*. New York: Ford's National Library, 1886.

Klatzy, Sheila R. "Patterns of Contact with Relatives." *Monography Series*. New York, 1973.

Knabenshue, S. S. "Irish Emigration." *U.S. Consular Reports*, no. 297 (January 1905): 24–25.

Knobel, Dale T. *Paddy and the Republic: Ethnicity and Nationality in Antebellum America*. Middletown, Connecticut: Wesleyan University Press, 1986.

———. "Paddy and the Republic: Popular Images of the American Irish, 1820–60." Ph.D. dissertation, Northwestern University, 1976.

———. "A Vocabulary of Ethnic Perception: Content Analysis of the American Stage Irishman." *Perspectives in American History* 4 (1970).

Kolm, Richard. "Documentation: Ethnicity and Ethnic Groups: Research Needs." *International Migration Review* 8 (Spring 1974): 59–67.

Lane, Robert. "James Jeffrey Roche and the

Boston Pilot." *New England Quarterly* 33 (September 1960): 341–63.

Lass, William E. *From the Missouri to the Great Salt Lake*. Nebraska: Nebraska State Historical Society, 1969.

Latrobe, C. J. *The Rambler in North America in 1832–1833*. 2 vols. 1836.

Laumann, Edward O. *Bonds of Pluralism*. New York: Wiley-Interscience, 1973.

———. *Prestige and Association in an Urban Community*. New York: Bobbs-Merrill, 1966.

———. *Social Stratification*. New York: Bobbs-Merrill, 1970.

Lazerson, Marvin. *Origins of the Urban School: Public Education in Massachusetts, 1870–1915*. Cambridge: Harvard University Press, 1971.

Leaming, R. E. "Study of a Small Group of Irish-American Children." *Psychological Clinic* 15 (March 1923): 18–40.

Lebow, Richard Ned. *White Britain and Black Ireland: The Influence of Stereotypes on Colonial Policy*. Philadelphia: Ishi Publications, 1977.

Lecky, W. "American Celt and His Critics." *Catholic World* 63 (January 1896): 55–69.

Lecky, W. "Irish in America." *Catholic World* 63 (1896): 355.

Lee, Brother Basil Leo. *Discontent in New York City, 1861–1865*. Washington, D.C, 1943.

LeRee, P. de. *The American Republican Songster*. New York: n.p., 1843.

Leslie, Sir Shane. "Celt, the Saxon, and the New Scene." *Living Age* 293 (June 9, 1917): 586–94.

———. "German and Irish Element in the American Melting Pot." *Dublin Review* 163 (October 1918): 258–83.

Levin, Jack. *The Functions of Prejudice*. New York: Harper and Row, 1975.

Levy, Mark R., and Michael S. Kraemer. *The Ethnic Factor*. New York: Simon and Schuster, 1973.

Lieberson, Stanley. *Ethnic Patterns in American Cities*. New York: Free Press of Glencoe, 1963.

Light, Ivan H. *Ethnic Enterprise in America*. Berkeley: University of California Press, 1972.

Limpus, Lowell M. *History of the New York Fire Department*. New York: Dutton, 1940.

Linehan, John C., and T. H. Murray. *Irish Schoolmasters in the American Colonies, 1640–1775*. Washington, D.C.: American-Irish Historical Society, 1898.

Linehan, John J. "The Society of the Friendly Sons of St. Patrick." *American Irish Historical Society Journal* 7 (1907): 183–88.

"Lists of Servants Who Sailed from Dublin, 1746–1747, on the *Eruyal*, and Arrived in Philadelphia." *Pennsylvania Magazine of History and Biography* 26 (1902): 287.

Litt, Edgar. *Ethnic Politics in America*. Glenview, Illinois: Scott, Foresman, 1970.

Littlejohn, Edward. "An American Letter." *Dublin Review*, no. 441 (Autumn 1947): 119.

Litwak, Eugene. "Geographic Mobility and Extended Family Cohesion." *American Sociological Review* 25 (1960): 385–94.

Lockhart, Audrey. *Some Aspects of Emigration from Ireland to the North American Colonies between 1660 and 1775*. New York: Arno Press, 1976.

London, H. "The Irish and American Nativism in New York City, 1843–47." *Dublin Review* 240 (Winter 1967): 378–94.

Loneregan, Thomas S. "The Irish Chapter in American History." *American Irish Historical Society Journal* 11 (1912): 109–21.

Lowe, David. "St. Patrick's Day, 1961." *Commonweal* 74 (April 21, 1962): 98–99.

Luckingham, Bradford. "Benevolence in Emergent San Francisco: A Note on Immigrant Life in the Urban Far West." *Southern California Quarterly* 55 (Winter 1973): 431–33.

———. "Immigrant Life in Emergent San Francisco." *Journal of the West* 12 (October 1973): 600–17.

Lyell, C. *A Second Visit to the United States of America*. 3 volumes. London: 1849.

MacCabe, James. *Secrets of the Great City: A Work Descriptive of the Virtues and Vices, the Mysteries, Miseries, and Crimes of New York City*. Philadelphia: National, 1868.

MacDonagh, Oliver. "Irish Emigration to the

United States of America and the British Colonies during the Famine." In *The Great Famine*, edited by Robert Dudley Edwards and T. Desmond Williams. Dublin: Browne and Nolan, 1956.

———. "The Irish Famine Emigration to the United States." *Perspectives in American History* 10 (1976): 379–82.

———. "The Irish in Victoria, 1851–91: A Demographic Essay." *Historical Studies: Papers Read before the Irish Conference of Historians*. Dublin: Gill and Macmillan, 1971.

MacManus, Seamus. *The Story of the Irish Race*. New York: Irish Publishing Co., 1921.

Madden, Richard R. *The United Irishmen, Their Lives and Times*. London: Catholic, 1860.

Maginnis, Thomas Hobbs, Jr. *The Irish Contribution to America's Independence*. Philadelphia: Diore Publishing Co., 1913.

Magnuson, Ed. "The Re-Greening of America: A New Wave of Irish Immigrants Is Showing Its Muscle." *Time* 133 (March 20, 1989): 30.

Maguire, Edward J., ed. *Reverend John O'Hanlon's, The Irish Emigrant's Guide for the United States: A Critical Edition with Introduction and Commentary*. New York: Arno Press, 1976.

Maguire, John Francis. *The Irish in America*. London: Longmans, Green, 1868.

Mahoney, Dorah. *Six Months in a House of Correction*. Boston: 1835.

Maisel, A. Q. "Irish Among U.S." *Reader's Digest* 66 (May 1955): 161–66.

Man, Alban P., Jr. "Labor Competition and the New York Draft Riots of 1863." *Journal of Negro History* 36 (October 1951): 375–405.

Manning, Biship T. "Irish Currents in America." *Information* 67 (March 1953): 10–15.

Mannion, John J. *Irish Settlements in Eastern Canada*. Toronto: University of Toronto Press, 1974.

Maquire, E. "Irish in America." *Historical Bulletin* 35 (November 1956): 22–30.

Marron, V. *My American Visit*. Dublin: Clonmore and Reynolds, 1951.

Martin, Asa. "The Temperance Movement in Pennsylvania prior to the Civil War." *Penn Magazine of History and Biography* 49 (1925): 195–230.

Marty, E. M. "Ethnicity: The Skeleton of Religion in America." *Church History* 41 (1972).

May, Henry Farnham. *Protestant Churches and Industrial America*. New York: Scribner's, 1949.

Mayo-Smith, R. *Emigration and Immigration*. New York: Scribner's, 1898.

McCabe, James D. *New York by Sunlight and Gaslight*. New York, 1881.

McCaffrey, Lawrence J. "The Conservative Image of Irish-America." *Ethnicity* 2 (1975):271–80.

———. *The Irish Diaspora in America*. Bloomington: Indiana University Press, 1976.

———. "Pioneers of the Ghetto." *Illinois Quarterly* 34 (1971): 31–42.

McCartan, Patrick. *With De Valera in America*. New York: Brentano's, 1932.

McCarthy, J. "The Gra-a-nd Parade." *American Heritage* 20, no. 2 (1969): 54–59.

McCarthy, Justin. *A History of Our Own Times*. New York: A. L. Burt, 1887.

McDonnell, Virginia B. *The Irish Helped Build America*. New York: Julian Messner, 1968.

McElroy, Robert McNutt. "Address." *American Irish Historical Society Journal* 13 (1914): 72–80.

McGee, T. D'Arcy. *History of the Irish Settlers in North America*. Boston: Donnahoe, 1852.

———. *The Irish Position in British and Republican North America*. Montreal: Longmoore, 1866.

McQuade, Molly. "Irish-American Siamsa (High School for the Humanities, New York)." *Dance Magazine* 63 (August 1989).

McSeveney, Samuel T. "Ethnic Groups, Ethnic Conflicts, and Recent Quantitative Research in American Political History." *International Migration Review* 7, no. 1 (Spring 1973): 15–33.

Meehan, Thomas F. "Archbishop Hughes and the Draft Riots." *United States Catholic *Historical Society Historical Records and Studies* 1 (1900): 171–90.

———. "First Irish Emigrant Society." *U. S. Catholic* 2: 202–211.

———. "First Irish Emigrant Society, 1817." *U.S. Catholic Historical Society* 6, pt. 2: 267–88.

Meister, Richard J., ed. *Race and Ethnicity in Modern America.* Lexington, Massachusetts: D. C. Heath, 1974.

Merritt, E. Percival. "Sketches of the Three Earliest Roman Catholic Priests in Boston." *Publications of the Colonial Society of Massachusetts* 25.

Merwick, Donna. *Boston Priests.* Cambridge: Harvard University Press, 1973.

Merwin, H. C. "Irish in American Life." *Atlantic Monthly* 77 (March 1896): 289–301.

Miller, David W. "Irish Catholicism and the Great Famine." *Journal of Social History* 9 (Fall 1975): 81–98.

Miller, Kerby A. *Emigrants and Exiles: Ireland and the Irish Exodus to North America.* New York: Oxford University Press, 1985.

Miller, Kerby A., Bruce Boling, and David N. Doyle. "Emigrants and Exiles: Irish Cultures and Irish Emigration to North America, 1790–1922." *Irish Historical Studies* 22 (September 1980): 97–125.

Miller, W. C. "Irish-Americans." *A Comprehensive Bibliography for the Study of American Minorities* 1: 381–422. New York: New York University Press, 1976.

Mitchell, Albert Gibbs, Jr. "Irish Family Patterns in Nineteenth-Century Ireland and Lowell, Massachusetts." Ph.D. dissertation, Boston University Graduate School, 1976.

Modell, John, and Tamara K. Hareven. "Urbanization and the Malleable Household: An Examination of Boarding and Lodging in America Families." *Journal of Marriage and the Family* 35 (1976).

Mohl, Raymond A. "Education as Social Control in New York City, 1784–1825." *New York History* 51 (April 1970): 219–37.

Monroe, Day. *Chicago Families.* Chicago: University of Chicago Press.

Moody, Theodore William. "Irish and Scotch-Irish in Eighteenth-Century America." *Studies: An Irish Quarterly Review* 35 (1946): 123–40.

Mooney, Thomas. *Nine Years in America: In a Series of Letters to His Cousin, Patrick Mooney.* Dublin: McGlashan, 1850.

Morehouse, Frances. "The Irish Migration of the 'Forties.'" *American Historical Review* 33 (April 1928): 579–92.

Morgan, J. H. "Ethnoconsciousness and Political Powerlessness: Boston's Irish." *Social Science* 53 (1978).

Morganthau, Tom. "The Jittery 'Other Illegals': European-Born Aliens Also Face Hard Choices." *Newsweek* 110 (October 5, 1987).

Moriarty, Thomas Francis. "The Truth Teller and Irish Americans of the 1820's." *American Catholic Historical Society Records* 75 (March 1964): 39–52.

Morrissey, J. "Mike Barry's Personal Newspaper." *Catholic Digest* 25 (October 1961): 123–28.

Morrow, R. L. "Negotiation of the Anglo-American Treaty of 1870." *American Historical Review* 39 (July 1934): 663–81.

Morse, Samuel Finley Breese. *Imminent Dangers to the Free Institutions of the United States through Foreign Immigration.* New York: Clayton, 1835.

Moynihan, Daniel P., ed. *On Understanding Poverty.* New York: Basic Books, 1969.

Moynihan, Kenneth James. "History as a Weapon for Social Advancement: Group History as Told by Jewish, Irish, and Black American, 1892–1950." Ph.D. dissertation, Clark University, 1973.

Mulloy, M. J. *Irish in America 1000 Years before Columbus.* Boston: Angel Guardian Press, 1906.

Munroe, Day. *Chicago Families: A Study of Unpublished Census Data.* Chicago: Chicago University Press, 1932.

Murphy, J. J. "Call for Irish-American Honest Self-Appraisal." *Homiletic and Pastoral Review* 54 (March 1954): 509–13.

Murphy, John C. "Attitudes of American Catholics toward the Immigrant and the Negro." Master's thesis, The Catholic University of America, 1940.

Murphy, Richard C., and Lawrence J. Mannion. *The History of the Society of the Friendly Sons of Saint Patrick in the City of New York, 1784 to 1955.* New York: Society of the Friendly Sons of St. Patrick of New York City, 1962.

Murphy, Thomas A. "Freedom's Indivisibility." *The Recorder: Irish-American Historical Society* 36 (1975): 23–27.

Murray, Charles A. *Travels in North America.* London: n.p., 1854.

Murray, K. "Voluntary Association among the Irish." Master's thesis, The Catholic University of America, 1967.

Murray, Thomas Hamilton. "The Irish Chapter in the History of Brown University." *American Irish Historical Society Journal* 2 (1899).

Muscatine, Doris. *Old San Francisco: The Biography of a City from Early Days to the Earthquake.* New York: Putnam, 1975.

Myers, A. C. *Immigration of the Irish Quakers into Pennsylvania, 1692–1750.* Pennsylvania: Swarthmore, 1902.

Myers, G. *History of Bigotry in the United States.* New York: Random House, 1943.

Myers, John M. *San Francisco's Reign of Terror.* Garden City, New York: Doubleday, 1966.

Nam, Charles B. "Nationality Groups and Social Stratification in America." *Social Forces* 37 (1959): 328–33.

"The 'Native American' Riots of 1844." *American Catholic Historical Researches* 8 (1891): 89–90.

Neal, Larry, and Paul Uselding. "Immigration, a Neglected Source of American Economic Growth: 1790 to 1792." *Oxford Economic Papers,* series 2, vol. 24 (1972): 68–88.

Nelson, Murray. "Ethnic Studies Programs: Some Historical Antecedents." *Social Studies* 68 (May/June 1977): 104–8.

Nevin, D. D. "Irish and Scotch in the United States." *Mecreburg Review* 3: 239.

Newman, William M. *American Pluralism, a Study of Minority Groups and Social Theory.* New York, 1973.

Nolte, William Michael. "The Irish in Canada, 1815–1867." Ph.D. dissertation, University of Maryland, 1975.

Noonan, Carroll J. *Nativism in Connecticut, 1829–1860.* Washington, D.C.: The Catholic University of America Press, 1938.

Nuesse, Celestine J., and Thomas J. Harte. *The Sociology of the Parish.* Milwaukee: Bruce Publishing Company, 1951.

Nunis, Doyce B., ed. *San Francisco Vigilance Committee of 1856.* Los Angeles, 1971.

O'Brien, C. G. O. "The Emigrant in New York." *Nineteenth Century* 16: 530–49.

O'Brien, George. "Irish in the American Melting-Pot." *Studies: An Irish Quarterly Review* 35 (September 1946): 343–50.

O'Brien, Michael J. "Chapter of Irish Charity in Thanksgiving History." *American Irish Historical Society Journal* 18 (1919): 163–68.

———. "The Commander-in-Chief's Guard." *American Irish Historical Society Journal* 27 (1928): 172–75.

———. *George Washington's Associations with the Irish.* New York: Kennedy, 1937.

———. *A Hidden Phase of American History.* New York: Dodd, Mead and Company, 1919.

———. "How the Descendants of Irish Settlers in America Were Written into History as 'Anglo-Saxons' and 'Scotch-Irish.'" *American Irish Historical Society Journal* 18 (1919): 99–109.

———. "Immigration, Land, Probate, Administration, Baptismal, Marriage, Burial, Trade, Military, and Other Records of the Irish in America in the Seventeenth and Eighteenth Centuries." *American Irish Historical Society Journal* 14 (1915): 163–268.

———. "An Interesting Example of the Extent of Irish Emigrations to the American Colonies." *American Irish Historical Society Journal* 27 (1928): 179–83.

———. "Irish in America in the Eighteenth Century." *Catholic World* 164 (October 1946): 58–65.

———. "The Irish in the American Colonies." *American Irish Historical Society Journal* 22 (1923).

———. *Irish Firsts in American History: Delivered at the Hotel LaSalle under the Auspices of the Illinois Chapter, April 28, 1917.* New York: Irish American Historical Society, 1917.

———. "Irish Pioneers and Schoolmasters in Butler County, Pennsylvania." *Ameri-*

can *Irish Historical Society Journal* 18 (1919): 198–204.

———. "Irish Schoolmasters in the American Colonies." *American Irish Historical Society Journal* 25 (1926): 35–61.

———. "Items Culled from the National Gazette and Literary Register." *American Irish Historical Society Journal* 27 (1928): 184–89.

———. "Some Examples of the 'Scotch-Irish' in America." *American Irish Historical Society Journal* 14 (1915): 269–79.

———. "Some Irish School Masters of Old New York and a Few Irish School Mistresses of Its Early Days." *Recorder* 3, no. 7 (December 1926): 6–8.

———. "Washington's Irish Friends." *American Irish Historical Society Journal* 25 (1926): 344–68.

O'Brien, S. "Dreamers." *Commonweal* 20 (June 1, 1934): 127–28.

O'Connor, F. "Opinion: On Writing about America." *Mademoiselle* 64 (April 1967).

O'Connor, R. C. "The Irish Element in American." *American Irish Historical Society Journal* 9 (1910): 451–62.

O'Connor, Sister Mary Catherine. "The Good Earth of My Ancestors." *Catholic World* 189 (May 1959): 101–5.

O'Dea, John. *History of the Ancient Order of Hibernians and Ladies' Auxiliary*. Philadelphia: Keystone Printing Co., 1923.

O'Donnell, Elliot. *The Irish Abroad*. New York: Putnam and Sons, 1915.

O'Donnell, John Hugh. "The Catholic Church in Northern Indiana, 1830–1857." *The Catholic Historical Review* 25 (1941): 134–45.

O'Donoghue, D. J. *Geographical Distribution of Irish Ability*. New York: Benziger, 1906.

O'Donovan, Jeremiah. *A Brief Account of the Author's Interview with His Countrymen*. Pittsburgh: The Author, 1864. Many later editions.

———. *Irish Immigration in the United States: Immigrant Interviews*. Pittsburgh: The Author, 1864.

O'Donovan, Patrick. "In Search of the Irish." *Observer*. (August 24, 1969): 7.

O'Dwyer, George Francis. "Irish Names in New England Records." *American Irish Historical Society Journal* 19 (1920): 89–91.

O'Dwyer, George. "Irish Migrations to America, 1861–1865." *American Irish Historical Society Journal* 30 (1932): 118–21.

O'Fahey, Charles J. "Reflections on the St. Patrick's Day Orations of John Ireland." *Ethnicity* 2 (1975): 244–57.

O'Farrell, Charles. "Irish Family Names Anglicised and Altered." *American Irish Historical Society Journal* 22 (1923): 157–60.

O'Flanagan, Harry. "Ireland's First Ambassador to the United States." *The Recorder: Irish-American Historical Society* 36 (1975): 76–77.

O'Gara, James. "The Irish in America." *Commonweal* 78 (July 12, 1963): 415.

O'Grady, Joseph P. *How the Irish Became American*. New York: Twayne Publishers, 1973.

O'Hanlon, John. *Irish-American History of the United States*. Riverside, New Jersey: Benziger, Bruce and Glencoe, 1903.

O'Kane, J. M. "The Ethnic Factor in American Urban Civil Disorders." *Ethnicity* 2, no. 3 (1975): 230–43.

O'Malley, F. W. "American Sons of th'Ould Sod." *American Mercury* 18 (September 1929): 25–33.

O'Meara, James. *Vigilance Committee of 1856*. San Francisco: n.p., 1887.

O'Meara, John Baptiste. "The Missions of the Irish Race in the United States." *American Irish Historical Society Journal* 10 (1911): 105–13.

O'Neil, Daniel J. *The Study of Irish Politics in American Universities: Some Recommendations*. Tuscon: University of Arizona, 1971.

O'Neill, William L. "The Contradictory Ethnics." *New Republic* 167 (September 9, 1972): 25–26.

O'Shea, J. J. "Irish Leaven in American Progress." *Forum* 27 (May 1899): 285–96.

O'Sheel, S. "Irish in America." *American Mercury* 27 (December 1932): 501.

Oglac, Sean. *Yanks in Corrigdown*. New York: Shamrock Guild, 1957.

Onahan, William James. *The Day We Celebrate*. Chicago: Dunn, 1982.

Opler, M. K., and J. L. Singer. "Ethnic Differences in Behavior and Psycho-Pathology: Italian and Irish." *International Journal of Social Psychiatry* 2 (1956): 11–22.

Orel, Harold, ed. *Irish History and Culture*. University of Kansas Press, 1976.

Orr, Hector. *The Native American: A Gift for the People*. Philadelphia: 1845.

Osofsky, Gilbert. "Abolitionist, Irish Immigrants, and the Dilemmas of Romatic Nationalism." *American Historical Review* 80, pt. 2 (October–December, 1975): 889–912.

Page, Thomas Walker. "The Transportation of Immigrants and Reception Arrangements in the Nineteenth Century." *Journal of Political Economy* 19 (November 1911): 732–49.

Park, Robert E. *The Immigrant Press and Its Control*. New York: Harper, 1922.

Park, Robert E., and Herbert A. Miller. *Old World Traits Transplanted*. New York: Harper, 1921.

Park, Robert Ezra. *Race and Culture*. New York: Free Press, 1950.

Parr, G.J. "The Welcome and the Wake, Attitudes in Canada West Toward the Irish Famine Migration." *Ontario Historical Society Journal*.

Parsons, Wilfrid, S.J. "Early Catholic Publishers of Philadelphia." *Catholic Historical Review* 24 (June 1938): 141–52.

Passi, Michael M. "Immigrants and the City: Problems of Interpretation and Synthesis in Recent White Ethnic History." *Journal of the Ethnic Studies* 4, no. 2 (Summer 1976): 61–72.

Paul, Rodman W. *Mining Frontiers of the Far West*. New York: Holt, Rhinehart and Winston, 1963.

Pearse, P.H. "Irish Legend." *Living Age* 310 (July 30, 1921): 302–5.

Pessen, Edward, ed. *Three Centuries of Social Mobility in America*. Lexington, Massachusetts: D. C. Heath 1974.

Peters, Clarence A., comp. *The Immigration Problem*. New York: H. W. Wilson, 1948.

Pettigrew, Thomas F. "Ethnicity in American Life: a Socio-Psychology Perspective." In *Ethnic Groups in the City: Culture, Institutions, and Power*, edited by Otto Feinstein. Lexington, Massachusetts: D. C. Heath, 1971.

Phillips, Mary MacDonough. "The Irish Host at the Castle Gate." *The Recorder: Irish-American Historical Society* 36 (1975): 88–94.

Philpott, Thomas Lee. *The Slum and the Ghetto: Neighborhood Deterioration and Middle Class Reform: Chicago, 1880–1930*. New York: Oxford University Press, 1978.

Piggott, M. M. "Irish Pioneers of the Upper Mississippi Valley." *American Irish Historical Society Journal* 9 (1910): 301–30.

Pocock, Roger. "Nine Men Who 'Discovered' America." *Cornhill Magazine* 163 (1931): 354–61.

Poland, D. S. "Educational Achievement and Ethnic Group Membership." *Comparative Educational Review* 17 (1973): 362–74.

Pomeroy, Ear. *The Pacific Slope*. New York: Alfred A. Knopf, 1968.

Potter, G. W. *To the Golden Door*. Boston: Little, Brown, 1960.

Pratt, John W. "Religious Conflict in the Development of the New York City Public School System." *History of Education Quarterly* 5 (June 1965): 110–20.

Pratt, Julius W. "John L. Sullivan and Manifest Destiny." *New York History* 14 (1933): 213–34.

President's Commission on Immigration and Naturalization. *Whom We Shall Welcome*. Washington, D.C.: Government Printing Office, 1953.

Preston, William Jr. *Aliens and Dissenters*. Cambridge: Harvard University Press, 1963.

Purcell, Richard J. "Education and Irish Schoolmasters in Colonial Massachusetts." *Catholic Educational Review* 33 (1935): 467–79.

———. "Education and Irish Schoolmasters in Maryland's National Period." *Catholic Educational Review* 32 (1934): 198–207.

———. "Education and Irish Teachers in Colonial Maryland." *Catholic Educational Review* 32 (1934): 143–53.

———. "Education and Irish Teachers in

Early Kentucky." *Catholic Educational Review* 34 (1936): 360–69.

———. "Education and Irish Teachers in Massachusetts, 1789–1865." *Catholic Educational Review* 34 (1936): 87–96, 159–66.

———. "Irish Educational Contribution to Colonial Pennsylvania." *Catholic Educational Review* 37 (1939): 425–39.

———. "Irish Educational Contribution to Pennsylvania in the National Period." *Catholic Educational Review* 38 (1940): 467–80, 537–49.

———. "Pioneer Irish Educators in Tennessee." *Catholic Educational Review* 34 (1926): 406–13.

———. "Rhode Island's Early Schools and Irish Teachers." *Catholic Educational Review* 32 (1934): 402–15.

———. "Schools and Early Irish Teachers in New Hampshire." *Catholic Educational Review* 32 (1934): 608-18

———. "Some Early Teachers in Connecticut." *Catholic Educational Review* 32 (1934): 332–38.

———. "Vermont: Schools and Early Irish Teachers." *Catholic Educational Review* 33 (1935): 277–81.

———. "The United States of America, the Irish Immigrant, the Famine, and the Irish American." *Irish Ecclesiastical Record* 1974.

Rae, G. "The Irish in America." *Information* 76 (March 1962): 16–26.

Reilly, A. J. "Irish Americans." In *One America*, edited by F. Brown and J. Roucek. New York: Prentice Hall, 1945.

———. "Irish Americans." In *Our Racial and National Minorities* edited by F. Brown and J. Roucek. New York: Prentice Hall, 1939.

Reilly, D. "Irishmen in American Science." *Ave Maria* 74 (1951): 167–70.

Reilly, J. "The American Bar and the Irish Pub: A Study in Comparisons and Contrasts." *Journal of Popular Culture* 10: 573–78.

Reynolds, Frank L. "The Ancient Order of Hibernians." *Illinois Catholic Historical Review* 4, (July 1921): 22–23.

Riach, Douglas C. "Black and Blackface on the Irish Stage, 1830–1860." *Journal of American Studies* 7: 231–41.

———. "Daniel O'Connell and American Anti-Slavery." *Irish Historical Studies* 20 (March 1976): 3–25.

Rice, Arnold S. *The Ku Klux Klan in American Politics*. Washington: Public Affairs, 1962.

Richardson, James. *The New York Police: From Colonial Times to 1901*. New York: Oxford University Press, 1970.

Richardson, Leon Burr. *William E. Chandler, Republican*. New York: 1940.

Riis, Jacob. *The Making of an American*. New York: Harper and Row Publishers, 1966.

Riley, Patrick G. D. "Exercising Human Rights." *The Recorder: Irish American Historical Society* 36 (1975): 145–55.

Rischin, Moses. *Immigration and the American Tradition*. Indianapolis: Bobbs-Merrill, 1976.

———. "Immigration, Migration, and Minorities in California: A Reassessment." *Pacific Historical Review* 41 (February 1972).

Roberts, Edward F. *Ireland in America*. New York and London: G. P. Putnam's Sons, 1931.

Roberts, K. L. "Rising Irish Tide" *Saturday Evening Post* 192 (February 14, 1920): 3–4.

Roche, James Jeffrey. "Irish Ability in the United States." *American Irish Historical Society Journal* 7 (1907): 17–32.

Roche, John P. "Latter-Day Puritans From Erin." *The American Irish* by William V. Shannon, *Reporter* 30, no. 4 (March 26, 1964).

Rodechko, James Paul. "Irish-American Journalist and Catholicism: Patrick Ford of the Irish World." *Church History* 39 (December 1970): 524–40.

———. *Patrick Ford and His Search for America: A Case Study of Irish-American Journalism, 1870–1913*. New York: Arno Press, 1976.

Rooney, William A. "The Degreening of the American Irish." *Business Week* (September 9, 1972): 15.

Rose, A. J. "Irish Migration to Australia in

the Twentieth Century." *Irish Geography* 4 no. 1 (1959): 79–84.

Rose, Peter I. *They and We: Racial and Ethnic Relations in the United States*. New York: Random House, 1974.

Ross, Dorothy. "The Irish-Catholic Immigrant, 1880–1900, A Study in Social Mobility." Master's thesis, Columbia University, 1959.

Ross, E. A. "Celtic Tide." *Century* 83 (April 1914): 949–55.

———. "Irish Immigrants." In *Old World and the New*, ch. 2. New York: Century, 1914.

———. *The Old World in the New*. New York: Century, 1914.

Rossman, K. R. "The Irish in American Drama during the Nineteenth Century." *New York History* 21: 39–53.

Rowe, John. *The Hard-Rock Men: Cornish Miners and the North American Mining Frontier*. New York: Barnes and Noble, 1974.

Royce, Josiah. *Race Questions, Provincialism, and Other American Problems*. New York: Macmillan, 1908.

Russell, Francis. *The Great Interlude: Neglected Events and Persons from the First World War to the Depression*. New York: McGraw-Hill, 1964.

Ryan, Frederick Lynn. "Industrial Relations in the San Francisco Building Trades." Ph.D. dissertation, University of California, Berkeley, 1930.

Ryan, G. E. "Shanties and Shiftlessness: The Immigrant Irish of Henry Thoreau." *Eire-Ireland* 13 (1978): 54–78.

Ryan, John A. *Distributive Justice: The Right and Wrong of Our Present Distribution of Wealth*. Riverside, New Jersey: Macmillan, 1935.

———. *Social Doctrine in Action: A Personal History*. New York: Harper and Bros, 1941.

Ryan, Joseph, ed. *White Ethnics: Their Life in Working Class America*. Englewood Cliffs, New Jersey: Prentice-Hall, 1973.

Sadlier, Mrs. J. "Irish in the United States." *Catholic World* 6: 765.

Sandalls, K. F. "An Investigation of the Differential Fertility Patterns of Irish and Italian Americans." Master's thesis, Georgetown University, 1970.

Saveth, Edward N. *American Historians and European Immigrants*. 1948.

Scamehorn, Howard L., ed. *The Buckeye Rovers in the Gold Rush*. Athens, Ohio: Ohio University Press, 1965.

Schafer, Joseph. "Know-Nothingism in Wisconsin." *Wisconsin Magazine of History* 8 (September 1924): 3–21.

Scheider, David M. *History of Public Welfare in New York State, 1609–1866*. Chicago: University of Chicago Press, 1938.

Schlesinger, Arthur M. "The Influence of Immigration on American History." In *New Viewpoints in American History*, by Arthur M. Schlesinger. New York: Macmillan, 1922.

———. *The Rise of the City, 1878–1898*. New York: Macmillan, 1933.

Schlesinger, Arthur M., Jr. *The Coming of the New Deal*. Sentry, 1958.

———. *Orestes A. Brownson*. Boston: Little, Brown, 1939.

Schlossman, S. L. "The Culture of Poverty in Ante-Bellum Social Thought." *Science and Society* 38 (1974): 150–66.

Schmeckebier, Laurence F. *History of the Know Nothing Party in Maryland*. Baltimore: Johns Hopkins University Press, 1899.

Schneider, George. "Lincoln and the Anti-Know Nothing Resolutions." *McLean County Historical Society Transactions* 3 (1900).

Schorneman, F. "My Irish-American Friends." *Living Age* 314 (August 19, 1922): 487–89.

Seller, Maxine. *To Seek America: A History of Ethnic Life in the United States*. Englewood, New Jersey: Jerome S. Ozer, 1977.

Sengstock, Mary C. "Kinship in a Roman Catholic Ethnic Group." *Ethnicity* 2, no. 2 (June 1975): 134–52.

Sennet Richard. *Families against the City*. New York: Vintage Books, 1970.

Senning, John P. "The Know-Nothing Movement in Illinois, 1854–1856." *Illinois Historical Society Journal* 7 (April 1914): 7–33.

Shaloo, J. P. "United States Immigration

Policy, 1882–1948." In *Essays in Honor of George H. Blakeslee*, edited by Dwight E. Lee and G. E. McReynolds. N. p., 1949.

Shamrock Society of New York. *Emigration to America*. Dublin: Connely, 1817.

Shannon, Fred A. *The Farmer's Last Frontier: Agriculture, 1860–1897*. New York: Farrar, 1945.

Shannon, James P. *Roman Catholicism and the American Way of Life*. South Bend, Indiana: University of Notre Dame Press, 1960.

Shannon, William V. *The American Irish*. New York: Macmillan, 1963.

———. "Lasting Hurrah." *New York Times Magazine* (March 14, 1976): 11.

Shapiro, Deanne Ruth. "The New Ethnicity: Myth or Reality?" *Foundations* 19 (July–September 1976): 223–34.

Shaw, Douglas Vincent. *The Making of an Immigrant City: Ethnic and Cultural Conflict in Jersey City, New Jersey, 1850–1877*. New York: Arno Press, 1976.

Shepardson, F. W. "Scotch and Irish in America." *Dial* 33 (November 16, 1902): 325–26.

Shepperson, W. S. *British Emigration to North America*. Oxford: Basil Blackwell, 1957.

Shippen, Katherine B. *Passage to America: The Story of the Great Migrations*. New York: Harper, 1950.

Shrier, Arnold. *Ireland the American Emigration, 1850–1900*. New York: Russell and Russell, 1958.

Shumsky, Neil L. "Tar Flat and Nob Hill: A Social History of Industrial San Francisco in the 1870's." Ph.D. dissertation, University of California, Berkeley, 1972.

"Slight to Irish-Americans." *Review* 5 (July 9, 1921): 34.

Smith, G. "Why Send More Irish to America." *Nineteenth Century* 13: 913; *Edinburgh Review* 44: 49–74; 89: 221–68; 91: 1–62; 93: 475–98.

Smith, Abbot Emerson. *Colonists in Bondage: White Servitude and Convict Labor in America, 1607–1776*. New York: W. W. Norton, 1947.

Smith, Alson J., Rev. *The Christian Front*. Detroit: League for Peace and Democracy, 1939.

Smith, Drew L. *The Legacy of the Melting Pot: A Sociological-Historical Study*. North Quincy, Massachusetts: Christopher, 1971.

Smith, Duane A. *Rocky Mountain Mining Camps*. Indiana: Indiana University Press, 1967.

Smith, J. "Irish-American as a Citizen." *New England Magazine* 47 (August 1912): 257–73.

Smith, Timothy L. "Immigrant Social Aspirations and American Education, 1880–1930." *American Quarterly* 21 (Fall 1969): 523–43.

———. "New Approaches to the History of Immigration in Twentieth-Century America." *American History Review* 71 (1966): 1265–79.

———. "Progressivism in American Education, 1888–1900" *Harvard Educational Review* 31, no. 2 (Spring 1961): 168–73.

———. "Protestant Schooling and American Nationality, 1800- 1850." *Journal of American History* (1966–67): 679–95.

Smith, William Carlson. *Americans in the Making*. New York: D. Appleton-Century, 1939.

Smyth, W. P. "Emigration from Ireland." *U.S. Consular Reports* 33, no. 118 (1890): 537–38.

Solomon, Barbara Miller. *Ancestors and Immigrants: A Changing New England Tradition*. Cambridge: Harvard University Press, 1956.

"Sons of St. Patrick." *Newsweek* 63 (February 3, 1964): 68.

Sowell, Thomas. "Ethnicity in a Changing America." *Daedalus* 107 (Winter 1978): 213–37.

Spalding, Martin J. *Miscelleanea: Comprising Reviews, Lectures, and Essays on Historical, Theological, and Miscellaneous Subjects*. Louisville, Kentucky: n. p., 1855.

Spin, Melford. "The Acculturation of American Ethnic Groups." *American Anthropologist* 57 (1955).

Spoehr, Luther W. "Sambo and the Heathen Chinese: California's Racial Stereotypes in the Late 1870's." *Pacific Historical Review* 42 (May 1973): 185–204.

Spofford, Harriet Prescott. *The Servant Girl Question*. Boston, 1881.

"Sprouting 'Isms': Irish Zealots to Join Ranks of U.S. Fist Shakers." *Newsweek* 13 (March 13, 1939): 17.

"St. Nicholas and the Five Points." *Putnam's Magazine* 1 (May 1853): 509–12.

Stables, G. "With Irish Emigrants." *London Society* 41: 233.

Staski, Edward. "Alcohol Consumption among Irish-Americans and Jewish Americans: Contributions from Archaeology." Ph.D. dissertation, University of Arizona, 1983.

Steffens, L. "William J. Burns, Intriguer: The Keenest of Detectives and the Story of His Hardest Job." *American Magazine* 65 (April 1908): 617–20.

Stein, Rita F. *Disturbed Youth and Ethnic Family Patterns*. Albany: State University of New York Press, 1971.

Steinfels, Peter. "The Chase of the Irish Age." *Commonweal* 96 (March 17, 1972): 30.

Stephens, J. G. "Emigration from England and Ireland." *U.S. Consular Reports*, no. 289 (October 1904): 176.

Stephenson, George M. "Nativism in the Forties and Fifties with Special Reference to the Mississippi Valley." *The Mississippi Valley Historical Review* 9 (December 1922).

Stivers, Richard. "The Bachelor Group Ethic and Irish Drinking." Ph.D. dissertation, Southern Illinois University, 1971.

———. *A Hair of the Dog: Irish Drinking and American Stereotype*. Pennsylvania State University Press, 1976.

———. "Irish Ethnicity and Alcohol Use." *Medical Anthropology* 2: 121–36.

Stokes, I. N. Phelps, comp. *The Iconography of Manhattan Island, 1498–1909*. New York: McGraw-Hill, 1967.

Stouffer, Samuel A. *Communists, Conformists, and Civil Liberties: A Cross Section of the Nation Speaks Its Mind*. Garden City, New York: Doubleday, 1955.

Stover, John F. *American Railroads*. Chicago: University of Chicago Press, 1961.

Strong, Josiah. *Our Country*. Cambridge: Belknap Press of Harvard University Press, 1963.

Strout, Richard L. "The Rise of the Irish." *New Republic* 150 (January 18, 1964): 22–24.

Sullivan, Michael Xavier. "Some Irish Contributions to Early American History." *American Irish Historical Society Journal* 9 (1910): 196–205.

Suttles, Gerald D. *The Social Order of the Slum*. Chicago: University of Chicago Press, 1968.

Sweeney, Helen M. *The Golden Milestone, 1846–1896*. New York, 1896.

Swiney, D. "Emigration from Ireland." *U.S. Consular Reports* 57, no. 213 (January 1898): 235.

Taft, Donald R. *Human Migration: A Study of International Movements*. New York: Ronald Press, 1936.

Taylor, George Rogers. *The Transportation Revolution*. New York: Harper Torchbooks, 1968.

Taylor, Philip. *The Distant Magnet*. New York: Harper and Row, 1973.

Testimony as to the Origin of the Riots in the City of Louisville, Kentucky, the 6th of August, 1855. Lousiville, Kentucky: Hull. 1855.

Thernstrom, Stephan. *The Other Bostonians*. Cambridge: Harvard University Press, 1973.

———. *Poverty and Progress*. Cambridge: Harvard University Press, 1964.

———. "Urbanization, Migration, and Social Mobility in Late Nineteenth-Century America." In *Towards a New Past*, edited by Barton Bernstein. New York: Random House, 1967.

———. "Working-Class Mobility in Industrial America." In *Essays in Theory and History: An Approach to the Social Sciences*, edited by Melvin Richter. Cambridge: Harvard University Press, 1970.

Thernstrom, Stephan, and Peter Knights. "Men In Motion: Some Data and Speculations about Urban Population Mobility in Nineteenth-Century America." *Journal of Interdisciplinary History* 1 (Autumn 1970).

Thernstrom, Stephan, and Richard Sennet,

eds. *Nineteenth-Century Cities*. New Haven: Yale University Press, 1969.

Thistlewaite, Frank. "Migration from Europe Overseas in the Nineteenth and Twentieth Centuries." *Rapports du Xieme congres international des sciences historique Stockholm*. Stockholm, 1960.

Thomas, Thomas. *Migration and Economic Growth*. 1st ed. Cambridge: Harvard University Press. 1954. 2d ed. Cambridge University Press, 1976.

Thompson, Craig, and Allen Raymond. *Gang Rule in New York: The Story of a Lawless Era*. New York: Dial, 1940.

Tilby, A. Wyatt. *The English People Overseas*. Boston, 1912.

Todd, Helen M. "Why Children Work: The Children's Answer." *McClure's Magazine* 40 (April 1913): 68–79.

Tomasi, Lydio F. *The Ethnic Factor in the Future of Inequality*. Staten Island: Center for Migration Studies, 1973.

Touhill, Blanche M., ed. *Varieties of Ireland, Varieties of Irish-Americans*. St. Louis: n.p., 1976.

Troen, Selwyn K. *The Public and the Schools: Shaping the St. Louis System, 1838–1920*. Columbia, Missouri: University of Missouri Press, 1975.

Trout, Charles H. *Boston: The Great Depression and the New Deal*. New York: Oxford University Press, 1977.

Truxes, Thomas M. "Connecticut in the Irish-American Flaxseed Trade, 1750–75." *Eire-Ireland* 12 (Summer 1977): 34–62.

Tumin, Melvin M. *An Inventory and Appraisal of Research on Anti-Semitism*. New York: Freedom Books, 1961.

Ueda, Reed. *Avenues to Adulthood: The Origins of High School and Social Mobility in an American Suburb*. Cambridge: Cambridge University Press, 1987.

Valentine, Alan. *Vigilante Justice*. New York: Reynal and Company, 1956.

Van Duesen, Glyndon G. "Seward and the School Question Reconsidered." *Journal of American History* 52, no. 1 (September 1965): 313–19.

Varcados, Peter. "Labor and Politics in San Francisco, 1880–1892." Ph.D. dissertation, University of California, Berkeley, 1968.

Wakin, Edward. *Enter the Irish-American*. New York: Crowell, 1976.

Wald, Lillian E. *The House on Henry Street*. New York: Holt, 1915.

Waldrop, Judith. "Irish Eyes of America (Irish Population and U.S. Immigration)." *American Demographics* 11 (March 1989).

Walker, F. A. "American Irish and American German." *Scribner's Monthly* 6: 172–79.

Walling, George. *Recollections of a New Chief of Police*. New York: Caxton, 1888.

Walsh, E. J. "Language Problem of Irish Immigrants at the Time of the Great Famine." *St. Meinrad Essays* 12 (May 1959): 60–73.

Walsh, James. *Ethnic Militancy*. San Francisco: R & E Associates, 1972.

Walsh, James J. *Modern Progress and History*. Bronx, New York: Fordham University Press, 1912.

———. *The World's Debt to the Irish*. Boston: Stratford, 1926.

Walsh, James P. "American-Irish: West and East." *Eire-Ireland* 6 (1972).

———. "De Valera in the United States, 1919." *Records of the American Catholic Historical Society of Philadelphia* 63 (September–December 1962): 98–106.

———. "Regent Peter C. Yorke and the University of California, 1900–1912." Ph.D. dissertation, University of California, 1970.

Walsh, L. J. "Life among the Early Irish Immigrants." *Catholic World* 154 (March 1942): 716–21.

Walther, Thomas R. "Some Aspects of Economic Mobility in Barrett Township of Thomas County, 1885–1905." *Kansas Historical Quarterly* (1971): 281–87.

Wang, Peter H. "The Immigration Act of 1924 and the Problem of Assimilation." *Journal of Ethnic Studies* 2, no. 3 (Fall 1974).

Ward, Alan J. "America and the Irish Problem." *Irish Historical Studies* 16 (March 1968): 64–90.

Ward, David. *Cities and Immigrants*. New York: Oxford University Press, 1971.

———. "Emergence of Central Immigrant Ghettoes in American Cities, 1840–1920." *Association of American Geographers, Annals* 58 (1968): 343.

Ward, L. R. "Those Puritanic American Irish!" *Modern Age* 20: 94–100.

Warner, William Lloyd, ed. *Yankee City*. New Haven: Yale University Press, 1963.

Warner, William Lloyd, and J. O. Low. *The Social System of the Modern Factory: The Strike: A Social Analysis*. New Haven: Yale University Press, 1965.

Warner, William Lloyd, and Leo Strole. *The Social Systems of American Ethnic Groups*. New Haven: Yale University Press, 1945.

Warren, John H. *Thirty Years' Battle with Crime, or, The Crying Shame of New York, As Seen under the Broad Glare of an Old Detective's Lantern*. Poughkeepsie, New York: White, 1875.

Watkins, A. "Irish Players in America." *Craftsman* 21: 352–63.

Webb, Robert N. *America Is Also Irish*. New York: Putnam's, 1973.

Weber, Michael P., and Anthony E. Broadman. "Economic Growth and Occupational Mobility in Nineteenth Century Urban America: A Reappraisal." *Journal of Social History* 11 (Fall 1977): 52–74.

Weisz, Howard R. "Irish-American and Italian-American Educational Views and Activities, 1870–1900: A Comparison." Ph.D. dissertation, Columbia University, 1968. Published 1976, by Arno Press.

———. "Irish-American Attitudes and the Americanization of the English-Language Parochial School." *New York History* 53 (1972): 157–76.

Wessel, Bessie Bloom. *An Ethnic Survey of Woonsocket, Rhode Island*. New York: Arno Press and the New York Times, 1970.

Weyl, Nathaniel. *The Jew in American Politics*. New Rochelle, New York: Arlington House, 1968.

Wheeler, Thomas C. *The Immigrant Experience*. Baltimore: Penguin Books, 1971.

Wheman, Henry J. *Wehman's Irish Song Book*. New York: H. J. Wehman, 1887.

White, E. *Early Irish in America*. 1948.

White, J. "Irish in America." In *Sketches from America*. Low, 1870.

White, James A. *The Era of Good Intentions*. New York, 1978.

White, Lyman Cromwell. *300,000 New Americans*. New York: Harper, 1957.

Whyte, William F. "Race Conflicts in the North End of Boston." *New England Quarterly* 12 (December 1939): 623–42.

Wibberly, Leonard. *The Trouble with the Irish*. New York: Holt, 1956.

———. "Coming of the Green." *American Heritage* 9 (August 1958): 22–27.

———. *The Coming of the Green*. New York: Holt, 1958.

Willcox, W. F. "The Distribution of Immigrants in the United States." *Quarterly Journal of Economics* 20: 523–46.

Williams, Harold A. *History of the Hibernian Society of Baltimore, 1803–1957*. Baltimore: Hibernian Society of Baltimore, 1957.

Williams, Joseph H., S.J. *Whence the "Black Irish" of Jamaica?* New York: Deal Press, 1932.

Williamson, Jeffrey G. "Migration to the New World: Long Term Influences and Impact." *Explorations in Economic History* 2, no. 4 (Summer 1974): 357–89.

Wilson, James Q. "Generational and Ethnic Differences among Career Police Officers." *American Journal of Sociology* 69 (March 1964): 522–28.

Wittke, Carl. "The Irish." In *We Who Built America*. New York: Prentice-Hall, 1940.

———. *The Irish in America*. Louisiana State University Press, 1956.

Wolfinger, Raymond E. "Ethnic Voting." *American Political Science Review* 59 (1965): 896.

Woodbury, K. B., Jr. "Incident between the French Canadians and the Irish in the Diocese of Maine in 1906." *New England Quarterly* 40 (June 1967): 260–69.

Woods, Robert, ed. *The City Wilderness: A Settlement Study by Residents and Associates of the South End House*. Boston: Houghton Mifflin, 1898.

———. ed. *Americans in Process: A Settlement Study*. Boston: Houghton Mifflin, 1903.

Yetman, Norman R. "The Irish Experience in America." In *Irish History and Culture*, edited by H. Orel. Manhattan, Kansas: University of Kansas Press, 1976.

Yorke, Peter C. *America and Ireland: An Open Letter to Mr. Garrett W. McEnerney*. San Francisco: n. p., 1918.

Young, Edward. *Special Report on Immigration*. Washington, D.C.: U.S. Government Printing Office, 1872.

Young, John P. *San Francisco: A History of the Pacific Coast Metropolis*. 2 vols. San Francisco: 1912.

Young, Kimball. *Mental Differences in Certain Immigrant Groups*. Eugene, Oregon: University of Oregon Press, 1923.

Zenner, Walter P. "International Networks in a Migrant Ethnic Group." In *Migration and Anthropology*, edited by Robert F. Spencer. Seattle: University of Washington Press, 1970.

5. Politics

Abraham, E. H. "Ignatius Donnelly and the Apocalyptic Style." *Minnesota History* 46 (1978): 102–111.

Adams, John Gibbons. *Without Precedent, The Story of the Death of McCarthyism.* New York: W. W. Norton, 1983.

Addams, Jane. "Why the Ward Boss Rules." *The Outlook* 58 (April 2, 1898).

Ainley, Leslie. *Boston Mahatma: The Public Career of Martin Lomasney.* Boston: W. M. Prendible, 1949.

Alexander, De Alva Stanwood. *Four Famous New Yorkers.* New York: Henry Holt, 1923.

Allswang, John M. *Bosses, Machines, and Urban Voters.* Port Washington, New York: Kennikat Press, 1977.

———. *A House for All Peoples: Ethnic Politics in Chicago, 1890–1936.* Boston: Lexington Books, 1971.

Anderson, Jack, and Ronald W. May. *McCarthy: The Man, The Senator, The "Ism."* Boston: Beacon Press, 1952.

Angoff, D. "Curley and the Boston Irish." *American Mercury* 69 (November 1949): 619–27.

Arnold, Joseph L. "The Last of the Good Old Days: Politics in Baltimore, 1920–1950." *Maryland Historical Magazine* 71 (Fall, 1976): 443–48.

Bagenal, Philip H. *The American Irish and Their influence on Irish Politics.* London: K. Paul, Trench, 1882.

Barbrook, Alec. *God Save the Commonwealth.* Amherst: University of Massachusetts Press, 1973.

Barry, C. J. "Some Roots of American Nativism." *Catholic Historical Review* 44 (1958): 137–46.

Beals, C. *Brass-Knuckle Crusade: The Great Know-Nothing Conspiracy, 1800–1860.* New York: Hastings House, 1960.

Bean, William G. "An Aspect of Know-Nothingism: The Immigrant and Slavery." *South Atlantic Quarterly* 23 (October 1924): 319–34.

———. "Puritan Versus Celt, 1850–1860." *New England Quarterly* 7(1934): 70–89.

Becker, Richard E. "Edward Dunne, Reform Mayor of Chicago, 1905–1907." Ph.D. dissertation, University of Chicago, 1971.

Bell, S. *Rebel, Priest, and Prophet: A Biography of Edward McGlynn.* New York: Devin-Adair, 1937.

Berger, M. "Irish Emigrant and American Nativism As Seen by British Visitors, 1836–1860." *Dublin Review* 219 (1946): 174–86.

———. "Irish Emigrant and American Nativism As Seen by British Visitors, 1836–1860." *Pennsylvania Magazine History and Biography* 70 (1946): 146–60.

Becschloss, M. R. *Kennedy and Roosevelt.* New York: Norton, 1980.

Biles, Roger. *Big City Boss in Depression and War: Mayor Edward J. Kelly of Chicago.* DeKalb: Northern Illinois University Press, 1984.

Billington, R. A. *The Protestant Crusade, 1800–1860.* New York: Macmillan, 1938.

Birkhead, L. M. *Father Coughlin.* Kansas City, Missouri: n.p., 1940.

Bishop, Jim. *The Day Kennedy Was Shot.* New York: Funk and Wagnalls, 1971.

Blackmore, C. P. "Joseph B. Shannon Political Boss and Twentieth Century Jeffersonian." Ph.D. dissertation, Columbia University, 1954.

Bliven, Bruce. "Boston: The Irish in Politics." *The New Republic* 30 (May 24, 1922): 367–69.

Blodgett, G. T. "The Mind of the Boston Mugwump." *Mississippi Valley Historical Review* 48 (1962): 614–34.

Blum, John Morton. *Joe Tumulty and the Wilson Era*. Boston: Houghton Mifflin Company, 1951.

Bocock, J. P. "Irish Conquest of Our Cities." *Forum* 17 (April 1894): 185–95.

The Boston Pilot's Attempt to Sell Adopted Citizens to the Whig Party Exposed by a Catholic Citizen of Boston. Boston, 1853.

Bradlee, Benjamin C. *Conversations with Kennedy*. New York: W. W. Norton, 1975.

Bradley, D. S., and M. N. Zald. "From Commercial Elite to Political Administrator: The Recruitment of Mayors of Chicago." *American Journal of Sociology* 71 (1965): 153–67.

Brauer, Carl M. *John M. Kennedy and the Second Reconstruction*. New York: Columbia University Press, 1977.

Breen, Matthew P. *Thirty Years of New York Politics*. New York, 1899.

Brown, Edmund Gerald. *Reagan and Reality: The Two Californias*. New York: Praeger, 1970.

Brown, Stuart Gerry. *Presidency on Trial: Robert Kennedy's 1968 Campaign and Afterwards*. Honolulu: University Press of Hawaii, 1972.

Brown, Thomas N. "The Political Irish: Politicians and Rebels." In *America and Ireland, 1776–1976: The American Identity and the Irish Connection*, edited by David Noel Doyle and Owen Dudley Edwards. Westport, Connecticut: Greenwood Press, 1980.

Brownell, Blaine A., and Warren E. Stickle, eds. *Bosses and Reformers*. Boston: Houghton Mifflin, 1973.

Brusher, Joseph S. *Consecrated Thunderbolt: Father Yorke of San Francisco*. Hawthorne, New Jersey, 1973.

Bryce, James. *The American Commonwealth*. New York: Macmillan, 1921.

Buckley, Christopher. "The Reminiscences of Christopher A. Buckley." *San Francisco Bulletin*. September 1–November 26, 1917.

Buckley, J. P. "The New York Irish: Their View of American Foreign Policy, 1914–1921." Ph.D. dissertation, New York University. Published by Arno Press, 1976.

Buckley, William F., Jr. *The Unmaking of a Mayor*. New York: Viking, 1966.

Buckley, William F., Jr., et al. *McCarthy and His Enemies: The Record and Its Meaning*. Chicago: H. Regenery, 1954.

Buenker, John D. "Cleveland's New Stock Lawmakers and Progressive Reform." *Ohio History* 78 (Spring 1969).

———. "Edward F. Dunne: The Urban New Stock Democrat as Progressive." *Mid-America* 50 (1968): 2–21.

———. "The Illinois Legislature and Prohibition, 1877–1919." *Journal of the Illinois State Historical Society*, 62.

———. "The Mahatma and Progressive Reform: Martin Lomasney as Lawmaker, 1911–1917." *New England Quarterly*.

———. *Urban Liberalism and Progressive Reform*. New York: Charles Scribner's Sons, 1973.

———. "The Urban Political Machine and the Seventeenth Amendment." *Journal of American History* 56.

Buenker, John D. "The Urban Political Machine and Women Suffrage: A Study in Political Adaptability." *The Historian* 33.

Bugbee, James M. *City Government of Boston*. Baltimore: 1887.

Buhite, Russell D. *Patrick J. Hurley and American Foreign Policy*. Ithaca, New York: Cornell University Press, 1973.

Bullough, William A. "Chris Buckley and San Francisco: The Man and the City." In *The Irish in San Francisco*, edited by James P. Walsh. San Francisco: Irish Literary History Society, 1978.

———. "The Steam Beer Handicap: Chris Buckley and the San Francisco Municipal Election of 1896." *California Historical Quarterly* 54 (Fall 1975): 245–62.

Burchell, R. A. "Did the Irish and German Voters Desert the Democrats in 1920?: A Tentative Statistical Answer." *Journal of American Studies* 6: 153–64.

Burns, James McGregor. *Edward Kennedy and the Camelot Legacy*. New York: W. W. Norton, 1976.

———. *John F. Kennedy: A Political Profile*. New York: Harcourt, Brace, 1961.

Calkin, Homer L. "The United States Government and the Irish." *Irish Historical Studies* 9 (March 1954): 28–54.

Callow, Alexander B., Jr. "San Francisco's Blind Boss." *Pacific Historical Review* 25 (August 1956): 261–79.

———. *The Tweed Ring*. New York: Oxford University Press, 1966.

———, ed. *The City Boss in America*. New York: Oxford University Press, 1976.

Campbell, Ballard C. "Ethnicity and the 1893 Wisconsin Assembly." *Journal of American History* 62 (1975): 74–94.

Cannon, Joseph Gurney. *Uncle Joe Cannon: The Story of a Pioneer American*. New York: Holt, 1927.

Carleton, William G. "Kennedy in History: An Early Appraisal." *The Antioch Review* 24 (1964): 280–81.

———. "The Popish Plot of 1928: Smith-Hoover Presidential Campaign." *Forum* 112 (1949): 141–47.

Carney, Francis M., and H. Frank Way, Jr. *Politics, 1960*. San Francisco: Wadsworth, 1960.

Carroll, Leo E. "Irish and Italians in Providence, Rhode Island, 1880–1960." *Rhode Island History* 28 (August 1969): 67–74.

Carroll, M. C. "Behind the Lighthouse: The Australian Sojourn of John Boyle O'Reilly." Ph.D. dissertation, University of Iowa, 1955.

Carson, Oliver, and Ernest Sutherland Bates. *Hearst: Lord of San Simeon*. New York: Viking Press, 1936.

Carter, E. C. "A 'Wild Irishman' under Every Federalist Bed: Naturalization in Philadelphia, 1789–1806." *Pennsylvania Magazine of History and Biography* 94 (1970): 331–46.

Carter, P. A. "The Campaign of 1928 Reexamined: A Study in Political Folklore." *Wisconsin Magazine of History* 46 (1970): 263–72.

Carter, P. A. "The Other Catholic Candidate: The 1928 Presidential Bid of Thomas J. Walsh." *Pacific Northwest Quarterly* 55 (1964): 1–8.

Casey, John, and Jane S. Bowles. *Farley and Tomorrow*. Chicago: Riley and Lee, 1937.

Casey R. D. "The Scripps-Howard Newspapers in the 1928 Presidential Campaign." In *Quarterly Journal* 7: 207–31.

Chalmers, L. "Fernando Wood—Tammany Hall." *New York Hist. Soc. Quarterly* 52: 329–402.

Chapernowne, Henry. *The Boss: An Essay upon the Art of Governing American Cities*. New York: George H. Richmond, 1894.

"Charles Francis Murphy." *National Cyclopedia of American Biography*. 13. New York: James T. White, 1906, 574–75.

"Chicago Convention." *Spectator* 75 (September 28, 1895): 390.

Clark, M. J. "The Bigot Disclosed: 90 Years of Nativism." *Oregon Historical Quarterly* 75 (1974): 109–90.

Clark, Terry Nicholas. "The Irish Ethnic and Spirit of Patronage." *Ethnicity* 2 (1975): 330ff.

Clubb, Jerome M., and Howard W. Allen. "The Cities and the Election of 1928: Partisan Realignment?" *American Historical Review* 74.

Cohn, Roy. *McCarthy*. New York: New American Library, 1961.

Colburn, D. R. "Governor Alfred E. Smith and Penal Reform." *Political Science Quarterly* 91 (1976): 315–27.

Colburn, G. A. "Father Coughlin and American Foreign Policy: An Irishman's Quest for Revenge." In *The San Francisco Irish, 1850–1976*, edited by James P. Walsh. 113–25. San Francisco: Irish Literary and Historical Society.

Coleman, Charles H. *The Election of 1868*. New York: 1933.

Connable, Alfred, and Edward Silberfarb. *Tigers of Tammany*. New York: Holt, Rinehart, and Winston, 1967.

Connolly, Christopher P. *The Devil Learns to Vote: The Short Story of Montana*. New York: Covici, Friede, 1938.

Connors, R. J. "The Local Political Career of Frank Hague." Ph.D. dissertation, Columbia University, 1966.

Considine, J. L. "Father Yorke: Champion of Human Rights." *Ave Maria* (February 18, 1950): 200–208.

Cook, Fred J. *Nightmare Decade: The Life*

and Times of Senator Joe McCarthy. New York: Random, 1971.

Cornwell, Elmer E. "Bosses, Machines, and Ethnic Groups." *Annals of the American Academy of Political and Social Sciences*, 353.

———. "A Note on Providence Politics in the Age of Bryan." *Rhode Island History* 19.

———. "Party Absorption of Ethnic Groups: The Case of Providence, Rhode Island." *Social Forces*, 38.

Coughlin, Charles E. *An Answer to Father Coughlin's Antics*. Detroit: n.p., 1940.

———. *By the Sweat of Thy Brow*. Michigan: Radio League of the Little Flower, 1931.

———. *Eight Lectures on Labor, Capital, and Justice*. Royal Oak, Michigan: Radio League of the Little Flower, 1934.

———. *Money*. Detroit: Radio League of the Little Flower, 1936.

Coyle, Dr. John G. "American-Irish Governors of Pennsylvania." *American Irish Historical Society Journal* 14 (1915).

Creel, George. *Wilson and the Issues*. New York: Century, 1916.

Croker, Hon. Richard. "Tammany and the Democracy." *The North American Review* 154 (February 1892): 225–30.

Crooks, James B. *Politics and Progress: The Rise of Urban Progressivism in Baltimore, 1895 to 1911*. Baton Rouge: Louisiana State University Press, 1968.

Crosby, D. F. *God, Church, and Flag: Senator Joe McCarthy and the Catholic Church, 1950–57*. Chapel Hill: University of North Carolina Press, 1978.

Cuddy, Edward. "Irish-Americans and the 1916 Elections." *American Quarterly* 21 (1969): 228–43.

Cuddy, Edward Joseph. *Irish-America and National Isolationism: 1914–1920*. New York: Arno Press, 1976.

Cummings, S. "A Critical Examination of the Portrayal of Catholic Immigrants in American Political Life." *Ethnicity* 6 (1979): 197–214.

Curley, James Michael. *I'd Do It Again: A Record of All My Uproarious Years*. Englewood Cliffs, New Jersey: Prentice-Hall, 1957.

Curran, M. P. *The Life of Patrick Collins*. Norwood, Massachusetts: Norwood Press, 1906.

Curran, Thomas J. "Know Nothings of New York State." Ph.D. dissertation, Columbia University, 1963.

Curry, R. O. "The Union as it Was: A Critique of Recent Interpretations of Copperheads." *Civil War* 13:25–39.

Cusak, T. E. "Archbishop John Ireland and the Spanish-American War: Peacemaker or Bungler." Master's thesis, University of Notre Dame, 1974.

Curti, M. E. "Young America." *American Historical Review* 32 (October 1926): 34–55.

Cutler, John Henry. *Honey Fitz: Three Steps to the White House*. New York: Bobbs-Merrill, 1962.

Dahl, Robert A. *Who Governs?* New Haven, Connecticut: Yale University Press, 1970.

Dallas, Rita, and Jeanira Ratcliffe. *The Kennedy Case*. New York: Putnam, 1973.

Damore, Leo. *Cape Cod Years of John Fitzgerald Kennedy*. Englewood Cliffs, New Jersey: Prentice-Hall, 1967.

D'Arcy, W. *Fenian Movement in the United States: 1858–1886*. Washington, D.C.: The Catholic University of America Press, 1947. Reprinted by Russell and Russell, 1971.

Darling, Arthur B. *Political Changes in Massachusetts, 1824–1848*. New Haven, Connecticut: Yale University Press, 1925.

Davenport, John I. *The Election Frauds of New York City and Their Prevention*. New York, 1881.

———. *The Election And Naturalization Frauds in New York City 1860–1870*. New York, 1894.

David, Jay, ed. *A Kennedy Reader*. Indianapolis, Indiana: Bobbs-Merrill, 1967.

David, Lester. *Ted Kennedy: Triumphs and Tragedies*. New York: Grosset, 1972.

Davis, Allen F. "Jane Addams vs. The Ward Boss." *Journal of the Illinois State Historical Society* 53 (Autumn 1960): 257–65.

Day, J. Edward. *My Appointed Round: 929 Days as Postmaster General*. New York: Holt, Rinehart and Winston, 1965.

DeSantis, V. "American Catholics and Mc-

Carthyism." *Catholic Historical Review* 51 (1965): 1–30.

DesMarais, P. H. "John Ireland in American Politics, 1886–1906." Master's thesis, Georgetown University, 1960.

Desmond, Humphrey. *The Know Nothing Party*. Washington, D.C., 1904.

Deusner, C. E. "The Know-Nothing Riots in Louisville." *Register of the Kentucky Historical Society* 61 (1943): 122–47.

Devoy, John. *Recollections of an Irish Rebel: The Fenian Movement, Its Origin and Progress*. New York: Young, 1929.

Dinneen, Joseph F. *The Kennedy Family*. Boston: Little, Brown, 1959.

———. *The Purple Shamrock: The Honorable James Michael Curley of Boston*. New York: Norton, 1949.

Donnelly, Edward Lawrence, ed. *That Man Curley*. Boston: Donnelly, 1947.

Dorsett, Lyle W. *Franklin D. Roosevelt and the City Bosses*. Port Washington, New York: Kennikat Press, 1977.

———. *The Pendergast Machine*. New York: Oxford University Press, 1968.

Doyle, David. "American Catholics, Native Rights, and National Empires: Irish-American Reaction to Expansion, 1890–1905." Ph.D. dissertation, University of Iowa, 1975. Published by Arno Press, 1976.

Doyle, David Noel, and Owen Dudley Edwards, eds. *America and Ireland, 1776–1976: The American Identity and the Irish Connection*. Westport, Connecticut: Greenwood Press, 1980.

Doyle, T. F. "Negro in the Irish Empire." *Catholic World* 154:536–44.

Duncliff, William J. *The Life and Times of Joseph P. Kennedy*. New York: McFadden, 1965.

Dupree, A. H., and L. H. Fishell, eds. "An Eyewitness Account of the New York Draft Riots, July 1863." *Mississippi Valley Historical Review* 47: 472–79.

Eaton, Hon. Dorman B. "The Degeneration of Tammany." *The North American Review*, no. 154 (February 1892): 297–304.

Ebner, Michael H., and Eugene M. Tobin, eds. *The Age of Urban Reform*. Port Washington, New York: Kennikat Press, 1977.

Eisinger, P. K. "Ethnic Political Transition in Boston, 1884–1933." *Political Science Quarterly* 93: 217–39.

Ellison, William H., ed. "Memoirs of Honorable William M. Gwin." *California Historical Quarterly* 19 (March 1940): 1.

Erie, Steven P. "The Development of Class and Ethnic Politics in San Francisco, 1870–1910: A Critique of the Pluralist Interpretation." Ph.D. dissertation, University of California at Los Angeles, 1975.

———. "Politics, the Public Sector, and Irish Social Mobility, San Francisco 1870–1900." *Western Political Quarterly* 31, no. 2 (1978): 274–89.

———. *Rainbow's End: Irish-Americans and the Dilemmas of Urban Machine Politics, 1840–1985*. Berkeley: University of California Press, 1988.

Ernst, R. "The One and Only Mike Walsh." *New York Historical Society Quarterly* 36: 43–65.

"Europe's Latest Lesson in Irish-American Politics." *Current Opinion* 67 (September 1919): 148–50.

Fairlie, Henry. *The Kennedy Promise: The Politics of Expectation*. Garden City, New York: Doubleday, 1973.

Farley, James A. *Behind the Ballots: The Personal History of a Politician*. New York: Harcourt, 1938.

———. *Jim Farley's Story: The Roosevelt Years*. New York: McGraw-Hill, 1948.

Farrell, J. T. "Archbishop Ireland and Manifest Destiny." *Catholic Historical Review* 33 (1936): 269–301.

Fay, Paul B., Jr. *The Pleasure of His Company*. New York: Popular Library, 1966.

Fee, Joan L. "Party Identification among American Catholics, 1972, 1973." *Ethnicity* 3, no. 1 (March 1976): 53–69.

Feuerlicht, Roberta Strauss. *Joe McCarthy and McCarthyism: The Hate That Haunts America*. New York: McGraw-Hill, 1972.

Finegan, James E. *Tammany At Bay*. New York, 1933.

Fitzsimmons, Louise. *The Kennedy Doctrine*. New York: Random, 1972.

Fleming, Thomas J. "I Am the Law." *American Heritage* 20 (June, 1969): 33–34, 37.

Flynn, E. G. *I Speak My Own Piece*. New York: Masses and Midstream, 1955.

Flynn, Edward J. *You're the Boss*. New York: Viking Press, 1947.

Flynn, G. Q. *American Catholics and the Roosevelt Presidency*. Lexington: University of Kentucky Press, 1965.

———. "Franklin D. Roosevelt and American Catholics, 1932–36." Ph.D. dissertation, Louisiana State University, 1966.

Flynn, George A. *Roosevelt and Romanism: Catholics and American Diplomacy*. New York: Greenwood Press, 1976.

Ford, P. "Irish Vote in the U.S." *North American Review* 147: 185.

Fordyce, Wellington C. "Nationality Groups in Cleveland Politics." *The Ohio State Archaeological and Historical Quarterly* 46.

Foster, Mark S. "The Early Career of Mayor Frank Hague." Master's thesis, University of Southern California, 1968.

———. "Frank Hague of Jersey City: The Boss as Reformer." *New Jersey History* 85.

Franklin, Allan. *The Trail of the Tiger*. New York: EPKC, 1928.

Franklin, C. E. "The Irish Element in American Politics." *Donohoe's Magazine* 34 (February 1895).

Freidel, Frank. *Franklin Roosevelt: The Apprenticeship*. Boston: Little, Brown, 1952.

Fried, Richard M. *Men against McCarthy*. New York: Columbia University Press, 1976.

Fuchs, Lawrence H. *John F. Kennedy and American Catholicism*. New York: Meredith, 1967.

———. "Presidential Politics in Boston: The Irish Response to Stevenson." *New England Quarterly* 30 (December 1957): 534–37.

Fuller, Helen. *Year of Trial: Kennedy's Crucial Decisions*. New York: Harcourt, Brace and World, 1962.

Funchion, Michael Francis. *Chicago's Irish Nationalists, 1881–1890*. New York: Arno Press, 1976.

Gabriel, Richard A. *Ethnic Voting in Primary Elections: The Irish and Italian of Providence, Rhode Island*. Kingston, Rhode Island: Bureau of Government Research, n.d.

Gay, Constance M. "The Campaign of 1855 in Virginia and the Fall of the Know-Nothing Party." *Richmond College Historical Papers* 1 (1916): 309–25.

Genen, Arthur. "John Kelly, New York's First Irish Boss." Ph.D. dissertation, New York University, 1971.

Gerson, L. *The Hyphenate in Recent American Politics*. Lawrence, Kansas: University of Kansas Press, 1964.

Gleason, William. *Daley of Chicago: The Man, the Mayor, and the Limits of Conventional Politics*. New York: Simon and Schuster, 1970.

Godkin, E. L. "Irish Conspirators and the American Government." *Nation* 36: 419.

Golden, Harry. *Mr. Kennedy and the Negroes*. Cleveland: World, 1964.

Gore, L. *Joe Must Go*. New York: Messner, 1954.

Gosnell, Harold F. *Boss Platt and His New York Machine*. Chicago: University of Chicago Press, 1924.

———. *Machine Politics: Chicago Model*. Chicago: University of Chicago Press, 1937.

Gottfried, Alex. *Boss Cermak of Chicago: A Study of Political Leadership*. Seattle: University of Washington Press, 1962.

Graham, Frank. *Al Smith American*. New York: Putnam, 1945.

Graham, Otis L., Jr. *An Encore for Reform: The Old Progressives and the New Deal*. New York: New Viewpoints, 1974.

Green, Larry. "Daley's Chicago Machine Begins to Squeak, Rust." *Los Angeles Time* 1 (December 19, 1977): 18.

Green, M. B. *The Problem of Boston*. New York: Norton, 1966.

Green, Paul Michael. "Irish Chicago: The Multiethnic Road to Machine Success." In *Ethnic Chicago*, edited by Peter d'A Jones and Melvin G. Holli. Grand Rapids, Michigan: William B. Eerdmans, 1981.

Greenstein, Fred I. "The Changing Pattern of Urban Party Politics." *Annals* (1964): 1–13.

Greer, J. K. "The Schism in the Democratic Party and the Electon of 1860." *Louisiana Historical Quarterly* 13 (1930): 470–79.

Greer, Scott. "Catholic Voters and the Democratic Party." *Public Opinion Quarterly* 25 (Winter 1961): 611–25.

Grey, W. E. "Twenty Years of Irish Home Rule In New York." *Quarterly Review* 171 (July 1890): 260–86.

Griffith, Robert. *The Politics of Fear: Joseph R. McCarthy and the Senate*. Lexington: University of Kentucky Press, 1970 (Reissued at Amherst: University of Massachusetts Press,1987).

Griffith, Robert, and Athan Theoharis, eds. *The Specter: Original Essays on the Cold War and the Origins of McCarthyism*. New York: New Viewpoints, 1974.

Grossman, Richard L., ed. *Let Us Begin: The First 100 Days of the Kennedy Administration*. New York: Simon and Schuster, 1961.

Gudelunas, William A., Jr., and William G. Shade. *Before the Molly Maguires: The Emergence of the Ethnoreligious Factor in the Politics of the Lower Anthracite Region, 1844–1872*. New York: Arno, 1976.

Gusfield, Joseph R. *Symbolic Crusade: Status Politics and the American Temperance Movement*. Urbana: University of Illinois Press, 1963.

Haeger, John D., and Michael P. Weber. *The Bosses*. Saint Charles, Missouri: Forum Press, 1974.

Halberstam, David. *The Unfinished Odyssey of Robert Kennedy*. New York: Random House, 1968.

Hall, Sue G., comp. and ed. *The Spirit of Robert F. Kennedy*. New York: Gorsset and Dunlap, 1968.

Halloran, Matthew F. *The Romance of the Merit System: Forty-Five Years' Reminiscences of the Civil Service*. 1928.

Handlin, Oscar. *Al Smith and His America*. Boston: Little, Brown, 1958.

———. "The Immigrant in American Politics." In *Foreign Influences in American Life*, edited by David Frederick Bowers. New Jersey: Princeton University Press, 1944.

Hapgood, Norman, and Henry Moskowitz. *Up from the City Streets: Alfred E. Smith*. New York: Grosset and Dunlap, 1927.

Harris, S. H. "John Louis O'Sullivan and the Elections of 1844 in New York." *New York History* 44 (1960): 278–98.

Hattery, John W. "The Presidential Election Campaigns of 1928 and 1960: A Comparison of the *Christian Century* and *America*." *Journal of Church and State* 9 (1967): 36–50.

Heath, Jim F. *Decade of Disillusionment: The Kennedy-Johnson Years*. Bloomington: Indiana University Press, 1975.

Henderson, Thomas McLean. *Tammany Hall and the New Immigrants: The Progressive Years*. New York: Arno Press, 1976.

Hennessey, Michael E. *Twenty-Five Years of Massachusetts Politics: From Russell to McCall, 1890–1915*. Boston, 1917.

Hennessy, Maurice N. *I'll Come Back in the Springtime: John F. Kennedy and the Irish*. New York: Washburn, 1966.

Herlihy, David J. "Battle against Bigotry: Father Peter C. Yorke and the American Protective Association in San Francisco, 1893–97." *Records of the American Catholic Historical Society of Philadelphia* 62 (June 1951): 95–120.

Hernon, J. M., Jr. *Celts, Catholics, and Copperheads*. Ohio State University Press, 1968.

———. "Irish Religious Opinion on the American Civil War." *Catholic Historical Review* 49 (1957): 508–23.

Hersh, Burton. *The Education of Edward Kennedy: A Family Biography*. New York: Morrow, 1972.

Hichborn, Franklin. *"The System," As Uncovered by the San Francisco Graft Prosecution*. San Francisco: n.p., 1915.

Higham, J. "Another Look at Nativism." *Catholic Historical Review* 44 (1952): 147–58.

Hill, Gladwin. *Dancing Bear: An Inside Look at California Politics*. Cleveland: World, 1968.

A History of Election Riots in New Orleans and the Exposure of the Systemic Violence and Corruption of the Modern Democracy. New Orleans: American Party, 1856.

Hogan, P. E. "Americanism and the Catholic University of America." *Catholic Historical Review* 33 (1947): 158–90.

Holt, Michael. *Forging a Majority: The Formation of the Republican Party in Pittsburgh, 1848–1860*. New Haven, Connecticut: Yale University Press, 1969.

———. "The Politics of Impatience: The Origins of Know Nothingism." *Journal of American History* 60 (1973): 309–31.

An Honest Appeal to Every Voter: The Bible in the Schools. New York: American Republican Party, 1844.

Honan, William H. *Ted Kennedy: Profile of a Survivor*. Chicago: Quadrangle, 1972.

Howard, J. Woodford, Jr. "Frank Murphy and the Philippine Commonwealth." *Pacific Historical Review* 33 (February 1964): 45–68.

———. *Mr. Justice Murphy: A Political Biography*. Princeton: Princeton University Press, 1968.

Howe, Frederic C. "The Boss, the Party, and the System." In *The City: The Hope of Democracy*, New York: Scribner's Sons, 1914. 92–112.

———. *Confessions of a Reformer*. New York: Charles Scribner's Sons, 1925.

Huthmacher, J. Joseph. *Massachusetts, People and Politics, 1919–1933*. New York: Atheneum, 1969.

———. *Senator Robert F. Wagner and the Rise of Urban Liberalism*. New York: Atheneum, 1968.

———. "Urban Liberalism and the Age of Reform." *Mississippi Valley Historical Review* 49 (September 1962): 231–41.

Immigration and the Present Mode of Naturalization Dangerous to the South and the Union of the States. New Orleans: American Party, 1856.

"Irish Republicans and General Washington." *Historical Monthly* (Dawson's) 15: 201.

Issel, William. "Class and Ethnic Conflict in San Francisco Political History: The Reform Charter of 1898," *Labor History*, 18 (Summer 1977): 34–59.

Jackson, Joy J. *New Orleans in the Guilded Age*. Baton Rouge: Louisiana State University Press, 1969.

Jeffreys-Jones, Rhodri. "Massachusetts Labour and the League of Nations Controversy in 1919." *Irish Historical Studies* (Ireland), 19, no. 76 (1975): 396–416.

Jensen, Richard. "Party Coalitions in America, 1820s to 1870s." *Working Paper Series*, series 3, no. 1. Notre Dame University, Center for the Study of American Catholicism, 1978.

Johnson, W. M. "On the Outside Looking In: Irish, Italian and black Ethnic Politics in an American City." Ph.D. dissertation, Yale University, 1977.

Josephson, Matthew, and Hannah Josephson. *Al Smith: Hero of the Cities*. Boston: Houghton, Mifflin, 1969.

Kaiser, Robert Blair. *R.F.K. Must Die! A History of the Robert Kennedy Assassination and Its Aftermath*. New York: Dutton, 1970.

Kass, Alvin. *Politics in New York State, 1800–1830*. New York: Syracuse University Press, 1965.

Kaucher, Dorothy. *James Duval Phelan: A Portrait, 1861–1930*. Saratoga: Montalvo Association, 1965.

Kauer, Ralph. "The Workingmen's Party of California." *Pacific Historical Review* 12 (September 1944): 275–91.

Keefe, Thomas M. "Chicago's Flirtation with Political Nativism, 1854–1856." *Records of the American Catholic Historical Society of Philadelphia* 82 (1971): 131–58.

Kennedy on Approaching Next President. Washington, D.C.: Health Security Action Council, 1975.

Kennedy, Eugene. *Himself: The Life and Times of Mayor Richard J. Daley*. New York: Penguin Books, 1978.

———. *St. Patrick's Day With Mayor Daley and Other Things Too Good To Miss*. New York: Seabury Press, 1976.

———. "The Year That Shook Chicago." *The New York Times Magazine*. March 5, 1978.

"Kennedy as a 'Flawed Product': Reshaping Teddy's Image." *Esquire* (June 1970): 87–99.

Kennedy, John F. *The Burden and the Glory*. New York: Harper and Row, 1964.

———. *The Completed Kennedy Wit*. New York: Citadel, 1967.

———. *A Memory of John Fitzgerald Kennedy*. Dublin, Ireland: Wood Printing Works.

———. *President Kennedy's Program*. Washington, D.C.: Congressional Quarterly Service, 1961.

———. *To Turn the Tide*. New York: Harper, 1962.

———. "The Visit to Ireland." *Department of State Bulletin* 49 (July 22, 1963): 128–32.

Kennedy, Joseph P. *I'm For Roosevelt*. New York: Reynal, 1936.

Kennedy, P. W. "The Know-Nothing Movement in Kentucky: The Role of M. J. Spalding, Catholic Bishop of Louisville." *Filson Club Historical Quarterly* 38: 20–30.

Kennedy, Robert F. *Thirteen Days: A Memoir of the Cuban Missile Crisis*. New York: W. W. Norton, 1969.

Kennedy, Rose Fitzgerald. *Times to Remember*. Garden City, New York: Doubleday, 1974.

Kerr, William T., Jr. "The Progressives of Washington, 1910–1912." *Pacific Northwest Quarterly* 55.

Kilroe, Edwin P., Abraham Kaplan, and Joseph Johnson. "The Story of Tammany." In *Tammany: A Patriotic History, 1786–1924*. New York: New York County Democratic Committee, 1924.

King, Clyde L. *The Fenian Movement*. Boulder: University of Colorado, 1909.

Kleppner, Paul J. *The Cross of Culture*. New York: The Free Press, 1970.

———. "Lincoln and the Immigrant Vote: A Case of Religious Polarization." *Mid-America* 67 (July 1966): 176–95.

Koskoff, David E. *Joseph P. Kennedy: A Life and Times*. Englewood Cliffs, New Jersey: Prentice-Hall, 1974.

Kunth, P. F. "Nativism in California." Master's thesis, University of California, Berkeley, (1947).

Landis, Mark. *Joseph McCarthy, the Politics of Chaos*. Selinsgrove: Susquehanna University Press, 1987.

Lapomarda, V. "Maurice Joseph Tobin: The Decline of Bossism in Boston." *New England Quarterly*, 43: 365–66.

Lasky, Victor. *J.F.K.: The Man and the Myth*. New York: Macmillan, 1963.

———. *Robert F. Kennedy: The Myth and the Man*. New York: Trident, 1968.

Leary, William M., Jr. "Woodrow Wilson, Irish Americans, and the Elections of 1916." *Journal of American History* 54 (1968): 68–72.

Lee, John Hancock. *The Origin and Progress of the American Party in Politics*. Philadelphia, 1855.

Lens, Sidney. "Mayor Daley's Last Hurrah." *Progressive* 39, no. 4 (1975): 13–18.

Leslie, Shane. *The Irish Issue in Its American Aspect*. New York: Charles Scribner's Sons, 1917.

Leuchtenburg, William E. *Franklin D. Roosevelt and the New Deal*. New York: Harper and Row, 1963.

Levin, Murray Burton. *Kennedy Campaigning: The System and the Style as Practiced by Senator Edward Kennedy*. Boston: Beacon, 1966.

Levine, Edward M. *The Irish and Irish Politicians*. Notre Dame: University of Notre Dame Press, 1966.

Lichtman, A. J. *Prejudice and the Old Politics: The Presidential Election of 1928*. Chapel Hill: University of North Carolina Press, 1979.

Lieberson, Goddard. *John Fitzgerald Kennedy—As We Remember Him*. New York: Macmillan, 1965.

Lincoln, Evelyn. *Kennedy and Johnson*. New York: Holt, Rinehart, and Winston, 1968.

Link, Arthur S. "What Happened to the Progressive Movement in the 1920's." *American Historical Review* 64.

———. *Woodrow Wilson and the Progressive Era*. New York: Harper and Row, 1954.

Lippman, Theo., Jr. *Senator Ted Kennedy*. New York: W. W. Norton, 1976.

Lipset, Seymour Martin. "Three Decades of the Radical Right: Coughlinites, McCarthyites and Birchers." In *The Radical Right*, edited by Danial Bell. Garden City, New York: Anchor Books, 1964, 395 ff.

Lipset, Seymour Martin and Earl Raab, eds. *The Politics of Unreason: Right-Wing Extremism in America, 1790–1970*. New York: Harper and Row, 1970.

Litt, E. *Beyond Pluralism: Ethnic Politics in America*. Illinois: Scott, Foresman, 1970.

———. *The Political Culture of Massachusetts*. Cambridge: Harvard University Press, 1965.

Loeb, James, Jr. "The Catholic Vote." *Commonweal*, June 16, 1950.

Lohbeck, Don. *Patrick J. Hurley*. Chicago: Regnery, 1957.

London, H. "Irish Assimilation and the American Republican Party." *Dublin Review* 242 (Spring 1968): 65–74.

Lord, Donald C. *John F. Kennedy*. New York: Barron's, 1977.

Lorenz, J. D. *Jerry Brown: The Man on the White Horse*. Boston: Houghton Mifflin Company, 1978.

Loth, David. *Public Plunder: A History of Graft in America*. New York: Carrick and Evans, 1938.

Lowell, A. L. "Irish Agitation in America." *Forum* 4: 397.

Lowi, Theodore J. *At The Pleasure of the Mayor: Patronage and Power in New York City, 1898–1958*. New York: Free Press of Glencoe, 1964.

Luebke, Frederick C. *Ethnic Voters and the Election of Lincoln*. Lincoln: University of Nebraska Press, 1971.

Lunt, Richard D. *High Ministry of Government: The Political Career of Frank Murphy*. Detroit: Wayne State University Press, 1965.

Lynch, Denis. *Boss Tweed*. Boni, 1927.

Lynch, Jeremiah. *Buckleyism: The Government of a State*. San Francisco: n.p., 1889.

———. *The Life of David C. Broderick: A Senator of the Fifties*. New York: Baker and Taylor, 1911.

"Magic of Camelot Fades." *New York Times* (November 14, 1971): 401.

Magil, A. B. *The Truth About Father Coughlin*. Workers Library, 1935.

Manchester, William R. *Portrait of a President: John F. Kennedy in Profile*. Boston: Little, Brown, 1962.

Mandlebaum, S. J. *The Social Setting of Intolerance: The Know Nothings: The Red Scare and McCarthyism*. Illinois: Scott, Foresman, 1964.

Mann, Arthur. *La Guardia: A Fighter Against His Times*. Philadelphia: Lippincott, 1959.

———. *Yankee Reformers in the Urban Age*. Cambridge: Belknap Press of Harvard University Press, 1954.

Marcus, Sheldon. *Father Coughlin: The Tumultuous Life of the Priest of the Little Flower*. Boston: Little, Brown, 1973.

Marshall, Charles C. "An Open Letter to the Honorable Alfred E. Smith." *Atlantic Monthly* 139 no. 4, (April 1927): 541–49.

Martin, Ralph G. *The Bosses*. New York: Putnam, 1964.

Martin, Ralph G., and E. Plant. *Front Runner, Dark Horse*. Garden City, New York: Doubleday, 1960.

Matthews, J. "Politics of Bussing." *New Republic* 171 (November 7, 1974): 9–11.

Matusow, Allen J., ed. *Joseph McCarthy*. Englewood Cliffs, New Jersey: Prentice-Hall, 1970.

McAdoo, William Gibbs. *Crowded Years*. Boston and New York: Houghton, Mifflin, 1931.

McBride, P. W. *Culture Clash: Immigrants and Reformers, 1880–1920*. San Francisco: R and E Research Associates, 1975.

McCaffrey, Lawrence J. "Irish-American Politics: Power With or Without Purpose." In *The Irish in America: Emigration, Assimilation and Impact*, edited by P. J. Drury. *Irish Studies*, vol. 4. Cambridge: Cambridge University Press, 1985.

McCaffrey, Lawrence J., ed. *Irish Nationalism and the American Contribution*. New York: Arno Press, 1976.

McCarthy, J. *McCarthyism: The Fight for America*. New York: Devin-Adair, 1952.

McCarthy, Joe. *The Remarkable Kennedys*. New York: Dial, 1960.

McColley, Robert, ed. *Federalists, Republicans, and Foreign Entanglements, 1789–1815*. Englewood Cliffs, New Jersey: Prentice-Hall, 1969.

McConville, Mary St. Patrick. *Political Nativism in the State of Maryland, 1830–1860*. Washington, D.C.: The Catholic University of America Press, 1928.

McCormick, R. L. "Ethno-Cultural Interpretations of Nineteenth-Century American Voting Behavior." *Political Science Quarterly* 89 (1974): 351–77.

McGann, Agnes Geraldine. *Nativism in Kentucky to 1860*. Washington, D.C.: The Catholic University of America Press, 1944.

McGurrin, James. *Bourke Cockran.* New York: Charles Scribner's Sons, 1948.

McKean, Dayton D. *The Boss: The Hague Machine in Action.* Boston: Houghton, Mifflin, 1940.

McLaughlin, J. Fairfax. *The Life and Times of John Kelley, Tribune of the People.* New York: American News, 1885.

Meyer, K. "The Politics of Loyalty from La-Follette to McCarthy in Wisconsin, 1918–1952." Ph.D. dissertation, University of Wisconsin, 1972.

Meyerhuber, C. I. "U. S. Imperialism and Ethnic Journalism: The New Manifest Destiny as Reflected in Boston's Irish-American Press, 1890–1900." *Eire-Ireland* 9 (1974): 18–29.

Miller, Douglas T. *Jackson Aristocracy: Class and Democracy in New York: 1830–1860.* New York: Oxford University Press, 1968.

Miller, Zane L. *Boss Cox's Cincinnati: Urban Politics in the Progressive Era.* New York: Oxford University Press, 1968.

Moley, Raymond. *Masters of Politics.* New York: Funk and Wagnalls, 1949.

Moody, Sidney C., ed. *Triumph and Tragedy.* New York: Morrow, 1968

Moore, Edmund A. *A Catholic Runs for President, The Campaign of 1928.* New York: Ronald, 1956.

Moos, Malcolm, and Stephen Hess. *Hats in the Ring.* New York: Random, 1960.

Moran, Rev. Dennis Michael. "Anti-Catholicism in Early Maryland Politics, 1634–1718." Master's thesis, University of Notre Dame, 1949.

Moscow, Warren. *The Last of the Big-Time Bosses.* New York, 1971.

Moscow, Warren. *What Have You Done For Me, Lately? The Ins and Outs of New York City Politics.* Englewood Cliffs, New Jersey: Prentice-Hall, 1967.

Moskowitz, Henry. *Alfred E. Smith: An American Career.* New York: Seltzer, 1924.

Mugglebee, Ruth. *Father Coughlin of the Shrine of the Little Flower.* Garden City, New York: Garden City, 1933.

Mulkern, J. R. "The Know-Nothing Party in Massachusetts." Ph.D. dissertation, Boston University, 1963.

Murphy, C. "McCarthy and the Businessman." *Fortune* 49: 156–58, 180–94.

"Murphy Chieftain." *Outlook* 137 (May 7, 1924): 10–12.

"Murphy, the Terrible Ogre of American Politics." *Current Opinion* 55 (December, 1913): 403–4.

"Murphyizing New York State." *Nation* 92 (July 6, 1911): 4–5.

Murray, Michael James. "The Evolution of a City Boss: Ed Butler of St. Louis." Master's thesis, Northeast Missouri State University, 1975.

Mushkat, Jerome. *Tammany: The Evolution of a Political Machine, 1789–1865.* New York: Syracuse University Press, 1971.

Myers, Gustavus. *The History of Tammany Hall.* New York: The Author, 1901.

Nelli, Humbert S. "John Powers and the Italians: Politics in a Chicago Ward, 1896–1921." *The Journal of American History* 17 (June 1970): 74.

"New Irish Declaration of Independence." *Literary Digest* 52 (March 18, 1916): 702–3.

"The New York Campaign: The Outcome." *Outlook* 93 (November 13, 1909): 572–73.

"The New York City Vote Analyzed." *Nation* 81 (November 16, 1905): 394–95.

"The New York Election." *Living Age* 263 (December 4, 1909): 632–34.

"The New York Election." *Nation* 105 (November 8, 1917): 500.

"New York's Contested Election." *Outlook* 81 (December 23, 1905): 945–47.

"New York's Municipal Campaign." *Independent* 59 (October 19, 1905): 936–37.

"New York's Return to Tammany." *Literary Digest* 55 (November 17, 1917): 12–13.

Newfield, Jack. *Robert Kennedy.* New York: Dutton, 1969.

Nie, N. H. "Political Attitudes among American Ethnics: A Study of Perceptual Distortion." *Ethnicity* 1 (1974): 317–42.

Noonan, C. J. *Nativism in Connecticut, 1829–1860.* Washington, D.C.: The Catholic University, 1938.

Nugent, Walter T. K. *The Tolerant Populists: Kansas, Populism and Nativism.*

Chicago: University of Chicago Press, 1963.

Nunnerley, D. *President Kennedy and Britain*. New York: St. Martin's Press, 1972.

O'Brien, Michael. *McCarthy and McCarthyism in Wisconsin*. Columbia, Missouri: University of Missouri Press, 1980.

O'Connell, M. R. *Irish Politics and Social Conflict in the Age of the American Revolution*. Philadelphia: University of Pennsylvania Press, 1965.

O'Connor Len. *Clout: Mayor Daley and His City*. New York: Avon Books, 1975.

———. *Requiem: The Decline and Demise of Mayor Daley and His Era*. Chicago: Contemporary Books, 1977.

Odegard, Peter H. *Pressure Politics: The Story of the Anti-Saloon League*. New York: Columbia University Press, 1928.

O'Donnell, Kenneth P., and David F. Powers, with Joe McCarthy. *Johnny, We Hardly Knew You: Memories of John Fitzgerald Kennedy*. Boston: Little, Brown, 1972.

O'Donovan-Rossa, Jeremiah. *In Senate, Before Committee on Privileges and Elections, in the Matter of Petition of Jeremiah O'Donovan-Rossa, for Seat as Senator From Fourth Senate District, State of New York: Petition and Statement of Claimant, December 30th, 1871 and February 7th, 1872*. New York: Sackett, 1872.

O'Flaherty, Patrick. "James Huston, A Forgotten Irish-American Patriot." *Irish Sword* (Ireland), 11, no. 42 (1973): 39–47.

O'Grady, Joseph Patrick. "Anthony M. Keiley (1832–1905): Virginia's Catholic Politician." *Catholic Historical Review* 54 (1969): 613–35.

———. "Immigrants and the Politics of Reconstruction in Richmond, Virginia." *Records of the American Catholic Historical Society, Philadelphia*. 83 (1972): 87–101.

———. "The Irish." In *The Immigrants Influence on Wilson's Peace Policies*, edited by Joseph Patrick O'Grady. Lexington: University of Kentucky, 1967.

———. "The Irish-American Influence in the Rejection of the Phelps-Rosebery Extradition Treaty of 1886." Master's thesis, University of Notre Dame, 1958.

———. *Irish-Americans and Anglo-American Relations, 1880–1888*. New York: Arno Press, 1976.

———. "The Roman Questions in American Politics: 1885." In *Journal of Church and State*, 10 (1968): 365–77.

O'Grady, M. D. "The Role of Thomas J. Walsh in Senatorial Contests, 1913–1926." Ph.D. dissertation, University of Notre Dame, 1951.

O'Hare, Sister M., and Jeanne d'Arc, C.S.J. "The Public Career of Patrick A. Collins." Ph.D. dissertation, Boston College, 1959.

Oldham, E. M. "Irish Support of the Abolitionist Movement." *Boston Public Library Quarterly* 10 (1958): 175–87 (1958).

O'Leary, John. *Recollections of Fenians and Fenianism*. London: Downey, 1896.

O'Malley, Peter J. "Mayor Martin Kennelly of Chicago: A Political Biography." Ph.D. dissertation, University of Illinois at Chicago, 1980.

O'Neill, William L. *The Progressive Years*. New York: Dodd, Mead, 1975.

The Origin, Principles, and Purposes of the American Party. New Orleans: American Party, 1855.

Orth, Samuel P. *The Boss and the Machine*. New Haven: Yale Univeristy Press, 1919.

Oshinsky, David M. *Senator Joseph McCarthy and the American Labor Movement*. Columbia: University of Missouri Press, 1976.

Osofsky, G. "Abolitionists, Irish Immigrants, and the Dilemmas of Romantic Nationalism." *American Historical Review* 80 (October 1975): 889–912.

Overdyke, William Darrell. *The Know-Nothing Party in the South*. Baton Rouge: Louisiana State University Press, 1950.

Parenti, Michael. "Ethnic Politics and the Persistance of Ethnic Identification." *American Political Science Review* 61, no. 3 (September 1967): 717–26.

"The Passing of Boss Murphy." *World's Work* 63 (June 1924): 124–26.

Paterson, Isabel. "Murphy." *American Mercury* 14 (July 1928): 347–54.

Peden, J. R. "Charles O'Conor and the 1872 Presidential Election." *The Recorder* 37 (1976): 80–90.

Peel, Roy V. *The Political Clubs of New York City*. New York and London: G. P. Putnam's Sons, 1935.

Peel, Roy V., and Thomas C. Donnelly. *The 1928 Campaign: An Analysis*. New York: Smith, 1951.

"A Peep into Murphy's Brain." *Literary Digest* 63 (March 7, 1914): 516–17.

Perkins, Frances. *The Roosevelt I Knew*. New York: The Viking Press, 1946.

Peterson, P. L. "Stopping Al Smith: The 1928 Democratic Primary in South Dakota." *South Dakota History* 4 (1974): 439–54.

Phelan, James D. "Municipal Conditions in San Francisco." *Arena* 17 (June 1897): 989–95.

Pike, James A. *A Roman Catholic in the White House*. Garden City, New York: Doubleday, 1960.

Piper, R. M. "The Irish in Chicago." Master's thesis, University of Chicago, n.d.

Polsby, N. "Towards an Explanation of McCarthyism." *Political Studies* 8: 250–71.

The Pope's Bull and the Words of Daniel O'Connell. New York: American Republican Party, 1856.

The Popish Intrigue: Fremont a Catholic!!! New Orleans: American Party, 1856.

"President and the Hyphen." *Literary Digest* 52 (March 18, 1916): 935.

Pringle, Henry F. *Alfred E. Smith: A Critical Study*. New York: Macy-Masius, 1927.

Proskauer, Joseph M. *A Segment of My Times*. New York: Farrar, Straus, 1950.

Quinlan, Anna. "Paul O'Dwyer Elects to Leave His Old Sod, Politics, and Is Moving on to New Ground." *New York Times* (September 21, 1977): 35.

Rakove, Milton L. *Don't Make No Waves—Don't Back No Losers, An Insiders Analysis of the Daley Machine*. Indiana: Indiana University Press, 1975.

———. *We Don't Need Nobody Sent, An Oral History of the Daley Years*. Indiana: Indiana University Press, 1979.

Redding, William M. *Toms Down, Kansas CIty and the Pendergast Legend*. New York, 1947.

Reeves, Thomas C. "McCarthyism: Interpretations Since Hofstadter." *Wisconsin Magazine of History* 60 (Autumn 1976): 42–54.

———, ed., *McCarthyism*. Hinsdale, Illinois: Dryden Press, 1973.

Reid, Sidney. "Tell It to Gaynor!" *Independent* 69 (August 19, 1910): 334–38.

Ridge, Martin. *Ignatius Donnelly: The Portrait of a Politician*. Chicago: University of Chicago Press, 1962.

Righter, Robert W. "Washington Bartlett: Mayor of San Francisco, 1883–1887." *Journal of the West* 3 (February 1964): 102.

Riordon, William L. *Plunkitt of Tammany Hall*. New York: E. P. Dutton, 1963.

Robinson, Edgar Eugene. *Machine Politics: A Study of Albany's O'Connells*. New Brunswick, New Jersey: Transactions Books, 1977.

Robinson, Edgar Eugene. *They Voted For Roosevelt: The Presidential Vote, 1932–1944*. Stanford, California: Stanford University Press, 1947.

Robinson, F. S. *Albany's O'Connell Machine*. New York: The Washington Park Spirit, 1973.

Rogin, M. *The Intellectuals and McCarthy*. Cambridge: MIT Press, 1967.

Roosevelt, Franklin D. *The Happy Warrior: Alfred E. Smith*. Boston and New York: Houghton, Mifflin, 1928.

Rorty, James, and Moshe Decter. *McCarthy and the Communists*. Boston: Beacon, 1954.

Rosebault, Charles J. "Tammany: New Ways of the Old Tiger." *World's Work* 48 (July 1924): 251–58.

Rosenthal, Herbert Hillel. "The Progressive Movement in New York State, 1906–1914." Ph.D. dissertation, Harvard University, 1955.

Ross, Douglas. *Robert F. Kennedy: Apostle of Change*. New York: Pocket, 1968.

Rovere, Richard H. *Senator Joe McCarthy*. New York: Harcourt, Brace, 1959.

Royko, Mike. *Boss: Richard J. Daley of Chicago*. New York: Dutton, 1971.

Rozwenc, Edwin, ed. *Roosevelt, Wilson, and the Trusts*. Boston: Heath, 1950.

Russell, F. "Honey Fitz." *American Heritage* 19 (August 1968): 28–31.

Rutherford, J. R. *Secret History of the Fenian Conspiracy*. London: Kegan Paul, 1877.

Ryan, Thomas G. "Ethnicity in the 1940 Presidential Election in Iowa: A Quantitative Approach." *Annals of Iowa* 43 (Spring 1977): 615–35.

Salinger, Pierre, et al., eds. *An Honorable Profession: A Tribute to Robert F. Kennedy*. Garden City, New York: Doubleday, 1968.

Salter, J. T. *Boss Rule*. New York: Whittlesey House, McGraw-Hill Book, 1935.

Sarbaugh, Timothy J. "Culture, Militancy, and De Valera: Irish Republicanism in California, 1900–1936." Master's thesis, San Jose State University, 1980.

———. "Irish Republicanism vs Pure Americanism: California's Reaction to Eamon De Valera's Visits." *California History* (Summer 1981): 158–72.

———. "Kennedy and American Catholics." Unpublished Ph.D. dissertation, University of Chicago, 1987.

Satrem, Wallace S., and Herbert Kaufman. *Governing New York City: Politics in the Metropolis*. New York: Sage, 1964.

Schaeffer, Joseph. "Who Elected Lincoln?" *The American Historical Review* 47.

Schlesinger, Arthur M., Jr. *Kennedy or Nixon: Does it Make Any Difference?* New York: Macmillan, 1965.

———. *A Thousand Days: John F. Kennedy in the White House*. Boston: Houghton Mifflin, 1965.

Schurz, Carl. *The Spoils System*. Altemus, 1896.

Scisco, Louis D. *Political Nativism in New York State*. New York: Columbia University Press, 1901.

Sevareid, Eric, ed. *Candidates 1960*. New York: Basic Books, 1959.

Sexton, Patricia Cayo, and Brendan Sexton. *Blue Collars and Hard-Hats: The Working Class and the Future of American Politics*. New York: Random, 1971.

Shannon, William V. *The American Irish: A Political and Social Portrait*. New York: Collier Books, 1974.

———. *The Heir Apparent: Robert Kennedy and the Struggle for Power*. New York: Macmillan, 1967.

———. "The Lasting Hurrah." *The New York Times Magazine*, March 14, 1976.

Sharrow, W. B. "John Hughes and a Catholic Response to Slavery in Antebellum America." *Journal of Negro History* 571: 254–69.

Shaw, William V. "The Men Who are Governing New York City." *Review of Reviews* 41 (March 1910): 300–7.

Shea, J. G. "The Anti-Catholic Issue in the Late Election: The Relation of Catholics to Political Parties." *American Catholic Quarterly Review* 12 (1881): 705–13.

Sherman, Richard B. "The Status Revolution and Massachusetts Progressive Leadership." *Political Science Quarterly* 78.

Short, K. R. M. *The Dynamite War: Irish American Bombers in Victorian Britain*. Dublin: Bill and Macmillar, n.d.

"'Silent Charles,' the Mayor Maker." *Literary Digest* 81 (May 17, 1924): 38–44.

Silva, Ruth Carided. *Rum, Religions, and Votes: 1927 Reexamined*. University Park: Pennsylvania State University Press, 1962.

Skelton, Isabel. *The Life of Thomas D'Arcy Mcgee*. Gardenvale, Canada: Garden City Press, 1925.

Smith, Alred E. *Campaign Addresses of Governor Alfred E. Smith, Democratic Candidate for President, 1928*. New York: Lyon, 1929.

Smith, Sister Mary Sean. "The Influence of the Irish Vote in Chicago in the Elections of 1844, 1888, and 1892." Master's thesis, University of Notre Dame, 1958.

Smith, William David. "Alfred E. Smith and John F. Kennedy: The Religious Issue during the Presidential Campaigns of 1928 and 1960." Ph.D. dissertation, Southern Illinois University, 1964.

Society of California Pioneers. *In Memorium: James Phelan*. San Francisco, 1893.

Sorensen, Theodore C. *Kennedy*. New York: Harper and Row, 1965.

———. *The Kennedy Legacy*. New York: Macmillan, 1969.

"The Sources of Tammany's Power." *Outlook* 73 (February 21, 1903): 419–21.

Speed, John Gilmer. "Purchase of Votes: How Votes are Bought in New York City." *Harper's Weekly* 49 (March 18, 1905): 386, 388.

70 Bibliography

Spivak, John L. *Shrine of the Silver Dollar*. Modern Age, 1940.

Stave, Bruce M. *The New Deal and the Last Hurrah*. Pittsburgh: University of Pittsburgh Press, 1970.

———, ed. *Urban Bosses, Machines and Progressive Reformers*. Lexington: Heath, 1972.

Stebbins, Charles M. *Tammany Hall: Its History, Organization and Methods*. Brooklyn: Stebbins, 1921.

Steele, Robert V. P. *When Even Angels Wept: The Senator Joseph McCarthy Affair—A Story Without a Hero*. New York: Morrow, 1973.

Steinke, J. "The Rise of McCarthyism." Master's thesis, Univeristy of Wisconsin, 1960.

Stoddard, Lothrop. *Master of Manhattan: The Life of Richard Croker*. New York: Longmans, Green, 1931.

Stowe, Lyman Beecher. "The New York Mayoralty Campaigning: Why It Is a National Issue." *Outlook* 118 (October 31, 1917): 332–33.

Strange, D. C. "Al Smith and the Republican Party at Prayer: The Lutheran Vote, 1928." *Review of Politics* 32: 347–64.

Straton, H. H. and F. M. Szasz. "The Reverend John Roach Straton and the Presidential Campaign of 1928." *New York State History* 69: 200–17.

Swanberg, W. A. *Citizen Hearst: A Biography of William Randolph Hearst*. New York: Charles Scribner's Sons, 1961.

Swanstrom, Roy. "The Reform Administration of James D. Phelan, Mayor of San Francisco." Master's thesis, University of California, Berkeley, 1949.

Sweeney, K. "Rum, Romanism, Representations and Reform: Coalition Politics in Massachusetts, 1847–1853." *Civil War History* 22: 116–37.

Syndergaard, R. "Wild Irishmen and the Alien and Sedition Acts." *Eire-Ireland* 9: 17–24.

Syrett, Harold, ed. *The Gentleman and the Tiger: The Autobiography of George B. McClellan, Jr*. Philadelphia: Lippincott, 1956.

"Tackling the Tammany Tiger." *Literary Digest* 70 (August 13, 1921): 10.

"Tammany's Confidence Game." *Outlook* 81 (October 7, 1905): 296–97.

"The Tammany Man." *Harper's Weekly* 46 (March 15, 1902): 332.

"Tammany and the Masses." *Independent* 53 (May 30, 1901): 1264–65.

"Tammany's Mixed Allies." *Nation* 77 (October 29, 1903): 335–36.

"Tammany's Return to Power." *Outlook* 117 (November 14, 1971): 401.

"The Tammany Victory: Its Meaning." *Outlook* 75 (November 14, 1903): 625–28.

"Tammany's Waterloo." *Literary Digest* 67 (November 15, 1913): 927–29.

Tanzer, Lester, ed. *The Kennedy Circle*. Washington, D.C.: Luce, 1961.

Tarr, Joel A. "J. R. Walsh of Chicago: A Case Study in Banking and Politics, 1881–1905." *Business History Review* 41 (1966): 451–66.

———. *A Study in Boss Politics: William Lorimer of Chicago*. Urbana: University of Illinois Press, 1971.

Terry, Edmund. "How Murphy Works." *Harper's Weekly* 53 (October 18 and 25, 1913): 10–11, 22–23.

Thelan, D. and E. Thelan. "Joe Must Go: The Movement to Recall Senator Joseph McCarthy." *Wisconsin Magazine of History* 49 (1966): 185–209.

Theoharis, Athan G. *Seeds of Repression, Harry S. Truman and the Origins of McCarthyism*. Chicago: Quadrangle Books, 1971.

Thompson, Charles Willis. "The Persistence of Tammany." *New York Times Magazine*. February 19, 1924.

———. "The Three Musketeers of French Lick." *New York Times Magazine*. December 9, 1923.

Thompson, Robert E. and Hortense Myers. *Robert F. Kennedy: The Brother Within*. New York: Macmillan, 1962.

"Times on Kennedy Legacy." *New York Times* (November 22, 1973): 46.

Tinkcom, Harry Marlin. *The Republicans and Federalists in Pennsylvania, 1790–1901*. Pennsylvania Historical and Museum Commission, 1950.

Toledano, Ralph and Victor Lasky. *Seeds of Treason*. London, 1950.

Toledo Committee, Unitarian Fellowship for Social Justice. *Coughlin Defiles Lincoln.* Ohio, 1940.

Tull, Charles J. *Father Coughlin and the New Deal.* Syracuse: Syracuse University Press, 1965.

Tulley, G. *F.D.R., My Boss.* New York: Scribner's, 1949.

Tumulty, Joseph P. *Woodrow Wilson as I Know Him.* Literary Digest, 1925.

Turner, George Kibbe. "Tammany's Control of New York by Professional Criminals." *McClure's* 33 (June 1909): 117–34.

Tuska, Benjamin. "Know Nothingism in Baltimore, 1854–1869." *Catholic Historical Review* 11 (1925): 217–51.

Van Nostrand, A. D. "The Lomasney Legend." *New England Quarterly* 21.

Vanden, Heuval, J. William, and Milton Gwirtzman. *On His Own: Robert F. Kennedy, 1964–1968.* Garden City, New York: Doubleday, 1970.

Villard, Oswald. "The New York Mayoralty Election." *Nation* 105 (October 25, 1917): 448–49.

Voss, Earl H., et al. *The New Frontiersmen.* Washington, D.C.: Public Affairs Press, 1961.

Wallace, William Kay. *The Passing of Politics.* New York: Macmillan, 1924.

Walsh, James P. "Abe Ruef Was No Boss: Machine Politics, Reform, and San Francisco." *California Historical Quarterly* 51 (Spring 1972): 3–16.

———. "De Valera in the United States, 1919." *Records of the American Catholic Historical Society of Philadelphia* 63 (September–December, 1962): 98–106.

———. *Ethnic Militancy: An Irish Catholic Prototype.* San Francisco: R and E Associates, 1972.

———, ed. *The Irish: America's Political Class.* New York: Arno Press, 1976.

———. "Peter Yorke and Progressivism in California, 1908." *Eire-Ireland* 10 no. 2: 73–81.

"The War on Murphy." *Literary Digest* 63 (February 21, 1914): 361–63.

Ward, Louis B. *Father Charles E. Coughlin: An Authorized Biography.* New York: Tower Publishers, 1933.

Warms, W. Axel. "Charles Francis Murphy, Human Being." *New York Times Magazine* (February 22, 1914): 5.

Warner, Emily Smith, and Daniel Hawthorne. *The Happy Warrior: A Biography of My Father Alfred E. Smith.* Garden City, New York: Doubleday, 1956.

Warren Commission. *Report of the Warren Commission on the Assassination of President Kennedy.* New York: Bantam Books, 1963.

Watkins, Arthur Vivian. *Enough Rope: The Inside Story of the Censure of Senator Joe McCarthy by His Colleagues, The Controversial Hearings that Signaled the End of a Turbulent Career and a Fearsome Era in American Public Life.* Englewood Cliffs, New Jersey: Prentice-Hall, 1969.

Weinbaum, P. O. "Temperance, Politics and the New York City Riots of 1857." *New York Historical Society Quarterly* 59 (1975): 246–70.

Weiss, Nancy J. *Charles Francis Murphy, 1858–1924: Respectability and Responsibility in Tammany Politics.* Northhampton, Massachusetts, 1968.

Wendt, Lloyd, and Herman Kogan. *Bosses in Lusty Chicago.* Bloomington: Indiana University Press, 1971.

———. *The Story of Bathhouse John and Hinky Dink.* New York: Garden City, 1944.

Werner, Morris R. *Tammany Hall.* Garden City, New York: Doubleday, Doran, 1928.

Whalen, Richard J. *The Founding Father: The Story of Joseph P. Kennedy.* New York: New American Library, 1964.

Wheeler, Everett P. "Tammany Hall." *Outlook* 105 (September 13, 1913): 73–81.

"Where it Leaves Murphy." *Nation* 97 (August 21, 1913): 158.

White Theodore H. *The Making of the President—1960.* New York: Atheneum, 1961.

Whitman, John H. A. "The Influence of Know-Nothingism in the Pivoted States in 1860." Master's thesis, University of Notre Dame, 1927.

"Why Hylan?" *Nation* 113 (November 23, 1921): 587.

Wicker, Tom. *JFK and LBJ: The Influence*

of Personality Upon Politics. New York: William Morrow, 1968.

Wilkie, James, and Rod McKuen, eds. *Quotations of Robert F. Kennedy: "I Dream Things That Never Were. . . and Say Why Not."* Los Angeles: Stanyan Books, 1970.

Williams, David A. *David C. Broderick*. San Marino: The Huntington Library, 1969.

Williams, Hal R. *The Democratic Party and California Politics, 1880–1896*. Stanford: Stanford University, 1973.

Wolfinger, Raymond. "The Development and Persistence of Ethnic Voting." *The American Political Science Review* (December 1965): 896–908.

Wood, Gordon S. "The Massachusetts Mugwumps." *New England Quarterly* 33 (1960): 435–51.

Zeiger, Henry A. *Robert F. Kennedy: A Biography*. Des Moines, Iowa: Meredith, 1968.

Zink, Harold. *City Bosses in the United States*. New York: Macmillan, 1939.

Zolot, H. M. "The Issue of Good Government and James Michael Curley: Curley and the Boston Scene from 1897–1918." Ph.D. dissertation, State University of New York, 1975.

6. Religion

Abel, Theodore. *Protestant Home Missions to Catholic Immigrants*. New York: Institute of Social and Religious Research, 1933.

Abell, Aaron I. *American Catholicism and Social Action, 1865–1950*. Garden City, New York: Hanover House, 1960.

———. "The Catholic Factor in Urban Welfare: The Early Period, 1850–1880." *The Review of Politics* 11 (July 1949): 289–324.

———. "Monsignor John A. Ryan: An Historical Interpretation." *The Review of Politics* 8 (January 1946): 128–34.

———. "Origins of Catholic Social Reform in the United States: Ideological Aspects." *The Review of Politics* 11 (July 1949): 294–309.

Abramson, Harold J. *Ethnic Diversity in Catholic America*. Wiley, New York. 1973.

———. "Ethnic Diversity Within Catholicism: A Comparative Analysis of Contemporary and Historical Religion," *Journal of Social History,* 4 (1970–71):359–88.

———. "The Religio-Ethnic Factor and the American Experience." *Ethnicity* 2 (1975): 163–77.

Agonite, Joseph A. "Ecumenical Stirrings: Catholic-Protestant Relations during the Episcopacy of John Carroll." *Church History* 45 (September 1976): 358–73.

———. "The Papers of John Carroll." *Catholic Historical Review* 63 (1977): 583–92.

Ahern, Patrick H. *Catholic Heritage in Minnesota, North Dakota, and South Dakota*. 1964.

———. *The Catholic University in America, 1887–1896*. Washington: Catholic University of America Press, 1948.

Ahern, J. *The Life of John J. Keane: Educator and Archbishop, 1839–1918*. Milwaukee: Bruce Publishing Co., 1955.

Allen, William. *Report on Popery Accepted by the General Association of Massachusetts, June, 1844*. Boston, 1844.

Angela, Sister Mary. *Sown in Granite: Glimpses of Events and People Associated with the Life of Benedict Joseph Fenwick*. Worcester, Massachusetts: n.p., 1963.

"Anti-Catholic Movements in the United States." *Catholic World* 22 (March 1876): 810–22.

"The Anti-Catholic Riots of 1844 in Philadelphia." *American Catholic Historical Researches* 13 (April 1896): 50–64.

"The Anti-Catholic Spirit of the Revolution." *American Catholic Historical Researches* 6 (October 1889): 146–78.

Arnold, Walter. "Catholic America, by John Cogley." *The New York Times Book Review* (March 11, 1973).

Augustine, Mary. *American Opinion of Roman Catholicism in the Eighteenth Century*. New York, 1936.

Backes, Ramond C. "Catholicism in Capital City: A History of St. Peter's Parish, Jefferson City, Missouri, 1828–1913." Master's thesis, St. Paul Seminary, 1956.

Bainton, Roland. *Christian Attitudes toward War and Peace*. Nashville: Abingdon Press, 1960.

Barrett, Patricia. *Religious Liberty and the American Presidency*. New York: Herder and Herder, 1963.

Barry, Coleman J. *The Catholic Univeristy of America 1903–1909: The Rectorship of Denis J. O'Connell*. Washington, D.C.: The Catholic University of America Press, 1950.

Barton, Bruce. *Angels of the Battlefield.* Philadelphia: Catholic Arts, 1897.

Bell, Daniel, ed. *The Radical Right.* Garden City, New York: Doubleday, 1964.

Bell, Stephen. *Rebel, Priest and Prophet: A Biography of Dr. Edward McGlynn.* Westport, Connecticut: Hyperion Press, 1937.

Bennett, William Harper. *Catholic Footsteps in Old New York.* New York: Schwartz, Kirwin and Fauss, 1909.

Berg, J. F. *Lecture: Delivered in the Music Fund Hall on Tuesday, November 26, 1850, in Answer to Archbishop Hughes on the Decline of Protestantism.* Philadelphia, 1850.

Berger, John Gerald. *A History of St. Brendan's Parish, The Village of Green Isle and Minnesota's First Irish Settlement.* Privately published, 1966.

Betz, Eva Kelly. *Priest, Patriot, and Leader: The Story of Archbishop Carroll.* New York: Benziger, 1960.

Biever, B. F. "Religion, Culture and Values: A Cross Cultural Analysis of Motivational Factors in Native Irish and American Irish Catholicism." Ph.D. dissertation, University of Pennsylvania, 1965. Published by Arno, 1976.

Billington, Ray Allen. "Anti-Catholic Propoganda and the Home Missionary Movement, 1800–1860." *Mississippi Valley Historical Review* 22 (December 1935): 361–84.

———. "Maria Monk and Her Influence." *Catholic Historical Review* 22 (October 1936): 283–96.

———. *The Protestant Crusade, 1800–1860: A Study of the Origin of American Nativism.* New York: Macmillan, 1938.

Bland, Sister Joan. *Hibernian Crusade, the Story of the Catholic Total Abstinence Union of America.* Washington, D.C.: The Catholic Univeristy of America Press, 1951.

Blanshard, Paul. *American Freedom and Catholic Power.* Boston: Beacon Press, 1949.

———. *The Irish and Catholic Power: An American Interpretation.* Boston: Beacon Press, 1953.

Blessing, Patrick J. *The British and Irish in Oklahoma.* Norman, Oklahoma: University of Oklahoma Press, 1980.

———. "Culture, Religion and the Activities of the Committee of Vigilance, San Francisco, 1856." *Working Papers* 8, no. 3 (1980). Charles and Margaret Hall Cushwa Center for the Study of American Catholicism, University of Notre Dame.

Blied, Benjamin. *Catholics and the Civil War.* Milwaukee, 1945.

Bliven, Bruce. "The Blooding Boss and the Musical Mayor." *American Heritage* 11 (December 1959): 8–11, 100–4.

Boardman, Anne Cawley. *Such Love is Seldom.* New York: Harper and Brothers, 1950.

Boardman, H. A. *The Intolerance of the Church of Rome.* Philadelphia, 1845.

Bocock, J. P. "The Irish Conquest of Our Cities," *Forum* 17: 186–95.

Borden, Morton. *Parties and Politics in the Early Republic, 1789–1815.* New York: Thomas Y. Crowell, 1967.

Boucher, Arline, and John Tehan. *Prince of Democracy: James Cardinal Gibbons.* New York: Doubleday, Hanover House, 1962.

Bouquillon, Thomas. *Education: To Whom Does it Belong?* Baltimore: John Murphy, 1892.

Bowler, Sister Mareilla. "A History of Catholic Colleges for Women in the United States of America." Ph.D. dissertation, The Catholic University of America, 1933.

Boyce, J. *The Satisfying Influence of Catholicity on the Intellect and Senses.* New York, 1851.

Brainerd, Thomas. *Our Country Safe From Romanism.* Philadelphia, 1843.

Brann, Rev. Henry A. *Most Reverend John Hughes.* New York: Dodd, Mead, 1892.

Brewer, Eileen M. "Beyond Utility: The Role of the Nuns in the Education of American Catholic Girls, 1860–1920." Ph.D. dissertation, University of Chicago, 1984. Published by Loyola, University of Chicago Press, 1987.

Bric, Rev. James J. "An Account of Catholicity in Public Institutions of Boston." *Records of the American Catholic Historical Society 1883–1885* 1–2 (Philadelphia, 1887).

Broderick, Francis L. *Right Reverend New*

Dealer: John A. Ryan. New York: Macmillan, 1963.

Browne, Henry. *The Catholic Church and the Knights of Labor.* Washington, D.C.: The Catholic University of America Press, 1949.

———, ed. "The Archdiocese of New York a Century Ago: A Memoir of Archbishop Hughes, 1838–1858." *The Historical Records and Studies Series* 39–40: 1952.

Brownlee, W. C. *Letters in the Roman Catholic Controversy.* New York, 1834.

———. *Popery: An Enemy to Civil and Religious Liberty, and Dangerous to Our Republic.* New York, 1836.

———. *The Religion of the Ancient Irish and Britons, Not Roman Catholic and The Immortal St. Patrick Vindicated From the False Charge of Being a Papist.* New York, 1841.

Brusher, Joseph S. *Consecrated Thunderbolt: Father Yorke of San Francisco.* New Jersey: Hawthorne, 1973.

Buczek, D. S. "Polish American Priests and the American Catholic Hierarchy: A View from the Twenties." *Polish American Studies* 33, no. 1 (1976): 34–43.

Buetow, Harold A. *Of Singular Benefit: The Story of Catholic Education in the United States.* New York: Macmillan, 1970.

Bultena, Louis. "Church Membership and Church Attendance in Madison, Wisconson." *American Sociological Review* 14 (1949).

Bunson, Maggie. "Catholics in the Revolution: Commodore John Barry." *Our Sunday Visitor Magazine* 64, no. 4 (February 8, 1976).

Burns, James A. *The Catholic School System in the United States.* New York: Benziger Brothers, 1908.

Burns, James A. *The Principles, Origins and Establishment of the Catholic School System in the United States.* 1912.

Burns, James A., and Bernard J. Kohlbrenner. *A History of Catholic Education in the United States.* New York: Benziger Brothers, 1937.

Burton, Katherine. *Children's Shepherd: The Story of John Christopher Drumgoole, Father of the Homeless and Founder of the Mission of the Immaculate Virgin.* New York: Kennedy, 1954.

Byrne, Edward J. "Anti-Catholicism in National Politics." Master's thesis, The Catholic University of America, 1928.

———. "The Religious Issue in National Politics." *Catholic Historical Review* 14 (1928): 329–69.

Byrne, Very Rev. William, ed. *History of the Catholic Church in the New England States.* Boston, 1899.

Cadden, J. P. *Historiography of the American Catholic Church, 1785–1943.* Washington D.C.: The Catholic University of America Press 1944.

Caldicott, Thomas F. *Hannah Corcoran: An Authentic Narrative of Her Conversion from Romanism: Her Abduction from Charlestown, and the Treatment She Received during Her Absence.* Boston, 1853.

Callahan, Nelson J. *A Case for Due Process in the Church: Father Eugene O'Callaghan, American Pioneer of Dissent.* Staten Island: Alba House, 1971.

Campbell, Thomas. *The Only True American School System.* New York: Messenger Office, 1901.

Campion, D. R. "Survey of American Social Catholicism, 1930–1940." Master's thesis, St. Louis University, 1949.

Carey, Mathew. *The Calumnies of Verus: Or, Catholics Vindicated from Certain Old Slanders Lately Revived; In a Series of Letters Published in Different Gazettes at Philadelphia.* Philadelphia: Johnston & Justice, 1792.

———. *The Olive Branch: Or Faults on Both Sides, Federal and Democratic.* Philadelphia: Author, 1815.

———. *Review of the Evidence of the Legendary Tale of a General Conspiracy of the Roman Catholics of Ireland.* Philadelphia, 1834.

———. *A Roland for an Oliver: Letters on Religious Persecution.* Philadelphia, 1826, 1829.

Carey, P. *History of the Church in Nebraska. Vol. I. The Church on the Northern Plains 1838–1874.* Bruce, Milwaukee, 1966.

———. *History of the Church in Nebraska. Vol II. The Church on the Fading Frontier 1864–1910.* Bruce, Milwaukee, 1966.

———. *History of the Church in Nebraska. Vol. III. Catholic Chapter in Nebraska Immigration.* Bruce, Milwaukee, 1966.

———. "John England and Irish-American Catholicism, 1815–1842: A Study of Conflict." Ph.D dissertation, Fordham University, 1975.

———. *A National Church: Catholic Search for Identity, 1820–1829.* Center for the Study of American Catholicism. Working Paper Series No. 3. University of Notre Dame, 1977.

———. "Voluntaryism: An Irish Catholic Tradition." *Church History* 48, no. 1 (1979): 49–62.

Carey, Patrick. *An Immigrant Bishop: John England's Adaptation of Irish Catholicism to American Republicanism.* Yonkers, New York: United States Catholic Historical Society, 1982.

———. "The Laiety's Understanding of the Trustee System, 1785–1855." *Catholic Historical Review* 64 (July 1978).

———. "Two Episcopal Views of Lay-Clerical Conflicts, 1785–1860." *Records of American Catholic Historical Society of Philadelphia* 87, nos. 1–4 (March–December 1976).

Carsody, Charles J. "American Catholic Religious Education: From 1776 to the Eve of the Vatican." *Listening* 11 (September 1976): 142–60.

Casey, William V., and P. Nobile, eds. *The Berrigans.* New York: Avon, 1971.

Catholicism in America: A Series of Articles from the Commonweal. New York: Harcourt, Brace, 1953.

Cavanaugh, John William C.S.C. *Spiritual Contribution of Ireland to America: Sermon of the Very Reverend Cavanaugh, C.S.C.D.D., to the National Convention of the Ancient Order of Hibernians, Detroit, July 19, 1921.* 1921.

Cerny, Karl Hubert. "Monsignor John A. Ryan and the Social Action Department: An Analysis of a Leading School of American Catholic Social Thought." Ph.D. dissertation, Yale University, 1955.

Chapman, J. L. *Americanism Versus Romanism: Or, The Cis-Atlantic Battle Between Sam and the Pope.* Nashville, 1856.

Cheever, George B. *The Right of the Bible in Our Public Schools.* New York, 1854.

Christ, Frank L., and Gerard E. Sherry. *American Catholicism and the Intellectual Ideal.* New York: Appleton, 1961.

Christina, Sister M. I., H.M. "Study of the Catholic Family Through Three Generations." *The American Catholic Sociological Review* 3 (1942).

Ciesluk, Joseph E. *National Parishes in the United States.* Washington, D.C.: The Catholic University of America Press, 1944.

Clancy, R. J. "Francis Patrick Kenrick and the Oxford Movement in America." Master's thesis, University of Notre Dame, 1932.

Clark, Mary Ann. *Great American Catholics.* Notre Dame, Indiana: Ave Maria Press, 1976.

Clarke, R. A. *Lives of the Deceased Bishops of the Catholic Church in the United States* 3. Clarke, New York, 1888.

Clarke, Thomas J. *Parish Societies.* Washington, D.C.: The Catholic University of America Press, 1943.

Code, Joseph. *Dictionary of the American Hierarchy.* New York: Longmans, Green, 1940.

Cogley, John. *Catholic America.* New York: Dial, 1973.

———. "The Irish Invasion." In *Catholic America*, edited by John Cogley. Dial Press, New York (1973): 28–51.

———. "Varieties of Catholicism." In *Catholic America*, edited by Philip Gleason. Dial Press, New York (1973): 143–67.

———. "Varieties of Catholicism." In *Majority and Minority*, edited by N. Yetman and C. H. Steele. Boston: Allyn-Bacon (1975): 252–60.

Conniff, James C. G. *Bishop Sheen Story.* New York: Fawcett, 1953.

Connors, Edward M. *Church-State Relationships in Education in the State of New York.* Washington, D.C: The Catholic University of America Press, 1951.

Constantius, Brother. "The Christian Brothers in the United States." *The Catholic Educational Review* (April 1911): 313–21.

Conway, Katherine E., and Mable Ward Cameron. *Charles Francis Donnelly: A Memoir with an Account of the Hearings On a Bill for the Inspection of Private Schools in Massachusetts in 1888–1889.* New York: White, 1909.

Coogan, M. Jane. *The Price of Our Heritage* 2 vols. Dubuque, Iowa: Mount Carmel Press, 1978.

Cooke, Terence Cardinal. "A Journey to the Edge." *Recorder: Irish-American Historical Society* vol. 36 (1975): 67–75.

Cooney, Sean Devin. "Intrinsic and Extrinsic Factors of Job Satisfaction and Job Dissatisfaction among Irish Catholic Priests." Ph.D. dissertation, Fordham University, 1974.

Corish, Patrick J., ed. *The United States of America; Vol. 6, A History of Irish Catholicism.* Dublin: Gill and Macmillan, 1970.

Corrigan, Patrick. *What The Catholic Church Most Needs in the United States.* New York: The American News, 1884.

Corrigan, Raymond. *The Church and the Nineteenth Century.* Milwaukee: Bruce, 1938.

Costello, Rev. Charles Agustine. "The Episcopate of the Right Reverend Josue M. Young, Bishop of Erie, Pennsylvania, 1854–1866." Master's thesis, University of Notre Dame, 1951.

Cronin, Bernard C. *Father Yorke and the Labor Movement in San Francisco, 1900–1910.* Washington, D.C.: The Catholic University of America Press, 1943.

Crosby, Donald F. "Angry Catholics: Catholic Opinion of Senator Joseph R. McCarthy, 1950–57." Ph.D. dissertation, Brandeis University, 1973.

———. *God, Church and Flag: Senator Joseph R. McCarthy and the Catholic Church, 1950–1957.* Chapel Hill: University of North Carolina Press, 1977.

Crosby, Donald P. "The Catholic Bishops and Senator Joseph McCarthy." *Religious American Catholic Historical Society* 86 (March–December 1975): 132–48.

Cross, Andrew B. *Priests' Prisons for Women.* Baltimore, 1854.

Cross, Robert D. "The Changing Image of the City Among American Catholics." *Catholic Historical Review* 48 (April 1962): 33–52.

———. *The Emergence of Liberal Catholicism in America.* Cambridge, Massachusetts: Harvard University Press, 1958.

———. "Origins of the Catholic Parochial Schools in America." *Amer. Benedictine Rev.* 16 (1965): 194–209.

———ed. *The Church and the City.* New York: Bobbs-Merrill, 1967.

Curley, Michael J. "The Aim of Catholic Education." *The Catholic Educational Review* 12, no. 1 (June 1916): 18–26.

Curran, E. R. "Conservative Thought and Strategy in the School Controversy, 1891–1893." *Notre Dame Journal of Education* 7 (1974): 144–62.

Curran, Rev. Edward Lodge. *Orthodox Americanism.* Brooklyn, New York: International Catholic Truth Society, 1945.

Curran, Francis X., S.J. *Catholics in Colonial Law.* Chicago: Loyola University Press, n.d.

———. "Some Problems of an Historian of the American Church." *Catholic Historical Society: Records and Studies Series* 44 (1956).

Curran, Robert Emmett. "Michael Augustine Corrigan and the Shaping of Conservative Catholicism in America, 1878–1902." Ph.D. dissertation, Yale University, 1974. Published in New York by Arno Press, 1978.

Curry, Lenord. *Protestant-Catholic Relations in America.* Lexington: University Press of Kentucky, 1972.

Cusack, Mary Francis. *Nun of Kenmare: An Autobiography.* Boston: Ticknor, 1889.

Cusack, Thomas Edward. "Archbishop John Ireland and the Spanish-American War: Peacemaker or Bungler." Master's thesis, University of Notre Dame, 1974.

Cutler, J. H. *Cardinal Cushing of Boston.* Hawthorn, New York, 1970.

Dabney, Virginius. *Dry Messiah: The Life of Bishop Cannon.* New York: Knopf, 1949.

Dahm, Charles W. *Power and Authority in the Catholic Church: Cardinal Cody in Chicago.* Notre Dame, Indiana: University of Notre Dame Press, 1982.

Daniel O'Connell and the Committee of the Irish Repeal Association of Cincinnati. Cincinnati, 1963.

Day, Edward C.S.R. "The Catholics Gamble on Revolution: Land of the Unfree in 1776." *Ligurian* 64 (January 1976): 34–39.

Deming, Angus. "The American Connection." *Newsweek* 86 (December 2, 1976): 52.

Denig, John. *The Know Nothing Manual, or Book for Americans, No. 1, in which the Native American Platform and Principles as Adopted by the Know Nothings are Set Forth and Defended . . . Together with Dissertations on Romanism.* Harrisburg, Pennsylvania, 1855.

Dever, Joseph. *Cushing of Boston.* Boston: Humphries, 1965.

Devine, George. *American Catholicism: Where Do We Go From Here?* Englewood Cliffs, New Jersey: Prentice-Hall, 1976.

Deye, Rev. Anthony H. "Archbishop John Baptist Purcell of Cincinnati: Pre-Civil War Years." Ph.D.dissertation, University of Notre Dame, 1959.

A Dialogue Between Dominie and Patrick: Or, the Bible vs. Papacy. Albany. New York, 1860.

Diffley, Jerome Edward. "Catholic Reaction to American Public Education, 1792–1852." Ph.D. dissertation, University of Notre Dame, 1959.

Dignan, Patrick J. *A History of the Legal Incorporation of Catholic Church Property in The United States, 1784–1932.* Washington, D.C.: The Catholic University of American Press, 1933.

Dinneen, Maurice. *The Catholic Total Abstinence Movement in the Archdiocese of Boston.* Boston: E. L. Grimes, 1908.

Dohen, D. *Nationalism and American Catholicism.* Sheed and Ward, New York. 1967.

Dolan, Jay P. *The American Catholic Experience.* New York: Doubleday, 1987.

———. "American Catholics and Revival Religion, 1850–1900." *Horizons* (Spring 1976): 39–57.

———. *Catholic Revivalism: The American Experience, 1830–1900.* Notre Dame: University of Notre Dame Press, 1978.

———. *The Immigrant Church: New York's Irish and German Catholics, 1815–1865.* Baltimore: Johns Hopkins University Press, 1975.

———. "Immigrants in the City: New York's Irish and German Catholics." *Church History* 41, no. 3 (September 1972): 354–68.

Donohoe, J. M. *The Irish Catholic Benevolent Union.* Washington, D.C.: The Catholic University of America Press, 1953.

Donovan, Joseph P., C.M. "Is This Parish Typical?" *The Homiletic and Pastoral Review* 49 (1948–1949).

Dorchester, Daniel. *Romanism Versus the Public School System.* New York: Phillips and Hunt, 1888.

Douglass, H. Paul. *The Church in a Changing City.* New York: George H. Doran, 1937.

———. *One Thousand City Churches.* New York: Harper & Bros., 1926.

———. *The St. Louis Church Survey.* New York: George H. Doran, 1924.

Downing, Sister Mary Omer, S.C. "An Investigation of Church 'Leakage' in an Urban Industrial Parish in Cleveland, Ohio." Master's thesis, The Catholic University of America, 1941.

Dreadful Scenes in the Awful Disclosures of Maria Monk. New York, 1836.

Duclos, W. E. "Crisis of an American Catholic Modernist: Toward the Moral Absolutism of William L. Sullivan." *Church History* 41, no. 3 (1972): 369–84.

Duffy, Francis P. *Father Duffy's Story.* Garden City, New York: Doubleday, 1919.

Duggan, Thomas B. *The Catholic Church in Connecticut.* New York, 1930.

Durkin, Joseph T. *Georgetown University.* New York: Doubleday, 1964.

Dwyer, John T. *Condemned to the Mines: The Life of Eugene O'Connell, 1815–1891, Pioneer Bishop of Northern California and Nevada.* New York: Vantage Press, 1976.

Dyrud, Keith P., Michael Novak, and Rudolph J. Vecoli, eds. *The Other Catholics.* Salem, New Hampshire: Ayer, 1978.

Egan, Maurice Francis. *The Disappearance of John Longworthy.* 1890.

Egan, Patrick K. *The Influences of the Irish on the Catholic Church in America in the Nineteenth Century.* Dublin: National University of Ireland, 1968.

Ellis, John Tracy. *American Catholicism.* Chicago: University of Chicago Press, 1956.

———. *American Catholics and the Intel-*

lectual Life. Chicago: Heritage Foundation, 1956.

———. "American Catholics and the Intellectual Life." *Thought* 30 (Autumn 1955).

———. "Cardinal Gibbons and New York." *Catholic Historical Society: Historical Records and Studies Series* 39–40 (1952).

———. *Catholics in Colonial America.* Baltimore: Benectine Studies, 1965.

———. "Church and State in the United States: A Critical Appraisal." *Catholic Historical Review* 38 (1952): 285–316.

———. *Documents of American Catholic History.* Milwaukee: Bruce, 1956.

———. "An English Visitor's Comments on the American Religious Scene, 1846." *Church History* (March 1967): 36–44.

———. *The Formative Years of the Catholic University.* Washington, D.C.: American Catholic Historical Association, 1946.

———. *John Lancaster Spalding.* Milwaukee: Bruce, and the National Catholic Educational Association, 1961.

———. *The Life of James Cardinal Gibbons: Archbishop of Baltimore, 1834–1921.* Milwaukee: Bruce, 1952.

———. *Perspectives in American Catholicism.* Baltimore: Helicon, 1963.

———. "Saint Patrick in America." *American Benedictine Review* 12 (December 1961): 415–29.

———, ed. *The Catholic Priest in the United States: Historical Investigations.* Brookline: Boston University, 1971.

England, John. *The Works of the Right Rev. John England, First Bishop of Charlestown* 5 Baltimore, 1849.

Erbacher, Sebastian Anthony. "Catholic Higher Education for Men in the United States, 1850–1866." Ph.D. dissertation, The Catholic University of America, 1931.

Esslinger, Dean. "American Catholics and Neutrality, 1914–1917." Master's thesis, University of Notre Dame, 1966.

Evans, J. B. "Irish Priests in Early Florida." *American Irish Historical Society Journal* 32 (1931): 74–78.

Ewens, Mary. O.P. "The Leadership of Nuns in Immigrant Catholicism." In *Women and Religion in America*, edited by Rosemary Radford Ruther and Rosemary Skinner Keller. *The Nineteenth Century.* San Francisco: Harper and Row, 1981.

Ewens, Mary. "The Role of the Nun in Nineteenth-Century America." Ph.D. dissertation, University of Minnesota, 1971.

Familiar Letters to J. B. Fitzpatrick, Catholic Bishop of Boston, By an Independent Irishman. Boston, 1854.

Farley, John M. *The Life of John Cardinal McCloskey.* New York, 1918.

"Fear of Catholicism in Colonial Pennsylvania." *American Catholic Historical Researches* 17 (April 1900): 74–77.

Fell, M. L. *The Foundations of Nativism in American Textbooks, 1783–1860.* Washington D.C.: The Catholic University of America Press, 1941.

Felts, Joseph B. *The Ecclesiastical History of New England.* Boston, 1855, 1862.

Fenton, J. H. *Salt of the Earth: An Informal Portrait of Richard Cardinal Cushing.* New York: Coward-McCann, 1951.

Fichter, Father Joseph H. *Dynamics of a City Church.* Chicago, 1951.

———. *Parochial School: A Sociological Analysis.* South Bend, Indiana: University of Notre Dame Press, 1958.

Finn, Brendan A. *Twenty-Four American Cardinals.* Boston: Humphries, 1948.

Flick, Ella Marie. *The Life of Bishop McDevitt.* Philadelphia, Pennsylvania: Dorrance, 1940.

Flynn, Austin. "The School Controversy in New York, 1840–1842, and its Effect on the Formulation of Catholic Elementary School Policy." Ph.D. dissertation, University of Notre Dame, 1962.

Flynn, George Q. *American Catholics and the Roosevelt Presidency: 1932–1936.* Lexington: University Press of Kentucky, 1968.

———. *Roosevelt and Romanism: Catholics and American Diplomacy, 1937–1945.* New York: Greenwood Press, 1975.

Fogarty, Gerald P. *The Vatican and the Americanist Crisis: Denis J. O'Connell, American Agent in Rome, 1885–1903.* Rome: University of Gregoriana, 1974.

Foik, Paul J. "Anti-Catholic Parties in American Politics, 1776–1860." *Records of the American Catholic Historical Society of Philadelphia* 26 (March 1925): 41–69.

———. "Pioneers Efforts in Catholic Journalism in the United States." *Catholic Historical Review* 1 (1915): 259–60.

Foley, Rev. Wilfrid. "Patrick N. Lynch, Catholic Bishop and Confederate Statesman." Master's thesis, University of Notre Dame, 1930.

Folk, P. J. "The Beginnings of Irish Catholic Journalism in America." *Catholic Historical Review* 5: 377–81.

Forster, William Patrick. "Michael J. O'Shaughnessy and His Reform Program: A Catholic Businessman's Interpretation of the Papal Design for a New Social Order." Master's thesis, University of Notre Dame, 1965.

Fosselman, David H. *Transitions in the Development of a Downtown Parish: A Study of Adaptations to Ecological Change in St. Patrick's Parish, Washington, D.C.* Washington, D.C.: The Catholic University of America Press.

Fuchs, Lawrence H. *John F. Kennedy and American Catholicism.* New York: Meredith, 1967.

A Full and Complete Account of the Late Awful Riots in Philadelphia. Philadelphia: Perry, 1865.

Funchion, Michael F. "Irish Chicago; Church, Homeland Politics and Class: The Shaping of an Ethnic Group, 1870–1900." In *Ethnic Chicago*, edited by Peter d'A. Jones and Martin G. Holli. Grand Rapids: Eerdmans, 1981.

Gaffey, James P. "The Changing of the Guard: The Rise of Cardinal O'Connell of Boston." *Catholic Historical Review* 59, no. 2 (1973): 225–44.

———. "The Life of Patrick William Riordan: Second Archbishop of San Francisco, 1841–1914." Ph.D. dissertation, The Catholic University of America, 1965.

———. "Patterns of Ecclesiastical Authority: The Problem of Chicago Succession, 1865–1881." *Church History* 42 (1973): 257–70.

Gannon, Robert I., S.J. *The Cardinal Spellman Story.* Garden City, New York: Doubleday, 1962.

Gardiner, Harold C. *Catholic Viewpoint on Censorship.* New York: Hanover House, 1958.

Garesche, Edward F. *Social Organization in Parishes.* New York: Benziger Bros., 1921.

Garraghan, Gilbert J. *The Catholic Church in Chicago, 1673–1871.* Chicago, 1921.

Ghelardi, Robert. *Power and Authority in the Catholic Church: Cardinal Cody in Chicago.* Notre Dame, Indiana: University of Notre Dame Press, 1981.

Gibbons, James Cardinal. *Discourses and Sermons.* Baltimore: Murphy, 1908.

———. *The Faith of Our Fathers.* Baltimore: Murphy, 1876.

———. *Our Christian Heritage.* Baltimore: Murphy, 1889.

———. *A Retrospect of Fifty Years.* Baltimore: Murphy, 1916.

Gibbs, J. C. *History of the Catholic Total Abstinence Union of America.* Philadelphia, 1907.

Gillard, John T., S.S.J. *The Catholic Church and the American Negro.* Baltimore: St. Joseph's Society, 1929.

Gladden, Washington. "The Anti-Catholic Crusade." *Century Magazine* 47 (March 1894): 789–95.

Glanz, Dr. Rudolph. *Jew and Irish: Historic Group Relations and Immigration.* New York: Waldon Press, 1966.

Gleason, Philip. "The Bicentennial and Other Milestones; Anniversary Assessments of American Catholicism." *Communion, International Catholic Review* 3 (Summer 1976): 115–35.

———. "Greeley Watching." *Review of Politics* 40 (1978).

———. "Immigration and American Catholic Intellectual Life." *The Review of Politics* 26 (April 1964): 150–59.

———. "The Main Sheet Anchor: John Carroll and Catholic Higher Education." *Review of Politics* 38 (October 1976): 576–613.

———. "Thanks to the Irish." *America* (May 14, 1966).

———, ed. *Catholicism in America.* New York: Harper and Row, 1970.

———, ed. *Contemporary Catholicism in*

the United States. Notre Dame, Indiana: University of Notre Dame Press, 1969.

Goarty, Patrick W. *The Economic Thought of Monsignor John A. Ryan.* Washington, D.C.: The Catholic University of America Press, 1953.

Godfrey, A. W. "Irish Catholic Was Beautiful." *America* 123 (December 5, 1970): 493.

Good, Patricia K. "Irish Adjustment to American Society: Integration or Separation? A Portrait of an Irish-Catholic Parish, 1863–1886 (Pittsburgh)." *Records of the American Catholic Historical Society of Philadelphia* 86 (March–December 1975): 7–23.

Graham, Sister Clara. *Works to the King: Reminiscences of Mother Seraphine Ireland.* St. Paul, Minnesota: North Central, 1950.

Grant, Dorothy Fremont. *John England . . . American Christopher.* Milwaukee: Bruce, 1949.

Greeley, Andrew M. *The American Catholic.* New York: Basic Books, 1977.

———. "American Catholics—Making it or Losing It?" *The Public Interest,* no. 28 (Summer 1973).

———. *The Catholic Experience: An Interpretation of the History of American Catholicism.* Garden City, New York: Doubleday, 1967.

———. "Catholicism in America: Two Hundred Years and Counting: A Personal Interpretation." *Critic* 34 (Summer 1976).

———. "Catholic Social Acitivism—Real or Rad/Chic." *NCR's Opinion Magazine* (February 7, 1975).

Greeley, Andrew M. and Peter H. Rossi. *The Education of Catholic Americans.* Chicago: Aldine, 1966.

Greeley, Andrew M., William C. McCready, and Kathleen McCourt. *Catholic Schools in a Declining Church.* Kansas City: Sheed and Ward, 1976.

Green, James Jeremiah. "The Impact of Henry George's Theories on American Catholics." Ph.D. dissertation, University of Notre Dame, 1956.

Greene, James J. "American Catholics and the Irish Land League." *Catholic Historical Review* 25: 1949.

Griffen, C. S. "Converting the Catholics: American Benevolent Societies and the Ante-Bellum Crusade Against the Church." *Catholic Historical Review.* 47 (1961): 325–41.

Griffin, Martin J. *Catholics and the American Revolution.* Ridley Park: M. J. Griffin, 1907–11.

———. "The Irish Catholics and the Revolution." *American Catholic Historical Researches* 6 (October 1910): 340–42.

———. "Religion of the Early Irish Immigrants to Pennsylvania." *American Catholic Historical Researches* 7 (April 1911): 170–72.

Grozier, R. J. *The Life and Times of John Carroll, Archbishop of Baltimore.* New York: Encyclopedia, 1966.

Guilday, Peter. *A History of the Councils of Baltimore.* New York: Macmillan, 1932.

———. "Trusteeism." *Historical Records and Studies* 18 (1928): 9.

———. *The Life and Times of John England, First Bishop of Charleston, (1786–1842).* New York: American Press, 1927.

———. "Two Catholic Best Sellers." *America* 54 (November 30, 1935): 177–79.

———, ed. *The National Pastorals of the American Hierarchy, 1791–1919.* Washington, D.C.: National Catholic Welfare Council, 1923.

Guminga, Theodore C., Archdiocese of St. Paul. "Catholic Immigrants in Northeast Minneapolis and Their Parishes." Master's thesis, St. Paul Seminary, 1959.

Gurn, Joseph. *Charles Carroll of Carrollton, 1737–1832.* New York: P. J. Kennedy and Sons, 1932.

Gwynn, Aubrey, S.J. "The First Irish Priests in the New World." *Studies* 21 (1932): 213–28.

Hackett, J. D. *Bishops of the United States of Irish Birth or Descent.* American Irish Historical Society. New York, 1936.

Hafen, LeRoy, and W. J. Ghent. *Broken Hand.* Denver, 1946.

Haggerson, M. E. "The History of the Diocese of Mobile from 1826–1859." University of Notre Dame. Masters thesis, 1942.

Hale, Charles. *A Review of the Proceedings*

of the Nunnery Committee of the Massachusetts Legislature. Boston, 1855.

Hall, James. *The Catholic Question, From the Western Monthly Magazine*. Cincinnati, 1835.

Hampsey, Sr. Mary Emmanuel. "The Catholic Reaction to the Homestead Strike of 1892." Master's Thesis, University of Notre Dame, 1960.

Hanchett, William. "The Question of Religion and the Taming of California, 1849–1854." *California Historical Society Quarterly* 32 (June 1953).

Handlin, Oscar. "Immigrant in American Politics" In *Foreign Influences in American Life*, edited by David F. Bowers. Princeton: Princeton University Press, 1944, 84–98.

Hanley, Thomas O'Brien, S.J. *Charles Carroll of Carrollton: The Making of a Revolutionary Gentleman*. Washington, D.C.: The Catholic University of America Press, 1970.

———, ed. *The John Carroll Papers*. 3 vols. Notre Dame: Notre Dame University Press, 1976.

Hanna, Mary T. *Catholics and American Politics*. Cambridge: Harvard University Press, 1979.

Hannah Corcoran, the Missing Girl of Charlestown. The Mysterious Disappearance Unraveled. The Convent and the Confessor. Attempt at Abduction Foiled! A Full and Complete Report of the Riot at Charlestown. Boston, 1853.

Hassard, John R. G. *Life of the Most Reverend John Hughes, First Archbishop of New York*. New York: Appleton, 1866.

Haughey, M. C. J. "A Candle Lighted." *American Catholic Historical Society Review* 64 (1953): 113–20.

Hayes, F. H. *Michigan Catholicism in the Era of the Civil War*. Lansing: Centennial Observance Commission, 1965.

Haynes, George H. "The Causes of Know-Nothing Success in Massachusetts." *American Historical Review*, 3 (October 1897): 67–82.

Healey, Robert C. *A Catholic Book Chronicle*. New York: P. J. Kennedy, 1951.

Heming, H. H. *The Catholic Church in Wisconsin*. Milwaukee, The Catholic Historical, 1895.

Hencken, Hugh O'Neill. "The 'Irish Monastery' at North Salem, New Hampshire." *New England Quarterly* 12 (1939): 429–42.

———. "What are Pattee's Caves? Are They the Remains of a Medieval Irish Monastery In New Hampshire As Is Claimed?" *Scientific American* 163 (1940): 258–59.

Heney, Francis J. "Parts of the Story of the Prosecution." *The Liberator* (July 24, 1909): 3–4.

Hennessey, James J. *American Catholics: A History of the Roman Catholic Community in the United States*. New York: Oxford University Press, 1981.

———. "The Distinctive Tradition of American Catholicism." In *Catholicism in America*, edited by Philip Gleason. New York: Harper and Row, 28–44.

———. "An Eighteenth Century Bishop: John Carroll of Baltimore." *Archivium Historiae Pontificiae* 16 (1978): 171–204.

Henthorne, Sister M. Evangela. *The Career of the Right Reverend John Lancaster Spalding, Bishop of Peoria, as President of the Irish Catholic Colonization Association of the United States, 1879–1892*. Urbana, Illinois: University of Illinois, 1932.

Hernon, J. M., Jr. "Irish Religious Opinion on the American Civil War." *Catholic Historical Review* 49 (1957): 508–23.

Hitchcock, James. "Secular Clergy in Nineteenth Century America: A Diocesan Profile." *Records of the American Catholic Historical Society of Philadelphia* 88 (March–December 1977).

Hogan, Peter E. *The Catholic University of America, 1896–1903: The Rectorship of Thomas J. Conaty*. Washington, D.C.: The Catholic University of America Press, 1949.

Holden, Vincent F., C.S.P. *The Yankee Paul: Isaac Thomas Hecker*. Milwaukee: Bruce, 1958.

Holmes, J. D. "Irish Priests in Spanish Natchez." *Journal Miss. Hist.* 29 (1967): 169–80.

Howe, M. A. DeWolf. *The Life and Labors of Bishop Hare*. Sturgis and Walton, 1911.

Howlett, W. J. *Life of the Right Reverend*

Joseph P. MacHebeuf. Pueblo, Colorado, 1908.

Hueston, Robert Francis. *The Catholic Press and Nativism, 1840–1860*. New York: Ayer, 1976.

Hughes, Emmett John. *The Church and Liberal Society*. Princeton: Princeton University Press, 1944.

Hughes, John. *Archbishop Hughes in Reply to General Cass, and in Self-Vindication*. New York, 1854.

———. *The Catholic Chapter in the History of the United States*. New York, 1852.

———. *Complete Works of the Most Rev. John Hughes, D.D., Archbishop of New York*. New York: Kehoe, 1866.

———. *Controversy Between Rev. Messrs. Hughes and Breckenridge on the Subject: "Is the Protestant Religion the Religion of Christ?"* Philadelphia, 1833.

———. *The Conversion and Edifying Death of Andrew Dunn*. Philadelphia, 1828.

———. *The Decline of Protestantism and Its Causes*. New York, 1850.

———. *A Discussion of the Question, is the Roman Catholic Religion in Any or in All its Principles of Doctrines, Inimical to Civil or Religious Liberty?* Philadelphia, 1836.

———. *Kirwan Unmasked*. New York, 1848.

Hughes, William H. *Three Great Events in the History of the Catholic Church in the United States*. Detroit: W. H. Hughes, 1890.

Hyde, Douglas. *No Thurus go Hamerica: No, Imeasg Na Ngaedheal Ins Oilean Ur*. Baile Atha Cliath, Oifig Diuolta Foillseachain Rialtais, 1937.

Ireland, John. "The Catholic Church and the Saloon." *North American Review*. October 1894.

Ireland, John. *The Church and the Age*. Baltimore: Murphy, 1894.

Ireland, John. *The Church and Modern Society*. St. Paul: Pioneer Press, 1905.

Irick, M. A. "Early Catholicity in the Sandusky Region Prior to 1847." Masters thesis, University of Notre Dame, 1939.

Ives, J. M. "The Catholic Contribution to Religious Liberty in Colonial America." *Catholic Historical Review* 21 (1935): 283–98.

Jacoby, George Paul. *Catholic Child Care in Nineteenth Century New York*. Washington, D.C., 1941.

Jendrus, Sr. Rose Ethel. "Bishop Spalding and His Position with Respect to the Higher Education of Women." Master's thesis, University of Notre Dame, 1946.

Jolly, Ellen Ryan. *Nuns of the Battlefield*. Providence, Rhode Island: Providence Visitor Press, 1927.

Kane, John Joseph. *Catholic-Protestant Conflicts in America*. Chicago: Regnery, 1955.

———. "Catholic Separatism." *Commonweal* 58 (June 26, 1953): 293–96.

Kantowicz, Edward. *Corporation Sole: Cardinal Mundelein and Chicago Catholicism*. Notre Dame, Indiana: University of Notre Dame Press, 1983.

Keefe, Thomas M. "The Catholic Issue in the Chicago Tribune before the Civil War." *Mid-America* 57 (1975): 227–45.

Kehoe, Lawrence, ed. *Complete Works of the Most Reverend John Hughes, First Archbishop of New York*. New York: Catholic Publication House, 1864.

Kelligar, William Lee, Archbishop of Omaha. "The Career of Bishop James O'Connor, Vicar Apostolic of Nebraska." Master's thesis, St. Paul Seminary, 1953.

Kelly, George Anthony. *The Catholic Church and the American Poor*. Staten Island, New York: Alba House, 1976.

——— *Catholics and the Practice of the Faith: A Census Study of the Diocese of Saint Augustine*. Washington, D.C.: The Catholic University of America Press, 1946.

Kelly, J., and A. W. McClure. *The School Question: A Correspondence Between Rev. J. Kelly . . . and Rev. A. W. McClure, Jersey City*. New York, 1853.

Kelly, M. G. "Irish-Catholic Colonies and Colonization Projects in the United States, 1795–1860." *Studies: An Irish Quarterly Review* 29 (1940): 95–110, 447–65.

Kelly, Sister Mary Gilbert. *Catholic Immigrant Colonization Projects in the United*

States, 1815–1860. New York: United States Catholic Historical Society, 1939.

Kenneally, James J. "The Burning of the Ursuline Convent, A Different View." *Catholic Historical Review* 59 (1973): 225–44.

Kenneday, Grace. *Father Clement, A Roman Catholic Story.* Boston, 1827.

Kenney, William J. "The Work of Father John J. Burke, 1917–1922." Ph.D. dissertation, St. Paul's College, Washington, D.C.

Kerrison, Raymond. *Bishop Walsh of Maryknoll, A Biography.* New York: G. P. Putnam's Sons, 1962.

Kincheloe, Samuel C. *The American City and Its Church.* Chicago: Friendship Press, 1938.

Kinzer, Donald L. *An Episode in Anti-Catholicism: The American Protective Association.* Seattle: University of Washington Press, 1964.

Kirkfleet, Cornelius. *The Life of Patrick Augustine Feehan, Bishop of Nashville, First Archbishop of Chicago, 1829–1902.* Chicago: Matre, 1922.

Kirlin, Joseph. *Catholicity in Philadelphia.* Philadelphia, 1909.

Kirwin, (pseudo. of Nicholas Murray). *Letters to the Right Rev. John Hughes, Roman Catholic Bishop of New York.* New York, 1855.

Know-Nothing: A Poem for Natives and Aliens. Boston, 1854.

Know-Nothing Songster. Compiled and Composed by "A Native." Boston, 1854.

The Know-Nothings. Cause and Effect. Boston, 1854.

The Know-Nothings. An Exposure of the Secret Order of Know Nothings; the Most Ludicrous and Startling Yankee "Notion" Ever Conceived. New York, 1854.

Koenig, Rev. Msgr. Harry C., ed. *A History of the Parishes of the Archdiocese of Chicago* 2 Vols., Chicago: Archdiocese of Chicago, 1980.

Kotre, John N. *The Best of Times, the Worst of Times: Andrew Greeley and American Catholicism, 1950–1975.* Chicago: Nelson-Hall, 1978.

Krugler, John D. "Lord Baltimore, Roman Catholics, and Toleration: Religious Policy in Maryland during the Early Catholic Years." *Catholic Historical Review* 65, no. 1 (January 1979).

Kunkel, Sr. Norlene Mary. "Bishop Bernard J. McQuaid and the Catholic Education." Ph.D. dissertation, University of Notre Dame, 1974.

———. "Christian Free School's Bishop Bernard McQuaid's 19th Century Plan." *Notre Dame Journal of Education* 7, no. 1 (1976): 18–27.

Kwitchen, Sister Mary Augustine. "James Alphonsus McMaster, A Study in American Thought." Master's thesis. The Catholic University of America, 1949.

La Forest, Brother Laurian. "Character Education According to Bishop Spalding." Master's thesis, University of Notre Dame, 1948.

Lally, Francis J. *The Catholic Church in a Changing America.* Boston: Little, Brown, 1962.

Lannie, Vincent P. "Catholics, Protestants and Public Education." In *Catholicism in America*, edited by P. Gleason. New York: Harper and Row, 1970, 45–57.

———. *Public Money and Parochial Education: Bishop Hughes, Governor Seward, and the New York School Controversy.* Cleveland: Press of Case Western Reserve University, 1968.

Lannie, Vincent P., and Bernard C. Diethorn. "For the Honor and Glory of God: The Philadelphia Bible Riots of 1840." *History of Education Quarterly* 8 (1968): 44–106.

Larkin, Emmet. *The Catholic Church and the Creation of the Modern Irish State.* Philadelphia: American Philosophical Society, 1975.

———. *The Consolidation of the Roman Catholic Church in Ireland, 1860–1870.* Chapel Hill, North Carolina: University of North Carolina Press, 1987.

———. *The Historical Dimensions of Irish Catholicism.* New York: Arno Press, 1976.

———. *The Making of the Roman Catholic Church in Ireland, 1850–1860.* Chapel Hill, North Carolina: University of North Carolina Press, 1980.

———. *The Roman Catholic Church in Ire-*

land and the Fall of Parnell, 1888–1891. Chapel Hill, North Carolina: University of North Carolina Press, 1979.

Lauer, James O. "The Contemporary American Attitude Towards Catholic Emancipation." Master's thesis, The Catholic University of America, 1930.

Leahy, William. *The Catholic Church in New England.* Boston, 1899.

Lehman, Leo Herbert. *The Soul of a Priest: My Conversion to the Pauline Succession.* New York: Liozeaux, 1942.

Leiffer, Murray H. *City and Church in Transition.* Des Moines: Willet and Clark, 1938.

Lenski, Gerhard. *The Religious Factor.* New York: Doubleday, Anchor Books, 1963.

Leonard, Henry B. "Ethnic Conflict and Episcopal Power: The Diocese of Cleveland, 1847–70." *Catholic Historical Review* 62: 338–407.

Leslie, S. "Celt: The Saxon and the New Scene." *Dublin Review* 160 (1917): 286–92.

———. "German and Irish Element in the American Melting Pot." *Dublin Review* 163 (1918): 258–83.

Leslier, Sir Shane. "Lost Irish in the U.S.A.: The Church in the Deep South." *Tablet* 211 (February 1, 1958): 103–4.

Liebert, John L., Archdiocese of St. Paul. "Sketch of the Life of Patrick John Ryan, Archbishop of Philadelphia, 1884–1911." Master's thesis, St. Paul Seminary, 1950.

Linehan, J. C., and T. H. Murray. *Irish Schoolmasters in the American Colonies, 1640–1775.* American Irish Historical Society, Washington, 1898.

Linkh, R. M. *American Catholicism and European Immigrants (1900–1924).* Center for Migration Studies, Staten Island, New York, 1975.

Liptak, Dolores Ann. "European Immigrants and the Catholic Church in Connecticut, 1870–1920." Ph.D. dissertation, University of Connecticut, 1978.

Liston, Sister M. Victorine. "Objectives in Education as Set Forth By Bishop Spalding." Master's thesis, University of Notre Dame, 1934.

Lord, Robert H., and John E. Sexton, and Edward T. Harrington. *History of the Archdiocese of Boston* 3 vols. New York: Sheed and Ward, 1944.

Lovejoy, C. J. *Memoir of Rev. Charles T. Torrey.* Boston: Jewett, 1847.

Lucey, Reverend William L., S.J. *Catholic Journalism in New England: 1855–1900.* Reprint from the *New England Social Studies Bulletin,* May 1953.

Lucey, Robert E. "The Catholic Church in Texas." In *The Catholic Church, U.S.A.,* edited by Louis J. Putz. Chicago: Fides, 1956.

Luebke, Frederick C. "Church History from the Bottom Up." *Reviews in American History* 4, no. 1 (March 1976): 68–72.

MacDonald, Fergus. *The Catholic Church and Secret Societies in the U.S.* New York: U.S. Catholic Historical Society, n.d.

MacDonald, Robert Rigg. "Father Charles Owen Rice: The Study of a Catholic Radical." Master's thesis, University of Notre Dame, 1966.

Malone, Sylvester L. *Dr. Edward McGlynn.* New York: Ayer, 1918.

Maly, Raymond John. "The Catholic Labor Alliance: A Laboratory Test of Catholic Social Action" Master's thesis, University of Notre Dame, 1950.

Marcus, Sheldon. *Father Coughlin: The Tumultous Life of the Priest of the Little Flower.* Boston: Little Brown, 1973.

Marie, Sister Leo. "Trends in Catholic Population in the United States." *American Catholic Sociological Review* (1942).

Mattingly, Sr. Mary Ramona. *The Catholic Church on the Kentucky Frontier, 1795–1812.* Washington, D.C.: The Catholic University of America Press, 1936.

Maurin, Peter. *Radical Christian Thought: Easy Essays.* New York: Sheed and Ward, 1936.

Maury, Reuben. *The Wars of the Godly.* McBride, 1928.

Maynard, T. *The Story of American Catholicism* 2 Vols. Doubleday, New York, 1960.

Maynard, Theodore. *Great Catholics in American History.* Garden City, New York: Hanover House, 1957.

———. "Lost Land: How American Catholicism Was Cast In An Urban Mold." *Commonweal* 34 (September 26, 1941): 533–36.

———. *Orestes Brownson: Yankee, Radical, Catholic*. New York: Macmillan, 1943.

———. *The Study of American Catholicism* 2 vols. New York: Doubleday, Image Books, 1960.

McAllister, L. G. *Thomas Campbell (1763–1854), Man of the Book*. Bethany, St. Louis, Missouri: n. p., n. d.

McAvoy, Reverend Thomas T., C.S.C. "Americanism, Fact and Fiction." *The Catholic Historical Review* 31 (July 1945): 133–53.

———. "Bishop John Lancaster Spalding and the Catholic Minority." *Review of Politics* 12 (January 1950): 3–19.

———. "The Catholic Minority in the United States, 1789–1821." *U.S. Catholic Historical Society: Historical Records and Studies Series* 39–40 (1952).

———. *Father O'Hara of Notre Dame: The Cardinal Archbishop of Philadelphia*. Notre Dame, Indiana: University of Notre Dame, 1967.

———. "The Formation of the Catholic Minority in the United States, 1820–1860." *The Review of Politics* 10 (1948): 13–24.

———. *A History of the Catholic Church in America*. Notre Dame: University of Notre Dame Press, 1969.

———. "The Irish Clergyman." In *A History of Irish Catholicism: The U.S.A.*, edited by Patrick J. Cornish. Vol. 6, pt. 11 (Dublin: Gill and Macmillan, 1970).

———. *Irish Clergyman in the United States*. Philadelphia: Records American Catholic Historical Society, 75–6–38, 1964.

———. "Orestes A. Brownson and Archbishop John Hughes in 1860." *Review of Politics* 24 (January 1962): 19–47.

———. "Public School vs. Catholic Schools and James McMaster." *The Review of Politics* 28, No. 1 (January 1966): 19–46.

———. *Roman Catholicism and the American Way of Life*. University of Notre Dame, Notre Dame, Indiana, 1960.

———. "The War Letters of Father Peter Paul Cooney or the Congregation of Holy Cross." Master's thesis, University of Notre Dame, 1930.

McAvoy, T. T., and T. N. Brown. *History of Irish Catholicism, Vol. 6, Part 2, The United States of America*. Dublin: Gill and Macmillan, 1970.

McCadden, Joseph J. "Bishop Hughes Versus the Public School Society of New York." *Catholic Historical Review* 50 (1964): 188–207.

———. "New York's School Crisis of 1840–1842: Its Irish Antecedents," *Thought*, 41 (Winter 1966): 561–88.

McCaffrey, Augustine, F.S.C. *Youth in a Catholic Parish*. Washington, D.C.: The Catholic University of America Press, 1969.

McCaffrey, James. *History of the Catholic Church in the Nineteenth Century*. Dublin and Waterford: M. H. Gill and Son, 1909.

McCaffrey, L. J. "Catholicism and Irish Identity." *Holy Cross Quarterly* 6 (1974): 1–4, 72–80.

McCarthy, Jay David. "Orestes A. Brownson—A Catholic Voice on the Civil War, 1861–1864." Master's thesis, University of Notre Dame, 1956.

McCray, Sister Mary Gertrude. "Evidences of Catholic Interest in Social Welfare in the United States, 1830–1850." Master's thesis, University of Notre Dame, 1937.

McCready, William C. "Faith of Our Fathers: A Study of the Process of Religious Socialization." Ph.D. dissertation, Chicago Circle Campus: University of Illinois, 1972.

McCullough, A. M. *The Experience of Seventy Years*. Minneapolis: Tribune Job Press, Minneapolis, 1895.

McDaniel, Issac. "Orestes A. Brownson on Irish Immigrants and American Nativism." *The American Benedictine Review* 32, no. 2 (June 1981): 122–39.

McDonald, R. R. "Father Charles Owen Rice: The Study of a Catholic Radical." Master's thesis, University of Notre Dame, 1966.

McDonnell, T. P. "Catholic Press Reporting on Northern Ireland." *Holy Cross Quarterly* 6, nos. 1–4 (1974): 68–71.

McEniry, Sister Blanche Marie. *Woman of*

Decision: The Life of Mother Mary Xavier Mehegan 1825–1915, Founders of the Sisters of Charity of Saint Elizabeth, Convent, New Jersey. New York: McMullen, 1953.

McGee, Thomas D'Arcy. *The Catholic History of North America*. Boston, 1855.

McGuire, C. D., ed. *Catholic Builders of the Nation*. Boston: Continental Press, 1923.

McKeown, Elizabeth. "War and Welfare, A Study of American Catholic Leadership." Ph.D. dissertation, University of Chicago, 1972.

———. "Catholic Identity in America." In *America in Theological Perspective* (New York: Seabury, 1976): 56–68.

McKeown, H. C. *The Life and Labors of Most Reverend John Joseph Lynch, First Archbishop of Toronto*. J. A. Sadlier, Montreal, and Toronto. 1886.

McLoughlin, Emmet. *People's Padre*. Boston: Beacon Press, 1963.

McManamin, Francis J. *The American Years of John Boyle O'Reilly, 1870–1890*. New York: Arno, 1976.

McNamara, Robert F. "Trusteeism in the Atlantic States, 1785–1863." *The Catholic Historical Review* 30 (1944): 139.

McNeal, Patricia F. *The American Catholic Peace Movement, 1928–1972*. New York: Ayer, 1978.

Mead, Margaret. "How Religion Has Fared in the Melting Pot." In *Religion and Our Racial Tensions*, edited by Willard L. Sperry. Cambridge: Harvard University Press, 1945.

Meagher, Walter J., and William J. Grattan. *The Spires of Fenwick: The History of the College of the Holy Cross, 1843–1963*. New York: Vantage, 1966.

Meehan, Thomas F. "Catholic Literary New York, 1800–1840." *Catholic Historical Quarterly* 4 (1919): 399–414.

———. "The Catholic Press." In *Catholic Builders of the Nation*, edited by C. D. McGuire. Boston: Continental Press, 1923.

———. "The First Catholic Monthly Magazines." *U.S. Catholic Historical Society: Historical Records and Studies Series* 31 (1940).

Meiring, Bernard Julius. "Educational Aspects of the Legislation of the Councils of Baltimore, 1829–1884." Ph.D. dissertation, University of California, Berkeley, 1963.

Melville, Annabelle M. *John Carroll of Baltimore: Founder of the American Catholic Hierarchy*. New York: Scribner's, 1955.

Meng, John J. "Cahensylism: The Second Chapter, 1891–1901." *The Catholic Historical Review*, 32 (1946): 321.

Merwick, Donna. *Boston Priests, 1848–1910: A Study of Social and Intellectual Change:* Cambridge: Harvard University Press, 1973.

Messbarger, Paul R. "Midwestern Catholicism: Two Portraits." *Catholic Mind* 74, no. 1306 (October 1976): 39–450.

———. "Midwestern Catholicism: Two Portraits." *Listening* 11 (Winter, 1976): 68–82.

Metzger, Charles H. *Catholics and the American Revolution*. Chicago: Loyola University Press, 1962.

———. "Some Catholic Tories in the American Revolution." *Catholic Historical Review* 4 (January 1950): 408–27.

Meyers, Mary Ann. "The Children's Crusade: Philadelphia Catholics and the Public Schools, 1840–1844." *Records of the American Catholic Historical Society of Philadelphia* 75 (1964): 103–27.

Michonneau, G. *Revolution in a City Parish*. Oxford: Blackfriars, 1949.

Misner, Barbara. "Highly Respectable and Accomplished Ladies: Early American Women Religious, 1790–1850." *Working Paper Series*, no. 3 (Spring, 1978). Charles and Margaret Hall Cushwa Center for the Study of American Catholicism, University of Notre Dame.

Mitchell, Rev. James H., A.M. *Rt. Rev. John Loughlin, D.D.* Brooklyn, New York: The Golden Jubilee Committee, 1891.

Mitchell, Rev. Philip Joseph. "A Study of Orestes A. Brownson's Views on the Know-Nothing Movement." Master's thesis, University of Notre Dame, 1945.

Mol, J. J. "Immigrant Absorption and Religion." *International Migration Review* 5 (Spring 1971): 62–70.

Monk, Maria. *Awful Disclosures of the Hotel*

88 Bibliography

Dieu Nunnery of Montreal. New York, 1836.

Moody, Joseph N., ed. *Church and Society: Catholic Social and Political Thought and Movements, 1789–1950*. New York: Arts, 1953.

Moore, Justus E. *The Warnings of Thomas Jefferson: Or, a Brief Exposition of the Dangers to Be Apprehended to Our Civil and Religious Liberties From Presbyterianism*. Philadelphia, 1844.

Moore, Tom. *Travels of an Irish Gentleman in Search of a Religion*. New York, 1835.

Moran, D. M. *Anti-Catholicism in Early Maryland Politics: The Puritan Influence*. Records of the American Catholic Historical Society, 61 (1950): 139–54.

———. *Anti-Catholicism in Early Maryland Politics: The Protestant Revolution*. Records of the American Catholic Historical Society, Philadelphia. 61 (1950): 213–36.

Moran, Michael. "The Writings of Francis Patrick Kenrick, Archbishop of Baltimore (1797–1863)." *Records of the American Catholic Historical Society* 41 (1930): 248.

Morgan, J. H. "Ethnoconsciousness and Political Powerlessness: Boston's Irish." *Social Science* 53 (1978).

Moriarity, T. F. "Agitation in the United in Behalf of Catholic Emanicipation as Seen Through The Truth Teller, 1825–1830." Master's thesis, University of Notre Dame, 1958.

Morrissey, Timothy Hughes. "Archbishop John Ireland and the Fairbault-Stillwater School Plan of the 1890's: A Reappraisal." Ph.D. dissertation, University of Notre Dame, 1975.

———. "A Controversial Reformer: Archbishop John Ireland and His Educational Belief." *Notre Dame Journal of Education* 7 (Spring 1976): 63–75.

Moynihan, J. H. "Archbishop Ireland." *Acta et Dicta* 6 (1933): 12–35.

———. *The Life of Archbishop John Ireland*. New York: Harper, 1953.

Mulvaney, Bernard G., C.S.V. "How Catholics and Non-Catholics Differ in Fertility," *The American Catholic Sociological Review*, VII (1946).

Murnion, Philip J. *The Catholic Priest and the Changing Structure of Pastoral Ministry, New York, 1920–1970*. New York: Ayer, 1978.

Murphy, Edward F. *Yankee Priest*. Garden City, New York: Doubleday, 1952.

Murphy, John C. *An Analysis of the Attitudes of American Catholics Toward the Immigrant and the Negro, 1825–1925*. Washington, D.C.: The Catholic University of America Press, 1940.

Murphy, Sister Francis Ellen. "Orestes A. Brownson's 'The Convert' As a Record of American Spiritual Experience in the 1840's." Master's thesis, University of Notre Dame, 1946.

Murray, John Courtney. *We Hold These Truths*. New York: Sheed and Ward, 1960.

Murray, P. F. "Calendar of the Overseas Missionary Correspondence of All Hallows College, Dublin, 1842–77." Master's thesis, University College, Dublin, 1956.

Musselman, G. Paul. *The Church on the Urban Frontier*. Connecticut: The Seabury Press, 1960.

Myers, *History of Bigotry in the United States*. New York: Capricorn, 1960.

National Pastorals and Annual Statements of the Hierarchy of the United States. *Our Bishops Speak, 1919–1951*. Milwaukee: Bruce, 1952.

Neuwein, Reginald H., ed. *Catholic Schools in Action*. Notre Dame: University of Notre Dame Press, 1966.

Nolan, Hugh. *The Most Reverend Francis Patrick Kenrick, Third Bishop of Philadelphia, 1830–1851*. Philadelphia: American Catholic Historical Society of Philadelphia, 1948.

Noonan, Carroll John. "Nativism in Connecticut, 1829–1860." Ph.D. dissertation, The Catholic University of America, 1938.

Noonan, D. P. *Passion of Fulton Sheen*. New York: Dodd, Mead, 1972.

Novak, Michael. *The Open Church*. New York: Macmillan, 1964.

Nuesse, Celestine J., and Thomas J. Harte. *The Sociology of the Parish*. Milwaukee: Bruce, 1951.

O'Brien, David J. "American Catholicism

and the Diaspora." *Cross-Currents*. 16: 307–24.

———. *American Catholics and Social Reform, The New Deal Years*. New York: Oxford University Press, 1968.

O'Brien, Joseph L. *John England Bishop of Charleston: The Apostle of Democracy*. New York: O'Toole, 1934.

O'Connell, Marvin Richard. *John Ireland and the American Catholic Church*. St. Paul: Minnesota: Minesota Historical Society Press, 1988.

O'Connell, Rev. Jeremiah J. *Catholicity in the Carolinas and Georgia, 1820–1857*. New York: Sadlier, 1879.

O'Connell, William Cardinal. *Recollections of 70 Years*. Cambridge: Houghton Mifflin, 1934.

O'Daniel, V. F. *The Rt. Rev. Edward Dominic Fenwick, O.P.* New York: Putset, 1920.

———. *Very Rev. Charles Hyacinth McKenna, O.P.* New York: Holy Name Bureau, 1917.

O'Dea, Thomas F. *American Catholic Dilemma*. New York: Sheed and Ward, 1961.

———. *The Catholic Crisis*. Boston: Beacon Press, 1968.

———. "The Catholic Immigrant and the American Scene." *Thought* 31 (1956): 251–70.

Odegard, P. H. "Catholicism and Elections in the United States." In: *Religion and Politics*, edited by P. H. Odegard. Rutgers, New Brunswick, New Jersey, 1960.

O'Donnell, John H. "The Catholic Church in Northern Indiana, 1830–1857." *Catholic Historical Review* 25 (1939): 135–45.

———. *The Catholic Hierarchy of the United States*. Washington, D.C.: The Catholic University of America Press, 1940.

O'Dwyer, George Francis. "Ann Glover, First Martyr to the Faith in New England." *United States Catholic Historical Society Records and Studies* 15 (1921): 70–78.

———. *The Irish Catholic Genesis of Lowell*. Lowell, Massachusetts, 1920.

O'Fahey, C. J. "Reflections on the St. Patricks Day Orations of John Ireland." *Ethnicity* 2, no. 3: 244–51.

O'Gorman, Thomas. *A History of the Roman Catholic Church in the United States*. New York: Christian Literature, 1895.

O'Grady, John. *Catholic Charities in the United States*. Washington, D.C.: National Conference of Catholic Charities, 1930.

O'Hara, Edwin V., and Richard J. Purcell. *Archbishop Ireland: Two Appreciations*. Minneapolis: College of St. Thomas, 1948.

O'Hearn, D. J. *Fifty Years at St. Johns Cathedral 1847–1897*. St. Johns Central, Milwaukee, 1898.

O'Kane, Murray. *Catholic Pioneers of America*. Philadelphia, 1882.

O'Mahony, T. "The Irish Churches and the Credibility Gap." *America* 127 (1972): 440–42.

O'Meara, J. B. "The Mission of the Irish Race in the United States." *American Irish Historical Society Journal* 10 (1911): 105–13.

O'Neill, Daniel. "St. Paul's Priests, 1850–1930: Recruitment, Ethnicity, and Americanization." In *An American Church*, edited by David J. Alvarez. Moraga, California: Saint Mary's College of California, 1979.

———. "St. Paul's Priests, 1851–1900: Recruitment, Formation, and Mobility." Ph.D. dissertation, University of Minnesota, 1979.

O'Neill, James M. *Catholicism and American Freedom*. New York: Harper and Brothers, 1952.

———. "Church and State in the United States." *U.S. Catholic Historical Society, Historical Records and Studies* 37 (1948).

O'Neill, Tomas. *Fiontan O Leathlobhair*. Baile Atha Claith, Morainn, 1962.

O'Reilly, B. *John McHale, His Life, Times and Correspondence* 2 vols. New York and Cincinnati: F. Pustet and Company, 1890.

O'Rourke, Williams. *The Harrisburg 7 and the New Catholic Left*. New York: Thomas Y. Crowell, 1972.

O'Shea, John J. *The Two Kenricks*. Philadelphia, 1904.

Onahan, William. "A Chapter of Catholic Colonization." *Acto Et Dicta* (July 1917).

Ong, Walter J., S.J. *Frontiers in American Catholicism.* New York: Macmillan, 1957.

Oursler, Fulton and Will. *Father Flanagan of Boys Towns.* New York, 1949.

Overmoehle, M. H. "The Anti-Clerical Activities of the Forty-Eighters in Wisconsin, 1848–1860." Ph.D. dissertation, St. Louis University, 1941.

Pallen, Conde Benoist. *The Catholic Church and Socialism: A Solution of the Social Problem.* St. Louis, Missouri: Freiburg B. Herder, 1890.

Paluszak, Sister Mary Cecilia. "The Opinion of the Catholic Telegraph on Contemporary Affairs and Politics." Master's thesis, The Catholic University of America, 1940.

Pare, B. *The Catholic Church in Detroit 1701–1888.* Detroit: Gabriel Richard Press, 1951.

Pargellis, Stanley. *Father Gabrial Richard.* Detroit: Wayne State University Press, 1950.

Pelotte, Donald E. *John Courtney Murray: Theologian in Conflict.* New York: Paulist Press, 1976.

Pfeffer, Leo. *Church, State, and Freedom.* Boston: Beacon Press, 1953.

Phelan, T. P. *Catholics in Colonial Days.* Gale Research, Detroit, 1935. Reprint. 1977.

"The Philadelphia Anti-Catholic Riots of 1844." *American Catholic Historical Researches* 7 (July 1911): 231–33.

Pike, James A. *A Roman Catholic in the White House.* Garden City, New York: Doubleday, 1960.

Powers, Rev. Joseph Leo. "The Knights of Labor and the Church's Attitude on Secret Societies." Master's thesis, University of Notre Dame, 1943.

Pratt, J. W. "Religious Conflict in the Development of the New York City Public School System." *History of Education Quarterly* 5: 110–20.

Purcell, Richard J. "Education and Irish Schoolmasters in Maryland National Period." *Catholic Education Review* 32 (1934): 198–207.

———. "Education and Irish Schoolmasters in Colonial Massachusetts." *Catholic Education Review* 33 (1935): 467–79.

———. "Education and Irish Teachers in Colonial Maryland." *Catholic Education Review* 32 (1934): 143–53.

———. "Education and Irish Teachers in Early Kentucky." *Catholic Education Review* 34 (1936): 360–69.

———. "Education and Irish Teachers in Massachusetts 1789–1865." *Catholic Education Review* 34 (1936): 87–96, 159–66.

———. "Irish Educational Contribution to Pennsylvania in the National Period." *Catholic Education Review* 38 (1940): 467–80, 537–49.

———. "John A. Ryan: Prophet of Social Justice." *Studies: An Irish Quarterly Review* 35 (June 1946): 153–74.

———. "Missionaries from All Hallow's (Dublin) to the United States, 1842–1865." *Records of the American Catholic Historical Society of Philadelphia* 53 (December 1942): 204–49.

———. "Pioneer Irish Educators in Tennessee." *Catholic Education Review* 34 (1936): 406–13.

———. "Rhode Islands Early Schools and Irish Teachers." *Catholic Education Review* 34 (1936): 402–15.

———. "Schools and Early Irish Teachers in New Hampshire." *Catholic Education Review* 32 (1934): 608–18.

———. "Some Early Teachers in Connecticut." *Catholic Education Review* 32 (1934): 332–38.

———. "Vermont: Schools and Early Irish Teachers." *Catholic Education Review* 33 (1935): 277–81.

Putnam, G. H. "The London Times and the American Civil War." *Magazine of History* 22 (April 1916): 131–44.

Putz, Louis J., C.S.C. *The Catholic Church, U.S.A.* Chicago: Fides, 1956.

Quigley, Martin, Jr., and Msgr. Edward M. Connors. *Catholic Action in Practice.* New York: Random House, 1963.

Quinlan, Richard J. "Growth and Development of Catholic Education in the Archdiocese of Boston." *The Catholic Historical Review* 22 (1937): 27–41.

Quirk, Robert E. *The Mexican Revolution*

and the Catholic Church, 1910–1929. Bloomington: Indiana University Press, 1973.

Ray, Mary Augustina. *American Opinion of Roman Catholicism in the Eighteenth Century.* New York, 1936.

Reilly, Daniel F. *The School Controversy (1891–1893).* Washington, D.C.: The Catholic University of America Press, 1943.

Reilly, Patricia Ann, Sr. M. "The Administration of Parish Schools in the Archdiocese of New York, 1800–1900." *U.S. Catholic Historical Society: Historical Records and Studies Series* 44 (1956).

Reily, John T. *Collections in the Life and Times of Cardinal Gibbons* 10 vols. Martinsburg, West Virginia, and McSherrystown, Pennsylvania, 1890–1903.

Reuss, Francis X. "Some Recollections of Rev. Patrick Rafferty, Missionary of the Diocese of Philadelphia." *Records of the American Catholic Historical Society* 7 (1897): 397.

Reynolds, F. L. "The Ancient Order of Hibernians." *Illinois Catholic Historical Review* 4 (1921): 22–33.

Reynolds, I. A., ed. *The Works of the Right Rev. John England.* Baltimore: John Murphy, 1849.

Rice, Madeline Hooke. *American Catholic Opinion in the Slavery Controversy.* Gloucester, Massachusetts: Peter Smith, 1964.

Riley, Arthur J. *Catholicism in New England to 1788.* Washington, D.C: The Catholic University of America Press, 1936.

Roche, Douglas J. *The Catholic Revolution.* New York: McKay, 1968.

Roche, James Jeffrey. *Life of John Boyle O'Reilly.* London: Cassell, 1891.

Roddy, Edward Creaves. "The Catholic Newspaper Press and the Quest for Social Justice, 1912–1920." Ph.D. dissertation, Georgetown University, 1961.

Rogers, Rev. Patrick. *Father Theobald Mathew: Apostle of Temperance.* New York and Toronto: Longmans, Green, 1945.

Roohan, James E. *American Catholics and the Social Question, 1865–1900.* New York: Arno Press, 1976.

Roohan, James E. "American Catholics and the Social Question, 1865–1900." *U.S. Catholic Historical Society: Historical Records and Studies* 43 (1955).

Rosenberg, Carroll. *Religion and the Rise of the American City: The New York City Mission Movement, 1912–1970.* Ithaca, New York: Cornell University Press, 1971.

Rothensteiner, Rev. John. *History of the Archdiocese of St. Louis.* St. Louis: Blackwell Wielands, 1928.

Rourke, Ulick J. *The Life and Times of the Most Rev. John McHale, Archbishop of Tuam and Metropolitan.* New York: P. J. Kennedy, 1883.

Rousseau, R. "Bishop John England and American-Church State Theory." Ph.D. dissertation, St. Paul University, 1969.

Roy, Ralph Lord. *Apostles of Discord: A Study of Organzied Bigotry and Disruption of the Fringes of Protestantism.* Boston: Beacon, 1953.

Russo, N. J. "Three Generations of Italians in New York City: Their Religious Acculturation." *International Migration Review,* 3:2:3–17. 1969.

Ryan, Alvan S., ed. *The Brownson Reader.* New York: Ayer, 1955.

Ryan, Msgr. John A. *The Catholic Church and the Citizen.* New York: Macmillan, 1928.

———. *The Church and Labor.* New York: Macmillan, 1920.

Ryan, Msgr. John A., and M. F. X. Millar. *The State and the Church.* New York: Macmillan, 1922.

Sadlier, Mary Anne. *Confessions of an Apostate* n.p., 1903.

Sanders, J. W. *The Education of an Urban Minority: Catholics in Chicago, 1833–1965.* Oxford University, New York. 1977.

———. *Nineteenth Century Boston Catholics and the School Question.* Center for the Study of American Catholicism. Working Paper Series, no. 2. University of Notre Dame. 1977.

Sandman, E. A. "James Alphonsus McMaster and the Controversy over Papal Infallibility." Master's thesis, University of Notre Dame, 1943.

Schaefer, Marvin R. "The Catholic Church

in Chicago: Its Growth and Administration." Ph.D. dissertation, University of Chicago, 1929.

Schavinger, Joseph Herman. *Profiles: In Action: American Catholics in Public Life*. Milwaukee: Bruce, 1966.

Schmeckebier, Laurence F. *History of the Know Nothing Party in Maryland*. Baltimore, Maryland: Johns Hopkins Press, 1899.

Schnepp, Gerald J., S.M. "Economic Status and Leakage." *The American Catholic Sociological Review* 4 (1943).

———. *Leakage from a Catholic Parish*. Washington, D.C.: The Catholic University of America Press, 1942.

———. "Nationality and Leakage?" *The American Catholic Sociological Review* 3 (1942): 154–63.

Schroll, Agnes Claire. *The Social Thought of John Lancaster Spalding, D. D.* Washington, D.C. The Catholic University of America Press, 1944.

Schuler, Paul Julian. "The Reaction of American Catholics to the Foundations and Early Practices of Progressive Education in the United States, 1892–1917." Ph.D. dissertation, University of Notre Dame, 1970.

Selekman, S. K. "Wave of the Past: Lessons of the Anti-Catholic Movement in the United States." *Menorah Journal* 31 (January 1943): 18–33.

Shade, William J. *Before the Molly Maguires: The Emergence of the Ethno-Religious Factor in the Politics of the Lower Anthracite Region, 1844–1872*. New York: Arno, 1976.

Shanabruch, Charles. *Chicago's Catholics: The Evolution of an American Identity*. Notre Dame, Indiana: University of Notre Dame Press, 1981.

Shannon, James P. *Catholic Colonization on the Western Frontier*. New Haven: Yale University Press, 1957.

Sharp, John K. *History of the Diocese of Brooklyn, 1853–1953: The Catholic Church on Long Island*. New York: Fordham University Press, 1954.

Shaughnessy, Gerald. *Has the Immigrant Kept the Faith?* New York: Macmillan, 1925.

Shaw, Richard. *Dagger John: The Unquiet Life and Times of Archbishop John Hughes of New York*. New York: Paulist, 1977.

Shea, John Gilmary. *The Catholic Church in Colonial Days*. New York: John G. Shea, 1892.

———. *History of the Catholic Church in the United States* 4 vols. New York: John G. Shea, 1892.

———. *Life and Times of the Most Rev. John Carroll*. New York: John G. Shea, 1888.

———. "The Progress of the Church in the United States." *American Catholic Quarterly Review* 9 (July 1884).

Sheen, Fulton John. *Wit and Wisdom of Bishop Fulton J. Sheen*. Englewood Cliffs, New Jersey: Prentice-Hall, 1968.

Sheerin, John B., C.S.P. *Never Look Back: The Career and Concerns of John J. Burke*. New York: Paulist Press, 1975.

Sheppard, J. Havergal. "The Irish in Protestant Denominations in America." *American Irish Historical Society Journal* 9 (1910): 92–109.

———. "Irish Preachers and Educators in the Early History of the Presbyterian Church in America." *American Irish Historical Society Journal* 24 (1925): 162–74.

Sisters of Reparation of the Congregation of Mary. *"Blessed are the Merciful": The Life of Mother Mary Zita (1844–1917), Foundress*. New York: n.p., 1953.

Skerrett, Ellen. "The Catholic Dimension." *The Irish in Chicago*, edited by Lawrence J. McCaffrey, et al. Urbana: University of Illinois Press, 1987.

———. "The Development of Catholic Identity among Irish Americans in Chicago, 1880–1920." In *From Paddy to Studs: Irish-American Communities in the Turn of the Century Era, 1880–1920*, edited by Timothy J. Meagher. New York: Greenwood Press, 1986.

Sloan, Raymond P. *On a Shoestring and a Prayer: The Story of Mother Alice, O.S.F. "Doctor of Sick Hospitals."* New York: Doubleday, 1964.

Smith, Albert Edward, and Vincent de P. Fitzpatrick. *Cardinal Gibbons: Churchman and Citizen*. Baltimore, Maryland: O'Donovan, 1921.

Smith, H. Shelton, Robert T. Handy, and Lefferts A. Loetscher. *American Christianity* 3 vols. New York: Charles Scribner's Sons, 1960.

Smith, Rev. John Talbot. *The Catholic Church in New York*. New York: Hall and Locke, 1905.

Smith, Timothy L. "Congregation, State, and Denomination: The Forming of the American Religious Structure." *William & Mary Quarterly* 25, series 3 (April 1968): 155–76.

Smylie, James H. "Catholics and Immigrants." *Christian Century* 80 (1963): 1396–99.

"Some Implications of Population Trends to the Christian Church." *The American Catholic Sociological Review* 3 (1942).

Spalding, J. L. *The Life of the Most Reverned M. J. Spalding, Archbishop of Baltimore*. New York: Benziger, 1873.

———. *The Religious Mission of the Irish People and Catholic Colonization*. New York: The Catholic Publication Society, 1880.

Spalding, Thomas W. *Martin John Spalding: American Churchman*. Washington, D.C.: The Catholic University of America Press, 1973.

Stack, John F. Jr. *International Conflict in an American City: Boston's Irish, Italians and Jews, 1935–1944*. Westport: Greenwood, 1979.

Stephenson, George M. "Nativism in the Forties and Fifties with Special Reference to the Mississippi Valley." *The Mississippi Valley Historical Review* 9 (December 1922).

Stock, Leo Francis. "The Irish Parliament and the American Revolution." *U.S. Catholic Historical Society: Records and Studies Series* 39 (1939).

Stokes, Anson Phelps. *Church and State in the United States*. New York: Harper and Brothers, 1950.

Stout, H. S. "Ethnicity: The Vital Center of Religion in America." *Ethnicity* 2 (1975): 204–24.

Sturges, W. K. "Bishop and His Architect: The Story of the Building of Baltimore Cathedral." *Liturgical Arts* 17 (February 1949): 53–57.

Sugrue, Thomas. *A Catholic Speaks His Mind on America's Religious Conflict*. New York: Harper, 1952.

Sweeney, Leo, C. M. "A Continuous Survey of a Highly Mobile Urban Parish." *The Homilectic and Pastoral Review* 44 (1943–44).

Swidler, Arlene. "Catholics and the 1876 Centennial." *The Catholic Historical Review*, 62, no. 3 (July 1976).

Szarnicki, Henry A. *Michael O'Connor, First Catholic Bishop of Pittsburgh, 1843–1860*. Pittsburgh: Wolfson, 1975.

Taves, Ann. "Relocating the Sacred: Roman Catholic Devotions in Mid-Nineteenth Century America." Ph.D. dissertation, University of Chicago, 1983.

Taylor, M. C. *A History of the Foundations of Catholicism in Northern New York*. New York: U.S. Catholic Historical Society (Monog. series 32) 1976.

Tehan, A. B., and J. Tehan. *Prince of Democracy: James Cardinal Gibbons*. New York: Doubleday, 1962.

Thompson, Joseph J., ed. *The Archdiocese of Chicago, Antecedents and Development*. Des Plains, Illinois: St. Mary's Training School Press, 1920.

Thompson, Mary P. "Anti-Catholic Laws in New Hampshire." *Catholic World* 51 (April–May 1890): 22–30, 185–97.

Tiffany, George E. "The Changing Church and the Changing Frontier." *U.S. Catholic Historical Society: Records and Studies Series* 35 (1946).

Tifft, Thomas W. "Toward a More Humane Social Policy: The Work and Influence of Monsignor John O'Grady." Ph.D. dissertation, The Catholic University of America, 1979.

Tourscher, F. E. *The Hogan Schism and Trustee Troubles in St. Mary's Church Philadelphia: 1820–1829*. Philadelphia: P. Reilly, 1930.

Treat, Roger L. *Bishop Sheil and the C.Y.O.* New York: Julian Messner, 1951.

Trent, James W., with Jenette Golds. *Catholics in College: Religious Commitment and the Intellectual Life*. Chicago: University of Chicago Press, 1967.

The Trial of the Convent Rioters. Cambridge, Massachusetts: 1834.

Trial of John R. Buzzell before the Supreme Judicial Court of Massachusetts for Arson and Burglary in the Ursuline Convent at Charlestown. Boston, 1834.

Trial of John R. Buzzell, the Leader of the Convent Rioters, for Arson and Burglary Committed on the Night of the 11th of August, 1834, by the Destruction of the Convent on Mount Benedict, in Charlestown, Massachusetts. Boston, 1834.

Trisco, Robert Frederick. *Catholic in America 1776–1976.* Washington, D.C.: National Conference of Catholic Bishops Commission for Bicentennial, 1976.

———. *The Holy See and the Nascent Church in the Middle Western United States, 1826–1850.* Rome, Georgia: Gregorian University Press, 1962.

Van Deusen, G. G. "Seward and the School Question Reconsidered." *Journal of American History* 52, no. 1 (1965): 313–19.

Wagener, Sister M. Gabrieline. "A Study of Catholic Opinion on Federal Aid to Education, 1870–1945." Ph.D. dissertation, 1963.

Walch, Timothy G. "Catholic Education in Chicago and Milwaukee, 1840–1890." Ph.D. dissertation, Northwestern University, 1975.

Walsh, Gerald Groveland, S.J. "Church and State in the United States." *U.S. Catholic Historical Society: Records and Studies Series* 37 (1948).

Walsh, H. L. *Hallowed Were the Gold Dust Trails.* Santa Clara, California: University of Santa Clara, 1946.

Walsh, James J. *The Popes and Science.* New York: Fordham University Press, 1911.

Walsh, James Joseph. *A Catholic Looks at Life.* Boston: Stratford, 1928.

———. *Our American Cardinals.* New York: D. Appleton, 1926.

Walsh, James P., and Timothy Foley. "Father Peter C. Yorke, Irish-American Leader." *Studia Hibernica*, no. 14: 90–103.

Walsh, John Patrick. "The Catholic Church in Chicago and the Problems of an Urban Society, 1893–1915." Ph.D. dissertation, University of Chicago, 1948.

Walsh, Reverend Louis S. *Historical Sketch of the Growth of Catholic Parochial Schools in the Archdiocese of Boston.* Newton Heights, Massachusetts: Press of St. John's Industrial School, 1901.

Wangler, T. E. "John Ireland and the Origins of Liberal Catholicism in the United States." *Catholic Historical Review* 56 (1971): 617–29.

Warkov, S., and A. M. Greeley. "Parochial School Origins and Educational Achievement." *American Sociology Review* 31 (1966): 406–14.

Wayman, Dorothy G. *Cardinal O'Connell of Boston.* New York: Farrar, Straus, 1955.

Weber, F. J. *America's Catholic Heritage: Some Bicentennial Reflections, 1776–1976.* Boston: St. Paul's Editions, 1976.

———. "Catholicism in Colonial America." *Homiletic and Pastoral Review* 65 (1965): 842–51.

———. "John Tracy Ellis, Historian of American Catholicism." *The American Benedictine Review* 17 (1966): 467–78.

Weber, Francis J., ed. *The Religious Heritage of Southern California: A Bicentennial Survey.* Los Angeles: Interreligious Council of Southern California, 1976.

———, ed. *Some California Catholic Reminiscences for the United States Bicentennial.* Los Angeles: Knights of Columbus, 1976.

Weigel, Gustave, S.J. "The Present Embarrassment of the Church." In *Religion in America*, edited by John Cogley. New York: Meridian, 1958.

Weisz, H. R. "Irish-American and Italian-American Educational Views and Activities, 1870–1900: A Comparison." *New York History* 53 (1972): 157–76.

Wescott, Thompson. "A Memoir of the Very Rev. Michael Hurley, D.C., O.S.A." *Records of the American Catholic Historical Society of Philadelphia* 1 (1884–86): 165–212.

Westoff, Charles F., and Larry Bumpass. "Revolution in Birth Control Practices of United States Roman Catholics." *Science* 179 (January 1973).

Whalen, Sister Mary Rose Gertrude. "Some Aspects of the Influence of Orestes A. Brownson on His Contemporaries." Ph.D. dissertation, University of Notre Dame, 1933.

Whitley, Edward, C.S.P. "John J. Burke, C.S.P., and Mexican Church-State Relations, 1927–1929." Ph.D. dissertation, St. Paul's College.

Will, Allen Sinclair. *Life of Cardinal Gibbons, Archbishop of Baltimore*. 2 vols. New York: Dutton, 1922.

Williams, Michael. *American Catholics in the War*. Washington, D.C.: National Catholic War Council, 1921.

Wills, Garry. *Bare Ruined Choirs*. New York: Doubleday, 1972.

———. *Politics and Catholic Freedom*. Chicago: Regnery, 1964.

Winter, M. M. "The Beginning of Catholicity in Minnesota." Master's thesis, University of Notre Dame, 1930.

Woehler, Brother Francis Borgia. "Bishop Spalding's Position Concerning Intellectual Culture." Master's thesis, 1944.

Wolters, Gilbert Francis, O.S.B. *A Socio-Economic Analysis of Four Rural Parishes*. Washington, D.C.: The Catholic University of America Press, 1938.

Wood, Rev. Thomas O. "The Catholic Attitude Toward the Social Settlement Movement: 1886–1914." Master's thesis, University of Notre Dame, 1958.

Woodbury, K. A. "An Incident Between the French-Canadians and the Irish in the Diocese of Maine, 1906." *New England Quarterly* 40 (1967): 260–68.

Zwierlein, Frederick J. "Catholic Beginnings in the Diocese of Rochester." *The Catholic Historical Review* 1 (1916): 282–98.

———. "Know Nothingism in Rochester, New York." *U.S. Catholic Historical Society Records and Studies* 14 (May 1920).

———. *Letters of Archbishop Corrigan to Bishop McQuaid and Allied Documents*. Rochester, New York: The Art Printshop, 1946.

———. *The Life and Letters of Bishop McQuaid, Prefaced with the History of Catholic Rochester before His Episcopate*. 3 vols. Rochester, New York: The Art Printshop, 1926.

———. *Theodore Roosevelt and Catholics, 1882–1919*. St. Louis: The Catholic Central Verein, 1956.

7. Labor

Abbott, Edith. "The Wages of Unskilled Labor in the United States, 1850–1900." *Journal of Political Economy* 13, no. 3 (June 1905): 321–67.

———. *Women in Industry*. New York: Arno Press and the New York Times, 1969.

Abell, A. I. "Catholic Reaction to Industrial Conflict: The Arbitral Process, 1885–1900." *Catholic Historical Review* 41(1955): 385–84, 87.

Adams, Graham, Jr. *Age of Industrial Violence, 1910–1915*. New York: Columbia University Press, 1966.

American Committee for Protection of Foreign Born. *Charles A. Doyle: Framed by Immigration Authorities: The Story of An American Trade Unionist*. New York: Author, 1949.

Anrowitz, Stanley. *False Promises*. New York: McGraw-Hill, 1973.

Anspach, M. R. "The Molly Maguires in the Anthracite Coal Regions of Pennsylvania 1850–1890." *Now and Then* 11 (1954): 25–34.

Aurand, H. W. "The Anthracite Strike of 1887–1888." *Pennsylvania History* 35 (1968): 172–173.

———. *From the Molly Maguires to the United Mine Workers: The Social Ecology of an Industrial Union, 1869–1897*. Philadelphia, Pennsylvania: Temple University Press, 1971.

Barbash, Jack. "Ethnic Factors in the Development of the American Labor Movement in Industrial Research Association." *Interpreting the Labor Movement*, 1952.

Barnes, Charles B. *The Longshoremen*. New York: Survey, 1915.

Barrett, Tom. *The Mollies Were Men*. New York: Vantage, 1969.

Beers, P. B. "The Molly Maguires." *American History Illustrated* 1 (1966): 12–22.

Bennett, John. "Iron Workers in Woods Run and Johnstown: The Union Era, 1865–1895." Ph.D. dissertation, University of Pittsburgh.

Bernstein, Irvin. "Forces Affecting the Growth of the American Labor Movement." In *Labor in a Changing America*, edited by William Haber. New York: Basic Books, 1960.

Berthoff, R. "The Social Order of the Anthracite Region, 1825–1902." *Pennsylvania Magazine of History and Biography* 89 (1965): 261–91.

Betten, Neil. *Catholic Activism and the Industrial Worker*. Gainesville: University Presses of Florida, 1976.

Biever, Bruce Francis. *Religion, Culture, and Values: Native Irish and American Irish Catholicism*. New York: Arno Press, 1976.

Bimba, Anthony. *The Molly Maguires*. New York: International Publishers, 1932.

Bishop, J. Leander. *History of American Manufacturers*. Philadelphia, 1868.

"Bitter Rain on St. Pat's Parade." *Maclean's* 96 (March 28, 1983).

Bland, J. *Hibernian Crusade: The Story of the Catholic Total Abstinence Union of America*. Washington, D.C: The Catholic University Press, 1951.

Broderick, John T. *Pulling Together*. Schenectady: Robson and Adee, 1922.

Broehl, W. G. *The Molly Maguires*. Cambridge, Massachusetts: Harvard University Press, 1964.

Brooks, J. G. *Impressions of the Anthracite Coal Troubles*. *Yale Review* 6 (1897): 306–11.

Browne, Henry Joseph. *The Catholic Church*

and the Knights of Labor. Washington, D.C.: The Catholic University, 1949.

———. "Terence V. Powderly and the Church—Labor Difficulties of the Early 1880's." *Catholic Historical Review* 32 (April 1946): 1–27.

Carman, H. J. et al., ed. *The Path I Trod: The Autobiography of T. V. Powderly.* New York: Columbia University, 1940.

Chalker, F. "Irish Catholics in the Building of the Ocmulgee and Flint Railroad." *Georgia Historical Quarterly* 54 (1970): 507–16.

Chalmers, H. II. *How the Irish Built the Erie.* New York: Bookmen, 1964.

Coleman, J. *Men and Coal.* New York: Farrar and Rhinehart, 1943.

Coleman, J. Walter. *The Molly Maguire Riots.* Richmond: Garrett and Massie, 1936.

Commons, John R. *History of Labor in the United States, 1896–1932* 4 vols. New York: Macmillan, 1935.

Congress. Joint Committee on Printing. *Biographical Directory of the American Congress, 1774–1961: The Continental Congress and the Congress of the United States.* Washington, D.C.: Government Printing Office, 1961.

Cox, LaWanda F. "The American Agriculture Wage Earner, 1865–1900." *Agricultural History* 22 (April 1949).

Cronin, B. C. *Father Yorke and the Labor Movement in San Francisco, 1900–1910.* Washington, D.C.: The Catholic University, 1943.

D'Arcy, William. *The Fenian Movement in the United States: 1858–1886.* Washington, D.C., 1947.

Dancis, B. "Social Mobility and Class Consciousness: San Francisco International Workers Association in the 1880s." *Journal of Social History* 11 (1978): 75–98.

Danhof, Clarence. "Farm-Making Costs and the Safety Valve: 1850–1860." *Journal of Political Economy* 49 (June 1941).

Davis, James J. *The Iron Puddler: My Life in the Rolling Mills and What Came of It.* Indianapolis, Indiana: Bobbs-Merrill, 1922.

Degler, Carl N. "Labor in the Economy and Politics of New York, 1850–1860: A Study of the Impact of Early Industrialism." Ph.D. dissertation, Columbia Univeristy, 1952.

Dewees, F. P. *The Molly Maguires: The Origin, Growth and Character of the Organization.* Burt Franklin, New York, 1877.

Dubnoff, S. J. "The Family and Absence from Work: Irish Workers in a Lowell, Massachusetts Cotton Mill, 1860." Ph.D. dissertation, Brandeis University, 1975.

Ehrlich, R. L. ed. *Immigrants in Industrial America 1850–1920.* Charlottesville, Virginia: University of Virginia.

Emmons, David M. *The Butte Irish: Class and Ethnicity in an American Mining Town, 1875–1925.* Urbana: University of Illinois Press, 1989.

England, C.D., ed. *The Molly Maguires of Pennsylvania, or Ireland In America: A True Narrative, Told by Ernest W. Lucy, U.S.A.* London, n.p., 1883.

Ernst, R. "Economic Nativism in New York City during the 1840's." *New York History* 29 (1848): 170–86.

Fenton, Edwin. *Immigrants and Unions: A Case Study.* New York: Arno Press, 1975.

Fetherling, Dale. *Mother Jones: The Miner's Angel.* Illinois: Southern Illinois University Press, 1974.

Finley, Joseph E. *The Corrupt Kingdom: The Rise and Fall of the United Mine Workers.* New York: Simon and Schuster, 1972.

Foner, P. S., and A. J. Lane. "James McParlan and the Molly Maguires." *Science and Society* 31 (1967): 77.

Frost, Richard H. *Mooney Case.* Stanford: Stanford University Press, 1968.

Fuller, Levi Varden. "The Supply of Agricultural Labor as a Factor in the Evolution of Farm Organization in California." Ph.D. dissertation, University of California, Berkeley, 1939.

Gates, Paul W. "Frontier Estate Builders and Farm Laborers." In *The Frontier in Perspective,* Walker D. Wyman and Clifton B. Kroeber. Madison: University of Wisconsin Press, 1965.

George, Henry. *The Condition of Labor.* London: S. Sonnenschein, 1898.

Gittleman, H. M. "No Irish Need Apply: Patterns of Responses to Ethnic Discrimination in the Labor Market." *Labor History* (Winter 1973): 56–68.

———. "Waltham System and the Coming of the Irish." *Labor History* (Fall 1967): 227–53.

———. *Workingmen of Waltham*. Baltimore: Johns Hopkins University Press, 1974.

Gluck, Elsie. *John Mitchell, Miner: Labor's Bargain with the Gilded Age*. New York: Day, 1929.

Goarty, P. W. *The Economic Thought of Monsignor John A. Ryan*. Washington, D.C.: The Catholic University, 1953.

Gompers, Samuel. *Seventy Years of Life and Labor: An Autiobiography*. New York: Dutton, 1925.

Goodrich, C. L. *The Miner's Freedom: A Study of the Working Life in a Changing Industry*. Boston: Marshall Jones, 1925.

Gordan, M. "Irish Immigrant Culture and the Labor Boycott in New York City, 1880–1886." in *Immigrants in Industrial America, 1850–1920*, edited by R. L. Ehrlich. Charlottesville, Virginia: University of Virginia, 1977, 111–22.

———. "The Labor Boycott in New York City, 1880–1886." *Labor History* 16, no. 2: 184–229.

Goulden, Joseph C. *Meany*. New York: Atheneum, 1972.

Gowaskie, J. M. "John Mitchell: A Study in Leadership." Ph.D. dissertation, The Catholic University of America, 1968.

Greeley, Andrew M. "Occupational Choice among the American-Irish." *Eire-Ireland* 7, no. 1:3–9.

Green, A. "The Death of Mother Jones." *Labor History* 1 (1960): 68–80.

Green, V. R. "The Molly Maguire Conspiracy in the Pennsylvania Anthracite Region 1862–1879." Master's thesis, University of Rochester, 1960.

Griffen, C. "Occupational Mobility in Nineteenth Century America: Problems and Possibilities." *Journal of Social History* 5 (1972): 310–30.

———. "The "Old" Immigration and Industrialization: A Case Study." *Immigrants in Industrial America*, edited by R. L. Ehrlich. Charlottesville: University of Virginia Press, 1977, 176–204.

———. "Workers Divided: The Effect of Craft and Ethnic Differences in Poughkeepsie, New York, 1850–1880." In *Nineteenth-Century Cities*, edited by S. Thernstrom and R. Senett. New Haven: Yale University Press, 1969, 49–96.

Groneman, C. "The Bloody Ould Sixth: A Social Analysis of a Mid-Nineteenth Century New York Working Class Community." Ph.D. dissertation, University of Rochester, 1973.

———. "Working Class Immigrant Women in Mid-Nineteenth Century New York: The Irish Woman's Experience." *Journal of Urban History* 4, no. 3 (1978): 255–73.

Gudelunas, W. A., Jr., and W. G. Shade. *Before the Molly Maguires: The Emergence of the Ethno-Religious Factor in the Politics of the Lower Anthracite Region, 1844–72*. New York: Arno Press, 1976.

Hanna, Hilton E., and Joseph Balesky. *The "Pat" Gorman Story: Picket and the Pen*. Yonkers: American Institute of Social Science, 1960.

Heald, Morrell. "Business Attitudes Toward European Immigration, 1800–1900." *Journal of Economic History* 13 (1953): 291.

Heaton, Herbert. "Industrial Immigrant in the United States, 1783–1812." *American Philosophical Society Proceedings* 45 (1951): 519.

"Hibernian." (Molly Maguires). *Blackwood's Magazine* 254 (July 1943): 30–35.

Higgs, Robert. "Race, Skills, and Earnings: American Immigrants in 1909." *Journal of Economic History* 31, no. 2 (June 1971): 420–28.

Higham, John. *Strangers in the Land*. New York: Atheneum, 1969.

Hill, J. *Politics, Labor and George Meany*. *Commonwealth* 10, no. 2 (1975): 47–49.

Hourwich, Isaac A. *Immigration and Labor*. New York: AMS, 1922.

House of Representatives. Communication on Foreign Relations. *Trial of American Citizens for Fenianism Report*. Washington, D.C.: Government Printing Office, November 25, 1876.

Hurley, John. "The Irish Immigrant in the Early Labor Movement, 1820–1862." Master's thesis, Columbia University, 1959.

"The Irish Connection." *Newsweek* 101 (March 21, 1983).

"Irish Mafia." (Molly Maguires). *Times Literary Supplement* (February 11, 1965): 106.

Itter, W. A. "Conscriptions in Pennsylvania During the Civil War." Master's thesis, University of Southern California, 1941.

———. "Early Labor Troubles in the Schuylkill Anthracite Region." *Pennsylvania History* 1 (1934): 28–37.

James, E. T. "T. V. Powderly: A Political Profile." *Pennsylvania Magazine of History and Biography* 99 (1975): 443–59.

Johnson, Malcolm. *Crime on the Labor Front*. New York: McGraw, 1950.

Jones, Mary Harris. *The Autobiography of Mother Jones*. Chicago: Charles H. Kerr, 1976.

———. *Autobiography of Mother Jones*, edited by M. F. Parton. Chicago: Charles H. Ken, 1925.

Karson, Marc. *American Labor Unions and Politics, 1900–1918*. Carbondale: Southern Illinois University Press, 1958.

Kelley, William D. *Speech of Hon. William D. Kelley, of Pennsylvania, on Protection to American Labor: Delivered in the House of Representatives, January 31, 1866*. Washington, D.C.: Congressional Globe Office, 1866.

Kildeen, C. E. "John Siney: The Pioneer of American Industrial Unionism and Industrial Government." Ph.D. dissertation, University of Wisconsin, 1942.

Klacznska, Barbara. "Why Women Work: A Comparison of Various Ethnic Groups—Philadelphia, 1910–1930." *Labor History* 17 (Winter 1976): 73–87.

Knight, R. E. L. *Industrial Relations in the San Francisco Bay Area 1900–1918*. University of California, Berkeley, 1960.

Lane, A.J. "Recent Literature in the Molly Maguires." *Science & Society* 30 (Summer 1966): 309–19.

Laurie, B. et al. "Immigrants and Industry, The Philadelphia Experience, 1850–1880." In *Immigrants in Industrial America 1850–1920*, edited by R. L. Ehrlich. Charlottesville, Virginia: 1977, 123–50.

Lazerow, J. "The Workingman's Hour: The 1886 Labor Uprising in Boston." *Labor History* 21, no. 2 (1980): 200–220.

Leonard, J. de L. *Catholic Attitudes Towards American Labor*. Ph.D. dissertation, Columbia University, 1940.

Lewis, Arthur H. *Lament for the Molly Maguries*. New York: Harcourt, 1964.

Logan, S. C. *A City's Danger and Defense: On Issues and Results of the Strikes of 1877*. Pennsylvania: Scranton, 1887.

Lucy, E. W. *The Molly Maguire of Pennsylvania or Ireland in America*. London: G. Bell and Sons, 1882.

Man, A. P., Jr. "Labor Competition and the New York Draft Riots of 1863." *Journal of Negro History* 36 (1951): 375–405.

McAvoy, Thomas T. "The Formation of the Catholic Minority." In *Catholicism in America*, edited by P. Gleason. New York: Harper and Row, 1970.

———. *American Catholics and the Second World War*. South Bend, Indiana: University of Notre Dame Press, 1944.

———. "The Catholic Minority after the Americanist Controversy, 1899–1917: A Survey." *Review of Politics* 10 (1948): 13–34.

———. *The Great Crisis in American Catholic History*. Chicago: Regnery, 1957.

———. *Roman Catholicism and the American Way of Life*. South Bend, Indiana: University of Notre Dame Press, 1960.

McCarthy, C. A. *The Great Molly Maguire Hoax: Based on Information Suppressed 90 Years*. Wyoming, Pennsylvania: Cro-Woods, 1969.

McDonald, David J., and Edward A. Lynch. *Coal and Unionism: A History of the America Coal Miners' Unions*. Silver Springs, Maryland: Lynald, 1939.

McDonald, Grace. *History of the Irish in Wisconsin in the Nineteenth Century*. Washington, D.C., 1954.

Miller, E. W. "The Southern Anthracite Region: A Problem Area, 1820–1952." *Economic Geography* 31 (1955): 331–50.

Montgomery, David. *Beyond Equality*. New York: Alfred A. Knopf, 1967.

Montgomery, David. "The Irish and the American Labor Movement." In *America and Ireland 1776–1976*, edited by David Noel Doyle and Owen Dudley Edwards.

Westport, Connecticut: Greenwood Press, 1980.

———. "The Irish Influence in the American Labor Movement." Notre Dame: Charles and Margaret Hall Cushwa Center, 1984. Reprint of Hibernian Lecture at the University of Notre Dame, 11 October 1984.

Morse, J. T. "Molly Maguire Trials." *American Law Review* 11 (1877): 233–60.

Musselman, B. L. "Working Class Unity and Ethnic Division: Cincinnati Trade Unionists and Cultural Pluralism." *Cincinnati Historical Society Bulletin* 34, no. 1 (1976): 121–43.

O'Brien, D. "American Catholics and Organized Labor in the 1930's." *Catholic Historical Review* 52, no. 3 (1966): 323–49.

O'Connor, Richard. *The First Hurrah: A Biography of Alfred E. Smith*. New York: Putnam, 1970.

O'Hanlon, John M. *Historical Sketches of Organized Labor of the State of New York*. Albany, New York: New York State Federation of Labor, 1923.

Oshinsky, D. M. *Senator Joseph McCarthy and the American Labor Movement*. Columbia: University of Missouri, 1976.

Parsons, T. "McCarthyism and American Social Tensions." *Yale Review* 44 (1954): 226–45.

Patterson, J. F. *Reminiscenses of John Maguire after Fifty Years of Mining*. Publications of Historical Society of Schuylkill County 4 (1913/14): 321.

Pinkerton, A. *The Molly Maguires and the Detectives*. New York: G. W. Dillingham, 1877.

Pinkowski, E. *John Siney: The Miners Martyr*. Philadelphia: Sunshine Press, 1963.

Powderly, Terence V. *The Path I Trod, An Autobiography*. New York: Columbia University Press, 1940.

Powers, J. L. *The Knights of Labor and the Church's Attitude on Secret Societies*. Master's thesis, University of Notre Dame, 1943.

Raffaele, J. F. "Mary Harris Jones and the United Mine Workers." Master's thesis, University of North Carolina, 1964.

Rhodes, J. F. "The Molly Maguires in the Anthracite Region of Pennsylvania." *American History Review* 15:3:547–561. 1910.

Rodechko, J. "Irish-American Society in the Pennsylvania Anthracite Region 1870–1880." In *The Ethnic Experience in Philadelphia*, edited by J. E. Bodner. Lewisburg, Pennsylvania: Bucknell University, 1973, 19–38.

Roney, Frank. *Frank Roney, Irish Rebel and California Labor Leader: An Autobiography*. Berkeley, California: University of California Press, 1931.

Ryan, Frederick Lynn. "Industrial Relations in the San Francisco Building Trades." Ph.D. dissertation, University of California, Berkeley, 1933.

Ryan, Msgr. John A. *The Church and Labor*. New York: Macmillan, 1920.

Schlegel, M. W. "The Workingman's Benevolence Association: First Union of Anthracite Miners." *Pennsylvania History* 10 (1943): 243–67.

Schroll, A. C. "Bishop John Lancaster Spalding and Quadragesimo." *Anno American Benedictine Review* 7 (1956): 248–62.

Shannon, F. A. "A Postmortem on the Labor-Safety-Valve Theory." *Agricultural History* 19 (1945): 31–37.

Sheetz, Carson Park. "History of Labor Unions in Sacramento from 1848 to 1899." Master's thesis, University of California, Berkeley, 1933.

Shumsky, N. L. "Frank Roney's San Francisco—His Diary: April, 1975–March, 1976." *Labor History* 17, no. 2 (1976): 245–64.

"Smiling Irish Eyes (Irish American Politicians and Aid to Northern Ireland)." *Time* 127 (March 24, 1986).

Spalding, J. L. *Socialism and Labor, and Other Arguments, Social, Political, and Patriotic*. Chicago: A. C. McClurg, 1902.

Steel, E. "Mother Jones in the Fairmont Field 1902." *Journal of American History* 57 (1970): 290–307.

Stroh, P. "The Catholic Clergy and American Labor Disputes." Ph.D. dissertation, The Catholic University of America, 1939.

Suffern, Arthur E. *The Coal Miner's Struggle for Industrial Status: A Study of the Evolution of Organized Relations and In-*

dustrial Principle in the Coal Industry. New York: Macmillan, 1926.

Sullivan, W. A. "The Industrial Revolution and the Factory Operatives in Pennsylvania." *Pennsylvania Magazine of History & Biography* 1954, no. 78: 476–77.

———. *The Industrial Worker in Pennsylvania 1800–1840*. Harrisburg: Pennsylvania Historical and Museum Commission, 1955.

———. "Philadelphia Labor: During the Jackson Era." *Pennsylvania History* 15 (1948): 1–16.

Swejda, G. J. *Irish Immigrants Participation in the Construction of the Erie Canal*. United States Office of Archaeology and Historic Preservation, 1969.

Thompson, E. "Mines and Plantations and the Movements of Peoples." *American Journal of Sociology* 37 (1932): 603–611.

Turnback, W. M. "The Attitudes of T. V. Powderly Toward Minority Groups." Master's thesis. The Catholic University of America, 1950.

Tygiel, Jules E. "Workingmen in San Francisco, 1880–1891." Ph.D. dissertation, University of California at Los Angeles, 1978.

Ware, Norman Joseph. *The Industrial Worker, 1840–1860*. Boston: Houghton Mifflin, 1924. Reprinted: Peter Smith, Gloucester, Massachusetts, 1965.

8. Nationalism

Adams, G. H. "Our State Department and Extradition." *American Law Review* 20 (1886): 540–52. 1886.

Akenson, Donald Harmon. *The United States and Ireland.* Cambridge, Massachusetts: Harvard University Press, 1973.

"An American Report on the Irish Terror." *The Literary Digest* 69, no. 18 (April 23, 1921): 11.

Anderson, Sir Robert. *Sidelights on the Home Rule Movement.* New York: Dutton, 1906.

Bagenal, Philip H. *The American-Irish and Their Influence on Irish Politics.* London: K. Paul, Trench, 1882.

Berthoff, Rowland T. "The Social Order of the Anthracite Region, 1825–1902." *Pennsylvania Magazine* 89 (July 1965).

Blake, Nelson M. "The United States and the Irish Revolution, 1914–1922." Ph.D. dissertation, Clark University, 1936.

Branningan, C. J. "The Luke Dillon Case and the Welland Canal Explosion of 1900: Non-Events in the History of the Niagra Frontier Region." *Niagra frontier* 24, no. 2 (1977): 36–44.

Brecher, John. "The IRA's Angels (Irish-American Support for the IRA)." *Newsweek* 97 (May 18, 1981).

Bromage, Mary C. "De Valera's Mission to America." *South Atlantic Quarterly* 50 (October 1951): 499–513.

Brown, S. A. J. "The Irish Question in Anglo-American Relations, 1914–1922." Ph.D. dissertation, Bradford University, 1977.

Brown, T. N. "Nationalism and the Irish Peasant 1800–1848." *Review of Politics* 15, no. 4 (1956): 403–45.

Brown, Thomas N. *Irish American Nationalism.* Philadelphia: Lippincott, 1966.

Brown, Thomas N. "The Origins and Character of Irish American Nationalism." *The Review of Politics* 18, no. 3 (1956): 327–57.

Buckley, Benjamin Clyde. "The Fenians and Anglo-American Relations after the Civil War." Master's thesis, Kansas State University, 1973.

Buckley, John Patrick. "The New York Irish: Their View of American Foreign Policy, 1914–1921." Ph.D. dissertation, New York Univeristy, 1974.

Calkin, H. L. "The United States Government and the Irish." *Irish Historical Studies* 9 (1954): 28–52.

Carroll, Francis M. *American Opinion and the Irish Question, 1910–1923.* Dublin: Gill and Macmillan, 1978.

———, ed. *The American Commission on Irish Independence, 1919: the Diary, Correspondence and Report.* Dublin: Irish Manuscripts Commission, 1985.

Cassidy, M. A. "The History of the Fenian Movement in the United States, 1848–1866, and its Background in Ireland and America." Master's thesis, University of Buffalo, 1941.

Clark, D. I. *Irish Blood: Northern Ireland and the American Conscience.* Port Washington, New York: 1977.

———. "Letters from the Underground: The Fenian Correspondence of James Gibbons." *Records of the American Catholic Historical Society* 81 (1970): 83–88.

———. "Militants of the 1860's: The Philadelphia Fenians." *Pennsylvania Magazine of History and Biography* 95 (1971): 98–108.

Cohalan, D. F. "Our Economic Interest in Ireland." *Forum.* 65 (1921): 59–67.

———. "Our Foreign Policy." *Forum.* 65 (1921): 187–96, 317–47.

Colton, K. E. "Parnell's Mission to Iowa." *Annals of Iowa: A Historical Quarterly* 22 (1940): 312–27.

Costigan, G. "The Tragedy of Charles O'Connor: An Episode in Anglo-Irish Relations." *American Historical Review* 49, no. 1 (1943): 32–54.

Creigton, R. J. "Influence of Foreign Issues on American Politics." *International Review* 13 (1882): 182–90.

Cronin, S. *The McGarrity Papers: Revelations of the Irish Revolutionary Movement in Ireland and America, 1900–1940*. Tralee, Kerry: Anvil, 1972.

Cronin, Sean. *Washington's Irish Policy, 1916–1986*. Dublin: Anvil, 1986.

Cuddy, Edward. "Irish-American Propagandists and American Neutrality, 1914–1917." *Mid-America* 49, no. 4 (October 1967): 252–75.

———. "Irish-Americans and the 1916 Elections: An Episode of Immigrant Adjustment." *American Quarterly* 21 (1969): 228–43.

Cuddy, H. "The Influence of the Fenian Movement on Anglo-American Relations, 1860–1872." Ph.D. dissertation, St. Johns University, 953.

Cuddy, J. E. "Irish-America and National Isolationism: 1914–1920." SUNY at Buffalo. Ph.D. dissertation, Suny at Bufffalo, 1965. Reprinted by Arno, 1976.

Curti, Merle E. "George N. Sanders, American Patriot of the Fifties." *The South Atlantic Quarterly* 27 (January 1928).

D'Arcy, W. *The Fenian Movement in the United States, 1858–1886*. Washington, D.C.: The Catholic University of America Press, 1947. Reprinted by Russell and Russell, 1971.

Davidson, Sara. "Bernadette Devlin: An Irish Revolutionary in Irish America." *Harper's* 240 (January 1970): 78–87.

Davis, H. A. "Fenian Raid on New Brunswick." *Canadian Historical Review* 36 (December 1955): 316–34.

De Valera, Eamonn. *Ireland's Request to the Government of the United States of America for Recognition as a Sovereign Independent States*. Washington, D.C.: Irish Diplomatic Mission, 1920.

Denieffe, Joseph. *A Personal Narrative of the Irish Revolutionary Brotherhood: Giving a Faithful Report of the Principle Events from 1855 to 1867*. New York: Gael, 1906.

Denison, Major George T. *The Fenian Raid on Fort Erie with an Account of the Battle of Ridgeway*. Toronto, Ontario: June 1866.

Devoy, John. *Devoy's Post Bag, 1871–1928*. Dublin, Ireland: Fallon, 1948.

———. *Recollections of an Irish Rebel*. New York: Charles P. Young, 1929.

Donovan, H. D. A. "Fenian Memories in Northern New York." *American Irish Historical Society Journal* 28 (1930): 148–52.

Doyle, David Noel. *Irish Americans, Native Rights and National Empires*. New York: Arno Press, 1976.

Duff, John B. "The Politics of Revenge: Ethnic Opposition to the Peace Policies of Woodrow Wilson." Ph.D. dissertation, Columbia University, 1964.

———. "Versailles Treaty and the Irish-Americans." *Journal of American History* 55, no. 3 (December 1968): 582–98.

Dwyer, Thomas Ryle. "American Efforts to Discredit de Valera during World War II." *Eire-Ireland* 7, no. 2: 20–33.

———. *Irish Neutrality and the United States of America, 1939–1947*. New York: Rowman, 1977.

———. "The United States and Irish Neutrality, 1939–1945." Ph.D. dissertation, North Texas State University, 1973.

Edwards, O. D. "American Diplomats and Irish Coercion, 1880–83. *Journal of American Studies* 1, no. 2 (1967): 213–32.

"Eire: The American Connection." *Newsweek* 81 (January 22, 1973): 41.

Emmett, Thomas Addis. *Incidents of My Life: Professional-Literary-Social, with Services in the Course of Ireland*. New York: Putnam, 1911.

Fenian Brotherhood. *Proceedings of the First General Convention of the Fenian Brotherhood of the Pacific Coast Held in San Francisco, California, September, 1864*. San Francisco: George W. Stevens, 1864.

"Fenianism by One Who Knows." *Contemporary Review* 19 (1871): 301–16.

Fitzpatrick, J. "The Irish-American and Sinn Fein." *Triumph* 8 (October 1973): 13–16.

"Franklin and the Fenian 'Battle of Richards' Farm." *Vermont Historical Society, News and Notes* 4 (February 1953): 41–43.

"Friends of the I.R.A." *New Republic* 173 (October 18, 1975): 3–5.

Funchion, Michael F. "Chicago's Irish Nationalists, 1881–1890." Ph.D. dissertation, Loyola University of Chicago, 1973. Published by Arno Press, 1976.

———. "Irish Nationalists and Chicago Politics in the 1880's." *Eire-Ireland* 10, no. 2 (1975): 3–18.

———. "The Political and Nationalist Dimensions." In *The Irish In Chicago*, edited by Lawrence McCaffrey et al. Urbana: University of Illinois Press, 1987.

Gafney, T. St. John. *Breaking the Silence: England, Ireland, Wilson and the War.* Liveright, New York, 1931.

Galbraith, J. S. "United States, Britain and the Creation of the Irish Free State." *Atlantic Quarterly* 48 (October 1949): 566–74.

———. "United States and Ireland," 1916–1920. *South Atlantic Quarterly* 46 (1947): 192–203.

Gibson, Florence Elizabeth. *The Attitudes of the New York Irish Toward State and National Affairs, 1848–1892.* New York, 1951.

Green, E. R. R. "Fenians." *History Today* 8 (October 1958): 698–705.

Green, J. J. "American Catholics and the Irish Land League, 1879–1922." *Catholic Historical Review* 35 (1949): 19–42.

Griffin, G. W. H., and G. Christy. *The Fenian Spy or John Bull in America.* New York: Happy Hours, 1873.

Guptill, F. F. "A Popular Bibliography of the Fenian Movement." *Eire-Ireland* 4, no. 2: 18–25.

Hachey, T. E. "British War Propaganda and American Catholics, 1918." *Catholic Historical Review* 61 (1975): 48–66.

Hackett, Francis. *Ireland: A Study in Nationalism*, 1918.

"'Hands Off' to Irish-Americans." *The Literary Digest* 69, no. 18 (June 25, 1921): 18.

Harmon, Maurice, ed. *Fenians and Fenianism.* Dublin: Scepter Books, 1968.

Haupfuhrer, Fred. "A Week before St. Patrick's Day, American IRA Sympathizers Raise Irish Leader Garret Fitzgerald's Ire." *People's Weekly* 21 (March 19, 1984).

Hazel, M. V. "First Link: Parnell's American Tour, 1880." *Eire-Ireland* 15, no. 1 (1980): 6–24.

Hazel, Michael Victory. "Charles Stewart Parnell and the Creation of the Modern Irish State, 1874–1886." Ph.D. dissertatiion, The University of Chicago, 1974.

Hendrick, B. J. *The Life and Letters of Walter H. Page.* New York: Doubleday, Garden City, 1925.

Hernon, J. M. *Celts, Catholics, and Copperheads: Ireland Views the American Civil War.* Columbus: Ohio State University Press, 1968.

———. "The Irish Nationalists and the Southern Secession." *Civil War History* 4 (1966): 43–53.

———, "The Use of the American Civil War in the Debate Over Irish Home Rule." *American Historical Review* 69, no. 4 (1964): 1022–26.

Hillenbrand, Martin J. "Department of State's Position on Irish Crisis." *Department of State Bulletin* 66 (March 20, 1972): 448–50.

Holland, Jack. *The American Connection: U.S. Guns, Money and Influence in Northern Ireland.* New York: Viking, 1987.

Hoslett, Schuyler Dean. "The Fenian Brotherhood." *Americana* 34 (1940): 596–603.

Hunt, H. M. *The Crime of the Century or the Assassination of Dr. Patrick Henry Cronin.* Chicago: Kochersperger, 1889.

"I.R.A. in America." *Newsweek* 13 (June 12, 1939): 15.

"Ireland: Lifting the Green Curtain." *Time* 82 (July 12, 1963): 28–40.

"Irish Neutrality and U.S. Foreign Policy." *America* 104 (February): 684.

James, Sir Henry. *The Work of the Irish Leagues.* London and New York: Cassell, 1890.

Jamison, Alden. "Irish-Americans, the Irish Question and American Diplomacy, 1895–1921." Ph.D. dissertation, Harvard University, 1942.

Jeffrey-Jones, R. "Massachusetts Labor and

the League of Nation Controversy in 1919." *Irish Historical Studies* 19, no. 76 (1975): 396–416.

Jenkins, Brian. "The British Government Sir John A. McDonald and the Fenian Claims." *Canadian Historical Review* 41 (1968): 142–59.

———. *Fenians and Anglo-American Relations during Reconstruction.* Ithaca, New York: Cornell University Press, 1969.

Jones, W. D. "Made in New York: A Plot to Kill the Queen." *New York Historical Society Quarterly* 51 (1967): 311–25.

Kiernan, J. L. *Ireland and America, Versus England, From a Fenian Point of View.* G. W. Pattison, printer. Detroit, 1864.

Kilpatrick, James J. "Echoes of American Troubles Across the Sea." *Nations Business* 63 (December 1975): 9–10.

King, Clyde L. "The Fenian Movement." *Colorado University Studies* 6 (1908–09): 187–213.

Kirby, Peadar. "Getting the Irish Up: The Other Side of Reagan's Visit." *Commonweal* 3 (June 15, 1984): 358–60.

Kraus, M. *America and the Irish Revolutionary Movement in the Eighteenth Century: In the Era of the American Revolution*, edited by R. B. Morris. New York: Columbia University, 1939.

Langan, M. "General John O'Neill: Soldier, Fenian and Leader of Irish Catholic Colonization in America." Master's thesis, University of Notre Dame, 1937.

Laubenstein, W. J. *The Emerald Whaler: A Saga of the Sea and Men Who Risked All for Freedom.* Indianapolis: Bobbs-Merrill, 1960.

Leary, W. M. "Woodrow Wilson, Irish-America and the Election., 1916." *Journal of American History* 54 (1967): 57–72.

Leslie, Shane. *The Irish Issue in Its American Aspect: A Contribution to the Settlement of Anglo-American Relations during and After the Great War.* New York: Scribner's, 1917.

Mannion, L. R., ed. "Constitution and By Laws of the Fenian Brotherhood of Colorado Territory." *Eire-Ireland* 4, no. 2 (1969): 7–17.

Maxwell, K. R. "Irish-Americans and the Fight Treaty Ratification." *Public Opinion Quarterly* 31 (Winter 1967–68): 620–41.

McCaffrey, Lawrence J. *Irish Nationalism and the American Contribution.* New York: Arno Press, 1976.

———. "Irish Nationalism and Irish Catholicism: A Study in Cultural Identity." *Church History* 42, no. 4 (December 1974): 524–34.

McCartan, Patrick. *With De Valera in America.* New York: D. Fitzgerald, 1911.

McDonald, Marci. "Regan Returns to his Roots." *Maclean's* 97 (June 4, 1984).

McDonnell, T. P. "Catholic Press Reporting on Northern Ireland." *Holy Cross Quarterly* 6, nos. 1–4 (1974): 68–71.

McEnnis, J. T. *The Clan-na Gael and the Murder of Dr. Patrick Henry Cronin.* Chicago: F. J. Schittze and J. W. Iliff, 1889.

McGee, Thomas D'Arcy. *The Irish Position in Britain and In Republican North America.* Montreal, Quebec: Longmoore, 1866.

McGinley, C. *Irish-American's in Philadelphia and Their Involvement with the Irish Independence Movement.* Temple University, Paper History Dept. Seminar, 1966.

McManamin, F. G. "The American Years of John Boyle O'Reilly, 1870–1890." Ph.D. dissertation, The Catholic University of America, 1959. Reprinted by Arno, 1976.

McSweeney, E. F. *Ireland is an American Question.* New York: Friends of Irish Freedom, 1919.

"Message to Americans: 'Offer No Aid' to Irish Republican Army." *U.S. News and World Report* 96 (March 19, 1984).

Minnick, W. C. "Parnell in America." *Speech Monographs* 20 (1953): 38–48.

Mitchell, A. "The Fenian Movement in America." *Eire-Ireland* 2 (1967): 6–10.

Moody, Theodore William. "Irish-American Nationalism." *Irish Historical Studies* 15 (1966–67): 438–45.

———, ed. *The Fenian Movement.* Cork, Ireland: Mercier, 1968.

Moriarty, T. F. "The Irish-American Response to Catholic Emancipation." *The Catholic Historical Review* 66, no. 3 (1980): 353–73.

Moriarty, Thomas Francis. "Agitation in the United States in Behalf of Catholic Emancipation as Seen Through the Truth Teller,

1825–1830." Master's Thesis, University of Notre Dame, 1958.

Morrow, R. L. "The Negotiation for the Anglo-American Treaty of 1870." *American Historical Review* 39 (1934): 663–81.

Murray, Hugh T., Jr. "The Green and Red Unblending: The National Association for Irish Freedom, 1972–1975." *Journal of Ethnic Studies* 3 (Summer 1975): 2.

Neidhardt, W. S. "The American Government and the Fenian Brotherhood: A Study in Mutual Political Opportunism." *Ontario History* 6, no. 4 (1972): 27–44.

———. *Fenianism in North America*. University Park: Pennsylvania State University Press, 1975.

Noer, T. J. "American Government and the Irish Question during World War I." *South Atlantic Quarterly* 72 (Winter 1973): 95–114.

"Northern Ireland: Off the Deep End." *Time* 98 (November 1, 1971): 48.

O'Brien, Joseph. "William O'Brien and the Course of Irish Politics, 1881–1918." Ph.D. dissertation, Columbia University, 1972.

O'Broin, L. *Fenian Fever: An Anglo-American Dilemma*. New York: New York University, 1971.

O'Connell, Maurice R. *Irish Politics and Social Conflict in the Age of the American Revolution*. Philadelphia: University of Pennsylvania Press, 1965.

O'Connor, Thomas Power, and Robert McWade. *Gladstone-Parnell and the Great Irish Struggle*. Toronto, Ontario: Robertson, 1886.

O'Doherty, Katherine. *Assignment America: De Valera's Mission to the United States*. New York: De Tanko, 1957.

O'Donnell, Frank Hugh. "Fenianism Past and Present." *Contemporary Review*, 43 (May 1883): 747–66.

O'Donovan-Rossa, Jeremiah. *Rossa's Recollections 1858 to 1898*. New York: Mariner's Harbor, 1898.

O'Donovan-Rossa, Margaret. *My Father and Mother Were Irish*. New York: Devin-Adair, 1939.

O'Grady, Joseph P. "The Irish-American Influence on the Rejection of the Phelps-Rosebury Extradition Treaty of 1886." Master's thesis, University of Notre Dame, 1958.

———. "Irish-Americans and Anglo-American Relations, 1880–1888." Ph.D. dissertation, University of Pennsylvania, 1965.

———. "Irish-Americans, Woodrow Wilson and Self Determinations: A Re-Evaluation." *Records of American Catholic Historical Society of Philadelphia* 74 (1963): 159–73.

———, ed. *The Immigrant's Influence on Wilson's Peace Policies*. University Press of Kentucky, 1968.

O'Hara, M. M. *Chief and Tribune: Parnell and Davitt*. Dublin: Maunsel, 1919.

O'Leary, John. *Recollections of Fenians and Fenianism* 2 vols. London, 1896.

O'Mahony, T. P. "And Now for the Chaos in Dublin." *America* 13 (December 7, 1974): 367–68.

O'Reilly, J. B. "At Last." *North American Review* 142 (1886): 104–110.

———. "Ireland's Opportunity, Will It Be Lost." *American Catholic Quarterly Review* 7 (1882): 114–20.

O'Shiel, Kevin R. *The Making of a Republic*. Dublin, Ireland: Talbot, 1920.

Peiper, Ezra Henry. "The Fenian Movement." Ph.D. dissertation, University of Illinois, 1931.

Proceedings of the Centennial Commemoration of the Martyrdom of Robert Emmet by the Irish Nationalist of Ohio. Columbus, Ohio: 1903.

Reidy, James. "John Devoy," *American Irish Historical Society Journal,* 27 (1928): 413–25.

Rice, Sister M. Elizabeth Ann. "Diplomatic Relations Between the United States and Mexico, 1925–1929." Ph.D. dissertation, The Catholic University of America, 1959.

Riley, Kelly. "When Irish are Smiling: Instead of Leprechauns and Shamrocks this March 17, Celebrate Irish Contributions to America." *Instructor* 94 (March 1985).

Ryan, Desmond. *The Fenian Chief: A Biography of James Stephens*. Coral Gables, Florida: University of Miami Press, 1969.

———. *The Phoenix Flame: A Study of Fenianism and John Devoy*. London: Barder, 1937.

Sammon, P. J. "The History of the Irish National Federation of America." Master's thesis, The Catholic University of America, 1951.

Sarbaugh, Timothy J. "Culture, Militancy, and De Valera: Irish Republicanism in California, 1900–1936." Master's thesis, San Jose State University, 1980.

———. "Irish Republicanism vs Pure Americanism: California's Reaction to Eamon De Valera's Visits." *California History* (Summer, 1981): 158–72.

Savage, John. *Fenian Heroes and Martyrs*. Boston: Donahoe, 1868.

Savory, D. L. "The Irish Republic and Neutrality in 1941." *Contemporary Review* 196, no. 1 (1959): 164–66.

———. "The Irish Republic and Neutrality in 1941." *Contemporary Review* 196, no. 2: 221–224.

Schofield, W. G. *Seek for a Hero—The Story of John Boyle O'Reilly*. New York: Kennedy, 1956.

Self, E. "The Abuse of Citizenship." *North American Review* 136 (1883): 541–56.

Severance, Frank H. "The Fenian Raid of 1866." *Publications of the Buffalo Historical Society* 25 (1921).

Shannon, William V. "Northern Ireland and America's Responsibility." *The Recorder: Irish-American Historical Society* 36 (1975): 28–42.

Shore, L. *The Irish Issue in Its American Aspect*. New York: Scribners, 1917.

Short, K. R. M. *The Dynamite War: Irish-American Bombers in Victorian Britain*. Atlantic Highlands, New Jersey: Humanities Press, 1979.

Sowles, Edward A. "History of Fenianism and the Fenian Raid in Vermont." *Vermont Historical Proceedings* (1880).

Splain, J. J. "The Irish Movement in the United States Since 1911." In *The Voice of Ireland*, edited by John Heywood. Dublin, 1924.

Stacey, C. P. "Fenian Troubles and Canadian Military Development, 1865–1871." *Canadian Defense Quarterly* 13 (1936): 207–9.

Strauss, E. *Irish Nationalism and British Democracy*. London: Methuen, 1951. New York: Columbia University Press.

Sullivan, A. "The American Republic and the Irish National League of America." *American Catholic Quarterly Review* 9 (1884): 35–44.

———. "Constitutionalism, Revolution and Culture, Irish-American Nationalism in St. Louis, 1902–14." *Missouri Historical Society Bulletin* 28, no. 4 (1972): 234–45.

———. "Fighting for Irish Freedom: St. Louis Irish-Americans, 1918–1922." *Missouri History Review* 65 (1971): 184–206.

Sweeny, William Montgomery. "The Fenian Invasion of Canada, 1866." *American Irish Historical Society Journal* 23 (1924): 193–203.

Tansill, C. C. *America and the Fight for Irish Freedom, 1866–1922*. New York: Devin-Adair, 1957.

Tarpey, Sister Marie Veronica. "The Role of Joseph McGarrity in the Struggle for Irish Independence." Ph.D. dissertation, St. John's University, 1970.

Train, George F. *An American Eagle in a British Cage: Four Days in a Felon's Cell*. Cork, 1868.

"The 'Troubles' in Ulster May, Just May, Be Easing A Bit." *New York Times*, October 15, 1977.

Wade, M. "The French Parish and Survivance in 19th Century New England." *Catholic Historical Review* 36 (1950): 163–89.

Walker, Mabel Gregory. *The Fenian Movement*. Colorado Springs: R. Myles, 1969.

Walsh, J. P. "DeValera in United States, 1919." *Records of the American Catholic Historical Society of Philadelphia* 73 (1962): 92–107.

———. "Woodrow Wilson Historians vs. the Irish." *Eire-Ireland* 2, no. 2 (1967): 55–66.

Ward, Alan J. "America and the Irish Problem 1899–1921." *Irish Historical Studies* 16, no. 61 (1968): 64–90.

———. *Ireland and Anglo-American Relations, 1899–1921*. London: London School of Economics and Political Science, Weidenfeld and Nicolson, 1969.

Wheeler, Alexander E. "Reminiscences of the Fenian Raid." *York Pioneer and Historical Society Representative 62nd Year* (1931): 15–6.

Whittemore, C. P. *A General of the Revolution: John Sullivan of New Hampshire.* New York: Columbia University, 1961.

Winkler, I. "The Fenian Movement and Anglo-American Diplomacy in the Reconstruction Period." Master's thesis, New York University, 1936.

Yorke, Peter C. *America and Ireland: An Open Letter to Mr. Garret W. McEnerney.* San Francisco, 1918.

9. War and the Military

Adams, E. E. *Great Britain and the American Civil War* 2 vols. London, 1925.

Athearn, Robert G. *Thomas Francis Meagher: An Irish Revolutionary in America.* Boulder, Colorado, 1949.

Amory, Thomas Coffin. *The Military Services and Public Life of Major-General John Sullivan.* Boston, 1868.

Barton, George. *Angels of the Battlefield.* Philadelphia: The Catholic Arts, 1897.

Bennet, William Harper. "Some Pre-Civil War Irish Militiamen of Brooklyn, New York." *American Irish Historical Society Journal* 21 (1922): 172–80.

Benz, Francis E. *Commodore Barry, Navy Hero.* New York: Dodd, Mead, 1950.

Berkeley, G. F. H. *The Irish Battalion in the Papal Army of 1860.* Dublin, 1929.

Botton, Ramond B. "John Mitchel (1815–1875): Irish Pariot and Defender of the Southern Cause in the War Between the States." *Virginia Magazine of History* 60 (April, 1952): 326–28.

Boyle, C. A. "The Memorial to the Irish Brigade at Gettysburg." *Irish Sword* 4 (1959): 68–69.

Boyle, G. E. "The Eighteenth (or Royal Irish) Regiment of Foot in America 1767–1775." *Society of Army Historical Research Journal* 2, no. 8 (1923): 63–68.

Braxton, F. "Irish on Our Revolution." *National Republic* 19 (March 1932): 24–25.

Cavanaugh, Michael. *Memoirs of General Thomas Francis Meagher.* Worcester, Massachusetts: The Messenger Press, 1892.

Clark, W. B. *Gallant John Barry.* New York, 1938.

Clow, Richmond L. "General Philip Sheridan's Legacy: The Sioux Pont Campaign of 1876." *Nebraska History* 57 (Winter 1976): 461–77.

Cohalan, D. F. "General John Sullivan." *American Irish Historical Society Journal* 30 (1932): 25–29.

Condon, William H. *Life of Major-General James Shields, Hero of Three Wars and Senator from Three States.* Chicago: Blakerly Printing, 1900.

Conyngham, David Power. *The Irish Brigade and its Campaigns.* Boston: P. Donahoe, 1869.

Corby, William. *Memoirs of Chaplain Life, By Very Rev. W. Corby.* Notre Dame, Indiana: Scholastic Press, 1894.

Coyle, John G. "The Irish Brigade of France in the Champlain Valley." *American Irish Historical Society Journal* 16, no. 2 (1917): 126–35.

D. M. "Irish in the Seventh Cavalry." *Irish Sword.* 1(1953): 336–38.

Devoy, John. *Recollections of an Irish Rebel.* New York: Charles P. Young, 1929.

Dickson, Charles. "John Mitchel and the South." *Irish Sword* 3 (Winter 1958): 282–83.

Dillon, William. *Life of John Mitchel* 2 vols. London, 1888.

Dolan, John. "The Little Bighorn Fight." *The New York Herald* (July 23, 1876).

Doyle, L. F. "Irish Cavalcade." *Catholic World* 166: 522–29.

Duffy, F. P. *Father Duffy's Story.* New York: Doran, 1919.

Eno, Joel N. "Irish Revolutionary Soldiers in New York State and Elsewhere." *Americana* 21 (October 1927): 631–38.

Exercises as the Unveiling of the Tablet Commemorating the Men of Irish Birth or Lineage in the American Revolution. Philadelphia, Pennsylvania: 1926.

Fink, Leo Gregory. *Barry or Jones, Father of the United States Navy: Historical Reconnaissance*. Philadelphia: Jefferies, 1962.

Fisher, D. "Exporting Death to Ireland: Arms Purchased with American Donations." *Commonweal* 104 (June 10, 1977): 356–58.

Flick, E. M. E. *Chaplain Duffy at the 69th Regiment*. Philadelphia: Dolphin Press, 1935.

Ford, C. *Donovan of the O.S.S*. Boston: Little, Brown, 1970.

———. "The Formation of Meagher's Irish Brigade." *Irish Sword* 3 (1958): 162–65.

Galwey, T. F. "The Irish-American Element in the Union Army." *Illustrated Catholic Family Annual* (1890): 70–73.

Garland, J. L. "Irish Soldiers of the American Confederacy." *Irish Sword* 1 (1951–52): 174–80.

———. "Some Notes on the Irish during the First Month of the American Civil War." *Irish Sword* 5 (Summer, 1961): 23–40.

Gordon, George W. "General Patrick R. Cleburne, Dedication of a Monument to His Memory at Helena Arkansas, May 10th, 1891." *Southern Historical Society Papers* 18 (1890): 260–72.

Gorman, R. *Speeches of Thomas Francis Meagher*. New York: 1869.

Graves, Robert. *Sargeant Lamb's America (1776–77)*. New York: Random House, 1940.

Greene, Marc T. "American Irish in the World War." *American Irish Historical Society Journal* 22 (1923): 150–53.

Gregory, Sir William H. "England and the Confederacy: A Letter of Sir William Henry Gregory." *American Historical Review* 44 (October 1938): 56–60.

Griffen, M. I. J. *Commodore John Barry: Father of the American Navy*. Philadelphia. 1903.

Griffith, Arthur. *Catholics and the American Revolution* 3 vols. Philadelphia: 1909.

———. "The Irish Catholics and the Revolution." *American Catholic Historical Review* 6 (1910): 340–42.

———, ed. *Meagher of the Sword*. Dublin: M. H. Gill and Son, 1915.

Halpine, Charles G. *Baked Meats of the Funeral*. 1866.

———. *The Life and Adventures, Songs, Services, and Speeches of Private Miles O'Reilly 47 Regiment, New York Volunteers, From the Authentic Records of the New York Herald*. New York, 1864.

Haltigan, J. *Irish in the American Revolution, and Their Early Influence in the Colonies*. Washington, D.C.: Haltigan, 1908.

Hammer, Kenneth. *Biographies of the Seventh Cavalry, June 25th, 1876*. Colorado: Old Army Press, 1972.

Hanchett, William. *Irish, Charles G. Halpine in Civil War America*. Syracuse: Syracuse University Press, 1970.

Hardee, W. J. "Biographical Sketch of Major-General Patrick R. Cleburn." *Southern Historical Society Papers* 31 (1903): 151–63.

Harris, S. H. "John L. O'Sullivan Serves the Confederacy." *Civil War History* 10 (1964): 275–90.

Hasbrouck, J. E. "Some Irish Revolutionary Soldiers." *Recorder* 3 (May 1925): 9–12.

Hatch, K. "Saint Patrick's Battalion: Unlikely Victims of a Mexican War." *Ireland of the Welcomes* 26, no. 2 (1977): 32–35.

Hay, T. R. *Pat Cleburne, Stonewall Jackson of the West*. Jackson, Tennessee: McCowat-Mercer Press, 1959.

Hayes, J. D. and D. D. Maguire. "Charles Graham Halpine: Life and Adventures of Miles O'Reilly." *New York Historical Society Quarterly* 51 (1967): 326–44.

Heffernan, J. B. "Ireland's Contributions to the Navies of the American Civil War." *Irish Sword* 3 (Winter 1957): 81–87.

Hogan, Martin Joseph. *The Shamrock Battalion of the Rainbow: A Story of the "Fighting Sixty-Ninth."* New York and London: Appleton, 1919.

Holderith, George L. "Colonel James A. Mulligan and the Chicago Irish Brigade in the American Civil War." Master's thesis, University of Notre Dame, 1932.

Hunt, O. B. *The Irish and the American Revolution*. Philadelphia: Friendly Sons of St. Patrick, 1976.

Hutton, Brian, ed. "Two Letters from Fort Sumter." *Irish Sword* 5 (Summer 1962): 179–83.

The Irish Abroad and at Home: At the Court and in the Camp, with Souvenirs of "The Brigade." New York: D. Appleton, 1856.

"Irish among the Ohio Troops in the War of 1812." *The Recorder: American-Irish Historical Society* (1925).

Jolly, Ellen Ryan. *Nuns of the Battlefield.* Providence, Rhode Island: Providence Visitor Press, 1927.

Jones, Paul John. "Irish Brigade at Fredericksburg." *Catholic Digest* 27 (January 1963): 105–10.

———. *The Irish Brigade.* Washington, D.C.: Luce, 1969.

Kiger, J. H. "Federal Government Propoganda in Great Britain during the American Civil War." *Historical Outlook* 19 (May 1928): 204–9.

Kohl, Lawrence F., and Margaret Cosse Richard, eds. *Irish Green and Union Blue: The Civil War Letters of Peter Welsh.* New York: Fordham University Press, 1986.

Kwitchen, M. C. *James Alphonsus McMaster.* Washington, D.C.: The Catholic University of America Press, 1949.

Large, David. "An Irish Friend and the Civil War." *Bulletin of Friends Historical Association* 47 (Spring 1958): 20–29.

Larkin, P. O. "Irish Names in Colonial Military History." *American Catholic Quarterly* 33 (July 1908): 471–85.

Leech, Arthur Blenner Hassett. *Irish Rifleman in America.* New York: Van Nostrand, 1875.

Lonn, Ella. *Foreigners in the Confederacy.* Chapel Hill, North Carolina: Peter Smith, 1940.

———. *Foreigners in the Union Army and the Navy.* Baton Rouge, Louisiana: 1951.

Love, J. E. "The Autobiography of James E. Love." *Missouri Historical Society Bulletin* 6 (1950): 124–38, 400–11.

Lucey, C. *Harp and Sword: 1776.* San Francisco: American Irish Foundation, 1976.

———. "The Irish in the American Revolution." *Ireland of the Welcomes* 26, no. 1 (1977): 37–39.

Lucey, W. L. "The Diary of Joseph O'Hagen: J. J. Chaplain of the Excelsior Brigade." *Civil War History* 6 (1960): 402–9.

Lyons, W. F. *Thomas Francis Meagher.* New York, 1886.

MacDonagh, M. *History of the Ninth Regiment Massachusetts Volunteers.* Boston, 1899.

———. *Irish at the Front.* London and New York: Hooder and Stoughton, 1916.

———. "Irish Soldiers: Their Humor and Seriousness." *Minnesota History* 24 (1917): 46–54.

MacNamara, M. H. *The Irish Ninth in Bivouac and Battle.* Boston: Lee and Shepard, 1867.

Maher, Marty. *Bringing up the Brass, My Fifty-Five Years at West Point.* New York: McKay, 1951.

McCann, Sean. *The Fighting Irish.* London: Frewin, 1972.

McCormick, J. F., Jr. "The Irish Brigade." *Civil War Times Illustrated* 8 (1969): 36–46.

McCormack, R. G. "The San Patricio Deserters in the Mexican War." *The Americas* 8 (1951): 131–42.

McGillivary, Charles A. "Irish-Born Recipients of the U.S. Congressional Medal of Honor." *Irish Sword* 12 (Winter 1975): 149–51.

McNeill, Mary. *The Life and Times of Mary Ann McCracken, 1770–1866.* Dublin, 1960.

Meehan, J. B. *The Birthplace of General Philip Henry Sheridan.* Dublin, 1926.

Meehan, T. F. "Army Statistics of the Civil War." *United States Catholic Historical Society Records and Studies* 13 (1919): 129–39.

Mese, William A. "Colonel John Montgomery: An 'Irishman Full of Fight,' Commander-in-Chief of the Virginia Troops in the County of Illinois." *Illinois Catholic Historical Review* 5 (July 1922): 51–58.

Miller, Robert Ryal. *Shamrock and Sword: Saint Patrick's Battalion in the U.S.-Mexican War.* Norman, Oklahoma: University of Oklahoma Press, 1989.

Monaghan, Frank. "Stephen Moylan in the American Revolution." *Studies: An Irish Quarterly Review* 19 (September 1930): 481–86.

Monaghan, Jay. *Civil War on the Western Border, 1854–1865.* New York: Bonanza Books, 1955.

Mullen, T. J., Jr. "The Fighting Sixty-Ninth." *Eire-Ireland* 4, no. 4 (1969): 13–26.

———. *The Hibernia Regiment of the Spanish Army.* Gainsville, Florida: University of Florida, 1966.

———. "The Irish Brigades in the Union Army." *Irish Sword* 9, no. 34 (1969): 50–58.

———. "The 69th Regiment at Bull Run." *Irish Sword* 7, no. 26 (1965): 2–4.

Murdock, Eugene Converse. *Patriotism Limited, 1862–1865.* Kent, Ohio: Kent State University Press, 1967.

Murphy, W. S. "The Irish Brigade of France at the Seige of Savannah, 1779." *Georgia Historical Quarterly* 38 (1954): 307–21.

Murray, Rev. Thomas Hamilton. *History of the Ninth Regiment, Connecticut Volunteer Infantry, "The Irish Regiment," in the War of the Rebellion, 1861–1865.* New Haven, Connecticut: Price, Lee and Adkins, 1903.

———. *Irish Rhode Islanders in the American Revolution.* Providence: American-Irish Historical Society, 1903.

Nugent, Robert. "The Sixty-Ninth Regiment at Fredericksburg: General Nugent's Description of the Splendid Work that was Performed by the Irish Brigade before Marye's Heights, December 11–15, 1862." *American Irish Historical Society Journal* 1 (July 1916): 191–200.

O'Brien, Michael J. "Captain Patrick O'Flynn: Friend of General George Washington." *American Irish Historical Society Journal* 21 (1922): 92–102.

———. "Christopher O'Brien, Revolutionary Soldier." *American Irish Historical Society Journal* 27 (1928): 70–72.

———. "The Cumberland County Pennsylvania Militia in the Revolution." *American Irish Historical Society Journal* 21 (1922).

———. "Francis McDonnell: A Son of Erin, Captured the English Flag at Stone Point." *American Irish Historical Society Journal* 21 (1922): 118–20.

———. "George Washington's Virginia Regiment." *American Irish Historical Society Journal* 25 (1926).

———. *The Irish at Bunker Hill.* New York: Devin-Adair, 1969.

———. "Irish at the Front." *Catholic World* 124 (March 1927): 827–28.

———. "The Kelleys, Burkes, and Sheas of the Massachusetts Line." *American Irish Historical Society Journal* 21 (1922): 107–10.

———. "Major Patrick Carr and Captain Patrick McGriff: Two Gallant Officers of the Georgia Continental Line." *American Irish Historical Society Journal* 21 (1922): 93–96.

———. "Morgan's Riflemen at the Battle of Saratoga." *American Irish Historical Society Journal* 22 (1923): 154–76.

———. "The Murphy's in Virginia: Patrick Murphy: A Brave Soldier of the Virginia Continental Line." *American Irish Historical Society Journal* 21 (1922): 103–6.

———. "Patrick Hogan: Schoolmaster and Revolutionary Soldier." *American Irish Historical Society Journal* 21 (1922): 89–92.

———. "Patrick McCann: Hero of the Border." *American Irish Historical Society Journal* 21 (1922): 79–85.

———. "Proctor's Artillery in the Revolutionary War." *American Irish Historical Society Journal* 21 (1922): 176–78.

———. "The Record of Sergeant William Murphy." *American Irish Historical Society Journal* 24 (1925): 154–56.

———. "Sergeant Patrick Cavanaugh: A Brave Soldier of the Revolution." *American Irish Historical Society Journal* 21 (1922): 86–88.

———. "Some Stray Historical Tidbits of the American Revolution." *American Irish Historical Society Journal* 17 (1918): 121–36.

———. "The Virginia Regiment—Commanded by Colonel George Washington." *American Irish Historical Society Journal* 25 (1926): 110–15.

O'Callaghan, John Cornelius. *History of the Irish Brigades in the Service of France from the Revolution in France Under Louis XVI.* New York: P. O'Shea, 1874.

O'Connell, J. C. *Irish in the Revolution and Civil War.* Washington, D.C.: Trades Unionist Press, 1903.

O'Danachair, Caoimhim, ed. "A Soldier's Letters Home, 1863–74." *Irish Sword* 3 (Summer 1957): 57–64.

O'Dwyer, George Francis. "Captain James Howard, Colonel William Lithgow, Colonel Arthur Noble, and other Irish Pioneers of Maine." *American Irish Historical Society Journal* 19 (1920): 71–88.

O'Flaherty, P. "James Huston: A Forgotten Irish-American Patriot." *Irish Sword* 11, no. 43: 39–47.

O'Hara, Jane. "Going Great Guns for the Cause (Irish Northern Aid Committee)." *Macleans* 94 (November 23, 1981).

Onahan, William James. "The French-Irish Brigades in the War of Independence." *American Irish Historical Society Journal* 9 (1910): 416–20.

Oswald, Mrs. Charles F. "Captain Lawrence O'Brien, 1842–1923." *American Irish Historical Society Journal* 23 (1924): 133–43.

Pepper, George W. "Personal Recollections of General Thomas Francis Meagher." *Donahoe's Magazine* (May 1899).

Petty, A. Milburn. "History of the 37th Regiment: New York Volunteers." *American Irish Historical Society Journal* 36 (1937).

Phelan, Thomas P. "Thomas Fitzsimons: Patriot, Soldier, Statesman." *American Irish Historical Society Journal* 21 (1922): 157–64.

Power, W. "The Enigma of the Patricios." *Eire-Ireland* 4, no. 4 (1969): 7–12.

Power, Walter. "Facets of the Mexican War." *The Recorder: Irish American Historical Society* 36 (1975): 135–43.

Purcell, R. J. "Ireland and the American Civil War." *Catholic World* 115 (April 1922): 72–84.

———. "James Shields: Soldier and Statesman." *Studies: An Irish Quarterly Review* 21 (1932): 73–87.

Reed, Donald A. *Admiral Leahy at Vichy, France*. Chicago: Adams, 1968.

Reynolds, Frank. *Ireland's Important and Heroic Part in America's Independence and Development*. Chicago: Daleiden, 1925.

Rhett, Claudine. "Sketch of John C. Mitchel of Ireland: Killed Whilst in Command of Fort Sumter." *Southern Historical Society Papers* 10 (1882): 268–72.

Riach, Douglas C. "Daniel O'Connell and American Anti-Slavery." *Irish Historical Studies* 20 (March 1976): 3–25.

Rice, Howard C., Jr., and Anne S. D. Brown, eds. *The American Campaigns of Rochambeau's Army* 2 vols. Princeton: Princeton University Press, 1978.

Rogers, Fred B. *Soldiers of the Overland: Being Some Account of the Services of General Patrick Edward Connor and His Volunteers in the Old West*. San Francisco: Grabhorn, 1938.

Ryan, Ignatius L. "Confederate Agents in Ireland." *United States Catholic Historical Society, Historical Records and Studies* 26 (1936): 40–91.

Sheridan, F. "Influence of the Irish People in the Formation of the United States." *Illinois Catholic Historical Review* (1927): 377–81.

Sherman, Andrew M. "Washington and His Army in Morris County." *American Irish Historical Society Journal* 10 (1911).

Smith, H. F. "Mulligan and the Irish Brigade." *Journal Illinois State Historical Society* 56 (1963): 164–75.

Stock, L. F. "Catholic Participation in the Diplomacy of the Southern Confederacy." *Catholic Historical Review* 16 (April, 1930): 1–18.

Sweeny, William Montgomery. "Captain Wayne Reid—Irish Soldier and Novelist." *American Irish Historical Society Journal* 24 (1925).

———. "The Irish Soldier in the War With Mexico." *American Irish Historical Society Journal* 26 (1927): 255–59.

Tangwall, W. F. "Immigrants in the Civil War: Some American Reactions." Ph.D. dissertation, University of Chicago, 1962.

Utley, Robert M. *Frontier Regulars: The United States Army and the Indian, 1866–91*. New York: Macmillan, 1973.

VanDyke, M. A. "Timothy Murphy: The Man and the Legend." *New York Folklore* 2, nos. 1–2 (1976): 87–110.

Weist, Katherine M. "Ned Casey and His Cheyenne Scouts." *Montana Magazine of Western History* 27 (Winter 1977): 14–25.

"Where Irish-Americans Stand in the War." *Literary Digest* 56 (February 2, 1918): 10–11.

Woodruff, Charles A. "The Irish Soldier in the Civil War." *American Irish Historical Society Journal* 11 (1912): 154–59.

10. Biographies, Autobiographies, Reminiscences

Adams, Charles Francis, Jr. *Charles Francis Adams*. Boston: Houghton Mifflin, 1900.

Amory, Thomas Coffin. *Life of Governor James Sullivan*. Boston: 1895.

Anderson, Mary Jane. "From an Irish Farm to a Minnesota Homestead." *Gopher Historian* 21 (Spring 1967): 21–26.

Anderson, Mary Jane Hill. *Autobiography*. Minneapolis, Minnesota: 1934.

Andrews, Peter. *In Honored Glory*. New York: Putnam, 1966.

Arkus, Leon Anthony. *John Kane: Painter*. Pittsburgh, Pennsylvania: University of Pittsburgh Press, 1971.

Baker, Gladys. *I Had to Know*. New York: Appleton, 1951.

Bannon, John. *Life of John Mitchell*. Liverpool, n.d.

Barker, Charles A. *Henry George*. New York: Oxford University Press, 1955.

Basen, N. K. "Kate Richards O'Hare: The "First Lady" of American Socialism, 1901–1917." *Labor History* 21 (1980): 165–99.

Beck, Herbert H. "The Camerons of Donegal, 1775–1952." *Lancaster County Historical Society Papers* 56 (1952): 85–109.

Bell, S. Rebel. *Priest and Prophet: A Biography of Edward McGlynn*. New York: Devin-Adair, 1937.

Bigelow, John. *Retrospectives of an Active Life*. New York, 1909.

Birmingham, George A. *Connaught to Chicago*. London: James Nisbet, 1914.

———. *From Dublin to Chicago: Some Notes on a Tour in America*. New York: Doran, 1914.

Birmingham, Stephen. "From the Banks of the Shannon to the Banks of Wall Street." *U.S. Catholic* 39 (1974): 30–35.

———. *Real Lace: America's Irish Rich*. New York: Harper and Row, 1973.

Boulton, Agnes. *Part of a Long Story*. Garden City, New York: Doubleday, 1958.

Bourke, Marcus. *John O'Leary*. Athens, Georgia: University of Georgia Press, 1968.

Bowers, Claude G. *The Irish Orators*. Indianapolis: The Bobbs-Merrill Company, 1916.

Breen, Mathew. *Thirty Years of New York Politics*. New York: Author, 1899.

Broderick, Edwin B. "From the Bronx to Lisdoonvarna." *The Recorder: Irish American Historical Society* 36 (1975): 116–19.

Broderick, F. *Right Reverend New Dealer: Biography of Msgr Ryan*.

Brougham, John. *Life, Stories, and Poems of John Brougham*. Boston: Osgood, 1881.

Brown, Richard Howard. "I Am of Ireland." *The Recorder: Irish American Historical Society* 36 (1975): 123–34.

Browne, P. W. "Thomas Dongan: Soldier and Statesman: Irish-Catholic Governor of New York, 1683–1688." *Studies: An Irish Quarterly Review* 23 (1934): 489–501.

Brusher, Joseph S. *Concentrated Thunderbolt! Father Yorke of San Francisco*. Hawthorne, New Jersey, 1973.

Buckley, Christopher A. "The Reminiscences of Christopher A. Buckley." *San Francisco Bulletin* (September 1–November 26, 1917).

Buckley, William F., Jr. *Quotations from Chairman Bill at His Best.* New Rochelle, New York: Arlington House, 1970.

Burns, R. D. "James F. Byrnes." In *Uncertain Tradition*, edited by Norman A. Graebner. 223–44. New York: McGraw-Hill, 1961.

Buscareno, Vincent Charles. "Richard Burke, Jr.: His Relationship with His Father, Edmund Burke and their Joint Efforts in Behalf of the Irish Catholics, 1790–1793." Ph.D. dissertation, St. John's University, 1972.

Byrnes, James Francis. *All in One Lifetime.* New York: Harper, 1958.

Cadwalader, Mary H. "Charles Carroll of Carrollton: A Signer's Story." *Smithsonian* 6, no. 9 (1975): 64–71.

Camp, Charles L., ed. "T. Kerr: An Irishman in the Gold Rush." *California Historical Society Quarterly* 7 (September and December 1928).

Campbell, Tom Walter. *Four Score Forgotten Men.* Little Rock, Arkansas: Pioneer, 1950.

Carroll, M. C. "Behind the Lighthouse: The Australian Sojourn of John Boyle O'Reilly." Ph.D. dissertation, University of Iowa, 1955.

Cashman, D. B. *The Life of Michael Davitt: Founder of the National Land League.* Boston: Murphy and McCarthy, 1881.

Chickering, Allen. "Garrett W. McEnery." *Catholic Historical Society Quarterly* 22 (March 1942): 21.

Christian, Linda. *Linda: My Own Story.* New York: Crown, 1962.

Clarke, Joseph Ignatius Constantine. *My Life and Memories.* New York: Dodd and Mead, 1925.

Clemens, C. "John Boyle O'Reilly: Neglected New England Poet." *Poetlore* 54 (1948): 361–72.

Cleveland, Charles Blair. *Great Baseball Managers.* New York: Crowell, 1950.

Cohan, George M. *Twenty Years on Broadway, and the Years it Took to Get There.* New York, 1925. Reprinted in Westport, Connecticut: Greenwood, 1971.

Conroy, Frank. *Stop Time.* New York: Penguin Books, 1977.

Corbett, James J. *The Roar of the Crowd.* New York: G. P. Putnam's Sons, 1925.

Corry, John. *Golden Clan.* New York: Houghton Mifflin, 1977.

Cosgrave, Luke. *Theatre Tonight.* Hollywood, California: House-Warven, 1952.

Cox, James M. *Journey Through My Years.* New York, 1946.

Crosby, Bing. *Call Me Lucky.* New York: Simon and Schuster, 1953.

Crosby, Edward J. *Story of Bing Crosby: With a Forward by Bob Hope.* New York: World, 1946.

Cunningham, Anne Rowe, ed. *The Letters and Diary of John Rowe.* Boston, 1903.

Curran, M. P. *The Life of Patrick Collins.* Norwood, Massachusetts: Norwood Press, 1906.

Cudahy, P. *Patrick Cudahy: His Life.* Milwaukee: Burdick and Allen, 1912.

Cusack, Mary Francis. *From Killarney to New York, or How He Became a Banker.* Boston: O'Loughlin, 1886.

Dasent, Arthur Irwin. *John Thadeus Delane: Editor of the Times, His Life and Correspondence* 2 vols. New York, 1908.

Devoy, John. *Devoy's Post Bag, 1871–1928.* Dublin, Ireland: Fallon, 1948.

———. *Recollections of an Irish Rebel.* New York: Charles P. Young, 1929.

Digby, Margaret. *Horace Plunkett: Anglo-American Irishman.* New York: Blackwell, 1949.

Dillon, William. *Life of John Mitchel.* London: K. Paul Trench, 1888.

Dooley, Agnes W. *Promises to Keep: The Life of Doctor Thomas A. Dooley.* New York: Farrar, Straus, 1963.

Dooley, Thomas Anthony. *Doctor Tom Dooley: My Story.* New York: Ariel, 1962.

———. *Dr. Tom Dooley's Three Great Books: Deliver Us From Evil: The Edge of Tommorrow; The Night They Burned the Mountain.* New York: Farrar, Straus, 1960.

———. *The Night They Burned the Mountain.* New York: Farrar, Straus, 1960.

Durso, Joseph. *Days of Mr. McGraw.* Englewood Cliffs, New Jersey: Prentice-Hall, 1969.

Dye, Eva Emery. *McLoughlin and Old Oregon.* McClurg, 1900.

Ellis, Elmer. *Mr. Dooley's America: A Life of Finley Peter Dunne.* New York: Knopf, 1941.

Ellis, John Tracy. "Peter Guilday." *Catholic Historical Review* 33 (1947): 257–68.

Emmet, Thomas Addis. *Incidents of My Life: Professional-Literary-Social, with Services in the Cause of Ireland.* New York: Putnam, 1911.

———. *Memoir of Thomas Addis and Robert Emmet; With Their Ancestors and Immediate Family.* New York: Emmet, 1915.

Ernst, Robert. "The One and Only Mike Walsh." *New York Historical Society Quarterly* 36 (January 1952).

Everett, Barbara. "John Barry: Fighting Irishman." *American History Illustrated* 12, no. 8 (1977): 18–25.

Ewen, David. *Complete Book of American Musical Theatre.* New York: Holt, 1958.

Fahey, John. *The Ballyhoo Bonanza: Charles Sweeny and the Idaho Mines.* Seattle: University of Washington Press, 1971.

Fairbanks, Henry G. *Louise Imogen Guiney.* Albany, New York, 1972.

Farrell, James A. "Thomas Fitzsimmons: Signer of the Constitution." *Records of the American Catholic Historical Society of Philadelphia*, 1928.

Fetherling, Dale. *Mother Jones: The Miner's Angel.* Detroit: Southern Illinois University Press, 1974.

Fleischer, Nathaniel S. *John L. Sullivan: Champion of Champions.* New York: Putnam, 1951.

Flynn, Elizabeth Gurley. *The Rebel Girl: An Autobiography: My First Life (1906–1926).* New York: International, 1965.

Foley, W. "Patrick N. Lynch, Catholic Bishop and Confederation Statesman." Ph.D. dissertation, University of Notre Dame, 1930.

Ford, Corey. *Donovan of OSS.* Boston: Little, Brown, 1970.

Ford, Sister Mary Muriel. "Anthony Michael Keiley, 1832–1905." Master's thesis, The Catholic University of America, 1937.

Fowler, Gene. *Beau James: The Life and Times of Jimmy Walker.* New York: Viking, 1949.

Foxall, Raymond. *John McCormack.* Staten Island, New York: Alba, 1963.

Frawley, Mary Alphonsine. *Patrick Donahoe.* Washington, D.C.: The Catholic University of America Press, 1946.

Fredman, L. "Broderick: A Reassessment." *Pacific Historical Review* 30 (1961).

Freedland, Michael. *James Cagney.* New York: W. H. Allen, 1974.

French, William. *Some Recollections of a Western Ranchman, New Mexico, 1833–1899.* London, 1927.

Friendly Sons of St. Patrick: Samuel Hood and Others. Philadelphia: 1844.

Gaither, Grant. *Princess of Monaco: The Story of Grace Kelly.* New York: Holt, 1957.

Gallagher, Teresa. *Give Joy to My Youth: A Memoir of Dr. Tom Dooley.* New York: Farrar, Straus, 1965.

Gatchell, Joseph. *Disenthralled: Being Reminiscences in the Life of the Author.* Troy, New York: Tuttle, 1844.

Geiger, Mary V. *Daniel Carroll: A Framer of the Constitution.* Washington, D.C.: The Catholic University of America Press, 1943.

George, Henry. *The Condition of Labour.* London: S. Sonnenschein, 1898.

Gibson, William. *A Mass for the Dead.* New York: Atheneum, 1977.

Graham, Sheilah. *Beloved Infidel: The Education of a Woman.* London: Cassell, 1958.

———. *College of One.* New York: Viking, 1967.

———. *The Rest of the Glory.* New York: Coward-McCann, 1964.

Greco, Michael R. "The Crucible: Antebellum Boston's Impact on a 'Wayward Youth'." *Essex Institute Historical Collections* 3 (1975): 196–212.

Greenough, Charles Pelham. "The Experiences of an Irish Immigrant, 1681." *Mas-*

sachusetts Historical Society Proceedings 49 (1916): 99–106.

Greer, James K. *Colonel Jack Hays: Texas Frontier Leader and California Builder*. New York, 1952.

Gregory, Horace. *The House on Jefferson Street*.

Griffin, Martin I. J. "Anthony M. Keiley." *American Historical Researches* 22 (April 1905): 168–70.

Griffin, Richard T. "Big Jim O'Leary: Gambler Boss iv th' yards." *Chicago History* 5, no. 4 (1976–77): 213–22.

Guilday, Peter Keenan. "Gaetano Bedini: An Episode in the Life of Archbishop Hughes." *U.S. Catholic Historical Society: Historical Records and Studies* 23 (1933): 87–107.

Guilday, Peter. *The Life and Times of John Carroll*. New York: Encyclopedia Press, 1922.

Guiney, Louise Imogen. *Robert Emmet: A Survey of His Rebellion and of His Romance*. London: David Nutt, 1904.

Hackett, Francis. *American Rainbow Early Reminiscences*. New York: Liveright, 1970.

Hallinan, Vivian Moore. *My Wild Irish Rogues*. Garden City, New York: Doubleday, 1952.

Hardy, Osgood. "Was Patrick Egan a 'Blunder Minister'?" *Hispanic American Historical Review* 8 (1928): 65–81.

Haughery, M. Catharine Joseph. "A Candle Lighted: A Capsule Biography of Margaret Gaffney Haughery, (1813–1882)." *American Catholic Historical Society, Records* 64 (June 1953): 113–20.

Hennessey, M. E. "Men of Irish Blood Who Have Attained Distinction in American Journalism." *American Irish Historical Society Journal* 3 (1900) 62–77.

Herndon, Booton. *Ford: An Unconventional Biography of the Men and Their Times*. New York: Weybright, 1969.

Hibernicus. *Hibernicus: Or, Memoirs of an Irishman Now in America*. Pittsburgh, Pennsylvania: Cramer and Spear, 1828.

Higgins, Thomas G. *An Autobiography*. New York: Comet Press, 1965.

Hill, J. "Politics, Labor and George Meany." *Commonweal* 102 (April 11, 1975): 47–49.

Hogan, John J. *Fifty Years Ago*. Kansas City, Missouri: Hudson, 1907.

Hogan, Robert Goode. *Dion Boucicault*. New York: Twayne, 1969.

Hogan, Virginia. "A Matchless Old Man." *Western Folklore* 13 (January 1954): 1–6.

Howard, Maureen. *Facts of Life*. New York: Penguin, 1980.

Hutcheson, William L. *Portrait of an American Labor Leader*. New York: American Institute of Social Science, 1955.

Huthmacher, J. Joseph. "Charles Evans Hughes, and Charles Francis Murphy: The Metamorphosis of Progressivism." *New York History* 46.

Irvine, Alexander. *From the Bottom Up*. Garden City, New York: Doubleday, 1910.

———. *A Yankee with the Soldiers of the King*. New York: Dutton, 1923.

Irvine, Alexander Fitzgerald. *Fighting Parson*. Boston: Little, Brown, 1930.

Jackson, Horace M. *Family History of Michael Jackson: Emigrant from Ireland, Citizen of Hartford, Connecticut*. Kansas City, Missouri: 1909.

James, Edward T. "T. V. Powderly: A Political Profile." *Pennsylvania Magazine of History and Biography* 99, no. 4 (1975): 443–59.

Johnson, John. *The Life and Confession of John Johnson: The Murderer of James Murray*. New York: Brown and Tyrell, 1824.

Johnston, J. "Road to Hillsborough." *Biography News* 2 (January 1975): 54–56.

Joyce, P. J. "Memories of Father Yorke." *The Furrow* 2 (1951): 689–97.

Katz, Marjorie P. *Grace Kelly*. New York: Coward-McCann, 1970.

Kaucher, Dorothy. *James Duval Phelan: A Portrait, 1861–1930*. Saratoga, California: Montalvo Association, 1965.

Kaufman, Mervyn. *Father of Skyscrapers: A Biography of Louis Sullivan*. Boston: Little, Brown, 1969.

Kaye, Joseph. *Victor Herbert: The Biography of America's Greatest Composer of Romantic Music*. Freeport, New York: Books for the Libraries Press, 1970.

Kehoe, Michael P. "The Carroll Family in

Maryland." *American Irish Historical Society Journal* 9 (1910): 258–78.

Kelly, John B. *Born to Battle: A Veracious Chronicle*. Boston: Meadar, 1944.

Kirkfleet, Cornelius. *The Life of Patrick Augustine Feehan*. Chicago: 1922.

Kittler, Glenn D. *Wings of Eagles*. Garden City, New York: Doubleday, 1966.

Kohl, Lawrence F., and Margaret Cosse Richard, eds. *Irish Green and Union Blue: The Civil War Letters of Peter Welsh*. New York: Fordham University Press, 1986.

Lally, Mary Ellen. *Biography of John Lally: Inventor of the Genuine Lally Column*. Boston: n.p., 1950.

Lamparski, Richard. *Whatever Became of James Francis Byrnes?* New York: Crown, 1970.

Lane, Roger. "James Jeffrey Roche and the Boston Pilot." *New England Quarterly* 33 (September 1960): 341–63.

Lang, Lincoln Alexander. *Ranching with Roosevelt*. Philadelphia: Lippincott, 1926.

Langan, Sister Mary Martin. "General John O'Neill: Soldier Fenian, and Leader of Irish Catholic Colonization in America." Master's thesis, University of Notre Dame, 1937.

Larkin, Emmet. *"Big Jim" Larkin*. Chicago: Chicago Univeristy Press, 1966.

Lawlor, David S. *The Life and Struggle of an Irish Boy in America*. New York: Moffat, 1918.

Levine, Erwin. *Theodore Francis Green: The Rhode Island Years, 1906–1936*. Providence: Brown University Press, 1963.

Lewis, A. H. *Richard Croker*. New York: Life, 1901.

Lewis, Arthur H. *Those Philadelphia Kellys*. New York: William Morrow, 1977.

Lewison, E. R. *John Purroy Mitchel: The Boy Mayor of New York*. New York: Astra Books, 1965.

Lord, Daniel A. *Played by Ear? The Autobiography of Daniel A. Lord, S.J.* Chicago: Loyola University Press, 1955.

Love, George F., and Earnest Havemann. *I Never Thought We'd Make It*. New York: Harcourt, Brace, 1952.

Love, James Edwin. "The Autobiography of James E. Love." *Missouri Historical Society Bulletin* 6 (January 1950): 124–38.

Lucey, W. L. "Two Irish Merchants of New England." *New England Quarterly* 14 (December 1941): 633–45.

Lunt, R. D. *High Ministry of Government: The Political Career of Frank Murphy*. Detroit: Wayne State University Press, 1965.

MacManus, Seamus. *The Rocky Road to Dublin*. New York: Macmillan, 1938.

Magner, Dennis. *The Art of Taming and Educating the Horse . . . And the Story of the Author's Personal Experience*. Battle Creek, Michigan: Review and Herald, 1884.

———. *Magner's Story of Twenty Years as a Horse Trainer*. Battle Creek, Michigan: Magner, 1895.

Manter, Ethel. *Rocket of the Comstock: The Story of John William Mackay*. Caldwell: Caxton, 1950.

Markmann, Charles Lam. *The Buckley's: A Family Examined*. New York: Morrow, 1973.

Marling, Joseph M. "A Pioneer Priest of Western Missouri." *American Ecclesiastical Review* 133 (December 1955): 361–69.

Marryat, Frederick. *A Diary in America*. Philadelphia, 1839.

Marwood, Darlington. *Irish Orpheus: The Life of Patrick S. Gilmore: Bandmaster Extraordinary*. Philadelphia: Ovivier-Maney-Klein, 1950.

Mason, Arthur. *Ocean Echoes: An Autobiography*. New York: Holt, 1922.

McAllister, Lester Grover. *Thomas Campbell (1763–1854): Man of the Book*. St. Louis, Missouri: Bethany, 1954.

McCarthy, Justin. *An Irishman's Story*. New York: Macmillan, 1904.

McCarthy, Mary. *Memoirs of a Catholic Girlhood*, 1957.

McCarthy, Patrick Joseph. *Autobiographical Memoirs*. Providence, Rhode Island: Visitor, 1927.

McCormack, John. *John McCormack: His Own Life Story*. Boston: Small, Maynard, 1918.

McCormack, Lyly Foley. *I Hear You Calling Me*. Milwaukee, Wisconsin: Bruce, 1949.

McCullough, A. M. *The Experiences of Seventy Years*. Minneapolis, Minnesota: Tribune Job Press, 1895.

McCune, Wesley. *"Frank Murphy:" In Nine Young Men*. New York: Harper, 1947.

McGinty, G. W., and E. Conly. *Cullen Thomas Conly: American Irish Stowaway, 1820–1876*. Shreveport, Louisiana: Rushing, 1976.

McGraw, Blanche Sidall. *Real McGraw*. New York: McKay, 1953.

Mizener, Arthur. *The Far Side of Paradise (Fitzgerald Biography)* Boston: Houghton Mifflin, 1965.

Monahan, James, ed. *Before I Sleep: The Last Days of Dr. Tom Dooley*. New York: Farrar, Straus, 1961.

Montgomery, Hugh. *Hugh Montgomery: Or Experiences of an Irish Minister and Temperance Reformer*. New York: Phillips and Hunt, 1883.

Mooney, Thomas. *Nine Years in America*. Dublin: James McGlashan, 1850.

Morehouse, Ward. *George M. Cohan: Prince of the American Theater*. Philadelphia: Lippincott, 1943.

Morrell, Parker. *Diamond Jim*. New York, 1934.

Mugglebee, R. *Father Coughlin*. New York: Doubleday, 1963.

———. *Father Coughlin of the Shrine of the Little Flower*. Boston: L. C. Page, 1933.

Neale, Samuel. *Some Account of the Lives and Religious Labours of Samuel Neale, and Mary Neale, Formerly Mary Peisley, Both of Ireland*. London; Gilpin, 1845.

Nesbit, Robert C. *"He Built Seattle:" A Biography of Judge Thomas Burke*. Seattle: University of Washington Press, 1961.

Newman, Robert. *Princess Grace Kelly: The Fascinating Life Story of a Girl Who Made the Lead from the Philadelphia Suburb to a Royal Palace*. New York: Monarch, 1962.

Neylan, John Francis. "Garret W. McEnerney, 1865–1942." *California Law Review* 31 (January 1943): 1–2.

O'Brien, John Augustine. *The Sea Saga of Dynamite Johnny O'Brien*. Seattle, Washington: Lowman and Hanford, 1933.

O'Brien, M. "Senator Joseph McCarthy and Wisconsin: 1946–1957." Ph.D. dissertation, University of Wisconsin, 1971.

O'Brien, Michael Joseph. "The Diary of Master Joseph Tate of Somersworth, New Hampshire." *American Irish Historical Society Journal* 27 (1928): 314–20.

———. *Hercules Mulligan: Confidential Correspondent of General Washington*. New York: Kennedy, 1937.

———. "Irish Mariners in New England." *American Irish Historical Society Journal* 17 (1918): 149–90.

———. "Irish Property Owners and Businessmen of New York City in the Seventeenth and Eighteenth Centuries." *American Irish Historical Society Journal* 15 (July 1916): 243–77.

———. "Irish Sea-Captains of New London Who Commanded Privateers in the Revolution: The Career of Captain Michael Mellally." *American Irish Historical Society Journal* 22 (1923): 192–98.

———. "John McCurdy: Irish Pioneer in Connecticut." *American Irish Historical Society Journal* 22 (1923): 199–203.

———. "The Story of Old Leary Street, or Cortland Street—The Leary Family in Early New York History." *American Irish Historical Society Journal* 1 (April 1916): 112–17.

O'Brien, Sister Mary Celine. *I Charge Each of You: The Story of Thomas A. Dooley*. North Easton, Massachusetts: Holy Cross Press, 1966.

O'Connell, Morris. *John Ireland*. Minnesota: Minnesota Historical Society, 1988.

O'Connor, Michael Patrick. *The Life and Letters of M. P. O'Connor*. New York: Dempsey and Carroll, 1893.

O'Keane, J. *Thomas J. Walsh: A Senator from Montana*. New Hampshire: M. Jones, 1955.

Offen, Roy. *Cagney*. Chicago: Regenery, 1972.

Owens, James. *Recollections of a Runaway Boy, 1827–1903*. Pittsburgh, Pennsylvania: Keystone, 1903.

Packard, H. B. "From Kilkenny: The Background of an Intellectual Immigrant." *Eire-Ireland* 10 (1975).

Pahorezki, Sister M. Sevina. *The Social and*

Political Activities of William J. Onahan. Washington, D.C.: The Catholic University of America, 1942.

Papenfuse, Edward C. "An Undelivered Defense of a Winning Cause: Charles Carroll of Carrollton's Remarks on the Proposed Federal Constitution." *Maryland Historical Magazine* 71 (Summer 1976): 220–51.

Parke, John E. *Recollections of Seventy Years.* Boston: Rand, Avery, 1886.

Parslow, Virginia D. " 'Flowert' Coverlets." *New York History* 37 (July 1956): 337–41.

Paul, Sherman. *Louis Sullivan: An Architect in American Thought.* Englewood Cliffs, New Jersey: Prentice-Hall, 1962.

Pendergast, Thomas F. *Forgotten Pioneers: Irish Leaders in Early California.* San Francisco, 1942.

Phelan, Josephine. *The Ardent Exile: The Life and Times of D'Arcy McGee.* Toronto: Macmillan, 1951.

Pinkerton, William John. *His Personal Record.* Kansas City, Missouri: Pinkerton, 1904.

Pope, Alexander. "Chief Justice Timothy D. Hurley." *American Irish Historical Society Journal* 25 (1926): 307–14.

Pringle, Henry F. *Alfred E. Smith: A Critical Study.* New York: Macy-Masius, 1927.

———. *Up to Now: An Autobiography.* New York: Viking, 1929.

Purdy, Claire Lee. *Victor Herbert: American Music Master.* New York: Messner, 1945.

Pyle, Joseph. *The Life of James J. Hill.* New York: Doubleday, 1917.

Rainsford, William Stephen. *The Story of a Varied Life.* London: Allen and Unwin.

Reid, Elizabeth. *Wayne Reid: A Memoir of His Life, by Elizabeth Reid, His Widow.* London: Ward and Downey, 1890.

Reilly, Desmond. "An Irish-American Chemist: William James MacNeven, 1763–1841." *Chymia* 2 (1949): 17–26.

"Reminiscences of an Old-Time Journalist: The Late Patrick Donahoe, of Boston." *Records of the American Catholic Historical Society of Philadelphia* 15 (1904): 314–17.

Rice, Harold. *Within the Ropes: Champions in Action.* New York: Stephen-Paul, 1946.

Roche, J. J. *Life of John Boyle O'Reilly.* New York: Mershon, 1891.

Rodechko, J. P. "Patrick Ford and His Search for America: A Case Study of Irish-American Journalism, 1870–1913." Ph.D. dissertation, Univeirty of Connecticut, 1967. New York: Arno Press, 1976.

Rogers, Frank. "Mike Walsh: A Voice of Protest." Master's thesis, Columbia University, 1950.

Rogow, Arnold A. *James Forrestal: A Study of Personality, Politics and Policy.* New York: Macmillan, 1963.

Ronayne, Edmond. *Ronayne's Reminiscences.* Chicago: Free Methodist, 1900.

Roney, Frank. *Irish Rebel and California Labor Leader: An Autobiography,* edited by Ira B. Cross. Berkeley: University of California Press, 1931.

Rossa, M. O. *My Mother and Father were Irish.* New York: Devin Adair, 1939.

Rowe, K. W. *Matthew Carey: A Study in Economic Development. Johns Hopkins University Studies in History and Political Science,* series 51, no. 4. Baltimore, Maryland: 1933.

Ryan, Rev. John A. "Ethics and Political Intervention in the Field of Social Action." *Review of Politics* 3 (1941): 300–305.

———. *Social Doctrine in Action: A Personal History.* New York: Harper and Row, 1941.

Ryan, Thomas. *Recollections of an Old Musician.* New York: Dutton, 1899.

Sampson, William. *Memories.* Leesburg, 1883.

Scamehorn, Howard L., ed. *The Buckeye Rovers in the Gold Rush.* Athens: Ohio University Press, 1965.

Schroll, A. C. "John Lancaster Spalding and *Quadragesimo Anno.*" *American Benedictine Review* 7 (1956): 248–62.

Schwartz, J. A. "Al Smith in the Thirties." *New York History* 45 (1964): 310–30.

Shaler, Nathaniel Southgate. *The Autobiography.* Boston: Houghton Mifflin, 1909.

Shoebotham, H. Minar. *Anaconda: Life of Marcus Daly (1841–1900): The Copper King.* Harrisburg, Pennsylvania: Stackpole, 1956.

Shulin, Joseph I. *John Daly Burk: Irish Rev-*

olutionist and American Patriot. Philadelphia: American Philosophical Society, 1964.

Smith, Dennis. *Report from Engine Company 82.* New York: Saturday Review Press, 1972.

Smith, Ellen Hart. *Charles Carroll of Carrollton.* Cambridge, Massachusetts: Harvard University Press, 1942.

Smith, Mortimore. *William Jay Gaynor.* Chicago: Regnery, 1951.

Smyth, Thomas. *Autobiographical Notes, Letters and Reflections.* Charleston, South Carolina: Walter, Evans and Cogswell, 1914.

Snelling, Joseph. *Life of Joseph Snelling: Being a Sketch of His Christian Experience and Labors in the Ministry.* Boston: M'Leish, 1847.

Sparling, Christopher J. *The Irish-Canuck-Yankee.* Chicago: Donohue, 1910.

Steel, E. "Mother Jones in the Fairmont Field 1902." *Journal of American History* 57 (1970): 290–307.

Stolberg, B. "James F. Byrnes." *American Mercury* 62 (March 1946): 263–72.

Strong, L. A. G. *John McCormack.* New York: Macmillan, 1941.

Sullivan, Ed. "My Story." *Collier's* 138 (September 14, 1956): 19–24; (September 28, 1956): 67–71; (October 12, 1956): 96–100.

Sullivan, Jerry B. "Kate Shelley: An Irish Heroine of Iowa." *American Irish Historical Society Journal* 25 (1926): 195–201.

Sullivan, Joseph. *Becoming an American.* Boston: Badger, 1929.

Sullivan, Louis Henri. *Autobiography of An Idea.* New York: Dover, 1956.

Sullivan, Mark. *The Education of an American.* New York: Doubleday, Doran, 1938.

Sullivan, Sister Gabrielle. *Martin Murphy, Jr.: California Pioneer, 1844–1884.* Stockton, California: University of the Pacific Press, 1974.

Sweeney, Francis. *It Will Take a Lifetime.* Boston: Charles River Books, 1980.

Tippin, Ernest Elwood. *A Brief History of George Manton Tippin, Sr., of Ireland, York County, South Carolina, and Washington County, Indiana, and His Descendents.* Wichita, Kansas: Preston, 1952.

Toker, F. "James O'Donnell: An Irish Georgian in America." *Journal of Society Archival Historians* 29 (1970): 132–43.

Toole, Gerald. *An Autobiography of Gerald Toole: The State's Prison Convict.* Hartford, Connecticut: Case, Lockwood, 1862.

Tunney, James Joseph. "My Fights with Jack Dempsey." In *Aspirin Age*, edited by Isabel Leighton, 1919–41. New York: Simon and Schuster, 1949, 152–68.

Twombly, Wells. *Shake Down the Thunder: The Official Biography of Notre Dame's Frank Leahy.* Philadelphia: Chilton, 1974.

Valentine, Lewis J. *Night Stick: The Autobiography of Lewis J. Valentine: Former Police Commissioner of New York.* New York: Dial, 1947.

Van Riper, Guernsey. *Mighty Macs: Three Famous Baseball Managers.* Champaign, Illinois: Garrard, 1972.

Vlanov, Barry. *Incredible Crosby.* New York: Whittlesey House, 1948.

Waldrop, Frank C. *McCormick of Chicago: An Unconventional Portrait of a Controversial Figure.* Englewood Cliffs, New Jersey: Prentice-Hall, 1966.

Walsh, J. C. "Charles O'Conor." *American Irish Historical Society Journal* 27 (1928): 286–313.

Walsh, Louis J. *John Mitchel.* London: 1934.

Walsh, Townsend. *The Career of Dion Boucicault.* Bronx, New York: Blom, 1967.

Waters, Edward Neighbor. *Victor Herbert (1859–1924): A Life in Music.* New York: Macmillan, 1955.

Wayman, Dorothy G. *David I. Walsh: Citizen-Patriot.* Milwaukee, Wisconsin: Bruce, 1952.

Whitlock, Brand. *Forty Years of It.* New York: D. Appleton, 1914.

11. Women

A Voice from the Roman Catholic Laity: The Parochial School Question—An Open Letter to Bishop Keane, Rector of the New Catholic University at Washington, D.C. Boston: Arnold, 1890.

Abbot, Edith. *The Immigrant and the Community*. Chicago: University of Chicago Press, 1926.

———. "The Wages of Unskilled Labor in the United States, 1850–1900." *Journal of Political Economy* 13, no. 3 (June 1905): 321–67.

———. *Women in Industry*. New York: Arno Press and the New York Times, 1969.

Acklen, Jeanette T. *Tennessee Records; Bible Records and Marriage Bonds; Tombstone Inscriptions and Manuscripts, Historical and Biographical*. 2 vols. Nashville, Tennessee: Cullom and Ghertner, 1933.

Addams, Jane. *A New Conscience and an Ancient Evil*. New York: Macmillan, 1912.

Alcott, Louisa May. *Work: A Story of Experience*. Boston: Roberts Brothers, 1873.

Allston, Margaret. *Her Boston Experiences: A Picture of Modern Boston Society and People*. Boston: Curtis, 1899.

Anderson, Mary Jane. "From an Irish Farm to a Minnesota Homestead." *Gopher Historian* 21 (Spring 1967): 21–26.

Anthony, Katherine B. *Mothers Who Must Work*. New York: Survey Association, 1914.

Arensberg, Conrad M., and Solon T. Kimball. *Family and Community in Ireland*. 2d ed. Cambridge: Harvard University Press, 1967.

Barron, Milton L., ed. *The Blending American: Patterns of Intermarriage*. Chicago: Quadrangle Books, 1972.

Barton, George. *Angels of the Battlefield*. Philadelphia: The Catholic Arts Publishing, 1897.

Biddle, E. H. "The American Catholic Irish Family" in C. M. Mindel and R. Habenstein, editors, *Ethnic Families in America*. New York: Elsevier, 89–123.

Blanc, Marie Therese. *The Condition of Women in the United States: A Traveler's Notes*. Paris: A. Colin, 1895.

Bland, Sister Joan. "Hibernian Crusade: The Story of the Catholic Total Abstinence Union of America." Ph.D. dissertation, The Catholic University of America, 1951. Published by the Catholic University of America Press, 1954.

Blessing, Patrick J. "West among Strangers: Irish Migration to California, 1850–1880." Ph.D. dissertion, University of California, Los Angeles, 1977.

Bloomberg, Susan E., Mary Frank Fox, Robert M. Warner, and Sam Bass Warner, Jr. "A Census Probe into Nineteenth-Century Family History: Southern Michigan, 1850–1880." *Journal of Social History* 5, no. 1 (Fall 1971): 27–45.

Bolger, Stephen Garrett. "The Irish Character in American Fiction, 1830–1860." Ph.D. dissertation, University of Pennsylvania, 1971.

Bolton, C. K. *Scotch-Irish Pioneers in Ulster and America*. Boston: Bacon and Brown, 1910.

Bolton, Ethel. *Immigrants to New England, 1700–1775*. Salem, Massachusetts: Essex Institute, 1931.

Boucicault, Dion. *The Colleen Bawn; or, The Brides of Garry Owen*. New York: French, n.d.

———. *The Irish Heiress*. London: Andrews, 1842.

———. *The Streets of New York*. Chicago: Dramatic, n. d.

———. *West End; or, The Irish Heiress*. New York, n.p., n.d.

Bouvier, Leon F., and S. L. N. Rao. *Socio-Religious Factors in Fertility Decline*. Cambridge, Massachusetts: Ballinger, 1975.

Bowker, R. R. "In Re: Bridget." *Old and New* 1(1871): 497–501.

Bowler, Sister Mareilla. "A History of Catholic Colleges for Women in the United States of America." Ph.D. dissertation, The Catholic University of America, 1933.

Boyce, Rev. John [pseudo. Paul Peppergrass]. *Mary Lee, Or The Yankee in Ireland*. Baltimore: Patrick Donahoe, 1860.

Brace, Charles Loring. *The Dangerous Classes of New York and Twenty Years' Work among Them*. New York: Wynkoop, 1880.

Brandt, Lillian. *Five Hundred and Seventy-Four Deserters and Their Families: A Descriptive Study of Their Characteristics and Circumstances*. New York: Charity Organization Society, 1905.

Brannick, T. O. "A Study of Returned Immigrants in an Irish Rural Parish." Master's thesis, University College, Dublin, 1978.

Breecher, Catherine E. *The True Remedy for the Wrongs of Women, with a History of an Enterprise Having that for Its Object*. Boston: Phillips, Sampson, 1851.

Brewer, Eileen M. "Beyond Utility: The Role of the Nuns in the Education of American Catholic Girls, 1860–1920." Ph.D. dissertation, University of Chicago, 1984.

———. *Nuns and The Education of American Catholic Women, 1860–1920*. Chicago: Loyola University Press, 1987.

Brody, Hugh. *Inishkillane: Change and Decline in the West of Ireland*. New York: Schocken Books, 1974.

Brown, Alice. *Louise Imogen Guiney*. New York: Macmillan, 1921.

Buenker, John D. "The Urban Political Machine and Women Suffrage: A Study in Political Adaptability." *The Historian* 33.

Burns, James A. *The Catholic School System in the United States*. New York: Benziger Brothers, 1908.

———. *The Principles, Origins and Establishment of the Catholic School System in the United States*, 1912.

Burr, Rollin H. "A Statistical Study of Patients Admitted at the Connecticut Hospital for Insane from the Years 1868 to 1901." *Quarterly Publications of the American Statistical Association* 8, no. 62 (1903): 313–15, 327–29.

Burton, Katharine. *Mother Butler of Marymount*. New York: Longmans, Green, 1944.

Butler, Elizabeth Beardsley. *Women and the Trades*. New York: Charities Publication Committee, 1909.

Caldicott, Thomas F. *Hannah Corcoran: An Authentic Narrative of Her Conversion From Romanism: Her Abduction From Charlestown, and the Treatment She Received During Her Absence*. Boston, n.p. 1853.

Calkin, Homer L. "The Irish in Iowa." *Palimpsest*, 45, no. 2 (1964).

Campbell, Helen. *Prisoners of Poverty: Women Wage Workers, Their Trades and Their Lives*. New York: Roberts, 1887.

———. *Women Wage-Earners: Their Past, Their Present, and Their Future*. Boston: Roberts, 1893.

Carter, Hugh, and Paul G. Glick. *Marriage and Divorce: A Social and Economic Study*. Cambridge, Massachusetts: Harvard University Press, 1970.

Cassidy, James F. *The Woman of the Gael*. Boston: Stratford, 1922.

Chambers, George. *Tribute to the Principles, Virtues, Habits and Public Usefulness of the Irish and Scotch Early Settlers of Pennsylvania*. Chambersburg, Pennsylvania: Kieffer, 1856.

Christian, Linda. *Linda: My Own Story*. New York: Crown, 1962.

Christina, Sister M. I., H.M. "Study of the Catholic Family Through Three Generations." *The American Catholic Sociological Review* 3 (1942).

Chudacoff, Howard P. "Newlyweds and Family Extensions: The First Stage of Family Cycle in Providence, Rhode Island, 1864–1865 and 1879–1880." In *Family and Population in Nineteenth Century America*, edited by Tamara K. Hareven and Maris A. Vinovskis, 179–205. Princeton: Princeton University Press, 1978.

Clarke, Joseph I. C. *A Woman's Duel: Drama in Four Acts*. New York: n.p., n.d. (circa 1900).

Clarke, Richard H. "Catholic Protectories and Reformatories." *American Catholic Historical Quarterly* 20, no.79 (1895): 607–40.

Clyde, Rev. John C. *"Irish Settlement:" Genealogies, Necrology and Reminiscences of the Now Northampton County, Pennsylvania*. Frazer, Pennsylvania: Author, 1879.

Coad, Ralph G. "Irish Pioneers of Nebraska." *Nebraska History Magazine* 17 (1936): 171–77.

Cohler, B. J., and M. A. Lieberman. "Personality Change Across the Second Half of Life: Findings from a Study of Irish, Italian and Polish American Men and Women." In *Ethnicity and Aging*, edited by D. E. Gelfand and A. J. Kutjk. New York: Springer, 1979.

Connell, Kenneth Hugh. "Illegitimacy before the Famine." In *Irish Peasant Society*, 51–86. Oxford: Clarendon Press, 1968.

———. *Irish Peasant Society*. London: Oxford, Clarendon Press, 1968.

———. "The Land Legislation and Irish Social Life." *Economic History Review* 11, no.1 (1958): 1–7.

———. "Peasant Marriage in Ireland: Its Structure and Development Since the Famine." *Economic History Review* 2d series, 14 (1962): 502–23.

———. "Peasant Marriages in Ireland after the Great Famine." *Past and Present* 12 (November 1957): 16–91.

Conway, Katherine, and Mabel Ward Cameron. *Charles Francis Donnelly: A Memoir*. New York: James T. White, 1909.

Conway, Thomas G. "Women's Work in Ireland." *Eire-Ireland* 7, no. 1: 1–27.

Cotton, Jane Baldwin. *Maryland Calendar of Wills, 1635–1743*. 8 vols. Baltimore, Maryland: W. J. C. Dulany, 1901.

Coulter, Ellis Merton. *A List of the Early Settlers of Georgia*. Athens: University of Georgia Press, 1949.

Crane, Stephen. *George's Mother*. New York, n.p., 1896.

———. *Maggie: A Girl of the Street*. New York, n.p., 1892.

Cross, Andrew B. *Priests' Prisons for Women*. Baltimore, n.p., 1854.

The Cross and Shamrock or How to Defend the Faith: An Irish-American Tale of Real Life Descriptive of the Temptations, Sufferings, Trials, and Triumphs of the Children of St. Patrick, in the Great Republic of Washington. Boston: Patrick Donahoe, 1853.

Curran T. J. "The Irish Family in Nineteenth Century Urban America: The Role of the Catholic Church." *Working Papers*, series 6, no. 2. Center for Studies in American Catholicism, University of Notre Dame, 1979.

Cusack, Mary Frances. *Advice to Irish Girls in America*. New York: Pustet, 1886.

———. *Nun of Kenmare: An Autiobiography*. Boston: Ticknor, 1889. See Irene Eager below.

Daly, M. E. "Women in the Irish Workforce from Pre-Industrial to Modern Times." *Soathar: Journal of the Irish Labor History Society*, no. 7, Dublin, 1981.

Daniel, Anna S. "Tenement House Labor." *Journal of the American Social Science Association* 30 (1892): 73–85.

Darkness and Daylight, or Lights and Shadows of New York Life: A Woman's Story of Gospel, Temperance, Mission, and Rescue Work. Hartford, Connecticut: A. D. Worthington, 1892.

Davidson, Sara. "Bernadette Devlin: An Irish Revolutionary in Irish America." *Harper's* 240 (January 1970): 78–87.

Davis, Allen F. "Jane Addams vs. The Ward Boss." *Journal of the Illinois State Historical Society* 53 (Autumn 1960): 257–65.

Davis, William H. "The Relation of the Foreign Population to the Mortality Rates of Boston." In *Medical Problems of Immigration*. Easton, Pennsylvania: American Academy of Medicine, 1913, 50–85.

de la Fontaine, Elise. "Cultural and Psychological Implications in Case Work with Irish Clients." In *Cultural Problems in Social Case Work*. New York: Family Welfare Association of America, 1940, 21–37.

Delzell, Ruth. *The Early History of Women Trade Unionists of America*. Chicago: National Women's Trade Union League of America, 1919.

Deshon, George. *Guide for Catholic Young Women, Especially for Those Who Earn Their Own Living*. New York: Catholic Book Exchange, 1897.

Dickson, R. J. *Ulster Emigration to Colonial America, 1718–1775*. London: Routledge and Kegan Paul, 1966.

Diner, Hasia. *Erin's Daughters in America: Irish Women in the Nineteenth Century*. Baltimore: Johns Hopkins University Press, 1983.

Dinnerstein, Leonard, and Frederic C. Jaher, eds. *The Aliens: A History in Ethnic Minorities in America*. New York: Appleton Century-Crofts, 1970.

Dinsmore, J. W. *The Scotch-Irish in America*. Chicago: Winona, 1906.

Donelin, Mary C. "American Irish Women 'Firsts.'" *American Irish Historical Society Journal* 24 (1925): 215–21.

Donnelly, Eleanor C. "Women in Literature." *World's Columbian Catholic Congress*. Chicago: Hyland, 1893.

Dorr, Rheta Childe, and William Hard. "The Woman's Invasion." *Everybody's* 20, no.1 (1909): 82.

Drachsler, Julius. *Intermarriage in New York City*. New York: Columbia University, 1921.

Drake, Daniel. *Pioneer Life in Kentucky*. Cincinnati, Ohio: R. Clarke, 1870.

Drake, Michael. "Marriage and Population Growth in Ireland, 1750–1845." *Economic History Review* 16, 2d series (1963).

Drayton, John. *Memoirs of the American Revolution in South Carolina*. Charleston: Printed by A. E. Miller, 1821.

Dreadful Scenes in the Awful Disclosures of Maria Monk. New York, 1836.

Dublin, Thomas. *Women at Work: The Transformation of Work and Community in Lowell, Massachusetts, 1826–1860*. New York: Columbia University Press, 1979.

Dubnoff, Steven Jan. "The Family and Absence from Work: Irish Workers in a Lowell, Massachusetts Cotton Mill, 1860." Ph.D. dissertation, Browders University. Waltham, Massachusetts, 1975.

Eager, Irene. *The Nun of Kenmare*. Cork: Mercier Press, 1970 (see Mary Francis Cusack above).

Early, R. H. *Chronicles and Family Sketches, Embracing a History of Campbell County, Virginia, 1782–1926*. Lynchburg, Virginia: J. P. Bell, 1927.

Eggenschwiler, David. *The Christian Humanism of Flannery O'Connor*. Detroit, Michigan: Wayne State University Press, 1972.

Ellinger, Agnes. *A History of the Temperance Movement in Minnesota to 1865*. Minnesota Historical Society, St. Paul, 1933.

Ellington, George. *The Women of New York*. New York: Vanguard Press, 1940.

Ely, William. *Big Sandy Valley: A History of the People and Country from the Earliest Settlement to the Present Time*. Catlettsburg, Kentucky: Central Methodist, 1887.

Evans, E. E. "The Scotch-Irish: Their Cultural Adaptation and Heritage in the American Old West." In *Essays in Scotch-Irish History*. edited by E. R. R. Green. London: Routledge and Kegan Paul, 1969.

Evans, John Whitney. "A History of the Immaculate Heart of Mary Parish of Curry, Murray County, Minnesota." Master's thesis, St. Paul Seminary, 1957.

Ewen, David. *Complete Book of American Musical Theatre*. New York: Holt, 1958.

Ewens, Mary. "The Role of the Nun in Nineteenth-Century America." Ph.D. dissertation, University of Minnesota, 1971.

Ewens, Mary. O.P. "The Leadership of Nuns in Immigrant Catholicism." In *Women and Religion in America*, edited by Rosemary Radford Ruther, and Rosemary Skinner Keller. *The Nineteenth Century* 1. San Francisco: Harper and Row, 1981.

Feeley, Kathleen. *Flannery O'Connor: Voice of the Peacock*. New Brunswick, New Jersey: Rutgers University Press, 1972.

Fetherling, Dale. *Mother Jones: The Miner's Angel.* Carbondale: Southern Illinois University Press, 1974.

Fisher, Sydney George. *The Making of Pennsylvania.* Philadelphia, Pennsylvania: J. B. Lipincott, 1896.

Fiske, John. *Dutch and Quaker Colonies* 2. Boston and New York: Houghton, Mifflin, 1899.

Fitzgerald, Sister Mary Innocenta. *A Historical Sketch of the Sisters of Mercy in the Diocese of Buffalo, 1857–1942.* Buffalo: Mt. Mercy Academy, 1942.

Flanigan, James C. *Marriages of Hancock County, 1806–1943.* Hapeville, Georgia: Printed by Tyler, 1943.

Flynn, Elizabeth Gurley. *The Rebel Girl: An Autobiography, My First Life (1906–1926).* New York: International, 1965.

Ford, Henry Jones. *The Scotch-Irish in America.* Princeton: Princeton University Press, 1915.

Foster, Elene. "An Irish Mother: A Monologue." *Century* 63 (1903): 616–18.

Franklin, S. M. "Agnes Nestor of the Glove Workers: A Leader in the Women's Movement." *Life and Labor* 3, no. 12 (1913): 370–74.

Friedman, Melvin J., and Lewis A. Lawson, eds. *The Added Dimension: The Art and Mind of Flannery O'Connor.* New York: Fordham University Press, 1966.

Frounde, James A. "Romanism and the Irish Race in the United States." *North American Review* 129 (1879–80): 522–23.

Fulton, Eleanor Jane. *An Index to the Will Books and Interstate Records of Lancaster County, Pennsylvania, 1729–1850.* Lancaster, Pennsylvania: Intelligencer Printing, 1936.

Gaither, Grant. *Princess of Monaco: The Story of Grace Kelly.* New York: Holt, 1957.

Garland, Robert. *The Scotch-Irish in Western Pennsylvania.* Pittsburgh: Carnegie Library, 1923.

Gayarre, Charles. *History of Louisiana.* 4 vols. New Orleans: F. F. Hansell and Brothers, 1903.

Georgia. *Colonial Records of the State of Georgia.* 18 vols. Atlanta, 1904–8.

Gilman, Agnes Geneva, and Gertrude M. Gilman. *Who's Who in Illinois: Women-Makers of History.* Chicago: Electric, 1927.

Gilmer, George. *Sketches of Some of the First Settlers of Upper Georgia.* New York: D. Appleton, 1855.

Gittleman, H. M. "Waltham System and the Coming of the Irish." *Labor History* (Fall, 1967): 227–53.

Glasco, Laurence A. "The Life Cycles and Household Structure of American Ethnic Groups, Irish, Germans, and Native-Born Whites in Buffalo, New York, 1855." *Journal of Urban History* 1, no. 3 (May 1975): 339–64.

Glick, Paul C. "Intermarriage among Ethnic Groups in the United States." *Social Biology* 17 (December 1970).

Gmelch, George. *The Irish Tinkers: The Urbanization of an Itinerant People.* Menlo Park, California: Cummings, 1977.

Goldmark, Pauline. *Notes on an Industrial Survey of a Selected Area in New York City, with Respect to Sanitary Conditions in the Factories.* Albany: State Printers, 1912.

Gordon, Milton M. *Assimilation in American Life: The Role of Race, Religion and Natural Origins.* New York: Oxford University Press, 1964.

Graham, Sheilah. *Beloved Infidel: The Education of a Woman.* London: Cassell, 1958.

———. *College of One.* New York: Viking, 1967.

———. *The Rest of the Glory.* New York: Coward-McCann, 1964.

Graham, Sister Clara. *Works to the King: Reminiscences of Mother Seraphine Ireland.* St. Paul, Minnesota: North Central, 1950.

Gray, Madeline. *Margaret Sanger: A Biography of Birth Control.* New York: Richard Marek, 1979.

Gredel, Stephen. "Immigration of Ethnic Groups to Buffalo, Based upon Census of 1850, 1865, 1875, and 1892." *Niagara Frontier*, 1963, 42–56.

Green, A. "The Death of Mother Jones." *Labor History* 1 (1960): 68–80.

Green, E. R. R., ed. *Essays in Scotch-Irish*

History. London: Routledge and Kegan Paul, 1969.

Green, S. S. *Scotch-Irish in America*. Worcester, Massachusetts: Hamilton, 1865.

Greer, Colin, ed. *Divided Society: The Ethnic Experience in America*. New York: Basic Books, 1974.

Griffen, Clyde, and Sally Griffen. "Family and Business in a Small City, Poughkeepsie, New York, 1850–1880." *Journal of Urban History* 1, no. 3 (1975): 316–38.

Groneman, Carole. "The Bloody Ould Sixth: A Social Analysis of a Mid-Nineteenth Century New York Working Class Community." Ph.D. dissertation, University of Rochester, 1973.

———. "'She Earns as a Child—She Pays as a Man': Women Workers in a Mid-Nineteenth-Century New York Community." In *Immigrants in Industrial America, 1850–1920*, edited by Richard L. Ehrlich, 33–46. Charlottesville: University Press of Virginia, 1977.

———. "Working Class Immigrant Women in Mid-Nineteenth Century New York: The Irish Woman's Experience." *Journal of Urban Studies* 4, no. 3 (1978): 255–74.

Guilfoy, William H. *The Influence of Nationality upon the Mortality of a Community, with Special Reference to the City of New York*. New York: Department of Health of the City of New York, 1917.

Guiney, Louise Imogen. *Lover's Saint Ruth's and Three Other Tales*. Boston: Copeland and Day, 1894.

———. *The Martyr's and Shorter Peoms*. Boston: Houghton Mifflin, 1900.

———. "Woman in American Literature." *Century Magazine*, 1890.

Guiney, Grace, ed. *Letters of Louis Imogen Guiney*. 2 vols. New York: Harper and Brothers, 1926.

Hadsell, William L. "A Sociological Study of Certain Irish Organizations and Families of New York." Master's thesis, Columbia University, 1910.

Haines, M. R. "Fertility and Marriage in a Nineteenth-Century Industrial City: Philadelphia, 1850–1880." *Journal of Economic History* 40, no. 1 (1980): 151–58.

Hale, Charles. *A Review of the Proceedings of the Nunnery Committee of the Massachusetts Legislature*. Boston, n.p., 1850.

Hale, John P. *Trans-Allegheny Pioneers*. Cincinnatti: Graphic Press, 1886.

Hale, Sara Josepha. *"Boarding Out": A Tale of Domestic Life*. New York: Harper and Brothers, 1846.

Handlin, Oscar, ed. *Children of the Uprooted*. New York: George Braziller, 1966.

Hanna, C. A. *The Scotch-Irish; Or the Scot in North Britain, North Ireland, and North America*. 2 vols. New York: Putnam, 1902.

Hannan, Damian, and Louise A. Katsiaouni. *Traditional Families? From Culturally Prescribed to Negotiated Roles in Farm Families*, no. 87. Economic and Social Research Institute, Dublin, 1977.

Hanratty, Marie Felicitia. "A Study of Early Irish Contributions to the Growth of St. Louis, 1804–1840." Master's thesis, St. Louis University, 1933.

Hareven, Tamara K., ed. *Family and Kin in Urban Communities, 1700–1930*. New York: New Viewpoints, 1977.

Hareven, Tamara K., and Mavis A. Vinovskis. "Marital Fertility, Ethnicity and Occupation in Urban Families: An Analysis of South Boston and the South End in 1880." *Journal of Social History* 3 (1975): 69–93.

Harris, Louisa. *Behind the Scenes; or Nine Years at the Four Courts*. St. Louis: A. R. Flemming, 1893.

Healy, Kathleen. *Frances Warde: American Founder of the Sisters of Mercy*. New York: Seabury Press, 1973.

Heer, David M. "The Marital Status of Second-Generation Americans." *American Sociological Review* 26, no. 2 (1961): 233–41.

Hendin, Josephine. *The World of Flannery O'Connor*. Bloomington, Indiana: Indiana University Press, 1970.

Henney, Nella Braddy. *Anne Sullivan Macy: The Story behind Helen Keller*. Garden City, New York: Doubleday, Doran, 1933.

Henry, Alice. "Mrs. Winifred O'Reilly: A Veteran Worker." *Life and Labor* 1911, 132–36.

———. *Women and the Labor Movement.* New York: George H. Doran, 1923.

Herrick, Christine Terhune. "Which Is Mistress?" *Ladies Home Journal* 3, no.5 (1886): 7.

Herron, Sister Mary Eulilia. *The Sisters of Mercy in the United States: 1843–1928.* New York: Macmillan, 1929.

Hill, Joseph A. "Comparative Fecundity of Women of Native and Foreign Parentage of the United States." *Quarterly Publications of the American Statistical Association* 8, no. 104 (1913): 583–604.

The History of Dublin, New Hamshire. Boston: Printed by J. Wilson and Son, 1855.

History of the Sisters of Notre Dame de Namur by the Pioneer Sister. Lowell, Massachusetts: St. Patrick's Convent, n.d.

Holland, Josiah G. *History of Western Massachusetts.* 2 vols. Springfield, Massachusetts: S. Bowles, 1855.

Holt, Hamilton. *The Life Stories of Undistinguished Americans as Told by Themselves.* New York: James Pott, 1906, 143–49.

Howe, George. *History of Presbyterian Church in South Carolina.* 2 vols. Columbia, South Carolina: Duffie and Chapman, 1870–83.

Hughes, Thomas P., ed. "Genealogies of Columbia County, New York." *American Ancestry* 2 (1887).

Humphreys, Alexander J. "The Family in Ireland." In *Comparative Family Systems.* Boston: Houghton Mifflin, 1965.

Hurd, Charles Edwin. *Genealogy and History of Representative Citizens of the Commonwealth of Massachusetts.* Boston: New England Historical, 1902.

Hurley, Doran. *Herself: Mrs. Patrick Crowley.* New York: Longmans, Green, 1939.

Hutchinson, Edward P. *Immigrants and Their Children, 1850–1950.* New York: Russel and Russell, 1956.

Immigration Commission, Reports of the (Dillingham Commission). *Occupations of the First and Second Generations of Immigrants in the United States: Fecundity of Immigrant Women.* Washington, D.C.: Government Printing Office, 1911.

International Migration Review. New York: Center for Migration Studies. *Women in Migration* 18, special issue (Winter 1984).

Irish Feminist Information. *Missing Pieces—Women in Irish History* 1. *Since the Famine.* Dublin: Irish Feminist Information Center, 1983.

"Irish Girls in Lowell." *Boston Pilot.* August 16, 1851.

Jackson, Pauline. "Women in Nineteenth Century Irish Immigration." *International Migration Review. Women in Migration* 18, special issue (Winter 1984).

James, Janet W. ed. *Women in American Religion.* Philadelphia: University of Pennsylvania Press, 1980.

Johnson, J. F. *Scots and Scotch-Irish in America.* New York: Lerner, 1966.

Johnson, James H. "Marriage and Fertility in Nineteenth Century Londonderry." *Journal of the Statistical and Social Inquiry Society of Ireland* 20, part 1 (1958).

Jolly, Ellen Ryan. *Nuns of the Battlefield.* Providence, Rhode Island: Providence Visitor Press, 1927.

Jones, Mary Harris. *The Autobiography of Mother Jones,* edited by M. F. Parton. Original edition, Chicago: Charles H. Kerr, 1925. New paperback edition, Chicago: Charles H. Kerr, 1976.

Jones, W. D. "Made in New York: A Plot to Kill the Queen." *New York Historical Society Quarterly* 51 (1967): 311–25.

Jordan, John Woolf. *Colonial and Revolutionary Families of Philadelphia.* 2 vols. New York and Chicago: Lewis, 1911.

———. *Genealogy and Personal History of the Allegheny Valley.* 3 vols. New York: Lewis Historical, 1913.

———. *Genealogy and Personal History of Northern Pennsylvania.* 3 vols. New York: Lewis Historical, 1913.

———. *Genealogy and Personal History of Western Pennsylvania.* 3 vols. New York: Lewis Historical, 1915.

Kane, Eileen. "Man and Kin in Donegal: A Study of Kinship Functions in a Rural Irish and Irish-American Community." *Ethnology* 1, no. 1 (1974): 91–108.

Katzman, D. M. *Seven Days a Week: Women and Domestic Service in Industrializing America.* New York: Oxford University Press, 1978.

Keehan, Sister Martha Julie. "The Irish Catholic Beneficial Societies Founded between 1818 and 1869." Master's thesis, The Catholic University of America, 1953.

Keep, G. R. C. "Some Irish Opinion on Population and Emigration." *Irish Ecclesiastical Record* 84 (1955): 377–86.

Kelley, M. E. J. "Women and the Labor Movement." *North American Review* 166, no. 4 (1898): 408–17.

Kellor, Frances A. "The Immigrant Woman." *Atlantic* 100, no. 3 (1907): 401–7.

———. *Out of Work: A Study of Employment Agencies*, 130. New York: G. P. Putnam, 1904.

Kelly, Richard J. "Emigration and Its Consequences." *New Ireland Review* 21, no. 5 (1904): 257–67.

Kenneally, James J. "Catholics and Woman Suffrage in Massachusetts." *Catholic Historical Review* 53.

Kennedy, Robert E., Jr. *The Irish*. Berkeley: University of California Press, 1973.

———. *The Irish: Emigration, Marriage and Fertility*. Berkeley: University of California Press, 1973.

———. "Selective Migration and the Acculturation of Immigrants: The Overseas Irish Family." *Working Paper* 1, series 4. Center for the Study of American Catholicism, University of Notre Dame, 1978.

Kennedy, Rose Fitzgerald. *Times to Remember*. Garden City, New York: Doubleday, 1974.

Kennedy, Ruby Jo Reeves. "Single or Triple Melting-Pot? Intermarriage Trends in New Haven, 1870–1940." *American Journal of Sociology* 49 (1944): 333.

Kennelly, Karen. "Mary Molloy: Women's College Founder." In *Women of Minnesota: Selected Biographical Essays*, edited by Barbara Stuhler and Gretchen Kreuter, 136–54. St. Paul: Minnesota Historical Society Press, 1977.

Kenney, Mary E. "Organization of Working Women: Address." *World's Congress of Representative Women*. 2 vols. Chicago, 1893.

Kiser, Clyde V., Wilson H. Grabill, and Arthur A. Campbell. *Trends and Variations in Fertility in the United States*. Cambridge, Massachusetts: Harvard University Press, 1968.

Klacznska, Barbara. "Why Women Work: A Comparison of Various Ethnic Groups—Philadelphia, 1910–1930." *Labor History* 17 (Winter 1976): 73–87.

Klatzy, Sheila R. "Patterns of Contact with Relatives." *Monography Series*. New York, 1973.

Kleinberg, Susan. "Technology's Stepdaughter: The Impact of Industrialization upon Working-Class Women, Pittsburgh, 1865–1890." Ph.D. dissertation, University of Pittsburgh, 1973.

Kneeland, George. *Commercialized Prostitution in New York*. New York: Century, 1917.

Kolbenschlag, Madonna. "Women and the Future of Irish Catholicism." *The Christian Century* 101 (April 18, 1984): 401–5.

Kraditor, Aileen S. *The Ideas of the Woman Suffrage Movement, 1890–1920*. New York: Columbia University Press, 1965.

Kuczynski, R. R. "The Fecundity of the Native and Foreign-Born Population in Massachusetts." *Quarterly Journal of Economics* 15 (1901): 4, 11–14, 17–19.

Kulp, George B. *Families of the Wyoming Valley*. 3 vols. Wilkes-Barre, Pennsylvania: E. B. Yordy, 1885–90.

Lamb, Martha J. *History of New York City*. 2 vols. New York: A. S. Barnes, 1877–96.

Larcom, Lucy. "Among Lowell Mill Girls: A Reminiscence." *Atlantic* (1881): 593–612.

Lash, Joseph. *Helen and Teacher: The Story of Helen Keller and Anne Sullivan Macy*. New York: Delacorte, 1980.

Leach, D. E. *The Northern Colonial Frontier, 1607–1763*. New York: Holt, Rinehart and Winston, 1966.

Leaming, R. E. "Study of a Small Group of Irish-American Children." *Psychological Clinic* 15 (March 1923): 18–40.

Lee, Francis Bazley. *Genealogical and Memorial History of the State of New Jersey*. New York: Lewis Historical, 1910.

Lee, Joseph. "Marriage and Population in Pre-Famine Ireland." *Economic History Review* 21 (1968): 283–95.

———. "Women and the Church Since the Famine." In *Women in Irish Society: The Historical Dimension*, edited by O. Mac-

Curtain and D. O. Corrain. Dublin: Arlen House, 1978.

Lehmann, William C. *Scotch-Irish Contributions to Early American Life and Culture*. Port Washington, New York: Kennikat Press, 1978.

Levine, Susan. "Honor Each Noble Maid: Women Workers and the Yonkers Carpet Weavers Strikes of 1885." *New York History* 62 (1981): 153–76.

Lewis, Arthur H. *Those Philadelphia Kellys*. New York: William Morrow, 1977.

"Lists of Servants Who Sailed from Dublin, 1746–1747, on the *Eruyal*, and Arrived in Philadelphia." *Pennsylvania Magazine of History and Biography* 26 (1902): 287.

Litwak, Eugene. "Geographic Mobility and Extended Family Cohesion." *American Sociological Review* 25 (1960): 385–94.

Lockhart, Audrey. *Some Aspects of Emigration from Ireland to the North American Colonies Between 1660 and 1775*. New York: Arno Press, 1976.

Loughnane, Mary Fionula. "Through Irish Eyes: A Mainly Women's Perspective on the Influence of Women and Men in Irish Families." Ph.D. dissertation, University of Michigan, 1983.

Lucey, Rev. William L., S.J. "Louise Imogen Guiney and Her 'Songs at the Start.'" *Records of the American Catholic Historical Society of Philadelphia* 66 (March 1955): 53–63.

Lynch, Elizabeth C. "Margaret Gaffney Haughery." *American Irish Historical Society Journal* 28 (1930): 153–54.

MacCurtain, Margaret, and D. O. Corrain, eds. *Women in Irish Society: The Historical Dimension*. Dublin, 1978.

MacDonald, Elspeth. "Hired Girls I Have Met." *Success* (1907): 334–35.

MacLochlain, Alf. "Social Life in Country Clare, 1800–1850." *Irish University Review* 2, no. 1 (1972): 55–78.

Mahoney, Dorah. *Six Months in a House of Correction*. Boston, n.p., 1835.

Mann, Ralph Emerson, II. "The Social and Political Structure of Two California Mining Towns, 1850–1870." Ph.D. dissertation, Stanford University, 1970.

Manning, Caroline. *The Immigrant Woman and Her Job*. Washington, D.C.: U.S. Woman's Bureau, 1930.

Martin, T. "The Race That God Made: A Memoir by An Architect's Granddaughter." *Kansas Quarterly* 6 (1974).

Massachusetts Bureau of Labor. *Trained and Supplementary Workers in Domestic Service, Prepared in Collaboration with the Women's Educational and Industrial Union, Boston, Massachusetts*. Boston: Wright and Potter, 1966.

Mattis, Mary Catherine. "The Irish Family in Buffalo, New York, 1855–1875: A Socio-Historical Analysis." Ph.D. dissertation, Washington University, 1975.

McDonald, Mary Lucy. *By Her Fruits . . . Sister Mary Joseph Lynch . . . Sister of Mercy, 1846–1898*. Farmington Hills, Massachusetts: R. S. M., 1981.

McEniry, Sister Blanche Marie. *Woman of Decision: The Life of Mother Mary Xavier Mehegan (1825–1915), Founders of the Sisters of Charity of Saint Elizabeth, Convent, New Jersey*. New York: McMullen, 1953.

McGraw, Blanche Sidall. *Real McGraw*. New York: McKay, 1953.

McKelvey, A. J. "Kate: The 'Good Angel' of Oklahoma." *American* 66, no.6 (1908): 587–93.

McKeon, Sister Francis Joseph. "The Formation of the Catholic Total Abstinence Union of America." Master's thesis, The Catholic University of America, 1946.

McNeill, Mary. *The Life and Times of Mary Ann McCracken, 1770–1866*. Dublin, 1960.

Meister, Richard J., ed. *Race and Ethnicity in Modern America*. Lexington, Massachusetts: D. C. Heath, 1974.

Messenger, John C. *Inis Beag: Isle of Ireland*. New York: Holt, Rinehart and Winston, 1969.

Messenger, John C. "Sex and Repression in an Irish Folk Community." In *Human Sexual Behavior*. New York: Basic Books, 1971.

Michaelson, Evelyn K., and Walter Goldschnidt. "Female Roles and Male Dominance among Peasants." *Southwestern Journal of Anthropology* 27 (1971): 330–52.

Michels, Eileen Manning. "Alice O'Brien: Volunteer and Philanthropist." In *Women of Minnesota: Selected Biographical Essays*, edited by Barbara Stuhler and Gretchen Kreuter, 136–54. St. Paul: Minnesota Historical Society Press (1977).

Miller, David W. "Irish Catholicism and the Great Famine." *Journal of Social History* 9, no. 1 (1975): 81–98.

Misner, Barbara. "Highly Respectable and Accomplished Ladies: Early American Women Religious, 1790–1850." *Working Paper Series*, no. 3 (Spring, 1978). Charles and Margaret Hall Cushwa Center for the Study of American Catholicism, University of Notre Dame.

Mitchell, Albert Gibbs, Jr. "Irish Family Patterns in Nineteenth-Century Ireland and Lowell, Massachusetts." Ph.D. dissertation, Boston University Graduate School, 1976.

Mitchell, Brian C. "Educating Irish Immigrants in Antebellum Lowell." *Historical Journal of Massachusetts* 11(1983): 94–103.

Modell, John, and Tamara K. Hareven. "Urbanization and the Malleable Household: An Examination of Boarding and Lodging in America Families." *Journal of Marriage and the Family* 35 (1976).

Moloney, Maurice T. "The Irish Pioneers of the West and Their Descendants." *American Irish Historical Society Journal* 8 (1909): 209–16.

Monaghan, Patricia, ed. *Unlacing: Ten Irish-American Women Poets*. n.p.: Firewood Press, 1988.

Monk, Maria. *Awful Disclosures of the Hotel Dieu Nunnery of Montreal*. New York, 1836.

Monroe, Day. *Chicago Families*. Chicago: University of Chicago Press, 1932.

Moore, Marguerite. "A New Woman's Work in the West of Ireland." *Catholic World* 64, no. 382 (1897): 451–59.

More, Louise Boland. *Wage Earners' Budgets: A Study of Standards and Cost of Living in New York City*. New York: Henry Holt, 1907.

Morgan, M., and H. H. Gordon. "Immigrant Families in an Industrial City: A Study of Households in Holyoke, 1880." *Journal of Family History* 4 (1979).

Mosher, Eliza. "Health of Criminal Women." *Boston Medical And Surgical Journal* 108 (1882): 316–17.

Mulvaney, Bernard, C.S.V. "How Catholics and Non-Catholics Differ in Fertility." *The American Sociological Review* 7 (1946): 124–27.

Myfanwy, Morgan, and Hilda H. Golden. "Immigrant Families in an Industrial City: A Study of Households in Holyoke, 1880." *Journal of Family History* 4, no. 1 (1979): 59–68.

Naughten, Thomas. "The Exodus of the Irish." *Westminster Review* 157 (1902): 85–88.

Neale, Samuel. *Some Account of the Lives and Religious Labours of Samuel Neale, and Mary Neale, Formerly Mary Peisley, Both of Ireland*. London: Gilpin, 1845.

Nestor, Agnes. *Woman's Labor Leader*. Rockford, Illinois: Bellevue Books, 1954.

Newman, Robert. *Princess Grace Kelly: The Fascinating Life Story of a Girl Who Made the Leap From the Philadelphia Suburb to a Royal Palace*. New York: Monarch, 1962.

Niehaus, Earl F. *The Irish in New Orleans: 1800–1860*. Baton Rouge: Louisiana State University Press, 1965.

Nims, Marion R. *Women in the War: A Bibliography*. Washington, D.C., 1918. Originally published by the U.S. Council of National Defense, Committee on Women's Defense Work, Government Printing Office, Washington, D.C., 1918.

Nolan, Janet A. *Ourselves Alone: Women's Emigration from Ireland, 1885–1920*. Lexington: University Press of Kentucky, 1989.

Oakes, Mary J. "Organized Voluntarism: The Catholic Sisters in Massachusetts, 1870–1940." *American Quarterly* 10 (1978): 652–80.

O'Brien, Michael J. "An Authoritative Account of the Earliest Irish Pioneers in New England." *American Irish Historical Society Journal* 18 (1919).

———. "Irish Marriages in New England." *American Irish Historical Society Journal* 17 (1918).

O'Connor, Sister Mary Catherine. "The Good Earth of My Ancestors." *Catholic World* 189 (May 1959): 101–5.

O'Dwyer, George Francis. "Ann Glover, First Martyr to the Faith in New England." *United States Catholic Historical Society Records and Studies* 15 (1921): 70–78.

O'Mahoney, Katharine O'Keefe. *Famous Irish Women*. Lawrence, Massachusetts: Lawrence, 1907.

O'Malley, Austin. "Irish Vital Statistics in America." *Studies* 7 (1918): 631.

O'Reilly, Bernard. *The Mirror of True Womanhood: A Book of Instruction for Women in the World*. New York: Peter F. Collier, 1878.

O'Reilly, Kevin Richards. *Population Dynamics and Family Planning In Dublin, Ireland*. Dublin, Ireland: n.d. (circa 1980).

Opler, Marvin K. "Cultural Perspectives in Research on Schizophrenics." In *Culture and Social Psychiatry*. New York: Atherton (1967): 282–303.

Palmer, Walter B. "Woman and Child Workers in Cotton Mills." *Quarterly Publications of the American Statistical Association* 7, no. 94 (1911): 588–617.

Parsons, Elsie C. "Women's Work and Wages in the United States." *Quarterly Journal of Economics* 29, no. 2 (1915): 201–34.

Penny, Virginia. *The Employment of Women: A Cyclopaedia of Woman's Work*. Boston: Walker, Wise, 1863.

Perry, Lorinda. *The Millinery Trade in Boston and Philadelphia: A Study of Women in Industry*. Binghamton, New York: Vail-Ballou, 1916.

Pettigrew, Thomas F. "Ethnicity in American Life: A Socio-Psychology Perspective." In *Ethnic Groups in the City: Culture, Institutions, and Power*, edited by Otto Feinstein. Lexington: D. C. Heath, 1971.

Pope, Jesse Eliphalet. *The Clothing Industry in New York*. New York: Columbia University Press, 1905.

Price, C. A., and J. Zubrzycki. "The Use of Intermarriage Statistics as an Index of Assimilation." *Population Studies* 16 (1962).

Purcell, Richard J. "Maine: Early Schools and Irish Teachers." *Catholic Educational Review* 33 (1935).

Raffaele, J. F. "Mary Harris Jones and the United Mine Workers." Master's thesis, University of North Carolina, 1964.

Reid, Elizabeth. *Wayne Reid: A Memoir of His Life, By Elizabeth Reid, His Widow*. London: Ward and Downey, 1890.

"Report of the General Investigator of Women's Work and Wages." *Proceedings of the General Assembly of the Knights of Labor*, 1887.

Reports of the Immigration Commission (Dillingham Commission). 42 vols. Washington, D.C., 1911. See especially volumes 3, 10–12, 18, 28, 29–35, and 37.

Riis, Jacob. *The Battle with the Slum*. New York: Macmillan, 1902.

Rogers, Lucille. *Lights from Many Candles: A History of Pioneer Women in Education in Tennessee*. Nashville: McQuiddy, 1960.

Room, Robin. "Cultural Contingencies of Alcoholism: Variations Between the Nineteenth-Century Urban Ethnic groups in Alcohol-Related Deaths." *Journal of Health and Human Social Behavior*, 1968, 99–113.

Rose, Peter I. *They and We: Racial and Ethnic Relations in the United States*. New York: Random House, 1974.

Rossa, M. O. *My Mother and Father were Irish*. New York: Devin Adair, 1939.

Sadlier, Mary Anne. *Confessions of an Apostate*, 1903.

Sandalls, K. F. "An Investigation of the Differential Fertility Patterns of Irish and Italian Americans." Master's thesis, Georgetown University, 1970.

Sanger, William W. *The History of Prostitution: Its Extent, Causes, and Effects throughout the World*. New York: Harper and Brothers, 1859.

Sayers, Peig. *An Old Woman's Reflections*. London: Oxford University Press, 1962.

Scheper-Hughes, Nancy. *Saints, Scholars and Schizophrenics: Mental Illness in Rural Ireland*. Berkeley: University of California Press, 1979.

Schrier, Arnold. *Ireland and the American Emigration, 1850–1900*. Minnesota: University of Minnesota Press, 1958.

Schwertner, M. "Eleanor Donnelly: The Singer of Pure Religion." *Catholic World* 105 (June 1917): 352–60.

Scott, Bonnie Kime. "Woman's Perspectives in Irish-American Fiction from Betty Smith to Mary McCarhy." In *Irish-American Fiction: Essays in Criticism*, edited by Daniel J. Casey and Robert E. Rhodes. New York: AMS Press, 1979.

Seller, Maxine. "The Education of Immigrant Children in Buffalo, New York, 1890–1916." *New York History* 57 (1976): 183–99.

———. *To Seek America: A History of Ethnic Life in the United States*. Jerome S. Ozer, Publisher, 1977.

Shields, Thomas Edward. *The Education of Our Girls*. New York: Benziger, 1907.

Simkhovitch, Mary Kingsbury. *The City Worker's World*. Macmillan, 1917.

Sisters of Reparation of the Congregation of Mary. *"Blessed are the Merciful": The Life of Mother Mary Zita (1844–1917), Foundress*. New York: n.p., 1953.

Sloan, Raymond P. *On a Shoestring and a Prayer: The Story of Mother Alice, O.S.F.: "Doctor of Sick Hospitals."* New York: Doubleday, 1964.

Smith, Alice E. "The Sweetman Colony." *Minnesota History* 9 (1928): 340–41.

Smith, Doris. "American-Irish Women in Education." *Recorder* 39 (1973): 33–39.

Smith, Mary Roberts. "Almshouse Women." *Quarterly Publications of the American Statistical Association* 4, no. 31 (1895): 219–62.

Smith, Zilpha. *Deserted Wives and Deserting Husbands: A Study of 234 Families Based on the Experience of The District Committees and Agents of the Associated Charities of Boston*. Boston, 1901.

Solomon, Barbara M. *Ancestors and Immigrants: A Changing New England Tradition*. Cambridge, Massachusetts: Harvard University Press, 1956.

Spengler, Joseph J. *The Fecundity of Native and Foreign-Born Women in New England*. Washington, D.C.: Brookings Institute, 1930.

Spin, Melford. "The Acculturation of American Ethnic Groups." *American Anthropologist* 57 (1955).

Spoffard, Harry. *The Mysteries of Worcester, or Charley Temple and His First Glass of Liquor*. Worcester, Massachusetts: H. J. Clapp, 1846.

Spoffard, H. P. *The Servant Girl Question*. Boston: Houghton, Mifflin, 1881. Reprinted in New York: Arno Press, 1977.

Steel, E. "Mother Jones in the Fairmont Field 1902." *Journal of American History* 57 (1970): 290–307.

Stivers, Richard. *The Hair of the Dog: Irish Drinking and the American Stereotype*. University Park: Pennsylvania State University Press, 1979.

Stuhler, Barbara, and Gretchen Kreuther, eds. *Women of Minnesota: Selected Biographical Essays*. St. Paul: Minnesota Historical Society Press, 1977.

Stygar, Sister Mary Martina. "Saint Louis Immigrants From 1820–1860." Master's thesis, St. Louis University.

Sullivan, A. M. "Why Send More Irish Out of Ireland." *Nineteenth Century* (1883).

Sullivan, Jerry B. "Kate Shelley: An Irish Heroine of Iowa." *American Irish Historical Society Journal* 25 (1926): 195–201.

Sullivan, William A. *The Industrial Worker in Pennsylvania, 1800–1840*. Harrisburg: Pennsylvania Historical and Museum Commission, 1955.

Sumner, Helen. "History of Women in Industry in the United States." *Report on Conditions of Women and Child Wage Earners in the United States* 9, 61st Congress, 2d session, 1910–13. S. doc. 645.

Taylor, R. N. "Educated about Their Station." *Catholic World* 53, no. 314 (1891): 172–77.

Thompson, Warren S. *Ratio of Children to Women, 1920*. Washington, D.C.: Government Printing Office, 1931.

Todd, Helen M. "Why Children Work: The Children's Answer." *McClure's Magazine* 40 (April 1913): 68–79.

Toomy, Lily Alice. "The Organized Work of Catholic Women." *World's Congress of Representative Women* 1. Chicago: Rand McNally, 1894.

True, Ruth S. *Boyhood and Lawlessness*. New York, Surrey Associates, 1914.

Tucker, G. S. L. "Irish Fertility Ratios Before the Famine." *Economic History Review* 23, no. 2, 2d series (August 1970): 267–48.

Tuke, James H. "News from Some Irish Emigrants." *Nineteenth Century* 20 (1889): 434.

Turbin, C. "And We Are Nothing But Women: Irish Working Women in Troy." In *Women of America*, edited by C. R. Berkin and M. B. Norton. Boston: Houghton Mifflin, 1979.

Turner, George Kibbe. "The Daughters of the Poor." *McClure's* 16 (1909): 46, 59.

Tynan, Katharine. "The Higher Education for Catholic Girls." *Catholic World* 51 (1890): 616–21.

Urlin, R. Denny. "Remarks on the Middle Class (Female) Emigration Society." *Journal of the Statistical and Social Inquiry Society of Ireland* 25 (1863): 439–46.

Ussher, Arland. "The Boundary between the Sexes." In *The Vanishing Irish: The Enigma of the Modern World*, edited by James A. O'Brien. New York: McGraw-Hill, 1953.

Van Kleeck, Mary. *Women in the Bookbinding Trade*. New York: Survey Associates, 1913.

Vinyard, Jo Ellen M. "The Irish on the Urban Frontier: Detroit, 1850–1880." Ph.D. dissertation, University of Michigan, 1972.

Wakefield, Edward. *An Account of Ireland, Statistical and Political*, 2 vols. London: Longman, Hurst, Rees, Orme and Brown, 1812.

Walker, Francis. "Our Domestic Service." *Scribner's* 11, no.18 (1857): 273.

Walkowitz, Daniel J. "Working-Class Women in the Gilded Age: Factory, Community, and Family Life among Cohoes, New York, Cotton Workers." *Journal of Social History* 5, no. 49 (1972): 464–90.

Walsh, James J. "Mother Xavier Mehegan and Her Work." *Catholic World* 121, no. 725 (1925): 624–32.

West, Mary Allen. "Domestic Service." *Our Day* 4, no. 3 (1889): 401–15.

Westoff, Charles F., and Larry Bumpass. "Revolution in Birth Control Practices of United States Roman Catholics." *Science* 179 (January 1973).

White, P. L. "An Irish Immigrant Housewife on the New York Frontier." *New York History* 48 (1967).

Willett, Mable Hurd. *The Employment of Women in the Clothing Trades*. New York: Columbia University Press, 1902.

Williams, Blaine T. "The Frontier Family." In *Essays on the American West*, edited by Harold M. Hollingsworth and Sandra L. Myers. Austin: The University of Texas Press, 1969.

Wolfe, Albert Benedict. *The Lodging House Problem in Boston*. Cambridge, Massachusetts: Harvard University Press, 1913.

Women's Educational and Industrial Union Papers. "Immigrant Women and Girls in Boston: A Report." Schlesinger Library, Radcliffe College, Cambridge, Massachusetts, 1907, box 7, folder 49.

———. "Industrial Opportunities for Women in Cambridge, 1910." Schlesinger Library, Radcliffe College, Cambridge, Massachusetts, box 7, no. 15.

Wood, Rev. Thomas O. "The Catholic Attitude toward the Social Settlement Movement: 1886–1914." Master's thesis, University of Notre Dame, 1958.

Woods, Caroline H. *Women in Prison*. New York: Hurd and Houghton, 1869.

Woods, Robert A., and Albert J. Kennedy. *Young Working Girls: A Summary of Evidence from Two Thousand Social Workers*. Boston: Houghton Mifflin, 1913.

"Working Women in Chicago." *Seventh Biennial Report of the Bureau of Labor Statistics, 1892*. Springfield, Illinois: H. W. Rokker, 1893.

Wright, Carroll D. *The Working Girls of Boston*. Boston: Wright and Potter, 1889.

Wright, D. M. "The Making of Cosmopolitan California: An Analysis of Immigration, 1848–1870." *California History Society Quarterly* 70 (1940): 323–43.

Wyman, Lillie B. Chance. "Studies of Factory Life; Among the Women." *Atlantic Monthly* 62, no. 371 (1881): 315–21.

12. Writers, Literature, Criticism

Adams, R. "Irishman on Thoreau: A Stillborn of Walden." *New England Quarterly* 13 (December 1940): 697–99.

Adelman, M. "The Irish Observed: E. O'Connor's Novels." *Furrow* 2 (December 1961): 718–24.

Adelson, Ann. *The Little Conquerors.* New York: Random, 1960.

Alexander, Doris. *The Tempting of Eugene O'Neill.* New York: Harcourt, Brace and World, 1962.

Alfred, William. *Hogan's Goat.* New York: Farrar, Straus and Giroux, 1966.

Allen, Joan M. *Candles and Carnival Lights: The Catholic Sensibility of F. Scott Fitzgerald.* New York: New York University Press, 1975.

Antush, J. V. "Realism in the Catholic Novel." *Catholic World* 185 (July 1958): 267–79.

Appell, John J. "From Shanties to Lace Curtains: The Irish Image in Puck, 1876–1910." *Comparative Studies in Society and History* 13 (October 1971): 365–75.

Apseloff, Stanford S. *James T. Farrell: A Visit to Chicago.* Kent, Ohio: Kent State University Libraries, 1969.

Asch, Sholem. *East River.* New York: Putnam, 1946.

Asinof, Eliot. "Some Oedipus, Some Danny Boy." *The New York Times Book Review.* November 29, 1977. A review of *Flesh and Blood* by Pete Hamill.

Barthel, Joan. "Real Story, Dialogue added." *The New York Times Book Review.* November 29, 1977. A review of *Closing Time* by Lacy Fosburgh.

Beach, Joseph Warren. "James T. Farrell: The Plight of the Children." In *American Fiction 1920–1940.* New York: Macmillan, 1941.

———. "James T. Farrell: Tragedy of the Poolroom Loafer." In *American Fiction 1920–1940.* New York: Macmillan, 1941.

Beckley, Zoe. *A Chance to Live.* New York: Macmillan, 1918.

Beer, Thomas. *The Mauve Decade.* New York: Knopf, 1926.

Bennett, J. "Irish Music for Pentecost." *Catholic Digest* 32 (June 1968): 108–12.

Berlin, Ellin MacKay. *The Best of Families.* Greenwich, Connecticut: Fawcett, 1970.

———. *Lace Curtain.* Garden City, New York: Doubleday, 1948.

———. *Land I Have Chosen.* Garden City, New York: Doubleday, Doran, 1944.

Betts, J. R. "The Negro and the New England Conscience in the Days of John Boyle O'Reilly." *Journal of Negro History* 51 (October, 1966): 246–61.

Blake, Mary Elizabeth. *In The Harbour of Hope.* Boston: Little, Brown, 1907.

Blanc, Robert E. *James McHenry (1785–1845), Playwright and Novelist.* Philadelphia: University of Pennsylvania Press, 1939.

Bleakley, Sister M. Alcuin. "Clerical Norms in the Work of J. F. Powers." Master's thesis, University of Notre Dame, 1967.

Bledsoe, Thomas. "John Boyle O'Reilly: Poet-Prophet of Democracy." *Crisis* 52 (January 1945): 18–19.

Bogard, Travis. *Contour in Time: The Plays of Eugene O'Neill.* New York: Oxford University Press, 1972.

Bolger, Stephan Garrett. *The Irish Character in American Fiction, 1830–1860.* New York: Ayer Company, 1976.

———. "The Irish Character in American Fiction, 1830–1860." Ph.D. dissertation, University of Pennsylvania, 1971.

Boucicault, Dion. *Andy Blake; Or, The Irish Diamond*. New York: French, 1856.

———. *Arrah-na-poque, or the Wicklow Wedding: An Irish Drama in Three Acts*. Chicago: Dramatic, n.d.

———. *The Colleen Bawn; or, The Brides of Garry Owen*. New York: French, n.d.

———. *The Irish Heiress*. London: Andrews, 1842.

———. *The O'Dowd*. New York: French, 1909.

———. *The Poor of New York: A Drama in Five Acts*. New York: French, 1857.

———. *The Shaugram: An Original Drama in Three Acts Illustrative of Irish Life and Character*. London: Dicks, n.d.

———. *The Streets of New York*. Chicago: Dramatic, n.d.

———. *The Wearing of the Green*. New York: Happy Hours, n.d.

———. *West End; or, The Irish Heiress*. New York: n.d.

Bowen, Corswell, and Shane O'Neill. *The Curse of the Misbegotten: A Tale of the House of O'Neill*. New York: McGraw-Hill, 1959.

Boyce, Rev. John [pseudo. Paul Peppergrass]. *Mary Lee, Or The Yankee in Ireland*. Baltimore: Patrick Donahoe, 1860.

———. *Shandy McGuire, Or Tricks Upon Travellers Being a Story of the North of Ireland*. New York: Edward Dunigan and Brothers, 1851.

———. *The Spaewife, Or the Queen's Secret; A Story of the Reign of Queen Elizabeth*. 2 vols. Baltimore: Murphy, 1853.

Bradsher, Earl J. *Mathew Carey: A Study in American Literary Development*. New York: Columbia University Press, 1912.

———. *Mathew Carey: Editor, Author, Publisher*. New York: Columbia University Press, 1912.

Branch, Edgar M. "American Writer in the Twenties: James T. Farrell and the University of Chicago." *American Book Collector* 11 (Summer 1961): 25–32.

———. "Freedom and Determinism in James T. Farrell's Fiction." In *Essays on Determinism in American Literature*, edited by Sydney J. Krause. Kent, Ohio: Kent State University Press, 1964.

———. *James T. Farrell*. Minneapolis: University of Minnesota Press, 1963. University of Minnesota Pamphlets on American Writers, no. 29. Reprinted in *Seven Novelists in the American Naturalist Tradition*, edited by C. C. Walcutt. Minneapolis: University of Minnesota Press, 1974.

———. *James T. Farrell*. New York: Twayne, 1971.

Breslin, Howard. *Let Go of Yesterday*. New York: Whittlesey, 1950.

Breslin, Jimmy. *Can't Anyone Here Play This Game*. New York: Ballantine Books, 1970.

———. *Forsaking All Others*. New York: Fawcett Book Group, 1983.

———. *The Gang that Couldn't Shoot Straight*. New York: Viking, 1969.

———. *He Got Hungry and Forgot His Manners*. New York: Ticknor and Fields, 1988.

———. "Kennedy, Eugene. Day with Jimmy Breslin." *Critic* 33 (October–November, 1974): 18–29.

———. *Table Money*. New York: Ticknor and Fields, 1987.

———. *The World According to Breslin*. New York: McGraw-Hill, 1985.

———. *World Without End, Amen*. New York: Viking, 1973.

Breslin, Jimmy, and Dick Schaap. *.44: A Novel*. New York: New American Library, 1979.

Brinig, Myron. *Copper City*. London: Dobden-Sanderson, 1931.

———. *Footsteps on the Stair*. New York: Rinehart, 1950.

———. *Wide-Open Town*. New York: Farrar, 1931. Reprinted in New York: Farrar, Rinehart, 1950.

Brougham, John. *The Fine Ould Irish Gentleman*. Boston, Reed, 1845.

———. *Humorous Stories*. New York: Derby and Jackson, 1858.

———. *The Irish Emigrant*. London: Lacy, 1869.

———. *The Irish Yankee, Or, the Birthday of Freedom*. New York: French, 1856.

———. *Life in New York; or Tom and Jerry on a Visit.* New York: French, 1856.

———. *Life, Stories and Poems of John Brougham.* Boston: Osgood, 1881.

———. *The Lottery of Life: A Story of New York.* New York: Munro, 1885.

———. *Temptation; or, The Irish Emigrant.* New York: French, 1856.

Brown, Alice. *Louise Imogen Guiney.* New York: Macmillan, 1921.

Brown, Stephen J. *Ireland in Fiction: A Guide to Irish Novels, Tales, Romances, And Folklore.* New York: Barnes and Noble, 1969.

Browne, Joseph. "The Greening of America: Irish-American Writers." *Journal of Ethnic Studies* 2, no. 4 (Winter 1975): 71–76.

———. "John O'Hara and Tom McHale: How Green is Their Valley?" In *Irish-American Fiction: Essays in Criticism*, edited by Daniel J. Casey and Robert E. Rhodes. New York: AMS, 1979.

Browning, Preston M., Jr. *Flannery O'Connor.* Carbondale: Illinois University Press, 1974.

Brownson, Orestes A. *The Foreigner in America: A Comic in Four Acts.* Dubuque, Iowa: Author, 1870.

Brucolli, Matthew J. *The Composition of Tender is the Night: A Study of the Manuscripts.* Pittsburgh: University of Pittsburgh Press, 1963.

———. *F. Scott Fitzgerald: A Descriptive Bibliography.* Pittsburgh: University of Pittsburgh Press, 1972.

———. *John O'Hara : A Checklist.* New York: Random House, 1975.

———. *The O'Hara Concern: A Biography of John O'Hara.* New York: Random House, 1975.

Brucolli, Matthew J., and Jackson R. Bryer, eds. *F. Scott Fitzgerald in His Own Time: A Miscellany.* Kent, Ohio: Kent State University Press, 1971.

Bryer, Jackson R. *The Critical Reputation of F. Scott Fitzgerald: A Bibliographical Study.* Hamden, Connecticut: Archon Books, 1967.

———. "F. Scott Fitzgerald." In *Sixteen Modern Authors: A Survey of Research and Criticism*, edited by Jackson R. Bryer. New York: W. W. Norton, 1973.

Buckley, F. "Thoreau and the Irish." *New England Quarterly* 13 (September 1940): 389–400.

Bugg, Lelia Hardin. *Orchids.* St. Louis, Missouri: Herder, 1894.

———. *People of Our Parish.* Boston: Marlier, 1900.

———. *The Prodigal's Daughter.* New York: Benziger, 1898.

———. *The Varsity Story.* New York: Macmillan, 1948.

Butler, Robert James. "Christian and Pragmatic Visions of Time in the Lonigan Trilogy." *Thought* 55 (December 1980): 461–75.

———. "The Christian Roots of Farrell's O'Neill and Carr Novels." *Renascence* 34 (1982): 81–97.

———. "Parks, Parties and Pragmatism: Time and Setting in James T. Farrell's Major Novels." *Essays in Literature* 10 (Fall 1983): 241–54.

Byrne, Robert. *Memories of a Non-Jewish Childhood.* New York: L. Stuart, 1970.

———. *The Tunnel.* New York: Harcourt, Brace, Jovanovich, 1977.

———. *Writing Rackets.* New York: L. Stuart, 1969.

Callaghan, Morley. *Such Is My Beloved.* New York: Charles Scribner's Sons, 1934.

Callahan, John F. *The Illusions of a Nation: Myth and History in the Novels of F. Scott Fitzgerald.* Urbana, Illinois: University of Illinois Press, 1972.

Carey, Mathew. *Autobiographical Sketches: Letters (1–28) To the Editor of the New England Magazine.* Philadelphia, Pennsylvania, 1833–35.

———. *Autbiography.* Brooklyn, New York: E. L. Schwab, 1942.

———. *Vindici Hibernica: Ireland Vindicated: An Attempt to Develop and Expose a Few of the Multifarious Errors and Falsehoods Respecting Ireland.* Philadelphia: M. Carey, 1826.

Cargill, Oscar, ed. *O'Neill and His Plays: Four Decades of Criticism.* New York: New York University Press, 1961.

Carpenter, Frederick Ives. *Eugene O'Neill.* New York: Twayne, 1964.

Carroll, James. *Fault Lines*. Boston: Little, Brown, 1980.

———. *Firebird*. New York: New American Library, 1988.

———. *Madonna Red*. New York, 1987.

———. *Mortal Friends*. Boston: Little, Brown, 1978.

———. *Prince of Peace*. Boston: Little, Brown, 1984.

———. *Seventeen Commandments Not from Heaven but Earth*. New York: National Paperback Books, 1985.

———. *Supply of Heroes*. New York: E. P. Dutton, 1986.

Carroll, Martin Clement. *Behind the Lighthouse: The Australian Sojourn of John Boyle O'Reilly*. Ann Arbor, Michigan: University Microfilmm. 1955.

Carson, Edward R. *The Fiction of John O'Hara*. Pittsburgh: University of Pittsburgh Press, 1961.

Casey, Daniel J. "Heresy in the Diocese of Brooklyn: An Unholy Trinity." In *Irish-American Fiction: Essays in Criticism*, edited by Daniel J. Casey and Robert E. Rhodes. New York: AMS Press, 1979.

Casey, Daniel J., and Robert E. Rhodes, eds. *Irish-American Fiction: Essays in Criticism*. New York: AMS Press, 1979.

Casey, John. *Spartina*. New York: Knopf, 1989.

Clark, Barrett Harper. *Eugene O'Neill: The Man and His Plays*. New York: McBridge, 1936.

Clarke, Joseph I.C. *Luck: A Comedy in Three Acts*. New York: De Lacy and Willson, 1877.

———. *The Fighting Race, and Other Poems and Ballads*. New York: American News, 1911.

———. *Lady Godiva: A Play in Four Acts*. New York: French, 1902.

———. *Malmorda: A Metrical Romance*. New York: Putnam, 1893.

———. *New York at Antietam*. New York, 1920.

———. *Robert Emmet: A Tragedy of Irish History*. New York: Putnam, 1888.

———. *A Woman's Duel: Drama in Four Acts*. New York: n.p., n.d. (circa 1900).

Clary, James Mansfield, ed. *The Nebraska of Kate McPhelim Cleary*. Lake Bluff, Illinois: United Educators, 1958.

Cleary, James Masfield, ed. *Proud We Are Irish: Irish Culture and History as Dramatized in Verse and Song*. Chicago: Quadrangle, 1966.

Cleary, Kate. *Like a Gallant Lady*. Chicago: Way and Williams, 1897.

Clemens, Cyril. "John Boyle O'Reilly: Neglected New England Poet." *Poet Lore* 54 (Winter 1948): 361–72.

Colby, Frances Bainbridge. *The Black Winds Blow*. New York: Harrison-Hilton Books, 1940.

Connell, R. E. "Citizen of the Democracy of Literature." *Catholic World* 65 (September 1897): 751–59.

Connolly, James B. *Between Shipmates*. Ormond Beach, Florida: George A. Zabriskie, The Doldrums, 1953.

———. *The Book of the Gloucester Fishermen*. New York: John Day, 1927.

———. *Coaster Captain: A Tale of the Boston Waterfront*. New York: Macy-Masius, 1927.

———. "Conrad the Writer: An Appreciation of Joseph Conrad." *Columbia* (December 1924): 15–17.

———. *The Crested Seas*. New York: Charles Scribner's Sons, 1907.

———. *The Deep Sea's Toll*. New York: Charles Scribner's Sons, 1905.

———. *Gloucestermen*. New York: Charles Scribner's Sons, 1930.

———. *Hiker Joy*. New York: Charles Scribner's Sons, 1920.

———. *Jeb Hutton: The Story of a Georgia Boy*. New York: Charles Scribner's Sons, 1902.

———. "The Literary Ballyhoo." *Columbia* 11 (March 1932): 14–15.

———. *An Olympic Victor: A Story of the Modern Games*. New York: Charles Scribner's Sons, 1908. Simultaneous publication in Scribner's 44 (July 1908): 18–31; (August 1908): 205–17; (September 1908): 357–70.

———. *Open Water*. New York: Charles Scribner's Sons, 1910.

———. *Out of Gloucester*. New York: Charles Scribner's Sons, 1902.

———. *Running Free*. New York: Charles Scribner's Sons, 1917.

———. *Sea-borne: Thirty Years Avoyaging*. Garden City: Doubleday, Doran, 1944.

———. *The Seiners*. New York: Charles Scribner's Sons, 1904.

———. *Sonnie Boy's People*. New York: Charles Scribner's Sons, 1913.

———. *Steel Decks*. New York: Charles Scribner's Sons, 1925.

———. *A Tale of the Sea*. Boston: Boston Seaman's Friend Society, n.d.

———. *Tide Rips*. New York: Charles Scribner's Sons, 1922.

———. *The Trawler*. New York: Charles Scribner's Sons, 1914.

———. *On Tybee Knoll: A Story of the Georgia Coast*. New York: A. S. Barnes, 1905.

———. *Wide Courses*. New York: Charles Scribner's Sons, 1912.

Connolly, Myles. *The Bump on Brannigan's Head*. New York: Macmillan, 1950.

———. *Dan England: The Noonday Devil*. Milwaukee: Bruce, 1951.

———. *Mr. Blue*, n.c.: n.p., 1926. New York: Macmillan, 1928.

———. *The Reason for Ann and Other Stories*. New York: McMullen Books, 1953.

———. *Three Who Ventured*. Philadelphia, Pennsylvania: Lippincott, 1958.

Connors, Margaret E. "Historical and Fictional Stereotypes of the Irish." In *Irish-American Fiction: Essays in Criticism*, edited by Daniel J. Casey and Robert E. Rhodes. New York: AMS Press, 1979.

Conroy, Frank. *Stop-Time*. New York: Viking Press, 1967.

Conroy, Pat. *The Great Santini*. Boston: Houghton Mifflin, 1976.

——— *The Prince of Tides*. Boston: Houghton Mifflin, 1986.

Conway, Katherine E. "John Boyle O'Reilly." *Catholic World* 52 (1891): 117–18.

———. "John Boyle O'Reilly." *Catholic World* 53 (May, 1891): 198–218.

———. *Lalor' Maples*. Boston: Flynn, 1900.

———, ed. *Watchwords from John Boyle O'Reilly*. Boston: Joseph George Cupples, 1891.

Costello, Mark. *The Murphy Stories*. Urbana: University of Illinois Press, 1973.

Crane, Stephen. *George's Mother*. New York, 1896.

———. *Maggie: A Girl of the Street*. New York, 1892.

Cronin, Harry C. *Eugene O'Neill: Irish and American: A Study in Cultural Context*. New York: Arno Press, 1976.

Cross, K. G. W. *F. Scott Fitzgerald*. New York: Grove, 1964.

Cullinan, Elizabeth. *A Change of Scene*. Boston: Curley, distributed by Magna Print, 1982.

———. *House of Gold*. Boston: Houghton Mifflin, 1970.

———. *The Time of Adam*. Boston: Houghton Mifflin, 1971.

———. *Yellow Roses*. New York: Viking, 1977.

Curley, Thomas F. "Catholic Novels and American Culture." *Commentary* 36 (July 1963): 34–42.

———. *It's A Wise Child*. New York: New Author's Guild, 1960.

———. *Nowhere Man*. New York: Holt, Rinehart and Winston, 1967.

———. *Past Eve and Adam's*. New York: Atheneum, 1962.

Curran, Joseph M. *Hibernian Green and the Silver Screen: The Irish and American Movies*. New York: Greenwood Press, 1989.

Curran, Mary Doyle. *The Parish and the Hill*. Boston: Houghton Mifflin, 1948.

Currie, Ellen. *Available Light*. New York: Washington Square Press, n.d.

Davis, Dorothy S. *Men of No Property*. New York: Charles Scribner's Sons, 1956.

Day, James M. *Paul Horgan*. Austin, Texas: Steck-Vaughn, 1967.

Deasy, Mary. *The Boy Who Made Good*. Boston: Little, Brown, 1955.

———. *Cannon Hill*. Boston: Little, Brown, 1949.

———. *The Celebration.* New York: Random House, 1963.

———. *The Corioli Affair.* Boston: Little, Brown, 1954.

———. *Devil's Bridge.* Boston: Little, Brown, 1952.

———. *Ella Gunning.* Boston: Little, Brown, 1950.

———. *The Hour of Spring.* Boston: Little, Brown, 1948.

———. *O'Shaugnessy's Day.* Garden City: Doubleday, 1957.

Degnan, James P. "J. F. Powers: Comic Satirist." In *Irish-American Fiction: Essays in Criticism*, edited by Daniel J. Casey and Robert E. Rhodes. New York: AMS Press, 1979.

Dever, Joseph. *A Certain Widow.* Milwaukee: Bruce, 1951.

———. *No Lasting Home.* Milwaukee: Bruce, 1947.

———. *Three Priests.* Garden City: Doubleday, 1958.

Dillon, David. "Priests and Politicians: The Fiction of Edwin O'Connor." In *Irish-American Fiction: Essays in Criticism*, edited by Daniel J. Casey and Robert E. Rhodes. New York: AMS, 1979.

Dineen, Joseph Francis. *The Alternate Case.* Boston: Little, Brown, 1958.

———. *The Anatomy of a Crime.* New York: Charles Scribner's Sons, 1954.

———. *Queen Midas.* Boston: Little, Brown, 1958.

———. *In Sin and Splendor.* New York: R. M. McBride, 1932.

———. *Underworld U.S.A.* New York: Farrar, Strauss and Cudahy, 1956.

———. *Ward Eight.* New York: Harper and Brothers, 1936.

Dolan, Regina. "Mathew Carey: Citizen and Publisher." *American Catholic Historical Society, Records* 65 (June 1954): 116–28.

Donleavy, J. P. *Are You Listening, Rabbi Low?* London: Viking, 1987.

———. *The Beastly Beatitudes of Balthazar B.* New York: Delacorte Press, 1968.

———. *The Destinies of Darcy Dancer: Gentleman.* New York: Delacorte Press/S. Lawrence, 1977.

———. "An Expatriate Looks at America." *Atlantic* 238 (December 1976).

———. *A Fairy Tale of New York.* New York: Delacorte Press/S. Lawrence, 1973.

———. *The Ginger Man.* Paris: Olympia Press, 1955.

———. *Meet My Maker the Mad Molecule.* Boston: Little, Brown, 1964.

———. *The Onion Eaters.* London: Eyre and Spottswoode, 1971.

———. *The Saddest Summer of Samuel S.* New York: Delacorte Press, 1966.

———. *A Singular Man.* Boston: Little, Brown, 1963.

———. *The Unexpurgated Code: A Complete Manual of Survival and Manners.* New York: Delacorte Press/S. Lawrence, 1975.

Donleavy, J. P., and Charles G. Masinton. *J. P. Donleavy: The Style of His Sadness and Humor.* Bowling Green, Ohio: Bowling Green University Popular Press, 1975.

Donnelly, Eleanor C., ed. *Round Table of Representative American Catholic Novelists.* New York: Benziger Brothers, 1896.

Dooley, Roger B. *Days Beyond Recall.* Milwaukee: Bruce, 1949.

———. *Flashback.* Garden City: Doubleday, 1969.

———. *Gone Tomorrow.* Milwaukee: Bruce, 1961.

———. *The House of Shanahan.* Garden City: Doubleday, 1952.

———. *Less Than the Angles.* Milwaukee: Bruce, 1946.

Douglas, Ann. "James T. Farrell: The Artist Militant." *Dissent* (Spring 1980): 214–16.

———. "*Studs Lonigan* and the Failure of History in Mass Society: A Study in Claustrophobia." *American Quarterly* 26 (Winter 1977): 487–505.

Drake, Robert. *Flannery O'Connor: A Critical Essay.* Grand Rapids, Michigan: Eerdmans, 1966.

Driscoll, Charles B. *Kansas Irish.* New York: Macmillan, 1943.

Driskell, Leon V., and Joan T. Britain. *The External Crossroads: The Art of Flannery O'Connor.* Lexington, Kentucky: University Press of Kentucky, 1971.

Drummond, Edward J. "Catholic Criticism in America: Studies of Brownson, Azarias, and Egan with an Essay for Catholic Critics." Ph.D. dissertation, University of Iowa, 1942.

Duggan, George Chester. *The Stage Irishman: A History of the Irish Play and Stage Characters From the Earliest Times.* New York: Blom, 1969.

Dunne, Finley Peter. *Dissertations by Mr. Dooley.* New York: Harper and Brothers, 1906.

———. *Familiar Stories for Children.* New York: Hurst, 1914.

———. *Observations by Mr. Dooley.* New York: R. H. Russell, 1902. Reprinted in New York by Greenwood Press, 1969.

———. *Philosopher Dooley Discourses On Bicycling.* Chicago: n.p., n.d. circa 1896.

———. *Mr. Dooley on the Choice of the Law.* Compiled by Edward J. Bander. Charlottesville, Virginia: Michie, 1963.

———. *Mr. Dooley on the Freedom of the Sieze.* New York: n.p, 1917.

———. *Mr. Dooley in the Hearts of His Countrymen.* Boston: Small, Maynard, 1899.

———. *Mr. Dooley at His Best,* edited by Elmer Ellis. New York: Charles Scribner's Sons, 1938.

———. *Mr. Dooley on Ivrything and Ivrybody.* Selected by Robert Hutchinson. New York: Dover Publications, 1963.

———. *Mr. Dooley: On Making a Will and Other Necessary Evils.* New York: Charles Scribner's Sons, 1919.

———. *Mr. Dooley: Now and Forever, Created by Finlay Peter Dunne.* Selected by Louis Filler. Stanford, California: Academic Reprints, 1954.

———. *Mr. Dooley in Peace and In War.* Boston: Small, Maynard, 1898. Reprint introduction by Paul Green. Urbana: University of Illinois Press, 1988.

———. *Mr. Dooley Remembers: The Informal Memoirs of Finley Peter Dunne,* edited by Philip Dunne. Boston: Little, Brown, 1963.

———. *Mr. Dooley Says.* New York: Charles Scribner's Sons, 1910.

———. *Mr Dooley on Timely Topics of the Day.* New York: n.p, 1905.

———. *Mr. Dooley's Opinions.* New York: Russell, 1901.

———. *Mr. Dooley's Philosophy.* New York: Russell, 1900.

———. *What Dooley Says.* Chicago: Kazmar, 1899.

Dunne, John Gregory. *Dutch Shea Jr.* New York: Harper, 1984.

———. *Harp.* New York: Simon and Schuster, 1989.

———. *Quintana and Friends.* New York: Washington Square Press, 1988.

———. *Red, White and Blue.* New York: Simon and Schuster, 1987.

———. *Studio.* New York: Limelight Editions, 1985.

———. *True Confessions: A Novel.* New York: E. P. Dutton, 1977.

———. *Vegas.* New York: Random House, 1974.

Dunphy, Jack. *Dear Genius: A Memoir of My Life with Truman Capote.* New York: McGraw-Hill, 1987.

———. *First Wine: A Novel.* Baton Rouge: Louisiana State University Press, 1982.

———. *John Fury: A Novel in Four Parts.* New York: Harper and Brothers, 1946. Reissued Ayer, 1976.

———. *The Murderous McLaughlins.* New York: McGraw-Hill, 1988.

———. *Nightmovers.* New York: Morrow, 1967.

Dyer, Henry Hopper. "James T. Farrell's Studs Lonigan, and Danny O'Neill Novels." Ph.D. dissertation, University of Pennsylvania, 1965.

Earls, Michael S. J. *From Bersabee to Dan: And Other Ballads.* Worcester: Holy Cross College, 1926.

———. *Manuscripts and Memoirs: Chapters in Our Literary Tradition.* Milwaukee: Bruce, 1935.

———. *Marie of the House D'Anters.* New York: Benziger Brothers, 1916.

———. *Melchoir of Boston.* New York: Benziger Brothers, 1910.

———. *Stuore.* New York: Benziger Brothers, 1911.

———. *Under College Towers: A Book of Essays.* New York: Macmillan, 1926.

———. *The Wedding Bells of Glendalough*. New York: Benziger Brothers, 1913.

Eble, Kenneth Eugene. *F. Scott Fitzgerald*. New York: Twayne, 1963.

Egan, Maurice Francis. *The Adventurers*. n. p, 1922.

———. *Belinda: A Story of New York*. H. L. Kilner, 1901.

———. *The Best Stories by the Foremost Catholic Authors*. New York: Benziger Brothers, 1910.

———. *The Boys in the Block*. New York: Benziger Brothers, 1897.

———. *In a Brazilian Forest; and Three Brave Boys*. H. L. Kilner, 1898.

———. *The Chatelaine of the Roses: A Romance of St. Bartholomew's Night, and Other Tales*. H. L. Kilner, 1897.

———. *Commemorative Tribute to Maurice Francis Egan*. American Academy of Arts and Letters, 1924.

———. *On the Construction of Patmore's Odes*, n. p, 1899.

———. *The Corona Readers*. Ginn, 1900.

———. *The Disappearance of John Longworthy*. Office of the Ave Maria, 1890.

———. *The Dream of Gerontius*. Longmans, Green, 1903.

———. *Everybody's Saint Francis*. T. F. Unwin, 1913.

———. *The Flower of the Flock, and The Badgers of Belmont*. New York: Benziger Brothers, 1895.

———. *From the Land of St. Laurence: Sketches of French and American Life*. B. Herder, 1898.

———. *A Garden of Roses: Stories and Sketches*. T. B. Noonan, 1887.

———. *A Gentleman*. New York: Benziger Brothers, 1893.

———. *Irish Literature*. Bigelow, Smith, 1904.

———. *The Ivy Hedge*. New York: Benziger Brothers, 1914.

———. *Jack Chumleigh at Boarding School*. H. L. Kilner, 1899.

———. *Jasper Thorn: A Story of New York Life*. H. L. Kilner, 1897.

———. *Lectures on English Literature*. W. H. Sadlier, 1889.

———. *The Leopard of Lancianus: And Other Stories*. H. L. Kilner, 1898.

———. *Life Around Us*. Pustet, 1921.

———. *The Life Around Us: A Collection of Stories*. F. Pustet, 1885.

———. *The Life and Labors of Pope Leo XIII: With a Summary of His Important Letters, Addresses, and Encyclicals*. Rand McNally, 1903.

———. *A Marriage of Reason*. John Murphy, 1893.

———. *Modern Novels and Novelists*. W. H. Sadlier, 1888.

———. *Onward and Upward: A Year Book Compiled From the Discourses of Bishop Keane*. John Murphy, 1902.

———. *Recollections of a Happy Life*. New York: Doran, 1924.

———. "How Perseus became a star." In *A Round Table of Representative American Catholic Novelists, at Which is Served a Feast of Excellent Stories*. New York: Benziger Brothers, 1897.

———. *Selections from the Prose and Poetry of John Henry Newman*. Houghton, Mifflin, 1907.

———. *Some Pleasant Tales for Boys and Girls*. C. Wildermann, 1898.

———. *Songs and Sonnets*. Dan F. Gillan, 1879.

———. *Songs and Sonnets: And Other Poems*. Benziger Brothers, 1898.

———. *Studies in Literature: Some Words about Chaucer and Other Essays*. B. Herder, 1899.

———. *The Success of Patrick Desmond*. Office of the Ave Maria, 1893.

———. *The Vocation of Edward Conway*. Benziger Brothers, 1896.

———. *The Watson Girls: A Washington Story*. H. L. Kilner, 1900.

———. *The Watsons of the Country*. H. L. Milner, 1909.

———. *The Wiles of Sexton Maginnis*. Century, 1909.

Eggenschwiler, David. *The Christian Humanism of Flannery O'Connor*. Detroit, Michigan: Wayne State University Press, 1972.

Ellis, Elmer. *Mr. Dooley's America: A Life

of Finley Peter Dunne. Hamden, Connecticut: Archon Books, 1941.

Engle, Edwin A. *The Haunted Heroes of Eugene O'Neill*. Cambridge, Massachusetts: Harvard University Press, 1953.

Falk, Doris A. *Eugene O'Neill and the Tragic Tension: An Interpretative Study of the Plays*. New Brunswick, New Jersey: Rutgers University Press, 1958.

Fanning, Charles. "Finley Peter Dunne and Irish-American Realism." In *Irish-American Fiction: Essays in Criticism*, edited by Daniel J. Casey and Robert E. Rhodes. New York: AMS Press, 1979.

———. *Finley Peter Dunne and Mr. Dooley: The Chicago Years*. Lexington: University Press of Kentucky, 1978.

———. "The Literary Dimension." In *The Irish in Chicago*, edited by Lawrence J. McCaffrey, et al. Urbana and Chicago: University of Illinois Press, 1987.

———, ed. *Mr. Dooley and the Chicago Irish: The Autobiography of a Nineteenth-Century Ethnic Group*. New York: Arno Press, 1976. Reprint The Catholic University Press of America, 1987.

———, ed. *The Exiles of Erin: Nineteenth-Century Irish-American Fiction*. Notre Dame: University of Notre Dame Press, 1989.

Fanning, Charles, and Ellen Skerrett. "James T. Farrell and Washington Park." *Chicago History* 7, no. 2 (Summer 1979): 80–91.

Farr, Finis. *O'Hara: A Biography*. Boston: Little, Brown, 1973.

Farrell, James T. *An American Dream Girl*. New York: Vanguard, 1950.

———. *Bernard Clare*. New York: Vanguard, 1946.

———. *Boarding House Blues*. New York: Paperback Library, 1961.

———. *A Brand New Life*. Garden City, New York: Doubleday, 1968.

———. *Calico Shoes and Other Stories*. New York: Vanguard, 1934.

———. *Can All This Grandeur Perish?* New York: Vanguard, 1937.

———. *Can All This Grandeur Perish? And Other Stories*. New York: Vanguard, 1937.

———. *Childhood Is Not Forever*. Garden City, New York: Doubleday, 1969.

———. *A Dangerous Woman: And Other Stories*. New York: Vanguard, 1957.

———. *The Death of Nora Ryan*. Garden City, New York: Doubleday, 1978.

———. *The Dunne Family*. Garden City: Doubleday, 1976.

———. *Ellen Rogers*. New York: Vanguard, 1941.

———. *The Face of Time*. New York: Vanguard, 1953.

———. *The Fate of Writing in America*. New York: New Directions, 1946.

———. *Father and Son*. New York: Vanguard, 1940. Reprinted by Arno Press, 1976.

———. *French Girls are Vicious: And Other Stories*. New York: Vanguard, 1955.

———. *Gas House McGinty*. New York: Vanguard, 1933.

———. *Guillotine Party and Other Stories*. New York: Vanguard, 1935.

———. *Invisible Swords*. Garden City: Doubleday, 1971.

———. *Judith*. Athens, Ohio: Duane Schneider Press, 1969. Limited to 300 copies.

———. *Judith and Other Stories*. Garden City, New York: Doubleday, 1973.

———. *The League of Frightened Philistines: And Other Papers*. London: Routledge, 1947.

———. *The Life Adventurous: And Other Stories*. New York: Vanguard, 1947.

———. *Literature and Morality*. New York: Vanguard, 1947.

———. *Lonely for the Future*. Garden City, New York: Doubleday, 1966.

———. *A Misunderstanding*. New York: House of Books, 1949.

———. *More Stories*. Garden City, New York: Doubleday, 1946.

———. *My Days of Anger*. New York: Vanguard, 1943.

———. *The Name Is Fogarty: Private Papers on Public Matters*. New York: Vanguard, 1950.

———. *New Year's Eve/1929*. New York: Smith, 1967.

———. *No Star is Lost*. New York: Vanguard, 1938.

———. *Olive and Mary Ann*. New York: Stonehill, 1978.

———. *$1,000 a Week: And Other Stories*. New York: Vanguard, 1942.

———. *Poet of the People: An Evaluation of James Whitcomb Riley (with Jeannette Nolan and Horace Gregory)*. Bloomington: Indiana University Press, 1951.

———. *Reflections at Fifty*. New York: Vanguard, 1954.

———. *Reflections on Literary Criticism*. New York: Vanguard, 1936.

———. *The Road Between*. New York: Vanguard, 1949.

———. *The Short Stories of James T. Farrell*. New York: New American Library, 1946.

———. *The Short Stories of James T. Farrell*. New York: Vanguard, 1937.

———. *Side Street and Other Stories*. New York: Paperback Library, 1961.

———. *The Silence of History*. Garden City, New York: Doubleday, 1963.

———. *Sound of a City*. New York: Paperback Library, 1962.

———. *Studs Lonigan: James T. Farrell's Masterpiece Complete*. New York: Avon Books, 1977.

———. *Studs Lonigan: A Trilogy*. New York: Vanguard, 1935 (*Young Lonigan, The Young Manhood of Studs Lonigan, and Judgement Day*.)

———. *This Man and This Woman*. New York: Vanguard, 1951.

———. *Tommy Gallagher's Crusade*. New York: Vanguard, 1939.

———. *To Whom It May Concern: And Other Stories*. New York: Vanguard, 1944.

———. *What Time Collects*. Garden City, New York: Doubleday, 1964.

———. *When Boyhood Dreams Come True*. New York: Vanguard, 1946.

———. *When Time Was Born*. New York: Smith, 1966.

———. *A World I Never Made*. New York: Vanguard, 1936.

———. *Yet Other Waters*. New York: Vanguard, 1952.

———. *Young Lonigan: A Boyhood in Chicago Streets*. New York: Vanguard, 1932.

Fast, Howard Melvin. *Place in the City*. New York: Harcourt, Brace, 1937.

Fawcett, Edgar. *The Evil That Men Do*. New York: Bedford, 1889.

Feeley, Kathleen. *Flannery O'Connor: Voice of the Peacock*. New Brunswick, New Jersey: Rutgers University Press, 1972.

Finn, B. A. "John Boyle O'Reilly, 1844–1944." *Catholic World* 159 (August, 1944): 410–16.

Fitzgerald, F. Scott. *Afternoon of an Author*. New York: Charles Scribner's Sons, 1957.

———. *Afternoon of an Author: A Selection of Uncollected Stories and Essays*. Introduction and notes by Arthur Mizener. New York: Charles Scribner's Sons, 1958.

———. *All the Sad Young Men*. New York: Charles Scribner's Sons, 1926.

———. *The Apprentice Fiction of F. Scott Fitzgerald*. New Brunswick, New Jersey: Rutgers University Press, 1965.

———. *The Basil and Josephine Stories*. New York: Charles Scribner's Sons, 1973.

———. *The Beautiful and the Damned*. New York: Charles Scribner's Sons, 1922.

———. *Bits of Paradise: 21 Uncollected Stories by F. Scott and Zelda Fitzgerald*. New York: Charles Scribner's Sons, 1974.

———. *Borrowed Time*. London: Grey Walls, 1951.

———. *The Crack-Up*. New York: Laughlin, 1945.

———. *Dear Scott/Dear Max: The Fitzgerald-Perkins Correspondence*. New York: Charles Scribner's Sons, 1971.

———. *The Diamond as Big as the Ritz: And Other Stories*. New York: Editions for the Armed Services, 1941.

———. *Flappers and Philosophers*. New York: Charles Scribner's Sons, 1920.

———. *The Great Gatsby*. New York: Charles Scribner's Sons, 1925.

———. *The Indispensible F. Scott Fitzgerald*. New York: Book Society, 1949.

———. *The Last Tycoon: An Unfinished*

Novel. New York: Charles Scribner's Sons, 1941.

———. *Letters*. New York: Charles Scribner's Sons, 1963.

———. *The Pat Hobby Stories*. New York: Charles Scribner's Sons, 1962.

———. *The Portable F. Scott Fitzgerald*. New York: Viking, 1945.

———. *Scott Fitzgerald: Letters to His Daughter*. New York: Charles Scribner's Sons, 1965.

———. *The Stories of F. Scott Fitzgerald: A Selection of 28 Stories*. Introduction by Malcolm Cowley. New York: Charles Scribner's Sons, 1951.

———. *Tales of Jazz Age*. New York: Charles Scribner's Sons, 1922.

———. *Taps at Reveille*. New York: Charles Scribner's Sons, 1935.

———. *Tender Is the Night*. New York: Charles Scribner's Sons, 1934. With the author's final revisions, edited by Malcolm Cowley. New York: Charles Scribner's Sons, 1951.

———. *This Side of Pardise*. New York: Charles Schribner's Sons, 1920.

———. *The Vegetable: Or, From President to Postman*. New York: Charles Scribner's Sons, 1923.

Fitzgerald, F. Scott, and Andrew Turnbull. *Scott Fitzgerald*. New York: Charles Scribner's Sons, 1962.

Flaherty, Joe. *Fogarty and Company*. New York: Coward, McCann, and Geoghegan, 1973.

———. *Tin Wife*. New York: Simon and Schuster, 1983.

Flanagan, Thomas. *Tenants of Time*. New York: Dutton, 1988.

Fleming, Thomas J. *All Good Men*. Garden City, New York: Doubleday, 1961. Reprinted by Ayer, 1976.

———. *The God of Love*. New York: Doubleday, 1963.

———. *The Good Shepherd*. New York: Doubleday, 1974.

———. *King of the Hill*. New York: New American Library, 1966.

———. *The Officer's Wives*. New York: Doubleday, 1981.

———. *Promises to Keep*. New York: Doubleday, 1978.

———. *Romans, Countrymen and Lovers*. New York: Morrow, 1969.

———. *Rulers of the City*. New York: Doubleday, 1977.

———. *The Sandbox Tree*. New York: Morrow, 1970.

———. *Time and Tide*. New York: Simon & Schuster, 1987.

Floyd, Virginia L. "Eugene O'Neill's 'New England' Cycle—The Yankee Puritan and New England Irish Catholic Elements in Five Autobiographical Plays Of Eugene O'Neill." Ph.D. dissertation, Fordham University, 1971.

Flynn, Dennis, ed. *James T. Farrell: On Irish Themes*. Philadelphia, Pennsylvania: University of Pennsylvania Press, 1982.

Foik, Paul J. "The Beginnings of Irish Catholic Journalism in America." *Catholic Historical Review* 5 (January 1920): 377–81.

———. *Pioneer Catholic Journalism*. New York: United States Catholic Historical Society, 1930.

Frazer, Winifred Dusenbury. *Love as Death in the Iceman Cometh: A Modern Treatment of An Ancient Theme*. Gainsville, Florida: University of Florida Press, 1967.

Fremantle, A. "Four American Catholic Essayists." *Commonweal* 49 (December 10, 1948): 225–28.

Friedman, Melvin J., and Lewis A. Lawson, eds. *The Added Dimension: The Art and Mind of Flannery O'Connor*. New York: Fordham University Press, 1966.

Frohock, William M. "James T. Farrell: The Precise Content." In *The Novel of Violence in America*, 1920–50. Dallas: Southern Methodist University Press, 1958.

Gassner, John. *O'Neill: A Collection of Critical Essays*. Englewood Cliffs, New Jersey: Prentice-Hall, 1964.

Geddes, Virgil. *The Melodramadness of Eugene O'Neill*. Brookfield, Connecticut: Brookfield Players, 1934.

Gelb, Arthur, and Barbara Gelb. *O'Neill*. New York: Harper and Row, 1973.

Gelfant, Blanche H. "James T. Farrell: The Ecological Novel." In *The American City Novel*. Norman: University of Oklahoma Press, 1954.

Gibson, William. *A Mass for the Dead.* New York: Atheneum, 1977.

———. *The Miracle Worker.* New York: Bantam Books, 1977.

Gill, Brendan. *The Day the Money Stopped.* Garden City: Doubleday, 1957.

———. *The Malcontents.* New York: Harcourt, Brace, Jovanovich, 1973.

———. *The Trouble of One House.* Garden City: Doubleday, 1950.

———. *Ways of Loving.* New York: Harcourt, Brace, Jovanovich, 1974.

———, ed. *States of Grace: Eight Plays by Philip Barry.* New York: Harcourt, Brace, Jovanovich, 1975.

Gillilan, Strickland W. *Including Finnegan: A Book of Gillilan Verse.* Chicago: Forbes, 1910.

Gilroy, Frank Daniel. *About Those Roses, or, How Not To Do a Play and Succeed, and the Text of the Subject Was Roses.* New York: Random House, 1965.

Glicksberg, Charles I. "The Criticism of James T. Farrell." *Southwest Review* 35 (Summer 1950): 189–96.

Goldhurst, William. *F. Scott Fitzgerald and His Contemporaries.* Cleveland, Ohio: World, 1963.

Goldstein, David. *My Boston Pilot Column.* Boston: Diocese of Boston, 1952.

Gordon, Mary. *Chase of the Wild Goose: The Story of Lady Eleanor Butler and Miss Sarah Ponsonby.* New York: Ayer, 1975. Reprint of the 1936 edition.

———. *The Company of Women.* New York: Ballantine Books, 1986.

———. *Final Payments.* New York: Random House, 1978.

———. "I Can't Stand Your Books: A Writer Goes Home (Irish-American Literature)." *The New York Times Book Review* (December 11, 1988).

———. *Men and Angels.* New York: Ballantine Books, 1986.

———. *The Other Side.* New York: Grossman, 1989.

———. *Temporary Shelter.* New York: Ballantine Books, 1988.

Grattan, C. Hartley. "James T. Farrell: Moralist." *Harper's* 209 (October 1954): 93–98.

Grebstein, Cheldon N. *John O'Hara.* New York: Twayne, 1966.

Greeley, Andrew M. "The American Irish since the Death of Studs Lonigan." *Critic* 29 (May–June 1971): 27–33.

———. *Ascent into Hell.* New York: Warner Books, 1984.

———. *The Cardinal Sins.* New York: Warner Books, 1984.

———. *Death in April.* New York: Warner Books, 1984.

Gregory, Horace. "James T. Farrell: Beyond the Provinces of Art." *New World Writing: Fifth Mentor Selection.* New York: New American Library, 1954.

Guiney, Louise Imogen. *Blessed Edmund Campion.* Benziger Brothers, 1908.

———. *Brownies and Bogies.* D. Lothrop, 1888.

———. *Carmen.* Boston: Little, Brown, 1896.

———. *Concerning Me and the Metropolis,* n.p, 1896.

———. *The Divine Comedy of Dante Alighieri.* Houghton, Mifflin, 1893.

———. *"England and Yesterday": A Book of Short Poems.* G. Richards, 1898.

———. *Goose-Quill Papers.* Roberts Brothers, 1885.

———. *Happy Ending: The Collected Lyrics of Louise Imogen Guiney.* Houghton, Mifflin, 1909. Reissued in New York: Greenwood Press, 1979.

———. *Hurrell Froude: Memoranda and Comments.* Methuen, 1904.

———. *James Clarence Mangan: His Selected Poems.* Lamson, Wolffe, John Lane, 1897.

———. *Lover's Saint Ruth's and Three Other Tales.* Boston: Copeland and Day, 1894.

———. *The Martyr's Idyl and Shorter Poems.* Boston: Houghton Mifflin, 1900.

———. *The Mount of Olives: And Primitive Holiness Set Forth in the Life of Paulinus: Bishop of Nola.* H. Frowde, 1902.

———. *Patrins.* Boston: Copeland and Day, 1897.

———. *Recusant Poets.* Sheed and Ward, 1939.

———. *Robert Emmet: A Survey of His Rebellion and of His Romance.* D. Nutt, 1904.

———. *Robert Louis Stevenson.* Boston: Copeland and Day, 1895.

———. *The Secret of Fourgereuse: A Romance of the Fifteenth Century.* Marlier, Callanan, 1898.

———. *Some Poems of Lionel Johnson: Newly Selected.* E. Mathews, 1912.

———. *Sonrab and Rustum: And Other Poems.* Houghton, Mifflin, 1899.

———. *Three Heroines of New England Romance.* Little, Brown, 1894.

———. *The White Sail: And Other Poems.* Tichnor, 1887.

———. "Woman in American Literature." *Century Magazine*, 1890.

Guiney, Grace, ed. *Letters of Louis Imogen Guiney.* 2 vols. New York: Harper and Brothers, 1926.

Hackett, Francis. *The Green Lion.* Garden City: Doubleday, Doran, 1936.

———. *That Nice Young Couple.* New York: Boni and Liveright, 1925.

———. *Queen Anne Boleyn.* Garden City: Doubleday, Doran, 1939.

Halliday, Samuel B. *The Little Sweeper or Life Among the Poor.* New York: Phinney, Blakeman and Mason, 1861.

Halpine, Charles G. *Baked Meats of the Funeral.* New York: Carleton, 1866.

———. *The Life and Adventures, Sons, Services and Speeches of Private Myles.* New York: Carleton, 1854.

———. *The Patriot Brothers; or, The Willows of the Golden Vale.* Dublin: n.p, n.d.

Hamill, Pete. *Flesh and Blood.* New York: Random House, 1977.

———. *The Gift.* New York: Random House, 1973.

———. *A Killing For Christ.* New York: New American Library, 1968.

Handlin, Oscar, ed. *Children of the Uprooted.* New York: George Braziller, 1966.

Hendin, Josephine. *The World of Flannery O'Connor.* Bloomington, Indiana: Indiana University Press, 1970.

Higgins, George V. *A City on a Hill.* New York: Knopf, 1975.

———. *Cogan's Trade.* New York: Knopf, 1974.

———. *The Digger's Game.* New York: Knopf, 1973.

———. *Dreamland.* Boston: Little, Brown 1977.

———. *The Friends of Eddie Coyle.* New York: Knopf, 1972.

———. *The Judgement of Deke Hunter.* Boston: Little, Brown, 1976.

Hindus, Milton. *F. Scott Fitzgerald: An Introduction and Interpretation.* New York: Holt, Rinehart and Winston, 1968.

Hogan, Robert Goode. *Dion Boucicault.* New York: Twayne, 1969.

Horgan, Paul. *The Common Heart.* New York: Harper and Brothers, 1942.

———. *The Devil in the Desert.* New York: Longmans, Green, 1952.

———. *A Distant Trumpet.* New York: Farrar, Straus and Cudahy, 1960.

———. *Everything To Live For.* New York: Farrar, Straus and Giroux, 1968.

———. *Far From Cibola.* New York: Harper and Brothers, 1938.

———. *The Fault of Angels.* New York: Harper and Brothers, 1933.

———. *Figures in the Landscape.* New York: Harper and Brothers, 1940.

———. *Give me Possession.* New York: Farrar, Straus and Cudahy, 1957.

———. *A Lamp on the Plains.* New York: Harper and Brothers, 1937.

———. *Lingering Walls.* London: Constable, 1936.

———. *Main Line West.* New York: Harper and Brothers, 1936.

———. *Memories of the Future.* New York: Farrar, Straus and Giroux, 1966.

———. *No Quarter Given.* New York: Harper and Brothers, 1935.

———. *One Red Rose for Christmas.* New York: Longmans, Green, 1952.

———. *The Peach Stone: Stories from Four Decades.* New York: Farrar, Straus and Giroux, 1967.

———. *The Saint-Maker's Christmas.* New York: Farrar, Straus and Cudahy, 1955.

———. *Things as They Are.* New York: Farrar Straus, 1964.

———. *Toby and the Nighttime.* New York: Ariel Books, 1963.

———. *Whitewater.* New York: Farrar, Straus and Giroux, 1970.

Hough, H. B. "Kilkenny Boy." *New Republic* 164 (February 6, 1971).

Howard, Maureen. *Before My Time.* Boston: Little, Brown, 1974.

———. *Bridgeport Bus.* Harcourt, Brace and World, 1965.

———. *Expensive Habits.* New York: Summit Books, 1986.

———. *Facts of Life.* New York: Penguin Books, 1980.

———. *Grace Abounding.* New York: Penguin Books, 1983.

———. *Not a Word about Nightingales.* New York: Penguin Books, 1980.

Howe, Irving. "James T. Farrell-The Critic Calcified." *Partisan Review* 14 (September–October 1947): 545–46.

Huffman, Frederick J. *The Great Gatsby: A Study.* New York: Charles Scribner's Sons, 1962.

Hunt, George W. "William Kennedy's Albany Trilogy." *America* 150 (May 19, 1984).

Hurley, Doran. *Herself: Mrs. Patrick Crowley: A Romantic Tale.* New York: Longmans, Green, 1939.

———. *Monsignor.* New York: Longmans, Green, 1939.

———. *The Old Parish.* New York: Longmans, Green, 1938.

Hurst, Fannie. *God Must Be Sad.* Garden City, New York: Doubleday, 1961.

Irish, Marie, and Willis N. Bugbee. *St. Patrick's Day, Plays and Pieces.* Syracuse, New York: Bugbee, 1932.

Jessup, G. H. *Gerald French's Friends.* New York, 1889.

Kazin, Alfred. *F. Scott Fitzgerald: The Man and His Work.* New York: World, 1951.

———. *On Native Grounds.* New York: Reynal and Hitchcock, 1942.

Keenan, Henry Francis. *The Money Makers: A Social Parable.* New York: Appleton, 1885.

Kennedy, Patrick. *Legendary Fictions of the Irish Celts.* London: Macmillan, 1866.

Kennedy, William. *Billy Phelan's Greatest Game.* New York: Penguin Books, 1983.

———. *Ironweed.* New York: Penguin Books, 1984.

———. *The Ink Truck.* New York: Viking, 1984.

———. *Legs.* New York: Penguin Books, 1983.

———. *Quinn's Book.* New York: Viking, 1988.

Kesey, Ken. *Kesey's Garage Sale.* New York: Viking, 1973.

———. *One Flew over the Cuckoo's Nest.* New York: Viking, 1962.

———. *Sometimes a Great Notion.* New York: Viking, 1962.

La Hood Marvin J., ed. *Tender is the Night: Essays in Criticism.* Bloomington, Indiana: Indiana University Press, 1969.

Latham, Aaron. *Crazy Sundays: F. Scott Fitzgerald in Hollywood.* New York: Viking, 1971.

Lathrop, G. P. "John Boyle O'Reilly as a Poet of Humanity." *Century Magazine* 43, n.s, 21 (December 1891): 313–15.

Laughlin, Clara E. *Just Folks.* New York: Macmillan, 1910.

———. *Travelling through Life.* Boston: Houghton Mifflin, 1934.

Lavin, Mary. *Happiness and Other Stories.* Boston: Houghton Mifflin, 1970.

Lawrence, Elwood P. "The Immigrant in American Fiction, 1890–1920." Ph.D. dissertation, Western Reserve University, 1943.

Leech, Clifford. *Eugene O'Neill.* New York: Grove, 1963.

Lehan, Richard D. *F. Scott Fitzgerald and the Craft of Fiction.* Carbondale, Illinois: Southern Illinois University Press, 1966.

Leslie, Frank. *There's a Spot in My Heart.* New York: Simon & Schuster, 1947.

Lockridge, Ernest. *Twentieth Century Interpretations of the Great Gatsby.* Englewood Cliffs, New Jersey: Prentice-Hall, 1968.

Lovett, Robert Morse. "James T. Farrell." *English Journal* 5 (May 1937): 347–54.

Lucey, Rev. William L., S.J. "Louise Imogen Guiney and Her 'Songs at the Start.'" *Records of the American Catholic Historical Society of Philadelphia* 66 (March 1955): 53–63.

———. "The Record of an American Priest: Michael Earls, S.J., 1873–1937." *The American Ecclesiastical Review* 137 (1957).

Lyman, Kenneth Cox. "Critical Reaction to the Irish Drama on the New York Stage, 1900–1958." Ph.D. dissertation, University of Wisconsin, 1966.

Lynch, William James. "The Theory and Practice of the Literary Criticism of James T. Farrell." Ph.D. dissertation, University of Pennsylvania, 1966.

MacGowen, Michael. *The Hard Road to Klondike*. Translated by Valentin Iremonger. London: Routledge and Kegan Paul, 1962.

Madden, Mary Anne. *See* Mary Anne Sadlier.

Maier, Eugene F. J. "Mathew Carey, Publicist and Politician (1760–1839)." *Records of the American Catholic Historical Society* 39 (1928): 71–154.

Marchand, Margaret. *Pilgrims on the Earth*. New York: Crowell, 1940.

Marcuson, Lewis R. "The Irish, the Italians and the Jews: A Study of Three Nationality Groups as Portrayed in American Drama between 1920 and 1960." Ph.D. dissertation, University of Denver, 1966.

Marriner, Ernest Cummings. *Jim Connolly and the Fishermen of Gloucester: An Appreciation of James Brendan Connolly*. Waterville, Maine: Colby College Press, 1949.

Martin, Carter W. *The True Country: Themes in the Fiction of Flannery O'Connor*. Nashville, Tennessee: Vanderbilt University Press, 1969.

Martin, Clement Carroll. "Behind the Lighthouse: The Australian Sojourn of John Boyle O'Reilly." Ph.D. dissertation, State University of Iowa, 1955.

Masinton, Charles G. *J. P. Dunleavy: The Style of his Sadness and Humor*. Bowling Green, Ohio: Bowling Green University Popular Press, 1977.

Matthews, Brander. *Vignettes of Manhattan*. New York: Harper, 1894.

McCarthy, Mary. *Birds of America*. New York: New American Library, 1971.

———. *Cast a Cold Eye*. New York: Harcourt Brace, 1950.

———. *A Charmed Life*. New York: Harcourt Brace, 1955.

———. *The Company She Keeps*. New York: Simon & Schuster, 1942.

———. *The Group*. New York: Harcourt, Brace, and World, 1963.

———. *The Grove of Academe*. New York: Harcourt Brace, 1952.

———. *How I Grew*. New York: Harcourt Brace Jovanovich, 1988.

———. *Memories of a Catholic Childhood*. New York: Harcourt Brace Jovanovich, 1957. Reissued in 1972.

———. *The Oasis*. New York: Random House, 1949.

———. *Occasional Prose: Essays*. New York: Harcourt Brace Jovanovich, 1985.

———. *A Source of Embarrassment*. London: W. Heinemann, 1950.

———. *Winter Visitors*. New York: Harcourt, Brace, and World, 1970.

McClure, Rev. William J. "Irish-American Poetry." *Illustrated Celtic Monthly* (July 1880): 8–10.

McGarry, Kevin. "Jim Connolly: From Aran to America." *Irish Digest* (1962): 50–53.

McGrath, Harold. *The Adventures of Kathlyn*. Indianapolis: Bobbs-Merrill, 1914.

———. *Arms and the Woman*. New York: Doubleday and McClure, 1899.

———. *The Blue Rajah Murder*. Garden City: Doubleday, Doran, 1930.

———. *Captain Wardlaw's Kitbags*. Garden City: Garden City Publishing, 1923.

———. *The Carpet from Bagdad*. Indianapolis: Bobbs-Merrill, 1911.

———. *The Changing Road*. Garden City: Doubleday, Doran, 1928.

———. *The Drums of Jeopardy*. Garden City: Doubleday, Page, 1920.

———. *Dueces Wild*. Indianapolis: Bobbs-Merrill, 1913.

———. *The Enchanted Hat*. Indianapolis: Bobbs-Merrill, 1908.

———. *The Girl in His House*. New York: Harper and Brothers, 1918.

———. *The Goose Girl*. Indianapolis: Bobbs-Merrill, 1909.

———. *The Green Complex*. Garden City: Doubleday, Doran, 1930.

———. *The Green Stone*. Garden City: Doubleday, Page, 1924.

———. *The Grey Cloak*. Indianapolis: Bobbs-Merrill, 1903.

———. *Half a Rogue*. Indianapolis: Bobbs-Merrill, 1906.

———. *Hearts and Masks*. Indianapolis: Bobbs-Merrill, 1905.

———. *The Luck of the Irish*. New York: Harper and Brothers, 1917.

———. *The Lure of the Mask*. Indianapolis: Bobbs-Merrill, 1908.

———. *The Man on the Box*. Indianapolis: Bobbs-Merrill, 1904.

———. *The Man with Three Names*. Garden City: Doubleday, Page, 1920.

———. *The Million Dollar Mystery*. New York: Grosset and Dunlap, 1915.

———. *The Other Passport*. Garden City: Doubleday, Doran, 1931.

———. *The Pagan Madonna*. Garden City: Doubleday, Page, 1921.

———. *Parrot and Company*. Indianapolis: Bobbs-Merrill, 1913.

———. *Pidgin Island*. Indianapolis: Bobbs-Merrill, 1914.

———. *The Place of Honeymoons*. Indianapolis: Bobbs-Merrill, 1912.

———. *The Princess Elopes*. Indianapolis: Bobbs-Merrill, 1905.

———. *The Puppet Crown*. Indianapolis: Bobbs-Merrill, 1900.

———. *The Ragged Edge*. Garden City: Doubleday, Page, 1922.

———. *A Splendid Hazard*. Indianapolis: Bobbs-Merrill, 1910.

———. *The Sporting Spinster*. Garden City: Doubleday, Page, 1926.

———. *We All Live Through It*. Garden City: Doubleday, Page, 1927.

———. *The World Outside*. Garden City: Doubleday, Page, 1923.

———. *The Voice in the Fog*. Indianapolis: Bobbs-Merrill, 1915.

McGuane, Tom. *The Bushwhacked Piano*. New York: Simon & Schuster, 1971.

———. *Ninety-two in the Shade*. New York: Farrar, Straus and Giroux, 1973.

———. *The Sporting Club*. New York: Simon and Schuster, 1968.

McHale, Tom. *Alinsky's Diamond*. Philadelphia: Lippincott, 1974.

———. *Farragan's Retreat*. New York: Viking, 1971.

———. *The Lady from Boston*. Garden City: Doubleday, 1978.

———. *Principato*. New York: Viking, 1970.

McHenry, James. *The Betrothed of Wyoming*. Philadelphia: n. p., 1830.

———. *The Hearts of Steel*. Philadelphia: A. R. Poole, 1825.

———. *Meredith; or, The Mystery of the Meschianza*. Philadelphia: n.p., 1831.

———. *McHenry's Irish Tales*. Glasgow: Cameron and Ferguson, 1901.

———. *O'Halloran; or, The Insurgent Chief*. Philadelphia: Carey and Lea, 1824.

———. *The Spectre of the Forest; or, The Annals of the Housatonic*. New York: E. Bliss, and E. White, 1823.

———. *The Wilderness; or, Braddock's Times*. New York: E. Bliss, and E. White, 1823.

———. *The Wilderness; or, The Youthful Days of Washington*. London: A. K. Newman, 1823.

McInerney, Ralph. *Gate of Heaven*. New York: Harper and Row, 1975.

———. *Jolly Rogerson*. Garden City: Doubleday, 1967.

———. *The Priest*. New York: Harper and Row, 1973.

———. *Roberson at Bay*. New York: Harper and Row, 1976.

McIntyre, John. *Ashton-Kirk: Criminologist*. Philadelphia: Penn, 1918.

———. *Ashton-Kirk: Investigator*. Philadelphia: Penn, 1910.

———. *Ashton-Kirk: Secret Agent.* Philadelphia: Penn, 1912.

———. *Ashton-Kirk: Special Detective.* Philadelphia: Penn, 1914.

———. *Blowing Weather.* New York: Century, 1923.

———. *The Boy Tars of 1812.* Philadelphia: Penn, 1907.

———. *Drums in the Dawn.* Garden City: Doubleday, Doran, 1932.

———. *Ferment.* New York: Farrar and Rinehart, 1937.

———. *Fighting King George.* Philadelphia: Penn, 1905.

———. *In the Dead of Night.* Philadelphia: J. B. Lippincott, 1908.

———. *In Kentucky with Daniel Boone.* Philadelphia: Penn, 1913.

———. *In the Rockies with Kit Carson.* Philadelphia: Penn, 1913.

———. *In Texas with Davy Crockett.* Philadelphia: Penn, 1914.

———. *The Museum Murder.* Garden City: Doubleday, Doran, 1929.

———. *On the Borders with Andrew Jackson.* Philadelphia: Penn, 1915.

———. *The Ragged Edge: A Tale of Ward Life and Politics.* New York: McClure, Phillips, 1902.

———. *Shot Towers.* New York: Frederick A. Stokes, 1926.

———. *Signing Off.* New York: Farrar and Rinehart, 1938.

———. *"Slag."* New York: Charles Scribner's Sons, 1927.

———. *Stained Sails.* New York: Frederick A. Stokes, 1928.

———. *Steps Going Down.* New York: Farrar and Rinehart, 1936.

———. *The Street Singer.* Philadelphia: Penn, 1908.

———. *With John Paul Jones.* Philadelphia: Penn, 1906.

———. *The Young Continentals at Bunker Hill.* Philadelphia: Penn, 1910.

———. *The Young Continentals at Lexington.* Philadelphia: Penn, 1909.

———. *The Young Continentals at Monmouth.* Philadelphia: Penn, 1912.

———. *The Young Continentals at Trenton.* Philadelphia: Penn, 1911.

———. *A Young Man's Fancy.* New York: Frederick A. Stokes, 1925.

———. *Young Patriots at Lexington.* New York: Hearthstone, 1949.

McKenney, Ruth. *All About Eileen.* New York: Harcourt, Brace, 1952.

———. *Jake Home.* New York: Harcourt, Brace, 1943.

———. *The Loud Red Patrick.* New York: Harcourt, Brace, 1947.

———. *Love Story.* New York: Harcourt, Brace, 1950.

———. *The McKenneys Carry On.* New York: Harcourt, Brace, 1940.

———. *Mirage* New York: Farrar, Straus and Cudahy, 1950.

———. *My Sister Eileen.* New York: Harcourt, Brace, 1938.

McMurtry, Larry. *All My Friends are Going to Be Strangers.* New York: Simon & Schuster, 1972.

———. *Horseman, Pass By.* New York: Harper, 1961.

———. *The Last Picture Show.* New York: Dial Press, 1966.

———. *Leaving Cheyenne.* New York: Harper and Row, 1963.

———. *Lonesome Dove.* New York: Simon & Schuster, 1980.

———. *Moving On.* New York: Simon & Schuster, 1970.

———. *Terms of Endearment.* New York: Simon & Schuster, 1975.

McNamara, Edward. *Once Over Deadly.* New York: Abelard-Schuman, 1958.

——— (as Ward Thomas). *Stranger in the Land.* Boston: Houghton Mifflin, 1949.

———. *A Waste of Shame.* New York: Vanguard, 1967.

McKenzie, Barbara. *Mary McCarthy.* New York: Twayne, 1966.

McManamin, Rev. Francis G., S.J. *The American Years of John Boyle O'Reilly, 1870–1890.* New York: Arno, 1976.

McSorley, Edward. *Kitty, I Hardley Knew You.* Garden City, New York: Doubleday, 1959.

———. *Our Own Kind*. New York: Harper, 1946.

———. *The Young McDermott*. New York: Harper, 1949.

Meade, James. *Up The Republic! A Novel of the Irish Easter Rebellion*. New York: Exposition, 1952.

Meehan, Thomas F. "Catholic Literary New York, 1800–1840." *Catholic Historical Review* (1918): 399–414.

Mehling, Rev. Theodore John. "The Letters of Louise Imogen Guiney to Reverend Daniel E. Hudson, C.S.C." Master's thesis, University of Notre Dame, 1935.

Meline, Mary Miller. *Charteris: A Romance*. Philadelphia: J. B. Lippincott, 1968.

———. *In Six Months; or, The Two Friends*. Kelly, Piet, 1874.

———. *Mobrays and the Harringtons: A Novel of American Life*. Baltimore: Baltimore, 1884.

———. *The Montarges Legacy: A Tale*. P. F. Cunningham, 1970,

Merrill, William S. *Catholic Archbishop in American Colonies Before 1774*. Washington, D.C.: The Catholic University of America Press, 1917.

Messbarger, Paul R. "American Catholic Dialogue, 1884–1900: A Study of Catholic Fiction." Ph.D. dissertation, University of Minnesota, 1969.

———. *Fiction with a Parochial Purpose: Social Uses of American Catholic Literature, 1884–1900*. Boston: Boston University Press, 1971.

Miller, James E. *F. Scott Fitzgerald: His Art and His Technique*. New York: New York University Press, 1964.

Miller, Jordan Yale. *Eugene O'Neill and the American Critic: A Bibliographical Checklist*. Hamden, Connecticut: Archon, 1974.

———. *Playwright's Progress: O'Neill and the Critics*. Chicago: Scott Foresman, 1965.

———. *Twentieth Century Interpretations of the Iceman Cometh: A Collection of Critical Essays*. Engelwood Cliffs, New Jersey: Prentice-Hall, 1968.

Miller, Wayne Charles, ed. *A Gathering of Ghetto Writers, Irish, Italian, Jewish, Black, and Puerto Rican*. New York: New York University Press, 1972.

Miller, William D. *A Harsh and Dreadful Love*. New York: Liveright, 1973.

Mitchell, Richard. "Studs Lonigan: Research in Morality." *Centennial Review* 6 (Spring 1962): 202–14.

Mizeher, Arthur, ed. *F. Scott Fitzgerald: A Collection of Critical Essays*. Englewood Cliffs, New Jersey: Prentice-Hall, 1963.

Morgan, Al. *Minor Miracle*. New York: Dodd and Mead, 1961.

Muller, Gilbert J. *Nightmares and Visions: Flannery O'Connor and the Catholic Grotesque*. Athens, Georgia: University of Georgia Press, 1972.

Murphy, Clyde F. *The Glittering Hill*. Cleveland, Ohio: World, 1944.

Murphy, Maureen. "Elizabeth Cullinan: Yellow and Gold." In *Irish-American Fiction: Essays in Criticism*, edited by Daniel J. Casey and Robert E. Rhodes. New York: AMS Press, 1979.

Norstedt, Johann A. "Irishmen and Irish-Americans in the Fiction of J. P. Dunleavy." In *Irish-American Fiction: Essays in Criticism*, edited by Daniel J. Casey and Robert E. Rhodes. New York: AMS Press, 1979.

O'Brien, Darcy. *The Silver Spooner*. New York: Simon and Schuster, 1981.

———. *A Way of Life, Like Any Other*. New York: Norton, 1977.

O'Brien, Fitz-James. *Collected Stories*, edited by Edward J. O'Brien. New York: A and C Boni, 1925.

———. *The Diamond Lens*. Philadelphia: H. Altemus, 1909.

———. *The Diamond Lens with Other Stories*. Ed. William Winter. New York: Charles Scribner's Sons, 1855.

———. *What Was It? And Other Stories*. London: Ward, and Downey, 1889.

O'Connell, Barry. "The Lost World of James T. Farrell's Short Stories." In *Irish-American Fiction: Essays in Criticism*, Daniel J. Casey and Robert E. Rhodes. New York: AMS Press, 1979.

O'Connor, Edwin. *All in the Family*. Boston, 1966.

———. *Benjy: A Ferocious Fairy Tale*. Boston: Little, Brown, 1957.

———. *The Best and the Last of Edwin O'Connor.* Ed. Arthur Schlesinger, Jr. Boston: Little, Brown, 1970.

———. *The Edge of Sadness.* Boston: Little, Brown, 1961.

———. *I Was Dancing.* Boston, 1964.

———. *The Last Hurrah.* Boston: Little, Brown, 1956.

———. *The Oracle.* New York: Harper and Row, 1951.

O'Connor, Flannery. *The Complete Stories.* New York: Farrar, Straus and Giroux, 1971.

———. *Everything That Rises Must Converge.* New York: Farrar, Straus and Giroux, 1971.

———. *A Good Man is Hard to Find, and Other Stories.* New York: Harcourt, 1955.

———. *Mystery and Manners.* New York: Farrar, Straus, and Giroux, 1969.

———. *The Violent Bear It Away.* New York: Farrar, Straus, and Giroux, 1960.

———. *Wise Blood.* New York: Farrar, Straus & Giroux, 1962.

O'Gadhra, Nollaig. *John Boyle O'Reilly.* Dublin, 1976.

O'Hara, John. *All the Girls He Wanted: And Other Stories.* New York: Avon, 1950.

———. *And Other Stories.* New York: Random House, 1968.

———. *Appointment in Samarra.* New York: Harcourt, Brace, 1934.

———. *Assembly.* New York: Random House, 1961.

———. *The Big Laugh.* New York: Random House, 1962.

———. *Butterfield 8.* New York: Harcourt, Brace, 1935.

———. *The Cape Cod Lighter.* New York: Random House, 1962.

———. *The Doctor's Son: And Other Stories.* New York: Harcourt, Brace, 1935.

———. *Elizabeth Appleton.* New York: Random House, 1963.

———. *The Ewings.* New York: Random House, 1972.

———. *A Family Party.* New York: Random House, 1956.

———. *The Farmer's Hotel.* New York: Random House, 1951.

———. *Files on Parade.* New York: Harcourt, Brace, 1939.

———. *Five Plays.* New York: Random House, 1961.

———. *From the Terrace.* New York: Random House, 1958.

———. *Good Samaritan: And Other Stories.* New York: Random House, 1974.

———. *The Hat on the Bed.* New York: Random House, 1963.

———. *Hellbox.* New York: Random House, 1947.

———. *Here's O'Hara: Three Novels and Twenty Short Stories.* New York: Duell, Sloan, and Pearce, 1946.

———. *Hope of Heaven.* New York: Harcourt, Brace, 1938.

———. *The Horse Knows the Way.* New York: Random House, 1964.

———. *The Instrument.* New York: Random House, 1967.

———. *The Lockwood Concern.* New York: Random House, 1965.

———. *Lovey Childs: A Philadelphian's Story.* New York: Random House, 1969.

———. *Ourselves to Know.* New York: Random House, 1960.

———. *Pal Joey.* New York: Duell, Sloan, and Pearce, 1940.

———. *Pipe Night.* New York: Duell, Sloan, and Pearce, 1945.

———. *A Rage to Live.* New York: Random House, 1949.

———. *Sermons and Soda Water.* New York: Random House, 1960.

———. *Ten North Frederick.* New York: Random House, 1955.

———. *The Time Element: And Other Stories.* New York: Random House, 1972.

———. *Waiting for Winter.* New York: Random House, 1966.

O'Malley, Frank. "James T. Farrell." In *Fifty Years of the American Novel: A Christian Appraisal*, edited by Harold C. Gardiner. New York: Charles Scribner's Sons, 1951.

O'Meara, Walter. *The Grand Portage.* Indianapolis: Bobbs-Merrill, 1951.

O'Neal, Charles. *The Three Wishes of Jamie McRuin*. New York, 1949.

O'Neill, Eugene Gladstone. *The Complete Works of Eugene O'Neill*. 2 vols. New York: Boni and Liveright, 1924.

———. *Hughie*. New Haven, Connecticut: Yale University Press, 1959.

———. *Long Day's Journey into Night*. New Haven, Connecticut: Yale University Press, 1956.

———. *A Moon for the Misbegotten: A Play in Four Acts*. New York: Random House, 1952.

———. *More Stately Mansions*. New Haven, Connecticut: Yale University Press, 1964.

———. *Plays*, 3 vols. New York: Random House, 1941.

———. *Plays*, 5 vols. New York: Boni and Liveright, 1925–26.

———. *The Plays of Eugene O'Neill*. New York: Charles Scribner's Sons, 1934.

———. *Ten "Lost" Plays*. New York: Random House, 1964.

———. *Thirst: Other One Act Plays*. Boston: Gorham, 1914.

———. *A Touch of the Poet*. New Haven, Connecticut: Yale University Press, 1957.

O'Reilly, John Boyle. *The City Streets*, n.p.: n.d.

———. *The Golden Secret*; or, *Bond and Free*. Melbourne: Cole: n.d.

———. *In Bohemia*. Boston: Pilot, 1886.

———. "John Boyle O'Reilly to a Friend." *Atlantic* 66 (October 1890): 572–74.

———. *The John Boyle O'Reilly Memorial Presented to the City of Boston, Dedicated June Twentieth, Eighteen Hundred Ninety-Six*. Boston: M. T. Callanan, 1896.

———. *The King's Men: A Tale of Tomorrow*. New York: Charles Scribner's Sons, 1884.

———. *Life of John Boyle O'Reilly*. Boston: J. S. Hyland, 1891.

———. *A Memorial to Crispus Attucks, Samuel Maverick, James Caldwell, Samuel Grey, and Patrick Carr, from the City of Boston*. Boston: City Council, 1889.

———. *Moondyne: A Story from the Underworld*. Boston: Roberts Brothers, 1883.

———. *The Poetry and Song of Ireland*. Boston: Gay Brothers, 1887.

———. *Roses*. Boston: Oliver Ditson, 1917 (score).

———. *Selected Poems*. Boston: P. J. Kenedy and Sons, 1913.

———. *Selected Poems of John Boyle O'Reilly*. Boston: H. M. Caldwell, 1904.

———. *Songs From The Southern Seas, and Other Poems*. Boston: Roberts Brothers, 1873.

———. *Songs, Legends, and Ballads*. Boston: Pilot, 1882.

O'Reilly, Myles. See Charles G. Halpine.

Orvell, Miles. *Invisible Parade: The Fiction of Flannery O'Connor*. Philadelphia, Pennsylvania: Temple University Press, 1972.

Ostenso, Martha. *O River, Remember*. New York: Dodd, 1943.

Phelan, Francis. *Four Ways of Computing Midnight*. New York: Atheneum, 1985.

Piper, Henry Dan, ed. *The Great Gatsby: The Novel, The Critics, The Background*. New York: Charles Scribner's Sons, 1970.

Pooley, Eric. "A Hard Place to Leave (Farrell's Irish Saloon)." *New York* 19 (April 21, 1986).

Porter, Bernard H. *The First Publications of F. Scott Fitzgerald*. Denver: Swallow, 1960.

Power, Crawford. *The Encounter*. New York: Sloane, 1950.

Powers, James Farl. *Lions, Harts, Leaping Does: And Other Stories*. New York: Time, 1963.

———. *Look How the Fish Live*. New York: Knopf, 1975.

———. *Morte d'Urban*. Garden City, New York: Doubleday, 1962.

———. *The Presence of Grace*. New York: Books for Libraries Press, 1956.

———. *Prince of Darkness: And Other Stories*. Garden City, New York: Doubleday, 1947.

———. *Wheat That Springeth Green.* New York: A. A. Knopf, 1988.

Powers, John R. *Do Black Patent Leather Shoes Really Reflect Up?* New York: Warner Books, 1982.

———. *The Last Catholic In America.* New York: Saturday Review Press, 1973.

Rank, Hugh. *Edwin O'Connor.* New York: Twayne, 1974.

———. "The Image of the Priest in American Catholic Fiction, 1945–1965." Ph.D. dissertation, University of Notre Dame, 1969.

Ready, William. *The Poor Hatter.* Chicago: Regnery, 1958.

Reaver, Joseph Russell. *An O'Neill Concordance.* Detroit, Michigan: Gale, 1969.

Reese, John Henry. *Sheehan's Mill.* Garden City, New York: Doubleday, Doran, 1943.

Reid, Wayne. *Boy Hunters of the Mississippi.* New York, 1852.

Reilly, Bernard. *College Boy.* New York: Benziger Brothers, 1899.

———. *Passing Shadows.* New York: Benziger Brothers, 1897.

Reilly, J. J. "Celtic Poe." (Fitz-James O'Brien) *Catholic World* 110 (March, 1920).

Reiter, Irene Morris. "A Study of James T. Farrell's Short Stories and Their Relation to His Longer Fiction." Ph.D. dissertation, University of Pennsylvania, 1964.

Rhodes, Robert E. "F. Scott Fitzgerald: 'All My Fathers.' " In *Irish-American Fiction: Essays in Criticism*, edited by Daniel J. Casey and Robert E. Rhodes. New York: AMS Press, 1979.

Riley, James Whitcomb. *Back-Yard Sketches: And Other Writings.* Carlton and Hollenbeck, 1895.

———. *Christy of Rathglin: An Entertaining and Exciting Story of the Life of An Irish Lad.* Boston: C. M. Clark, 1907.

———. *Green Fields and Running Brooks.* Indianapolis: Bobbs-Merrill, 1895.

———. *Songs of Two Peoples.* Boston: Estes and Lauriat, 1898.

———. *Spanish American War Songs.* Sidney A. Witherbee, 1898.

———. *The Transmitted Word.* Dorchester Press, 1893.

———. *The Works of James Whitcomb Riley.* Indianapolis: Bobbs-Merrill, 1892.

Robbins, J. A. *James T. Farrell Literary Essays: 1954–1974.* New York: Kennikat Press, 1976.

Robinson, Henry Morton. *The Cardinal.* New York: Simon & Schuster, 1950.

———. *The Great Snow.* New York: Simon & Schuster, 1947.

———. *The Perfect Round.* New York: Harcourt, Brace, 1945.

———. *Waters of Life.* New York: Simon & Schuster, 1960.

Roche, James Jeffrey. *Life of John Boyle O'Reilly: Together With His Complete Poems and Speeches, Ed., By Mrs. John Boyle O'Reilly.* New York: Cassell, 1891.

———. *Songs and Satires.* Boston: Ticknor, 1887.

———. *The Story of Filibusters: To Which is Added the Life of Colonel David Crockett.* London: T. Fisher Unwin, 1891.

Roddan, Rev. John T. *John O'Brien, Or, The Orphan of Boston: A Tale of Real-Life.* Boston: P. Donahoe, 1850.

Rosenfield, Paul. "Beyond the World of Fiction: No More Heroes for Hamill." *Los Angeles Times Book Review* (January 1, 1978).

Rossman, Kenneth R. "The Irish in American Drama in the Mid-Nineteenth Century." *New York History* 21 (1940): 39–53.

Ryan, S. P. "The Catholic Novelist in the U.S.A." *Catholic World* 188 (February 1959): 388–93.

Sadlier, Mary Anne. *Benjamin; or The Pupil of the Christian Brothers.* P. J. Kennedy, 1852

———. *Bessy Conway; or, The Irish Girl in America.* P. J. Kennedy, 1863.

———. *The Blakes and Flanagans: A Tale, Illustrative of Irish in the United States.* D. and J. Sadlier, 1858.

———. *The Confederate Chieftains: A Tale of the Irish Rebellion of 1641.* D. and J. Sadlier, 1860.

———. *Confessions of an Apostate.* New York: P. J. Kennedy, 1903.

———. *Con O'Regan; or, Emigrant Life in the New World*. D. and J. Sadlier, 1885.

———. *The Daughter of Tirconnell: A Tale of the Reign of James the First*. D. and J. Sadlier, 1863.

———. *Elinor Preston; or, Scenes at Home and Abroad*. D. and J. Sadlier, 1861.

———. *The Family*. D. and J. Sadlier, 1875.

———. *The Fate of Father Sheehy: A Tale of Tipperary Eighty Years Ago*. Excelsior Catholic, 1903.

———. *The Hermit of the Rock of Cashel: A Tale of Landlordism in Tipperary*. Cameron and Ferguson, 1850.

———. *The Life of Saint Elizabeth of Hungary: Duchess of Thuringia*. D. and J. Sadlier, 1854.

———. *The Lost Son*. D. and J. Sadlier, 1885.

———. *MacCarthy More or, The Fortunes of an Irish Chief in the Reign of Queen Elizabeth . . . .* D. and J. Sadlier, 1885.

———. *New Lights; or, Life in Galway: A Tale*. D. and J. Sadlier, 1885.

———. *The Old House by the Boyne; or Recollections of an Irish Borough*. D. and J. Sadlier, 1885.

———. *Old and New; or, Taste versus Fashion*. D. and J. Sadlier, 1863.

———. *The Orphan of Moscow; or The Young Governess*. D. and J. Sadlier, 1849.

———. *The Poems of Thomas D'Arcy McGee; with Copious Notes; with an Introduction and Biographical Sketch*. D. and J. Sadlier, 1902. Reissued by P. H. Brady, 1978.

———. *The Red Hand of Ulster; or the Fortunes of Hugh O'Neill*. P. Donahue, 1850.

———. "Shan Dempsey's Story." In *A Round Table of the Representative American Catholic Novelists, at Which is Served a Feast of Excellent Stories*. New York: Benziger Brothers, 1897.

———. *Tales and Stories*. D. and J. Sadlier, 1866.

———. *The Vendetta; and other Tales*. D. and J. Sadlier, 1862.

———. *Willy Burke; or, The Irish Orphan in America*. Thomas B. Noonan, 1850.

Sanborn, Alvan F. *Meg Macintyre's Raffle: And Other Stories*. Boston: Copeland and Day, 1896.

———. *Moody's Lodging House*. Boston: Copeland and Day, 1895.

Sanborn, Ralph V., and Barrett H. Clark. *A Bibliography of the Works of Eugene O'Neill*. New York: Random House, 1931.

Schaaf, Barbara C. *Mr. Dooley's Chicago*. Garden City, New York: Doubleday, 1977.

Schofield, William Grenough. *Seek for a Hero . . . The Story of John Boyle O'Reilly (1844–90)*. New York: Kennedy, 1956.

Schwartz, Arthur. *A Tree Grows in Brooklyn: A Musical Play*. New York: Harper, 1951.

Scott, Bonnie Kime. "Woman's Perspectives in Irish-American Fiction from Betty Smith to Mary McCarthy." In *Irish-American Fiction: Essays in Criticism*, edited by Daniel J. Casey and Robert E. Rhodes. New York: AMS Press, 1979.

Shain, Charles E. *F. Scott Fitzgerald*. Minneapolis, Minnesota: University of Minnesota Press, 1961.

Shafer, Ingrid H. *Eros and the Womanliness of God: Andrew Greeley's Romances of Renewal*. Chicago: Loyola University Press, 1986.

Sheaffer, Louis. *O'Neill: Son and Playwright* 1. Boston: Little, Brown, 1968.

———. *O'Neill: Son and Artist* 2. Boston: Little, Brown, 1973.

Sheed, Wilfrid. "The Good Word: There Is No (Irish) Mafia." *The New York Times Book Review*, (April 1, 1973).

———. *People Will Always Be Kind*. New York: Farrar, Straus, and Giroux, 1973.

———. *Square's Progress*. New York: Farrar, Straus and Giroux, 1965.

Simon, Myron. *Ethnic Writers in America*. New York: Harcourt, Brace, Jovanovich, 1972.

Sinclair, Upton. *King Coal*. New York: Macmillan, 1918.

Singer, D. "Hawthorne and the Old Irish."

New England Quarterly 42 (September 1969): 425–32.

Skinner, Richard Dana. *Eugene O'Neill: A Poet's Quest*. New York: Longmans, Green, 1935.

Sklar, Robert. *F. Scott Fitzgerald: The Last Tycoon*. New York: Oxford University Press, 1967.

Smith, Betty. *Joy In the Morning*. New York: Harper, 1963.

———. *Tomorrow Will be Better*. New York: Harper, 1948.

———. *A Tree Grows In Brooklyn*. New York: Harper and Brothers, 1947.

Smith, Dennis. *The Final Fire*. New York: Saturday Review Press, 1975.

———. *Report from Engine Company 82*. New York: Saturday Review Press, 1972.

Speer, Roderick S. "The Bibliography of Fitzgerald's Magazines 'Essays.' " *Fitzgerald/Hemingway Annual*, 1969.

Spofford, Mrs. Harriet Prescott, Miss Louise Imogen Guiney, and Miss Alice Brown. *Three Heroines of New England Romance*. Boston: Little, Brown, 1895.

Stephens, Martha. *The Question of Flannery O'Connor*. Baton Rouge, Louisiana: Louisiana State University Press, 1973.

Stern, Milton R. *The Golden Moment: The Novels of F. Scott Fitzgerald*. Urbana, Illinois: University of Illinois Press, 1970.

Stewart, Ramona. *Casey*. Boston: Little, Brown, 1968.

Sugrue, Thomas. *Such is The Kingdom*. New York, 1940.

Sullivan, James W. *Tenements Tales of New York*. New York: Holt, 1895.

Sylvester, Harry. *Big Football Man*. New York: Farrar and Rinehart, 1933.

———. *Dayspring*. New York: Appleton-Century, 1945.

———. *Dearly Beloved*. New York: Duell, Sloan, and Pearce, 1942.

———. *A Golden Girl*. New York: Harcourt, Brace, 1950.

———. *Moon Gaffney*. New York: H. Holt, 1947.

Tanner, Edward Everett. *Around the World With Auntie Mame*. New York: Harcourt, Brace, 1958.

——— (with Dorothy Erskine). *The Pink Hotel*. New York: Putnam, 1957.

———. *First Lady: My Thirty Days Upstairs in the White House, by Martha Dinwiddie Butterfield as Told to Patrick Dennis*. New York: W. Morrow, 1964.

———. *Genius*. New York: Harcourt, Brace, 1962.

———. *How Firm a Foundation*. New York: Morrow, 1968.

———. *The Joyous Season*. New York: Harcourt, Brace and World, 1965.

———. *Little Me: The Intimate Memoirs of that Great Star of Stage, Screen, and Television, Belle Poitrine, as Told to Patrick Dennis*. New York: Dutton, 1961.

———. *Paradise*. New York: Harcourt, Brace and Jovanovich, 1971.

——— (as Patrick Dennis). *Auntie Mame: An Irreverent Escapade*. New York: Vanguard, 1955.

——— (as Patrick Dennis). *Guestward Ho! By Barbara Hooton, as Indiscreetly Confided to Patrick Dennis*. New York: Vanguard, 1957.

———. *Tony*. New York: Dutton, 1966.

——— (as Virginia Rowans). *House Party*. New York: Crowell, 1954.

——— (as Virginia Rowans). *Love and Mrs. Sergent*. New York: Ferrar, Straus, and Cudahy, 1961.

——— (as Virginia Rowans). *The Loving Couple*. New York: Crowell, 1956.

——— (as Virginia Rowans). *Oh! What a Wonderful Wedding*. New York: Crowell, 1953.

Tebbel, John William. *Voice in the Streets*. New York: Dutton, 1954.

Thorp, Willard. "Catholic Novelists in Defense of Their Faith, 1829–1865." *Proceedings of the American Antiquarian Society: At The Semi-Annual Meeting Held in Boston, April 17, 1968* 78, part I. Worcester, Massachusetts, 1968.

Tiernan, Frances Christine Fisher. *After Many Days: A Novel*. D. Appleton, 1894.

———. *Aurora: A Novel*. J. B. Lippincott, 1886.

———. *Autumn Leaves: Verse and Story*. William H. Young, 1899.

———. *Bonny Kate: A Novel.* D. Appleton, 1878.

———. *By the Tiber.* D. H. Allen, 1881.

———. *A Comedy of Elopement.* D. Appleton, 1893.

———. *Ebb-Tide: And Other Stories.* D. Appleton, 1872.

———. *Grapes and Thorns; or a Priest's Sacrifice.* Christian Press Asociation, 1909.

———. *Heart of Steel: A Novel.* D. Appleton, 1883.

———. *The House of Yorke.* Catholic Publication Society, 1872.

———. *The Life Beyond.* F. H. Revell, 1892.

———. *San Salvador: A Novel.* Houghton, Mifflin, 1892.

———. *The Secret Request.* "Ave Maria" Office, 1915.

———. *Signor Monaldini's Niece.* Roberts Brothers, 1880.

———. *Six Sunny Months.* Catholic Publication Society, 1878.

———. *Two Coronets.* Houghton Mifflin, 1889.

———. *Valerie Aylmer: A Novel.* D. Appleton, 1900.

———. *A Winged Word: And Other Sketches and Stories.* Catholic Publication Society, 1873.

Tiusanen, Tino. *O'Neill's Scenic Images.* Princeton, New Jersey: Princeton University Press, 1968.

Toole, John Kennedy. *A Confederacy of Dunces.* Baton Rouge: Louisiana State University Press, 1980.

Tornquist, Egil. *A Drama of Souls: Studies in O'Neill's Super-Naturalistic Technique.* New Haven, Connecticut: Yale University Press, 1969.

Townsend, Edward W. *Chimmie Fadden, Major Max: And Other Stories.* New York, 1895.

Trowbridge, J. T. "Recollections of Halpine." *Independent* 55 (February 12, 1903): 357–59.

Tully, Jim. *Biddy Brogan's Boy.* New York: Charles Scribner's Sons, 1942.

———. *Blood on the Moon.* New York: Coward-McCann, 1931.

———. *The Bruiser.* New York: Greenberg, 1936.

———. *Circus Parade.* New York: A. and C. Boni, 1927.

———. *A Dozen and One.* Hollywood: Murray and Gee, 1943.

———. *Emmett Lawler.* New York: Harcourt, Brace, 1922.

———. *Jarnegan.* New York: A. and C. Boni, 1926.

———. *Ladies in the Parlor.* New York: Greenberg, 1935.

———. *Laughter in Hell.* New York: A. and C. Boni, 1932.

———. *Shadows of Men.* Garden City, New York: Doubleday, 1930.

———. *Shanty Irish.* New York: Boni, 1928.

Turnbull, Andrew Winchester. *Scott Fitzgerald.* New York: Charles Scribner's Sons, 1962.

Turner, Clarence Steven. "Man's Spiritual Quest in the Plays of Eugene O'Neill." Ph.D dissertation, University of Texas, 1962.

Walcutt, Charles C. "James T. Farrell: Aspects of Telling the Whole Truth." In *American Literary Naturalism, A Divided Stream.* Minneapolis: University of Minnesota Press, 1956.

———. *John O'Hara.* Minneapolis: University of Minnesota Press, 1969.

Wald, Alan M. *James T. Farrell: The Revolutionary Socialist Years.* New York: New York University Press, 1978.

Walsh, Thomas. *Dangerous Passenger.* Boston: Little, Brown, 1959.

Walsh, Townsend. *The Career of Dion Boucicault.* Bronx, New York: Blom, 1967.

Ward, Leo Richard. *Holding Up the Hills.* New York: Sheed and Ward.

Wedge, George F. "Two Bibliographies: Flannery O'Connor, J. F. Powers." *Critique* 2 (Fall 1958): 59–70.

Weinberg, Daniel E. "Viewing the Immigrant Experience in America Through Fiction and Autobiography: With a Select Bibliography." *History Teacher* 9, no. 3 (1976): 109–32.

White, James Addison. "The Era of Good Intentions: A Survey of American Catholics' Writing Between the Years 1880–1915." Ph.D. dissertation, University of Notre Dame, 1956.

Wickham, Joseph F. "John Boyle O'Reilly." *America* 13 (1915): 425–26.

Winther, Sophus Keith. *Eugene O'Neill: A Critical Study*. New York: Russell and Russell, 1961.

Wittke, Carl Frederick. "The Immigrant Theme on the American Stage." *Mississippi Valley Historical Review* 39 (September 1952): 211–32.

Wolle, Francis. "Fitz-James O'Brien in Ireland and England, 1828–1851." *American Literature*, 14 (November 1942).

———. *Fitz-James O'Brien: A Literary Bohemian of the Eighteen-Fifties*. Boulder, Colorado: University of Colorado Press, 1944.

Wood, Michael. "Tougher Than Hammett." *The New York Times Book Review*, October 21, 1977. Review of *True Confessions*, by John Gregory Dunne.

Zimmerman, George Denis. *Songs of Irish Rebellion: Political Street Ballads and Rebel Songs, 1780–1900*. Hatboro, Pennsylvania: Folklore Associates, 1967.

13. Scotch-Irish

Archives of Maryland. 30 vols. Baltimore: Maryland Historical Society, 1883–1919.

Ackerly, Mary D., and Lula E. J. Parker. *Our Kin: The Genealogies of Some of the Early Families Who Made History in the Founding and Development of Bedford County.* Lynchburg, Virginia: Bell, 1930.

Acklen, Jeanette T. *Tennessee Records; Bible Records and Marriage Bonds; Tombstone Inscriptions and Manuscripts, Historical and Biographical.* 2 vols. Nashville, Tennessee: Cullom and Ghertner, 1933.

Ardery, Mrs. W. B. *Kentucky Records* 1 and 2. Lexington, Kentucky: Keystone Printery, 1926, 1932.

Armour, William C. *Scotch-Irish Bibliography of Pennsylvania.* Nashville, Tennessee, 1897.

Barna, F. "The Frontiersman as Ethnic: A Brief History of the Scotch-Irish." In *Ethnic Groups in the City*, edited by O. Feinstein. Boston: D. C. Heath, 1971.

Beckett, J. C. *Protestant Dissent in Ireland, 1687–1780.* London: Faber and Faber, 1948.

Bolton, C. K. *Scotch-Irish Pioneers in Ulster and America.* Boston: Bacon and Brown, 1910.

Bolton, Ethel. *Immigrants to New England, 1700–1775.* Salem, Massachusetts: Essex Institute, 1931.

Bowen, Clarence Winthrop. *The History of Woodstock.* 8 vols. Connecticut: Windham, 1926–43.

Bradley, A. G. "Ulster Scot in the United States." *19th Century* 71 (1912): 1121–33.

Chalkley, L. *Chronicles of the Scotch-Irish in Virginia.* 3 vols. Baltimore: Genealogical, 1980. Original edition, 1912.

Chambers, George. *Tribute to the Principles, Virtues, Habits and Public Usefulness of the Irish and Scotch Early Settlers of Pennsylvania.* Chambersburg, Pennsylvania: Kieffer, 1856.

Charleston Free Library. *Index to Wills of Charleston County, South Carolina, 1671–1868.* South Carolina University Library, 1950.

Clarke, Desmond. *Arthur Dobbs, Esquire (Governor of North Carolina), 1689–1765.* London: Bodley Head, 1958.

Clemens, William Montgomery. *Virginia Wills Before 1799.* Pompton Lakes, New Jersey: Biblio, 1924.

Clyde, Rev. John C. *"Irish Settlement": Genealogies, Necrology and Reminiscences of the Now Northampton County, Pennsylvania.* Frazer, Pennsylvania: Author, 1879.

Cocke, W. R., III. *Hanover County Chancery Wills and Notes. A Compendium of Genealogical, Biographical and Historical Material Contained in Cases of the Chancery Suits.* Columbia, Virginia: W. R. Cocke, III, 1940.

The Collections of the History of Albany: From Its Discovery to the Present Time, With . . . Biographical Sketches, Etc. 4 vols. Albany, New York, 1865–71.

Colonial Records of the State of Georgia. 18 vols. Atlanta, 1904–08.

Coolidge, R. D. "Scotch-Irish in New England." *New England Magazine* 42 (1910): 747–50.

Corbitt, David L. *The Formation of the North Carolina Counties*: Raleigh, North Carolina, 1950.

Cotton, Jane Baldwin. *Maryland Calendar of Wills, 1635–1743.* 8 vols. Baltimore, Maryland: W. J. C. Dulany, 1901.

Coulter, Ellis Merton. *A List of the Early*

Settlers of Georgia. Athens: University of Georgia Press, 1949.

Coyle, J. G. "The Scot, the Ulster Scot and the Irish." *American Irish Historical Society Journal* 12 (1913): 103–11.

Craig, Neville B. *History of Pittsburgh.* Pittsburgh, Pennsylvania: J. R. Weldin, 1851.

Davidson, Robert. *History of the Presbyterian Church in the State of Kentucky.* New York: R. Carter, 1847.

Dickie, A. A. "Scotch-Irish Presbyterian Settlers in Southern Wisconsin." *Wisconsin Magazine of History* 31(1948): 291–302.

Dickson, R. J. *Ulster Emigration to Colonial America, 1718–1775.* London: Routledge and Kegan Paul, 1966.

Dinsmore, J. W. *The Scotch-Irish in America.* Chicago: Winona, 1906.

Documents Relating to the Colonial History of New York, 1663–1778. 15 vols. Albany, New York, 1853–87.

Doddridge, Joseph. *Notes on the Settlement and Indian Wars of the Western Parts of Virginia and Pennsylvania, 1763–1783.* Wellsburg, Virginia: Printed at the office of the *Gazette* for the author, 1824.

Drake, Daniel *Pioneer Life in Kentucky.* Cincinnati, Ohio: R. Clarke, 1870.

Drayton, John. *Memoirs of the American Revolution in South Carolina.* Charleston: A. E. Miller, 1821.

Dunaway, Wayland. *The Scotch-Irish of Colonial Pennsylvania.* Chapel Hill: University of North Carolina Press, 1944.

"Early Irish Settlers in Maine and New Hampshire." *Sprague's Journal of Maine History* 10 (1922): 29–31.

Early, R. H. *Chronicles and Family Sketches: Embracing a History of Campbell County, Virginia, 1782–1926.* Lynchburg, Virginia: J. P. Bell, 1927.

Eaton, Samuel J. M. *Lakeside: A Memorial of the Planting of the Church in Northwestern Pennsylvania.* Pittsburgh: Presbyterian Board of Coalportage, 1880.

Eid, Leroy V. "The Colonial Scotch-Irish: A View Accepted Too Readily." *Eire-Ireland* 21, no. 4 (1986): 81–105.

Ely, William. *Big Sandy Valley: A History of the People and Country from the Earliest Settlement to the Present Time.* Catlettsburg, Kentucky: Central Methodist, 1887.

Evans, E. E. "Old Ireland and New England." *Ulster Journal of Achaelogy* 12 (1949): 104–12.

———. "A Pennsylvanian Folk Festival." *Ulster Folklife* 5 (1959): 14–19.

———. "The Scotch-Irish in the New World: An Atlantic Heritage." *Journal of the Royal Society of Antiquaries of Ireland* 95 (1965): 39–49.

———. "The Scotch-Irish: Their Cultural Adaptation and Heritage in the American Old West." In *Essays in Scotch-Irish History*, edited by E. R. R. Green. London: Routledge, and Kegan Paul, 1969.

Farson, W. V. "Henry McCullough and His Irish Settlement." *North Carolina Booklet* 22 (1924): 32–39.

Fisher, Sydney George. *The Making of Pennsylvania.* Philadelphia: J. B. Lippincott, 1896.

———. *Pennsylvania: Colony and Commonwealth.* Philadelphia: H. T. Coates, 1897.

Fisk, W. L. "The Scotch-Irish in Central Ohio." *Ohio Archaeological Quarterly* 25 (1948): 518–30.

Fiske, John. *Dutch and Quaker Colonies.* 2 vols. Boston and New York: Houghton Mifflin, 1899.

———. *Old Virginia and Her Neighbors.* 2 vols. Boston and New York: Houghton Mifflin, 1897.

Flanigan, James C. *Marriages of Hancock County, 1806–1943.* Hapeville, Georgia: Tyler, 1943.

Foote, William H. *Sketches of Virginia* (two series). Philadelphia: W. S. Martien, 1850, 1855.

Ford, Henry Jones. *The Scotch-Irish in America.* Princeton: Princeton University Press, 1915.

French, J. H. *Gazetteer of the State of New York.* Syracuse, New York: R. P. Smith, 1860.

Fulton, Eleanor Jane. *An Index to the Will Books and Interstate Records of Lancaster County, Pennsylvania, 1729–1850.* Lancaster, Pennsylvania: Intelligencer Printing, 1936.

Futhey, J. Smith. *Upper Octorara Presbyterian Church*. Philadelphia: H. B. Ashmead, 1870.

Futhey, J. Smith, and Gilbert Cope. *History of Chester County, Pennsylvania*. Philadelphia: L. H. Everts, 1881.

Garland, Robert. *The Scotch-Irish in Western Pennsylvania*. Pittsburgh: Carnegie Library, 1923.

Gayarre, Charles. *History of Louisiana*. 4 vols. New Orleans: F. F. Hansell and Brothers, 1903.

Gibson, William J. *History of Huntingdon Presbytery*. Bellefonte, Pennsylvania: Bellefonte Press, 1874.

Gilman, Marcus Davis. *The Bibliography of Vermont*. Burlington: Free Press, 1897.

Gilmer, George. *Sketches of Some of the First Settlers of Upper Georgia*. New York: D. Appleton, 1855.

Glasgow, Maude. *The Scotch-Irish in Northern Ireland and the American Colonies*. New York: Putnam, 1936.

Gordon, Thomas F. *History of New Jersey*. Trenton: D. Fenton, 1834.

Goss, Winifred Lane. *Colonial Gravestone Inscriptions in the State of New Hampshire*. Dover, New Hampshire, 1942.

Green, E. R. R., ed. *Essays in Scotch-Irish History*. London: Routledge, and Kegan Paul, 1969.

———. "Queenborough Township: Scotch-Irish Emigration and the Expansion of Georgia, 1763–1776." *William and Mary Quarterly* 17 (1960): 183–99.

———. "The Scotch-Irish and the Coming of the Revolution in North Carolina." *Irish Historical Studies* 7 (1955): 77–86.

———. "Scotch-Irish Emigration, an Imperial Problem." *Western Pennsylvania Historical Magazine* 35 (1952): 193–209.

———, ed. "The Strange Humors that Drove the Scotch-Irish to America, 1729." *William and Mary Quarterly* 12 (1955): 112–23.

Green, S. S. *Scotch-Irish in America*. Worcester, Massachusetts: Hamilton, 1865.

Greenleaf, Jonathan. *Ecclesiastical History of Maine*. Portsmouth, New Hampshire: H. Gray, 1821.

Hale, John P. *Trans-Allegheny Pioneers*. Cincinnati: Graphic Press, 1886.

Hall, B. H. *History of Eastern Vermont*. New York: D. Appleton, 1958.

Hamilton, Peter J. *Colonial Mobile*. Boston and New York: Houghton Mifflin, 1910.

Hanna, C. A. *The Scotch-Irish; Or the Scot in North Britain, North Ireland, and North America*. 2 vols. New York: Putnam, 1902.

Harlow, Henry A. *History of the Presbytery of Hudson*. Middletown, New York: Stivers, Slauson and Boyd, 1888.

Hatfield, E. F. *History of Elizabeth (N.J.)*. New York: Carlton and Lanahan, 1868.

Hiner, M. "The Scotch-Irish and Academies in the Transallagheny Frontier." Master's thesis, University of West Virginia, 1933.

Historical Collections of the Georgia Chapters, D.A.R. 4 vols., 1929–32.

The History of Dublin, New Hampshire. Boston: J. Wilson and Son, 1855.

Holland, Josiah G. *History of Western Massachusetts*. 2 vols. Springfield, Massachusetts: S. Bowles, 1855.

Hough, Franklin B. *Papers Relating to Pemaquid and Parts Adjacent in the Present State of Amine*. Blanny: Weed, Parsons, 1856.

Howe, George. *Presbyterian Church in South Carolina, History of*. 2 vols. Columbia: Duffie and Chapman, 1870–1883.

Howe, Henry. *Historical Collections of Ohio*. 2 vols. Cincinnati: State of Ohio, 1908.

———. *Historical Collections of Virginia*. Charleston, South Carolina: Babcock, 1845.

Hudson, Charles. *History of the Town of Lexington, Middlesex County, Massachusetts: From Its First Settlement to 1868*. 2 vols. Boston: Wiggin and Lunt, 1868.

Hurd, Charles Edwin. *Genealogy and History of Representative Citizens of the Commonwealth of Massachusetts*. Boston: New England Historical, 1902.

Ireland, O. S. "The Ethnic-Religious Dimensions of Pennsylvania Politics, 1778–1779." *William and Mary Quarterly* 30 (1933): 423–48.

Jefferson, Thomas. *Notes on Virginia*. Philadelphia: Prichard and Hall, on Market Street, between Front and Second Streets, 1778.

Johnson, J. F. *Scots and Scotch-Irish in America*. New York: Lerner, 1966.

Johnson, Thomas Cary. *Virginia Presbyterianism and Religious Liberty*. Richmond: Presbyterian Committee of Publication, 1907.

Jones, Maldyn D. "Scotch-Irish." In *The Harvard Encyclopedia of American Ethnic Groups*, edited by Stephan Thernstrom. Cambridge: Harvard University Press, 1980.

Jones, U. J. *Early Settlement of the Juniata Valley*. Harrisburg, Pennsylvania: Harrisburg Publishing, 1899.

Jordan, John Woolf. *Colonial and Revolutionary Families of Philadelphia*. 2 vols. New York and Chicago: Lewis Historical, 1911.

———. *Genealogy and Personal History of the Allegheny Valley*. 3 vols. New York: Lewis Historical, 1913.

———. *Genealogy and Personal History of Northern Pennsylvania*. 3 vols. New York: Lewis Historical, 1913.

———. *Genealogy and Personal History of Western Pennsylvania*. 3 vols. New York: Lewis Historical, 1915.

———. *Historic Homes and Institutions and Genealogical Memoirs of the Lenigh Valley*. 2 vols. New York and Chicago: Lewis Historical, 1905.

Kegley, Frederick Bittle. *Kegley's Virginia Frontier: The Beginnings of the Southwest: The Roanoke of Colonial Days, 1740–1783*. Roanoke, Virginia: Southwest Virginia Historical Society, 1938.

Keith, Charles Penorse. *Chronicles of Pennsylvania from the English Revolution to the Peace of Aix-La-Cahpelle, 1688–1748*. Philadelphia: Patterson and White, 1917.

Kenrohan, J. W. "Ulster Pilgrim Fathers: An Irish Mayflower." *Landmark* 2 (1920): 691–94.

Kephart, H. *Our Southern Highlanders*. New York: MacMillan, 1921.

Kercheval, Samuel. *History of the Valley of Virginia*. Winchester, Virginia: S. H. Davis, 1833.

Kittochtinny Historical Society. *Papers*. Chambersburg, Pennsylvania, 1900.

Klett, Guy S. *Presbyterians in Colonial Pennsylvania*. Philadelphia: University of Pennsylvania Press, 1937.

———. "Scotch-Irish Pioneering along the Susquehanna River." *Pennsylvania History* 20 (1953): 165–79.

Kulp, George B. *Families of the Wyoming Valley*. 3 vols. Wilkes-Barre, Pennsylvania: E. B. Yordy, 1885–90.

La Far, Mable Freeman, and Caroline Price Wilson. *Chatham County, Georgia, Abstracts of the Will of 1773–1817*. Washington, D.C.: National Genealogical Society, 1936.

Lamb, Martha J. *History of New York City*. 2 vols. New York: A. S. Barnes, 1877–96.

Lancaster County Historical Society. *Historical Papers and Addresses*. Lancaster, Pennsylvania, 1897–1919.

Latimer, W. T. "Ulster Emigration to America." *Journal of the Royal Society of Antiquaries of Ireland* 32 (1902): 388–92.

Leach, D. E. *The Northern Colonial Frontier, 1607–1763*. New York: Holt-Rinehart-Winston, 1966.

Lee, Francis Bazley. *Genealogical and Memorial History of the State of New Jersey*. New York: Lewis Historical, 1910.

Lehmann, William C. *Scotch-Irish Contributions to Early American Life and Culture*. Port Washington, New York: Kennikat Press, 1978.

Lemon, J. T. *The Best Poor Man's Country: A Geographical Study of Early Southeastern Pennsylvania*. Baltimore: Johns Hopkins University Press, 1972.

Leyburn, J. G. "The Melting Pot: The Ethnic Group that Blended, the Scotch-Irish." *American Heritage* 22 (1970): 97–101.

———. *The Scotch-Irish*. Chapel Hill: University of North Carolina Press, 1962.

Linehan, J. C. "The Irish-Scots and the Scotch-Irish." *Granite Monthly* 11 (1888): 50–57, 85–95.

Linn, John Blair. *Annals of Buffalo Valley, Pennsylvania*. Harrisburg, Pennsylvania: L. S. Hart, 1877.

Littell, John. *Family Records or Genealogies*

of the First Settlers of Passaic Valley. Feltville, New Jersey: D. Felt, 1851.

Little, George Thomas. *Genealogical and Family History of the State of Maine.* 4 vols. New York: Lewis Historical, 1909.

Lodge, H. C. "The Distribution of Ability in the United States." *Century Magazine* 42 (1891): 687–94.

Logan, John J. *History of the Upper Country.* Charleston: S. G. Curtenay, 1859.

Loudon, Archibald. *Narratives of the Outrages Committed by the Indians.* 2 vols. Carlisle, Pennsylvania: From the press of A. Loudon (Whitehall), 1808–11.

Lunceford, Alvin Mell. *Early Records of Taliaferro County, Georgia.* Crawfordville, Georgia, 1956.

MacCracken, H. M. "The Scotch-Irish in America and in New York." *New York State Historical Association Proceedings* 11 (1912): 104–22.

MacLeod, W. C. "Celts and Indians." In *Beyond the Frontier*, edited by P. Bohannan. New York: Natural History Press, 1967.

Magruder, James Mosby. *Index of Maryland Colonial Wills, 1634–1777, at Land Office, Annapolis, Maryland.* 3 vols. Annapolis, 1933.

———. *Magruder's Maryland Colonial Abstracts: Wills, Accounts and Inventories, 1772–1777.* 5 vols. Annapolis, 1934.

Manwaring, Charles William. *A Digest of the Early Connecticut Probate Records.* 3 vols. Hartford, Connecticut: R. S. Peck, 1904–06.

Marshall, W. F. *Ulster Sails West.* Belfast, Ireland: Quota Press, 1943.

Martin, John H. *Chester and Its Vicinity.* Philadelphia: W. H. Pile and Sons, 1877.

McAdams, Mrs. Harry K. *Kentucky Pioneer and Court Records.* Lexington, Kentucky: Keystone Printery, 1929.

McAlarney, Mathias W. *History of the Sesqui-Centennial of Paxtang Church, September 18, 1890.* Harrisburg, Pennsylvania: Harrisburg Publishing, 1890.

McCall, Hugh. *History of Georgia.* 2 vols. Savannah: Seymour and Williams, 1811–16.

McClung, John A. *Sketches of Western Adventure, 1755–1794.* Dayton: O. L. F. Caflin, 1854.

McCrady, E. *The History of South Carolina Under Royal Government.* New York: Macmillan, 1899.

McWhorter, Lucullus Virgil. *The Border Settlers of Northwestern Virginia from 1768 to 1795.* Hamilton, Ohio: Republican, 1915.

Meade, William. *Old Churches, Ministers, and Families of Virginia.* 2 vols. Philadelphia: J. B. Lippincott, 1898.

Meginness, John F. *Otzinachson; Or a History of the West Branch Valley of Susquehanna.* Philadelphia: H. B. Ashmead, 1857.

Mell, A. R. W. *Revolutionary Soldiers Buried in Alabama.* Montgomery, Alabama, 1904.

Michigan Pioneer and Historical Society. *Collections.* Lansing, Michigan, 1874–1915.

Mills, R. *Statistics of South Carolina.* Charleston, South Carolina: Hurlbut and Lloyd, 1826.

Moffatt, J. Scotch-Irish in the Up-Country. *South Atlantic Quarterly* 33 (1934): 137–51.

Moody, T. W. "Irish and Scotch-Irish in 18th Century America." *Studies* 35: 123–140.

———. "The Ulster Scots in Colonial and Revolutionary America." *Studies* 34 (1945): 52–69.

Morrison, Leonard A. *History of Windham in New Hampshire, 1719–1883.* Boston, Massachusetts: Cupples, Upham, 1883.

Munsell, Joel. *The Annals of Albany.* 10 vols. Albany, New York: J. Munsell, 1850–59.

———. *Collections on the History of Albany.* 4 vols. Albany, New York: J. Munsell, 1865–71.

Narragansett. *The Narragansett Historical Register.* 9 vols. Providence, Rhode Island: Narragansett Historical, 1882–91.

Nelson, William. *Church Records in New Jersey.* Paterson, New Jersey: Paterson History Club, 1904.

Nevin, Alfred. *Encyclopedia of the Presbyterian Church in the United States of America.* Philadelphia: Presbyterian Encyclopedia, 1884.

Noyes, Sybil, Charles Thornton Libby, and Walter Goodwin Davis. *Genealogical Dictionary of Maine and New Hampshire*. Portland, Maine: South-Worth-Anthoensen Press, 1928–39.

O'Brien, M. J. "An Alledged First Census of the American People: A Criticism of William H. Clemen's Book." *American Irish Historical Society Journal* 29 (1930–31).

———. "How the Descendants of Irish Settlers in America were Written into History as Anglo-Saxons and Scotch-Irish." *American Irish Historical Society Journal* 18 (1919): 99–109.

———. "Irish in the Surrogate's Records Ulster County, New York." *American Irish Historical Society Journal* 26 (1927): 129–36.

———. "The Scotch-Irish Myth." *American Irish Historical Society Journal* 24 (1925): 142–53.

———. "Shipping Statistics of the Philadelphia Custom House, 1733–1774; Refute the Scotch-Irish Theory." *American Irish Historical Society Journal* 22 (1923): 132–41.

———. "Some Examples of the 'Scotch-Irish' in America." *American Irish Historical Society Journal* 14 (1915): 269–79.

O'Callaghan, E. B., ed. *Documentary History of New York*. 4 vols. Albany, New York. 1849–51.

O'Connell, J. D. *The Scotch-Irish Delusions in America*. Washington, D.C., 1897.

O'Neall, John B. *Biographical Sketches of the Bench and Bar of South Carolina*. Charleston, South Carolina: S. G. Courtenay, 1859.

O'Neall, John B., and J. A. Chapman. *Annals of Newberry*. Newberry, South Carolina: Aull and Houseal, 1892.

Olds, Fred A. *Abstract of North Carolina Wills from about 1760 to about 1800*. Oxford, North Carolina: Privately printed by "The Orphan's Friend," 1925.

Osmond, J. *History of Luzerne Presbytery*. Philadelphia: Presbyterian Historical Society, 1897.

Owen, Mary. *Old Salem*. Winston-Salem, North Carolina: Lithographed by Winston Printing, 1941.

Owen, Thomas. *History of Alabama and the Dictionary of Alabama Biography*. Chicago: S. J. Clarke, 1921.

Parker, Edward L. *History of Londonderry, New Hampshire*. Boston: Perkins and Whipple, 1851.

Patterson, A. W. *History of the Back Woods*. Pittsburgh: Author, 1843.

Pennsylvania Scotch-Irish Society. *First [Through Fifth] Annual Meeting[s] and Banquet[s]*. Philadelphia: Allen, Lane, and Scott, 1890–94.

Pepper, George W. *Under Three Flags*. Cincinnati, Ohio: Curtis and Jennings, 1899.

Perceval-Maxwell, M. *The Scottish Migration to Ulster in the Reign of James I*. London: Routledge and Kegan Paul, 1973.

Perrin, W. H. *Southwest Louisiana, Biographical and Historical*. New Orleans, Louisiana: Gulf, 1891.

Perrin, W. H., J. C. Battle, and G. C. Kniffen. *A History of Kentucky*. Louisville, Kentucky: F. A. Battey, 1886.

Perry, A. L. *Scotch-Irish in New England*. Boston, 1891.

Phillips, J. D. "George Duncan: Emigrant to Londonderry, New Hampshire and Founder of the Duncan Families of New England." *Essex Institute Historical Collection* 86 (1950): 156–247.

Pillsbury, H. "Scotch-Irish and the History of Londonderry." *Americana* 21 (1922): 547–57.

Pope, Charles Henry. *The Pioneers of Maine, and New Hampshire, 1623–1660*. Boston: C. H. Pope, 1908.

Putnam, A. W. *History of the Middle Tennessee*. Nashville, Tennessee: Printed for the author, 1859.

Ray, Worth S. *The Lost Tribes of North Carolina*. 3 parts. Baltimore: Southern Book, 1956.

Records of Philadelphia Presbytery and of the Synods of New York and Philadelphia, 1706–1788. Philadelphia, 1841.

Revill, Janie. *A Compilation of the Original Lists of Protestant Migrations to South Carolina, 1763–1773*. Columbia, South Carolina: State, 1939.

Ridlon, G. T. *Saco Valley Settlements and Families: Historical, Biographical and Genealogical*. Portland, Maine: Author, 1895.

Roche, J. J. "The Scotch-Irish and Anglo-Saxon Fallacies." *American Irish Historical Society Journal* 2 (1899): 89–92.

Rupp, I. Daniel. *Early History of Western Pennsylvania*. Pittsburgh: D. W Kauffman, 1846.

Shepardson, F. W. "Scotch and Irish in America." *Dial* 33 (1902): 325–26.

Smith, J. "The Scotch-Irish: An Inquiry into the New and Mysterious Race that Sprang from a Hyphen." *Illustrated American* 18 (1895): 354–60.

———. "The Scotch-Irish Shibboleth Analyzed and Rejected." *American Irish Historical Society Journal* 1 (1898).

Smith, Joseph. *History of Jefferson College*. Pittsburgh: J. T. Shryock, 1857.

———. *Old Redstone (Presbytery), or Historical Sketches of Western Presbyterianism*. Philadelphia: Lippincott, Grambo, 1854.

Spencer, Alfred. *Spencer's Roster of Native Sons*. Bath, New York: Courier Press, 1941.

Stearns, Ezra Scollay. *Genealogical and Family History of the State of New Hampshire*. 4 vols. New York: Lewis, 1908.

Stearns, J. F. *Newark: Historical Discourses Relating to the First Presbyterian Church*. Newark, New Jersey: Daily Advertiser Office, 1853.

Stevens, William B. *History of Georgia*. 2 vols. New York: D. Appleton, 1847.

Stewart, Robert Armistead. *Index to Printed Virginia Genealogies*. Richmond, Virginia: Old Dominion Press, 1930.

Stille, Charles. *Major Anthony Wayne and the Pennsylvania Line*. Philadelphia: J. B. Lippincott, 1893.

Stone, F. D. "First Congress of Scotch-Irish in America." *Pennsylvania Magazine of History and Biography* 14 (1890): 68–71.

Stone, James Kent. *An Awakening and What Followed*. Notre Dame, Indiana: Ave Marie Press, n.d.

Summers, Lewis Preston. *Annals of Southwest Virginia, 1769–1800*. Abingdon, Virginia: L. P. Summers, 1929.

Survey of the Manuscript Collections in the New York Historical Society. New York, 1941.

Swem, Earl Gregg. *Virginia Historical Index*. 2 vols. Roanoke, Virginia: Stone Printing and Manufacturing, 1934.

Swope, Belle M. *History of Middle Spring Presbyterian Church, Middle Spring, Pennsylvania, 1783–1900*. Newville, Pennsylvania: Times Steam Print House, 1900.

Thompson, Zadock. *History of Vermont: [Natural, Civil, and Statistical, In Three Parts]*. Burlington, Pennsylvania: N.P., 1900.

Tinsley, H. D. *History of North Creek, Ohio County, Kentucky; With a Genealogy and Biographical Section*. Frankfort, Kentucky: Roberts Printing, 1953.

Torrence, Clayton. *Old Somerset on the Eastern Shore of Maryland*. Richmond, Virginia: Whittet and Shepperson, 1935.

———. *Virginia Wills and Administrations, 1632–1800; An Index of Wills Recorded in Local Courts of Virginia, 1632–1800*. Richmond, Virginia: William Boyd Press, 1931.

Turner, Douglas K. *History of Neshaminy Presbyterian Church of Warwick, Hartsville, Bucks County, Pennsylvania, 1726–1876*. Philadelphia: Culbertson and Bache, Printers, 1876.

Turner, Orsamus. *History of the Pioneer Settlements of Phelps and Gorham's Purchase, and Morris' Reserve*. Rochester, New York: W. Alling, 1851.

———. *Pioneer History of the Holland Purchase of Western New York*. Buffalo, New York: Jewett, Thomas, 1849.

Ullery, Jacob G. *Men of Vermont: An Illustrated Biographical History*. Brattleboro, Vermont: Transcript Publishing Co., 1894.

Van Meter, Benjamin Franklin. *Genealogies and Sketches of Some Old Families Who Have Taken Prominent Part in the Development of Virginia and Kentucky, Especially*. Louisville, Kentucky: J. P. Morton, 1901.

Van Voorhis, John S. *The Old and New Monongahela*. Pittsburgh: Nicholson Printer, 1893.

Waldenmaier, Inez. *A Finding List of Virginia Marriage Records Before 1853*. Washington, D.C., 1955

Wall, C. A. *North Worcester: Its First Settlers and Old Farms*. Worcester, Massachusetts: Printed by the author, 1890.

———. *Reminiscences of Worcester: From the Earliest Period*. Worcester, Massachusetts: Tyler and Seagraves, 1877.

Wallace, E. M. "Early Farmers in Exeter." *Wisconsion Magazine of History* 8 (1925): 415–22.

Watson, John F. *Annals of Philadelphia*. 2 vols. Philadelphia: Whiting and Thomas, 1856–57.

Wayland, John W. *Virginia Valley Records: Genealogical and Historical Materials of Rockingham County and Related Regions*. Strasburg, Virginia: Shenandoah Publishing House, 1930.

Weatherford, W. D. *Pioneers of Destiny: The Romance of the Appalachian People*. Birmingham, Alabama: Vulcan Press, 1955.

Weis, Frederick Lewis. *The Colonial Clergy of Maryland, Delaware and Georgia*. Lancaster, Massachusetts: Society of the Descendants of the Colonial Clergy, 1950.

———. *The Colonial Clergy of Virginia, North Carolina and South Carolina*. Boston, Massachusetts: Publications of the Society of the Descendants of the Colonial Clergy, 1955.

White, William P. *The Presbyterian Church in Philadelphia*. Philadelphia: Allen, Lane and Scott, 1895.

Whitehead, William A. *Contributions to the Early History of Perth Amboy and Adjoining Country*. New York: D. Appleton, 1856.

———. *East Jersey Under the Proprietary Governments*. Newark, New Jersey: M. R. Dennis, 1875.

Whitney, Seth H. *Kennebec Valley: Early History of the Valley*. Augusta, Georgia: Sprague, Burleigh and Flint,1887.

Williams, E. M. "The Scotch-Irish in Pennsylvania." *Americana* 17 (1923): 374–87.

Williamson, William D. *History of the State of Main*. 2 vols. Hallowell: Glazier, Masters and Smith, 1839.

Willis, W. "Scotch-Irish Immigration to Maine and Presbyterianism in New England." *Collections Maine Historical Society*. 1st series, no. 6 (1859): 1–37.

Willis, William. *History of Portland From 1632 to 1864*. Portland, Maine: Bailey and Noyes, 1865.

Wilson, A. E. *Paddy Wilson's Meeting House in Providence Plantations, 1791–1839*. Boston: Pilgrim Press, 1920.

Wilson, Samuel M. *Catalogue of Revolutionary Soldiers and Sailors of the Commonwealth of Virginia—Warrants Granted by Virginia*. Frankfort, Kentucky: Compiled by S. M. Wilson from official records in the Kentucky state land office, 1953.

Wing, Conway P. *History of the First Presbyterian Church of Carlisle, Pennsylvania*. Carlisle, Pennsylvania: Valley Sentinel Office, 1877.

Wittke, Carl. "The Colonial Emigration from Ireland: The Irish and the Scotch-Irish." In *We Who Built America*, edited by Carl Wittke. Cleveland: Case Western Reserve, 1967.

Wyman, Thomas Bellows. *Charlestown, Middlesex County, The Genealogies and Estates Of, 1629–1818*. 2 vols. Boston: D. Clapp and Son, 1879.

14. Irish in Places, by Regions and States

Regions

Frontier

Baxter, Maurice G. "Encouragement of Immigration to the Mid-West During the Civil War." *Indiana Magazine of History* 46 (1950).

Browne, H. J. "Archbishop Hughes and Western Colonization." *Catholic Historical Review* 36 (October 1950): 257–85.

Butler, T. A. *The Irish on the Prairie.* New York: D. and J. Sadlier, 1874.

Dwyer, Bishop R. J. "The Irish in the Building of the Inter-Mountain West." *Irish Ecclesiastical Review* 87 (June 1957): 401–19.

Henthorne, Evangela. *The Irish Catholic Colonization Association of the United States: Its Origin and Development Under the Leadership of the Rt. Rev. John Lancaster Spalding, Bishop of Peoria, President of the Association, 1879–1892.* Champaign, Illinois: Twin City, 1932.

Jenkins, Thomas J. *Six Seasons in Our Prairies and Six Weeks in Our Rockies.* Louisville, Kentucky: C. A. Rodgers, 1884.

Kelley, Sister Mary G. *Catholic Immigrant Colonization Projects in the United States, 1815–1860.* New York, 1939.

———. "Irish Catholic Colonies and Colonization Projects in the United States, 1795–1860," *Studies: An Irish Quarterly Review* 29 (1940): 95–110; 447–65.

Kelly, William, J. P. *An Excursion to California Over the Prairie, Rocky Mountains, and Great Sierra Nevada.* 2 vols. London: Chapman and Hall, 1851.

Luebke, F. C. "Ethnic Group Settlement on the Great Plains." *Western Historical Quarterly* 8 (1977): 405–30.

McAvoy, Thomas T., C.S.C. "Americanism and Frontier Catholicism." *Review of Politics* 5 (1943).

Moloney, Maurice T. "The Irish Pioneers of the West and Their Descendants." *American Irish Historical Society Journal* 8 (1909): 209–16.

O'Dwyer, Riobard, N. T. *Who Were My Ancestors? A Genealogy of Eyeries Parish, Castletownbere Co. Cork.* Astoria, Illinois: Stevens, 1976.

O'Grady, John. "Irish Colonization in the United States." *Studies: An Irish Quarterly Review* 19 (September 1930): 387–407.

Onahan, William. "A Chapter of Catholic Colonization." *Acto Et Dicta* (July 1917).

Piggott, M. "Irish Pioneers of the Upper Mississippi Valley." *American Irish Historical Society Journal* 9 (1910): 301–30.

Schob, David E. *Hired Hands and Plowboys.* Chicago: University of Illinois Press, 1975.

Shannon, James P. *Catholic Colonization on the Western Frontier.* New Haven, Connecticut: Yale University Press, 1957.

Socolofsky, Homer E. "William Scully: His Early Years in Illinois, 1850–1865." *Journal of the West* 4, no. 1 (1965): 41–55.

———. "William Scully's Irish and American Lands." *Western Historical Quarterly* 9, no. 2 (April 1978): 149–61.

Spalding, J. L. *The Religious Mission of the Irish People and Catholic Colonization.* New York: The Catholic Publication Society, 1880.

Stephenson, George M. "Nativism in the Forties and Fifties with Special Reference to the Mississippi Valley." *The Mississippi Valley Historical Review* 9 (December 1922).

Still, B. "Patterns of Mid-Nineteenth Census Urbanization in the Middle West." *Mississippi Valley Historical Review* 28 (1941).

Walsh, J. P. "American-Irish: West and East." *Eire-Ireland* 6 (1971).

Williams, Blaine T. "The Frontier Family." In *Essays on the American West*, edited by Harold M. Hollingsworth and Saudrs L. Myres. Austin: The University of Texas Press, 1969.

Winther, Oscar O. *The Transportation Frontier.* New York: Holt, Rhinehart, and Winston, 1964.

Wyman, Walker D., and Clifton B. Kroeber, eds. *The Frontier In Perspective.* Madison: University of Wisconsin, 1957.

New England

Appel, John J. "The New England Origins of the American Irish Historical Society." *The New England Quarterly.*

Bean, W. G. "Puritan Versus Celt." *New England Quarterly* 7 (1934): 70–89.

De Goesbriand, Louis. *Catholic Memoirs of Vermont and New Hampshire.* Burlington: Vermont Press of R. S. Styles, 1886.

Goodwin, William Brownell. *The Ruins of Great Ireland in New England.* Boston: Meader, 1946.

Hansen, M. L. "The Second Colonization of New England." *New England Quarterly* 2 (1929).

Jacobus, D. L. "Irish in New England Before 1700." *New England Historical and Genealogical Register* 90 (1936): 165–67.

"New Ireland in New England." *The Recorder: American-Irish Historical Society* 1, no. 1 (1939).

O'Brien, Michael J. "An Authoritative Account of the Earliest Irish Pioneers in New England." *American Irish Historical Society Journal* 18 (1919).

———. "Irish Marriages in New England." *American Irish Historical Society Journal* 17 (1918).

———. *Pioneer Irish in New England.* New York: Kennedy, 1937.

Ryan, G. E. "Shanties and Shiftlessness: The Immigrant Irish of Henry Thoreau." *Eire-Ireland* 13 (1978).

Singer, David. "Hawthorn and the 'Wild Irish'." *New England Quarterly* 42 (1969): 425–32.

Solomon, Barbara M. *Ancestors and Immigrants: A Changing New England Tradition,* Cambridge: Harvard University Press, 1956.

South

Cobb, Irvin Shresbury. "The Lost Irish Tribes in the South." *Tennessee Historical Magazine.* 2d series (1931): 115–24.

———. *The Lost Irish Tribes in the South.* Washington, D.C.: Friends of Irish Freedom, National Bureau of Information, 1919.

Gallagher, Hugh S. "Cape Blanco." *American Irish Historical Society Journal* 30 (1932): 92–96.

Harper, Jared, and Charles Hudson. "Irish Traveler Cant in its Social Setting." *Southern Folklore Quarterly* 37, no. 2 (1973): 101–14.

Hernon, Joseph M. "The Irish Nationalists and Southern Secession." *Civil War History* 12 (1966): 43–53.

Kenney, Michael. "The Irish in 'The South.'" *Studies: An Irish Quarterly Review* 22 (1933): 89–100.

Leslie, Sir Shane. "Lost Irish in the U. S. A.: The Church in the Deep South." *Tablet* 211 (February 1, 1958): 103–4.

McDonald, Forrest, and Grady McWhiney. "The Celtic South." *History Today* 30 (1980): 11–15.

McGinty, Garnie. "Some Irish Footprints among the Tall Pines." *Louisiana History* 4 (1963): 273–89.

O'Brien, Michael J. "A Glance at Some Pioneer Irish in the South." *American Irish Historical Society Journal* 7 (1907): 45–58.

States

Alabama

Kenny, Michael. *Catholic Culture in Alabama: Spring Hill College, 1830–1930.* New York, 1931.

Lipscomb, Oscar Hugh. "The Administration of John Quinlan, Second Bishop of Mobile, 1859–1883." *Records of the American Catholic Historical Society* 78 (1967): 3–163.

———. "The Administration of Michael Portier, First Bishop of Mobile, 1829–1859." Ph.D. dissertation, The Catholic University of America, 1965.

Arizona

Jackson, W. Turrentine. *Treasure Hill.* Tuscon: University of Arizona Press, 1963.

California

Averback, Alvin. "San Francisco's South of Market District, 1850–1950: The Emergence of a Skid Row." *California Historical Quarterly* 53 (Fall 1973): 199–200.

Bancroft, Hubert Howe. *Popular Tribunals.* 2 vols. Santa Barbara: Wallace Hebberd, 1970.

Bisceglia, Louis R. "The Fenian Funeral of Terence Bellow McManus." *Eire-Ireland* 14, no. 3 (1979).

———. "Irish Identity in the Mother Lode." *Working Papers in Irish Studies.* Northeastern University Press, 1986.

———. "Primary Sources of Anti-English Activities in California, 1916–36." *Southern California Quarterly* 64 (1982): 227–37.

Blessing, Patrick J. "Culture, Religion and the Activities of the Committee of Vigilance, San Francisco, 1856." *Working Papers*, series 8, no. 3 (1980), Charles and Margaret Hall Cushwa Center for the Study of American Catholicism, University of Notre Dame.

———. "West Among Strangers: Irish Migration to California, 1850–1880." Ph.D. dissertation, University of California, Los Angeles, 1977.

Breatnach, Seamus. "Should Irish Eyes Be Smiling?" *San Francisco* 12 (August 1970): 27–29.

Breatnac, S. "The Difference Remains." In *The San Francisco Irish*, edited by J. P. Walsh. San Francisco: Irish Literary Historical Society, 1978.

Brusher, Joseph S. *Consecrated Thunderbolt: Fr. Yorke of San Francisco.* Hawthorne: Wagner, 1973.

———. "Peter C. Yorke and the A.P.A. in San Francisco." *Catholic Historical Review* 37 (July 1951): 129–50.

Bullough, William A. "Chris Buckley and San Francisco: The Man and the City." In *The Irish in San Francisco*, edited by James P. Walsh, San Francisco: Irish Literary History Society, 1978.

———. "The Steam Beer Handicap: Chris Buckley and the San Francisco Municipal Election of 1896." *California Historical Quarterly* 54 (Fall 1975): 245–62.

Burchell, R. A. "The Gathering of a Community: The British-born of San Francisco in 1852 and 1872." *Journal of American Studies* 10 3: 279–312.

———. *San Francisco Irish, 1848–1880.* Berkeley: University of California Press, 1980.

Calhoon, F. D. *49er Irish.* Hicksville, New York, 1977.

Callow, Alexander, B., Jr. "San Francisco's Blind Boss." *Pacific Historical Review* 25 (August 1956): 261–79.

Camp, Charles L., ed. "T. Kerr: An Irishman in the Goldrush." *California Historical Quarterly* 7 (September and December 1928).

Clawson, Marion. "What It Means to Be a Californian: Migration to California, 1870–1945." *California Historical Quarterly* 24 (June 1945).

Cleland, Robert Glass. *The Irvine Ranch.* San Marino: The Huntington Library, 1966.

Connolly, James. "The Historical Place of Irishmen in California." *American Irish Historical Society Journal* 3 (1900).

Cronin, Bernard C. *Father Yorke and the La-*

bor Movement in San Francisco, 1900–1910*. Washington, D.C.: The Catholic University of America Press, 1943.

Cross, Ira B., ed. *Frank Roney: An Autobiography*. New York: Arno Press, 1976.

Crowley, George T. "The Irish in California." *Studies* 25 (1936).

Dancis, Bruce. "Social Mobility and Class Consciousness: San Francisco's International Workmen's Association in the 1880's." *Journal of Social History* 11 (Fall 1977): 75–98.

Decker, Peter. *Fortunes and Failures*. Cambridge: Harvard University Press, 1978.

———. "Social Mobility on the Urban Frontier: The San Francisco Merchants, 1850–1880." Ph.D. dissertation, Columbia University, 1974.

DeFord, Mariam Allen. *They Were San Franciscans*. Caldwell, Idaho: Caxton, 1941.

Donnelly, Mark. "The Irish Among Us." *Westways* (Automobile Club of Southern California), March 1988, 36–37.

Dowling, Patrick J. *California and the Irish Dream*. San Francisco: Golden Gate Publishers, 1988.

Drury, Clifford M. "Church-Sponsored Schools in Early California." *Pacific Historian* 20 (1976).

Dwyer, Bishop R. J. "The Irish in the Building of the Inter-Mountain West." *Irish Ecclesiastical Review* 87 (1957): 401–9.

Dwyer, John T. *Condemned to the Mines: The Life of Eugene O'Connor, 1815–1891, Pioneer Bishop of Northern California and Nevada*. New York: Vantage, 1976.

Dwyer, Joseph J. "The Liberating of San Francisco: A Review of the Battle." *Cosmopolitan Magazine* 43 (August 1907): 442–44.

Erie, S. P. "The Development of Class and Ethnic Politics in San Francisco 1880–1910: A Critique of the Pluralist Interpretation." Ph.D. dissertation, University of California, Los Angeles, 1975.

———. "Politics and Public Sector and Irish Social Mobility, San Francisco, 1870–1900." *Western Political Quarterly* 31 (1978): 274–89.

Fahey, Frank W. "Dennis Kearney, Demagogue." Ph.D. dissertation, Stanford University, 1956.

Fenian Brotherhood. *Proceedings of the First General Convention of the Fenian Brotherhood of the Pacific Coast Held in San Francisco California, September, 1864*. San Francisco: George W. Stevens, 1864.

Gaffney, James P. *Citizen of No Mean City: Archbishop Patrick Riordan of San Francisco, 1891–1914*. Wilmington, Delaware: Consortium, 1976.

Graves, J. A. *Celts Who Have Helped Build Up Los Angeles*. Los Angeles, 1916.

Gribben, Arthur, and Marsha Maguire, comps. *Irish Cultural Directory for Southern California*. Los Angeles: University of California Mythology Center, 1985.

Guinn, J. M. "Los Angeles in the Later Sixties and Early Seventies." *Publications of the Historical Society of Southern California* 64 (1887).

Herlihy, D. J. "Battle Against Bigotry: Father Yorke and the American Protective Association in San Francisco, 1893–1897." *Records of American Catholic Historical Society* 62 (1951): 95–120.

Hurley, Mark J. *Church-State Relationships in Education in California*. Washington, 1948.

Hurt, Peyton. "The Rise and Fall of the 'Know-Nothings' in California." *California Historical Society Quarterly* 9 (March and June 1930): 16–49, 99–128.

"The Irish in California." *Proceedings of the American Irish Historical Society* 15 (1916).

Isetti, Ronald Eugene. *Called to the Pacific: A History of the Christian Brothers in the San Francisco District, 1868–1944*. Moraga, California: St. Mary's College, 1979.

Issel, W. "Class and Ethnic Conflict in San Francisco's Political History: The Reform Charter of 1898." *Labor History* 18 (1977): 341–59.

Kauer, Ralph. "The Workingman's Party of California." *Pacific Historical Review* 12 (September 1944): 275–91.

King, Joseph A. *The Irish Lumberman-Farmer: Fitzgeralds, Harrigans, and Others*. Lafayette, California: n.p., 1982.

Long, J. H. "A Factual Study of the Influence of Reverend P. B. Yorke on Education." Master's thesis, The Catholic University of America, 1932.

Luckingham, Bradford F. "Associational Life on the Urban Frontier: San Francisco, 1848–1856." Ph.D. dissertation, University of California, Davis, 1968.

———. "Benevolence in Emergent San Francisco: A Note on Immigrant Life in the Urban Far West." *Southern California Quarterly* 55 (Winter 1973): 431–33.

———. "Immigrant Life in Emergent San Francisco." *Journal of the West* 12 (October 1973): 600–17.

———. "Religion in Early San Francisco." *Pacific Historian* 17 (1973).

Lummis, Keith. "Some Old California Documents." *Masterkey* 52, no. 3 (1978).

Mann, Ralph Emerson II. *After the Gold Rush: Society in Grass Valley and Nevada City, California, 1849–1870*. Stanford: Stanford University Press, 1982.

———. "The Decade after the Gold Rush: Social Structure in Grass Valley and Nevada City, California, 1850–1860." *Pacific Historical Review* 41 (November 1972): 494–95.

———. "The Social and Political Structure of Two California Mining Towns, 1850–1870." Ph.D. dissertation, Stanford University, 1970.

McCabe, Charles. "Is there a Real Jerry?" *San Francisco Chronicle* (March 1, 1976).

———. "Jerry and God." *San Francisco Chronicle* (July 2, 1976).

———. "Who is this Guy?" *San Francisco Chronicle* (April 10, 1975).

McGinty, Brian. "The Green and The Gold." *The American West* 15, no. 2 (March/April 1978): 18–21; 65–69.

McGowan, Edward. *Narrative of Edward McGowan, Including Full Account of the Author's Adventures and Perils While Persecuted by the San Francisco Vigilance Committee in 1856*. San Francisco: n.p., 1857.

McGowan, Joseph A. *History of the Sacramento Valley*, 2 vols. New York: Lewis, 1961.

McKevitt, Gerald. *The University of Santa Clara: A History 1851–1977*. Stanford: Stanford University Press, 1979.

Monaghan, Jay. *Australians and the Gold Rush*. Berkeley: University of California Press, 1966.

Morgan, Sister Mary Evangelist. *Mercy: Generation to Generation*. San Francisco: Fearon Publishers, 1957.

Muscatine, Doris. *Old San Francisco: The Biography of a City From Early Days to the Earthquake*. New York: Putnam's, 1975.

Myers, John M. *San Francisco's Reign of Terror*. Garden City, New York: Doubleday, 1966.

O'Connor, R. C. "The Irish in California." *American Irish Historical Society Journal* 15 (1916).

O'Donnell, L. A. "From Limerick to the Golden Gate: An Odyssey of an Irish Carpenter." *Studies: An Irish Quarterly* 68 (1979): 76–91.

Pendergast, Thomas F. *Forgotten Pioneers: Irish Leaders in Early California*. San Francisco: Trade Pressroom, 1942.

Peterson, Richard H. "The Frontier Thesis and Social Mobility on the Mining Frontier." *Pacific Historical Review* 44, no. 2 (1975): 52–67.

Posner, R. M. "The Lord and the Drayman: James Bryce vs Dennis Kearney." *California Historical Quarterly* 50 (1971).

Pyeatt, Ralph. "The Story of Murpheys." *Pacific Historian* 19 (1975).

Quigley, Dr. Hugh. *The Irish Race in California and on the Pacific Coast*. San Francisco: A. Roman, 1878.

Quinn, Charles R. *History of Downey*. Downey, California: Elena Quinn, 1973.

Richards, Sherman L. "A Demographic History of the West: Butte County, California, 1850." *Papers of the Michigan Academy of Science: Arts and Letters* 46 (1961).

Roney, F. *Irish Rebel and California Labor Leader: An Autobiography*, edited by I. B. Cross. Berkeley: University of California Press, 1931.

Ryan, Frederick Lynn. "Industrial Relations in the San Francisco Building Trades." Ph.D. dissertation, University of California, Berkeley, 1930.

Sarbaugh, Timothy. "Culture, Militancy, and De Valera: Irish Republicanism in

California 1900–1936." Master's thesis, San Jose State University, 1980.

———. *Exiles of Confidence: The Irish-American Community of San Francisco, 1880–1920*. In *From Paddy to Studs: Irish American Communities at the Turn of the Century Era, 1880 to 1920*, edited by Timothy J. Meager. New York: Greenwood Press, 1986.

———. "Father Yorke and the San Francisco Waterfront, 1901–1916." *The Pacific Historian* (Fall 1981): 29–35.

———. "Irish Republicanism vs Pure Americanism: California's Reaction to Eamon De Valera's Visits." *California History* (Summer 1981): 158–72.

Saxton, Alexander. *The Invisible Enemy: Labor and the Anti-Chinese Movement in California*. Berkeley: University of California Press, 1971.

Seager, Robert. "Some Denominational Reactions to Chinese Immigration to California, 1865–1892." *Pacific Historical Review* 28 (1959): 49–66.

Senkewicz, Robert Michael. "American and Catholic: The Premature Synthesis of the San Francisco Irish." In *An American Church*, edited by D. J. Alvarez. Moraga, California: St. Mary's College, 1979.

———. "Business and Politics in Gold Rush San Francisco, 1851–1856." Ph.D. dissertation, Stanford University, 1974.

Shumsky, Neil L. "Frank Roney's San Francisco Diary." *Labor History* 17, no. 2 (April 1975–March 1976).

———. "Tar Flat and Nob Hill: A Social History of Industrial San Francisco in the 1870s." Ph.D. dissertation, University of California, Berkeley, 1972.

Stack, R. E. "The McCleers and the Birneys: Irish Immigrant Families into Michigan and the California Gold Fields, 1820–1893." Ph.D. dissertation, St. Louis University, 1972.

Star, Kevin. "Jerry Brown: The Governor as Zen Jesuit." In *The San Francisco Irish, 1850–1876*, edited by James P. Walsh. San Francisco: Irish Literary and Historical Society, 1979.

Sullivan, Gabrielle. *Martin Murphy Jr.: A Californian Pioneer, 1844–1884*. Atherton: Holt, 1974.

Tamony, P. "Western Words: Malarkey: TAD, and Its San Francisco Roots." *Western Folklore* 33 (April 1974): 158–62.

Thomas, Lately. *Between Two Empires: Life Story of California's First Senator, William McKendree Gwin*. Boston: 1969.

Trost, Richard H. *The Mooney Case*. Stanford, California, 1968.

Tygiel, Jules E. "Workingmen in San Francisco, 1880–1901." Ph.D. dissertation, University of California at Los Angeles, 1978.

Varcados, Peter. "Labor and Politics in San Francisco, 1880–1892." Ph.D. dissertation, University of California, Berkeley, 1968.

Walsh, Henry L., S.J. *Hallowed Were the Gold Dust Trails*. University of Santa Clara Press, 1946.

Walsh, James P., *Ethnic Militancy*. San Francisco: R and E Associates, 1972.

———. "Peter Yorke and Progressivism in California, 1908." *Eire-Ireland* 10 (1975).

———. "Regent Peter C. Yorke and the University of California, 1900–1912." Ph.D. dissertation, University of California, 1970.

———, ed. *The San Francisco Irish, 1850–1976*. San Francisco: Irish Literary and Historical Society, 1978.

Walsh, James P., and Timothy Foley. "Father Peter C. Yorke: Irish-American Leader." *Studia Hibernica* (Ireland) 14 (1974).

Walters, Donald E. "The Feud Between California Populist T. V. Cator and Democrats James Maguire and James Barry." *Pacific Historical Review* 27 (1958): 281–98.

Weber, Francis J. *Catholic Footprints in California*. California: Hogarth Press, 1970.

———. "Irish-Born Champion of the Mexican-Americans." *California Historical Society Quarterly* 49 (1970).

Wever, Francis J. *California Catholicism*. Los Angeles, 1975.

Weyer, Sister Anita. "Joseph Scott: A Life of Service." *Southern California Quarterly* 48 (September 1966): 241–64.

Williams, D. A. *David C. Broderick*. San Marino, California: Huntington Library, 1969.

Williams, Mary Floyd. *History of The San Francisco Committee of Vigilance of 1851*. New York: Da Copa Press, 1969.

Wright, D. M. "The Making of Cosmopolitan California: An Analysis of Immigration, 1848–1870." *California History Society Quarterly* 70 (1940): 323–43.

Colorado

Leonard, S. J. "The Irish, English, and Germans in Denver, 1860–90." *Colorado Magazine* 54.

Connecticut

Duggan, Rev. Thomas. *The Catholic Church in Connecticut*. New York: States History, 1930.

Duffy, Joseph. "Nineteenth-Century Images of Hartford's Irish-Catholic Community: (1827–1861)." *Eire-Ireland* 21, no. 2 (Summer 1986): 1–12.

Hall, Edward A. "The Irish Pioneers of the Connecticut Valley." *American Irish Historical Society Journal* 4 (1904).

"Irish Settlers in Connecticut." *American Irish Historical Society Journal* 24 (1925).

Jackson, Horace M. *Family History of Michael Jackson: Emigrant from Ireland, Citizen of Hartford, Connecticut*. Kansas City, Missouri, 1909.

Kennedy, R. J. "Single or Triple Melting Pot: Intermarriage in New Haven 1870–1950." *American Journal of Sociology* 58 (1952).

Liptak, Dolores Ann. "European Immigrants and the Catholic Church in Connecticut, 1870–1920." Ph.D. dissertation, University of Connecticut, 1978.

McManus, Thomas. *Historical Sketch of the Catholic Church in Hartford*. Hartford: Clark and Smith, 1880.

Munich, Austin Francis. *The Beginnings of Roman Catholicism in Connecticut*. New Haven: Yale University Press, 1935.

Noonan, C. J. *Nativism in Connecticut 1829–1860*. Washington, D.C: The Catholic University of America Press, 1938.

O'Brien, Michael J. "The Connecticut Irish in the Revolution." *American Irish Historical Society Journal* 22 (1923).

———. "The Irish in New London, Connecticut in the Seventeenth and Eighteenth Centuries." *American Irish Historical Society Journal* 22 (1923): 183–91.

———. "Irish Pioneers in Hartford County, Connecticut." *American Irish Historical Society Journal* 27 (1928).

———. "Irish Pioneers of New London." *American Irish Historical Society Journal* (1927).

———. "Irish Settlers in Connecticut in the Seventeenth and Eighteenth Centuries." *American Irish Historical Society Journal* 24 (1925): 125–41.

O'Connell, John J. "The Abolition Movement in Connecticut: 1830–1850." Master's thesis, Trinity College, Hartford, 1976.

O'Connell, Philip. "Some County Cavan Priests in Connecticut." *Breifne* 2 (1965): 485–94.

Parmet, Robert D. "The Know-Nothings in Connecticut." Ph.D. dissertation, Columbia University, 1966.

Purcell, Richard J. "Some Early Teachers in Connecticut." *Catholic Educational Review* 32 (1934): 332–38.

Stone, Frank Andrews. *The Irish in Connecticut*. Storrs: Parousia Press, 1975.

Delaware

O'Brien, Michael J. "Irish Pioneers in Delaware." *American Irish Historical Society Journal* 18 (1919).

Purcell, Richard J. "Irish Settlers in Early Delaware." *Pennsylvania Magazine of History and Biography* 16.

Georgia

Callahan, Helen. "A Study of Dublin: The Irish in Augusta." *Richmond County History* 5 (1973): 5–14.

Chalker, Russell. "Irish Catholics in the Building of the Okmulgee and Flint Railroad." *Georgia Historical Quarterly* 54, no. 4 (Winter 1970): 508–16.

Crimmins, John D. "One Hundredth Anniversary of the Founding of the Hibernian Society of Savannah, Georgia." *American Irish Historical Society Journal* 11 (1912).

"The Irish in Atlanta, Georgia." *American Irish Historical Society Journal* 30 (1932).

Muller, E. "Roving the South with the Irish Horse Traders: Once a Year They Meet in Atlanta to Bury Their Dead." *Reader's Digest* 39 (July 1941): 59–63.

O'Brien, Michael J. "The Dooly's of Georgia." *American Irish Historical Society Journal* 22 (1923): 179–81.

Illinois

Allswang, John M. *A House for All People: Ethnic Politics in Chicago, 1890–1936*. Lexington: University Press of Kentucky, 1971.

Barry, Patrick T. *The First Irish in Illinois*. Chicago: Chicago Newspaper Union, 1902.

———. "First Irish in Illinois." *American Irish Historical Society Journal* 4 (1904) 95–108.

Becker, Richard E. "Edward Dunne: Reform Mayor of Chicago, 1905–1907." Ph.D. dissertation, University of Chicago, 1971.

Biles, Roger. *Big City Boss in Depression and War: Mayor Edward J. Kelly of Chicago*. DeKalb: Northern Illinois University Press, 1984.

Brewer, Eileen M. "Beyond Utility: The Role of the Nuns in the Education of American Catholic Girls, 1860–1920." Ph.D. dissertation, University of Chicago, 1984.

Buenker, John D. *Urban Liberalism and Progressive Reform*. New York: Charles Scribner's Sons, 1973.

Cook, Frederick Francis. *Bygone Days in Chicago: Recollections of the "Garden City" of the Sixties*. Chicago: McClurg, 1910.

Cressey, Paul F. "Population Succession in Chicago, 1898–1930." *The American Journal of Sociology* 44 (1938–39).

Dahm, Charles W. *Power and Authority in the Catholic Church: Cardinal Cody in Chicago*. Notre Dame, Indiana: University of Notre Dame Press, 1982.

Dillion, Patrick J. "History of Irish Immigration to the United State: The Irish in Chicago." *Christus Rex* 12 (1958): 51–59.

Fanning, Charles and Ellen Skerrett." James T. Farrell and Washington Park." *Chicago History* 7, no. 2 (Summer 1979): 80–91.

Fanning, Charles, Ellen Skerrett, and John Corrigan. *Nineteenth Century Chicago Irish: A Social and Political Portrait*. Chicago: Center for Urban Policy, Loyola University of Chicago, 1980.

Farrell, J. T. "World I Grew Up In: Chicago's South Side." *Commonweal* 83 (February 25, 1966): 606–7.

French, Charles, ed. *Biographical History of the American-Irish in Chicago*. Chicago: American Biographical, 1897.

Fleming, George. "Canal at Chicago." Ph.D. dissertation, The Catholic University of America, 1950.

Flinn, John J. *History of the Chicago Police from the Settlement of the Community to the Present Time*. Chicago: Police Book Fund, 1887.

Funchion, Michael F. "Chicago's Irish Nationalists, 1881–1890." Ph.D. dissertation, Loyola, University of Chicago, 1973.

———. "Irish Chicago: Church, Homeland, Politics, and Class—The Shaping of an Ethnic Group, 1870–1900." In *Ethnic Chicago*, edited by Peter d'A. Jones and Melvin G. Holli. Grand Rapids: William B. Erdmans, 1981.

———. "Irish Nationalists and Chicago Politics in the 1880s." *Eire-Ireland* 10, no. 2 (1975): 3–18.

Gaffey, James P. "Patterns of Ecclesiastical Authority: The Problem of Chicago Succession, 1865–1881." *Church History* 42 (1973): 257–70.

Gallery, Mary Onahan, ed. "The Diaries of William J. Onahan." *Mid-America* 14 (1931): 152–77.

Gates, Paul W. *The Illinois Central Railroad and Its Colonization Work*, 1934.

Gleason, William F. *Daley of Chicago*. New York: Simon and Schuster, 1970.

Greeley, Andrew M. "Looking Backward: Commodore Barry Country Club in Twin Lakes, Wisconsin." *Chicago History* 8, no. 2 (1979): 112–19.

Green, Paul Michael. "Irish Chicago: The

Multiethnic Road to Machine Success." In *Ethnic Chicago*, edited by Peter d'A. Jones and Melvin G. Holli. Grand Rapids, Michigan: William B. Eerdmans, 1981.

"Haymarket: A Tribute to Early Irish Policemen." *Sceal* (Newsletter of the Chicago Irish Folklore Society) 2, no. 2 (1981).

Keefe, Thomas M. "The Catholic Issue in the Chicago Tribune before the Civil War." *Mid-America* 57 (1975): 227–45.

———. "Chicago's Flirtation with Political Nativism, 1854–1856." *Records of the American Catholic Historical Society of Philadelphia* 82 (1971): 131–58.

Kirkfleet, Cornelius. *The Life of Patrick Augustine Feehan: Bishop of Nashville, First Bishop of Chicago, 1829–1902*. Chicago: Matre, 1922.

Koenig, Msgr. Harry C., ed. *A History of the Parishes of the Archdiocese of Chicago*, 2 vols. Chicago: Archdiocese of Chicago, 1980.

Kantowicz, Edward. "Church and Neighborhood." *Ethnicity* 7, no. 4 (December 1980).

Levine, Edward M. *The Irish and Irish Politicians*. Notre Dame, Indiana: University of Notre Dame Press, 1966.

Lubell, S. "The Chicago Irish." In *The Future of American Politics,* edited by Samuel Lubell. New York: Harper, 1952.

McCaffrey, Lawrence, et al. *The Irish in Chicago*. Urbana and Chicago: University of Illinois Press, 1987.

McCullough, L. E. "Irish Music in Chicago: An Ethnomusicological Study." Ph.D. dissertation, Loyola University of Chicago, 1978.

McGoorty, J. P. "Early Irish of Illinois." *Illinois Historical Society Transactions* 34 (1927): 54–64.

McGorty, John P. "The Early Irish in Illinois." *Illinois Catholic Historical Reveiw* 10 (July 1927): 26–37.

O'Dwyer, George Francis. "Irish Colonization in Illinois." *Illinois Catholic Historical Review* 3 (July 1920): 73–76.

O'Malley, Peter J. "Mayor Martin Kennelly of Chicago: A Political Biography." Ph.D. dissertation, University of Illinois at Chicago, 1980.

Onahan, W. J. "Irish Settlements in Illinois." *Catholic World* 33 (1881): 157–62.

Overton, Richard C. *Burlington West: A Colonization History of the Burlington Railroad*, 1941.

Pierce, Bessie Louise. *A History of Chicago*. 3 vols. Chicago: Alfred A. Knopf, 1937–57.

Piper, R. M. "The Irish in Chicago." Master's thesis, University of Chicago, n.d.

Sanders, James W. *The Education of an Urban Minority: Catholics in Chicago, 1833–1965*. New York: Oxford University Press, 1977.

Senning, J. P. "The Know-Nothing Movement in Illinois." *Journal of the Illinois Historical Society* 7 (1914–15).

Shanabruch, Charles. *Chicago's Catholics: The Evolution of an American Identity*. Notre Dame, Indiana: University of Notre Dame Press, 1981.

Skerrett, Ellen. "The Catholic Dimension." In *The Irish in Chicago*, edited by Lawrence J. McCaffrey, et al. Urbana: University of Illinois Press, 1987.

———. "The Development of Catholic Identity among Irish Americans in Chicago, 1880–1920." *From Paddy to Studs: Irish American Communities in the Turn of the Century Era, 1880 to 1920*, edited by Timothy J. Meager. New York: Greenwood Press, 1986.

Smith, M. S. "The Influence of the Irish Vote in Chicago and the Elections of 1884, 1888 and 1892." Master's thesis, University of Notre Dame, 1958.

Thompson, Joseph J. "The Irish in Early Illinois." *Illinois Catholic Historical Review* 2 (October 1919): 223–38.

———. "The Irish in Chicago." *Illinois Catholic Historical Review* 3 (October 1920): 196–216.

Walsh, James B., ed. *The Irish: America's Political Class*. New York: Arno Press, 1976.

Walsh, John Patrick. "The Catholic Church in Chicago and the Problems of an Urban Society, 1893–1915." Ph.D. dissertation, University of Chicago, 1948.

Zorbaugh, Harvey Warren. *The Gold Coast and the Slum: A Sociological Study of Chi-

cago's Near North Side. Chicago: University of Chicago Press, 1929.

Indiana

Esslinger, Dean Robert. "The Urbanization of South Bend's Immigrants, 1850–1880." Ph.D. dissertation, University of Notre Dame, 1972.

Lang, E. "Irishmen in Northern Indiana before 1850." *Mid-America* 36 (July 1954): 190–98.

Iowa

Bowers, William L. "Crawford Township, 1850–70: A Population Study of a Pioneer Community." *Iowa Journal of History* 58 (January 1960).

Calkin, H. L. "The Irish in Iowa." *Palimpsest* 45 (1964): 33–96.

Carey, Sister Mary Helen. "The Irish Element in Iowa to 1865." Master's thesis, The Catholic University of America, 1944.

Colton, Kenneth E. "Parnell's Mission in Iowa." *Annals of Iowa: A Historical Quarterly* 22 (1940): 312–27.

"Irish in Iowa." *The Palimpsest* 45 (January 1954).

Price, Eliphalet. "The Trial and Execution of Patrick O'Connor at the Dubuque Mines." *Palimpsest* 1 (1920): 86–97.

Schmitz, Diocese of Sioux Falls. "Wexford, Iowa, 1851–1876." Master's thesis, Saint Paul Seminary, 1959.

Sullivan, J. B. "Kate Shelley: An Irish Heroine of Iowa." *American Irish Historical Society Journal* 25 (1926): 195–201.

Thorne, Mildred. "A Population Study of an Iowa County in 1850," *Iowa Journal of History* 57 (1959).

Van Der Zee, Jacob. *The British in Iowa.* Iowa City: State Historical Society of Iowa, 1922.

Kansas

Martin, T. "The Race That God Made Mad: A Memoir by an Architect's Granddaughter." *Kansas Quarterly* 6, no. 2 (1974): 105–14.

Walther, Thomas R. "Some Aspects of Economic Mobility in Barrett Township of Thomas County, 1885–1905." *Kansas Historical Quarterly* (1971): 281–87.

Kentucky

Anneken, Sister Mary Gemma. "A Study of the Growth of Catholicism in Covington, Kentucky, 1830–1868." Master's thesis, University of Notre Dame, 1946.

Ardery, Mrs. W. B. *Kentucky Records* 1, 1926; 2, 1932. Lexington, Kentucky: Keystone Printery.

Deusner, C. E. "The Know-Nothing Riots in Louisville." *Register of the Kentucky Historical Society* 61 (1943): 122–47.

Ellis, William E. "Patrick Henry Callahan: A Kentucky Democrat in National Politics." *Filson Club Historical Quarterly* 51, no. 1 (1977): 17–30.

Fitzpatrick, Edward. "Early Irish Settlers in Kentucky." *American Irish Historical Society Journal* 2 (1899).

Godwin, Parke. "Secret Societies—The Know-Nothings." *Putnam's Monthly* 5 (January 1855): 94–95.

Hutcheon, Wallace S. "The Louisville Riots of August, 1855." *Kentucky Historical Society Register* 69 (1971): 150–72.

Kennedy, P. W. "The Know-Nothing Movement in Kentucky: The Role of M. J. Spalding, Catholic Bishop of Louisville." *Filson Club Historical Quarterly* 38 (20–30).

Koester, L. "Louisville's Bloody Monday, August 6, 1955." *The History Bulletin* 25 (1948).

Linehan, John C. "Irish Pioneers and Builders of Kentucky." *American Irish Historical Society Journal* 3 (1900).

Loester, Leonard. "Louisville's 'Bloody Monday'—August 6, 1855." *The Historical Bulletin* 26 (March 1948): 53–54, 62–64.

"The Louisville Riots." *Washington National Era,* August 16, 1855.

"The Louisville Riots—The Tragic Side of Know-Nothingism." *New York Times,* August 8, 1855.

McGann, A. G. *Nativism in Kentucky to*

1860. Washington, D.C.: The Catholic University of America Press, 1944.

O'Brien, Michael J. *Irish Pioneers in Kentucky*. A series of articles published in the *Gaelic American*. New York: James Thompson, 1912.

Ousley, Stanley, Jr. "The Irish in Louisville." Master's thesis, University of Louisville, 1974.

Ousley, Stanley. "The Kentucky Irish American." *Filson Club Historical Quarterly* 53, no. 2 (1979): 178–95.

Purcell, Richard J. "Education and Irish Teachers in Early Kentucky." *Catholic Educational Review* 34 (1936): 360–69.

Spalding, Brother Martin John. "Biography of a Kentucky Town—An Historical, Cultural and Literary Study of Bardstown." Master's thesis, University of Notre Dame, 1940.

Louisiana

McGinty, G. W., and E. Conly. *Cullen Thomas Conly: American Irish Stowaway 1820–1876*. Shreveport, Louisiana: Rushing, 1976.

Neu, I. "From Kilkenny to Louisiana: Notes on Eighteenth–Century Irish Emigration." *Mid-America* 49 (April 1967): 101–14.

Niehaus, Earl F. *The Irish in New Orleans, 1800–1860*. Baton Rouge: Louisiana State University Press, 1965.

———. "The Irish in New Orleans, 1803–1862." Ph.D. dissertation, Tulane University, 1961.

———. "Paddy on the Local Stage and in Humor: The Image of the Irish in New Orleans, 1830–1862." *Louisiana History* 5 (1964): 117–34.

Reinders, Robert C. "The Louisiana American Party and the Catholic Church." *Mid-America* 40 (1958): 218–28.

Maine

Baker, Margaret J. "The Irish in Lewiston, Maine: A Search for Security on the Urban Frontier, 1850–1880." *Maine Historical Society Quarterly* 13, no. 1/A special (1973): 3–25.

O'Brien, Michael J. "The Early Irish in Maine." *American Irish Historical Society Journal* 10 (1911).

———. "The Lost Town of Cork, Maine." *American Irish Historical Society Journal* 12 (1913).

O'Dwyer, George F. "Irish Pioneers of Maine." *American Irish Historical Society Journal* 19 and 20 (1920–21).

Purcell, Richard J. "Maine: Early Schools and Irish Teachers." *Catholic Educational Review* 33 (1935).

Woodbury, K. B., Jr. "Incident Between the French Canadians and the Irish in the Diocese of Maine in 1906." *New England Quarterly* 40 (June 1967): 260–69.

Maryland

Dodd, Jill Siegal. "Social Change and the Working Class Community in Antebellum Baltimore." Ph.D. dissertation, Harvard University, 1977.

Garonzik, Joseph. "The Racial and Ethnic Make-Up of Baltimore Neighborhoods, 1850–70." *Maryland Historical Magazine* 71 (Fall 1976): 396–402.

"The Irish in Baltimore." *American-Irish Historical Society, Recorder* 9, no. 2 (1936).

"Irish Pioneers in Maryland." *American Irish Historical Society Journal* 14 (1915).

McGinty, Brian. "The Truth of a Good Country: The Irish in America (Early Maryland Colony)." *Early American Life* 121 (December 1981): 76–86.

McKenrick, Carl Ross. "New Munster." *Maryland Historical Magazine* 35 (1940): 147–59.

O'Brien, Michael J. "The Irish in Maryland, 1778." *American Irish Historical Society Journal* 24 (1925).

———. "The Irish in Montgomery and Washington Counties, Maryland, in 1778." *American Irish Historical Society Journal* 24 (1925): 157–61.

———. "New Munster, New Ireland County, Maryland." *American Irish Historical Society Journal* 22 (1923): 30–44.

Purcell, Richard J. "Education and Irish Schoolmasters in Maryland's National Period." *Catholic Educational Review* 32 (1934): 198–207.

———. "Irish Colonists in Colonial Maryland." *Studies: An Irish Quarterly Review* 23 (1932): 279–94.

Raley, R. L. "Irish Influence in Baltimore Decorative Arts, 1785–1815." *Antiques* 79 (March 1961): 276–79.

Schmeckebier, Laurence F. *History of the Know Nothing Party in Maryland*. Baltimore: Johns Hopkins University Press, 1899.

Scully, D. J. "Irish Influence in the Life of Baltimore." *American Irish Historical Society Journal* 7 (1907).

Tuska, B. "Know Nothingism in Baltimore, 1854–1860." *Catholic Historical Review* 11 (1925): 217–51.

Williams, H. A. *History of the Hibernian Society of Baltimore, 1830–1957*. Baltimore: Hibernian Society of Baltimore, 1957.

Massachusetts

Ackland, Thomas. "The Kelts of Colonial Boston." *American Irish Historical Society Journal* 7 (1907).

Baum, D. "The 'Irish Vote' and Party Politics in Massachusetts, 1860–1876." *Civil War History* 26 (1980): 117–141.

Bliven, Bruce. "Boston: What Have the Irish Done?" *New Republic* 30 (May 10, 1922): 307–9.

Brayley, Arthur Wellington. *The Complete History of the Boston Fire Department*. Boston, 1889.

———. *Schools and Schoolboys: Old Boston*. Boston, 1894.

Breen, T. H., and Stephen Foster. "Moving to the New World: The Character of Early Massachusetts Immigration." *William and Mary Quarterly* 30, no. 2 (1973): 189–222.

Brown, H. La Rue. "Massachusetts and the Minimum Wage." *Annals of the American Academy of Political and Social Science* 48 (July 1913).

Bushee, Frederick A. "The Growth of the Population of Boston." *American Statistical Association*, no. 46 (June 1899): 241–72.

Chesbrough, E. S. *Tabular Representation of the Present Condition of Boston*. Boston, 1851.

Cohen, Morris H. "Worcester Ethnics." *Holy Cross Quarterly* 5, nos. 3–4: 42–47.

Cole, Donald G. *Immigrant City*. Chapel Hill: University of North Carolina Press, 1963.

Creveling, Harold. "A Cultural Geography of Worcester, Massachusetts." Ph.D. dissertation, Clark University, 1953.

Cullen, James B. *Story of The Irish in Boston*. Boston: Cullen, 1899.

Darling, A. B. "Jacksonian Democracy in Massachusetts, 1824–1848." *American Historical Review* 29 (1924): 187–271.

Donovan, George Francis. "The Irish in Massachusetts before 1700." *Historical Bulletin* 8 (March 1930): 43–45, 53.

———. *The Pre-Revolutionary Irish in Massachusetts*. Menasha, Wisconsin: George Banta, 1932.

———. "The Pre-Revolutionary Irish in Massachusetts, 1620–1775." Ph.D. dissertation, St. Louis University, 1931.

Doyle, John E. "Chicopee's Irish (1830–1875)." *Historical Journal of Massachusetts* 3, no. 1 (1974): 13–23.

Dublin, Thomas. *Women at Work: The Transformation of Work and Community in Lowell, Massachusetts, 1826–1860*. New York: Columbia University Press, 1979.

Dubnoff, Steven Jan. "The Family and Absence From Work: Irish Workers in a Lowell, Massachusetts Cotton Mill, 1860." Ph.D. dissertation, Browders University, Waltham, Massachusetts, 1975.

Dubovik, P. N. "Housing in Holyoke and Its Effects on Family Life, 1800–1910." *Historical Journal of Western Massachusetts* 4 (1975).

Dwight, Thomas. "The Attach on Freedom of Education in Massachusetts." *American Catholic Quarterly Review* 12 (October 1888): 545–55.

"Early Irish Settlers at Worcester, Massachusetts." *American Irish Historical Society Journal* 18 (1919).

Eisinger, P. K. "Ethnic Political Transition in Boston, 1884–1933." *Political Science Quarterly* 93: 217–39.

Emery, Susan L. *A Catholic Stronghold and Its Making: A History of St. Peter's Parish, Dorchester, Massachusetts, and of Its First Rector, The Rev. Peter Ronan, P.R.* Boston: George H. Ellis, 1910.

Eno, Arther L. Jr., ed. *Cotton Was King.* Lowell: Lowell Historical Society, 1976.

Forbes, H. A., and H. Lee. *Massachusetts Help to Ireland during the Great Famine.* Milton, Massachusetts: Forbes House, 1967.

Friedman, D. J. *White Militancy in Boston.* Lexington, Massachusetts: Lexington Books, 1973.

Gearan, Mari Margaret. *The Early Irish Settlers in the Town of Gardner, Massachusetts.* Fitchburg, Massachusetts: 1932.

Gesualdi, Louis. " 'Research Note': A note on Boston's racial problems." *Sociological Inquiry* 52 (1982): 255–57.

Gitelman, Howard M. *Workingmen of Waltham.* Baltimore: Johns Hopkins University Press, 1974.

Handlin, Oscar. *Boston's Immigrants: A Study in Acculturation.* Cambridge, Massachusetts: Belknap Press of Harvard University Press, 1959.

Hareven, T. K., and M. Vinovskis. "Marital Fertility, Ethnicity and Occupation in Urban Families: An Analysis of South Boston and the South End in 1880." *Journal of Urban History* 1 (1975): 293–315.

Hunnewell, James F. *A Century of Town Life: A History of Charlestown, 1775–1887.* Boston: Little, Brown, 1888.

Hunter, R. J. "Dublin to Boston, 1719." *Eire/Ireland* 6 (1971): 18–24.

"Irish Girls in Lowell." *Boston Pilot* 16 (August 1851): 7.

Kenneally, James J. "Catholics and Woman Suffrage in Massachusetts." *Catholic Historical Review* 53.

Kenngott, G. F. "Irish in Massachusetts." In *Record of a City*, edited by F. F. Kenngott. New York: Macmillan, 1912.

Knights, Peter. *The Plain People of Boston, 1830–1860: A Study in City Growth.* New York: Oxford University Press, 1971.

Kuczynski, R. R. "Fecundity of the Native and Foreign Born Population in Massachusetts." *Quarterly Journal of Economics* 16 (1901).

Lane, Robert. *Policing the City, Boston, 1822–1885.* Cambridge: Harvard University Press, 1967.

Langtry, Albert P., ed. *Metropolitan Boston.* New York: Lewis Historical, 1929.

Lankevich, George J., ed. *Boston: A Chronological and Documentary History, 1602–1970.* Dobbs Ferry, New York: Oceana, 1974.

Lee, Thomas Z. "The Charitable Irish Society of Boston." *American Irish Historical Society Journal* 24 (1925).

Linehan, John C. "Irish Pioneers in Boston and Vicinity." *American Irish Historical Society Journal* 3 (1900).

Linehan, Mary Lessey. "The Irish Settlers of Pelham, Massachusetts." *American Irish Historical Society Journal* 3 (1900).

Litt, Edgar. *The Political Cultures of Massachusetts.* Cambridge: Massachusetts Institute of Technology, 1965.

"Looking Back at Old Cambridge, Massachusetts." *American Irish Historical Society Journal* 7 (1907).

Lynch, John E. "Early Irish Settlers in Worcester, Massachusetts." *The Recorder, American Irish Historical Society* 10 (1939).

Marston, Sallie A. "Neighborhood and Politics: Irish Ethnicity in Nineteenth Century Lowell, Massachusetts." *Annals of the Association of American Geographers* 78 (September 1988): 414–33.

Massey, D. "Class, Racism and Bussing in Boston." *Annales* 8 (1976).

McCarthy, J. "Southie is My Home Town: Why the Irish Love South Boston." *Holiday* 35 (March 1964): 60–61.

Meagher, Timothy J. " 'The Grand Privilage of Our Public Schools': The Delayed Development of Parochial Education among Irish Catholics in Worcester." *Historical Journal of Massachusetts* 12 (January 1984).

———. " 'Irish All the Time': Ethnic Consciousness among the Irish in Worcester, Massachusetts, 1880–1905." *Journal of Social History* 19 (Winter 1985).

———. "Irish, American, Catholic, Irish–American Identity in Worcester, Massachusetts, 1880–1920." In *From Paddy to Studs: Irish–American Communities at the*

Turn of the Century Era, 1880 to 1920, edited by Timothy J. Meager. New York: Greenwood Press, 1986.

———. " 'Why Should We Care for a Little Trouble or a Walk Through the Mud': St. Patrick and Columbus Day Parades in Worcester, Massachusetts, 1845–1915." *New England Quarterly* 58 (March 1985).

Merk, Lois Bannister. "Boston's Historic Public School Crisis." *New England Quarterly* 31 (June 1958): 172–99.

Merwick, D. *Boston's Priests, 1848–1910*. Cambridge: Harvard University Press, 1973.

Millet, William W. "The Irish and Mobility Patterns in Northampton, Massachusetts, 1846–1883." Ph.D. dissertation, University of Iowa, 1980.

Mitchell, Albert Gibbs, Jr. "Irish Family Patterns in Nineteenth Century Ireland and Lowell, Massachusetts." Ph.D. dissertation, Boston University, 1976.

Mitchell, Brian C. "Educating Irish Immigrants in Antebellum Lowell." *Historical Journal of Massachusetts* 11(1983): 94–103.

———. "Immigrants in Utopia: The Early Irish Community of Lowell, Massachusetts, 1821–1861." Ph.D. dissertation, University of Rochester, 1981.

———. *The Paddy Camps: The Meaning of Community among the Irish in Lowell, Massachusetts, 1821–1861*. Urbana: University of Illinois Press, 1986.

———. " 'They Do Not Differ Greatly': The Pattern of Community Development among the Irish in Late Nineteenth Century Lowell, Massachusetts." *From Paddy to Studs: Irish American Communities at the Turn of the Century Era, 1880 to 1920*, edited by Timothy J. Meager. New York: Greenwood Press, 1986.

Morgan, John H. "Ethnoconsciousness and Political Powerlessness: Boston's Irish." *Social Science* 53, no. 3 (1978): 159–67.

———. "The Irish of South Boston." *Worldview* 18 (1975).

Morgan, M., and H. H. Gordon. "Immigrant Families in an Industrial City: A Study of Households in Holyoke, 1880." *Journal of Family History* 4 (1979).

Mulkern, John Raymond. "The Know-Nothing Party in Massachusetts." Ph.D. dissertation, Boston University, 1963.

Mullaney, K. F. *Catholic Pittsfield and Berkshire (Massachusetts)*. Pittsfield, Massachusetts: Press of the Sun Printing, 1897–1924.

O'Brien, Michael J. "Early Irish Names on the Ipswich Vital Records." *American Irish Historical Society Journal* 16 (1917).

———. "Irish Immigrants to New England—Extracts from the Minutes of the Selectmen of the Town of Boston, Massachusetts." *American Irish Historical Society Journal* 13 (1914): 177–87.

———. "Irish Names from Boston Probate Records." *American Irish Historical Society Journal* 15 (1916).

———. "The Pioneer Irish of Essex County, Massachusetts." *American Irish Historical Society Journal* 26 (1927).

———. "Pioneer Irishmen of Northhampton, Massachusetts." *American Irish Historical Society Journal* 17 (1918).

———. "Some Stray Historical Nuggets from the Early Records of Massachusetts Towns." *American Irish Historical Society Journal* 15 (1916): 172–90.

———. "Some Traces of the Irish Settlers in the Colony of Massachusetts Bay." *American Irish Historical Society Journal* 18 (1919).

O'Connor, Thomas H. "The Irish in Boston." *Urban and Social Change Review* 12, no. 2 (1979): 19–23.

O'Dwyer, George F. *The Catholic Genesis of Lowell*. Lowell, Massachusetts: Sullivan Brothers, 1920.

———. "Historical Gleanings from Massachusetts' Records." *American Irish Historical Society Journal* 18 (1919).

———. *Irish Catholic Genesis of Lowell*. Lowell, Massachusetts: Sullivan Brothers, 1920.

———. "The Irish in Ipswich, 1630–1700." *Catholic World* 115 (September 1922): 805–14.

O'Malley, Charles J. "American Irish Progress in Boston." *American Irish Historical Society Journal* 24 (1925).

Powers, V. E. "Invisible Immigrants: The Pre-Famine Irish Community in Worcester, Massachusetts from 1826 to 1860."

Ph.D. dissertation, Clark University, 1976.

Purcell, Richard J. "Education and Irish Schoolmasters in Colonial Massachusetts." *Catholic Educational Review* 33 (1935): 467–79.

Quincy, Josiah. *Municipal History of Boston*. Boston, 1852.

Rice, Franklin, ed. *The Worcester of Eighteen Hundred and Ninety Eight*. Worcester, Massachusetts: F. S. Blanchard, 1899.

Russell, F. "Why Massachusetts Loves the Kennedy's." *National Review* 22 (August 11, 1970).

Ryan, D. P. "Beyond the Ballot Box: A Social History of the Boston Irish, 1845–1917." Ph.D. dissertation, Boston University, 1979.

Stack, John F., Jr. *International Conflict in an American City: Boston's Irish, Italians and Jews, 1935–1944*. Westport, Connecticut: Greenwood, 1979.

Stegner, Wallace. "Who Persecutes Boston?" *Atlantic Monthly* 174 (July 1944).

Sweeney, K. "Rum, Romanism, Representations, and Reform: Coalition Politics in Massachusetts, 1847–1853." *Civil War History* 22 (1976): 116–37.

Thernstrom, Stephan. "Immigrants and Wasps: Ethnic Difference in Occupational Choice in Boston, 1890–1940." In *Nineteenth Century Cities*, edited by Stephan Thernstrom and Richard Sennett. New Haven, Connecticut, 1969.

———. "Irish Life in Yankee City." In *Catholicism in America*, edited by Philip Gleason. New York: Harper and Row, 1970.

———. *The Other Bostonians*. Cambridge: Harvard University Press, 1973.

———. *Poverty and Progress*. Cambridge: Harvard University Press, 1964.

Towne, W. Henry, and Michael J. O'Brien. "Early Irish Settlers at Worcester, Massachusetts." *American Irish Historical Society Journal* 18 (1919): 169–75.

Ueda, Reed T. *Avenues to Adulthood: The Origins of High School and Social Mobility in an American Suburb*. Cambridge, Massachusetts: Cambridge University Press, 1987.

———. "Class, Culture, and Education in Boston, Massachusetts, 1850–1930." Ph.D. dissertation, Harvard University, 1977.

Ward, D. "Nineteenth Century Boston: A Study in the Role of Antecedent and Adjacent Conditions in the Spatial Aspects of Urban Growth." Ph.D. dissertation, University of Wisconsin, 1963.

Warner, Sam Bass, Jr. *Streetcar Suburbs: The Process of Growth in Boston, 1870–1900*. New York: Atheneum, 1969.

Washburn, Charles. *Industrial Worcester*. Worcester, Massachusetts, 1917.

White, A. O. "Antebellum School Reform in Boston: Integrationists and Separatists." *Phylon* 34 (1973).

Whyte, W. F. "Race Conflicts in the North End of Boston from 1860 to the Present." *New England Quarterly* 12 (1939): 623–42.

Woods, R. A. "Irish in Boston." In *Americans in Process*, edited by R.A. Woods. Boston: Houghton, 1902.

Zolot, H. M. "The Issue of Good Government and James Michael Curley: Curley and the Boston Scene from 1897–1918." Ph.D. dissertation, State University of New York, Stoney Brook, 1975.

Michigan

Bloomberg, Susan E., Mary Frank Fox, Robert M. Warner, and Sam Bass Warner, Jr. "A Census Probe into Nineteenth-Century Family History: Southern Michigan, 1850–1880." *Journal of Social History* 5, no. 1 (Fall 1971): 27–45.

Kirk, Gordon Wilham, Jr. "The Promise of American Life: Holland, Michigan, 1847–1894." Ph.D. dissertation, Michigan State University, 1970.

Meagher, Rev. George Thomas. "A Study of the Influence of the Michigan Central Railroad on the Growth of the Catholic Church in Southern Michigan from 1840 to 1850." Master's thesis, University of Notre Dame, 1936.

Stack, Robert Edward. "The McCleers and the Birneys—Irish Immigrant Families—Into Michigan and the California Gold Fields, 1820–1893." Ph.D. dissertation, Saint Louis University, 1972.

Vinyard, Jo Ellen. "Inland Urban Immigrants: The Detroit Irish, 1850." *Michigan History* 55 (1973).

———. "The Irish on the Urban Frontier: Detroit, 1850–1880." Ph. D. dissertation, University of Michigan, 1972.

———. *The Irish on the Urban Frontier: Nineteenth Century Detroit, 1850–1880.* New York: Arno Press, 1976.

Minnesota

Anderson, M. J. "From an Irish Farm to a Minnesota Homestead." *Gopher Historian* 21 (1967): 21–26.

Benson, James K. "Irish and German Families and the Economic Development of Midwestern Cities, 1860–1895: St. Paul, Minnesota." Ph.D. dissertation, University of Minnesota, 1980.

Berger, John Gerald. *A History of St. Brendan's Parish: The Village of Green Isle and Minnesota's First Irish Settlement.* Privately published, 1966.

Deininger, M., and D. Marshall. "A Study of Land Ownership by Ethnic Groups from Frontier Times to the Present in a Marginal Farming Area of Minnesota." *Land Economics* 31 (1955): 160–351.

Egan, Howard Eston. "Irish Immigration to Minnesota, 1865–1890." *Mid-America* 12, no. 1 (October 1929): 133–66, and 12 (January 1930): 223–46.

Ellinger, Agnes. *A History of the Temperance Movement in Minnesota to 1865.* St. Paul, Minnesota: Minnesota Historical Society, 1933.

Evans, John Whitney. "A History of the Immaculate Heart of Mary Parish of Curry, Murray County, Minnesota." Master's thesis, St. Paul Seminary, 1957.

Flahavan, Edward J. "A Quarter Century of Alms: The Aid Given to the Diocese of St. Paul by the Society of the Propogation of Faith, (1850–1873)." Master's thesis, St. Paul Seminary, 1956.

Flanagan, Kieran Denis. "Emigration, Assimilation, and Occupational Categories of the Irish Americans in Minnesota, 1870–1900." Master's thesis, University of Minnesota, 1969.

Ireland, J. *Catholic Colonization in Minnesota.* St. Paul, Minnesota: Catholic Colonization Bureau of Minnesota, 1879.

"The Irish Colonies in Minnesota." *The Recorder, American-Irish Historical Society* 7, no. 2 (1934).

Kennelly, Karen. "Mary Molloy: Women's College Founder." In *Women of Minnesota: Selected Biographical Essays*, edited by Barbara Stuhler and Gretchen Kreuter. St. Paul: Minnesota Historical Society Press, 1977, 136–154.

Michaels, Eileen Manning. "Alice O'Brien: Volunteer and Philanthropist." In *Women of Minnesota: Selected Biographical Essays*, edited by Barbara Stuhler and Gretchen Kreuter. St. Paul, Minnesota: Minnesota Historical Society Press, 1977, 136–54.

Moudry, Richard Paul. "The Chapel of St. Paul: The Beginnings of Catholicity in St. Paul, Minnesota, 1840–1851." Master's thesis, St. Paul Seminary, 1950.

Qualey, C. C. "Some National Groups in Minnesota." *Minnesota History* 31 (1950): 18–32.

Regan, Ann. "The Irish." In *They Chose Minnesota*, edited by D. Holmquist. St. Paul, Minnesota, 1981.

Shannon, James P. "Bishop Ireland's Connemara Experiment." *Minnesota History* 35 (1956–57): 205–13.

Smith, Alice E. "The Sweetman Irish Colony." *Minnesota History* 9 (December 1928): 331–46.

Sweetman, J. *Farms for Sale in the Sweetman Catholic Colony of Murry County Minnesota.* St. Paul, Minnesota: Irish-American Colonization, 1885.

———. "The Sweetman Catholic Colony of Currie, Minnesota: A Memoir." *Acta et Dicta* 3 (1911): 41–61.

Tuke, J. H. "News from Some Irish Immigrants." *19th Century* 25: 431–37.

Winter, Sister Mary Meinrad. "The Beginnings of Catholicity in Minnesota." Master's thesis, University of Notre Dame, 1950.

Missouri

Atlantic and Pacific Railroad Company. *A Guide to Irish Settlements in Southwest Missouri.* St. Louis, 1875. Copy in Yale Western Americana Collection, Yale University.

Brown, A. T. *The Politics of Reform Kansas City Municipal Government, 1925–1950*. Kansas City: Community Studies, 1958.

Connolly, Christopher P. *The Devil Learns to Vote: The Short Story of Montana*. New York: Covici, Friede, 1938.

Dolan, Ellen Meara. *The St. Louis Irish*. St. Louis: 1967.

Dykstra, Arlen R. "Rowdyism and Rivalism in the St. Louis Fire Department, 1850–1857." *Missouri Historical Review* 69 (October 1974): 48–64.

Faherty, William B. *Dream by the River: Two Centuries of St. Louis Catholicism, 1766–1967*. St. Louis, 1973.

Hanratty, Marie Felicitia. "A Study of Early Irish Contributions to the Growth of St. Louis, 1804–1840." Master's thesis, St. Louis University, 1933.

Harrison, Ann. "Edward Butler." Master's thesis, Washington University, 1968.

Hayes, Sister Mary. "Politics and Government in Colonial St. Louis: A Study of the Growth of Political Awareness." Ph.D. dissertation, St. Louis University, 1972.

Hodes, Frederick Anthony. "The Urbanization of St. Louis: A Study of Urban Residential Patterns in the Nineteenth Century." Ph.D. dissertation, St. Louis University, 1973.

Kelleher, Daniel T. "St. Louis, 1916 Residential Segregation Ordinance." *Bulletin of the Missouri Historical Society* 26 (April 1970): 239–48.

McHugh, George J. "Political Nativism in St. Louis, 1840–1857." Master's thesis, St. Louis University, 1939.

O'Hanlon, John. *Life and Scenery in Missouri*. Dublin, 1890.

O'Leary, Cornelius F. "The Irish in the Early Days of St. Louis." *American Irish Historical Society Journal* 9 (1910): 206–13.

Reddig, W. *Tom's Town: Kansas City and the Pendergast Legend*. New York: Lippincott, 1947.

Stygar, Sister Mary Martina. "Saint Louis Immigrants from 1820–1860." Master's thesis, St. Louis University.

Sullivan, Margaret. "Constitutionalism, Revolution and Culture: Irish-American Nationalism in St. Louis, 1902–1914." *Missouri Historical Society Bulletin* 28, no. 4 (July 1972): 234–45.

———. "Fighting for Irish Freedom: St. Louis Irish-Americans, 1918–1922." *Missouri Historical Review* 65 (1971): 184–206.

———. "St. Louis Ethnic Neighborhoods, 1850–1930: An Introduction." *Bulletin of the Missouri Historical Society* 34 (January 1977): 64–76.

———. "Where Did All the Irish Go? The Irish in St. Louis, 1900–1925." Paper read at the annual meeting of the Organization of American Historians, 1976.

Thompson, Alice. "William Igoe: The Quiet Boss." Ph.D. dissertation, St. Louis University, 1981.

Towey, Martin G. "Kerry Patch Revisited: Irish Americans in St. Louis in the Turn of the Century Era." In *From Paddy to Studs: Irish American Communities at the Turn of the Century Era, 1880 to 1920*, edited by Timothy J. Meager. New York: Greenwood Press, 1986.

Towey, Martin G., and Margaret LoPiccolo Sullivan. "The Knights of Father Mathew: Parallel Ethnic Reform." *Missouri Historical Review* 75 (January 1981): 168–83.

Ward, Francis J. "Early Irish in St. Louis, Missouri." *American-Irish Historical Society Journal* 6 (1906): 47–50.

Montana

American Association for the Recognition of the Irish Republic. *Butte Chapter, Second Annual Convention, Butte, Feb 12, 1922*. Butte: Butte Independent, 1922.

Ancient Order of Hibernians. *Constitution and Byelaws of the AOH of America. Montana Territory, 1886*. Butte: Mining Journal, 1887. Copy in Irish Collection, University of Montana.

Dowling, Catherine. "Irish-American Nationalism, 1900–1916: Butte as a Case Study." Master's thesis, University of Montana, 1982.

Emmons, David M. "An Aristocracy of Labor: The Irish Miners of Butte, 1878–1914." *Labor History* 28 (Summer 1987): 275–306.

———. *The Butte Irish: Class and Ethnicity*

in an American Mining Town, 1875–1925. Urbana and Chicago: University of Illinois Press, 1989.

———. "Immigrant Workers and Industrial Hazards: The Irish Miners of Butte, 1880–1919." *Journal of American Ethnic History* 5 (Fall 1985): 41–64.

———. "The Orange and the Green in Montana: A Reconsideration of the Clark-Daly Feud." *Arizona and the West* 28 (Autumn 1986): 225–45.

Foot, Forrest. "The Senatorial Aspirations of William A. Clark." Ph.D. dissertation, University of California, Berkeley, 1941.

McPherson, James L. "Butte Miner's Union: An Analysis of Its Development and Economic Bargaining Position." University of Montana, Master's thesis, 1949.

Oberley, Edith Toole. "The Baron C. C. O'Keefe: The Legend and the Legacy." *Montana* 23, no. 3 (1973): 18–29.

Prodgers, Jeanette. "Father Jeremiah J. Callahan: Butte's First Irish Priest, 1898–1906." *Montana: The Magazine of Western History* 34 (1984): 42–49.

Shoebotham, H. Minar. *Anaconda: The Life of Marcus Daly, the Copper King.* Harrisburg, Pennsylvania: Stackpole, 1956.

Smith, Norma. "The Rise and Fall of the Butte Miners' Union, 1878–1914." Master's thesis, Montana State University, 1961.

Toole, K. Ross. "The Genesis of the Clark-Daly Feud." *Montana Magazine of History* 1 (1951): 21–33.

———. "Marcus Daly: A Study of Business in Politics." Master's thesis, University of Montana, 1948.

Wetzel, Kurt. "The Making of an American Radical: Bill Dunn in Butte." Master's thesis, University of Montana, 1970.

Nebraska

Casper, Henry W. *History of the Roman Catholic Church in Nebraska: Catholic Chapters in Nebraska Immigration.* 3 vols. Milwaukee: Bruce, 1966.

Coad, Ralph G. "Irish Pioneers of Nebraska." *Nebraska History Magazine* 17 (1936): 171–77.

Martin, Sister M. Aquinata. "Irish Catholic Colonization in the Diocese of Omaha, 1856–1890." Master's thesis, University of Notre Dame, 1932.

O'Neill, J. *O'Neill's Irish American Colonies in Nebraska,* n.p., 1896.

O'Dowd, Michael. *Irish Catholic Immigration to America.* Omaha, Nebraska: 1874.

Nevada

DeQuille, Dan. *The Big Bonanza.* New York: Alfred A. Knopf, 1967.

Gorman, Thomas K. *Diamond Jubilee of the Church in Nevada.* Reno, 1935.

Shepperson, Wilbur S. "The Foreign-Born Response to Nevada." *Pacific Historical Review* 39 (February 1970).

New Hampshire

Brennan, James F. "The Irish Pioneers and Founders of Peterborough, New Hampshire." *American Irish Historical Society Journal* 2 (1899).

———. "The Irish Settlers of New Hampshire." *American Irish Historical Society Journal* 9 (1910): 247–57.

———. "The Irish Settlers of Southern New Hampshire." *American Irish Historical Society Journal* 9 (1910).

"Early Irish Settlers in Maine and New Hampshire." *Sprague's Journal of Maine History* 10 (1922): 29–31.

The History of Dublin, New Hampshire. Boston: J. Wilson and Son, 1855.

Linehan, John C. "Early New Hampshire Irish." *American Irish Historical Society Journal* 3 (1900).

O'Brien, Michael J. "Irish Pioneers in New Hampshire." *American Irish Historical Society Journal* 25 (1926).

———. "Some Irish Names Culled from the Official Records of New Hampshire." *American Irish Historical Society Journal* 18 (1919).

Purcell, Richard J. "Schools and Early Irish Teachers in New Hampshire." *Catholic Educational Review* 32 (1934): 608–18.

Qurik, Robert D. "The Irish Element in New

Hampshire to 1865." Master's thesis, The Catholic University of America, 1936.

New Jersey

Connors, R. J. "The Local Political Career of Frank Hague." Ph.D. dissertation, Columbia University, 1966.

Foster, Mark S. "The Early Career of Mayor Frank Hague." Master's thesis, University of Southern California, 1968.

———. "Frank Hague of Jersey City: The Boss as Reformer." *New Jersey History* 85.

Mahoney, Willian H. "American-Irish Prominent in New Jersey State and Local Government." *American Irish Historical Society Journal* 21 (1922): 125–31.

———. "The Irish Element in Newark, New Jersey." *American Irish Historical Society Journal* 21 (1922).

———. "Irish Footsteps in New Jersey Sands." *American Irish Historical Society Journal* 26 (1927): 247–54.

———. "The Irish in Princeton, New Jersey." *American Irish Historical Society Journal* 27 (1928): 314–20.

———. "Irish Settlers in Union County, New Jersey." *American Irish Historical Society Journal* 28 (1930).

———. "The Melting Pot: Irish Footsteps in New Jersey." *American Irish Historical Society Journal* 25 (1926).

———. "Some Seventeenth-Century Irish Colonists in New Jersey." *American Irish Historical Society Journal* 26 (1927): 242–46.

O'Brien, Michael J. "The Irish in New Jersey Probate Records." *American Irish Historical Society Journal* 27 (1928).

———. "Some Early Irish Settlers and Schoolmasters in New Jersey." *American Irish Historical Society Journal* 11 (1912).

Purcell, Richard J. "Irish Settlers in Early New Jersey." *The Recorder, American Irish Historical Society Journal* 13 (1914): 1.

Shaw, Douglas Vincent. *The Making of an Immigrant City: Ethnic and Cultural Conflict in Jersey City, New Jersey, 1850–1977*. New York: Arno Press, 1976.

Vesey, Maxwell. "When New Brunswick Suffered Invasion." *Dalhouse Review* 19 (1939): 197–204.

New York

Albion, Robert G. *The Rise of New York Port, 1815–60*. New York: Scribner's, 1939.

Alfred, W. "Ourselves Alone: Irish Exiles in Brooklyn." *Atlantic* 27 (March 1971): 53–58.

Asbury, Herbert. *The Gangs of New York*. New York: A. A. Knopf, 1928.

Bannon, Theresa. *Pioneer Irish of Onondaga County, New York, 1776–1847*. New York: G. P. Putnam's Sons, 1911.

Barnes, David M. *The Draft Riots in New York, July 1863; The Metropolitan Police: Their Services during Riot Week, Their Honorable Record*. New York: Baker and Godwin, 1863.

Bayor, R. H. *Neighbors in Conflict: The Irish, Germans, Jews and Italians of New York City, 1929–41*. Baltimore: Johns Hopkins University Press, 1978.

Beadles, John Asa. "The Syracuse Irish, 1812–1928: Immigration, Catholicism, Socioeconomic Status, and Irish Nationalism." Ph.D. dissertation, Syracuse University, 1974.

Bennett, William Harper. *Catholic Footsteps in Old New York*. New York: Schwartz, Kerwin and Fauss, 1909.

———. *Handbook to Catholic Historical New York City*. New York: Schwartz, Kerwin and Fauss, 1927.

Bernard, W. F. *Forty Years at the Five Points*. New York: Five Points House of Industry, 1893.

Bernstein, Iver. *The New York City Draft Riots*. New York: Oxford University Press, 1990.

Brace, C. L. *The Dangerous Classes of New York and Twenty Years Work among Them*. New York: Wynkoop, 1880.

Burke, O. "New York's Irish: Pictures." *Jubilee* 6 (March 1959): 6–15.

Camann, H. *The Charities of New York, Brooklyn and Staten Island*. New York: Hurd and Houghton, 1868.

Carpenter, Niles. *Nationality, Color, and Economic Opportunity in the City of Buf-*

falo. New York: University of Buffalo, 1927.

Casey, Daniel J. "Heresy in the Diocese of Brooklyn: An Unholy Trinity." *New York Affairs* 4, no. 4 (1978): 73–86.

Coffey, John Joseph. "A Political History of the Temperance Movement in New York State, 1808–1920." Ph.D. dissertation, Pennsylvania State University, 1976.

The Collections of the History of Albany: From Its Discovery to the Present Time, With . . . Biographical Sketches, Etc. 4 vols. Albany, New York, 1865–71.

Collins C. W. "Alexander MacComb," *York State Tradition* 28:3 (1974) 18–20.

Cook, A. *The Armies of the Streets: The New York Draft Riots of 1863*. Lexington, Kentucky: University Press of Kentucky, 1974.

Cook, Adrian. "Ashes and Blood: The New York City Draft Riots." *American History Illustrated* 12 (August 1977): 30–40.

Costello, A. *Our Firemen: History of the New York Fire Department*. New York, 1887.

———. *Our Police Protectors: History of the New York Police*. New York, 1884.

Coyle, John G. "Irish Militiamen in New York Province." *American Irish Historical Society Journal* 15 (1916).

Crapsey, Edward. *The Nether Side of New York*. New York: Sheldon, 1872.

Crimmins, John D. *St. Patrick's Day: Its Celebration in New York, 1737–1845*. n.p., n. d.

Curran, T. J. "Know Nothings of New York State." Ph.D. dissertation, Columbia University, 1963.

Cusack, M. F. *Advice to Irish Girls in America*. New York: Pustet 1886.

———. *From Killarney to New York or How Thade Became a Banker*. New York: Pustet, 1886.

Dallas, Gregor. "New York, 1856." *History Today* 37 (December 1987).

Danaher, Franklin M. "Early Irish in Old Albany, New York." Paper read before the American-Irish Historical Society, 1903.

Deacy, Jack. "The I.R.A.: New York Brigade." *New York Magazine* (March 13, 1972) 40–43.

Dolan, Jay. "Immigrants in the City: New York Irish and German Catholics." *Church History* 41 (1974): 354–68.

Donovan, Herbert D.A. "Fenian Memories in Northern New York." *American Irish Historical Society Journal* 23 (1924).

Dowling, Victor James. "Irish Pioneers in New York." *American Irish Historical Society Journal* 8 (1909): 117–39.

Doyle, R. D. "The Pre-Revolutionary Irish in New York, 1643–1775." Ph.D. dissertation, St. Louis University, 1932.

Dupree, A. H., and L. H. Fishell, eds. "An Eyewitness Account of the New York Draft Riots, July 1863." *Mississippi Valley Historical Review* 47: 472–79.

"Emigrants in Niagara, 1847." *Niagara Historical Society Publication* 31 (1918): 34–41.

Ernst, Robert. "Economic Nativism in New York City During the 1840s." *New York History* 29 (1948): 170–86.

———. *Immigrant Life in New York*. Port Washington, New York: Ira J. Friedman, 1965.

Fitzpatrick, F. E. "Irish Immigration to New York from 1865–1880." Master's thesis, The Catholic University of America, 1948.

Flaherty, Joe. *Chez Joey: The World of Joe Flaherty*. New York: Coward, McGann, and Geoghegan, 1974.

———. "The Men of Local 1268: God Bless Them All, The Last of a Bad Breed." *New York Magazine* (March 13, 1972) 56–58.

Genen, Arthur. "John Kelly: New York's First Irish Boss." Ph.D. dissertation, New York University, 1971.

Gerard, James. *The Impress of Nationalities upon the City of New York*. New York: Columbia University, 1951.

Gibson, F. E. *The Attitudes of New York Irish Toward State and National Affairs, 1848–1892*. New York: Columbia University, 1951.

Glasco, Laurence Admiral. "Ethnicity and Social Structure: Irish, Germans and Native-Born of Buffalo, New York, 1850–1860." Ph.D. dissertation, State University of New York at Buffalo, 1973.

———. "The Life Cycles and Household

Structure of American Ethnic Groups, Irish, Germans, and Native-Born Whites in Buffalo, New York, 1855." *Journal of Urban History* 1, no. 3 (May 1975): 339–64.

Gordon, Michael. "Irish Immigrant Culture and the Labor Boycott in New York City, 1880–1886." In *Immigrants in Industrial America, 1850–1920*, edited by R. C. Ehrlich. Charlottesville: University of Virginia Press, 1977.

———. "Studies in Irish and Irish American Thought and Behavior in Guilded Age New York City." Ph.D. dissertation, University of Rochester, 1977.

Gredel, Stephen. "Immigration of Ethnic Groups to Buffalo." *Niagara Frontier* (Summer 1963): 42–56.

Griffen, Clyde. "Workers Divided: The Effect of Craft and Ethnic Differences in Poughkeepsie, New York, 1850–1880." In *Nineteenth Century Cities*, edited by Stephan Thernstrom and Richard Sennett. New Haven: Yale University Press, 1969.

Griffen, Clyde, and Sally Griffen. "Family and Business in a Small City, Poughkeepsie, New York, 1850–1880." *Journal of Urban History* 1, no. 3 (1975): 316–38.

———. *Natives and Newcomers: The Ordering of Opportunity in Poughkeepsie, New York, 1850–1880*. Cambridge: Harvard University Press, 1978.

Groneman, C. "She Earns as a Child—She Pays as a Man: Women Workers in a Mid-Nineteenth Century New York City Community." In *Immigrants in Industrial America, 1850–1920*, edited by R. C. Ehrlich. Charlottesville: University of Virginia Press, 1977.

Groneman, Carol Pernicone. "The Bloody Ould Sixth: A Social Analysis of a Mid-Nineteenth Century New York City Working Class Community." Ph.D. dissertation, University of Rochester, 1973.

Halsey, Francis Whitney. *The Old New York Frontier*. New York: Charles Scribner's Sons, 1901.

Hamill, Pete. "Notes on the New Irish: A Guide for the Goyim." *New York Magazine* (March 13, 1972): 33–39.

Harlow, Alvin F. *Old Bowery Days*. New York, 1931.

Harrigan, Margaret Connors. "Their Own Kind: Family and Community Life in Albany, New York, 1850–1915." Ph.D. dissertation, Harvard University, 1975.

Harris, S. H. "John Louis O' Sullivan and the Election of 1844 in New York." *New York History* 44 (1960): 278–98.

Hastings, Hugh. "Irish Stars in the Archives of the New York Province." *American Irish Historical Society Journal* 9 (1910).

Hughes, Thomas P., ed. "Genealogies of Columbia County, New York." *American Ancestry* 2 (1887).

"Irish Players in New York." *Outlook* 99: 801.

"Irish Property Owners of Old New York." *American Irish Historical Society Journal* 15 (1916).

Kortenaar, Henry Ten. "Irish Power on First Avenue." *Commonweal* 90 (May 23, 1969): 278–79.

Linehan, John C. "The Society of the Friendly Sons of St. Patrick in the City of New York," *American Irish Historical Society Journal* 7 (1907): 183–95.

Lippard, George. *New York: Its Upper Ten and Lower Million*. Cincinnati, Ohio: Mendenhall, 1854.

Maguire, Edward J. "Gleanings of New York Irish Records." *American Irish Historical Society Journal* 3: (1900).

Man, A. P. "The Irish in New York in the Early Eighteen-Sixties." *Irish Historical Studies* 7 (September 1950): 87–108.

Mattis, Mary Catherine. "The Irish Family in Buffalo, New York, 1855–1875: A Socio-Historical Analysis." Ph.D. dissertation, Washington University, 1975.

McCarthy, J. "Gra-a-nd Parade: New York City's Saint Patrick's Day Parade." *America Heritage* 20 (February 1969): 54–59.

McManus, Terence. "A Few Outstanding Figures of Irish Ancestry at the Bench and Bar of New York." *American Irish Historical Society Journal* 23 (1924).

Meehan, Thomas F. "A Bit of New York History." *American Irish Historical Society Journal* 7 (1907).

———. "New York's First Irish Emigrant Society." *U.S. Catholic Historical Society, Records and Studies* 6 (1913): 202–11.

———. "Pioneer Times in Brooklyn." *U.S. Catholic Historical Society, Records and Studies* 3 (1904): 115–30.

"Memorial to the Irish Emigrant Society of New York." 41st Congress. 3d Session, *House Misc. Doc., #69, F 6*, 1871.

Miller, Douglas T. "Immigration and Social Stratification in Pre-Civil War New York." *New York History* 49 (1968): 157–68.

Moynihan, Daniel Patrick. "The Irish." In *Beyond the Melting Pot*, edited by Daniel Patrick Moynihan and Nathan Glazer. Cambridge: MIT Press, 1963.

———. "Irish of New York." *Commentary* 36 (1963): 93–107.

———. "When the Irish Ran New York." *Reporter* 24 (June 8, 1961): 32–34.

Murphy, R. C., and L. Mannion. *The History of the Society of the Friendly Sons of St. Patrick in the City of New York, 1784–1955*. New York: Murphy and Mannion, 1962.

O'Brien, Michael J. "The Carrolls in the Old New York." *American Irish Historical Society Journal* 22 (1923): 84–95.

———. "Early Irish Settlers in the Champlain Valley." *Recorder* 4 (September 1927): 104.

———. "In Old New York: The Irish Deceased: In Trinity and St. Paul's Churchyards." *American Irish Historical Society Journal* 27 (1928).

———. "The Irish Burghers of New Amsterdam and Freemen of New York." *American Irish Historical Society Journal* 17 (1918).

———. "Irish Colonists in New York." *New York State Historical Association*, 1906.

———. "The Irish and Dutch in Albany, New York, Colonial Records." *American Irish Historical Society Journal* 26 (1927).

———. "The Irish in the Dutch Records of the City of New York." *American Irish Historical Society Journal* 27 (1928).

———. "The Irish in Old New York." *The Recorder* 3 (1926): 6.

———. "Irish Schoolmasters in the City of New York." *American Irish Historical Society Journal* 27 (1928).

———. "Irish Settlers in Orange County, New York." *American Irish Historical Society Journal* 27 (1928).

———. "Irish Settlers in Queen's County, City of New York." *American Irish Historical Society Journal* 27 (1928).

———. "Some Pre-Revolutionary Ferrymen of Staten Island." *American Irish Historical Society Journal* 15 (1916).

———. "The Ulster County, New York Irish in the Surrogate's Records." *American Irish Historical Society Journal* 22 (1923): 129–36.

O'Driscoll, Felicity. "Political Nativism in Buffalo." *Records of the American Catholic Historical Society* (September 1937).

O'Gorman, Richard. "New York City in 1859: A Letter... to William Smith O'Brien (1 January 1859)." *New York History* 34 (January 1953): 85–90.

Purcell, Richard J. "Immigration from the Canal Era to the Civil War." In *History of the State of New York*, edited by Alexander C. Flick, 10 vols. New York: Columbia University Press, 1935.

———. "Irish Contribution to Colonial New York." *Studies: An Irish Quarterly Review* 27 (1928): 41–60.

———. "Irish Cultural Contribution in Early New York." *Catholic Educational Review* 35 (1937): 449–60, and 36 (1938): 28–42.

———. "The Irish Emigrant Society of New York." *Studies: An Irish Quarterly Review* 27 (December 1938): 585–87.

———. "Irish Residents in Albany, 1783–1865." *The Recorder* 12 (1950): 1

———. "The New York Commissioners of Emigration and Irish Immigrants, 1847–1860." *Studies* 37 (March 1948): 29–42.

Purcell, Richard J., and John F. Poole. "Political Nativism in Brooklyn." *American Irish Historical Society Journal* 32 (1940).

Quillen, Isaac J. "A History of the Five Points to 1890." Master's thesis, Yale University, 1932.

Riis, J. A. "Irish in New York." In *Battle With the Slum*, edited by J. A. Riis. Boston: Houghton, 1900.

Rosenwaile, Ira. *Population History of New York City*. New York: Syracuse University Press, 1972.

Rowley, William E. "The Irish Aristocracy of Albany, 1798–1878." *New York History* 52, no. 3 (July 1971): 275–304.

Schwartz, J. "Morrisiania's Volunteer Fireman, 1848–1874: The Limits of Local Insititutions in a Metropolitan Age." *New York History* 55 (1974).

"Some Irish Arrivals in New York in 1810–1811." *The Recorder, American Irish Historical Society Journal* 2, no. 2 (1923).

"Some Irish Arrivals in New York, Philadelphia, and Baltimore in 1811." *The Recorder, American Irish Historical Society Journal* 3, no. 6.

Svefda, G. J. *Irish Immigrant Participation in the Construction of the Erie Canal.* Washington, D.C.: Office of Archealogy and Historic Preservation, 1969.

Thompson, Craig, and Allen Raymond. *Gang Rule in New York: The Story of a Lawless Era.* New York: Dial, 1940.

Tracy, P. "Irish Power on First Avenue." *Commonweal* 90 (May 23, 1969): 278–79.

Walling, G. *Recollections of a New York Chief of Police.* New York: Caxton, 1888.

Ward, Samuel Dexter. "New York City in 1842." *New York Historical Society Quarterly* 21, no. 4 (October 1937).

Webber, J. E. "Visit of the Irish Players to New York." *Cand. Magazine* 38.

Weinbaum, P. O. "Temperance, Politics and the New York City Riots of 1857." *New York Historical Society Quarterly* 59 (1975): 246–70.

White, P. L. "An Irish Immigrant Housewife on the New York Frontier." *New York History* 48 (1967).

North Carolina

Corbitt, David L. *The Formation of the North Carolina Counties.* Raleigh, North Carolina, 1950.

Green, E. R. R. "The Scotch-Irish and the Coming of the Revolution in North Carolina." *Irish Historical Studies* 7 (1955): 77–86.

Hannon, W. B. "Irish Builders in North Carolina." *The Recorder* (1925).

"Irish Named Counties In North Carolina." *American Irish Historical Society Journal* 10 (1911): 324–26.

Ray, Worth S. *The Lost Tribes of North Carolina.* 3 parts. Baltimore, Maryland: Southern Book Company, 1956.

Semmes, Lt. Raphael. "Extracts from the County Records of Guilford County, North Carolina." *The Recorder, American-Irish Historical Society* 3 (1925).

Smith, J. E., Jr. "Thomas Burke: Governor of North Carolina." *American Irish Historical Society Journal* 28 (1930): 61–64.

Williams, V. Faison. "Henry McCullough and His Irish Settlement." *North Carolina Booklet* 22 (1924): 32–39.

Ohio

Bartha, Stephen J. "A History of Immigrant Groups in Toledo." Master's thesis, Ohio State University, 1945.

Callahan, Nelson J., and William F. Hickey. *Irish-Americans and Their Communities of Cleveland.* Cleveland: Ethnic Heritage Studies, 1978.

Dannenbaum, J. "Immigrants and Temperance Ethnocultural Conflicts in Cincinnati, 1845–1900." *Ohio History* 87 (1978): 125–39.

Geary, James W. "Towards the 'Lace Curtain': The Irish in Cleveland in the Immediate Post-Civil War Era." *Ethnic Forum* 2 (1982): 60–76.

Leonard, Henry B. "Ethnic Conflict and Episcopal Power: The Diocese of Cleveland, 1847–1870." *Catholic Historical Review* 62 (1976): 388–407.

Pap, M. "The Irish Community of Cleveland." In *Ethnic Communities of Cleveland: A Reference Work*, edited by M. Pap. Cleveland: John Carroll University, 1973.

Rogers, V. A. "The Irish in Cincinnati, 1860–1870." Master's thesis, University of Cincinnati, 1972.

Oklahoma

Brown, Thomas Elton. *Bible Belt Catholicism: A History of the Roman Catholic Church in Oklahoma, 1905–1945.* New York: United States Catholic Historical Society, 1977.

Blessing, Patrick J. *The British and Irish in*

Oklahoma. Norman: University of Oklahoma Press, 1980.

Lohbeck, Don. *Patrick J. Hurley.* Chicago: Henry Regnery, 1956.

McNamee, John, ed. *Breaking the Cake of Custom. (Sermons of Noted Irish-Born Tulsa Parish Priest, Rev. James McNamee).* Tulsa: Privately Printed, 1978.

Michalicka, Brother John. "First Catholic Church in Indian Territory, 1872: St. Patrick's Church at Atoka." *Chronicles of Oklahoma* 1, no. 4 (Winter 1972): 479–85.

White, James D. *Tulsa Catholics.* New York: Carlton Press, 1978.

Oregon

Barry, Bob. *From Shamrocks to Sagebrush.* Lakeview, Oregon: Examiner, 1969.

"Disbandment of the United Irishmen of Portland, Oregon." *Oregonian* (February 14, 1880).

Feller, Daniel M. *Get a Job: Occupational Structure and Social Mobility in Portland, Oregon, 1860–1880.* N.p., n.d. Microfilm copy in collection of Oregon Historical Society, Portland, Oregon, circa 1970.

"Irish Bend, Benton County." *Oregon Historical Quarterly* 46.

"The Irish and the Democratic Party." *Oregonian* (March 10, 1855).

"Irish Land League Holds Meeting in Portland." *Oregonian* (July 24, 1882).

"The Irish and the Vote." *Oregonian* (May 12, 1874).

Kazin, Michael. *Irish Families in Portland, Oregon, 1850–1880* (1975). Copy in rare books collections of Oregon Historical Society, Portland, Oregon.

Kilkenny, Judge John. *Shamrock and Shepherds: The Irish of Morrow County.* Oregon: Morrow County Historical Society, 1968.

"The Portland Branch of the Irish Land League Has Meeting. Letter from Governor Thayer." *Oregonian* (November 2, 1881).

"Portland Irish-Americans Meet and Pass Resolutions Denouncing Proposed Arbitrary Treaty with England." *Oregonian* (April 27, 1908).

"Portland's First Census." *Oregonian* (March 23, 1930).

Robbins, William Grover. "The Far Western Frontier: Economic Opportunity and Social Democracy in Early Roseburg, Oregon." Ph.D. dissertation, University of Oregon, 1969.

———. "Opportunity and Persistence in the Pacific Northwest: A Quantitative Study of Early Roseburg, Oregon." *Pacific Historical Review* 39 (1970).

———. "Social and Economic Change in Roseburg, Oregon, 1850–1880." *Pacific Northwest Quarterly* (April 1973): 80–87.

Schiwek, Joseph A. *Report on Demolished Historic Sites in 1960s Urban Renewal Area.* n. p. 1974. Copy in collection of Oregon Historical Society, Portland, Oregon.

Pennsylvania

Adams, Don R. "Workers on the Brandywine." *Working Papers for the Regional Economic History Center* 3 (1980).

Alexander, John K. "Poverty, Fear and Continuity: An Analysis of the Poor in Late Eighteenth-Century Philadelphia." In *The Peoples of Philadelphia*, edited by Allen F. David and Mark H. Jaller. Philadelphia: Temple University Press, 1973.

Allison, Milton M. "Iffly: 'Ghost Town.'" *Western Pennsylvania Historical Magazine* 35 (June 1952).

Anspach, M. R. "The Molly Maguires in the Anthracite Coal Regions of Pennsylvania, 1850–1890. *Now and Then* 2 (1954): 25–54.

Armour, William C. *Scotch-Irish Bibliography of Pennsylvania.* Nashville, Tennessee, 1897.

Aurand, H. W. "The Anthracite Strike of 1887–1888." *Pennsylvania History* 35 (1968).

Barrett, J. P. "The Life and Death of an Irish Neighborhood." *Philadelphia Magazine* 61 (1970).

———. *The Sesqui-Centennial History of St. Denis Parish.* Haverstown, Pennsylvania: St. Denis Parish, 1875.

Bennett, John. "Iron Workers in Woods Run and Johnstown: The Union Era, 1865–1895." Ph.D. dissertation, University of Pittsburgh, 1978.

Berthoff, R. "The Social Order of the Anthracite Region, 1825–1902." *Pennsylvania Magazine of History and Biography* 89 (1965): 261–91.

Blumin, Stuart. "Mobility and Change in Antebellum Philadelphia." In *Nineteenth Century Cities*, edited by Stephan Thernstrom and Richard Sennett. New Haven: Yale University Press, 1969.

Bodner, John, ed. *The Ethnic Experience in Philadelphia*. Lewisburg, Pennsylvania: Bucknell University Press, 1977.

Burstein, Alan Nathan. "Residential Distribution and Mobility of Irish and German Immigrants in Philadelphia, 1850–1880." Ph.D. dissertation, University of Pennsylvania, 1975.

Cales, Edgar B. "The Organization of Labor in Philadelphia, 1850–1870." Ph.D. dissertation, University of Pennsylvania, 1940.

Carter, E. C. "A 'Wild Irishman' Under Every Federalists Bed: Naturalization in Philadelphia, 1789–1806." *Pennsylvania Magazine of History and Biography* 94 (1970): 331–46.

Chalkley, L. *Chronicles of the Scotch-Irish in Virginia*. 3 vols. Baltimore: Genealogical, 1980. Original edition, 1912.

Clark, Dennis J. "The Adjustment of Irish Immigrants to Urban Life: The Philadelphia Experience, 1840–1870." Ph.D. dissertation, Temple University, 1970.

———. "Babes in Bondage: Indentured Irish Children in Philadelphia in the Nineteenth Century." *Pennsylvania Magazine of History and Biography* 101, no. 4 (1977): 475–86.

———. "Eireannach Eigin: William J. Bradley (1892–1981), Sinn Fein Advocate." *Eire-Ireland* 18, no. 2 (Summer 1983): 116–126.

———. "Ethnic Enterprise and Urban Development." *Ethnicity* 5, no. 2 (1978): 108–18.

———. "Intrepid Men, Three Philadelphia Irish Leaders, 1880–1920." In *From Paddy to Studs: Irish American Communities at the Turn of the Century Era, 1880 to 1920*, edited by Timothy J. Meager. New York: Greenwood Press, 1986.

———. *The Irish in Philadelphia*. Philadelphia: Temple University Press, 1973.

———. *The Irish Relations: Trials of an Immigration Generation*. East Brunswick, New Jersey: Fairleigh Dickinson University Press, 1982.

———. "Kellyville: An Immigrant Enterprise." *Pennsylvania History* 39, no. 2 (January 1972).

———. "Militants of the 1860s: The Philadelphia Fenians." *Pennsylvania Magazine of History and Biography* 95 (1971): 98–108.

———. "Muted Heritage: Gaelic in an American City." *Eire-Ireland* 6 (1971).

———. "News from the Old Country: Irish Newspapers in Philadelphia, 1820–1970." Unpublished paper delivered at the annual meeting of the *Organization of American Historians*, St. Louis, April 1976.

———. "The Philadelphia Irish: Persistent Presence." In *The Peoples of Philadelphia*, edited by A. F. Davis and M. H. Haller. Philadelphia: Temple University Press, 1973.

Clemens, William Montgomery. *Virginia Wills Before 1799*. Pompton Lakes, New Jersey: Biblio, 1924.

Cocke, W. R., III. *Hanover County Chancery Wills and Notes. A Compendium of Genealogical, Biographical and Historical Material Contained in Cases of the Chancery Suits*. Columbia, Virginia: W. R. Cocke, III, 1940.

Coleman, J. W. *The Molly Maguire Riots: Industrial Conflict in the Pennsylvania Coal Region*. Richmond, Virginia: Garrett and Massie, 1936. Reprinted by Arno Press, 1969.

Coyle, Dr. John G. "American-Irish Governors of Pennsylvania." *American Irish Historical Society Journal* 14: 1914–15.

Davis A. F., and M. H. Haller, eds. *The Peoples of Philadelphia: A History of Ethnic Groups and Lower Class Life, 1790–1940*. Philadelphia: Temple University Press, 1973.

Desmond, H. J. "Obstructions to Irish Immigration to Pennsylvania, 1736." *American Catholic Quarterly* 21: 485.

Feldberg, Michael. "The Crowd in Philadelphia History: A Study in Ethnic Conflict." *Labor History* 15 (1974): 323–36.

———. *The Philadelphia Riots of 1844: A Study of Ethnic Conflict.* New York: Greenwood Press, 1975.

Fennell, Dorothy E. "Western Insurrection: The Popular Classes, Culture, and Ideology of Western Pennsylvania, 1780–1800." Ph.D. dissertation, University of Pittsburgh, Pennsylvania, 1977.

Good, P. K. "Irish Adjustment to American Society: Integration or Separation? A Portrait of an Irish-Catholic Parish, 1863–1886." *Record of the American Catholic Historical Society of Philadelphia* 86 (1975): 7–23.

Griffen, Martin I. J. "Religion of the Early Irish Immigrants in Pennsylvania." *American Catholic Historical Researches* 7 (April 1911): 170–72.

Hackett, James Dominick. "Philadelphia Irish." *American Irish Historical Society Journal* 30 (1932).

Hollingsworth, G. "Irish Quakers in Colonial Pennsylvania: A Forgotten Segment of Society." *Journal of the Lancaster County Historical Society* 79 (1975): 150–62.

Holt, Michael. *Forging A Majority: The Formation of the Republican Party in Pittsburgh, 1848–1860.* New Haven, Yale University Press, 1969.

"The Irish Settlement in the Forks of the Delaware." *Penn Germania* 1 (August 1912).

Kane, John Joseph. "The Irish Immigrant in Philadelphia, 1840–1880: A Study in Conflict and Accommodation." Ph. D. dissertation, University of Pennsylvania, 1950.

———. "Philadelphia Irish." *Information* 69 (March 1955).

Lannie, V. P., and B. C. Diethorns. "For the Honor and Glory of God: The Philadelphia Bible Riots of 1840." *History of Education Quarterly* 8 (1968).

Laurie, Bruce. "Immigrants in Industry: The Philadelphia Experience, 1850–1880." In *Immigrants in Industrial America, 1850–1920*, edited by R. C. Ehrlich. Charlottesville: University of Virginia Press, 1977.

———, ed. *Working Peoples of Philadelphia, 1800–1850.* Philadelphia: Temple University Press, 1980.

Lemon, James T. *The Best Poor Man's Country.* Baltimore: Johns Hopkins University Press, 1972.

Lewis, A. H. *Those Philadelphia Kellys: With a Touch of Grace.* New York: Morrow, 1977.

Light, D. B., Jr. "Class, Ethnicity and Urban Ecology in a Nineteenth Century City: Philadelphia Irish, 1840–1890." Ph.D. dissertation, University of Pennsylvania, 1979.

Martin, A. "The Temperance Movement in Pennsylania Prior to the Civil War." *Pennsylvania Magazine of History and Biography* 49 (1925).

McCabe, J. *Secrets of a Great City.* Philadelphia: National, 1868.

McGivern, E. P. "Ethnic Identity and Its Relation to Group Norms: Irish-Americans in Metropolitan Pittsburgh." Ph.D. dissertation, University of Pittsburgh Press, 1979.

Monahan, K. "The Irish Hour: An Expression of the Musical Taste and the Cultural Values of the Pittsburgh Irish Community." *Ethnicity* 4 (1977).

Myers, A. C. *Immigration of the Irish Quakers into Pennsylvania, 1692–1750.* Pennsylvania: Swarthmore, 1902.

Myers, Albert Cook. *Quaker Arrivals at Philadelphia, 1692–1750: Being a List of Certificates of Removal Received at Philadelphia Monthly Meeting of Friends.* 2d ed. Baltimore: Southern Book, 1957.

Nevin, Alfred. *Men of Mark of the Cumberland Valley, 1776–1876.* Philadelphia: Fulton Publishing, 1876.

O'Brien, Michael J. "Early Pittsburgh, Pennsylvania." *American Irish Historical Society Journal* 13 (1914): 205–8.

———. "The Cumberland County, Pennsylvania Militia in the Revolution," *American Irish Historical Society Journal* 21 (1922): 121–24.

———. "Irish Pioneers in Berks County Pennsylvania." *American Irish Historical Society Journal* 27 (1928).

———. "Irish Settlers in Pennsylvania." *American Irish Historical Society Journal* 6 (1906).

Purcell, Richard J. "Irish Educational Contribution to Colonial Pennsylvania." *Catholic Educational Review* 37 (1939): 425–39.

Rhodes, J. F. "The Molly Maguires in the Anthracite Region of Pennsylvania." *American Historical Review* 3 (1910): 547–61.

Rodechko, James. "Irish-American Society in the Pennsylvania Anthracite Region, 1870–1880." In *The Ethnic Experience in Pennsyvania*, edited by John E. Bodner. Lewisburg, 1973.

Runcie, J. "Hunting the Nigs in Philadelphia: The Race Riot of 1834." *Pennsylvania History* 39 (1972).

Schwartz, Sally. "Ethnicity in Pennsylvania, 1681–1800." Ph.D. dissertation, Harvard University, 1977.

Smith, G. B. "Footloose and Fancy Free: The Demography and Sociology of a Runaway Class in Colonial Pennsylvania, 1771–1776." Master's thesis, Bryn Mawr, 1971.

Vinyard, J. M. "On the Finge in Philadelphia." *Journal of Urban History* 1 (1975).

Walsh, Victor. "'Across the Big Water': Irish Community Life in Pittsburgh, 1850–1885." Ph.D. dissertation, University of Pittsburgh, 1983.

———. "A Fanatic Heart: The Cause of Irish American Nationalism in Pittsburgh during the Gilden Age." *Journal of Social History* 15 (Winter 1981): 187–203.

Warner, Sam Bass, Jr. *The Private City: Philadelphia in Three Periods of Its Growth*. Philadelphia: University of Pennsylvania Press, 1968.

Works Progress Administration. "The Irish in Pennsylvania." *Works Progress Administration Historical Survey, Ethnic Survey*, 1938–41; 8 rolls, roll no. 8.

Rhode Island

Cornwell, E. E., Jr. "Party Absorption of Ethnic Groups: The Case of Providence, Rhode Island." *Social Forces* 38 (1960).

Carroll, Leo E. "Irish and Italians in Providence, Rhode Island, 1880–1960." *Rhode Island History* 28 (August 1969): 69–74.

Cosgrove, John I. "The Irish in Rhode Island, To and Including the Revolution." *American Irish Historical Society Journal* 11 (1912): 365–85.

Gabriel, R. A. *Ethnic Voting in Primary Elections: The Irish and Italians of Providence, Rhode Island*. Kingston, Rhode Island: Bureau of Government Research, 1969.

Lee, Thomas Z. "The Irish in Rhode Island." *American Irish Historical Society Journal*, 15 (1916).

———. "The Irish of Rhode Island Colony in Peace and War." *American Irish Historical Society Journal* 15 (1916): 156–67.

McCanna, Francis I. "Study of History and Jurisdiction of Rhode Island." *American Irish Historical Society Journal* 22 (1923).

Mott, Frank L. "Portrait of an American Mill Town: Demographic Response to Mid-Nineteenth Century Warren, Rhode Island." *Population Studies* 26 (March 1972).

Murray, Thomas Hamilton. "Commerce Between Ireland and Rhode Island." *American Irish Historical Society Journal* 6 (1906): 31–45.

———. "The Irish Vanguard of Rhode Island." *American Irish Historical Society Journal* 4 (1904).

———. MSS. *A Rhode Island Thousand: Being a List of Ten-Hundred Men and Women of Birth and Lineage Who Contributed to the Upbuilding of the Colony and State* 2, 1908.

———. "Sketches of an Early Irish Settlement in Rhode Island." *American Irish Historical Society Journal* 2 (1899).

O'Brien, Michael J. "Obituary Notices in the Providence, Rhode Island, Newspapers." *American Irish Historical Society Journal* 25 (1926).

Purcell, Richard J. "Irish Builders of Colonial Rhode Island." *Studies: An Irish Quarterly Review* 24 (1935): 289–300.

———. "Rhode Island's Early Schools and Irish Teachers." *Catholic Educational Review* 32 (1934): 402–15.

Pryor, E. T., Jr. "Rhode Island Family Structure 1875 and 1960." In *Household and Family in Past Time*, edited by P. Laslett and R. Walls. Cambridge, England: Cambridge University Press, 1972.

Walsh, Sister Mary E. "The Irish In Rhode Island From 1800–1865." Master's thesis, The Catholic University of America, 1937.

Wessell, B. B. *An Ethnic Survey of Woonsocket, Rhode Island*. Chicago: University of Chicago Press, 1931.

Wheeler, Robert A. "Fifth Ward Irish: Immigrant Mobility in Providence, 1850–1870." *Rhode Island History* (Spring 1973).

South Carolina

Carroll, Kenneth L. "The Irish Quaker Community at Camden." *South Carolina Historical History Magazine* 77, no. 2 (1976): 69–83.

Cosgrave, John I. "The Hibernian Society of Charlestown, South Carolina." *American Irish Historical Society Journal* 25 (1926).

Melvin, Patrick. "John Barnwell and Colonial South Carolina." *Irish Sword* (Ireland) 11, no. 42 (1973): 4–20; no. 43 (1978): 129–41.

O'Brien, Michael J. "The Irish in Charleston, South Carolina." *American Irish Historical Society Journal* 25 (1926): 134–46.

———. "Irish in South Carolina." *American Irish Historical Society Journal* 25 (1926).

———. "'Limerick Plantation' Berkeley County, South Carolina." *American Irish Historical Society Journal* 25 (1926).

———. "Marriage Notices Published in the South Carolina Gazette." *American Irish Historical Society Journal* 25 (1926).

Reville, Janie. *560 Irish Immigrants Who Came to South Carolina in 1768*. Columbia, South Carolina, 1937.

Tobin, William A. *The Irish in South Carolina*. Florence, South Carolina: Stricklin, n.d.

Walsh, Patrick. "The Irish in South Carolina, Georgia, Alabama, Louisiana, and Tennessee." *American Irish Historical Society Journal* 3 (1900).

South Dakota

Harney, Sister Mary Carmel. "History of Catholic Education in South Dakota, 1880–1931." Master's thesis, University of Notre Dame, 1932.

Kelly, Sister Mary James. "Two Decades of Catholic Church History in the South Dakota Country, 1839–1859." Master's thesis, University of Notre Dame, 1932.

Tennessee

Acklen, Jeanette T. *Tennessee Records; Bible Records and Marriage Bonds; Tombstone Inscriptions and Manuscripts, Historical and Biographical*. 2 vols. Nashville, Tennessee: Cullom and Ghertner, 1933.

Caper, G. M., Jr. "Yellow Fever in Memphis in the 1870s." *Mississippi Valley Historical Review* 24 (1938).

Clayton, L. W. "The Irish Peddler Boy and the Old Deery Inn." *Tennessee Historical Quarterly* 31 (1977): 149–60.

Polly, Owen. "Is It True What They Say about the Irish?" *West Tennessee Historical Society Papers* 32 (1978): 120–32.

Purcell, Richard A. "Pioneer Irish Educators in Tennessee." *Catholic Educational Review* 34 (1926): 406–13.

Roper, James E. "Paddy Meagher, Tom Hurling and The Bell Tavern." *West Tennessee Historical Society Papers* 31 (1977): 5–32.

Stanton, William M. "The Irish of Memphis (since 1819)." *West Tennessee Historical Society Papers* 6 (1952).

Texas

Almonte, Juan N. "Statistical Report on Texas." *Southwestern Historical Quarterly* 28 (1924–25).

Baker, B. Kimball. "The Saint Patricks Fought for their Skins and Mexico." *Smithsonian* 8, no. 12 (1978).

Barr, Alwyn. "Occupational and Geographic Mobility in San Antonio, 1870–1900." *Social Science Quarterly* 51(1970): 396–403.

Blackburn, George M., and Sherman L. Richards. "A Demographic History of the West: Nueces County, Texas, 1850." *Prologue* (Spring 1972).

Fitzmaurice, M. A. "Four Decades of Catholicism in Texas, 1820–1860." Master's thesis, The Catholic University of America, 1926.

Flannery, J. B. *The Irish Texans*. San Antonio, 1980.

Herbert, R. B. *San Patricio de Hiberniae: The Forgotten Colony*. Texas, n. p., 1981.

Huson, Hobart. *Refugio: A Comprehensive History of Refugio from Aboriginal Times to 1953*. Houston: Guardsman, 1953.

"The Irish in Texas." *The Recorder* 4, no. 5 (1931).

La Fleur, Sister Mary Monica. "The Immigration Factor in the Growth of the Diocese of Galveston: 1841–1874." Master's thesis, University of Notre Dame, 1965.

Lathrop, Barnes F. *Migration into East Texas, 1835–1860*. Austin, 1949.

Linehan, John C. "Irish Pioneers in Texas." *American Irish Historical Society Journal* 2 (1899).

Lucey, Robert E. "The Catholic Church in Texas." In *The Catholic Church, U.S.A.*, edited by Louis J. Putz. Chicago: Fides, 1956.

McBeath, J. J. "The Irish Empressarios of Texas." Master's thesis, The Catholic University of America, 1953.

McGrath, Sister Paul of the Cross. *Political Nativism in Texas, 1825–1860*. Washington, n.p., 1930.

Miller, Robert Ryal. *Shamrock and Sword: Saint Patrick's Battalion in the U.S.-Mexican War*. Norman, Oklahoma: University of Oklahoma Press, 1989.

Newton, Ada L. K. "The Anglo-Irish House of the Rio Grande." *Pioneer America* 5, no. 1 (1973): 33–38.

Muir, Andrew Forest. "Humphrey Jackson: Alcalde of San Jacinto, 1784–1833." *Southwestern Historical Quarterly* 68 (1965): 361–65

Oberste, William H. *Texas Irish Empresarios and Their Colonies*. Austin, Texas: Von Boeckmann-Jones, 1953.

Rice, Bernadine. "Irish in Texas." *American Irish Historical Society Journal* 30 (1932).

Roche, Richard. *The Texas Connection*. Wexford, Ireland: County Wexford Heritage Committee, 1989.

Utah

Baskin, R. N. *Reminiscences of Early Utah*. n.p., 1914.

Dwyer, Robert J. "The Irish in the Building of the Intermountain West." *Utah Historical Quarterly* 35, no. 3 (July 1957): 221–35.

———. "Lawrence Scanlan, Pioneer Bishop of Salt Lake." *Utah Historical Quarterly* 20 (1952): 135–58.

———. *The Story of the Cathedral of the Madeleine*. Salt Lake City, 1936.

Rogers, Fred B. *Soldiers of the Overland*. San Francisco, 1938.

Vermont

Cunningham, P. "Irish Catholics in a Yankee Town: A Report About Brattheboro, 1847–1898." *Vermont History* 44 (1976).

O'Brien, Michael J. "Stray Historical Items from the Green Mountain State." *American Irish Historical Society Journal* 18 (1919).

Purcell, Richard A. "Vermont: Schools and Early Irish Teachers." *Catholic Educational Review* 33 (1935): 277–81.

Virginia

Ackerly, Mary D., and Lula E. J. Parker. *Our Kin: The Genealogies of Some of the Early Families Who Made History in the Founding and Development of Bedford County*. Lynchburg, Virginia: J. P. Bell, 1930.

Chalkley, L. *Chronicles of the Scotch-Irish in Virginia*. 3 vols. Baltimore: Genealogical, 1980. Original edition, 1912.

Clemens, William Montgomery. *Virginia Wills Before 1799*. Pompton Lakes, New Jersey: The Biblio Company, 1924.

Cocke, W. R., III. *Hanover County Chancery Wills and Notes. A Compendium of Genealogical, Biographical and Historical Material Contained in Cases of the Chancery Suits*. Columbia, Virginia: W. R. Cocke, III, 1940.

Greer, George Cabell. "Early Immigrants to Virginia (1623 to 1666) Collected by George Cabell Greer, Clerk, Virginia State Land Office, from the Records of the Land Office, in Richmond." *American Irish Historical Society Journal* 13 (1914).

Lawless, Joseph T. "Some Irish Settlers in

Virginia." *American Irish Historical Society Journal* 2 (1899).

Linehan, John C. "Early Irish Settlers in Virginia." *American Irish Historical Society Journal* 4 (1904).

O'Brien, Michael J. "Burke's Garden, Virginia." *American Irish Historical Society Journal* 22 (1923).

———. "Callaghan, Virginia." *American Irish Historical Society Journal* 22 (1923).

———. "Extracts from Virginia Church Records." *American Irish Historical Society Journal* 18 (1919).

———. "Extracts from Virginia Marriage Records." *American Irish Historical Society Journal* 13 (1914).

———. "Grantees of Lands in the Colony and State of Virginia—Copied from the County Records in Virginia." *American Irish Historical Society Journal* 13 (1914).

———. "Land Grants to Irish Settlers of Virginia." *American Irish Historical Society Journal* 24 (1925).

———. "Pioneer Irish Families in Virginia." *American Irish Historical Society Journal* 25 (1926).

———. "Pioneer Irish Settlers in Rockingham County, Virginia." *American Irish Historical Society Journal* 27 (1928).

———. "Some First Families of Virginia." *American Irish Historical Society Journal*, 26 (1927).

———. "Virginia Irish in the Revolution." *American Irish Historical Society Journal*, 27 (1928).

O'Grady, J. P. "Anthony M. Keiley (1832–1905): Virginia'a Catholic Politician." *Catholic Historical Review* 54 (1969).

———. "Immigrants and the Politics of Reconstruction in Richmond, Virginia." *Records of the American Catholic Historical Society* 83 (1972).

Sweeny, William A. "Some Virginia Records." *American Irish Historical Society Journal* 28 (1930).

Sweeny, William J. "Some Pioneer Irishmen of Virginia and North Carolina." *The Recorder* 2, no. 6 (1924).

Sweeny, William M. "Virginia County Records." *American Irish Historical Society Journal* 30 (1932).

Washington, D.C.

Borchert, James. "The Rise and Fall of Washington's Inhabited Alleys: 1852–1872." *Columbia Historical Society Records* 48 (1971–72): 267–88.

Hickey, Mathew E. "Irish Catholics in Washington Up to 1860." Master's thesis, The Catholic University of America, 1933.

McGirr, Newman F. "The Irish in the Early Days of the District . . ." *Columbia Historical Society, Records* (1949): 48–49.

O'Brien, Michael J. "Some Interesting Notes on Washington, D.C." *American Irish Historical Society Journal* 13 (1914): 227–29.

Wisconsin

Carroon, R. G. "John Gregory and the Irish Immigration to Milwaukee." *Historical Messenger for the Milwaukee County Historical Society* 27 (1971): 51–64.

Buck, James S. *Pioneer History of Milwaukee*. Milwaukee, Wisconsin, 1876.

Coleman, Peter J. "Restless Grant County: America on the Move." *Wisconsin Magazine of History* 66 (Autumn 1962).

Conzen, Kathleen N. *Immigrant Milwaukee, 1836–1860*. Cambridge: Harvard University Press, 1976.

Curti, Merle. *The Making of An American Community*. Stanford: Stanford University Press, 1959.

Desmond, Humphrey J. "Early Irish Settlers in Milwaukee." *American Irish Historical Society Journal* 29 (1930–31).

Geiger, John O. "Humphrey J. Desmond: Catholic, Citizen, Reformer (Milwaukee)." Ph.D. dissertation, Marquette University, 1972.

Kohn, Sister Mary Laurentine. "The Catholicity in Manitowoc County with Background of Wisconsin, from 1818 to 1940." Master's thesis, University of Notre Dame, 1942.

McDonald, M. J. "The Irish in the North Country." *Wisconsin Magazine of History* 40 (1956): 126–40.

McDonald, Sister M. Justille. *History of the Irish in Wisconsin in the Nineteenth Cen-*

tury. Washington, D.C.: The Catholic University of America Press, 1954.

Scanlon, Charles M. "History of the Irish in Wisconsin." *American Irish Historical Society Journal* 13 (1914).

Schafer, Joseph. *Four Wisconsin Counties*. Madison: State Historical Society of Wisconsin, 1927.

———. "Know-Nothingism in Wisconsin." *Wisconsin Magazine of History* 8 (1925): 3–21.

Wallace, E. M. "Early Farmers in Exeter." *Wisconsin Magazine of History* 7 (June 1925): 415–22.

Whelan, L. F. "Them's They: Story of Monches, Wisconsin." *Wisconsin Magazine of History* 24 (September 1940): 39–55.

Section II
Manuscript Collections

Alabama

Birmingham

Birmingham Public Library, Archives and Manuscripts Department, 2020 Park Place, Birmingham, Alabama 35203

Immigration and naturalization records from the Tenth Circuit Court, 1887–1911.

Samford University, Special Collections, Harwell G. Davis Library, 800 Lakeshore Drive, Birmingham, Alabama 35209

Assorted scattered materials on Ireland, including the Albert E. Casey Collection of Irish Materials, which includes birth, marriage, and death records from Ireland—of potential value to genealogists.

Mobile

Mobile Public Library, Special Collections, 704 Government Street, Mobile, Alabama 36602

A major southern genealogical collection, which includes 4,500 microfilms of copies of manuscript schedules of the federal census rolls and more than 1,000 family histories.

Chancery Archives, Catholic Diocese of Mobile, P.O. Box 1966, Mobile, Alabama 36601

Useful collection of records of parishes in the diocese from 1704 to 1834. Including records of baptisms, marriages, and funerals. One document entitled "Register of Catholicity, 1834," lists all Catholics living in North Alabama. Many of the records are in French, Spanish, or Latin.

Quinlan, John, 1859–83. Records. Records of the second bishop of Mobile, John Quinlan, a native of Ireland.

Montgomery

Alabama Department of Archives and History, 624 Washington Avenue, Montgomery, Alabama 36104.

Small scattered collection of materials of Irish and Scotch-Irish interest; includes a few letters to and from emigrants.

Alaska

Anchorage

Anchorage Library, Archives and Manuscript Department, Anchorage, Alaska 99504

Harris, Richard Tighe. 750 items, 1853–1969. Papers of the co-founder of Juneau, Alaska, from a County Down background.

Fairbanks

Catholic Diocese of Fairbanks, Diocesan Archives, 1316 Peger Road, Fairbanks, Alaska 99701

Although no real "archives" yet exists in the formal sense, items on the history of the archdiocese are being collected, materials on Irish Americans are included. Of specific interest are notes and papers of Dermot O'Flanagan, a pastor of the archdiocese (1933–50) and then bishop of Juneau, and numerous notes on other clergy of Irish extraction. Holy Ghost Fathers from Ireland have been working in the archdiocese for the past ten years; at present some scattered papers but no specific collections cover their activities.

Arizona

Mesa

Mesa Branch Genealogical Library, 464 East 1st Avenue, Mesa, Arizona 85204

A major branch of the Genealogical Library of the Church of the Latter Day Saints in Salt Lake City. Holds thousands of microfilm rolls of vital statistical records for the United States, and hundreds of volumes of family histories. Moreover, items not on hand, including microfilm copies of vital records from Ireland, can be rapidly acquired from the main branch in Salt Lake City via interlibrary loan.

Tucson

Arizona Historical Society Library, Manuscripts Division, 949 E. Second Street, Tucson, Arizona 85719

Walsh, Eileen, 1886–1963. Papers, 1864–1963; ca. 2 ft. Irish-born resident of Tucson, Arizona. Family correspondence and diaries describing Mrs. Walsh's travels in Europe and the United States and life in southern Arizona.

California

Berkeley

University of California at Berkeley, Bancroft Library, Manuscript Division, Berkeley, California 94720

Manuscripts focusing on the history of California, Irish writers, the Western region, together with collections of papers of persons prominent in literature, politics, and the professions. Includes papers of a great number of prominent Irish immigrants and Irish Americans, among them the Murphy family, John Francis Neyland, James D. Phelan, Thomas Crowley, James Riordan, Scanlon family, and Samuel Fleming Sinclair. A wide range of manuscripts, notes, and letters by participants and victims of various vigilante activities in the mid-nineteenth century, chiefly in San Francisco. Also materials on Irish-born Dennis Kearney and the Workingman's Party of the late 1870s.

O'Faolain, Sean. Papers, 1900–. Irish short story writer and man of letters. One of the most important literary and political figures of twentieth-century Ireland. Included in this extensive collection are the manuscripts of many of his novels, unpublished manuscripts, and papers. Researchers interested in viewing specific items should see the librarian.

Plunkett, Sir Horace Curzon, 1854–1932. Papers, 1881–1932; ca. 77 ft. Correspondence, diaries, extracts of diaries (prepared by Margaret Digby), and obituaries of Irish-born Sir Horace C. Plunkett, who spent some time as a rancher in Wyoming (1877–89) before returning to Ireland and becoming active in reform of Irish agriculture and politics.

Yeats, William Butler, 1865–1939. One portfolio, 1908–34. Letters from the Irish poet chiefly to Mabel Dickinson, relating to Yeats's work with the Abbey Theatre and his encounters with Mrs. Patrick Campbell, Winston Churchill, Lady Gregory, George Bernard Shaw, and John M. Synge.

Bancroft Library, Regional Oral History Office, University of California, Berkeley, California 94720

This program contains the following two oral interviews of interest to researchers of the Irish experience in America.

Crowley, Thomas. Water transportation owner. Father and mother from Ireland. Boyhood on San Francisco waterfront. Comments on the Port of San Francisco. Open for research use.

Gallagher, Mary. I.W.W. sympathizer. The interview contains information on the I.W.W. in Chicago. Leavenworth cases, 1918; defense witness in California criminal syndicalism cases; work for Tom Mooney's pardon; work for Warren K. Billings's pardon.

Downey

Downey Historical Society, P.O. Box 554, Downey, California 90241

Materials relating to the history of Downey and to its founder, John G. Downey, Roscommon-born politician and businessman; the only Irishman ever to become governor of a state, California. Photographs, miscellaneous deeds, bills of sale, and personal correspondence of early settlers.

Los Angeles

University of California at Los Angeles, Oral History Program, 136 Powell Library, 405 Hilgard Avenue, Los Angeles, California 90024

This program contains at least one oral history interview of interest for research on the Irish experience in America.

Starkie, Walter Fitzwilliam. University professor, literary historian, romance linguist, expert in folklore and mythology. Interview conducted November 1970–February 1971: nine tapes (14.5 hours). 465 pp. edited transcript.

University of California at Los Angeles, University Research Library, Department of Special Collections, 405 Hilgard Avenue, Los Angeles, California 90052

Manuscripts, documents, photographs, pamphlets on history of Los Angeles, California, and the West. Includes materials on prominent Irish Americans in these areas.

University of California at Los Angeles, William Andrews Clark Memorial Library, 2520 Cimarron Street, Los Angeles, California 90018

Major collections of manuscripts on English literature, history, economics, and theology. Includes a collection on Oscar Wilde and the 1890s.

Sacramento

California Office of the Secretary of State, California State Archives, 1020 O Street, Sacramento, California 95814

Manuscript records of the branches and divisions of the California state government, documenting government activities and providing information on many individuals and organizations. Outstanding collection of records of California's pre-Civil War militia companies, many with large numbers of Irish-born members. State census manuscripts of 1852 shows place of birth and place of last residence, thus making it possible to trace migration patterns of Irish to California at the time. Papers and reports on John G. Downey, Roscommon-born politician and businessman and the only Irishman ever to become governor of a state—California.

The Chancery, Diocese of Sacramento, P.O. Box 1706, Sacramento, California 95808

O'Connell, Bishop Eugene. Carbon copies of extensive correspondence written between 1861 and 1871 by Bishop Eugene O'Connell of Sacramento to All Hallows College Drumcondra, Dublin, Ireland, concerning the large numbers of priests from that college who emigrated to California. The originals of these letters are at All Hallows College, Dublin, Ireland.

San Diego

Diocesan Office for Apostolic Ministry/ Alcala Park, P.O. Box 80428, San Diego, California 92138

Correspondence files between the Los Angeles and San Diego bishops where there is some reference to the formation of the Society of the Friendly Sons of St. Patrick. Also files of the Irish religious orders of men and women, and diocesan priests who helped in the formation of the diocese in 1936. Orders on file are: Irish Franciscan Brothers, Galway; Sisters of St. Clare of Newry, County Down; Sisters of Mercy of Ireland, Sligo; Irish Presentation Sisters, County Kerry; Irish Presentation Sisters, Kilkenny; Sisters of Mercy, Galway.

San Francisco

Chancery Archives, Archdiocese of San Francisco, 445 Church St., San Francisco, California 94114

A virtually complete file of the San Francisco *Monitor* from 1867 to the present is held here. The *Monitor* was founded in 1858 as an Irish newspaper, and contains much Irish news. Irish information can be found scattered throughout correspondence files, 1853–1952, though information for the early years is relatively sparse. Personal files of deceased diocesan priests, 1853–1973, contain much information by and about Irish-born priests.

California Historical Society Library, 2909 Jackson Street, San Francisco, California 94109

Scattered private papers of Irish in nineteenth-century California; includes a letter and some papers written by Jasper O'Farrell, the Irish immigrant surveyor who laid out the City of San Francisco in the late 1840s. The extensive collection of private papers of prominent San Franciscans is essential for studies of the impact of the Irish on the society and economy of nineteenth-century California. Among other specifically Irish items are letters of Teresa Lawlor, William McBride, James McCardle, and James O'Neal.

Sutro Library, San Francisco Branch of California State Library, 480 Winston Drive, San Francisco, California 94132

Useful general collection of primary value to those doing genealogical work or interested in local history.

San Marino

The Huntington Library, 1151 Oxford Road, San Marino, California 91108

Vast collections on British and American history and literature. Items of value to researchers on Ireland and Irish Americans include Irish estate records: most extensive collection of nineteenth-century Irish landlord records in the United States; papers of the 1856 Committee of Vigilance.

Santa Clara

University of Santa Clara, Michael Orradre Library, Santa Clara, California 95053

Various announcements of the Convention of the Ancient Order of Hibernians and Ladies' Auxiliary, and the minutes of these meetings. A four-drawer pamphlet file containing general material. Approximately 2,500 volumes of books on the Irish in the United States and abroad. These books are interfiled in the collection, but a separate card catalog is also maintained. An extensive collection of periodicals and newspapers, including the *Irish Times* (1859–present) and the *Dublin Review* (1838–1923). Special Hibernian library collection.

Stanford

Hoover Institute on War, Revolution and Peace, Archives, Stanford University, Stanford, California 94305

James O. Healy collection on contemporary Irish history; includes letters by Sean T. O'Kelly, late president of Ireland, Bulmer Hobson, and Joseph McGarrity. Also holds a collection of Roger Casement materials, and the Ann Monday Collection of items on the North of Ireland conflict since 1969. Frank O'Connor called this Stanford collection "the finest library [in the United States] about Ireland between 1916 and 1962."

Sunnyvale

Sunnyvale Historical Society and Museum Association, Sunnyvale Historical Museum, Sunnyvale Avenue and California Street, Sunnyvale, California 94088

Photography, oral history interviews, and general material relating to one of the original settlers of the area, Irish-born Martin Murphy, Jr., who brought his family overland to California before statehood and played an important part in the early development of the region.

Canal Zone

Balboa Heights

Canal Zone Library-Museum, The Panama Collection, Box "M", Balboa Heights, Canal Zone

General materials relating chiefly to the Panama Canal and Canal Zone. The annual reports of the board of directors of the Panama Railroad, 1852–1951 and the diaries and reminiscences of men engaged in the construction of the railroad and canal; includes some material on Irish Americans and Irish immigrants.

Colorado

Boulder

University of Colorado, Libraries, Western History Collections, Boulder Campus, Boulder, CO 80302

General holdings on the settlement and development of Colorado and the Rocky Mountain region since 1860. Among the records are manuscript collections on mining, politics, labor, and a variety of local and regional activities. Of particular importance for the study of the Irish in the western mining industry are the following:

Industrial Workers of the World. Papers and minute books.

Western Federation of Miners. Papers, especially the "Decision in the Case of the Butte Miners' Union, March 1915." Executive Board, minute books. Local unions' financial records. Michigan Defense Fund.

Colorado Springs

Colorado College Library, Special Collections, Colorado Springs, Colorado 80903

Sinton Family. Letters, 1818–1956. In part, transcripts (typewritten) 1940–56 by J. Ronald H. Greeves in Ireland, from originals in private hands. Letters, chiefly 1818–69, of the Sinton (formerly O'Brien) family of Ann (Greeves) O'Brien, who immigrated from Ireland. Many of the letters written by Greeves family members describe conditions in Ireland between 1818 and 1843.

Denver

Colorado Division of State Archives and Public Records, 1313 Sherman Street, Denver, Colorado 80203

An extensive collection of public records of the state of Colorado. Since these include naturalization records (1862 to the early twentieth century) and military records (1861–1949) they are of value to students researching the experiences of Irish immigrants who settled in the area. The archives also holds copies of the Colorado state census of 1885 and manuscript schedules of federal censuses for period 1860–1910. Also an extensive collection of vital records (many including an index) of birth, marriage, divorce, and death records.

Denver Public Library, Western History Department and Genealogical Division, 1357 Broadway, Denver, CO 80203

The Western history department houses one of the finest libraries in the nation of materials on all phases of the development of states west of the Mississippi River. Particularly strong on the gold and mining rushes. Includes much material of value to those researching the story of the Irish in the West. The genealogy division of the library houses numerous notebook files on Colorado pioneers, manuscripts, and genealogical charts. These include a great many individuals of Irish birth and descent.

Connecticut

Hartford

Chancery Office, Archdiocese of Hartford, 134 Farmington Ave., Hartford, Connecticut 06105

Scattered letters generally regarding the attitudes of diocesan clergy toward Fenianism in the mid-1860s. General correspondence between bishops and pastors.

Connecticut State Library, History and Genealogy Archives, 231 Capital Avenue, Hartford, Connecticut 06106

Scattered materials on Irish immigrants including about 20 boxes of naturalization records and records of ethnic surveys by the Works Progress Administration. The latter includes interviews and notes on interviews of Irish immigrants during the 1930s.

New Haven

Yale University Libraries, Beinecke Rare Book and Manuscript Library, 121 Wall Street, New Haven, Connecticut 06520

American literature collection includes a large collection on Eugene O'Neill, Irish-American playwright.

Platt, Thomas Collier, 1833–1910. Pa-

pers, 1851–1915. Businessman and U.S. representative and senator, New York. Material relating to patronage for Irish Americans and his support of the American Protective Association.

Yale University Libraries, Sterling Memorial Library, Vertical Files Collection, 120 High Street, New Haven, Connecticut 06520

The Crawford Theatre Collection of journals, scrapbooks, production materials, and photographs on individual performers; includes materials on Irish Americans in the theater from mid-nineteenth century to the present.

New London

Connecticut College, Library, Department of Special Collections, Mohegan Avenue, New London, Connecticut 06320

A small collection of manuscripts including letters of Eugene O'Neill.

Delaware

Greenville

Eleutherian Mills Historical Society, P.O. Box 3630, Greenville, Wilmington, Delaware

Overall collection concentrates on business and economic materials. Many of the individual collections, especially the duPont deNemours and Company records, include extensive materials covering activities of Irish immigrant workers.

Kenny, Reverend Patrick. Irish priest. Diary, personal notes and parochial records for period 1805–28.

District of Columbia

Washington, D.C.

The Catholic University of America, Department of Archives, Manuscripts, and Museum Collections, 6th and Michigan Ave., NE, Washington, D.C. 20064

Labor history materials, including papers of leaders of the Knights of Labor, Congress of Industrial Organizations, American Federation of Labor, and United Mine Workers; records of Catholic social welfare organizations in the United States; history materials and papers of Catholic clergy. All of these include materials generated by and about Irish Americans. Among the more useful materials are the following:

Fenian Brotherhood. Papers, ca. 1855–1920; ca. 2 ft. Selected papers from the estate of Jeremiah O'Donovan Rossa documenting Fenian activities in the United States and Ireland. Four boxes were deposited by William D'Arcy, who used them for his study of the Fenians in the United States. Fifteen letters from James Stephans and letters and papers of John Mitchel, Charles Kickham, John O'Mahony, and O'Donovan Rossa. The collection contains much information on the Fenian movement in Ireland collected but unused by D'Arcy in his study.

Geary, James Aloysius. Papers, 1903–58; ca. 3 ft. Professor of Celtic and Comparative Linguistics (active in Irish societies and affairs). Correspondence, research notes, articles, printed matter.

Guilday, Peter. Papers, ca. 1914–47; ca. 40 feet and 9 rolls of microfilm. Professor of Church History. Correspondence, research files, and printed material, including photostats and transcripts from the Congregation of the Propaganda Fidei in Rome (from ca. 1600), the Irish Dominican Archives, and the Irish College in Rome.

Hughes, Archbishop John. Manuscripts and correspondence relating to the activities of the mid-nineteenth-century archbishop of New York.

Irish College in Rome. Papers, 1830–49; 3 rolls of microfilm. Papers of the Irish College in Rome relating to the Church in America.

O Donovan Rossa, Jeremiah. Papers; microfilm.

Powderly, Terence Vincent. Papers, 1864–1933; ca. 90 ft. Grand Master Workman of the Knights of Labor. Commissioner General of Immigration. Correspondence, reports, photos, and printed matter relating to his career in immigration (1883–1930).

Purcell, Richard Joseph. Papers, ca. 1920–50; ca. 20 ft. History professor. Historiographer of the American Irish Historical Society of New York. Lectures, articles, correspondence, and immigration research files; includes many transcribed immigrant letters.

Archives, Georgetown University, 37th and O Streets, N.W., Washington, D.C. 20057

The total collection of almost 2,000 linear feet of materials contains a great deal of interest to students of the Irish in America. Among the most useful are:

Crimmins, John D., 1844–1917. Papers; 0.25 ft. New York financier and philanthropist, of Irish descent and active in such organizations as the Friendly Sons of St. Patrick and the American Irish Historical Society. Correspondence and printed ephemera.

Dolan, Thomas F. Papers; 2.0 ft. Illinois politician of Irish descent. Letters from a variety of correspondents including James A. Farley.

Early, John, S.J., 1814–73. Papers; 0.75 ft. President of Georgetown University, 1858–66 and 1870–73.

Healy, Patrick F., S.J., 1839–1910. Papers; 1 ft. President of Georgetown University, 1873–82. Correspondence, diaries, and manuscripts.

McCarthy, Eugene. Papers; 400 ft. A collection of materials dealing with Senator Eugene J. McCarthy's (1916–   ) bid for presidency in 1968.

Maguire, Bernard A., S.J., 1818–86. Papers; 0.25 ft. Correspondence and manuscripts of Irish-born Bernard A. Maguire, S.J., president of Georgetown University from 1853 to 1858 and from 1866 to 1870.

Maynard, Sara Casey, ?–1945. Papers; 0.5 ft. Correspondence, manuscripts, and artwork belonging to Sara Casey Maynard, wife of the poet Theodore Maynard.

Meehan, Thomas F., 1854–1943? Papers; 0.25 ft. American journalist of Irish descent. The collection includes correspondence to Meehan, some of it from such Irish nationalists as James Stephens and John O'Leary.

O'Neill, Scannell. Papers; 0.25 ft. Editor and journalist of Irish descent. His correspondence includes letters from such Irish writers as Douglass Hyde and Katherine Tynan.

Shea, John Gilmary, 1824–92. Papers; 25 ft. Historian and journalist whose father was born in Ireland. Correspondence, manuscripts, and autograph collection.

Walsh, Edmund A., S.J., 1882–1956. Papers; 21 ft. Historian and expert on foreign affairs; founded the School of Foreign Service at Georgetown University. Correspondence and manuscripts.

Library of Congress, Manuscript Division, Library of Congress Annex, 2nd Street and Independence Avenue, S.E., Washington, D.C. 20540

Hotze, Henry. Papers, 1860–65; 3 vols. A letter book contains letters of Hotze, the editor of the *Index* (London) to Confederate agents in Ireland.

Ireland. Parliament. House of Commons. Debates, 1776–89; 82 vols. Verbatim shorthand report of debates (45 vols.) together with a longhand transcript thereof (37 vols.), made by or for Sir Henry Cavendish.

Lansing, Robert. 1864–1928. Papers, 1890–1933; 20 ft. Statesman, cabinet officer, and author. Correspondence, clippings, photos, memorabilia, MS. of book, diaries, scrapbooks, and desk books. The papers mainly deal with the years 1914–20, during which Lansing was counsel to the State Department and secretary of state, and give information on American foreign relations during World War I and the peace conference, with data on Lansing's relations with President Wilson and with various foreign diplomats and statesmen. Includes material on the Lusitania affair, the Mexican crisis, the arming of merchantmen, and the Irish rebellion.

Madison, James. Papers; 8 vols. Considerable correspondence exists between Madison and the earl of Donoughmore and the marquis of Clanricarde, which establishes that there was a close working relationship among them.

Matteson, David Maydole. Manuscript. Unpublished manuscript carefully documenting riots in American cities since late colonial days. Probably the best guide available to nineteenth-century rioting. Includes many incidents identified as "Irish riots." Manuscript Division, no. 7356.

McDermott, Michael. Recollections on

Ireland and Irish-America. Manuscript Division Ms 2-15-1000.

National Library of Ireland Collection. Microfilm copies of 1,400 items in the National Library of Ireland relating to the United States.

Pickett Papers (Confederate State Department Papers). Letters from Confederate agents in Ireland. Box H, nos. 23-25, letters of Bishop P. N. Lynch. Box N, nos. 55, reports of Robert Dowling. Box N, no. 56, reports of Lt. J. L. Capston. Box N, no. 57, reports of Rev. Fr. John Bannon. Box N, no. 58, letters of Capt. J. F. Lalor.

Sampson, William. Papers relating to Ireland and America, 1806-49.

Stephens, James. 2 ft; 78 items. Literary collections of Halsted B. Vanderpoel, manuscripts of James Stephens, Irish poet and writer, together with correspondence, literary manuscripts, galley proofs, and printed matter.

Florida

Pensacola

University of West Florida, John C. Pace Library, Pensacola, Florida 32504

Jones, Charles W. Family papers of Irish-born United States senator cover legal, political, and personal matters.

Sullivan, J. J., and son. Business and legal papers, general correspondence, 1885-1929.

Georgia

Atlanta

Archives, Archdiocese of Atlanta, 756 West Peachtree Street, N.W., Atlanta, Georgia 30308

The archdiocese was created in 1956 and most of the earlier materials are in the Diocese of Savannah. The most interesting item at Atlanta is the almost complete files of the parish newspaper, *St Anthony's Catholic News,* from 1935 to 1962. The official organ of the Catholic Layman's Association of Georgia, created in the early 1930s to combat anti-Catholic prejudice, the newspaper documents efforts by Irish-Americans to deal with religious bigotry.

Emory University Library, Robert W. Woodruff Library, Special Collections Department, Atlanta, Georgia 30322

Wesleyan Collection hold many letters from Ireland over the nineteenth century.

Milledgeville

Georgia College Library, Flannery O'Connor Collection, 231 West Hancock Street, Milledgeville, Georgia 31061

A collection of 135 manuscripts and letters of Georgian Irish-American writer Flannery O'Connor. Also includes four audio recordings, five motion pictures, critical writings, clippings, photographs, and memorabilia.

Hawaii

Honolulu

Hawaii State Archives, Iolani Palace Grounds, Honolulu, Hawaii 96813

General collection covering a number of Irish immigrants. Includes immigration records (1842-1900); court records since 1842; marriage records since 1842; and naturalization records (1844-94).

Illinois

Berwyn

Order of Servants of Mary, Eastern Province, Provincial Archives, 3401 South Home Avenue, Berwyn, Illinois 60402

Records of the province and administration of the Eastern Province of Semites (1967–75); its predecessor, the Our Lady of Sorrows Province (1870–1967); records of the Novene of Our Sorrowful Mother (1937–75); personal papers of deceased members; and records of houses that have been closed. Some records refer to foundations made in Ireland.

Carbondale

Southern Illinois University of Carbondale, Morris Library, Special Collections, Carbondale, Illinois 62901

A large collection of materials pertaining to 20th-century American, British, and Irish authors (especially expatriates) and theater, particularly political theater and that of the Irish Renaissance. Among the more useful are the following:

The Holy Door. Records, 1964–66; ca. 285 items. Business papers of a little magazine in Dublin, Ireland, edited by Brian Lynch. Includes items on Aidan Higgins, Brian Higgins, Patrick Kavanagh, Anthony Kerrigan, Thomas Kinsella, John Montague, and Desmone O'Grady.

Lavin, Mary (Walsh), 1912–   . Papers, 1953–64; 6 ft. Irish author. Manuscripts of short stories and a small collection of miscellaneous papers.

O'Riordan, Conal O'Connell, 1874–1948. Correspondence 1907–23; ca. 80 items. Irish author and playwright. Letters to O'Riordan, especially after he became director of the Abbey Theatre, Dublin, in 1909. Correspondents include Lord Dunsany, George Bernard Shaw, and William Butler Yeats.

Robinson, Lennox, 1886–1958. Papers, 1904–58; 17 ft. Irish playwright, author, critic, producer and lecturer. Correspondence; manuscripts of Robinson's plays, essays and anecdotes, newspapers columns, short stories, lectures, and music; Robinson's personal library; literary manuscripts of A. E. (George William) Russell, Frank Dermody, Isabella Augusta (Persse) Gregory, Frank J. Hugh O'Donnell, and William Butler Yeats. The items relate chiefly to Robinson's literary career and activities as manager-director at the Abbey Theatre, Dublin, Ireland. Correspondents include William C. Allgood, Robert Bell, Robert J. Brophy, Flora S. Cornwall, Christabel Childers, Edward Gordon Craig, Edith S. Dodd, Nora (Robinson) Dorman, Gerard Fay, Miss E. M. Fry, Oliver St. John Gogarty, W. F. Hessey, Rutherford Mayne (Samuel Waddell), Sean O'Casey, Frank J. Hugh O'Donnell, Sean O'Faolain, Donal O'Kelley, Mary Devenport O'Neill, Sean O'Sullivan, Tom Robinson, George William Russell, David Sears, Charlotte Shaw, George Bernard Shaw, and James Stephens.

Stuart, Francis, 1902–   . Papers, 1932–71; ca. 3 ft. Irish author. Unpublished novels and other writings and notebooks. Correspondents include Maud Gonne, Compton Mackenzie, Liam O'Flaherty, and Ezra Pound.

Tynan, Katharine (Hinkson), 1861–1931. Papers, 1882–1955; 3 ft. Irish poet, author, and critic; major figure in the Irish Renaissance movement. Correspondence; manuscripts, typescripts, and proof of articles and poems. Correspondents include Padraic Colum, Lady Gregory, John O'Leary, Sir Horace Plunkett, James Stephens, and Lady Wilde.

Chicago

Chicago Historical Society Library, Clark Street at North Avenue, Chicago, Illinois 60614

An important collection for anyone interested in the Irish in Chicago and Illinois. Among the major collections specifically dealing with Ireland and the Irish are the following:

Fitzpatrick, John, 1872–1946. Papers, 1890–1965; 8 ft. Labor organizer. Chiefly correspondence received by Fitzpatrick as president of Chicago Federation of Labor; also papers relating to the Journeyman Horse Shoers' Union and to Fitzpatrick's unsuccessful candidacy for mayor of Chicago on the Labor party ticket in 1919. Most papers dated 1913–30. Includes materials relating to

Chicago labor, Chicago civic matters and political affairs, the Labor party of Cook County and of the United States, Brookwood Resident Workers' College of Katonah, N.Y., William Zebulon Foster, Chicago and Illinois teachers' organizations and school matters, Negroes in labor, socialism and communism and their relevance to the labor movement, Irish freedom, and Russian relief in the early 1920s; correspondence of Samuel Gompers, William Green, and Frank Morrison, of the American Federation of Labor, and Edward Nockels, of the Chicago Federation of Labor.

Irish Fellowship Club of Chicago. Records, 1910–65; 1 ft. Correspondence, minutes, membership data, and other papers. Includes material relating to speeches delivered before the Irish Fellowship Club, Irish-American attitudes on Irish Home Rule (1917–22), Irish neutrality during World War II, preparations for Eamon de Valera's visit (1939) to Chicago, and annual St. Patrick's Day parades and dinners; papers (1915–65) of the Illinois Chapter of the American Irish Historical Society, the Illinois Republican Council (1923–65), and the Ulster-Irish Liberty Legion (1950–65); and Faherty with his father, Michal J. Faherty. Other correspondents include Liam T. Cosgrave, William T. Cosgrave, and Eamon de Valera.

Mulligan, James A., 1830–64. Papers, 1849–1900; 1400 items and 9 v. U.S. Army colonel, lawyer, and journalist. Correspondence, diary, account books, student notebook, Martin James Russell, the Irish Brigade (23rd Illinois Infantry), the Irish and Catholics in Chicago and their role in the Civil War. Includes records of the executive committee of the Irish Brigade (April–June 1861); accounts of law firms of which Mulligan was a member; papers concerning Mulligan's Chicago Catholic newspaper, *The Western Tablet;* correspondence of Henry S. Fitch, a Catholic priest, and personal and family correspondence of Mulligan's wife, Marian Nugent Mulligan, and her brother, James Nugent, containing material on the Civil War and on affairs at New Creek, W.Va.

Miscellaneous Irish materials. Letters and reminiscences of Peter Casey and Frank Conlan [Frank Murphy].

The Newberry Library, 60 West Walton Street, Chicago, Illinois 60610
Outstanding collection of general materials useful to the student of the Irish at home or in the United States. Of particular interest are numerous records of railroad companies that employed a great many Irish in the Midwest and far West over the nineteenth century. Also holds the world's finest collection of United States city and county directories, invaluable items for researchers interested in tracing Irish immigrants across the United States.

The University of Chicago Library, Department of Social Collections, 1100 East 57th Street, Chicago, Illinois 60637
Account books, 18th–19th centuries; 22 vols. Miscellaneous account books, chiefly American, including account book (1778–91) kept at Temple Patrick, Ireland.

Clarke, Adam, 1760–1832. Letters, 1794–1828; 59 items. Methodist clergyman and theologian. Letters from Clarke to his wife covering his travels over various church circuits and including information on church affairs, various Methodist church conferences, his experiences in the English provinces, the squalid living conditions of the Irish peasants, and an epidemic that struck London in the spring of 1814. Includes two letters to his daughter.

D'Alton, John, 1792–1867. Papers (1830–67); ca. 12 ft. Irish antiquarian and barrister. 153 octavo MS. volumes used by D'Alton as notebooks and as indexes to printed and manuscript sources, and containing excerpts and transcripts from the sources; together with correspondence, miscellaneous notes, and commonplace book (ca. 1736) of Feidhlim O'Neill. Includes three MSS. of the late seventeenth and eighteenth centuries: Seuthrum Keitinn, "Forus Feasa or Eirinn" (Geoffrey Keating), *Elements of the history of Ireland*); "Life of Christ"; and Seuthrum Keitinn, "Eochairsciath an Aifrinn" (Geoffrey Keating, *Border-Shield of the Mass,* 1703)

The William M. Spencer manuscripts on French history, 1770–1840. Ca. 320 items. Letters (1807–13) from Napoleon Bonaparte to Gen. Henri Jacques Guillaume Clarke, duc de Feltre (1765–1818), containing instructions on military affairs; letters from J. B. Sorgniard, abbot of the diocese of Saint Brieuc, canon of the collegiate Church of Notre Dame de Lamballe, and royalist spy in Brittany (1790–1800), to Monseigneur Le Mintier, bishop of Treguier, concerning firsthand information on the fate of the Chouan rebels, preparations for the invasion of England and Ireland.

Mundelein

Chicago Archdiocesan Archives, St. Mary of the Lake Seminary, Mundelein, Illinois 60060

Eight of eleven ordinaries of Chicago and the majority of the clergy since the archdiocese was established in 1844 have been Irish-born or of Irish descent. The archdiocesan archives contain a great deal of material generated by and about these individuals. Cataloguing of materials is presently underway and has so far been completed up to 1926.

Springfield

Illinois State Historical Society, Old State Capitol Building, Springfield, Illinois 62706

Over four million items on all aspects of Illinois history, including papers of many Irish-American political leaders. Also records of education, religion, business, labor, and social groups. Among the more important recent materials are the notes and manuscripts of the Federal Writers' Project, 1935–44.

Hinch, Benjamin P. Correspondence, 1838–56; 102 items. Postmaster at New Haven, Illinois, and member of the 19th Illinois General Assembly. Letters concerning state and local politics in Gallatin Co., Illinois, received from U.S. representatives, members of the Illinois General Assembly, political associates, and constituents; together with letters (1838–55) from Hinch's brother, H. Hinch in St. Francisville, Louisiana, concerning his term as mayor of St. Francisville during the 1830s, flatboatmen, Irish rioting, fears of Negro insurrections, and economic and social conditions in West Feliciana parish.

King Family. Papers, 1798–1927; 2 ft. (2286 items). In part, transcripts (typewritten) and photocopies. Correspondence, journals, genealogical notes, and other papers of David King (1794–1877), his wife, Sarah Ann (Denniston) King (1805–77), and their children, John Nevin King (1827–1915), Charles Speer King (b. 1832), Campbell Denniston King (1828–84), William Henry King (b. 1840), David King, Jr. (b. 1838), James Stuart King (b. 1831), Joseph Rush Hays King (b. 1846), Lucie Stuart King (b. 1842), and Thomas Clark King (1834–66). Contains detailed descriptions of Irish immigration.

Miscellaneous Irish materials. Papers covering the murder of Dr. Patrick Cronin; McConnell family papers and Dr. James Mahon letters.

Indiana

Indianapolis

Indiana Historical Society, 140 N. Senate Avenue, Indianapolis, Indiana 46204

A broad collection of materials on the settlement of the Northwest territory, Indiana territory, Indiana from the eighteenth century to the present day. Includes many letters, diaries, account books, and business records written by Irish Americans or about Irish Americans. See especially the papers of John Dowling and the letters by Anne Faussett Dwyer, Andrew Erskine, Hugh D. Gallagher, and Joseph Hewitt.

Indiana State Library, 140 N. Senate Avenue, Indianapolis, Indiana 46204

A collection of personal papers and other manuscripts relating to Indiana. Of particular value for the study of the Irish in the region are the manuscripts on wars, especially the War of 1812, the Mexican War and the Civil War. Many items on politics cover the Irish contribution. See especially the four letters from Maloney and O'Conner families dated 1852 and 1860, which describe conditions and work in the United States and land problems in Ireland. Also personal papers of Mrs. Charles W. Ballard and Allen Hamilton.

Lafayette

Diocese of Lafayette in Indiana, Chancery Archives, 610 Lingle Avenue, Lafayette, Indiana 47902

Papers regarding the Diocese of Lafayette; records of the St. Joseph's Orphanage, 1876–1937. These papers and records contain general references to Irish clerics and inmates of the orphanage.

McMahon, Father John. Papers. Served as "spiritual director" of the Fenian Raid on Canada, 1866, and also as a priest in Fort Wayne diocese. After the Canadian government released him, he was assigned to St. Joseph Church, Reynolds.

O'Flaherty, Father Edward. Papers. Served as "spiritual director" of the Indiana Fenian Brotherhood, and was mainly associated with St. Bernard's in Crawfordsville.

St. Joseph Orphanage, 1876–1937. Papers. Many records on Irish orphans.

Notre Dame

University of Notre Dame, Archives, Box 513, Notre Dame, Indiana 46556

Extensive collection of holdings on American Catholicism. Particularly useful for students of the Irish experience in America are the nineteenth-century diocesan records and the personal collections of individual clergy and laymen. These include numerous letters on the Irish experience in various areas and comments on the Fenian Brotherhood.

Several uncalendared collections of prominent Irish Americans, including Frank C. Walker (New Deal political figure), Revs. William Corby and John W. Cavanaugh, and other priests active in the history of the University of Notre Dame. Papers of Francis O'Malley, Notre Dame professor and noted literary figure. One box of materials labeled Irish Republic, containing letters, clippings and printed materials relating to Ireland, Irish Americans, Irish independence movement, and Irish-American appeals, etc. Also holds a copy of the overseas correspondence of All Hallows College, Dublin—source of a great many Irish priests in nineteenth-century America—and a number of collections of diocesan records, including Cincinnati, Hartford, and New Orleans. All of these collections are presently being inventoried and calendared. Researchers should write for current status of specific collections. The following collections are of specific interest to researchers on Irish America.

Brownson, Orestes. Papers

Hagerty, James Edward, 1869–1946. Papers, 1918–45; 2 boxes. Professor of economics and sociology at Ohio State University. Correspondence and notes relating to Catholic teaching in social and economic affairs, together with some clippings of Msgr. John Augustine Ryan (1869–1945).

Ireland. Papers, 1844–1950; 2 packages and 2 reels of microfilm. Transcripts (typewritten), microfilm and photocopies of original documents in the archives of All Hallows Seminary near Dublin, Ireland. Correspondence from Irish priests working in the United States to members and officers of All Hallows Seminary, near Dublin, where they had been trained for missionary work. Includes an incomplete collection of the *Irish Bulletin* (1921), a mimeographed letter or report, and 46 broadsides and handbills, referring to the movement for Irish freedom.

McMahon, Joseph H., 1862–1939. Papers, 1892–95; 2 boxes. Roman Catholic clergyman of New York City, librarian, and a founder of the Catholic Summer School of America.

O'Donnell, Charles Leo, 1884–1934. Papers, 1896–1933; 3 boxes. Catholic clergyman, president of the University of Notre Dame, poet and literary critic. Personal correspondence and literary papers, including some items of Joyce Kilmer (1886–1918), and other personal papers. Open to investigators under restrictions accepted by the repository.

O'Malley, Austin, 1858–1932. Papers, 1897–98; 1 box. Oculist, physician, author, and professor of English at the University of Notre Dame. Chiefly papers concerning Catholic activities in colleges in 1895.

Diocesean records. Papers from the dioceses of Cincinnati, Hartford, and New Orleans; all include numerous letters by Irish priests and/or Irish immigrants.

Oral history project. Several oral history interviews relating to Catholic social action and the history of the university have been provided by Irish and Irish Americans.

Iowa

Des Moines

Iowa State Department of Archives and History, E. 12th Street & Grand Avenue, Des Moines, Iowa 50319, Phone: 515-281-5472

General collection, with scattered items of Irish interest. The most useful specific collection is the Scotch-Irish Society collection of clippings.

Dubuque

Archdiocesan Center, 1229 Mt. Loretta Avenue, P.O. Box 479, Dubuque, Iowa 52001

Personal letters of deceased priests. Parish files of legal documents concerning land grants. Letters from bishops to clergy and laity. Many of the writers or recipients of these letters were Irish or Irish-American.

Loras College, Wahlert Memorial Library, 14th and Alta Vista Streets, Dubuque, Iowa 52001

Connolly, Maurice, 1877-1921; 50 items. Political papers and other correspondence.

Iowa City

Iowa State Historical Society, Manuscript Collection, 402 Iowa Avenue, Iowa City, Iowa 52240

Useful general collection of items on the Irish in Iowa including manuscript schedules of the state census of 1856, some immigrant letters, and the records of the Ancient Order of Hibernians, 1884-1924.

Kansas

Abeline

The Dwight D. Eisenhower Library, Abeline, Kansas 67410

The Dwight D. Eisenhower Library, dedicated in May 1962, holds papers, books, and other materials relating to Eisenhower's career as military leader, educator, president, and statesman. Among the holdings are many manuscript collections relating to Irish Americans, including James C. Hagerty, press secretary to the president. A detailed listing of holdings is available from the library.

Hays

Ellis County Historical Society, Thomas More Prep Center for Research, 17th Street and Hall Street, Hays, Kansas 67601

Materials relating to all phases of Ellis County history, including papers of the short-lived town of Hays City, 1868; civil and criminal justice of the peace dockets of Big Creek Township, 1872-85; some papers of Irish-American Katheryn O'Loughlin McCarthy, first U.S. congresswoman from Kansas.

Lawrence

University of Kansas, Special Collections, Kenneth Spencer Research Library, Lawrence, Kansas 66045

An important collection for the study of the Irish in America and at home. Includes the James Joyce collection (900 items); the P. S. O'Hegarty Irish History collection (25,000 items), which includes materials on the Irish literary renaissance, specifically the Abbey Theatre; the William Butler Yeats family correspondence files (450 items).

Leavenworth

Leavenworth Public Library, 5th and Walnut, Leavenworth, Kansas 66048

Most useful items for Irish research are copies of the Kansas state census beginning in 1865.

Topeka

Kansas State Historical Society, 120 West Tenth Street, Topeka, Kansas 66612

Scattered items of value to research on the Irish in Kansas, including the Socolofsky collection, which covers some of Irish landlord William Scully's activities in Marion County, the Mary Bond papers, and the Francis Gerarty diaries.

Lease, Mary Elizabeth Clyens. Clippings, 1850–1933. Clippings and biographical material.

Kentucky

Frankfort

Archives Branch, Kentucky Department of Libraries and Archives, 300 Coffee Tree Road, P.O. Box 537, Frankfort, Kentucky 40602

Important collection of naturalization records, by county, beginning as early as 1783; includes many Irish immigrants who settled in Kentucky.

Louisville

The Filson Club, Manuscript Department, 118 Breckinridge Street, Louisville, Kentucky 40203

Davie, Preston, 1881–1967. Genealogical collections; 34 boxes. Information on the origins of the Preston and Patton families in Ireland, Scotland, and England.

Louisiana

Baton Rouge

Diocese of Baton Rouge, Catholic Life Center, 1800 S. Acadian Thruway, P.O. Box 2028, Baton Rouge, Louisiana 70821

Records of baptism, marriage, and burials from the civil parishes: Ascension (1772), Assumption (1793), East Baton Rouge (1793), East Feliciana (no church), Iberville (1773), Livingston (1839), Pointe Coupee (1728), St. Helena (no church), St. James (1770), Tangipahoa (1890), West Baton Rouge (1841), and West Feliciana (1849). Many of these records contain information on Irish immigrants.

Louisiana State Archives and Records, Office of Secretary of State, P.O. Box 94125, Baton Rouge, Lousiana 70804

Important source of information on nineteenth-century Irish immigration to New Orleans and the South; collections includes passenger lists for the Port of New Orleans, 1813–1903, together with an index for 1839 to 1849. Voter registration lists also available for 1898.

Louisiana State Library, 760 Riverside Mall, Baton Rouge, Louisiana 70821

Manuscripts and notes from the Works Progress Administration project on Louisiana; includes information on Irish activities in nineteenth-century Louisiana.

Louisiana State University Library, Department of Archives and Manuscripts, Room 202, Library, Baton Rouge, Louisiana 70803

Eggleston-Gildart-Roach family papers, 1825–1903. 285 items and 6 vols. Correspondence and diaries, one of a journey through England and Ireland in 1825.

New Orleans

New Orleans Public Library, Louisiana Division, 219 Loyola Avenue, New Orleans, Louisiana 70140

Useful general collection of manuscripts providing information on many Irish residents includes naturalization records (1827–1906); Charity Hospital admission books (1818–1900); voter registration records (1880–1978); extensive collection of New Orleans newspapers, beginning in 1802; city cemetery records, 1835 to 1935.

Tulane University Library, Special Collections Division, Howard-Tilton Memorial Library, New Orleans, Louisiana 70118

Of most Irish interest are the forty-eight volumes of naturalization records of Orleans parish, from 1845 to 1899; they include a great many records on Irish immigrants.

Maine

Portland

Diocesan Archives, Chancery Office, 510 Ocean Avenue, Woodfords P.O. Box H, Portland, Maine 04103
Healy, Bishop James A., 1876–1900. Miscellaneous and uncataloged letters. Letterpress books of correspondence.
Hurley Monsignor. Formerly vicar general of the diocese. Untitled manuscript of notations. Completed for Louis S. Walsh, presumably in 1906.
McCarthy, Charles, Jr., 1883–1917. Diaries.
Walsh, Louis S. Journal, "My Journey to Paris," 1789–1883.

Waterville

Colby College, Library, Special Collections, Waterville, Maine 04901
Healy Collection. Many first editions are included among the 8,000 volumes by and about Irish authors who wrote between 1880 and 1940. In addition, the collection contains secondary materials, periodicals, letters, manuscripts, a file of clippings, and microfilms of dissertations. Among the individual authors represented is George Bernard Shaw.

Maryland

Annapolis

Maryland State Archives, Hall of Records Commission, Box 828, Annapolis, Maryland 21404
The most useful items for the study of the Irish in the region are the land patent records, 1633–80; the naturalization records, 1858–1930; and the general papers on convicts and aliens arriving in colonial Maryland.

Baltimore

Maryland Historical Society Library, Manuscript Division, 201 West Monument Street, Baltimore, Maryland 21201
Associated Friends of Ireland in the City of Baltimore. Records, 1828–1829; 1 vol. Constitution, by-laws, and membership and officer lists of a group formed to support civil and religious liberty in Ireland; proceedings, constitution, and membership and officers lists (1828–29) of the Irish Emancipation Society of Maryland, a predecessor group.
Carroll, Charles. Papers. Collection of papers of prominent Irish Catholic family in colonial Maryland.
Clarke, Ambrose, d. 1810. Papers, 1793–1829; ca. 3 ft. Merchant and shipowner of Baltimore. Personal and business correspondence, letter book, business and cargo auction accounts. Correspondence includes comments on the effect of the Napoleonic wars on trade, the rights of neutral traders, and travel in Dublin, Ireland. Receipts for the construction of Clarke's house in Baltimore (1769–99).
Hall, Thomas John, 1883–1953. Papers, 1870–1940; 2 ft. Genealogist, registrar, and historian at St. James Church, Anne Arundel County, Maryland. Genealogical notes on the Waters family of Limerick, Ireland.
Stabler family. Papers, 1787–1921; 3 items and 8 vols. In part, handwritten transcripts. Correspondence of James Pleasants Stabler (1796–1840), relating to his trip to England and Ireland.
Miscellaneous Irish materials. Letters of John Crawford, McHenry family papers, Meyer family papers, and papers of David Bailey Warden and O. H. Williams.

Bethesda

Sisters of Mercy of the Union, Generalate Archives, 1000 Kentsdale Drive, Bethesda, Maryland 20034
Archives, manuscripts, and memorabilia tracing the history of the Sisters of Mercy, primarily in the United States but also in Ireland. Included are detailed records of the Sisters of Mercy of the Union beginning in 1929; letters, 1837–41, of Catherine McAuley, founder of the congregation; papers of members of the congregation, includ-

ing reminiscences of a Crimean War nurse, a diary of a nurse in the Spanish-American war, and a typescript of Civil War experiences; three early eighteenth-century illuminated manuscripts.

Emmitsburg

Daughters of Charity of St. Vincent de Paul, St. Joseph's Provincial House, South Seton Avenue, Emmitsburg, Maryland 21727
Manuscripts dealing with the history of the Sisters of Charity of St. Joseph in Emmitsburg since 1809, and papers of the congregation's founder, Elizabeth Ann Seton, 1786–1820. Additional materials consist of correspondence of American Catholic bishops, 1805–42, Civil War and Spanish-American War papers, and mission histories. Contains much material on Irish Americans in the Catholic Church.

Mount St. Mary's College, Hugh J. Phillips Library, Emmitsburg, Maryland 21717
Useful collection of materials dealing with Irish Catholicism in Maryland; includes journals, papers, and letters.

Massachusetts

Boston

Boston Public Library, Boston, Massachusetts 02117
Strong collection of books on the history of the Irish in America from the colonial period to the present. In addition to general histories, there are histories of the Irish in various parts of the country; biographies of famous Irish Americans; specialized histories of the education of the Irish, the Irish in government and politics, and the Irish in the labor movement; sociological studies on immigration, economic problems, and interaction with other ethnic groups (150 titles).

Strong general collection of the literary writers of the nineteenth century, including Conway, O'Reilly, Roche, and Sullivan, as well as the many writers of the twentieth century, including Finley Peter Dunne, Farrell, Fitzgerald, O'Hara, and O'Neill, along with biographical and critical works (500 titles).

In music the library has a large collection, including the works of Francis O'Neill, Victor Herbert, and others (100 titles).

Large collection of Massachusetts newspapers on microfilm, including those specifically Irish American: the Boston *Pilot* and the *Republic Miscellany,* O'Neill's *Irish Pictorial Weekly* and the *Irish Echo.* The *Irish Echo,* the journal of the Philo-Celtic Society of Boston, was published from 1886 to 1894; its four volumes chronicle the Irish language movement not only in the Boston area but throughout the country. Other periodicals include the *Journal* and the *Recorder* of the American Irish Historical Society and the publications of the Friends of Irish Freedom and the United Irish League of America.

Fred Allen (1894–1956) Collection. Consists of his personal library, together with five boxes of correspondence, scripts, records, tapes, and photographs.

Donn Byrne (1889–1928) Collection; ca. 600 items. Mostly letters or documents relating to his literary and personal life, and letters relating to Mrs. Donn Byrne; with index.

John Collins Archives. 46 file drawers. Papers relating to his two terms as mayor of Boston, 1960–67.

Edwin O'Connor (1918–68) Papers; ca. 400 items. Mostly letters from and to O'Connor, relating to his literary work; with index.

Stephen O'Meara Papers. Covering the period 1880–1918, from his years as manager and publisher of the *Boston Journal* through his two terms as police commissioner of Boston, this manuscript collection gives a vivid picture of Boston and Massachusetts of the time. Over 300 archival folders; with finding list.

John Boyle O'Reilly, 1844–90. Over fifty letters from and to O'Reilly on various topics.

Mary Boyle O'Reilly, 1875–1939. Over forty letters from and to her, regarding her literary work.

Ireland—Union to Free State. Over 30,000 original pamphlets together with thousands of press cuttings illustrative of struggles in Ireland from the Union to the Free State. Many individual items from much later dates; one whole section brings together pamphlets and other documents relating to the early phases of the present situation in Northern Ireland. Printed catalog of items in the collection is included.

Modern Irish History. Over 1,500 books, pamphlets, broadsides, leaflets, typed documents and letters, holograph letters, ephemera. From the Fenian period to the early days of the Irish Free state; encompasses Fenian and post-Fenian organizations at home and overseas, land disturbances, Parnell, home rule, the rise of the Labour party, the Easter Rising, the War of Independence, the Treaty, the Civil War, beginnings of the Free State. A large proportion of the material was written by principals of the movements.

Northern Ireland political literature, 1968–72. Edited from the collection in the Linenhall Library, Belfast. Eighty-three sheets of microfiche.

Special material on Irish history,, 1916–22. 280 postcards, mostly portraits of personalities involved.

Boston University, Department of Special Collections, Muger Memorial Library, 771 Commonwealth Avenue, Boston, Massachusetts 02213.

The Rare Book Collection. Contains volumes printed in Europe and America from the Renaissance to the present day. Especially important here for researchers of Irish Americana are the George Bernard Shaw works, which are supplemented by the extensive collection of Shaw correspondence in the library's special collections.

The Historical Manuscript Collection. Ten letters and manuscripts of several songs by Irish poet Thomas Moore (1779–1852).

The Richards Collection. Letters of W. B. Yeats. Typescript of *Mourning Becomes Electra* by Eugene O'Neill. Plans and papers of Sir Walter Raleigh, who had extensive estates in Co. Cork, Ireland.

The Military History Collections. Includes the working library and archives of the Massachusetts First Corps of Cadets and the Library of the Military Historical Society of Massachusetts. The former includes extensive records of day-to-day activity during the Lawrence Mill Strike of 1912 and the Boston Police Strike of 1919, both involving numerous Irish immigrants. The library of the Military Historical Society of Massachusetts contains some 1,500 volumes on the American Civil War, including regimental histories, military biographies, first-person accounts, and publications of veterans organizations. Many of these works provide coverage of Irish immigrants and their descendents.

History of Nursing Archives. Includes the papers of the Nursing Council of the United Community Services of Boston; the Massachusetts Nurses Association; and the Massachusetts League for Nursing. The papers of the Visiting Nurse Association of Boston, founded in 1886 as the Instructive District Nursing Association, includes reports, correspondence, records of cases and visits by the nurses, and photographs. Reports of this group's work during the Chelsea Fire of 1908 are particularly extensive. Many of these records are invaluable in providing insights into the lives of Irish nurses, women, and households in Boston over the period.

The Anderson Poetry Collection. Contains over 1,000 volumes of modern verse including works by Joyce Kilmer and James Joyce.

The Twentieth-Century Archives. Founded to collect papers of contemporary figures who have influenced public opinion during this era. Among Irish-American items are the following: Alistair Cooke's notes taken at Robert Kennedy's side as he lay mortally wounded in Los Angeles; extensive collections of manuscripts, drafts, documents, and correspondence of George Bernard Shaw; Gene Kelly's notes on performances of all kinds. Mary Lavin and Frank O'Connor are represented by extensive collections.

Specific collections of papers on the following Irish Americans or writers who have written about Irish America: Stephen Birmingham, Evan Connell, Mary Deasy, Thomas B. Dewey, Jack Dunphy, Thomas J. Fleming, James Leo Herlihy, Mary Kelly, Ed Lacy, Wilfred McCormick, William P. McGivern, Frank O'Connor, Richard O'Connor, Walter O'Meara, Eugene O'Neill, George Bernard Shaw, Wilfred Sheed, James Carroll, Pete Hamill, Shannon O'Cork, William V. Shannon, Gail Sheehy. Finally there are over four million documents recounting the long political career of the honorable John W. McCormick, Speaker of the United States House of Representatives, who served as a congressman from the time of Calvin Coolidge to that of Richard Nixon.

Manuscript Collections

Harvard University, Business School, Business School, Baker Library, Manuscripts Department, Soldiers Field Road, Boston, Massachusetts 02163

Over 1300 collections of business records on New England and the United States. Particularly useful for students of the Irish economic adjustment and Irish-American businessmen are the records of the credit investigation firm Dun and Company (later Dun and Bradstreet) which date from the 1840s and cover almost the entire country.

John F. Kennedy Presidential Library and Museum, Columbia Point, Boston, Massachusetts 02125

The John F. Kennedy Library is a presidential library administered by the National Archives and Records Administration; it was established to preserve and to make available to specialized scholars and the general public the documents and memorabilia of President Kennedy and his contemporaries in politics and government. The papers of President Kennedy were donated to the library in 1965 by the executors of the president's estate. The donation also included sizable collections of books and other printed material, audiovisual material, and memorabilia. It is the policy of the Kennedy Library to make its research facilities available on an equal basis to anyone who clearly needs to use its unique resources, within limits set by statute, deeds of gift, and deposit agreements.

President Kennedy's papers have been organized into four categories: Personal Papers, Pre-Presidential Papers, Presidential Papers, and Papers of the Post-Assassination Period. These papers are supplemented by additional, more specialized collections of personal or organizational papers; audiovisual materials; sound recordings; motion picture film; cartoons; and various private audiovisual collections. Detailed finding aids and indexes are available at the library.

Personal Papers; 20 ft, 5 rolls microfilm. These personal papers of John F. Kennedy have been assembled from collections previously scattered through other collections or located in separate places. The Harvard Records were donated by Harvard University; the "Athenia" records were donated by the State Department. Additional materials will be added from time to time, as received.

Biographical materials, 1 ft.; early years, 1 ft.; Harvard records, 1 ft.; Harvard notebooks, 1 ft.; Athenia records, 1 roll of microfilm; correspondence, 1943–52, 3 ft.; Boston office, 1940–56, 1 ft.; accounts and bills, 1941–58, 7 ft.; manuscripts, 5 ft.; senator's notes, 1 ft.; doodles, 2 ft.;

Pre-presidential Papers, 1947–60; 430 linear feet. The Pre-Presidential papers are the official papers from John F. Kennedy's legislative career and are organized into five series. The five major series are: the House of Representatives Files, 1947–1952 (39 feet); Political Campaigns (10 feet); Senate Files, 1953–1960 (321 feet); 1960 Campaign Files (55 feet); and Transition Files (5 feet).

Presidential Papers, 1961–63; 3351 linear feet. These papers include the President's Office Files maintained by John F. Kennedy's personal secretary, Mrs. Evelyn Lincoln, in the Oval Office of the White House; the National Security Files generated by the Special Assistant to the President for National Security Affairs, McGeorge Bundy; the White House Central Files which document general White House activities; a Subject File of all inactive correspondence, memoranda, and reports generated in the White House; Miscellaneous Presidential Files; and the White House Staff Files consisting of correspondence, memoranda, and reports relating to the issues and problems on which the staff member was working. Among the more useful papers here for researchers on Irish-America are the 11 linear feet of immigration/naturalization records and the papers of Ralph Dugan, Special Assistant to the President; Lawrence O'Brien, Special Assistant to the President for Congressional Relations; and Timothy Reardon, Administrative Assistant to the President.

Papers of the Post-Assassination Period 1963–74; 1310 linear feet. This group of papers reflects the world-wide reaction to the death of President John F. Kennedy and include the following: Condolence Correspondence to members of the Kennedy family and to American representatives abroad; Poetry; Music; Essays; Dedications; Church Services; Resolutions; and formal condolences of foreign governments, state assemblies, and national and international organizations.

Collections of Personal or Organizational Papers The Kennedy Library has also received the papers of a number of people active in public affairs, many of them friends and associates of President Kennedy or of Robert Kennedy. Others served in the Kennedy administration. Some had little or no connection with the careers of John or Robert

Kennedy. The library has also received papers or records of national foundations and organizations, such as the records of the Democratic National Committee. Among the more useful items here for study of the Irish in America are the collections covering the following individuals or institutions: John E. Byrne, press secretary to the Governor of Maine; Columbia University Bureau of Applied Social Research transcripts used in preparation of the study *Television and the Death of a President;* Democratic National Committee; Joseph Dolan, administrative assistant to Senator Robert Kennedy; William L. Dunfey, Democratic party worker in New Hampshire; Ralph Dungan, special assistant to the president, later ambassador to Chile; William Hartigan, assistant to President Kennedy, later assistant postmaster general; Edward M. Kennedy papers, chiefly senatorial files; Joseph P. Kennedy, father of President Kennedy; Robert F. Kennedy, attorney general, U.S. senator from New York; Robert F. Kennedy Memorial Foundation; Rose F. Kennedy, mother of President Kennedy; Dorothy O'Brien, Democratic party chairwoman, Northern District, Illinois; Thomas P. O'Neill, majority leader and speaker, House of Representatives; Scott Rafferty, Department of Justice, interview notes on civil rights; John Reilly, attorney, Department of Justice and commissioner; Edward Toomey, paper relating to the John F. Kennedy Medical Symposia series; Edward C. Welsh, executive secretary, National Aeronautics and Space Council.

Audiovisual Materials Approximately 30,000 still photographs, about 50 percent in color, made by White House photographers. Most are of public functions, such as official trips (except those to Paris and Vienna in 1961), and meetings and ceremonies at the White House and elsewhere. The collection also includes photographs of the president on vacation and of his family. Additionally, newspapers, magazines, wirepress agencies, and other organizations have donated substantial numbers of photographs to the library. Most photos cover the same events and subjects described above; but some extend back to the 1960 presidential campaign and earlier. Photographs of memorial services for the president are also included in these donations. A large part of these photographs are on microfilm; the majority are black and white. Contributors include the *New York Times, Newsweek, Look, Magnum, Black Star,* and *Wide World Photos.* Many of these photographs are subject to copyright and other restrictions. Individuals, many from foreign countries, donated snapshots taken at various occasions, places and dates. Often these photos are of the president traveling through the donor's area, or of local memorial services for the president.

Sound Recordings The heart of this collection is 244 tapes of presidential addresses and remarks recorded by White House Communications Agency, 1961–63. Private organizations, such as the members of the National Association of Broadcasters, have donated recordings of President Kennedy's speeches while in Congress and during the 1960 presidential campaign, tapes of the entire 1956 and 1960 Democratic National Conventions, and other political speeches and campaign advertisements. Some of these latter date back to 1944, but the bulk were recorded between 1952 and 1964. Almost all sound recordings in the library are available for duplication, although some are subject to copyright restrictions.

Motion Picture Film The major television networks, government organizations, White House photographers, and some private agencies and individuals have donated the bulk of this collection. Most of the network-donated footage covers the President in his official capacity: trips, meetings, ceremonial occasions, interviews and addresses. Some of the footage dates back to the 1950's and records John F. Kennedy's activities while a member of Congress. Much of this film is subject to copyright or other restrictions.

Cartoons Most of the cartoons in the library's collection were presented to John F. Kennedy at various times. The majority of the cartoons highlight issues of his career, his family, and reactions to the news of his assassination. Other cartoons in the collection date to 1876 and illustrate political issues of national, international, and local (Boston) interest. Among the cartoonists represented in the collection are Thomas Nast, D. R. Fitzpatrick, Low, "Norman," Herblock, and Hugh Haynie. Most of these cartoons are subject to copyright or other restrictions.

Various Private Audiovisual Collections Audiovisual records created or collected by various persons and institutions and deposited in the Kennedy Library, including the Berinsky Burton Photograph Collection; the Guggenheim Productions Film Collection; the Ernest Hemingway Collection; the Robert

F. Kennedy Collection; and the Victoria Schuck Collection.

Massachusetts State Archives, Massachusetts Secretary of State Office, Room 55, State House, Boston, Massachusetts 02133

Boston port passenger arrival lists, 1848–91, with a microfilm copy of a national archives index to same; vital records, birth, marriages, deaths for Boston, 1841 to 1890; manuscript schedules of federal censuses, 1790 to 1890; manuscript schedules of state censuses for 1855 and 1865.

Massachusetts State Library, 341 State House, Boston, Massachusetts 02133

Manuscripts of legislative and executive documents from colonial period to 1930, covering a great deal of activity by Irish politicians.

The South End Historical Society, Inc., 532 Massachusetts Avenue, Boston, Massachusetts 02118

Papers, photographs, and other materials relating to Boston's South End. Included is an architectural survey of buildings in the area as well as papers from local organizations, many Irish or Irish-American.

Archives, St. Vincent De Paul Society, 294 Washington, Boston, Massachusetts

Reports of the St. Vincent De Paul Society in Boston, 1869–90.

Albion (ship). Records, 1865–72; 109 items. Correspondence, accounts, bills, mortgage from Patrick McCullough, owner, of Attacumcussey, Ireland, to Nathaniel T. Glifford, agent, in New Bedford, Massachusetts.

Keefe, Richard. Diary, 1888. Special Agent, St. Vincent De Paul Conferences; also cases, 1889.

Lynch & Stoughton (New York). Letter books, 1783–92; 2 vols. New York Historical Society Collections. Correspondence of Dominick Lynch and Thomas Stoughton (partners in a firm of merchants) with merchants in Europe, especially Ireland.

Ring, Thomas. Correspondence cited as "Early Letters," 1860–70. Two volumes of Thomas Ring's correspondence: 1876–1880 and 1880–86, cited as "Ring Papers I" and "Ring Papers II." Letterpress books of Thomas Ring: 1891–92, 1894–97, cited as "Ring Papers III" and "Ring Papers IV."

Rutty, John, 1698–1775. Letters (microfilm copies), 1732–77; 9 ft. Author, composer, and professor at the University of Connecticut. Correspondence, college course work and notes, articles relating partly to Irish and English literature, books, book reviews, essays on Irish literature, letters written to editors, music written by Dr. Saul, plays, poems, short stories, doctoral dissertation on A. E. Coppard, photos, newspaper clippings, and other papers.

Sheehan, William Francis, 1859–1917. Papers, 1891–1919, 1939–1940; ca. 150 items. Lawyer, businessman, and New York State politician. Correspondence relating to Theodore Roosevelt, personal matters, the state of the Democratic party in New York and nationally, and local political matters. Correspondents include Archbishop Michael Corrigan, James W. Gerard, Arthur P. Gorman, E. H. Harriman, Daniel A. O'Gorman, John C. Spooner, Vice Presidennt Adlai E. Stevenson, and Henry L. Stimson.

South Carolina Historical Society. Papers, 1760–1907; ca. 2 ft. Travel journals, diaries, and memoirs, partly transcripts (typewritten). Diaries, journals, memories, and recollections of travels in the District of Columbia, Maryland, North Carolina, and Virginia; from Philadelphia, Pennsylvania to Charleston, South Carolina (1765); from Charleston, South Carolina to New Haven, Connecticut (1832); and in Ireland.

Townshend, George Townshend, 1st Marquis, 1724–1807. Correspondence, 1767–93. British army officer and lord-lieutenant of Ireland. Correspondence relating to Townshend's position as lord-lieutenant of Ireland and family affairs. Includes letters to Townshend from his sons at school.

Brighton

Roman Catholic Archdiocese of Boston, 2121 Commonwealth Avenue, Brighton, Massachusetts 02135

A large collection (80,000 items) of materials. Parish records, including baptismal, marriage, and confirmation records; diaries of parishes and individuals; official correspondence relating to administration, the establishment of parishes, theological problems, and philanthropic activities; collateral material on such topics as school social service agencies and the effect of Irish immigration on the establishment of parishes.

The collections in the archives are arranged into eight distinct record groups: records of bishops and archbishops; records of Auxiliary Bishops; records of the chancery; records of parishes; records of Institutions; records of Nondiocesan Agencies; personal papers; audio-visual materials; Among the individuals for whom extensive records are held are: Archbishop William O'Connell, Richard Cardinal Cushing, Bishop John Fitzpatrick (1846–66) and Bishop John Williams. These holdings are particularly valuable for almost any kind of background work on parish history or research involving the Catholic influence on Irish newcomers in Boston. An excellent and detailed survey by James M. O'Toole, *Guide to the Archives of the Archdiocese of Boston*. (Boston: Archdiocese of Boston, 1982), is available.

Cambridge

Widener Library, Harvard University, Cambridge, Massachusetts 02138

One of the world's great libraries. The entire collection is invaluable to students of Irish history, literature, and religion. Essential also for its collections of primary and secondary works on Irish Americans. Of particular importance are the following two collections:

Irish on the Continent. For several hundred years beginning around 600 A.D., Ireland was the center of learning in Western Europe. From Irish monasteries, scholars traveled all over the continent, founding monasteries and schools in France, Germany, Belgium, Italy, Switzerland, Austria, and a number of other countries. This effort produced a great many manuscripts: copies of the Bible, commentaries on the Bible, lives of saints, theological treatises, classical writings of ancient Greece and Rome, grammatical, astronomical, and geographical treatises, philosophical works, historical chronicles, and imaginative legends. Most of these works are in Latin, some in old Irish. A few Latin manuscripts have marginal notes in Old Irish.

As monasteries and schools on the continent were dissolved, the manuscripts found their way into the public libraries of cities and towns. The National Library of Ireland has attempted to locate these manuscripts throughout the World and copy them on microfilm. About 80 percent of the total are believed to have been located and copied. At present the total number of manuscripts located is 2,297. Widener Library has copies of all of these manuscripts, together with an extensive index.

British Museum Irish Collection. Also on hand at Widener Library is an impressive collection of microcopies of items on Irish history held by the British Museum. Those include items on Irish imports and exports in the seventeenth century, the Irish Brigade in France, 1671–1801, estate records, Poor Law Union records, and the health money rolls for Armagh and other locations.

Two extensive indexes, copies of which are available in the Government Documents and Microforms Division of Widener, are invaluable for locating items in both of the above collections.

Harvard University, Harvard Theatre Collection (Pusey Library), Cambridge, Massachusetts 02138

An impressive collection of materials on the development of the America Theatre. Irish performers, writers, and organizers—including Edward Harrigan—are represented in the collection. In addition, the following two collections hold Irish materials.

Cahill, Marie. Clipping file, 1870–1933. The clipping files of Harvard Theatre collections and the Frank Lenthall Collection (private) provide coverage of Miss Cahill's career.

Guinan, Mary Louise Ceilia. Clippings, 1844–1933. The Harvard Theatre Collection has clippings and programs relating to her performances.

Radcliffe College, Schlesinger Library, 10 Garden Street, Cambridge, Massachusetts 02138

Assorted manuscript collections on women born of Irish immigrant parents, including Leonara O'Reilly papers.

Chestnut Hill

Boston College, Special Collections, John J. Burns Library, 140 Commonwealth Avenue, Chestnut Hill, Massachusetts 02167

Extensive materials relating to the Irish Home Rule Movement, Boston history, and prominent Bostonians.

Butler family. Earls of Carrick papers, eighteenth–nineteenth centuries; 7 boxes. Deeds and land records of the estates of the earls of Carrick of Ireland.

Cahill, George. Papers, 1866–93; ca. 300 items. Leader in Irish independence movement. Correspondence, reports, collection lists, programs, and printed matter connected with Cahill's duties as member of the supervisory body of the Fenian Brotherhood and as secretary of the Quincy (Massachusetts) branch of the Irish Land League.

Cleeve, Brian Talbot, 1921– . Papers; 3 ft. Irish author. Correspondence, notes, and typescripts of published and unpublished writings in various drafts, with holograph corrections, galleys, clippings, juvenilia, photos, and other papers relating to Cleeve's career as novelist and short story and television writer from 1952 to 1960.

Collins, Patrick Andrew, 1871–1905. ca. 330 items. Chiefly the papers of this lawyer, political leader and diplomat. Correspondence, drafts of speeches and articles, clippings, memorabilia, and photos. A large group of letters, telegrams, and cables sent to Collins as president of the Irish Land League; also includes printed official league announcements. Other letters are from John Boyle O'Reilly, editor, poet, author, and lecturer, to Francis Henry Underwood, lawyer, editor, and author; letters chiefly to or from O'Reilly and Jeremiah O'Donovan Rossa, poet, editor, and leader in the Fenian and related organizations.

O'Donovan, Michael Francis/(Frank O'Connor) 1903–66. Papers, 1937–48; 1 ft. Personal and business correspondence, financial records, manuscripts of writings, and galleys, relating to his connection with Abbey Theatre and the Cuala Press; together with legal documents, photos, and other papers relating to his literary career as playwright and writer of short stories, under the pseudonym Frank O'Connor.

O'Reilly, John Boyle. Extensive collection of papers, manuscripts, letters, etc.

Lancaster

Haverhill Public Library, 99 Main Street, Lancaster, Massachusetts 01523

Alfred Poor Manuscript Collection gives background of all inhabitants of towns of Groveland and Branford for the year 1851, including details of birthplaces and names of parents for all Irish mill workers in the area at the time.

Salem

Essex Institute, 132 Essex Street, Salem, Massachusetts 01970

Many manuscript collections of papers of prominent nineteenth-century citizens of Massachusetts, many of whom violently opposed the Irish adjustment, especially to politics. Useful for Irish studies in that they provide insights into the attitudes of leaders of the larger society toward sons and daughters of Erin. Also some ships' passenger lists of Irish arrivals from Liverpool in mid-nineteenth century.

Waltham

American Jewish Historical Society Library, 2 Thornton Road, Waltham, Massachusetts 02154

Price, Samuel, 1886–1962. Papers, 1913–62; 2 ft. Rabbi of Beth El Temple, Springfield, Massachusetts. Correspondence and personal diaries describing the Irish War of Independence.

Worcester

College of the Holy Cross, Archives, 1 College Street, Worcester, Massachusetts 01610

Materials relating to the history of Holy Cross College, including holdings relating to the trustees, presidents, deans, treasurers, departments, honor societies, faculty, admissions, and publications. Includes a large amount of materials by and about Irish Americans. Particularly useful for studying the intellectual life of the nineteenth-century Boston Irish.

Boyce, Rev. John. "The Satisfying Influence of Catholicity on the Intellect and Senses," a lecture delivered before the Catholic Institute of New York on Friday evening, January 24, 1851.

Earls, Rev. Michael. Shaughnessy Collection. Letters of Earls to his family from Europe, 1897–98; notebooks, 1890, 1899–1900; miscellaneous letters. Earls's letters, 1910–16.

Guiney, Imogen. In the Grace Guiney Collection, 1899–1920. letters to Louise Imogen Guiney, catalogued alphabetically. The Gordon Collection of Guiney Letters, Portfolios. Correspondence of Guiney and Father W. Harmon van Allen.

Guiney, Patrick R. Miscellaneous papers.

Healy, Rev. Louis S., 1850–1900. James A. Healy, 1849, bishop of Boston. James A. Healy, copies of two diaries, 1849–91. James A. Healy, sermons, uncataloged.

Walsh, Rev. Louis S. Letters to his parents, 1876. Files on Rev. Thomas J. Conaty, Katherine E. Conway, William Henry, Cardinal O'Connell, Mary B. O'Reilly and letters to Michael Earls, S.J.

Michigan

Ann Arbor

Bentley History Library, The University of Michigan, 1150 Beal Avenue, Ann Arbor, Michigan 48109

A major resource for the study of the Irish in the region and throughout the United States. Several valuable finding aids are available at the library. Among the most useful collections are the following:

Immigration sources project. Letters and papers of various immigrants to Michigan; includes materials on many Irish.

William Narcissus Lyster Papers. 1839–61; 1 reel microfilm. Lyster was a missionary at a large parish of the Diocese of Michigan of the Protestant Episcopal Church. Sermons, poems, reports, and correspondence. Included are drafts of letters to his family in Ireland and to colleagues, primarily concerning his work and the communities to be visited.

Joseph McMahon Papers. 1832–1906; 25 items. McMahon lived in Manchester, Michigan. Correspondence and miscellaneous manuscripts. Relevant items include a letter of 1832 concerning immigration from Ireland to America and a description of conditions in Ireland.

Kerby A. Miller Collection, 1820–1978. Letters/reminiscences; 1 ft. Professor at the University of Missouri, Columbia, and at the Institute of Irish Studies, Belfast, Northern Ireland. These are letters and reminiscences of Irish immigrants to the United States and Canada, including two letters relating to the Irish in Michigan.

Most Holy Trinity Roman Catholic Church, Detroit. Records, 1834–69; 3 reels microfilm. Baptism, marriage, and burial registers. This parish was made up largely of Irish immigrants (Access restricted).

Cornelius William Tuomy (1877–1966) Papers. 1 ft. Correspondence, ledger books, and diary, 1870–1947.

Underwood family letters. These letters of the Underwood family of Lenawee County and of the Crandall family of Gratiot County include correspondence received from relatives in Ireland.

Detroit

Burton Historical Collection, Detroit Public Library, Detroit, Michigan 48202

Richard E. Elliot Papers. A major collection of papers of an individual who acted as an agent to bring Irish immigrants to Michigan. Includes twelve volumes of letterbooks and an immigrant register for the years 1851 to 1869.

Sacred Heart Seminary Library, 2701 Chicago Blvd., Detroit, Michigan 48206

Invaluable source for the study of the Irish in the Catholic Church in nineteenth-century Michigan. Includes church newspapers (1884–96), and manuscripts of Catholic Church records for Detroit and some surrounding areas, beginning in 1800. Also includes parish history collections, receipt books, and temperance society membership lists.

Wayne State University, Archives of Labor History and Urban Affairs, Walter P. Reuther Library, Detroit, Michigan 48202

An invaluable collection for study of the extensive Irish involvement in unionization and labor organizations throughout the country. Includes records from 1860 to the present. The official depository for the American Federation of State, County and Municipal Employees; American Federation of Teachers; Air Line Pilots Association; The Newspaper Guild; United Auto Workers; United Farm Workers; and a variety of state and local labor organizations. Includes a great many personal papers of union leaders, labor activists, and politicians. The Industrial Workers of the World papers are invaluable

Dearborn

Henry Ford Museum and Greenfield Village, Ford Archives, 20990 Oakwood Avenue, Dearborn, Michigan 48121

Personal papers and business files of Henry Ford, the son of an Irish immigrant from County Cork. Records from offices of the Ford Motor Company, as well as subsidiary companies owned by Henry Ford. Company records include information on production, public relations, sales and advertising, finance, subsidiaries, legal operations, international operations, organization, and administration. These include coverage of his establishment of a factory in County Cork in memory of his father. There are also personal papers of individuals associated with Henry Ford or the company, as well as nearly 400,000 photographs and 400 oral histories.

East Lansing

Michigan State University, Archives and Historical Collections, East Lansing, Michigan 48824

Dobbins family, 1882–1937. 29 folders. Letters from members of the Dobbins family living in Ireland.

Slafter family. Papers, 1855–91; 14 folders. Personal and business correspondence, deeds, receipts, and insurance policies of the family of William Slafter of Tuscola County, Michigan. Subjects include business, real estate transactions, farming and logging, the Fenians, the Civil War, and travel and conditions in Kansas and New England.

Lansing

Michigan State Archives, 3405 North Logan, Lansing, Michigan 48918

A valuable collection of vital governmental records for anyone interested in tracing the progress of Irish immigrants or their descendents in the state of Michigan. Includes tax assessment rolls; manuscript schedules of federal and state censuses; military records; state, county, and city records.

Olivet

Olivet College, Libraries, College Archives, Olivet, Michigan 49076

Records, photographs, and correspondence of writers, including Padric and Mary Colum, associated with the college in the 1930s and 1940s.

Minnesota

Minneapolis

Abbott-Northwestern Hospital, Corp., Sister Kenny Institute, Health Sciences Library, 810 East 27th Street, Minneapolis, Minnesota 55407

Material relating to the career of Sister Elizabeth Kenny and the founding of the institute named for her. Annual reports are included, as is material relating to the early treatment of poliomyelitis and the discovery of polio virus vaccines.

St. Paul

College of Saint Thomas, Library, 2115 Summit Avenue, St. Paul, Minnesota 55105

Houses the "Celtic Library," a collection of 4,800 titles of Irish and Scottish history and literature; also some miscellaneous items on Irish in America.

Byrne, James C. 1858–1942. 1894 and 1915; 3 items. Priest, ordained 1883. Two essays, "The Welfare of the Spirit" and "The Art of Description," and a compendium of clippings, primarily from the *Catholic Bulletin*.

Casey, Edward Francis, 1879–1962. Ca. 1911; 1 item. Priest, ordained 1912. Book of favorite poems plus class notes.

Cassidy, James F. n.d. 1 item. Student at the St. Thomas Military Academy or the College of St. Thomas. "Historical Notes," a compendium of class notes.

Dolphin, John F., 1861–1920. 1899–1903; 0.5 ft. Priest, ordained 1886. President of the College of St. Thomas, 1899–1903. Dolphin's correspondence files from his tenure as president of the college.

Flynn, Vincent J., 1901–56. 1928–57; 27 ft. Priest, ordained 1927. President of the College of St. Thomas, 1944–56. A collection of both personal papers and institutional records. Included are notes on and drafts of a number of Flynn's scholarly publications; the general administrative records of the College of St. Thomas and the St. Thomas Military Academy, 1944–56; papers documenting Flynn's membership in various scholarly, professional, fraternal, and civic organizations.

Foley, John P., 1877–1964. 1927–28; 13 items. Priest, ordained 1908. President of the College of St. Thomas, 1927–28. Correspondence, primarily with Dean R. R. Schumway of the University of Minnesota regarding the accreditation of the college.

Gallaghan, James S., 1883–1950. 1929–31; ca. 150 items. Priest, ordained 1910, and member of the Congregation of the Holy Cross; dean of discipline and student life at the College of St. Thomas, 1928–33. Part of Gallaghan's correspondence and related files are from his tenure as dean at the college.

Gillen, Marrhias J., 1882–1960. 1904–5; 13 items. Priest, ordained 1907. Chairman of the Department of Classical Languages at the College of St. Thomas, 1918–28. Class notebooks from Gillen's tenure at the St. Paul Seminary.

Ireland, John, 1838–1918, 1894–1961; 50 items. Priest, ordained 1861. Archbishop of St. Paul-Minneapolis, 1888–1918. Correspondence.

Keenan, Edward P., 1906–69. 1884–1961; 50 items. Priest, ordained 1931. Professor of English at the College of St. Thomas, 1934–69. Manuscript of Keenan's novel, *Burden Light,* and his "History of St. Paul Seminary"; correspondence, and an autograph collection from late nineteenth and early twentieth century English literature.

McSweeney, Edward, 1846–1943. Papers, 1888; 1 item. Priest; president of the College of St. Thomas, 1887–88. "Seminarian's Horarium 1888," handscript notebook including schedules for work, study, and meditation. Description of classes.

Moynihan, Humphrey, 1862–1943. 1908–24; ca. 70 items. Priest, ordained 1891. President of the College of St. Thomas, 1903–21. List of priests who graduated from the college and correspondence, primarily with students regarding payment of tuition at the college. A few documents from the (Rev. Thomas) Cullen administration of St. Thomas (1921–27) are also included with this collection.

Moynihan, James H., 1882–1959. Ca. 1934–46; ca. 50 items. Priest, ordained 1906. President of the College of St. Thomas 1933–44. Correspondence, 1934–35, regarding the College Athletic Board; a 1939 report on the College for American Council on Education; nine string-bound compendia (ca. 1930) of notes or reflections on religious subjects; ten bound notebooks (1940–46) containing notes for classes, spiritual reflections, and notes on Church history. Some Moynihan material is also included in the Flynn papers (see above).

O'Gorman, Thomas, 1843–1921. Papers, 1896; 15 items. Priest, ordained 1865. President of the College of St. Thomas 1885–87. Bishop of Sioux Falls, 1896–1921. Copies of correspondence regarding the "Columbian Catholic Summer School" and O'Gorman's elevation to the episcopacy.

O'Keefe, Timothy, 1895–1974. Papers, 1930–59; 3 ft. Professor of Education, 1922–65, and chairman of the department, 1935–59 at the College of St. Thomas. Lecture notes.

O'Shaughnessy, I. A., 1885–1973. Papers, 1938–62; 8 ft. Business executive. Graduate and benefactor of the College of St. Thomas. Photographs, commemorative notebooks, material on the dedication of the O'Shaughnessy Library, on O'Shaughnessy's papal orders, citations, medals, and the educational center, plus biographical clippings and correspondence.

Shannon, James P., 1921– . Papers, 1957, 1965–66; 15 items. Priest, 1946–69. President of the College of St. Thomas, 1956–66. Auxilliary bishop of St. Paul-Minneapolis, 1965–69. President of the Minneapolis Foundation, 1973– . Correspondence, certificates of congratulation sent to Shannon on his assuming the presidency of the college. Papal bull naming Shannon titular bishop-elect of Lacubaza and auxiliary to the archbishop of St. Paul.

Minnesota Historical Society, Division of Archives and Manuscripts, 1500 Mississippi Street, St. Paul, Minnesota 55101

A major collection of items of interest to Irish researchers. Includes naturalization records for 75 of Minnesota's 87 counties; records of the Great Northern and Northern Pacific Railway companies cover their efforts to bring immigrants to settle railroad land; Ignatius Donnelly papers; the working papers and productions of the Works Progress Administration during the Depression. Among the more prominent collections of Irish interest are the following:

Christie family. Papers, ca. 1823–1949; 14 ft. Correspondence, essays, articles, newspaper clippings, and other papers relating to the family of James C. Christie (d. 1890) and his wife Elizabeth (Reid) Christie, Irish immigrants of Wisconsin, Blue Earth County, Minnesota, and Bozeman, Montana, and to the related Stevens and Monahan families. Includes descriptions of nineteenth-century life in Arkansas, Colorado, Minnesota, Missouri, and Wisconsin, and activities of various business firms, religious, temperance, and political organizations.

Follet family. Papers, 1841–1912; 300 items and 1 vol. Correspondence, financial statements, and other papers of Frederick Follett (1804–91), journalist of Batavia, New York, his son Frederick M. Follet, a professional soldier, and other members of the family. The papers relate to the postal business at Batavia, New York, the Seneca Indians, Mormons in Utah, the Pony Express, the presidential election of 1860, the American Civil War, and the Fenian outbreaks.

Irish-American Colonization Company, Ltd., Dublin. Records, 1872–1909; 5 vols. and 3 boxes. Contracts, ledgers, daybooks, and other business records of a colonization company organized in Ireland in 1880 by John Sweetman to help Irishmen better their conditions by emigrating to the United States. Includes information on the purchase of land at Currie, Minnesota, from the Winona and St. Peter Railway Company, on John O'Brien's interest in the colonization company, and on the Murray County Cooperative Store Company.

Miscellaneous Irish materials. Papers and letters of Irish immigrants, including Mary Jane Hill Anderson autobiography and papers of Callahan and McBreath families.

Rahilly, Patrick H. Papers, 1874–1930; ca. 3 ft. State legislator of Lake City, Minnesota. Correspondence and clippings concerning the Catholic Church and the Irish in America, including copies of letters and speeches written by Rahilly and Ignatius Donnelly. Some letters deal with the Catholic Church and the Irish Independence movement. Correspondents include Ignatius Donnelly and Archbishop John Ireland.

Minnesota Historical Society, Oral History Collection, St. Paul, Minnesota

Oral history collections include the following interviews concerning the Irish in Minnesota.

Pierce Butler III, grandson of Justice Pierce Butler (1866–1939), Justice of the United States Supreme Court. This interview contains information on the Butler family since its arrival from Ireland in the late 1840s. Much of the interview concerns Mr. Butler's memories of his grandfather, Pierce Butler. Approximately one and one half hours. Restricted to those with Mr. Butler's specific written permission to use.

Mr. and Mrs. Eugene Casserly. Early settlers in Minnesota. The interview contains information on their early years in Minnesota after coming from Ireland, and comments on a recent trip to Ireland. Three cassettes, two hours.

Catherine Rowe Conzemius. Teacher in early Minnesota. The interview includes information concerning life in Minnesota, including farming, school discipline, prohibition, women's roles, and the Ku Klux Klan. Two cassettes.

Mississippi

Jackson

Catholic Diocese of Natchez-Jackson, 231 East Amite Street, Jackson, Mississippi 39205

Correspondence and diaries of two bishops of Irish origin: Bishop Thomas Heslin, 1889–1911, and Bishop John Edward Gunn, 1911–1924. All of the material of Bishop Heslin's administration is available. Most of Bishop Gunn's material has been processed and is also available. Materials from the many Irish priests who worked in this diocese, mainly correspondence, are in the archives. Also some materials on Irish settlements that followed the railroads; these include places as Sulpher Springs, Paulding, Bassfield, and Sullivan's Hollow.

Mississippi Department of Archives and History, 100 South State Street, Jackson, Mississippi 39205

Koger, J. T., (d. 1862). Correspondence, 1820–73; 1 reel microfilm. Methodist minister, chaplain in the 1st Mississippi infantry, and Confederate officer in the 41st Mississippi infantry, Company A. Correspondence of Koger, chiefly to his wife, concerning Methodist church affairs in the South and his experiences in the Civil War. Includes correspondence by members of Mrs. Koger's family, in particular Matthew Elder of Dublin, Ireland.

Missouri

Independence

Harry S. Truman Library, Independence, Missouri 64050

As an agency of the National Archives and Records Service, the Harry S. Truman Library is responsible for preserving, describing, and providing reference service on the papers of Harry S. Truman and other manuscripts in its custody. Included among the manuscript collections are materials donated to the library by persons of Irish extraction. Also of value in providing information on the Irish in America are the White House Files, which contain materials on prominent Irish Americans and on organizations such as the Society of the Friendly Sons of St. Patrick and the Ancient Order of Hibernians. Leading Manuscript Collections:

Boyle, William M., Jr. Papers, 1946–61; 1 ft. Chairman, Democratic National Committee.

Connelly, Matthew J. Files, 1945–53; 1 ft. Secretary to the President, 1945–53.

Galvin, Michael J. Papers, 1933–63; 10 ft. Undersecretary of Labor, 1949–53.

McCahill, William P. Papers, 1948–51; 1 ft. Executive secretary, President's Committee on Employment of the Physically Handicapped, 1949–62.

McGohey, John F. X. Papers, 1944–72; 5 ft. U.S. attorney for the Southern District of New York, 1944–49; U.S. district judge, Southern District of New York, 1949–70.

McGrath, J. Howard. Papers, 1943–52; 88 ft. U.S. senator from Rhode Island, 1947–49; chairman, Democratic National Committee, 1947–49; attorney general of the United States, 1949–52.

McGuire, Charles H. Papers, 1951–55; 1 ft. Director, National Shipping Authority, 1951–53; Director, Office of the National Shipping Authority and Government Aid, Maritime Administration, 1953–55.

Maher, Sister Patrick Ellen, 1922–64. 1 ft. Research materials relating to Harry S. Truman's political campaigns and to the work of the Truman Committee.

Matthews, Francis P., 1887–1952. 1932–52; 29 ft. Secretary of the Navy, 1949–51; Ambassador to Ireland, 1951–52. Correspondence, memoranda, reports, speech files, appointment schedules, newspaper clippings files, publications, and other materials, relating to Matthew's career.

Murphy, Charles S. Papers, 1947–67; 18 ft. Administrative Assistant to the President, 1947–50; Special Counsel to the President, 1950–53; Under Secretary of Agriculture, 1960–65; Chairman, Civil Aeronautics Board, 1965–68.

Murphy, Charles S. Files, 1948–53; 9 ft.

O'Connell, Joseph J., Jr. Papers, 1944–47; 2 ft. General Counsel, Department of the Treasury, 1944–47.

O'Gara, John E. Papers, 1919–61; 1 ft. Official, Central Intelligence Agency, 1949–61.

White House Office of Social Corresp. Files, 1945–53; 100 ft.

White House Social Office. Files, 1945–53; 42 ft.

There are also a number of microfilm collections.

Kennedy, John F. Papers; 1 reel microfilm. Papers concerning proposed dinner to be held January 30, 1964, in honor of John F. Kennedy. Property of Leo Wartgame.

McGrath, Earl J. Papers, 1949–53; 3 reels microfilm. U.S. Commissioner of Education, 1949–53. Property of Earl J. McGrath.

Malone, William M. Newspaper clipping files, 1940–57; 1 reel microfilm. Chairman, Democratic Central Committee, San Francisco County California. Property of William M. Malone.

The Truman Library also has transcripts of oral history interviews.

Connelly, Matthew J. 135 pages. Secretary to the President, 1945–53 (closed).

Curry, Charles F. 30 pages. Kansas City, Missouri, businessman and friend of Harry S. Truman.

Feeney, Joseph G. 63 pages. Administrative assistant to the president, 1952–53.

Keenan, Joseph G. 61 pages. International secretary, International Brotherhood of Electrical Workers.

Lawrence, David L. 40 pages. Mayor of Pittsburgh, Pennsylvania, 1946–59; governor of Pennsylvania, 1959–63.

Murphy, Charles S. 198 pages. Administrative assistant to the president, 1947–50; special counsel to the president, 1950–53.

Murphy, Harry E. 31 pages. Member of Battery D, 129th Field Artillery in World War I.

Sullivan, John L. 90 pages. Assistant secretary of the Navy for Air, 1945–46; undersecretary of the Navy, 1946–47; secretary of the Navy, 1947–49.

Walsh, Robert K. 208 pages. Reporter for the Washington, D.C. *Evening Star*, 1946–49.

Jefferson City

Missouri State Archives, Jefferson City, Missouri 65101

Petition for pardon and prisoners' papers on numerous Irish prisoners at state penitentiary in Jefferson City.

Adjutant General of Missouri, Records and Archives, 1717 Industrial Drive, Jefferson City, Missouri 65101

Holds military records and other materials on Missouri inhabitants who served in the armed forces of the Confederacy. Includes data on a large number of Irish immigrants.

St. Louis

Missouri Historical Society Archives, Jefferson Memorial Building, Lindell Blvd. at De Baliviere, St. Louis, Missouri 63112

Boyce, Joseph, 1841–1928. Papers, 1844–1919; ca. 120 items. Businessman of St. Louis, Missouri. Correspondence, insurance and business papers, bills of lading, steamboat items, genealogical material, and other papers. Includes letters of the Civil War and World War I periods, and relating to Father John Bannon (d. 1913), pastor of St. John's Catholic Church, St. Louis, Missouri, and Confederate chaplain, who later returned to Dublin, Ireland.

Chopin, Kate O'Flaherty. Papers, 1851–1904. Large collection of papers.

Fenian Brotherhood. Records, 1866–1921. Letters from leaders of the Fenian movement in America to the various circles throughout the United States; twelve manuscripts of speeches of John O'Keefe for the cause of Irish liberty. Writers of the letters include James Gibbons, James Keenan, Michael Kerwin, Richard McCloud, John O'Neill, and Frank Renehan.

Neill, Edward Duffield, 1823–93. Papers, 1827–1930; 13 vols. and 8 boxes. Presbyterian minister, educator, and historian. Correspondence, notes, scrapbooks, newspaper clippings, and other papers gathered by Neill as a student at Amherst and Andover, a home missionary in Illinois, a minister in St. Paul, the founder of churches in Minnesota, state superintendent of education and chancellor of the University of Minnesota, chaplain of the 1st Minnesota Volunteer Infantry and of the Philadelphia hospitals during the Civil War, and American consul at Dublin.

Taylor, James Wickes, 1819–93. Papers, 1852–94; 4 vols. and 13 boxes. Lawyer, consular officer, and journalist. Correspondence, articles, speeches, and newspaper clippings, reflecting Taylor's interest in all phrases of the development of the American and Canadian Northwest while he was a special agent and U.S. consul at Winnipeg. Papers relate to reciprocal relations of trade and transportation between the United States and Canada, the proposed annexation of Canada by the U.S., the Red River Rebellion of 1869–70, and the Fenian raid in 1871.

Washington University Libraries, Department of Rare Books and Special Collections, John M. Olin Library, Lindell and Skinner Blvds., St. Louis, Missouri 63130

O'Donnell, George Marion, 1914–62. Papers, 1932–61; 1718 items. Author and educator. Letters or manuscripts from authors John Berryman, James Laughlin, and Flannery O'Connor.

Ward, Mary Augusta (Arnold), 1851–1920. Papers, 4 boxes. British author. Drafts of two letters to unidentified correspondents relating to Irish Independence and to the National Union of Women Workers of Great Britain and Ireland.

University of Missouri at St. Louis, 8001 Natural Bridge Road, St. Louis, Missouri 63121

Useful general collection, best item of Irish interest is the Fellowship of America's *Loyal Irish Record Book 1929–1930*.

Oral History Program, University of Missouri at St. Louis, 8001 Natural Bridge Road, St. Louis, Missouri 63121

The immigrant in St. Louis project includes the following twelve interviews over life in the 1970s with Irish in St. Louis: Mary B. Bresnahan, Richard Conway, Monica Costello, Leo Fleming, Bert Gates, Nelly Gates, Thomas Kennedy, Ellen Manion, James J. Mullally, Vincent McDonald, John Stretch. Topics discussed include places of residence, work, time, reason and method of arrival, acculturation to St. Louis. Also holds twenty slides of Irish active in nineteenth-century Catholic churches in St. Louis.

Montana

Butte

World Museum of Mining, Butte, Montana 59701

The minute books of the Butte Workingmen's Union (1915–16) contain extensive listings of Irish immigrant miners, who predominated in the area at the time.

Butte/Silver Bow County Archives, Butte Public Library, Butte, Montana 59701

County files include mortuary records, which provide a great deal of genealogical information on Irish miners in the town and county. Works Projects Administration reports include the valuable *Report on Contageous Diseases, Silver Bow County, 1908–1912*, which provides detailed information on health conditions for Irish miners.

Crow Agency

Custer Battlefield National Monument, P.O. Box 39, Crow Agency, Montana 59022

Photographs, correspondence, Army records, diaries, documents, research notes and other items relating to the thirty-two Irishmen who died with General Custer in the Battle of the Little Big Horn.

Helena

Montana Historical Society Archives, 225 North Roberts Street, Helena, Montana 59620

A number of collections of papers on mining and miners—overwhelmingly Irish; also a number of general sources on immigration to the state. Among the more useful items are: Alice Gold and Silver Mining Company records; Anaconda Company papers; P. J. Brophy papers; Martin Hogan papers; Montana Council of Defense papers; Andrew O'Connell papers; Silver Bow County Board of Health: "Report on Sanitary Conditions in the Mines and Community, Silver Bow County, December 1908–April 1912" and "Report Showing Results of Inspection of Dwellings, Hotels, Rooming Houses, and Boarding Houses and Their Surroundings" (conditions of habitation for Irish miners); many local newspapers providing a great deal of information on Irish miners in the region around 1900.

Roman Catholic Diocese of Helena, 612 Harrison Avenue, Helena, Montana 59601

Records of the Roman Catholic Diocese of Helena, including records of parishes and institutions, correspondence of bishops, diaries of priests, and general historical data relating to the Roman Catholic Church in Montana. All items provide a great deal of information on the Irish in the mines in the region. Includes: Bishop John Brondel papers; "Butte Parish Boundaries"—1908 Report; Bishop John Carroll papers; Michael J. Hannan file; parish files of the predominantly Irish parishes of St. Lawrence O'Toole, St. Mary, and St. Patrick

Missoula

University of Montana, Library, K. Ross Toole Archives, Missoula, Montana 59812

Irish collection; microfilm copies of the following items essential to study of the Irish presence in mining and politics.

Ancient Order of Hibernians: general correspondence, 1894–1937; conferences and conventions, 1898–1948; financial records, 1882–1937; membership and dues ledgers, 1882–1937; reports, 1882–1937; minute books, 1884–1917 (Hibernian Hall board of trustees).

Robert Emmet Literary association: financial records, 1883–1946; minute books, 1882–1925.

Emmet Association and Ancient Order of Hibernian Committees, Proceedings of a Joint Meeting . . . for a monument to Thomas Francis Meagher, Butte, Jan 1, 1898.

Irish Volunteers of America: minute books, 1897, 1912–15; financial records, 1909, 1912–13.

Friends of Irish Freedom, organization, 1916, 1921.

American Association for the Recognition of the Irish Republic, miscellany, 1921–22.

Sunburst club, minute books, 1886–1900.

Murray, James E. Papers, 1919–60; 4 in. Senator from Montana, 1935–60; very active in Irish movement in the United States between 1919 and 1922; delegate to Irish Race Convention of 1919 in Philadelphia; national president of the American Association for Recognition of Irish Republic in 1922; member of Friends of Irish Freedom. The material pertaining directly to Ireland and the Irish in the United States is only a small segment of the much larger James E. Murray collection.

Senator Mike Mansfield papers, 1943–1989. Contain useful information on the senator's relationships with a number of Irish-American politicians, including Speaker of the House John McCormick and President John F. Kennedy.

Nebraska

Lincoln

Nebraska State Historical Society, 1500 R. Street, Lincoln, Nebraska 68505

Ancient Order of Hibernians / Hibernian Benevolent Society, 1 ft. The Lincoln division of the Hibernian Benevolent Society was organized in 1855. Its main function was to encourage immigration to the Lincoln area. Collection consists of one roll book relating to membership records, 1885–89.

Murphy family, 1823–1971. Ca. 400 items and 1 reel microfilm. The Murphy family of Nebraska began to emigrate to the New World in approximately 1830. After first settling in Canada, the family began to disperse south throughout the United States. A large number settled in the midwest. The Micheal Murphy family settled in Richardson County, Nebraska, in 1874; later, various members of the family moved to western Nebraska.

One box of manuscript material arranged in five series: correspondence, 1956–71; census and passenger lists, 1823–25; biographical data on various members of the Murphy family, undated; printed matter, undated; and miscellany, 1892–1903, undated. The bulk of the collection consists of census and passenger lists with a substantial amount of biographical data. Includes several maps that indicate the locations of the different members of the family in Ireland. A completed copy of the Thomas Murphy's genealogical study, *Murphy's Family Tree,* is on microfilm in the newspaper room under M53570.

Nebraska Historical Sketches Collection of term papers written for Nebraska History off-campus course taught at Walthill, Nebraska, September–November, 1960, and at Albion, February–May, 1961. Includes: Margaret M. Casey Anderson, "My Autobiography." Concerns the Tighe and Casey families—Irish immigrants. Celia M. Coffey, "Reminiscences." Mullin family; Irish in Nebraska; good on immigrant experience. Marcella Dougherty, "My Fabulous Family." Concerns the Irish immigrant family of Michael Dougherty. J. Paul Fritton, "History of Nebraska." Gibbons and Murphy families; Irish in Nebraska. Helen R. Mullin, "History of My People and Their Settlement in Nebraska." Lee and Hannigan families. Margaret Orr, "Nebraska History." Deals with the history of Michael Casey and John Tighe descendents. Life of Irish-Catholic pioneers.

University of Nebraska at Lincoln, Library, Special Collections Division, 303 Love Library, University of Nebraska, Lincoln, Nebraska 68588

Union Pacific Railroad papers. Much information on Irish role in constructing first cross-continental railroad.

Omaha

Union Pacific Historical Museum, 1416 Dodge Street, Omaha, Nebraska 68179

Miscellaneous collection of Union Pacific Railroad records; over 100,000 photographs and slides relating to railroads and various aspects of the American West and Midwest.

Archives, Archdiocese of Omaha, 100 N. 62nd St., Omaha, Nebraska 68132

An unprocessed and important collection of items of all kinds on the church in Nebraska, including letters from East Coast Irish immigrant families seeking aid in finding relatives who have disappeared; various Church records from the numerous Irish settlements in nineteenth-century Nebraska. See archivist for details.

Nevada

Carson City

Nevada Office of the Secretary of State, Division of State, County and Municipal Archives, 1807 North Carson Street, Carson City, Nevada 89710

Local and state government records from throughout Nevada since 1857. Also military records from posts throughout the state. Personal papers of Patrick McCarran, Irish-American U.S. senator from Nevada.

Elko

Northeastern Nevada Museum, 1515 Idaho Street, Elko, Nevada 89801

Materials relating to gambling and similar activities both in the United States and abroad; materials on Nevada, particularly the southern part of the state, including photographs, oral histories, maps, manuscripts, and motion pictures; archives of the University of Nevada at Las Vegas.

Reno

Archives of the Diocese of Reno-Las Vegas, Chancery Office, 515 Court Street, Reno, Nevada 89509

General Archival Records, 1860–present. The Irish played a large part in the early development of the Catholic Church in Nevada. The archives contain many items by and about prominent early Irish including Bishop Patrick Manogue of Virginia City, a miner turned priest, and state senator John O'Kane, who helped found a parish in the 1870s.

The collections have never been properly organized and are therefore very difficult to use. Researchers should contact the archivist for further information.

Oral History Project, University of Nevada, Reno, Reno, Nevada 89507
Oral history interview with James E. Hickey (1890–1969), politician. A pioneer and justice of the peace of Carson Valley. Discusses the hard winter of 1889–90 in Carson Valley; the history of Carson River mills; wood drives in Alpine County; politics of Douglas County; the work of the justice of the peace in Gardnerville, Nevada; observations on the marriage business in Douglas County; sketches of local figures.

New Jersey

Clifton

Roman Catholic Diocese of Paterson, Archives, 774 Valley Road, Clifton, New Jersey 07013
Records of the Diocese of Paterson, which encompasses Morris, Passaic, and Sussex Counties.

New Brunswick

Rutgers University, Library, New Brunswick, New Jersey 08901
Cobbett, William, 1763–18xx. Papers, 1792–1898; 77 items and 2 reels microfilm. English political journalist and essayist. Letters to Robert G. Harper, William Jackson, and James Oldden; copies of letters to James Abercrombie, Mathew Carey, Isaac Franklin, Thomas Jefferson, Elizabeth Langton, Timothy Pickering, N. Webster, and others; a copy of "To the collective wisdom" (1828), an essay written for the *Political register;* copies of portraits, caricatures, and examples of Cobbett's political satire; microfilm of letters, extracts, clippings, and other papers by or relating to Cobbett; printed material, including several biographical accounts of Cobbett and a notation of his death; Cobbett family letters, 1826–98. Places represented include Wilmington, Delaware; Philadelphia; London; Dublin; and Normandy, France.

Paterson

Paterson Public Library, 250 Broadway, Paterson, New Jersey 07501
Holland, John P. Papers, 1875–1900. Irish-born, former Christian Brother who invented the submarine to deal with England's powerful navy; letters, sketches, blueprints, and historical notes.

South Orange

Seton Hall University, Archives, South Orange, New Jersey 07079
Meagher McManus Collection; approximately 5,000 items. Mostly books but includes a number of Cromwellian notices proscribing Catholics in Ireland. Also holds a book found on Wolfe Tone when he died.
Archdiocese of New Jersey. Records. Archives of the Archdiocese of New Jersey going back to eighteenth century. Many references to Irish; Archbishop Corrigan's dispute with the Ancient Order of Hibernians, whom he regarded as a radical group.

Trenton

New Jersey Division of Archives and Record Management, New Jersey Department of State, 185 West Street, Trenton, New Jersey 08625
Useful general collection of vital records; important for anyone intending to trace Irish or other inhabitants. Includes military records, wills, deeds, marriage bonds, court records, passenger lists, records of the Morris Canal and files on railroads.

New Mexico

Santa Fe

New Mexico State Records Center and Archives, 404 Montezuma, Santa Fe, New Mexico 87503

General collection; important for research on the Irish are the naturalization records for 1870–1900.

New York

Albany

Albany Institute of History of Art, McKinney Library, 125 Washington Avenue, Albany, New York 12210

Albany Committee for Relief of Ireland. Records, 1847–48; 73 items. Reports and papers concerning shipments of food to Ireland during the Great Famine. Also records of contributions to the fund by residents of Albany.

New York State Department of Education, New York State Archives, Cultural Education Center, Empire State Plaza, Albany, New York 12230

State censuses, laws, election records, and papers of governors, including Alfred E. Smith. Also holds prison records and state censuses with many Irish entries. The most important larger collection on the Irish is the following:

Batcheller, George Sherman, 1836–1908. Papers, 1807–1943; 12 ft. Union Army officer, politician, and diplomat. Includes family letters, letters on the Fenian raids (June 6–10, 1866), and material relating to the Civil War.

Sisters of Mercy archives, 634 New Scotland Avenue, Albany, New York 12208

Two histories of the establishment of the Irish Sisters of Mercy in Albany in the 1860s; letters of sisters; official journals, financial records, blueprints and plans of churches and other institutions operated by the sisters, mainly in the Albany diocese; numerous photographs of church-related subjects.

Binghamton

State University of New York at Binghamton, University Library, Special Collections, Vestal Parkway East, Binghamton, New York 13901

Literary papers, including manuscripts, play scripts, notebooks, cassettes, pictures and letters of Padraic Colum, and papers of Mary Colum. The Mary Levin Collection includes her twenty-year correspondence, beginning in 1943, with Lord and Lady Dansany and other Irish writers.

Brooklyn

The Chancery Office, Diocese of Brooklyn, Archives, 75 Greene Avenue, Brooklyn, New York 11238

Correspondence of Bishop John Loughlin (1853–91) and Bishop Charles Edward McDonnell (1892–1921).

St. Francis College, James A. Kelly Local Historical Studies Institute, 180 Remsen Street, Brooklyn, New York 11201

A useful collection of Irish materials, including papers of Congressman John Rooney, minutes of the Friendly Sons of St. Patrick, John C. Malone papers, and a collection of Irish-American sheet music.

Buffalo

Diocese of Buffalo, Chancery Office, 35 Lincoln Parkway, Buffalo, New York 14222

Timon, Bishop. One original and one copy of Bishop Timon's diary (Bishop Timon was the first bishop of Buffalo).

State University of New York at Buffalo, Lockwood Memorial Library, Poetry Collection, Buffalo, New York 14214

James Joyce Collection. Manuscripts, letters, and photographs of James Joyce and a number of important English and American writers.

Geneva

Hobart and William Smith Colleges, Warren Hunting Smith Library, Geneva, New York 14456

Correspondence of Thornton Wilder and Mrs. Adaline Glashean concerning James Joyce's *Finnegans Wake*.

Hyde Park

Franklin D. Roosevelt Library, Hyde Park, New York 12538

Gray, David, 1870–1968. Papers, 1868–1962; 6 ft. Journalist and diplomat. Diplomatic and personal correspondence, memoranda, reports, and newspaper clippings, chiefly relating to Gray's service as U.S. minister to Ireland, 1940–47 (See also entry on University of Wyoming David Gray collection).

U.S. President's Committee on an Inquiry on Cooperative Enterprise in Europe. Records, 1936–37; 5 ft. Correspondence, memoranda, reports of field activities in Europe, transcripts of interviews, press releases, and a final report relating to the work of a committee charged with the responsibility of making a broad survey that would indicate the status and extent of cooperative enterprise and its effects on the economy and welfare of Europe. The committee spent ten weeks in Europe observing the operation of consumer cooperatives and interviewing cooperative employees and executives in Ireland and a number of other countries.

Ithaca

Cornell University, Libraries, M.P. Catherwood Library, Labor-Management Documentation Center, 144 Ives Hall, Ithaca, New York 14850

Over 8 million manuscripts and collective bargaining agreements. Included are records of six national labor unions, and five New York State labor organizations, and papers of numerous individuals important in labor relations. Invaluable for the study of the Irish in labor relations.

Cornell University, John M. Olin Library, Department of Manuscripts and University Archives, 101 Olin Library, Ithaca, New York 14853.

Crandall, Albert Rogers, 1861–63, 1912; 21 items. Civil War letters from encampments in Virginia to his cousins in Alfred Center, New York.

Crangle, Roland and Emily Elkus, 1898–1955; 1 1/2 ft. Scrapbooks (3 vols.) of Roland Crangle (1862–1945), attorney of Buffalo, and (1 vol.) of his wife, Emily Elkus Crangle (1878–).

Devereux Collection. 1800–1942; 309 pieces. Correspondence, typescript (1800–1839), of Devereux and Butler families; also William M. Morris and James Clapp on the suffering of Catholics in Ireland.

Devereux-Kernan Letters. 1800–1915; 405 pieces. The Kernan correspondence contains letters of Senator Francis Kernan.

Devereux, Nicholas, Collection. 1801–85; 560 pieces. Included are papers relating to early promotion of the Erie Railroad. Much information on Irish immigrant workers.

Griffin, William Joseph, 1863–1959. Oral History Interview, May 1958; 1 vol. (twenty-six page typescript carbon copy; original held by the Forest History Foundation, Inc., St. Paul, Minnesota).

Humphreys, Robert, 1845–92. 43 pieces. Carpenter Letters (1845–88) to Robert Humphreys in Dublin, Ireland, and Windsor, England, from his aunt and uncle, Honor and John Fleming, of Philadelphia.

Jackson, W. W. Rent book, 1785–1802; 1 vol. Yearly receipts for rent payments on a leasehold by James Glass, Armagh County, Ireland.

Kernan Family Collection, 1776–1922. 22 boxes. This collection of letters, clippings, speeches, and miscellaneous items relating to the activities of the Kernan family of Utica. Included is general coverage of Catholics in the Utica area, their strong religious beliefs and their work on the local canal.

Lewis, John Livy, 1813–89. Papers, 1810–1928; 1227 items and 2 vols. Personal and business correspondence, Masonic documents, and papers relating to temperance and education.

McNish Family, 1773–1853. 6 in. These additional papers of Alexander McNish included correspondence and legal papers dealing with politics and family matters, the latter including several from relatives in Ireland and in Ohio and Kentucky.

Smith, Goldwin, 1823–1910. Papers, 1820–1910; ca. 31 ft. Historian, journalist, and university professor. Correspondence and other papers chiefly relating to English, Canadian, and American political questions, including the Irish Home Rule struggle. Correspondents include W. Bourke Cochran, W. E. Gladstone, and Viscount Peel.

Stevenson Family, 1795–1846. 8 pieces. Include letters to Samuel Stevenson concerning conditions in Ireland, Missouri, and Alabama.

Tobin, James, 1834. 15 pp. From Canandaigua, February 13, 1834, to a friend in Ireland, describing economic, agricultural, political, and social conditions in the Canandaigua region in particular and in the United States in general, with comments on immigration, the development of transportation, and other aspects of American life.

Wilde, J. F. Correspondence, 1848, 1880; 2 items. Physician. Letters (1848) to solicitor Christopher McNally of Dublin.

Jamaica

St. John's University Library, Grand Central and Utopia Parkways, Jamaica, New York 11432

The American Friends of Irish Neutrality Papers, 1938–41; 5/6 ft., 109 items. Donated to St. John's University by Paul O'Dwyer, who turned over "every record I had concerning the American Friends of Irish Neutrality" and associated activities. This organization had its national headquarters in the Murray Hill Hotel, 112 Park Avenue, New York, New York. Its purpose was, in the words of Mr. O'Dwyer, "to keep the pressures off Ireland to enter World War II." Includes letters, membership and donation cards, minutes, press clippings, post cards, and printed mimeographed and typed materials of various kinds (speeches, releases, pamphlet, etc.).

The American League for an Undivided Ireland Papers, 1947–63; 2 1/4 ft., ca. 2,000 items. These papers were donated to St. John's University by Mr. Charles T. Rice, National vice-president and treasurer of the organization. In addition, there are organization notes, telegrams, press clippings, press releases, and various types of printed materials (U.S. congressional hearings, congressional record, congressional resolutions—all bearing on the organization's platform: to abolish the border between Eire and Northern Ireland). The bulk of the material covers the years 1947–58. There are only a few items after the death of the national president, Joseph Scott of Los Angeles, at the age of ninety. A feature of the papers is the extensive correspondence carried on between him and Mr. Rice in New York.

The Bernadette Devlin Papers. This collection contains documents, correspondence, etc., pertaining to the appeal from the decision of the magistrate's court, convicting Bernadette Devlin of excitement to riot and riotous behavior and disorderly conduct in the City of Londonderry, August 1969. Efforts to raise funds to defray expenses of appeal proceedings by Paul O'Dwyer. Application for a hearing by the European Commission on Human Rights, Strassbourg, France, August 8, 1970, including a statement of facts by Bernadette Devlin and signed by her.

O'Dwyer, Paul. Papers, 1970–77. ca. 3 ft., 18 manila envelopes. These papers were donated to St. John's University by Paul O'Dwyer (then president of the New York city council.) They deal with the troubles and disturbances in Northern Ireland and the efforts by Irish-American individuals and groups to find a solution for them.

New York

American Irish Historical Society, 991 Fifth Avenue, New York, New York 10028

Probably the finest American collection of materials on the Irish in the United States. Includes approximately 50,000 volumes together with manuscript collections and archival materials relating to Irish-American individuals, families and organizations. In addition to the seven major collections described below, the society holds many scattered items of interest, including William Butler Yeats's letter to playwright Seamus O'Brien, scrapbooks of American newspaper accounts of the Fenians, and items from the estate of Congressman Burke Cockran.

American Irish Historical Society Records, 1897–1974; 100 ft. The society's archives include minutes of council meetings, as well as general membership and committee meetings, business correspondence, financial records, annual reports, membership files, programs, invitations, photographs, and miscellaneous memorabilia.

Catholic Club of Greater New York Records, 1873–1957; 7 ft. Originally named the Xavier Union of New York City, the Catholic Club numbered among its members many of the most influential and wealthy Catholics in metropolitan New York. Its objectives were "to encourage virtue and Christian piety among educated Catholic young men," to promote the "moral improvement" of its members through literature and social activities. Records include minutes of meetings, financial reports, membership files, programs, invitations, and other miscellaneous memorabilia.

Friends of Irish Freedom Records, 1919–36; 11 ft. The Friends of Irish Freedom arose out of the First Irish Race Convention held in New York City in March 1916. Victor Herbert was national president, but it was Justice Daniel F. Cohalan who was the organization's real leader and spokesperson. The FOIF's primary objective, as stated in its constitution, was "to encourage and assist any movement that will tend to bring about the National Independence of Ireland." Various chapters sprang up throughout the United States. The FOIF was one of the foremost American Irish political groups operating in the United States during the 1920s and 1930s. Records included correspondence, registers of dues payments, financial records, minutes, and newsletters.

The Guild of Catholic Lawyers. Records. The Guild of Catholic Lawyers was organized in response to various problems many Catholics confronted in the practice of law. The purpose of the guild was the "mutual benefit, spiritual and temporal of the individual members, for the upholding of the noble standards and best traditions of the profession and for the consolidation of Catholic thought on questions affecting public welfare and morals." Records include minutes of meetings.

Society of the Friendly Sons of St. Patrick, 1803–1964; 26 ft. Instituted in 1784 to assist the "poor and distressed natives of Ireland," the Society of the Friendly Sons of St. Patrick is the oldest American Irish organization in the United States. Their records, largely financial, reflect the primary purpose of the society, fundraising for needy causes related to the Irish. Also included are materials relating to the annual dinners and yearbooks. Approximately four linear feet contain correspondence used by Richard C. Murphy in writing the history of the society, published in 1962, and the original drafts of the history.

Cohalan, Daniel Florence, Papers, 1891–1935; 11 ft. Appointed in 1911 as Supreme Court justice for the state of New York, Daniel F. Cohalan was an active member of the Democratic party and became closely associated with Charles F. Murphy, one-time head of Tammany Hall. Cohalan was a vigorous supporter of Irish independence and was a central figure in organizing the American Irish in support of this goal. This collection of correspondence and speeches documents his activities and associations with the Fenian leader John Devoy, Prime Minister Eamon de Valera, President Woodrow Wilson, the Clan Na Gael of New York, the Friends of Irish Freedom, the Friendly Sons of St. Patrick, the Catholic Club, and the Guild of Catholic Lawyers.

O'Callahan, Rev. Donald M. Papers, 1942–73; 4 ft. Correspondence relates to his activities with the Anci Clan Na Gael, the IRA Veterans Clubs, the Irish Republican Brotherhood, the American Irish Historical Society, the Friendly Sons of St. Patrick, the United Irish Counties Association, the American League for an Undivided Ireland, and the Irish Freedom League.

City University of New York, John Jay College of Criminal Justice, Library, 445 West 59th Street, New York, New York 10019

Materials relating to the U.S. criminal justice system, including a letter by John Jay; 3,000 volumes of trial transcripts from New York City criminal courts, 1890s–1920s. Papers of Lewis E. Lawes, warden of Sing Sing prison from 1920 to 1941.

Columbia University Libraries, Herbert H. Lehman Papers, 406 International Affairs Building, 420 West 118th Street, New York, New York 10027

Manuscripts, correspondence, oral history transcripts regarding Herbert J. Lehman; includes a wide assortment of materials on politics, civil rights, and McCarthyism.

Columbia University, The Oral History Collection, Box 20, Butler Library, New York, New York 10027

The Columbia University Oral History Project includes the reminiscences of prominent political figures, journalists, civic leaders, and their relatives and associates. The following interviews provide information of interest to researchers of the Irish-American experience: William Harvey Allen, 4 vols., 1950; William Hamilton Anderson, 1950; William Stiles Bennet, 2 vols., 1951; Robert S. Binkerd, 1949; Frederic René Coudert, 1950; John W. Davis, 1954; Samuel Dickstein, 1950; Edward J. Flynn, 1950; James W. Gerard, 1950; John Heffernan, 1950; John T. Hettrick, 2 vols., 1949; Arthur Krock, 1950; Jeremiah T. Mahoney, 1949; New York State Election of 1949, 2 vols., 1949; John Lord O'Brian, 1952; Joseph O'Mahoney, 1958; Geoffrey Parsons, 1949; Ferdinand Pecora, 6 vols., 1962; Herbert Claiborne Pell, 3 vols., 1951; William A. Pendergast, 6 vols., 1951; Joseph M. Proskauer, 1961; Lawson Purdy, 1948; Martin Saxe, 1949; Frederick Chauncey Tanner, 1950; James W. Wadsworth, 3 vols., 1952; Paul O'Dwyer, 1962; William O'Dwyer, 1962

Columbia University Libraries, Rare Book and Manuscript Library, 801 Butler Library, New York, New York 10027

Dale, Samuel Sherman, 1859–1935. Papers, 1810–1929; 24 vols. In part transcripts (typewritten). Correspondence, diaries (1887–1929) and other papers. Includes sixteen volumes of correspondence (1902–29) relating to weights and measures, the textile tariff, and other subjects; a catalog of Dale's books, an 1810 account book kept by Samuel Dale of Carncastle, Ireland; and two volumes of accounts (1839–56) of Thomas Dale.

Dunning, William Archibald, 1857–1922. Papers, 1781–1922; 16 boxes. Correspondence, journals, notes for lectures, articles, reviews, and books, memorabilia, and other papers of Dunning and other members of his family. Subjects of the notes include the British Empire and the U.S., England, and Ireland.

Kilroe Collection. A major source of primary materials on Tammany Hall from the 1780s to the 1920s, collected by lawyer Edwin Patrick Kilroe.

Mitchel and Purroy family papers, ca. 1830–1918; 811 items. Correspondence; mss. of writings; documents by and relating to John Mitchel (1815–75), Irish patriot; to his grandson, John Purroy Mitchel (1879–1918), mayor of New York City; to Mayor Mitchel's maternal grandfather, John B. Purroy; and to other members of the Mitchel and Purroy families.

Moore, George, 1852–1933. Papers, 1887–1928; 44 items. Irish author and journalist. Correspondence consisting of thirty-eight letters written to agents concerning the publication of Moore's works and four letters to the Marquise Clara Lanz; mss. include the first draft of the strike at Arlingford, a play, and portions of an early draft of *A Storyteller's Holiday* (1918).

Shaw, George Bernard, 1856–1950. Papers, 1933–40; 107 items. Papers on "The future of political science in America." Correspondence, mss., and documents relating to Shaw's speech, "The future of political science in America," which he delivered to the Academy of Political Science at the Metropolitan Opera House in New York, April 11, 1933, including the typescript prepared for publication by Dodd, Mead & Company, the radio broadcast by station WJZ, and the business affairs of the occasion itself.

Sutliff, Mary Louise, b. 1865. Papers, 1917–40; 49 items. Letters from Irish writers. Letters both from and about Irish poets, playwrights, and editors, written to Mary Sutliff, discussing Irish literature and Irish writers. Authors represented include Padraic Colum, O'Sullivan, and George Russell.

Willis, Henry Parker, 1874–1937. Papers, ca. 1910–37; ca. 10,000 items. Author, economist, and professor of banking at Columbia University. Correspondence, mss. of writings, speeches, reports, and memoranda. Much of the collection deals with the formation and early development of the Federal Reserve System. Includes material relating to the Phillipine National Bank, the banking inquiry of 1925, the Irish Banking Commission, and the Indian Currency Commission.

Yeats Family Papers, 1896–1940; 78 items. Correspondence, family photos, with annotations by Elizabeth C. Yeats, newspaper clippings, book reviews, and other printed material. Includes twelve letters (1918) from William Butler Yeats to Ellen Douglas Duncan, director of the Dublin Gallery of Modern Art, relating to public lectures containing comments on the unrest in

Ireland; thirty letters from Elizabeth C. Yeats to Mary L. Sutliff, dealing with publications of the Cuala Press, Dublin.

The New York Public Library, Manuscripts and Archives Division, Fifth Avenue and 42nd Street, New York, New York 10018

Cockran, William Bourke, 1854–1923. Papers, 1880–1923; 56 boxes. Lawyer and U.S. representative from New York City. Correspondence, speeches, lawyer's briefs (many with notes of comment by R. M. McElroy), legal papers, court register of cases (1880–94), newspaper clippings, and other papers. Includes genealogical charts of the Burke, Barry, and Knight families, records of cases as counsel for the sheriff of New York County, and material relating to congressional matters, Irish affairs, the Spanish-American War, the Boer War, World War I, and the Catholic Church. Correspondents include William Jennings Bryan, James C. Carter, Sir Roger Casement, Winston Churchill, William R. Churchill, William H. Clark, Grover Cleveland, Richard Croker, John Dillon, Patrick Ford, Moreton Frewen, Thomas P. Gill, Judge Martin J. Keogh, the 9th Duke of Marlborough, Charles F. Murphy, Thomas P. O'Connor, Sir Horace Plunkett, John Redmond, Thomas B. Reed, Theodore Roosevelt, Edward M. Shepard, Goldwin Smith, John C. Tomlinson, the American Commission on Irish Independence, and the United States Irish League of America.

Daly, Charles Patrick, 1816–99. Papers, 1716–1899; 48 boxes. Judge, of New York City. Correspondence (1829–97); travel diaries and notebooks (1851–81) relating to Europe and America; addresses, lectures, and writings on the history of law and judicial institutions, biographies of lawyers, Irish Americans and the Friendly Sons of St. Patrick, Sag Harbor and North Haven, New York, history of the New York Fire Department (1871), and other miscellaneous writings; legal and land papers; accounts and account book (1844–99); scrapbooks (1839–94) containing material on the Astor Place rioters (1849); and papers of Daly's wife, Maria (Lydig) Daly, including correspondence (1856–97) relating to women's war relief work and social affairs, accounts (1883–92), and papers (1894–1902) of Paul du Chaillu.

Dowden, Elizabeth Dickinson (West). Letters, 1913–31; 80 items. Wife of Irish editor and critic Edward Dowden (1843–1913) of Dublin, Ireland. Letters from Mrs. Dowden to Dr. Clara Barrus at West Park, New York, relating to personal and library matters, especially the writings of her husband. Covers public affairs, especially during World War I.

Fleming, Sampson Letter book, 1782–90; 1 vol. Letters from Montreal, Philadelphia, Beaver Hall, and New York City, to William Edgar, New York City, and to Friends and relatives in Ireland, Montreal, and elsewhere, relating to general business, personal matters, the Pennsylvania lottery, debts due from Mrs. Margaret Smith and William S. Smith, the ships Jay and the Empress of China (Later known as the Edgar), China trade, stock in the Bank of America, and other subjects. Includes accounts (1777) of the Deputy Commissary for Detroit and Canada.

George, Henry, 1839–97. Papers, 1854–1916; 20 boxes. Economist and reformer. Correspondence, diaries (1855–96), lectures, speeches, notes, manuscripts of George's writings, including a draft of *Progress and Poverty* (1879), pamphlets, newspaper clippings, and other papers. Contains much information regarding the appeal of his ideas to Irish Americans.

Kane, Whitford, 1882–. Papers, 1913–55; 1 box. Correspondence with Irish theater and literary figures, including Padraic Colum and Sean O'Casey.

Miscellaneous Irish materials. Padraig Cundun poems and papers; Sampson Fleming notebooks; letters of Thomas Francis Meagher.

Mitchel, Jane Verner. Letters, 1851–55; 1 vol. Transcripts (typewritten carbons): letters of Mrs. Mitchel, wife of the Fenian leader John Mitchel (1815–75), to Mary Thompson in Ireland, describing the life of the Mitchel family as political prisoners in Van Dieman's Land (Tasmania) and their escape and life in the U.S.

Morton, Levi Parsons, 1824–1920. Papers, 1868–1920; 16 boxes. Banker, vice-president of U.S., and governor of New York. Dispatch of the ship *Constellation* to the relief of Ireland, 1880.

O'Casey, Sean, 1880–1964. Papers, 1933–48; 149 items. Irish dramatist. Correspondence, pen and ink sketches, photos, and other papers. Most of the letters are to O'Casey's friend Jack Carney, and reflect O'Casey's interest in the progress of World

War II, contemporary Irish and English literature, the Irish labor movement, communism, Catholicism and Protestantism in Ireland, and music. Includes references to James Larkin and George Bernard Shaw.

Rodd Family Papers, 1826–59; ca. 60 items. Accounts of travel in Ireland.

Shaw, Albert, 1857–1947. Papers, 1874–1947; 200 ft. Editor, review of books. Contains manuscripts and unpublished reminiscences for a history of Ireland.

Smith Family Papers, 1769–1907. 2 boxes. Correspondence and miscellaneous papers concerning the Irish cause.

Wheeler, Everett Pepperell, 1840–1925. Papers, 1868–1925; 10 boxes. Lawyer and civil service reformer of New York City. Papers on the Irish question (1918–21).

New York University, Libraries, Tamiment Library, 70 Washington Square South, New York, New York 10012

Records of trade unions and old and new left groups. Papers of trade union leaders, many of them Irish born or of Irish background.

The Salvation Army, Archives Bureau, 120 West 14th Street, New York, New York 10011

A collection of materials concerning various aspects of the social work of the Salvation Army since 1880, including social relief work, rescue homes for single mothers, work with abandoned, abused, and delinquent children, slum work and settlement houses, and specialized work with alcoholics and drug addicts.

North Tarrytown

Rockefeller University, Rockefeller Archive Center, Hillcrest, Pocanatico Hills, North Tarrytown, New York 10591

Davis, Jackson, 1882–1947. Papers, 1898–1947; 40 items. Educator, of Henrico County, Virginia. Correspondence concerning conference on missionary societies in Great Britain and Ireland (1918).

Ogdensburg

Diocese of Ogdensburg, Archives, 622 Washington Street, Ogdensburg, New York 13669

General collection of materials concerning the Roman Catholic Diocese of Ogdensburg since 1872; also the mid-eighteenth century records of Fort La Presentation, a French and Indian settlement at Ogdensburg. Several parishes in this area were first settled by the Irish. These include Bombay, Hogansburg, Brasher Falls, Chateaugay, and Waddington. Although there is no section in the archives dealing with the Irish, many of the records refer to, or were generated by, clergy of Irish birth or descent.

Rochester

St. Bernard's Seminary, Library, 2260 Lake Avenue, Rochester, New York 14612

Materials by or about Bernard J. McQuaid, Thomas F. Hickey, John Francis O'Hern, Edward Mooney, James Edward Kearney, Fulton John Sheen, and Joseph Lloyd Hogan, all bishops of the Roman Catholic diocese of Rochester.

Syracuse

Canal Museum, Erie Blvd., East, Syracuse, New York 13202

A collection of materials on the Erie Canal, the New York State Barge Canal, and other New York canals, focusing primarily on their construction; covers the important role of Irish immigrants in building the canal.

North Carolina

Chapel Hill

University of North Carolina at Chapel Hill, Library, Manuscripts Department and Southern Historical Collection, Chapel Hill, North Carolina 27514

Brownrigg Family Papers, 1771–1886; 299 items. Family correspondence of various members of the Brownrigg family of Wicklow County, Ireland; Chowan, Pasquotank, and Hertford counties, North Carolina; and Mississippi; including Richard Brownrigg of Ireland; the brothers John and Thomas Brownrigg; Thomas's wife, Ruth; their son, Gen. Richard Thomas Brownrigg (b. 1793), and daughter, Priscilla Elizabeth Brownrigg, who married the Hon. John L. Bailey. The material concerns health, education, travels, and business, and includes letters (1784–94) from John Brownrigg written from Jamaica and Ireland to his friends and relatives in North Carolina.

Hughes Family Papers, 1790–1910; 410 items. Correspondence, miscellaneous account books, personal notebooks, sermons, clippings, deeds, wills, and bills (chiefly 1820–67) of the members of the Hughes family and relatives in South Carolina, Georgia, Mississippi, Louisiana, and Ireland.

Southern Historical Collection. Includes letters and papers of Irish immigrants, including the Griffin family papers; the Hugh McGavock papers.

Sproul, Andrew J. Papers, 1845–90; 54 items. Letters received by Sproul in Ohio from his mother and other relatives in Ireland; letters to his wife while he served with the 16th Ohio Volunteer Infantry in the lower Mississippi Valley (1861–63); pocket memorandum books.

Steele, Ephraim. Correspondence, 1755–1877; 75 items. Merchant and landowner, at Carlisle, Pennsylvania. Correspondence, mainly 1773–1823, received by Steele from relatives and friends in Ireland, North and South Carolina, and elsewhere.

Whittle, Lewis Neale. Papers, 1826–1919; ca. 800 items. Engineer, lawyer, and Confederate Army officer, of Macon, Georgia. Chiefly letters (1834–72) to Whittle from family and friends, and Whittle family correspondence with Powers, Griffin, and Potter connections in Virginia and Georgia. Includes letters from Episcopal clergymen such as Stephen Elliott, Alexander Gregg, and Francis M. Whittle, bishop of Virginia; officers in the U.S. Navy; relatives in Ireland, (1826, 1837, 1858–59); and Confederate soldiers in Georgia, Virginia, and Kentucky (1861–65).

Charlotte

Public Library of Charlotte and Mecklenburg County, 310 North Tryon Street, Charlotte, North Carolina 28202

Extensive library of Scotch-Irish materials, includes cardfiles of many families who settled in the area.

Durham

Duke University, Archives, 341 Perkins, Duke University, Durham, North Carolina 27706

Angelesey, Henry William Paget, 1st Marquis of, 1768–1854. Papers, 1830; 59 items. British Army officer and statesman. Letters to Lord Angelesey during his service as lord lieutenant of Ireland, chiefly relating to Irish politics, and to British foreign and domestic affairs.

Billmyer Family papers, 1832–1906; 998 items. Correspondence of the West Virginia family, whose seat was at Shepherdstown, Jefferson County. Includes letters from Henry E. Unself, a suitor of Mrs. David Billmyer, written from New Orleans (1854–55) describing the city, its theatrical and social life, and such events as the yellow fever epidemics, the rise of the Know-Nothing party, and the Irish uprising.

Carew, Sir Benjamin Hallowell, 1760–1834. Papers, 1794–1831; 55 items. British naval officer. Papers relating to Carew's career, especially his service in the French Revolutionary and Napoleonic Wars and his command on the Irish coast.

Croker, John Wilson, 1780–1857. Papers, 1809–57; 2251 items. British politician, essayist, and admiralty official. Chiefly letters received by Croker and relating to his career as secretary to the admiralty and as a Tory politician; Catholic emancipation, the corn laws, the Crimean War, and Irish politics.

Darnley, John Bligh, 4th Earl of, 1767–1831. Papers, 1738–1858; 76 items. Member of the House of Lords. Chiefly letters from prominent English politicians discussing Catholic emancipation, the elections of 1818 and 1820, the Irish Parliament and the Act of Union, the state of Ireland (1831), the Napoleonic War, Russian trade with Great Britain after 1775, and agriculture in England.

Miscellaneous Irish materials. Papers of Francis Yates Aglionby; William Harty; Valentine Browne Lawless; McCullough-Hutchinson papers; McMullen family papers; Malet family papers; Moore family papers; Potts family papers; W. Ramage report on the state of Ireland (see Robert Dundas papers); Staunton family papers.

Greenville

East Carolina University, East Carolina Manuscript Collection, J.Y. Joyner Library, Greenville, North Carolina 27843

Salisbury, Frank C., 1875–1964. Papers, 1800–1964; 273 items. Newspaper editor and historian, of Morehead City, North Carolina. Material on Irish and Civil War songs.

Raleigh

Diocese of Raleigh, Chancery Office, 215 Gibbons Drive, Raleigh, North Carolina 27606

Organization of the archives began in summer 1977; still largely incomplete. Many references to a large number of Irish priests who served in the area from earliest days. The transcription and indexing of parish registers for North Carolina from 1820 to 1924 (when North Carolina became a diocese) is in progress. Information available on Irish Catholic members of parishes. Private papers of Miss Nannie Gary of Halifax, North Carolina, contain information on her ancestors who immigrated in the 1830s and 1840s.

Salisbury

Rowan County Public Library, 201 West Fisher Street, Salisbury, North Carolina 28144

Collection of court records, deeds, and wills. Many of them provide coverage of Irish immigrants, especially for later colonial period. Records on "Old Irish Town" settlement.

North Dakota

Bismark

State Historical Society of North Dakota, Liberty Memorial Building, Bismark, North Dakota 58505

Papers, notes, and reports of Works Progress Administration Historical Records Survey providing information on Irish role in settlement of North Dakota.

Richardton

Assumption Abbey, Archives, Richardton, North Dakota 58652

Records of the abbey and other Catholic institutions in the region, including James McLaughlin papers on Indian tribes.

Ohio

Canton

Malone College, Library, Canton, Ohio 44709

Shackleton, Richard, 1726–92. Letters, 1744–90; 234 items. Master of Baltimore School, County Kildare, Ireland. Correspondence between Shackleton and his father, a few letters to his mother, and seventy-two letters from Edmund Burke.

Cincinnati

Archdiocese of Cincinnati, Archdiocesan Archives, Mount St. Mary's Seminary, 5440 Moeller Avenue, Cincinnati, Ohio 45212

Chancery records and correspondence, 1822–1925. Correspondence arranged chronologically and alphabetically (usually by the sender of the letter) within each year. Annual parish reports begin with 1880. Nineteenth-century reports break down the parish census figures into English, German, French, and total number of parishioners. Since the Catholic church in Cincinnati was composed largely of Irish and German families, there is considerable correspondence of interest to researchers. Irish versus German conflicts are covered. Microfilm copies of the *Catholic Telegraph,* the archdiocesan newspaper. Work on the papers of the episcopacy of Archbishop McNicholas is still in process, but the material is available to researchers.

Cleveland

Western Reserve Historical Society, History Library, 10825 East Blvd., Cleveland, Ohio 44106

Useful general collection of manuscript schedules of federal censuses 1790 to 1900. Also copies of passenger lists for New York and Baltimore and some scattered diaries of prominent Irish immigrants. Among the more useful major collections of Irish interest are the following:

Blair, Mary Jane. Letters, 1866–67; 121 items. Letters written while on tour of Ireland and other European countries.

Goodrich Social Settlement (Cleveland, Ohio). Records, 1897–1960; 4 ft. Settlement House founded by Flora Stone Mather. Letters (1893–1909) of Miss Mather, and material relating to Irish in Appalachian communities served by the settlement.

Sullivan, William. Papers, 1851–91; 296 items. Correspondence, circular letters, reports, minutes, and other papers relating to the Irish Emigrant Aid Society of Ohio and to the Fenian Brotherhood, for which Sullivan was center of the Tiffin, Ohio, circle. Includes material on the Irish Parliamentary party and the Irish-American Club Company of Cleveland. Correspondents include Michael Cavenaugh, James W. Fitzgerald, H. O'C. MacCarthy, Edward O'Flaherty, John O'Mahoney, and William R. Roberts.

Columbus

Ohio Historical Society, Inc., Archives-Manuscripts Division, 1–71 and 17th Avenue, Columbus, Ohio 43211

Index to naturalization records for Franklin County, 1850–1906. Also the following major collections:

Bissell, Thomas. Papers, 1840. Letters, September 15 and November 13, 1840, to Thomas Bissell of Monaghan, Ireland, from relatives in East Liverpool, Ohio, urging him to come to America but warning him to beware of the "Yankees" and telling him of their circumstances in Ohio.

Kurtz, Charles L. Papers, 1869–99; 13 ft. A typescript inventory is available. These papers contain information on the Irish in Ohio.

Mooney, James. Papers. One ALS dated May 26, 1906, contains information on the Irish Land League.

Nugent, Jane White. Papers, 1804–26. These letters contain information on Ireland.

Society of Friends. Ohio Friends records, 1732–1937; 2 ft. Correspondence, minutes, vital records, deeds, indentures, testimonies, and other papers, of various Ohio meetings, and the New Garden Quarterly Meeting, Fountain City, Indiana. Includes communications with Friends in Dublin.

The Ohio Historical Society also possesses a political broadside titled "Citizen? under which flag?" (New York: Yale Publishing Co., 1888). The broadside is an appeal to Irish in favor of Harrison and Morton.

Kent

Kent State University, Libraries, Department of Special Collections, Kent, Ohio 44242

Materials relating to literature and theater, including papers of James Stephens.

Oberlin

Oberlin College, Archives, 420 Mudd Learning Center, Oberlin, Ohio 44074

Frost, Wesley, 1884–1968. Papers, 1891–1944; ca. 3 ft. Foreign service officer and teacher of international relations; U.S. minister and ambassador to Paraguay. Correspondence, 1917–43; writings on Frost's experience in the consular service in Ireland during World War I.

Youngstown

Diocese of Youngstown, Chancery Office, 144 West Wood Street, Youngstown, Ohio 44503
Titles of collections: Calvary Cemetery, Canton, Records; Catholic Social Services, Records; Bishop McFadden Collection; Msgr. J. Paul O'Connor, Files; Parish Files, 77 page inventory; Saint Ann's Parish, Marriage Files; Saint Augustine Parish; Saint Louis Orphanage, Records; Bishop Emmet M. Walsh, Papers.

Oklahoma

Oklahoma City

Oklahoma Department of Libraries, Archives and Records Division, 200 Northeast 18th Street, Oklahoma City, Oklahoma 73105
Barnard, Kate. Letters and papers, 1875–1930. Letters, both personal and official, of Irish-American reformer Kate Barnard.

Tulsa

McFarlin Library, Special Collections/Rare Books, University of Tulsa, 600 S. College, Tulsa, OK 74104
A major collection of materials for researchers interested in Irish and Irish-American writers. Among the holdings of the collection are the following:
Joyce, James. The major collection of Joyce primary materials in the Harriet Shaw Weaver collection described below. The Weaver collection is augmented by research works in the *James Joyce Archive.* The 63-volume *Archive* is a facsimile edition, which makes accessible nearly all known Joyce manuscripts, printer's galleys, and page proofs. This permits scholars to see Joyce's creative process at work and helps eliminate the guesswork that has surrounded errors in the published texts.

Fitzgerald, F. Scott. The Fitzgerald collection contains over 600 items. It includes first and variant editions of Fitzgerald's work and extensive secondary works by Sheila Graham, Arnold Gingrich, and Alfred Kazin. The collection is especially strong on Fitzgerald's contributions to magazines and other books. This aspect of the collection comprises approximately 250 items.
Harriet Shaw Weaver. The collection is the center of the Joyce holdings in the Department of Rare Books and Special Collections, and consists of more than 200 volumes. It includes works by and about Joyce. First editions of all of Joyce's writing published during his lifetime are included except for *Finnegan's Wake.* (However, this work is represented in the Edmund Wilson library by a copy heavily annotated in his hand.) Also present are numerous subsequent editions and translations of Joyce's writings (there are eighteen different editions of *Ulysses,* for example) and various critical studies which had been given to Miss Weaver by other publishers and authors.
Stephens, James. The James Stephens collection numbers over 61 items, including a book of *Two Essays,* which was number 10 of 19 inscribed and presented to some unknown person by Stephens prior to the submission of final page proofs to the printer.

Oregon

Portland

Archives of Portland, History and Archives Department, 2838 East Burnside, Portland, Oregon 97207
Extensive collection of materials on Catholic church in Oregon and throughout the Pacific Northwest, invaluable for any study of the Irish in these areas. Includes materials from parish archives, diocesan papers, and account books.

Oregon Historical Society, 1230 S.W. Park Avenue, Portland, Oregon 97205
Dobbs, Arthur, 1689–1764. Papers, 1683–1747; 1 folder and 80 ft. of micro-

244 Manuscript Collections

film. Irish author and statesman, and colonial governor of North Carolina. Photocopies of typewritten transcripts and microfilm made from originals in the Public Record Office of Northern Ireland, Belfast.

Estes, George. General papers. Correspondence and manuscripts on the Catholic Church, the Irish in Oregon, and on the Grand Orange Lodge.

Great Britain Board of Trade. Records, 1791–92; 25 ft. and 1 box. Reports, proposals, inquiries, and other documents relating to Irish immigration to the U.S.

Microfilm: Daniel M. Feller, *Get a Job: Occupational Structure and Social Mobility in Portland, Oregon, 1860–1880.* (Includes a section on Irish).

Pamphlets: Oliver Snoddy, "A Clan Na Gael Constitution and Ritual from Portland, 1916," and the "The Irish in Jordan Valley, Malheru County, Oregon."

Pennsylvania

Bloomsburg

Columbia County Historical Society, Bloomsburg State College, Bloomsburg, Pennsylvania 17815

Transcripts of two "Mollie Maguire" trials in the Columbia County Court House, 1866 and 1877, where, among others, organizer Pat Hester was tried.

Carlisle

United States Military History Institute, Carlisle Barracks, Carlisle, Pennsylvania 17013

An important and extensive collection of materials in military history which are vital to any effort to understand the experiences of one of the most important immigrant groups in the United States Army during the nineteenth century, the Irish. Especially strong on Civil War materials, but includes extensive materials on all aspects of recruiting and employing individuals in the U.S. Army and militia companies.

Harrisburg

Diocese of Harrisburg, Chancery Office, 4800 Union Deposit Road, Harrisburg, Pennsylvania 17105

General records of St. Patrick's Church in Carlisle, founded in 1779, and St. Patrick's Church in Harrisburg, built 1826–28. Both were founded because of support from the Irish immigrants working on the Pennsylvania Canal, which followed the Susquehanna River. There is a diocesan-owned Irish cemetery in Liverpool, Pennsylvania, about twenty-five miles north of Harrisburg, on the river. There lie buried Irish immigrants who dropped while working on the canal. Part of the anthracite coal field lies in this diocese. Northumberland and Columbia counties were once enormous producers, roughly 1870–1925.

Pennsylvania Historical and Museum Commission, Bureau of Archives and History, William Penn Memorial Museum and Archives Building, Box 1026, Harrisburg, Pennsylvania 17120

The Pennsylvania State Archives holds twenty-seven cartons of records created under the Federal Writers' Project; included are ethnic materials on different groups, probably assembled and created by the Historical Records Survey. One of the groups covered in this collection is the Irish. Much of this material has been microfilmed and is held also by the Balch Institute in Philadelphia.

Haverford

Haverford College Library, Quaker Collection, Haverford, Pennsylvania 19401

Friends, Society of. Haddonfield Monthly Meeting Records, 1808–1902; 1 ft., 345 items. Reports, minutes, certificates of removal and other papers of a subsidiary of the Philadelphia Yearly Meeting of Friends, located in Haddonfield, New Jersey. Includes copies of letters (1890–1951) from the Women's Meetings of Dublin Yearly Meetings.

Grace, John Patrick. 1874–1940. Papers, 1902–40; 12,077 items and 3 vols. Politician and journalist. Personal and legal papers. Includes material on Charleston and

South Carolina politics; the Charleston American, a newspaper founded by Grace; anti-English feeling at the time of World War I; American sympathy for Irish nationalism; enforcement of the Espionage Act against Grace for his wartime editorials; speculation in Florida property during the 1920s; Grace's speaking engagements on behalf of Alfred E. Smith (1928); his opposition to Roosevelt's nomination in 1932; his attitude toward events in the 1930s.

Holyoake, George Jacob, 1817–1906. Papers, 1873–1931; 355 items. British social reformer. Mostly letters from Holyoake to William H. Guignan, illustrating his career as a reformer. Includes information on the movement to improve workingmen's conditions, Irish reform, Holyoake's journey to the U.S. (1882), his religious views, and home rule for England and Ireland.

Iredell, James, 1751–99. Papers (1767–1890) of James Iredell, Sr., and James Iredell, Jr., Statesman and U.S. Supreme Court justice from Edenton, North Carolina. Correspondence, and business, political, family, and other papers, of Iredell, of his son (James Iredell, Jr., governor and U.S. senator from North Carolina), and of the Iredell family.

Johnston, Zachariah and Thomas. Papers, 1717–1858; 626 items and 7 vols. Planter and politician of Augusta and Rockridge counties, Virginia. Includes the journal (ca. 1717) of an Irish linen weaver, and a diary (1794) of travel in Kentucky.

McCullough family, 1820s–1900. Papers, McCullough-Hutchinson families. Papers of the McCullough and Hutchinson families of Fairfield County, North Carolina, including letters from relatives in Ireland covering religion and agriculture.

McMullen family papers, 1783–1969; 10,015 items and 38 vols. Family correspondence of a family in Ireland. Includes letters from relatives in Ireland, and from nuns of the Order of the Visitation of Holy Mary.

Melville, Henry Dundas, 1st Viscount, 1742–1811. Papers, 1790–1809; addition, 1799–1813; 364 items. British statesman. Correspondence and reports concerning the secret service, commerce, Rev. Thomas Peirson, and military affairs of India and Ireland.

Mencken, Henry Louis, 1880–1956. Papers, 1901–21; 5433 items. Drama critic for the *Baltimore Herald and Sun*. Magazine articles and newspaper clippings relating to Irish national theater.

Peel, Sir Robert Bart, 1788–1850. Correspondence, 1816–64. British statesman, of Tamworth, Staffordshire, England. Letters to and from Peel discussing the British colonial relationship to Gabon, the Irish economy, politics, and government in Great Britain, and the settlement of Peel's estate. Correspondents include Sir Francis Burdett, Sir Henry Goulburn, Lord Liverpool, John Spencer, Viscount Althrop, and Henry John Temple, 3d Viscount Palmerston.

Potts family papers, 1720–1925. 404 items. Papers of the Potts family of Ireland and Maryland, consisting primarily of letters of William Potts I and his son, William Potts II, merchants of Frederick, Maryland. Includes letters from members of the Potts family in Ireland.

Primrose, Sir Henry William, 1846–1923. Papers, 1864–1942; 259 items. British civil servant, of London, England. Includes about fifty items (1911–12) on the work of the Committee on Irish Finance, Irish home rule, and the loyalty of Catholic converts (1837).

Russell, John Russell, 1st Earl, 1792–1878. Papers, 1817–74; 115 items. British statesman and prime minister. Papers chiefly concerning Russell's political career during the 1830s and 1840s. Subjects include parliamentary reform and elections, the Corn laws, Irish politics, court reform, and Constantine Henry Phipps, 1st Marquis of Normandy.

Scattergood family. Papers, 1694–1903; ca. 2 ft. In part, transcripts (handwritten). Letters, documents, religious accounts, portraits, and other papers. Includes about 330 letters (1781–1814) of Thomas Scattergood (1748–1814), Friend's minister of Philadelphia, written to friends and family during his religious travels in New England, Virginia, North Carolina, England, Ireland, and Scotland.

Shackleton family. Papers, 1707–85; 1 ft., 82 items. Transcripts (handwritten). Chiefly correspondence of the Carleton, Chandlee, and Shackleton families of Ballitore, Ireland, Philadelphia and Kennett Sq., Pennsylvania, and York, England, exchanging news of family and friends. Correspondents include Thomas Carleton (1699–1792), Abraham Shackleton (1699–1771), Elizabeth (Carleton) Shackleton (1726–1824), Richard

Shackleton (1726–92), Roger Shackleton (d. 1766), and William Shackleton (1725–70).

Sheppard family papers, 1656–1887. Correspondence, accounts, deeds, marriage certificates, wills, extracts from minutes (1827–61) of Philadelphia Yearly Meeting concerning the Separation of 1827–28, and other papers. Includes material on the Wilburite controversy in Philadelphia, Ohio, and other Yearly Meetings. Correspondents include Nathan Cook, Joseph Kite, Mary Kite, James Wansborough, and other Irish Friends.

Townshend, George Townshend, 1st Marquis, 1724–1807. Papers, 1749–1800; 58 items. British Army officer. Chiefly correspondence concerning military appointments, administration of the British Army, and English and Irish politics. Townshend served as lord lieutenant of Ireland, 1767–72.

Wilbur, John. 1774–1856. Papers, 1831–73; 51 items. In part, transcripts (handwritten). Quaker leader. Letters by Wilbur together with eighteen miscellaneous letters, articles, and other papers concerning him written by relatives and supporters. The Wilbur letters include fourteen letters (1853–55) discussing a visit to England and Ireland.

Lewisburg

Bucknell University, Archives, Lewisburg, Pennsylvania 17837

Gogarty, Oliver St. John, 1878–1957. Papers, 1913–54; 5 ft. Irish-American author and surgeon. Correspondence, notebooks, and original drafts of poems; unpublished poems by Gogarty's contemporaries and autographed publications from his personal library. Includes material relating to the literary and theatrical world centered in Dublin, Ireland, in the early twentieth century; copies of Abbey Theatre plays by Gogarty; an anonymous poem, "Secret Springs of Dublin Song." Correspondents include A. E. (George William) Russell, Lord Dunsany, Lady Gregory, C. M. Grieve, George Moore, W. B. Yeats, and the artist Augustus John.

Shaw Society of America Records 1949–65. 3 ft. (ca. 1800 items). Correspondence, reports of William D. Chase, founder of the society; a facsimile of Shaw's will and other papers relating to the founding of the society in 1950 and the first three meetings. Includes autographs of Katherine Cornell, Marion Davies, Albert Einstein, Thomas Mann, Gene Tunney, and others.

Bucknell University, Ellen Clarke Bertrand Library, Lewisburg, Pennsylvania 17837

Over 2,000 manuscripts, letters, and memorabilia of Oliver St. John Gogarty; over 2,000 manuscripts, letters, and memorabilia items of George Bernard Shaw.

Philadelphia

Balch Institute for Ethnic Studies, 185 7th Street, Philadelphia, Pennsylvania 19106

Extensive collection of Irish materials, continually growing as a result of an active effort to expand the collection. Presently includes papers of Curtis family, 1845–47; the papers of historian Dennis Clark; Ignatius Donnelly papers, 1836–43; Costello family papers, 1827–74; reminiscences of San Francisco by Michael Doyle; letters of Daniel Polin and others; a number of Irish-American newspapers published between 1849 and 1951.

Chestnut Hill College, Logue Library, Philadelphia, Pennsylvania 19118

Shaw, George Bernard. Scattered letters of Shaw to James G. Huneker.

City Archives of Philadelphia, 522 City Hall Annex, Philadelphia, Pennsylvania 19107

Archives of the City of Philadelphia including records of the mayor's office, records of police, fire, health, and other departments. Records of overseers of the poor and prison inspectors. Also includes an extensive collection of naturalization applications, 1821 to 1911. Useful collection of reports by Guardians of the Poor. Ship and passenger lists, 1859–67.

Genealogical Society of Pennsylvania, 1300 Locust Street, Philadelphia, Pennsylvania 19107

Collection of census records, city directories, naturalization records, church records, cemetery records and wills; of value in tracing the experiences of Irish immigrants and others in Pennsylvania.

Historical Society of Pennsylvania, Manuscripts Department, 1300 Locust Street, Philadelphia, Pennsylvania 19107

Barry, John. Minute book of the Hibernia Fire Company.

Cruice, Robert Blake, d. 1899. Legal papers, 1884–98; 300 items. Physician, of Philadelphia. Materials relating to various estates of which Cruice was the executor and some items concerning property held by him in Ireland.

Gratz, Simon, 1840–1925. Miscellaneous section: autographs, 1533–1900. Forms part of the Gratz collections in Historical Society of Pennsylvania collections. Letters and papers of noted persons, mainly Americans. Papers relate to American diplomatic history and foreign relations, settlements in the West, the French and Irish Revolutions.

Martin, John Hill, 1823–1906. Papers, 1856–78; 3 vols. Philadelphia author and lawyer. Journal (ca. 1856) with extensive notes. Includes information on national and local events. Reflection on the riots in Philadelphia between the Native American party and the Catholic Irish.

Powell Family. Powell, Johnston, Taylor, and Cole papers, 1700–1925; 50,000 items. Papers of several allied families long prominent in Philadelphia, Newport, Rhode Island, and Jamaica, British West Indies. The bulk of these papers are those of Robert Johnston, including journals of travels in northern Europe and Russia (1814), Scotland (1810–13), and Ireland (1812).

Society of the Friendly Sons of St. Patrick of Philadelphia for the Relief of Emigrants from Ireland. Records, 1771–1910; 75 items. Book of rules, minutes referring to George Washington, thirty-two membership certificates in the Hibernian Society (1771–97), minutes (1813–1910), annual toasts (1853–80), and thirty-eight portraits.

Presbyterian Historical Society, 425 Lombard Street, Philadelphia, Pennsylvania, 19147

Main archives of the United Presbyterian Church in America. Essential for any study of the Scotch-Irish in the United States.

Scotch-Irish Foundation, Library and Archives, Balch Institute of Ethnic Studies, 18 South 7th Street, Philadelphia, Pennsylvania 19106

A major collection of miscellaneous materials for the study of the Scotch-Irish in the United States.

Ryan Memorial Library, American Catholic Historical Society, St. Charles Seminary, Overbrook, Philadelphia, Pennsylvania 19151

The American Catholic Historical Society, founded in 1884, is the oldest Catholic historical society in the United States. The founding members were predominantly Irish American. The society's collections contain substantial quality manuscript sources relevant to the Irish in America.

A major project presently underway has as its goal the preparation of subject checklists of source materials, one of which is to be a thorough finding aid for Irish-American materials scattered throughout perhaps fifty different record groups. A preliminary inventory is still being completed.

There are three manuscript collections that bear significantly on Irish-American organizations. The Molly Maguire Collection (Record Group 12) contains four items of correspondence, 1874–77, between the archbishop of Philadelphia and the bishop of Erie, discussing the "Millies." In one letter is a lengthy, detailed account of the group's activities. The Fenian Brotherhood Collection (Record Group 14) includes 407 manuscript items of the correspondence of this organization's officers between 1857 and 1870. The Martin I. J. Griffin Papers (Record Group 8) highlight the organization of the Irish Catholic Benevolent Union (Griffin was its Secretary and founder-editor of its *Journal*). There are 20 linear feet of manuscripts in the collection, which span the dates 1842–1911.

The other manuscript collections contain materials concerning Archbishop John Hughes, Rev. Patrick Reilly, John Timon Reilly, James J. Ryan, Thomas Joseph Shanahan, and many other Americans of Irish descent. The substantial portion of these manuscripts concern individuals who resided in the eastern United States, particularly Pennsylvania. They record the participation of Irish Americans in philanthropy, business, education, government, and religion.

The nonmanuscript collections, particularly a 10,000-item pamphlet collection and an extensive collection of nineteenth-century Catholic newspapers, contain a wealth of materials pertaining to Irish Americans.

Temple University, Urban Archives Center, Samuel Paley Library, Philadelphia, Pennsylvania 19122
United Neighbors Association Records, 1853–1969; 30 cu. ft. The United Neighbors Association, now called United Communities of Southeast Philadelphia, was the result of the 1946 merger of three settlement houses in southeast central Philadelphia: Workmen Place House, Stanfield House, and Southwark House. After a second merger in 1950, the House of Industry joined UNA, and Workman Place House and College Settlement were closed.

The records of the UNA are divided into two distinct groups: those of the predecessor agencies, which detail typical settlement house and relief activities from 1853 to 1950, and those of the UNA, which are primarily concerned with block organizations, home and school associations, community councils and urban renewal. The Philadelphia Society for Employment and Instruction of the Poor, a Quaker-sponsored agency organized in 1847, operated the House of Industry at Seventh and Catharine streets. The House of Industry operated a laundry, served as a station on the underground railroad for escaped slaves, was used as an emergency hospital, established a "ragged school," kindergarten, and nursery school, and provided a sewing room and dispensary for the Irish and later the Poles in the area. Detailed case records and relief rolls document this work. By the 1920s, when the neighborhood had become Italian, House of Industry activities were more typical of other settlement houses and included a variety of clubs and classes.

University Settlements. Records, 1838–1969; 26 cu. ft. University Settlements consisted of three houses: Dixon House, University House, and Western Community House. It served the Schuylkill area around South Street west of Broad Street, a strongly Irish neighborhood, and a portion of South Philadelphia, around Twenty-second and Moore Streets. In 1967, the agency broke its original ties with the University of Pennsylvania Christian Association and became Diversified Community Services.

Oral History Collection. The library holds a few taped interviews with Irish women. The Oral History Collection also holds a series of tapes, records broadcasts made over station KYW News/Radio, from October 6 to December 22, 1975, under the title "The Philadelphia Stories, a Bicentennial Contribution of Temple University." These broadcasts on the history and people of Philadelphia and the Philadelphia area by Temple University faculty, students, and others, were compiled by Professor Morris Vogel. Among the more useful for Irish research are: No. 15, Dr. Herbert Ershkowitz, "Irish Catholic Riots—1840s"; No. 16, Dennis Clark, "Why Did the Irish Come to America?"; No. 17, Dennis Clark, "How Did the Irish Get to Philadelphia?"; No. 18, Dennis Clark, "Irish Neighborhoods"; No. 19, Dennis Clark, "Irish and Politics"; No. 20, Dennis Clark, "Irish and Italians."

University of Pennsylvania, Special Collections, Van Pelt Library, 3420 Walnut Street, Philadelphia, Pennsylvania 19104
The Special Collections of the University of Pennsylvania Libraries houses a very broad range of historical research materials. Irish and Irish Americans are well represented in the collections in American drama, American history and American literature. Of specific interest to Irish researchers are the extensive holdings of manuscripts and papers of James T. Farrell in the American literature collection. The English literature holdings include a comprehensive collection of the works of Jonathan Swift. Finally, the American drama collection includes extensive materials on the Irish on the nineteenth-century American stage, especially in the Philadelphia region.

Pittsburgh

Catholic Diocese of Pittsburgh, Diocesan Historical Archives, 111 Blvd. of the Allies, Pittsburgh, Pennsylvania 15222
A collection of manuscripts, documents, and letters relating to the history of Roman Catholicism in western Pennsylvania and specifically to the Diocese of Pittsburgh, established in 1843.

University of Pittsburgh, Libraries, Archives of Industrial Society, Hillman Library, Pittsburgh, Pennsylvania 15260
A large collection of approximately 211 collections concentrating on the post-Civil War period, primarily in Pittsburgh and western Pennsylvania. Includes personal papers of politicians, labor leaders, business people, and records of companies, institutions, societies, labor unions, schools, churches, and government agencies.

Swarthmore

Swarthmore College, Friends Historical Library, Swarthmore, Pennsylvania 19081

Friends, Society of, Records, ca. 1660–1949; 69 vols. on 9 reels. Microfilm (positive) of abstracts in Eustace Street Meetinghouse, Dublin, and of original records in Friends Meetinghouse, Lisburn. Minutes of men's and women's business meetings and registers of births, deaths, marriages, and removals, for meetings in Balleyhagen, Carlow, Cork, Dublin, Edenderry, Grange, Limerick, Lisburn, Lurgan, Moate, Montmellick, Richhill, Tipperary, Ulster, Waterford, Wexford, Wicklow, and Youghal.

Swarthmore College. List of public Friends. 1656–1832; 18 items. An account, with names and occasional notes, of Friends in the ministry who came from Europe to America, and went from America to England and Ireland, 1656–1832; public Friends who visited New England, 1656–1824; lists of families of Friends in Falls Monthly Meeting, and in Horsham, Pennsylvania, Newport, Rhode Island, Solebury, Pennsylvania and Wrightstown, New Jersey; and a list of the ministry from Philadelphia, 1800–1812.

University Park

Pennsylvania State University, Libraries, Special Collections Division, W342 Pattee Library, University Park, Pennsylvania 16802

Materials relating primarily to nineteenth- and twentieth-century American and English literary history; American and Pennsylvania political, economic, labor, and social history. Included in literary papers are the papers of John O'Hara. Among union records are those of the United Steel Workers and the Pennsylvania AFL-CIO.

Carvill family. Papers, 1880–late 1920s; 3 ft. Business and personal correspondence, 6 diaries, deeds, business agreements, shipping accounts, bills, receipts, and other legal and shipping documents of an Irish family.

Gore-Booth, Eva, 1870–1926. Papers, 1868–1928; ca. 3 ft. Author, poet and artist, of Ireland and England. Letters, exercise books, watercolor paintings, pencil sketches, eight poems, part of a play, *The Death of Deirdre,* periodicals, clippings, and photos.

Harene family. Papers, 1834–77; ca. 2 ft. Documents, receipts and copies of letters of an Irish family. The majority of the papers are legal documents but include some interesting indentures.

Irish family papers (general). Papers, 1832–1935; ca. 11 ft. A seven-foot section of papers of about 190 influential Irish individuals; includes correspondence, diaries, notebooks, deeds, indentures, wills, leases, marriage settlements, clippings, exercise books, newspapers, insurance papers, birth certificates, bonds, mortgages, and receipts.

MacGillycuddy family. Papers, 1890s; ca. 2 ft. Correspondence, legal documents, pamphlets, and a will, of an Irish family. Chiefly documents and letters concerning the bankruptcy case, marriage, and marriage settlement of Denis C. MacGillycuddy.

Mount-Temple family. Property, 1884–96; ca. 2 ft. Indentures, sale and mortgage agreements, wills rentals, valuations, and other documents relating to the family's property in Dublin, Ireland.

Wilkes-Barre

King's College, D. Leonard Corgan Library, Special Collections, 14 West Jackson Street, Wilkes-Barre, Pennsylvania 18711

Manuscripts and tape recordings relating to the history, politics, religion, social life, and culture of the Wyoming Valley and the anthracite mining region of Pennsylvania. Included are papers and tapes on the art, folklore, ethnic groups, churches, and political activities of the area, as well as papers of local U.S. representative Daniel J. Flood. The George Korson Folklore Archive includes tapes and transcripts on the Irish-American experience.

Rhode Island

Providence

Diocese of Providence, Chancery Office, Cathedral Square, Providence, Rhode Island 02903
Manuscript entitled "Catholicism in Rhode Island: The Formative Era," by Drs. Patrick R. Conley and Matthew J. Smith.

Providence College, Phillips Memorial Library, College Archives, Eaton Street and River Avenue, Providence, Rhode Island 02918
Papers of Rhode Island political leaders of national significance, many of them Irish born or of Irish ancestry, such as John E. Fogarty and Robert E. Quinn. Also materials relating to ethnic communities including the Irish. William E. Walsh's Civil War diary and the Patrick T. Conley photograph collection.

Rhode Island State Archives, Room 43, State House, Providence, Rhode Island 02903
Manuscript schedules of state censuses; political records dating from colonial period; a wide variety of tax lists and vital records for the state.

South Carolina

Columbia

South Carolina Dept of Archives and History, 1430 Senate Street, Columbia, South Carolina 29211
Vast collection of records dating from the early colonial period including materials very valuable for researchers tracing Scotch-Irish and Irish immigrants; includes copies of records from the Public Records Office in London and the U.S. National Archives.

University of South Carolina, South Carolinian Library, Manuscripts Division, Columbia, South Carolina 29208
Bannon, John, 1829–1913. Papers, 1863–1927; 66 items. Chaplain, Confederate Army. Chiefly correspondence and other papers relating to Bannon's service as a chaplain in the Confederate Army and his assignment to Ireland as an agent to attempt to prevent the recruiting of Irish immigrants to the Union Army.
McDowell, Davison, 1784–1842. Papers, 1767–1838; 59 items and 1 vol. Business papers; correspondence with the family in Ireland; legal papers, including the will of Thomas Kirkpatrick of Ireland, indentures of Agnes Stitt, and accounts for settlement of Robert Kirkpatrick's estate; receipt and account book (1776–1812) from Georgetown, D.C.

Miscellaneous Irish materials. "Address to the Irishmen of Charleston, 1861." Letters by Robert Fullerton, William Hill, William Humphrey, and McCormick family—John and Ann. A manuscript, *The American Edgeworths: A Biographical Sketch of Richard Edgeworth, with Letters and Documents,* edited by Edgar E. Edgeworth.

Winthrop College, Dacus Library Archives, Rock Hill, South Carolina 29733
Useful collection for those interested in the genealogy of the Scotch Irish in the area. Includes records of Scotch-Irish festivals held in the area in 1980 and 1983, and records of the York County Multi-Ethnic Heritage Project for 1977. Extensive collection of Presbyterian Church records.

South Dakota

Aberdeen

Presentation Convent, Presentation Heights, Aberdeen, South Dakota 57401

The Presentation Sisters came to Dakota Territory in 1880 from George's Hill, Dublin, in response to an invitation of Bishop Marty, O.S.B., to teach Indian children. Subsequently, two motherhouses were established, one in Fargo, North Dakota, in 1883 and later the other in Aberdeen, South Dakota. Materials on their activities are presently being organized.

University of South Dakota, Richardson Archives, Vermillion, South Dakota 57069

Collection of materials on prominent citizens of Irish birth or background, in a number of areas including business and politics; also records of the Works Progress Administration Federal Writers' Project.

Tennessee

Knoxville

Knoxville-Knox County Public Library, McClung Historical Collection, 500 West Church Avenue, Knoxville, Tennessee 37902

Graham, Hugh, 1784–1865. Papers, 1805–86; ca. 1 ft. Merchant of Tazewell, Tennessee; Irish-born. Chiefly accounts, bills and notes, relating to Nenney and Graham Company and Chrisman and Stuarts Company, Tazewell, Tennessee; personal correspondence and legal documents, and information compiled by A. A. Kyle on the Graham, Kyle, and Nenney families.

Watterson family. Papers, 1780–1908; ca. 1 ft. Personal and business correspondence, legal documents, bills, receipts, and photos of an Irish family who settled in Hawkins County, Tennessee.

Nashville

Tennessee Department of Education, Library and Archives, Manuscript Section, 403 7th Avenue North, Nashville, Tennessee 37219

Eakin, William, 1810–49. Papers, 1828–65; 14 items and 1 vol. Businessman. Memoirs (to 1846) describing the family journey from Ireland to Tennessee in 1822, and the establishment of the family's mercantile and other businesses in Shelbyville and Nashville; old wills, slave deeds (1841–46), a few accounts, and some genealogical material on the Eakin family.

Tennessee State Library and Archives, 403 7th Avenue North, Nashville, Tennessee 37215

Useful for researchers interested in Scotch-Irish experience. Holds records of the Scotch Irish Congress of 1899.

Texas

Austin

Lyndon Baines Johnson Library and Museum, 2313 Red River, Austin, Texas 78705

The major collection of materials on the life of Lyndon Johnson includes his papers as president, collections of personal and organizational papers of individuals who knew or served with Johnson. Many of the manuscript collections are still being processed and some have been closed by the desire of the donor. Researchers should inquire about availability before visiting the library. For researchers on the Irish-American political experience, this collection is of primary importance for its coverage of Vice-President Johnson's relationship to President Kennedy.

Texas State Library, Archives Division, P.O. Box 12927, Capitol Station, Austin, Texas 78711

Useful records for exploring Irish plans and efforts to colonize Texas include records of the McMullen and McGloin colonies and passenger lists of arrivals. Also holds a variety of general records of value for researching the Irish experience in Texas, for example, naturalization records and voter registration records.

University of Texas at Austin, General Libraries, E. C. Barker Texas History Center, Austin, Texas 78712

Three collections of manuscripts identified as Irish and dating from pre-statehood. Also the following:

Rowntree, Joseph Gustave, 1879– . Papers, 1500–1958; 445 items. Correspondence; reminiscences; genealogical material on the Rountree and Rowntree families (Texas ranchers) in the U.S. and Ireland; writings, broadsides, and clippings.

Dallas

Dallas Historical Society, Research Center Library and Archives, Hall of State, Fair Park, Dallas, Texas 75226

A collection of materials on the history of Texas and Dallas; includes items on assassination of John F. Kennedy.

Utah

Salt Lake City

Church of Jesus Christ of Latter-Day Saints, Genealogical Library, 50 East North Temple, Salt Lake City, Utah 84150

The library is the hub of a worldwide system of genealogical activities. It holds 80,000 genealogical volumes on all countries of the world, many on Ireland, and over a half million microfilm rolls of genealogical records. The library holds microfilmed copies of many existing Irish land records, wills, birth, marriage, and death records, etc. This is the most useful collection of its kind in the world. Moreover, a series of published guides, available from the library, and helpful informed archivists on duty at the library make it easier in many cases to do Irish genealogical research in Utah than in Ireland. At present copies of the following records from Ireland are available.

Birth, Marriages and Deaths, 1845–present. Since January 1, 1864, all births, marriages and deaths in Ireland have been required to be registered. However, Protestant marriages were registered beginning as early as April 1, 1845. For the earlier years the library holds Phillimore's Parish Register Series of marriages and some banns in Ireland, arranged by county. The Genealogical Society has microfilm copies of all indexes to Irish Civil registration from the earliest to 1957. These microfilm copies of the actual records include births, 1864–81, 1900–55; marriages 1845–70; and deaths, 1864–70.

Registry of Deeds, 1708–1904. Includes a surname and county index of all deeds registered over the years of coverage.

Irish Probates, 1858–1900. Since 1857 probate cases have been filed and adjudicated in eleven district registries throughout the country, with a central office in Dublin. This system replaced a religious one managed by the Church of Ireland. Probate holdings have proved very useful in locating relatives of nineteenth-century Irish immigrants to the United States, especially those from a little higher up on the social scale. Unfortunately, many probate records were destroyed when the Irish Republican Army burned the Customs House in 1922. At present the Public Record Offices of Northern Ireland and the Republic of Ireland hold the will books for the period 1858–1900; the Genealogical Society library has copies of all of the wills from the Republic; those from Northern Ireland remain to be filmed. There is no comprehensive index to all wills but each separate book has its own index.

Census of Ireland, 1821–51 and 1900. Most of the actual manuscript census records for late nineteenth-century Ireland appear to have been destroyed. There are complete census records available for 1821, 1831, 1841, 1851, and 1900; the library holds microfilm copies of all of these.

Vermont

Montpelier

Vermont State Papers Division, Secretary of State's Office, Pavillion Building, 109 State Street, Montpelier, Vermont 05602

An impressive holding of state and local vital statistical records, mostly prior to 1900. Also pamphlets covering Irish riots in nineteenth-century Vermont.

Virginia

Richmond

Virginia Historical Society, 428 North Blvd., Richmond, Virginia 23221

Scott family papers, 1829–1937; 793 items. Diary (1866) of John Scott, concerning a voyage to Ireland and travels in Ireland and England. Persons represented include Isabella (Doherty) Scott, of Ballyshannon, Ireland, and New York City.

Tompkins family papers, 1792–1869; 2930 items. Correspondence on travels in Ireland.

Turner, Dawson, 1775–1858. Miscellanea curiosa, 1549–1834. Botanist and antiquary. In part, transcripts. Correspondence, diaries, poetry, religious writings, booklists, engravings, and other materials collected by Turner. Includes diaries of unidentified persons traveling in France and in Ireland.

Williamsburg

College of William and Mary, Earl Gregg Swan Library, Williamsburg, Virginia 23185

Hoffman, Samuel Owens. Letters, 1821–57; 145 items. Letters of Hoffman, of Baltimore, Maryland, to his wife, the former Louisa Gilmore, and his son, W. Gilmore Hoffman, in school at College Point, Flushing, New York. Includes descriptions of city renewal activities in Baltimore (1826); a chronicle of a trip through Ireland, England, and France (1830); and an account (1832) of the situation in Washington when Martin Van Buren's nomination as U.S. Minister to Great Britain was rejected by the U.S. senate.

Smith, Thomas, 1783–1841. Papers, 1783–1862; 1700 items. Resident of Powhatan County, Virginia. Correspondence, notes, and other papers of Smith, and of Mary and Thomas Smith of Warren County, Ohio. Includes genealogical charts used to trace ancestral lines through the Quaker and Scotch-Irish settlers of New Jersey and Pennsylvania, who began migrating to the Shenandoah Valley of Virginia in the 1730s.

Washington

Olympia

Washington State Archives, 12th and Washington Streets, Olympia, Washington 98504

Extensive collection of state and local materials dating from 1851; these include territorial census manuscripts, naturalization records, military records, and birth and death indexes.

Pullman

Washington State University Library, Archives and Special Collections, Pullman, Washington 99164

D'Arcy, Nicholas, Estate Papers, 1791–1869. Documents, notes, marriage records, land title agreements, and genealogical notes concerning life in the United States and the transfer of land in County Roscommon, Ireland.

Spokane

Gonzaga University, Crosby Library, Rare Book and Manuscript Collection, East 502 Boone Avenue, Spokane, Washington 99258

Papers of James Edward O'Sullivan, relating to the development of the Coulee Dam; also materials relating to Harry Lillis (Bing) Crosby and the Crosby family.

Tacoma

The Washington State Historical Society, 315 North Stadium Way, Tacoma, Washington 98403

Holds sixteen boxes of original manuscripts of the Federal Writers Project, including information on cities, towns, counties, and place names of Washington. Many of these studies and other special studies on pioneers and journalism contain information on ethnic groups in the state and therefore provide coverage of the Irish here. The files are indexed and available for use in the library.

West Virginia

Morgantown

West Virginia University, Library, Regional History Collection, Morgantown, West Virginia 26505

A large collection, 20,000 linear feet of personal papers, business records, state and local government and county records, photographs, oral history recordings, maps, unpublished genealogies and other assorted materials relating to the state of West Virginia and the upper Ohio Valley, Appalachia, the coal industry, and organized labor.

Since the Irish and their descendents played a large part in the development of the area and its industries, they are prominently featured in the collection. But since they are indexed under "immigration" rather than "Irish" it is difficult to find specific materials on the group. Nevertheless, this is an important collection.

Brooke family papers, 1856–1955; 3 boxes, 1 folder, 1 reel microfilm. Family of St. George Tucker Brooke, law professor. Correspondence, biographical materials, clippings, and photos; letters, ca. 1870, from James Harold in Ireland to his son James in New York.

Wheeling

Diocese of Wheeling-Charleston, Chancery Office, 1300 Byron Street, Wheeling, West Virginia 26003

Annual parish reports which are available for most Wheeling-Charleston parishes from 1865 to the present, with some reports missing from 1912 to 1933. These reports, prepared by the pastors of each parish, give a summary report of church activities, membership, ministry and finances.

Registers of baptisms, marriages and deaths are maintained in each parish of the diocese. In the diocesan archives at the chancery in Wheeling, there are microfilm copies of most of these parish registers up to 1968.

Some of the correspondence of the bishops and clergy of the diocese from 1895 to the present is in the diocesan archives. General papers of Irish priests who have served in the diocese since its beginning.

Wisconsin

La Crosse

Murphy Library, University of Wisconsin—La Crosse, La Crosse, Wisconsin 54601.

Oral history collection holds one interview of Irish interest: John MacDonald farmer.

Madison

The State Historical Society of Wisconsin, Archives Division, 816 State Street, Madison, Wisconsin 43706

In addition to those items listed below, the library also holds collections of papers on Joseph P. O'Donnell (1847–1906) and Maria

Maud Leonard McCreery (1883–1938). See also typescript entitled "Irish in Wisconsin."

Garrett, George A, 1888– . Papers, 1947–60; 3 boxes. Diplomat and public official. Correspondence and memorabilia kept by Garrett during his service as U.S. minister and ambassador to Ireland, 1947–51.

McCarthy, Charles, 1873–1921. Papers, 1906–53; 51 boxes. Political scientist, publicist, and first Wisconsin legislative reference librarian. Correspondence and other papers. Agricultural material (1913–21) includes correspondence with farm leaders and organizations, such as the National Agricultural Organization Society, and relates to the rural cooperative marketing movement, cooperative legislation, and organization, rural credit and land ownership, and standardization of farm products. Correspondence, beginning about 1913, with Sir Horace Plunkett concerns the rural cooperative movement in Ireland and Irish affairs after World War I.

Milwaukee

Marquette University, Memorial Library, Department of Special Collections and University Archives, 1415 West Wisconsin Avenue, Milwaukee, Wisconsin 53233

Cullen, Michael D., 1941– . Papers, 1962–77; 5 cu. ft. An Irish immigrant (1961) who founded the Casa Maria House of Hospitality in Milwaukee (1966) and was one of the Milwaukee 14 (1968), a group of antiwar and draft resistance activists who destroyed draft records and were subsequently convicted and imprisoned. Correspondence, manuscripts, audiotapes, newsletters, leaflets, and other printed material. Family correspondence and oral history interviews are restricted; other personal papers are closed for ten years from the date of origin.

Cardinal Strich College, Milwaukee, Wisconsin 53217

Holds a collection of Irish pedigrees on families in Ireland from the eleventh century to the end of the sixteenth century.

River Falls

University of Wisconsin—River Falls, River Falls, Wisconsin 54022

The oral history collection here holds a transcript dealing with "How the Irish Settlement Came to New Richmond, Wisconsin." This transcript consists of an interview with Belle Lundy, a native of New Richmond, eighty-eight years old. Belle describes briefly how her grandmother came to New Richmond from Maryborough, Queens County, Ireland. The remainder of the transcript is spent in discussing living patterns, Indian visits to the home, and lifestyle customs in New Richmond during the early part of Belle's life.

Wyoming

Cheyenne

Wyoming State Archives, Museums and Historical Department, Barrett Building, Cheyenne, Wyoming 82002

Extensive collection of governmental and vital records dating from 1869. Also large collection of diaries, pioneer narratives, private papers, and census records. Also holds the manuscripts of the work of the Works Progress Administration in the state during the 1930s.

Laramie

University of Wyoming Library, Division of Rare Books and Special Collections, Box 3334, University Station, Laramie, Wyoming 82071

David Gray Collection, 1870–1963. Correspondence, notes, clippings, photos, unpublished manuscripts. David Gray was born in Buffalo, New York, in 1870. After graduation from Harvard University he embarked on a career as a writer. In 1940, Roosevelt appointed him minister to Ireland, a position he held until 1947. His papers are particularly important for any study of Irish neutrality during World War II, where he played an adversarial role to de Valera for most of the period. He died in Sarasota, Florida, in 1968.

The correspondence and other materials in this collection described below mainly cover Gray's years as U.S. Minister to Ireland. (Researchers should see also entry above on Gray papers in Franklin D. Roosevelt Library, Hyde Park, New York.)

CORRESPONDENCE: The greater bulk of this collection is comprised of correspondence and includes approximately twenty years, from the thirties into the fifties; however, the majority of letters were written between 1940 and 1945. The letters are filed chronologically. Among the persons writing to Mr. Gray and receiving letters from Mr. Gray are included: Dean Acheson, Ray Atherton, Karl A. Bickel, Anthony Biddle, Carroll Binder, Anna Roosevelt Beottiger, Homer T. Bone, Parker Buhrman, James F. Byrnes, A. J. Cronin, John Cudahy, John F. Dulles, John C. Erhardt, James A. Farley, Stanley Field, Edward J. Flynn, Cameron Forbes, Chauncey J. Hamlin (Jr. and Sr.), W. A. Harriman, Cordel Hull, John F. Kennedy (handwritten, 1945), Joseph Kennedy, Thomas W. Lamont, Clarence Lea, John McCormack, Frank McDermot, Herbert Pell, Hugh Peterson, Quentin Reynolds, Reginald C. Robbins, Eleanor Roosevelt, Franklin Roosevelt, J. Hall Roosevelt, James Roosevelt, Mrs. Kermit Roosevelt, Archbishop Spellman, Adlai E. Stevenson, Robert B. Stewart, Julian Street, Daniel J. Tobin, Eamon de Valera, John Winant, William Woodward, Judge Wylie (handwritten letter concerning de Valera's trial in 1916), Robert R. Young, J. Flynn, Reginald C. Robbins, Hugh Peterson.

NEWSPAPER CLIPPINGS: Although many newspaper clippings are filed with the correspondence because they directly pertain to certain items mentioned in a letter, there are ten files comprised entirely of newspaper clippings dating from 1940 through 1958, plus one file of undated clippings. These pertain mainly to Irish topics, but also include items on the Roosevelts.

IRISH REPUBLICAN ARMY HUNGER STRIKES: One file containing information regarding the hunger strikes of 1942 through 1944 in the Irish Republican Army.

SINN FEIN: HISTORICAL BACKGROUND: One large file containing manuscripts containing background on Sinn Fein, the political organization.

SINN FEIN REBELLION HANDBOOK: One paperback book dated Easter, 1916.

CENSORSHIP: GALLEY SHEETS: One large folder containing galley sheets that illustrate the censorship that was prevalent in the Irish newspapers during the war years.

MANUSCRIPTS: Two large folders containing drafts of a manuscript written about the Irish history and the problems in contemporary Ireland, authored by David Gray.

PUBLICATIONS AND PAMPHLETS: One large folder containing a collection of publications on Irish home rule, partition, and other national problems.

CATHOLIC-PROTESTANT RELATIONS: One file containing a letter written in 1918 by a Catholic woman and telling of the hate for the Protestants. One copy of the *Ulster Protestant,* dated 1942, relating tales of horror about the Catholic Church and the priests.

Section III
Government Manuscripts and Publications

The importance of Ireland to the United States is reflected in the volume of documents on Ireland and its people scattered throughout federal government archives and depositories and in the number of publications covering Ireland or immigrants from Ireland produced by federal agencies. Reflecting the basic division of governmental materials, this section is divided into two parts: manuscripts (that is, original documents created by a department, usually during the normal course of its activities) and published sources, which includes Congressional committee hearings, documents, reports, statistical analyses, correspondence, and testimony presented before committees of the House or Senate.

Government Manuscript Record Groups

The National Archives and Records Center holds millions of cubic feet of government manuscripts loosely arranged in over 400 "record groups"—defined as a collection of records assembled from one or more bureaus or departments of the federal government. The current guide to those holdings is the publication by the National Archives and Records Service, *Guide to the National Archives of the United States* (Washington, 1974). The intent of this manuscript section is to provide a basic overview of manuscript collections most useful for research on Irish Americans. Where additional guides to specific groups of records are available, they are listed with the particular record group.

The record collections discussed below are selected for the information they provide on the Irish experience at home or in the U.S. They are arranged numerically, and the listing is obviously far from exhaustive; indeed, given the extent of the records and their constant expansion by the addition of newer records, it is clear that a definitive listing would be impossible to develop. It should be remembered that many of the manuscript collections have been microfilmed and copies are available through the main branch of the National Archives or the associated regional branches. For a useful listing of microfilmed documents, see the current *List of National Archives Microfilm Publications,* available from the National Archives. Since guides are constantly updated and new listings of various kinds developed, researchers interested in a particular record group should contact the National Archives directly.

Researchers interested in tracing individuals through government records will find invaluable the work by Meredith B. Colket, Jr., and Frank E. Bridgers, *Guide to Genealogical Records in the National Archives* (Washington: The National Archives and Records Service, 1964).

Record Group 10: National Commission on Law Observance and Enforcement

The National Commission on Law Observance and Enforcement was appointed by President Hoover on March 4, 1929, to inquire into "the problem of the enforcement of prohibition under the provisions of the Eighteenth Amendment of the Constitution." Each commissioner headed a committee that reported on one general aspect of criminal law enforcement to include prohibition; official lawlessness, the courts, the police, criminal justice and the foreign-born; prosecution; statistics of crime; juvenile delinquency; penal institutions; probation; parole.

Among these records are reports for the

1920s on the nativity of judges, law enforcement personnel, and the numbers of foreign-born, including Irish, involved in crime in major cities.

Record Group 11: General Records of the United States Government

Consists of the Constitution; the Bill of Rights and related records; laws of the US; international treaties; agreements; and proclamations; executive orders; rules and regulations of federal agencies; and electoral records.

Among these records is a listing of immigrants entering the U.S. for 1819–20. Extradition requests and papers on Irishmen whom the British government were attempting to extradite, mostly during the post-Civil War period. Records of negotiations between the U.S. and the British on a number of Irish matters, including recruitment and drafting of Irishmen for the Civil War.

Record Group 15: Veterans' Administration

Records on veterans' matters of all kinds: legal records, war risk insurance bonds, vocational-rehabilitation records, pension and land bounty claims—some dating from 1773—financial records on payment of persons, records from veterans' homes, the 1893 census schedules enumerating union civil war veterans. Irishmen are listed on a great many of these records, beginning with the Revolutionary War. Declarations for pensions and land grants as a result of service in various wars include statements providing birthplace, places of residence, affidavits by friends and officials to attest to service—all essential items for researchers attempting to explore the participation of Irish Americans in war or their postwar experiences.

Record Group 16: Office of the Secretary of Agriculture

The Department of Agriculture was established on May 15, 1862, and its duties have been steadily expanded; from simply distributing seeds and plants and engaging in educational activities, it now engages in research, education, marketing, disposal of surplus crops, and rural development. As a result of these last activities in rural development in the early part of the twentieth century, the department engaged in a lengthy correspondence with Sir Horace Plunkett—advocate of agricultural cooperative movements in early twentieth-century Ireland—relating to agriculture in Ireland and the impact of Irish agricultural techniques on American agriculture.

Record Group 20; Office of the Special Advisor to the President on Foreign Trade

These records include a number of reports made by U.S. consuls in Ireland on the foreign and internal trade of Ireland and Northern Ireland. They cover commercial and industrial aspects of the economies of these countries. Most of the records are for the period 1925 to 1935 and are thus invaluable for the study of the economy of modern Ireland during this most important period.

Record Group 21: District Courts of the United States

The records of the district and circuit courts system, established in 1789. The district courts were given exclusive original cognizance over civil cases of admiralty and maritime jurisdiction, of seizures, and of all suits against consuls and vice consuls. The circuit courts were to have jurisdiction over actions involving aliens or citizens of different states and, concurrent with the courts of the several states, equity suits where the matter in dispute was in excess of $500. The national bankruptcy acts of the mid-nineteenth century and later were added to the district courts, while the Judiciary Act of 1911 abolished the circuit courts and added their duties to those of the district courts.

The U.S. district court records for the District of Washington include naturalization records (1801–1926) and minute books (1801–63), in which there are many notations on naturalization. Many of these records provide information on the large number of Irish who lived in that area over the period.

Record Group 24: Bureau of Naval Personnel

While the Bureau of Naval Personnel was established in 1862, the records held by the organization date back to the earliest years of the establishment of the nation. Among the most useful are muster rolls, correspondence, records relating to naval officers, enlisted men and apprentices, records of the Bureau of Navigation, field establishments, and cartographic records.

The naval records also include muster rolls and personnel papers for sailors especially for the period 1846 to 1885. Since many of these records provide details of a person's career both before and after navy service, they are invaluable for studies in social history, especially for research in social mobility.

An extensive body of records in this collection deals with the naval career of Irish-born George Campbell Read (1787–1862).

See Chapter 4 of Meredith B. Colket, Jr., and Frank E. Bridgers, *Guide to Genealogical Records in the National Archives* (Washington: The National Archives and Records Service, 1964).

Record Group 26: United States Coast Guard

Personnel records, including registers of officers, 1790–1919; World War I cards for enlisted men (with surnames beginning with A through H) and honorable discharges, 1917–37; muster rolls, 1833–1932; officer personnel files, 1890–1929; records of general and summary courts-martial, 1906–41.

Case histories of individuals and vessels engaged in or suspected of smuggling rum, 1928–35, consisting of reports of seizures and court actions, copies of log entries, newspapers clippings, and correspondence. Similar and related records are among the correspondence files, 1910–41, and among those of the Intelligence Division. Records of the Public Relations Division, the Coast Guard Information Service, and predecessor agencies, 1916–46, include narrative and statistical reports and monographs of Coast Guard operations in the two World Wars; war diaries, 1942–45; miscellaneous reference materials.

Data on Irish immigrants are scattered among all of these records, especially those for the years 1933–41.

Record Group 29: Bureau of the Census

The Census Office was established in 1902 as a permanent bureau in the Department of the Interior; in 1954 it became known as the Bureau of the Census. National censuses began in 1790; the first nine decennial censuses were taken by U. S. district marshals. The 1790 census was submitted directly to the president, from 1800 to 1840 to the secretary of state, from 1850 to 1870, to the secretary of the interior, and from 1880, taken by enumerators and submitted to the census office.

The manuscript schedule of the federal population censuses are among the most valuable of resources for historians of the Irish experience in America. Particularly valuable for research on Irish death rates and economic progress in industry or agriculture are the non-population schedules of the census. The agricultural manuscripts among these non-population schedules provide data on a wide range of aspects of Irish engagement in agricultural activities, including farm tenure, farm values, population, investments in the property, and use of hired hands. The schedules of business activity provide an equally extensive range of data and allow precise studies of Irish involvement in business.

For discussion of the value of manuscript schedules of the federal census records for social history and genealogical research, see Meredith B. Colket, Jr., and Frank E. Bridgers, *Guide to Genealogical Records in the National Archives* (Washington: The National Archives and Records Service, 1964).

Record Group 32: United States Shipping Board

Established in 1916 and abolished by executive order in June 1933, the Shipping Board holds records on shipping of various kinds.

Among its duties were the determination of shipping requirements to facilitate trade between the United States and various foreign countries including Ireland. Information on Irish exports and imports is also included in these records.

Record Group 36: Bureau of Customs

The Customs Service, created by an act of July 31, 1789, became part of the Department of the Treasury when that department was established in September 1789.

Among other functions, the Bureau of Customs is responsible for the entrance and clearance of vessels and aircraft and the protection of passengers. It also assists other agencies in the control of persons entering or leaving the United States. The most useful records in this collection include records of port arrivals for the nineteenth century which include passenger lists for New York (1820–1919), Boston (1883–99), Baltimore (1829–1919), New Orleans (1820–97), Philadelphia (1835–99), and copies of lists for a large number of individuals arriving at other Atlantic and Gulf ports. In addition to the name and size of each ship, these records indicate date of arrival, the port of departure; the name, age, sex, and occupation of every passenger; the country of origin for each passenger, their destination, and passenger status (cabin or steerage).

An additional very valuable source for researching the relative wealth of individuals or groups of Irish and other arrivals is the passenger baggage lists held by the Bureau of the Customs for the years 1863 to 1871.

Extensive coverage of Irish shipping and the Irish export and import trade is also to be found in the records of this bureau. Laurence F. Schmeckebier, *The Customs Service* (Baltimore, 1924) provides a useful outline of the topic. For an extensive listing of copies of passenger lists, see National Archives Microfilm Publication, Pamphlet describing M 575, *Copies of Lists of Passengers Arriving at Miscellaneous Ports on the Atlantic and Gulf Coasts and at Ports on the Great Lakes, 1820–1873* (Washington, D.C., 1972); and National Archives Microfilm Publication, Pamphlet for microcopy No. 334, *A Supplemental Index of Passenger Lists of Vessels Arriving at Atlantic and Gulf Coast Ports (excluding New York), 1820–1874* (Washington, 1969).

Record Group 38: Office of the Chief of Naval Operations

The Office of the Chief of Naval Operations was established in March 1915, to coordinate naval operational activities. Under the office were the Office of Naval Intelligence, the Board of Inspection and Survey, and the Naval Communication Service; later the Hydrographic Office and the Naval Observatory were added.

The records of the Office of Naval Intelligence in this collection contain a considerable quantity of cartographic and other records on Ireland. They include manuscript and printed geographic surveys, which provide much information on army command areas, railroads, airfields, and charts of Irish harbors and the coastline, especially for the period since Irish independence in 1922.

For a useful overview see Henry P. Beers, "The Development of the Office of the Chief of Naval Operations," *Military Affairs,* vol. 10 and 11 (1946–47); and Vincent Davis, *Postwar Defense Policy and the U.S. Navy, 1943–46* (Chapel Hill, 1966).

Record Group 42: Office of Public Buildings and Grounds

These records begin in 1791 with the effort to plan for the building of a capital city. Among the records are the minutes correspondence registers of contributions and other documents relating to the building of the Washington Monument in the latter half of the nineteenth century. Among these are numerous records concerning the activities of the Know Nothing party and their relationship with Irish Americans.

Also found in this record group are the official papers of John Hoban (1762–1831) Irish-born architect who worked in Washington, D.C., and plans for a monument to be erected in the honor of Wexford-born John Barry (1745–1803), co-founder of the American Navy.

See National Archives Microfilm Publications, *Records of the District of Columbia Commissioners and the Offices Concerned with Public Buildings, 1791–1867*, M371, 27 rolls, DP.

Record Group 45: Naval Records Collection of the Office of Naval Records and Library

This collection began in 1882 when the librarian of the Navy Department began to collect naval documents relating to the Civil War. The collection has grown to hold records dating from 1691. Included are papers of all naval shore establishments from 1814 to 1911. Especially useful are the muster rolls and personnel records of naval personnel, many of them Irish-born. Also found here are originals and transcripts of logs, journals, and diaries of officers of the U.S. Navy at sea. Here we find the correspondence, reports and other materials relating to the career of Wexford-born John Barry (1745–1803), one of the founders of the American Navy.

National Archives Microfilm Publications: Many of the series of letters sent and received by the secretary of the navy before 1886 are available as microfilm publications. The "area file" for the period 1775–1910 has also been filmed.

See Chapter 4 of Meredith B. Colket, Jr., and Frank E. Bridgers, *Guide to Genealogical Records in the National Archives* (Washington: The National Archives and Records Service, 1964).

Record Group 46: United States Senate

This collection includes journals of legislative proceedings and minute books, bills and resolutions, committee records, reports and cartographic records. All of these collections date from the earliest days of the nation usually 1789. Many of the holdings covering Irish activities can be found by perusing the listing of published documents for dates of Senate events of Irish interest and tracing back to the committee records or other related documents.

Among the cartographic records is a statistical atlas of the United States, based on the results of the 1870 census, showing the distribution of Irish throughout the United States. An individual plate shows the Irish distribution on the Pacific Coast. There are also a number of maps of Ireland in these records, usually for the twentieth century.

A great many guides to this record group have been published for listing see the National Archives and Records Service, *Guide to the National Archives of the United States* (Washington, 1974), pp. 50–51.

Record Group 48: Office of the Secretary of the Interior

Includes almost 5,000 cubic feet of records dating between 1833 and 1964. Among these records are the records of the patents and miscellaneous division (1849–1943); records of the lands and railroads division (1849–1907); records of the Indian division (1898–1907); and cartographic records (1840–1923). Many of these provide wide and useful general information on Irish immigrants.

Of particular interest to researchers on the Irish-American experience is the collection of bounty land claims, prison and convict records, records of the government hospital for the insane and charitable institutions, and the extensive correspondence pertaining to the granting of pensions to Irishmen who served in the army and navy.

Record Group 49: Bureau of Land Management

This office was generally responsible for administering all public land transactions except surveying and mapping work. Among the most useful records for our purposes are the records relating to public land disposals (1796–1951). The records of the general land office held in this collection contain extensive data on the settlement of land by Irish immigrants. Since these records provide correspondence, naturalization information, and other documents to support an individual's application for land settlement they can be of considerable value for research on settlement of the land by Irish newcomers.

Record Group 50: Treasurer of the United States

Essentially the records of the banker of the federal government, established in 1789. The correspondence files hold a number of letters providing information on the Fenian movement.

Record Group 56: General Records of the Department of the Treasury

The Department of the Treasury had administrative control of immigration matters from most of the nineteenth century, and thus the "General Records of the Office of the Secretary" contain considerable information on general and specific questions regarding Irish immigration, correspondence with the commissioner general of immigration and his representatives in various ports, and letters to consuls in Ireland and Britain. This record group also includes copies of correspondence of the secretary of the treasury with collectors of customs, 1789–1833; letters received by the secretary from collectors of customs, 1833–1869; and copies of letters sent by the secretary to collectors of customs, 1789–1878.

All of the above correspondence and papers, which are indexed, include considerable amounts of information on Irish movement to the United States. Also in this record group are reports, correspondence, memoranda and other records of a number of Irish-American secretaries and under-secretaries, most notably Edward H. Foley (1948–53) and John L. Sullivan (1942–44).

See National Archives Microfilm Publications, Pamphlet describing M 575, *Copies of Lists of Passengers Arriving at Miscellaneous Ports on the Atlantic and Gulf Coasts and at Ports on the Great Lakes, 1820–1873* (Washington, 1972).

Record Group 59: General Records of the Department of State

Records of a department established by the president in 1789 to oversee matters pertaining to foreign affairs. Very valuable for Irish researchers. The most useful materials are: Diplomatic Correspondence, 1785–1906; Correspondence, 1789–1906; Miscellaneous Correspondence, 1784–1906; Records of Organizational Units, 1793–1961; and Records Relating to Special Subjects or Events.

These records, generally arranged alphabetically by country and thereafter chronologically, provide information on the social and economic conditions in Ireland; public opinion in Ireland on various topics; communications relating to the protection of United States seamen and military and ex-military men directed to American consular officers in Ireland at the ports of Dublin, Cork, Londonderry, Belfast, Galway, Limerick, Athlone, Ballymena, Sligo, and Lurgan; considerable correspondence on British attempts to extradite Irishmen for various crimes, usually political; efforts of various organizations and individuals to encourage Irish emigration; general character of emigrants; Civil War recruiting in Ireland; post-Civil War activity by Irish veterans; Fenian activity in the United States and in Ireland; correspondence regarding efforts by consular officials to find Irish relatives in the United States; detailed information on the recognition of an independent Ireland; payment of military pensions to returning emigrants. Also of value are some of the seventy volumes of "territorial papers" relating to the administration of United States territories before 1873 when many Irish immigrants could be found in these regions.

Considerable information concerning the flow of immigrants and particular problems associated with movement. Detailed information on the final recognition of the Irish Free State and a number of testimonials on the event. Consular dispatches and reports of Irish-born James Leander Cathcart (1767–1843), revolutionary soldier and consul at Tropoli, Madeira, and Tunis, and his special diplomatic correspondence from Tunis. Also consular dispatches and reports of Irish-born Daniel Clark (1766–1813), consul at New Orleans.

Among the more useful guides for our purposes are Daniel T. Goggin and H. Stephen Helton, compilers, *Preliminary Inventory of the General Records of the Department of State*, PI 157 (1963); and Natalia Summers, compiler, *List of Documents Relating to Special Agents of the Department of State, 1789–1906*, SL 7 (1951).

Record Group 60: General Records of the Department of Justice

The Department of Justice was established on June 22, 1870, to expand the legal and administrative duties of the attorney general, whose office was established in 1789. The duties of the department included providing means for the enforcement of Federal laws; representing the government in any court; supervising Federal penal institutions; detecting violations of Federal laws except those assigned to other agencies; administering immigration and naturalization laws and registration of aliens. The papers resulting from these activities are organized into a number of special collections, including the following: attorney general's records (1790–1870); opinions on questions of law (1817–1934); letters, sent and received (1818–1918).

These records provide a wide variety of data on Irish immigrants, including information on Fenian expeditions to invade the homeland and the shipping of arms from the United States during the period of Fenian activity and later; the indictment of persons implicated in Fenian activity and later; the indictment of persons implicated in Fenian plots; the course of action recommended by United States attorneys to prevent Fenian invasions of Ireland. The records for the First World War period contain essential items for the study of the revolutionary activities of various Irish groups, including predominantly Irish western mining organizations. Over the past several decades the department has been heavily involved in monitoring the collection of funds for possible use by radical organizations in Ireland and thus should hold some interesting records for researchers working on recent Irish-American affairs.

Record Group 63: Committee on Public Information

This agency was established by executive order on April 13, 1917, to release government news during World War I, sustain morale, and administer "voluntary" press censorship. After July 1, 1918, the work of the committee was curtailed until it went out of business on June 30, 1919.

Included in this record group are papers and correspondence on government efforts to influence Irish Americans and others to support World War II (Committee on Public Information). Also includes information on press censorship of Irish-American newspapers during the war.

Record Group 66: Commission of Fine Arts

Established in 1910, the duties of the Commission of Fine Arts included providing advice on all matters of art with which the Federal government was concerned. Thus it advises on the location of statues and monuments in the District of Columbia and on monuments erected by the United States elsewhere. Holds records of efforts to erect a memorial to John Barry (1745–1803) Irish-born co-founder of the U.S. Navy.

The records relating to the erection of statues and monuments before 1910 are generally found among records of the Office of Public Buildings and Grounds (Record Group 42).

Record Group 69: Work Projects Administration (WPA)

The Works Progress Administration was established on May 6, 1935, and after July 1, 1939, became known as the Work Projects Administration. The agency succeeded the Federal Emergency Relief Administration (FERA) and the Civil Works Administration (CWA) both established in 1933. Not until June 30, 1944, was the WPA liquidated. These records include the papers of a variety of agencies and are of incalculable value for researching the condition of Irish Americans and Irish-American residential areas of larger cities over a period of time (the 1930s) when these areas were undergoing rapid transition. Of particular importance are the Records of the WPA Federal Project No. 1, which included the theater and writers' projects and the Historical Records Survey up to 1936 when the Historical Records Survey was made an independent agency. The federal writers' project effort produced surveys of many cities, some of which give extensive accounts of Irish newcomers—for example, sections on the Irish in New York and the Irish in Philadelphia.

In addition, the Historical Records Survey provides inventories of archival and other materials in libraries and archives and is invaluable in locating original records for research in the areas for which records can be found—practically the entire country.

See Katherine H. Davidson, comp., *Pre-

liminary Inventory of the Records of the Federal Writers' Project, Work Projects Administration, 1935–1942 (1953).

Record Group 75: Bureau of Indian Affairs

Established in 1824, the Bureau of Indian Affairs is responsible for relations between the Federal government and Native Americans, usually those on reservations.

Scattered records on Irish Americans who served as agents to various tribes over the nineteenth century. See Edward W. Hill, compiler, *Preliminary Inventory of the Records of the Bureau of Indian Affairs*, PI 163 (2 volumes, 1965).

Record Group 79: National Park Service

The National Park Service was established in 1916 to oversee national parks and monuments. Among the records in this group are the records of the War Department relating to national parks, 1892–1937; and the records of the Potomac Company and the Chesapeake and Ohio Canal Company, 1785–1938. This latter collection holds extensive and unique information on Irish laborers working on the building of the Chesapeake and Ohio Canal. Records also include details of efforts to import Irish laborers in the 1780s and 1830s. Particularly useful are the details of the difficulty of getting newcomers from Cork and Longford to work together without violence.

See Edward E. Hill, compiler, *Preliminary Inventory of the Records of the National Park Service*, PI 166 (1966).

Record Group 80: General Records of the Department of the Navy

The department was established on April 30, 1798, to control naval affairs. Among the most useful records for our purposes are the records of the office of the secretary of the navy (1804–1959), which include papers on negotiations between the United States and the British government on Irishmen in the U.S. Navy, many of them deserters from the U.S. Navy. Notes and correspondence on opinions of Admiral William S. Sims, whose critical address in June 1921 on the "Irish Question" inspired an impressive reaction by Irish Americans. This record group also contains muster rolls and personnel records on naval personnel, including many Irish Americans.

Record Group 84: Foreign Service Posts of the Department of State

This record group includes the records of diplomatic posts, 1788–1945; and the records of consular posts (1790–1949). It should be remembered that many of the earlier records are incomplete (for a variety of reasons) and researchers should also consult the records maintained by the Department of State (see Record Group 59, above); in many cases their duplicate copies of these foreign service posts documents are more complete and the finding aids more comprehensive.

The records of diplomatic and consular posts consist of embassy, legation, and consular records of the following types: original signed instructions and copies of despatches; notes from the government of the country in which the post was located and copies of notes to it; copies of instructions and communications to subordinate consulates and despatches and reports from them; miscellaneous correspondence; passport records; records of births, marriages, and deaths of American citizens; listings of important events; notes of administrative changes; inventories of consular property. There are also records of arrival and departure of American vessels and descriptions of their cargoes, including comments on the state and attitudes of emigrants leaving for the United States. There are also registers and some card indexes. The records dated before 1912 are generally bound by series and thereunder chronologically; after 1912 they are arranged by year and thereunder by subject according to the decimal classification scheme of the Foreign Service.

Numerous records providing information on the Fenian movement can be found throughout this record group, especially in the correspondence between Canadian consular posts and Washington. Also of primary importance to students of the Irish is the information on the British reaction to the activities of the Irish in America and to riots involving the Irish in England, which can be found in the records held by consular and diplomatic posts throughout Ireland; these contain correspondence between those overseas posts and various United States agencies other than the Department of State, including these listed here. Belfast: 1864–1912, correspondence in; 1882–92, correspondence out; 1912–35, general files. Ballymena: 1904–7, correspondence out. Londonderry: 1858–88, correspondence out; 1902–21, correspondence out. Dublin: 1869–71, correspondence in; 1889–1912, correspondence in; 1868–1912, correspondence out; 1912–35, general correspondence. Cork: 1869–1912, correspondence in; 1912–35, general correspondence. London: 1831–1915, general notes between British government and U.S. legation; 1831–1915, consular correspondence; 1912–35, general files. Most files covering the Irish War of Independence and the Irish Civil War (1918–23) provide much information on the American reaction to those events.

See Mark G. Eckhoff et al., compilers, *List of Foreign Service Post Records in the National Archives,* SL 9 (1967). Many of these records are available in microfilm; see the current *List of National Archives Microfilm Publications* available from the National Archives. Also see Meredith B. Colket, Jr., and Frank E. Bridgers, *Guide to Genealogical Records in the National Archives* (Washington: The National Archives and Records Service, 1964).

Record Group 85: Immigration and Naturalization Service

The secretary of the treasury had general supervision over immigration between 1882 and 1891. In 1891 the Office of Superintendent of Immigration of the Department of the Treasury was established; it was designated a bureau in 1895. In 1903 the bureau became part of the Department of Commerce and Labor; from there it went to the Department of Labor, until 1933, when the Immigration and Naturalization Service was formed. In 1940 it was transferred to the Department of Justice.

Since 1891 the Immigration and Naturalization Service has administered laws relating to admission, exclusion, deportation, and naturalization of aliens; it investigates violations of those laws, patrols U.S. borders, supervises naturalization work in designated courts, and registers aliens. This is one of the most valuable collections of documents providing information on Irish and Irish Americans. The general records (1882–1932) provide details on deportations; emigration of felons; the volume of emigration from Ireland and methods of travel, including the volume of traffic handled by various steamship companies; area of origin, destination, occupations, financial position and background conditions of Irish migrants to the United States; notes on immigration and naturalization laws; the rights of Irish Americans returning for visits to their home society. The "passenger arrival records" from 1883 to the present contain microfilm copies of rosters of ship (and later airplane) passengers at Boston, Baltimore, New Orleans, New York, Philadelphia, and a number of minor ports.

This record group also includes historical data on the numbers of Irishmen committed to state penitentiaries in Pennsylvania during the 1880s and 1890s.

The case and correspondence files (1882–1938) provide information on appeals by individual Irish immigrants for reversals of nonadmittance decisions or deportation orders because of physical or mental disabilities or other violations of immigration laws.

Among the most useful records in this record group are the diaries of immigration officials at port cities, which comment on the conditions of arriving immigrants, frequently noting the relationship between arrivals and their relatives already in the United States and the contents of their baggage.

See Darrell H. Smith and H. Guy Herring, *The Bureau of Immigration* (Baltimore, 1924); and Meredith B. Colket, Jr., and Frank E. Bridgers, *Guide to Genealogical Records in the National Archives* (Washington: The National Archives and Records Service, 1964).

Record Group 90: Public Health Service

Approximately 1400 cubic feet of records, dated 1802 to 1965, consisting of the general records of the Public Health Service (1833–

1946); records of the quarantine divisions (1878–1936); records of venereal disease control organizations (1918–36).

These records provide information on the inspection and occasional quarantine of vessels arriving with immigrants from Ireland (1890–1927) and the medical condition of new arrivals (1931–34).

See Ralph Chester Williams, M.D., *The United States Public Health Service, 1798–1950*, Washington, D.C.: Government Printing Office, 1951.

Record Group 93: War Department Collection of Revolutionary War Records

This record group includes bound records (1775–98): letters, muster rolls, letter books of officers, rosters of state and continental troops; and unbound records (1775–84): records of military organizations arranged by state and thereunder by organization; compiled military service records and related indexes (1775–84): a single file of thousands of Revolutionary War officers and men containing one or more record cards with information on the individual, arranged by state and organization, indexed by number and name.

Much information on the Irish in Revolutionary America in the muster rolls, pay abstracts, organizational records, account books, and other materials. Since all of the names appearing in these records have been indexed, it is possible to trace individual Irish relatively rapidly or to examine Irish military activity in the Revolutionary era. Of particular value for Irish researchers are the war record and orderly books of Irish-born Edward Hand (1774–1802), who served as a general in the Revolutionary army.

See Chapter 5 of Meredith B. Colket, Jr., and Frank E. Bridgers, *Guide to Genealogical Records in the National Archives* (Washington: The National Archives and Records Service, 1964).

Record Group 94: Adjutant General's Office, 1780s–1917

On June 17, 1775, the Continental Congress appointed an Adjutant General of the Continental Army. Between then and 1821, the adjutant general was alternatively appointed and cashiered; but from 1821 to the present, the office has been in continuous existence. The Adjutant General's Office handled Army orders, correspondence, and other records, and it received final custody of almost all records concerning the military establishment, including personnel of the army and discontinued commands. Altogether there are at present about 39,000 cubic feet of records dated between 1783 and 1917 in this record group.

For our purposes this collection provides assorted information on Fenian activity; records of negotiations between British and U.S. government on problems associated with Civil War recruitment of Irishmen; muster rolls for volunteer and regular military and militia units (1784–1912), in which many Irish served; records covering the activities of Irish-born Richard C. Kerens (1842–1916), railroad builder and politician who managed transportation for the army in Arkansas and Indian Territory during the Civil War period; records of Union army general, Irish-born Thomas Francis Meagher (1823–67).

Record Group 95: Forest Service

Initially established in 1881 as the the Division of Forestry in the Department of Agriculture, its basic mission was to manage programs of land acquisition, fire control, state cooperation, promoting conservation, and managing the best use of grassland and forest. In this collection we find papers on the establishment of a commission in Ireland in 1908 to investigate the poor status of Ireland's forests, together with notes regarding the attempts to solve the problems thorough the passage of the Irish Forestry Act of 1928.

See Charlotte M. Ashby, compiler, *Preliminary Inventory of the Cartographic Records of the Forest Service*, PI 167 (1967); and Harold T. Pinkett, compiler, *Preliminary Inventory of the Cartographic Records of the Forest Service*, PI 18 (1969).

Record Group 98: United States Army Commands, 1784–1821

A relatively small collection of 48 cubic feet of materials consisting of letter books, registers of men furloughed, discharged and detailed, orderly and company books, and some correspondence. Useful for locating Irish immigrants who served over this period.

Record Group 107: Office of the Secretary of War

Established in 1789; by the outbreak of World War II the secretary of war had assumed responsibility for supervision of all activities of the War Department, including finances, equipment, training and operations, protection of seacoast harbors and cities, and execution of the National Defense Act of 1920. This collection of over 3,000 cubic feet of records reflects the changing scope of the office since its foundation.

For our purposes we find here papers and notes on many largely Irish units including the famed 69th Regiment of New York. Notes on negotiations between the U.S. and British governments on the attempts of Irishmen claiming to be British citizens and attempting to get releases after being drafted into the Union Army.

Records Group 109: War Department Collection of Confederate Records

This collection of 5,730 cubic feet consists of records of the Confederate States of America that were either captured or acquired upon the surrender of the Confederacy or by donation or purchase. Muster rolls, returns of various kinds, and paymaster vouchers on Confederate units, many of them including a large number of Irish, especially those from southern cities like New Orleans.

Correspondence and documents on the military career of Irish-born plantation owner, intellectual and Confederate General Patrick Ronayne Cleburne (1828–64), who died in the last major action of the Civil War.

See Chapter 6 of Meredith B. Colket, Jr., and Frank E. Bridgers, *Guide to Genealogical Records in the National Archives* (Washington: The National Archives and Records Service, 1964).

Record Group 110: Provost Marshal General's Bureau (Civil War)

Created in 1863 to administer all activities connected with enrolling and drafting men for military service, for detecting and arresting deserters, and to supervise the volunteer recruiting service. This collection of 1,582 cubic feet provides extensive information (1863–66) on individuals, many of them Irish, who served as substitutes for personnel drafted during the Civil War. Notes on negotiations between the U.S. and British governments on the attempts of Irishmen claiming to be British citizens and attempting to get releases after being drafted into the Union Army.

Record Group 111: Office of the Chief Signal Officer

This record group includes over 300,000 items in the Cartographic and Audiovisual Records, 1860–1954; includes numerous photographs of Irish servicemen and Irish units in the Brady Collection of Civil War pictures, most of which are held in this office.

Record Group 120: American Expeditionary Forces, 1917–23

Over 25,000 cubic feet of records dated between 1912 and 1929. Includes the Records of the AEF Tactical Units, 1917–19; and the Records of the American Forces in France, 1919–20. Both of these collections provide much information on the largely Irish Fighting 69th Regiment from New York.

Record Group 125: Office of the Judge Advocate General (Navy)

The offices of Solicitor and Judge Advocate General were established in 1865 to handle legal duties of the Navy and Marine Corps. In 1921, both offices were merged. Among the records (1799–1943) in this 2,687 cubic feet collection are general correspondence, personnel records relating to Navy and Marine Corps courts-martial, courts of inquiry, boards of investigation and inquest, and matters relating to desertions and discharges. Many of these records provide information on Irish immigrants who served in the Navy or Marine Corps at the time.

Record Group 127: United States Marine Corps

The U.S.M.C. was established on July 11, 1798 by an act that authorized the Commandant of the Corps to appoint an adjutant, a paymaster, and a quartermaster. From that small beginning, the records of the Corps have grown until at present there are over 2,300 cubic feet for the years 1798 to 1950 alone. Researchers on the Irish experience in America will find the muster rolls and extensive papers regarding the military records of many Irish who served in the U.S.M.C. at various times over the period of the records.

See Chapter 4 of Meredith B. Colket, Jr., and Frank E. Bridgers, *Guide to Genealogical Records in the National Archives* (Washington: The National Archives and Records Service, 1964).

Record Group 129: Bureau of Prisons

The Bureau of Prisons was established in the Department of Justice by an act of May 14, 1930. Records of the Superintendent of Prisons dating from 1907 were transferred to the Bureau.

Includes case files on federal prisons and paroles (1910–43) which hold applications for paroles, record of court commitments, release reports, criminal and social histories of prisoners, transcripts of minutes of parole board meetings and correspondence. Of particular value for researchers interested in Irish representation in federal prisons are the files and inspection reports from states with large Irish populations, for example, Massachusetts.

Record Group 130: White House Office

The White House Office was established by executive order on September 8, 1939. It maintains communication with the Congress, individual members of Congress, heads of executive agencies, the press and the general public. This collection also includes records maintained by various White House offices and officials before 1939 that were not regarded as personal papers by the presidents. Overall, there are 56 cubic feet of records dated between 1814 and 1959 in this record group.

Some records regarding presidential involvement in Irish matters scattered throughout this collection. See also notes in manuscript section of this guide regarding holdings of presidential libraries.

Record Group 153: Office of the Judge Advocate General (Army)

Over 5,500 cubic feet of records dated from 1800 to 1957. Among the most useful for our purposes are the notes on negotiations between the U.S. and British governments on the attempts by Irishmen to get releases from the military on the basis of claims to British citizenship or claims that they were recruited illegally into the Union Army.

Record Group 163: Selective Service System (World War I)

This agency was established on May 18, 1917, to register and induct men into the military service. Much of the management of the draft was left to the states, where local draft boards were established on the basis of one for every 30,000 people. There are 263 cubic feet of records in this record group dated between 1917 and 1939. The alien files of the Selective Service System (1917–19) hold an extensive file, indexed by name, of Irish immigrants and others who sought exemption from the draft on the basis of foreign citizenship.

Record Group 165: War Department General and Special Staffs

An extensive collection, consisting of over 10,000 cubic feet of records dated mostly between 1903 and 1948. For our purposes the collection of interest is the cartographic records relating to Ireland; includes maps of army recruiting areas, army command areas, and notes on the disposition of the Irish Republican Army in 1922.

Record Group 166: Foreign Agricultural Service

Initially established as a section of Foreign Markets in the Department of Agriculture in 1895 to collect information on production, consumption, and prices of foreign farm products. This collection of 961 cubic feet of records includes scattered notes and comments on Irish agriculture in the correspondence from representatives in Northern Ireland and the Irish Free State over the period 1921–38.

Record Group 188: Office of Price Administration

An extensive collection of records from an agency established to stabilize prices and rents and to manage supplies of vital commodities during World War II. The 8,860 cubic feet of record contain extensive data on prices, rents, banking, and other economic matters in Ireland during World War II.

Record Group 204: Office of Pardon Attorney

The Office of the Pardon Attorney, originally called the Office of Attorney in Charge of Pardons, was established in the Attorney General's Office by an act of March 3, 1891. The office had the responsibility for recommending action on federal pardon applications to the president. The records date from 1853 to 1946 and include endorsements, protests, and reports filed with requests for executive clemency, 1853 to 1946, with an index of cases for the period 1853 to 1889.

Among the files of interest to researchers on the Irish in America are the numerous requests for pardons forwarded by the military to the president during the Civil War; the records on the granting of pardons to participants in the Fenian "invasion" of Canada; and the records of pardons and commutations for "political prisoners" of the period immediately after World War I, including those of James "Big Jim" Larkin, Irish-born labor agitator pardoned in the mid-1920s.

Record Group 206: Solicitor of the Treasury

The Office of the Solicitor of the Treasury was created in 1830 to supervise legal proceedings involving the collection of debts due to the United States. The Case Files and Suit Records, 1791–1929, hold 110 linear feet of scattered records regarding suits involving Irish immigrants developing out of violations of the Alien Contract Law in 1895.

Record Group 208: Office of War Information

The Office of War Information was established in June 1942 to coordinate the government's war information program. There are 4,630 cubic feet of records dated between 1942 and 1948, with some dated as early as 1926. Many records of the Office of War Information Overseas Operations Branch are still maintained by the Department of State.

For our purposes this record group holds correspondence with various Irish-American organizations that were cooperating with the government in dissemination of information furthering U.S. involvement in World War II.

Record Group 241: Patent Office

The first patent board was established in 1791, but not until 1836 was the Patent Office established under the Department of

State; after a period under the Department of the Interior, it became part of the Department of Commerce in 1849. There are 18,681 cubic feet of records here dated between 1791 and 1923.

The most useful set of records here for those interested in the Irish experience in America are the plans, correspondence, and other papers regarding the granting of a patent to the former Irish Christian Brother John Philip Holland (1840–1914) for his invention of a submarine, with which he intended to destroy the might of the British Navy.

Record Group 257: Bureau of Labor Statistics

The Bureau of Labor Statistics originated as the Bureau of Labor on June 27, 1884, and became an independent Department of Labor without Cabinet status in 1888. From 1903 to 1913 it was part of the Department of Commerce and Labor; it was transferred to the present Department of Labor in 1913.

As the federal government's principal fact-finding agency in the field of labor economics, the bureau gathers and analyzes data and publishes reports concerning the labor force, employment, and unemployment, work stoppages, foreign labor conditions, and so forth. The entire collection is of untold value for any exploration of Irish work condition, stoppages, status, etc.

Record Group 391: United States Regular Army Mobile Units, 1821–1942

These records, consisting of almost 7,000 cubic feet, cover all the regular army mobile units from 1821, when there were only seven infantry regiments and four artillery units, until the beginning of World War II, where there were literally hundreds of units. They include some information on the Irish in the Mexican War and the Civil War. The "Cartographic and Audiovisual Records" include over a thousand pictures, paintings, and photographs of military men, many of them Irish.

These records are particularly useful for the study of the Fenian movement. They include a listing of Fenians who "invaded" Canada in 1866 and papers on the granting of paroles to many of them; also, the records of U.S. Army units that conducted operations to prevent the Fenian action. Particular interesting also are the records of army commands in the Far West over the second half of the nineteenth century, when the Irish-born provided the largest immigrant contingent in most posts and units, as indicated by the seventeen Irish immigrants who died with General Custer at the Battle of the Little Big Horn in 1873.

Many of the records of Thomas Francis Meagher (1823–1867), Irish-born Union army general, are also included in this record group.

Record Group 393: United States Army Continental Commands, 1821–1920

In 1921 the War Department divided the United States into two geographical Army commands—the Eastern and the Western departments. The names and jurisdictions of the new commands changed frequently after 1821, and new commands were created as the United States grew, until the entire country was dotted with commands and subdivisions. In 1920 this arrangement was stabilized by the division of the United States into nine corps areas.

Over 10,000 cubic feet of documents that comprise the primary records on the United States army between 1821 and 1920 and thus contain a great deal of information on the Irish in the military. In the collection are letter books and registers of letters received, with indexes; endorsements and telegrams; issuances; correspondence files, with indexes and record cards; reports; station books; rosters; returns; registers of deserters, discharges, furloughs, and prisoners. The Irish are well represented in all of these documents.

Published Government Documents

The staggering range and volume of United States government publications reflect the vastness and complexity of American society. Researchers attempting to use this monumental stockpile of paper must learn of the existence of particular documents of value to students of the Irish and then locate and acquire copies of particular items. These problems are intensified by the fact that publications on Ireland and the Irish, especially before independence in 1922, tend to be buried in reports of a more general nature.

It is possible, however, for a diligent researcher to find much of the material on a particular topic by searching the indexes listed below for events or general subjects that involved the Irish—for example, the Fenian movement, immigration, naturalization, or extradition. But in any extensive search for government publications it is advisable to consult a specialist, usually found on the staff of the U. S. Government depository branch at any major college or public library throughout the United States. The United States Code specifies that depository libraries must provide the general public with access and assistance in finding federal government documents.

Prior to embarking on a search for published government documents a very useful overview of the scope and availability of such documents can be acquired by surveying Daniel W. and Marilyn A. Lester, compilers, *Checklist of United States Public Documents, 1789–1976: A Dual Media Edition of the United States Superintendent of Documents' Public Documents Library Shelf Lists with Accompanying Indexes* (Arlington, Virginia: The United States Historical Documents Institute, 1978).

In attempting to locate specific published government documents today we are fortunate that over the past decade a commercial organization, the Congressional Information Service (CIS) and its Greenwood Press division have developed a number of indexes that together provide the most comprehensive coverage of such reports. The following are the most useful of these items:

1. CIS, U.S. CONGRESSIONAL COMMITTEE HEARINGS INDEX. Provides a comprehensive index to all published hearings from the early 1800s through 1969. It includes all bills and laws discussed and witnesses who testified before Congress on these items.

2. CIS U.S. SERIAL SET INDEX AND MICROFICHE. Comprehensive subject and name index to the complete U.S. Serial Set, which covers all numbered congressional reports and documents issued from 1789 through 1969.

3. CIS U.S. CONGRESSIONAL COMMITTEE PRINTS INDEX AND MICROFICHE COLLECTION. Provides subjects and names access to over 15,000 committee prints issued from the early 1800s to 1969. Prints are generally defined as background studies, analytical or statistical data, bill drafts, and statute compilations prepared and printed to aid congressional committees in their legislative and oversight activities.

4. CIS/INDEX TO PUBLICATIONS OF THE U.S. CONGRESS. This is the item that brings the listings in the above three indexes up to date. Covers all congressional prints, hearings, documents, and reports published by Congress since 1970. Also produces an annual volume, which provides monthly abstracts and indexes for the particular year and includes a fully indexed legislative history of all public laws.

Acquiring a copy of a document located in an index can be a challenge, since the means of distribution of publications is complex, in part determined by the chiefs of executive departments and agencies and in part determined by law. Most documents are published and can be found in any depository library, but others are mimeographed in only a few copies; still others are designated "for official use only" or produced for internal distribution only. The best procedure for nonexperts eager to find a publication is to request it from the librarian at the U.S. Government depository branch at any major college or public library throughout the United States. If a particular document is unavailable the librarian can request a copy from the designated regional depository for the area, or from a higher agency if necessary.

The listing of published government items provided below was generated by searching all four of the above CIS indexes under a variety of headings most likely to yield items on Ireland and the Irish in America. The reference numbers provided with each item vary with the type of document. An explanation of the meaning of those reference numbers is provided in the introduction to the four index volumes above. For our purposes it is sufficient that the reference numbers provided with each item below are detailed enough to allow a government documents librarian to locate the particular item.

It should be kept in mind that few published government documents appeared before the Civil War.

15th Congress, 1817–19

Encouragement to Irish emigrants to emigrate to Illinois territory of New York Irish Emigrant Association. *Misc.* 499 (15–1) ASP038.

Petitions of Irish Emigrant Association of New York, Philadelphia, Baltimore, and Pittsburgh. *H. doc.* 119 (15–1) 9.

30th Congress, 1847–49

Presidential message transmitting report on American citizens imprisoned in Ireland. *H. rp.* 19 (30–2) 540.

32d Congress, 1851–53

Proposals for transporting mail between Jersey City and Galway, Ireland. *H. rp.* 152 (32–1) 656.

34th Congress, 1855–57

To provide for carrying out first article of treaty with Her Majesty, Queen of United Kingdom of Great Britain and Ireland, of June 15, 1856, for surveying and marking border of Washington Territory and British possessions. *S. rp.* 251 (34–1) 837.

37th Congress, 1861–63

Famine in Ireland. Resolutions of Kentucky. *H. misdoc.* 23 (37–2) 1141.

Relief to starving population of Ireland. *H. rp.* 116 (37–2) 1145.

Resolutions of legislature of Kentucky on relief of Ireland. *S. misdoc.* 5 (37–2) 1124.

Resolutions of legislature of Wisconsin on relief of Ireland. *S. misdoc.* 51 (37–2) 1124.

39th Congress, 1865–67

Message of President on arrest of American citizens in Ireland. *H. exdoc.* 139 (39–1) 1267.

Message of President on release of Fenian prisoners. *H. exdoc.* 154 (39–1) 1267.

40th Congress, 1867–69

Arrest of American citizens in Great Britain and Ireland. *H. misdoc.* 46 (40–1) 1312.

Message of president on imprisonment of Warren and Costello in Great Britain for Fenianism. *H. exdoc.* 312 (40–2) 1346.

Message of president, on Messrs. Costello and Warren, naturalized citizens of United States, imprisoned in Great Britain for Fenianism. *H. exdoc.* 66 (40–3) 1374.

Message of president on trial and conviction of American citizens in England for Fenianism. *H. exdoc.* 157 (40–2) 1339.

Message of president transmitting papers on arrest and trial of Rev. John McMahon, Robert B. Lynch, and John Warren by government of Great Britain. *S. exdoc.* 42 (40–2) 1317.

Request for release of Rev. John McMahon, arrested during Fenian's attack on Canada. *H. rp.* 7 (40–2) 1357.

42d Congress, 1871–73

Joint resolution referred to Committee on Foreign Affairs, stating that no persons are in prison in Canada on account of complicity in Fenian invasion of June 1866. *H. misdoc.* 227 (42–2) 1527.

Message of president, transmitting correspondence on release of William G. Walpine, Fenian prisoner. *H. exdoc.* 114 (42–2) 1513.

44th Congress, 1875–77

Concurrent resolution proposing common unit of money and accounts for United States, Great Britain, and Ireland. *S. rp.* 39 (44–1) 1667.

Resolution proposing a common unit of money and accounts for United States of America and United Kingdom of Great Britain and Ireland. *S. misdoc* 35 (44–1) 1665.

46th Congress, 1879–81

Relief for Irish people. *H. rp.* 465 (46–2) 1935.

Report of commander of relief ship *Constellation*, which transported supplies to starving people of Ireland. *S. exdoc.* 215 (46–2) 1886.

47th Congress, 1881–83

Message of president on American citizens imprisoned in Ireland, 3 parts. *H. exdoc.* 155 (47–1) 2030.

Message of president on arrest and confinement in Ireland of certain citizens of United States. *S. exdoc.* 510 (47–1) 1990.

Message of president transmitting papers on alleged arrest and imprisonment in Ireland of Michael P. Boyton by Great Britain [at end of volume]. *S. exdoc.* 5 (47-sp) 1943.

49th Congress, 1885–87

Congratulations extended to William E. Gladstone and his associates on efforts to secure home rule in Ireland. *H. misdoc.* 249 (49–1) 2418; *H. misdoc.* 314 (49–1) 2418.

J. J. O'Neils' resolution concerning "home rule" in Ireland. *H. misdoc.* (49–1)

Mahoney's resolution on "home rule" in Ireland. *H. misdoc.* (49–1)

Mr. Blair's report from the Committee on Education and Labor, to accompany the petition to the United League of America, and resolutions to Mr. Gladstone and Mr. Parnell for their efforts to promote "home rule" in Ireland. *S. rp.* (49–1).

50th Congress, 1887–89

Ireland. Immigration from Europe, United States Labor Impact Review (50), 1888, HS 50-A.

Savage, George W. "Trade and Agriculture in Ireland." *U.S. Consular Reports*, August 1889.

51st Congress 1889–91

Irish Emigrant Society. "Immigration laws, immigrants' living and working conditions, and New York immigrant station established, investigation." (51–2), *H. rp.* v.2. n. 3472.

53d Congress 1893–95

Ashby, N. B. Agriculture in Ireland. *Consumer Report*, 1895, v. 47:47–51.

Piatt, A. D. "Agriculture Statistics of Ireland." *Consumer Report*, November 1895, v. 49:370–72.

54th Congress, 1895–97

Ashby, N. B., "Prices of Agriculture produced in Ireland." *Consumer Report*, July 1896, v. 51:523–4.

Tamey, J. B. "American Goods in Ireland." *Consumer Report*, August 1896, v. 51:768–69.

55th Congress, 1897–99

Application of convention relating to tenure and disposition of real and personal property, concluded between United States and Great Britain on March 2, 1899, to Irish Free State [correspondence between Department of State, American ambassador at London, and British Foreign Office].

Ashby, N. B. "Agricultural Statistics of Ireland." *Consumer Report*, May 1897, v. 54, no. 200–51-2.

Piatt, A. D. "Banking and railway statistics of Ireland, 1898." *Consumer Report*, September 1899 v. 61; no. 228:143–44.

Swiney, Daniel. "Emigration from Ireland." *Consumer Report*, June 1898, v. 57, no. 213: 235.

Wilbouer, Joshua. "Dublin, Agriculture in Ireland, cattle trade in Ireland" [article from *Irish Daily Independent*]. *Commercial Relations*, 1898, v. 2:801–5.

56th Congress, 1899–1901

Gallinger, J. H. Report from Committee on Pensions, favoring H. 3233, to increase pensions to Ireland. February 19, 1901. *S. rp.* 2341. (56–2) v. 5; 4067.

Gibson, K. R. Report from Committee on Invalid Pensions Amending H. 3233, to Increase Pensions to Ireland. Jan 15, 1901. *H. rp.* 2317 (56–2) v. 1; 4212.

Wilbour, Joshua. "Agricultural Statistics of Ireland, 1899." *Commercial Relations*, 1899. 1900 v. 2: 879.

58th Congress, 1903–5

Knabenshue, S. S. "Emigration." *Monthly Consumer Reports,*. June 1, 1905. no. 297.

Knabenshue, S. S. "Irish immigration." *Monthly Consumer and Trade Report*, July 1905. no. 298: 114–45

Manufacturer's Bureau. "Ireland." *Monthly Consumer and Trade Report*, August 1905, no. 299: 140–43.

Moe, A. K. "Irish Industries."

Moe, A. K. "Irish immigration statistics for 1904." *Monthly Consumer and Trade Report*, July 1905. No. 298: 97–99.

Piatt, A. D. "American Trade with Ireland." *Monthly Consumer Report*, December. 1904. no. 291:91–93.

Stephens, J. G. "Emigration from Ireland and England." *Monthly Consumer Report*, October 1904, no. 289.

Towvelle, W. W. "American products in Ireland." *Monthly Consumer and Trade Report*, February 1904, v. 74, no. 281:299–300.

60th Congress 1907–9

Moe, A. K. "Bernard Road Train in Ireland." *Monthly Consumer and Trade Report*, March 1908, no. 330:81–82.

Moe, A. K. "Labor conditions in Ireland, comparison of cost of living for workingmen in cities" [resume of report of British Board of Trade; transmitted by Moe]. *Monthly Consumer and Trade Report*, April 1908, no. 331:119–21.

61st Congress 1909–11

Armstrong, J. S., Jr. "Ireland, improved conditions demand more [agriculture] implements." *Monthly Consumer and Trade Report*, Feb. 1910, no. 353:64–66.

Brerton, Cloudesley. "Education in Ireland." *Education Bureau Report*, 1910, v. 1: 551–78.

Culver, H. S. "Improving Irish Agriculture." *Monthly Consumer and Trade Report*, June 1909, no. 345: 85–86.

Ireland. "Road systems, public, of foreign countries and of the several states" (63–1), 1913, JO817.

Knabenshue, S. S. "Ireland, good opening for American motorboat builders." *Monthly Consumer and Trade Report*, Nov. 1909, no. 350:76–75.

Moe, A. K. "Results of tobacco growing experiments in Ireland." *Monthly Consumer and Trade Report*, June, 1909, no. 345: 76–77.

64th Congress, 1915–17

Foreign Relations Committee. Senate. Clemency for Irish political prisoners, adverse report to accompany Senate Res. 236 and Senate Res. 237, and amendment proposed by Mr. Sterling, July 25, to Senate Res. 237 [requesting the president to ask British government to exercise clemency in treatment of Irish political prisoners, and requesting the president to advise U.S. ambassador to Great Britain to use his influence, unofficially, to obtain commutation of sentence of death of Sir Roger Casement, etc.] submitted by Mr. Stone, July 25, calendar day of July 27, 1916. *S. rp.* 740 (641) v. C, 6902.

Industrial Commission. Mining Conditions and Industrial Relations at Butte, Montana. *S. Doc.* 415 (64–1).

Irish-American Athletic Club. Federal departments and agencies programs, FY17 appropriations publications (64–1) (Feb.–May 1916), H141–0-B.

State Department. American citizens in Ireland in response to resolution, report relative to safety and well-being of American citizens in Ireland. June 13, 1916. *S. doc.* 462 (64–1) v. 43, 6953.

65th Congress, 1917–19

Foreign Affairs Committee. House. Irish question hearings on House J. Res. 356, requesting commissioners plenipotentiary of United States in international peace conference to present to said conference right of Ireland to freedom, independence, and self-determination: Dec. 12, 1918. *H. doc.* 1832 (65–3) v. 107; 7576.

Foreign Affairs Committee. House. Right of Ireland to self-determination. Report to accompany House J. Res. 375; submitted by Mr. Flood. Feb. 11, 1919. *H. rp.* 1054 (65–3) v. 2, 7455.

Ireland. Self-determination of Ireland, United States presentation to Versailles Conference, ratification (65–3), Dec. 12, 13, 1918, H192–1.

Irish Progressive League of New York. Irish government self-determination, United States presentation to Versailles Conference, authorization (65–3), Dec. 12, 13, 1918, H192–1.

Irish Women's Council of America. Irish government self-determination, United States presentation to Versailles Conference, authorization (65–3), Dec 12, 13, 1918, H192–1.

66th Congress, 1919–21

Foreign Affairs Committee. House. Government for Ireland, report to accompany House Con. Res. 57 [that Ireland have government of its own choice]; submitted by Mr. Proter. May 29, 1920. *H. rp.* 1063 (66–2) v. B, 7656.

Foreign Relations Committee. Senate. Representatives of Ireland at Paris report to accompany Senate Res. 48 [urging American Peace Commission to secure hearing for representatives of Irish Republic] submitted by Mr. Borah. June 5, 1919. *S. rp.* 6 (66–1) v. A, 7591.

Ireland. Independence movement recognition by United States and Great Britain, consular service review (66–2), Dec. 12,13,1919, H229–5.

Ireland. Independence of Ireland after World War I, proposal review (66–1), July–Sept. 1919, S159–0.

Irish National Bureau. Ireland and Great Britain, colonial policies and need for recognition of Irish independence, consular service review (66–1), Dec.12,13, 1919, H229–5.

State Department. Hearing for representatives of Ireland at Peace Conference, letter advising Senate that attention of M. Clemenceau, president of Peace Conference, had been invited to fall text of Senate resolution of June 6, 1919, requesting American Peace Commission to procure hearing for representatives of the people of Ireland. June 20, 1919. *S. Doc.* 35 (66–1) v. 14, 7609.

"Struggle of the Irish people." An address to Congress of U.S. adopted at January Session of Dail Eireann presented by Mr. Borah. 1921. *S. doc.* (66–3).

67th Congress, 1921–23

Ireland. Farmers' cooperation associations, review (67–4), January 16, 1923, S191–5.

Ireland. Foreign exchange rates stabilization conference, authorization (67–1), October 8, 1921, H290–9.

68th Congress, 1923–25

Christopher, F. A. "Ireland, its agricultural, industrial, and commercial resources." *Foreign and Domestic Commerce Bureau, Trade Bulletin*, 188; February 11, 1924.

Protesting drafts in the United Kingdom, Irish Free State, and Canada, compiled from reports of American Consular Office. November 1925.

69th Congress, 1925–27

King, M. R. "Typhus fever epidemiology." Public Health Service. October 28, 1927.

70th Congress, 1927–29

"Economic Survey of the Irish Free State." Foreign and Domestic Commerce Bureau. 1928.

Maranio, Enrique. "Irish participation in Bolivar's campaign." Pan American Union. 1927.

Park, William M. "Automotive industry and trade." Foreign and Domestic Commerce Bureau. 1928.

72d Congress, 1931–33

"Life expectancy and comparison." Public Health Service. June 1932.

75th Congress, 1937–38

"Air navigation arrangement between the U.S. and the Irish Free State." State Department. September 29 and November 4, 1937.

"Market for meteorological instruments in the Irish Free State." Foreign and Domestic Commerce Bureau. June 1937.

"Reciprocal trade agreement between the United States, United Kingdom, and Northern Ireland." State Department. November 17, 1938.

76th Congress, 1939–41

Electrical markets based on a report by Edwin J. King. Foreign and Domestic Commerce Bureau, Sept. 1939.

77th Congress, 1941–42

Authorizing the president to present to Eire on behalf of people of U.S. a statue of Commodore John Barry. *S. rp.* 1492 (76–3) 10429; *S. rp.* 79 (77–1) 10543; *H. rp.* 505 (77–1) 10554.

Ireland. Naval Academy midshipmen admission from Ireland, authorization (77–1), June 12, 1941, H975–0.121.

Maritime Commission to sell two merchant vessels to government of Ireland. *H. rp.* 1454 (77–1) 10558.

Midshipmen from the Irish Free State. Authorization of their appointment to the U.S. Naval Academy. 1941. *H. rp.* 4387.

Motion picture industry. *Foreign and Domestic Commerce Bureau, Industrial Reference Survey*, January–November 1941.

Radio market. *Foreign and Domestic Commerce Bureau, Industrial Reference Survey*, January–August 1941.

War Shipping Administration to sell or charter two merchant vessels to Government of Ireland. *S. rp.* 1553 (77–2) 10658.

79th Congress, 1945–46

Air transport services agreement. State Department, February 3, 1945.

Foreign Service of U.S.A. Summary of economic information. *International Reference Service*, July 1946.

Medical and sanitary data on Eire. *War Department, Technical Bulletin*, February 1946.

Motion picture equipment potentialities in Eire. *Foreign and Domestic Commerce Bureau*, April–Dec. 1945.

Northern Ireland. Tax conventions with Great Britain and Northern Ireland, ratification (79–1), May/June 1945, S760–6.

Northern Ireland. Tax conventions with Great Britain, and Northern Ireland, review (79–2), April 17, 1946, S806–5.

80th Congress, 1947–48

Aeronautical equipment [Ireland, Norway, Spain, Sweden, United Kingdom]. Foreign and Domestic Commerce Bureau, *Digest of International Developments*, June 1949.

Air transport services agreement. State Department, June 2–3, 1947.

Cheatan, C. B., and J. B. Gibbs. Tobacco market notes. Foreign Agricultural Relations Office, Jan. 22, 1948.

Communication from the president requesting funds for presentation to Eire of Statue of Commodore John Barry. *H. doc.* 412 (80–1) 11154.

Documentation, consular, and customs requirements for shipment. *Foreign and Domestic Commerce Bureau*, Aug. 1948.

Economic cooperation, agreement under Public Law 472. *State Dept.* June 28, 1948.

Economic review. *Foreign and Domestic Commerce Bureau*, Aug. 1948.

Electric industry. World trade in commodities. *Foreign and Domestic Commerce Bureau*, Nov. 1948.

European recovery program; country study. *Economic Cooperation Administration*, Feb. 1949.

Foreign Commerce yearbook series. *Foreign and Domestic Commerce Bureau*, Aug. 1948.

Foreign Service of U.S.A. Summary of current economic information. *Foreign and Domestic Commerce Bureau*. 1947.

Increase authorized appropriation for statue of Commodore John Barry to be presented to Eire. *S. rp.* 1760 (80–2) 11208; *H. rp.* 1972 (80–2) 11211.

Ireland. Political conditions and economic recovery problems. Background studies on European problems. H7232 lst session, 1947.

Market for leather and its products. *Foreign and Domestic Commerce Bureau*, Jan–July 1947.

Northern Ireland. Great Britain-United States petroleum agreement, ratification (80–1), June 1947, S835–9.

Northern trade agreement. Application of most favored nation treatment to areas under occupation or control agreement between United States, United Kingdom, and Northern Ireland. *State Dept.*, July 6, 1948.

Sanlerg, Arthur M. "Fish and products" [preliminary report done under provisions of Research and Marketing Act.] *Foreign Market Notes*, Foreign Agriculture Relations Office, Oct. 25, 1948.

Source of crude drugs and essential oils. *Foreign and Domestic Commerce Bureau, Industrial Reference Survey*, Jan–July 1947.

Wall, Harold E. "Living and office operating costs." *Foreign and Domestic Commerce Bureau*, Apr. 1949.

81st Congress 1949–51

Double taxation, Agreement on the taxes of estates of deceased persons. *State Dept.* September 13, 1949.

Double taxation. Agreement on the taxes of income. *State Dept.* September 13, 1949.

Economic cooperation agreement made under Public Law 472, 80th Congress. *State Dept.* February 17–18, 1950.

Economic information (summary). Foreign and Domestic Commerce Bureau, December 1949.

Economic review. Foreign and Domestic Commerce Bureau, July 1949.

Economic review for 1949. Foreign and Domestic Commerce Bureau, July 1950.

Footwear production and trade. *Foreign Domestic Commerce Bureau, World Trade in Commodities*, November 1949.

Foreign Affairs Committee. Senate. Unification hearing. April 28, 1950.

Friendship, commerce, navigation treaty and protocol. *State Dept.* January 21, 1950.

Gibbs, Barnard J. "U.S. tobacco in Ireland." *Foreign Market Notes, Foreign Agriculture Relation Office*, July 26, 1949.

Gibbs, J. Barnard. "Favorable market for U.S. tobacco continues in Ireland." Foreign Agricultural Relations Office, Foreign Market Notes, October 24, 1950.

Handicraft. Foreign and Domestic Commerce Bureau, July 1949.

Ireland. Europe recovery program extension authorization (81–1), February 1949, S892–1.

Ireland. Unification, sense of Congress resolution (81–2), April 28, 1950, H1292–2.

Naval stores. Foreign and Domestic Commerce Bureau, August 1949.

Northern Ireland. Irish political unification, sense of Congress resolutions (81–2), April, 28, 1950, H1292–2.

Northern Ireland. U.S. foreign policy decisions regarding Western Europe, 1948 docs compilation (81–1), 1974, H920–6.

Northern Ireland. U.S. foreign policy decisions regarding Western Europe, 1949 docs compilation (81–2), 1975, H920–13.

Ophthalmic products trade. International Trade Office, December 1949.

Paint, etc.—market. Foreign and Domestic Commerce Bureau, May 1950.

Paper industry. *Foreign and Domestic Commerce Bureau, World Trade in Commodities*, May 1950.

Passports and agreements. *State Dept.*, Aug. 1, 1949.

Ritter, Ann S. Trade-union organization. Labor Statistics Bureau, 1950.

Seed situation. Foreign and Domestic Commerce Bureau, August 1950.

Trade associations and importers [list of trade associations and Irish importers of ECA-financial machinery and equipment from the U.S.]. Economic Cooperation Administration, April 1948–December 1949.

Typewriter market. Foreign and Domestic Commerce Bureau, August 1949.

Veterinary medicines and biologicals market.

Foreign and Domestic Commerce Bureau, July 1949.

Wool textile industry. Foreign and Domestic Commerce Bureau, March 1950.

82d Congress, 1951–53

Consideration of resolution to provide for unity of Ireland. *H. rp.* 1004 (82–1) 11498.

Double taxation, convention. Senate Foreign Relations Committee (82–1). Apr. 12–13, 1957.

Economic cooperation agreement made under Public Law 472, 80th Congress. *State Dept.*, Apr. 20 and June 7, 1951.

General features of tariff and trade regulations. Foreign and Domestic Commerce Bureau, British Commonwealth Div. Nov. 1951.

Ireland. Tax conventions with South Africa, New Zealand, Norway, Ireland, Greece, and Canada, ratification (82–1), April 1951, S965–11.

Ireland. Unification, sense of Congress resolution, (82–1) Feb. 1951. H1313–2.

Ireland. U.S. foreign policy decisions regarding Western Europe, 1951 docs. compilation (82–2), 1985, H920–8.

Northern Ireland. U.S. foreign policy decisions regarding Western Europe, 1950 docs. compilation (82–1), 1977, H920–22.

Northern Ireland. U.S. foreign policy decisions regarding Western Europe, 1951 docs. compilation (82–2), 1985, H920–8.

Providing for representatives at unveiling of Commodore John Barry Memorial at Wexford, Ireland. Sept. 15, 1956. *H. rp.* 2409 (84–2) 11899.

Providing for unity of Ireland. *H. rp.* 875 (82–1) 11498.

Tariff and trade controls. Foreign and Domestic Commerce Bureau, British Commonwealth Div., Jan 1952.

83d Congress, 1953–55

Consular officers, convention and supplementary protocol. *State Dept.* May 1, 1950 and May 3, 1952.

Mutual security counterpart special account agreement. *State Dept.*, June 17, 1954.

84th Congress, 1955–57

Atomic energy cooperation for civil uses, agreement. *State Dept.*, Mar. 16, 1956.

Import tariff system. Foreign Bureau, Jan. 1955.

Morris, William J. Basic data on economy. Foreign Dept. Jan. 1955.

Providing for joint committee to represent Congress at unveiling for Commodore John Barry Memorial, Wexford, Ireland. *S. rp.* 2439 (84–2) 11889.

Guaranty of private investments. *State Dept.*, Oct. 5, 1955.

85th Congress, 1957–59

Ahern, F. E. Patent and trademark regulations. Foreign Commerce Bureau, September 1958.

Air transport services agreement. State Dept., March 4, 1958.

Black, Deane M. Preparing shipments to Ireland. Foreign Commerce Bureau, April 1957.

Economic developments, 1956. Foreign Commerce Bureau, British Commonwealth Div., May 1957.

Import tariff system. Foreign Commerce Bureau, British Commonwealth Div., March 1957.

Ireland. Nomination of Scott McLeod to be ambassador (85–1), 1957, S381–6.

Ireland. Nomination of Robert W. Scott McLeod to be United States ambassador (85–1), April/May 1957, S1220–5; Sfo–2.

Kendall, N. W. Civil Aviation. Foreign Commerce Bureau, August 1957.

Licensing and exchange controls. Foreign Commerce Bureau, January 1958.

Scholarship exchange program. State Dept., March 16, 1957.

Senate Foreign Relations Committee. Hearings on the nomination of Scott McLeod, ambassador. April 30–May 1, 1957.

Travagline, Vincent D. Establishing business. Foreign Commerce Bureau, May 1958.

86th Congress, 1959-61

Abdo, Albert N. Economy, basic data. Foreign Commerce Bureau, February 1959.

Abdo, Albert N. Living Conditions. Foreign Commerce Bureau, July 1959.

Adverse report on proposed agreement between United States and United Kingdom and Northern Ireland for cooperation on uses of atomic energy. *H. rp.* 662 (86-1) 12161.

Black, Deane M. Preparing shipments to Ireland [documents needed, labeling and marking, entry and warehousing, customs procedures]. Foreign Commerce Bureau, June 1960.

Establishing business. Foreign Commerce Bureau, British Commonwealth Div., June 1960.

Nuclear research and training equipment and materials, grant for procurement: agreement. State Dept., March 24, 1960.

87th Congress, 1961-63

Agricultural trade agreement. State Dept., May 3, 1962.

Atomic energy cooperation for civil uses. State Dept., Feb. 13, 1961.

Black, Deane M. Licensing and exchange controls. Foreign Commerce Bureau, January 1961.

Dobbins, Claude E. Livestock and meat industry. Foreign Agriculture Service, March 1962.

EEC membership application [seeks larger trading environment through EEC membership]. Commerce Dept. [reprint from Foreign Commerce Weekly] October 1961.

Establishing business. International Programs Bureau, Commerce Dept. December 1961.

Import tariff system. International Programs Bureau, Commerce Dept., December 1962.

Ireland. Nomination of Edward G. Stockdale to be United States ambassador (87-1), March 1961, S1430-12.

Irish Export Board. Sugar import quotas revision (87-2), May, June 1962, H19244-3; S1515-1.

Leslie, Edward A. Economic development. International Programs Bureau, Commerce Dept., April 1962.

Living conditions. International Programs Bureau, Commerce Dept., November 1961.

McMurray, Joseph P., Chairman of Federal Home Loan Bank Board. Heritage and future potentialities [an address given at the 62nd Anniversary dinner of the Society of Friendly Sons of St. Patrick] March 17, 1962.

Senate Foreign Relations Comm. Hearings on the nomination of Edward T. Stockdale for ambassador. Senate. (87-1), March 23-24.

88th Congress, 1963-65

Agreement on public liability for damage caused by N.S. *Savannah*. State Dept., June 18, 1964.

Atomic energy for civil uses, agreement. State Dept., August 7, 1963.

Beef and veal, trade agreement. February 25, 1964.

Educational data [compiled by Margaret L. King in collaboration with George A. Male]. Education Office, H.E.W., March 1963.

Ireland. Nuclear research and cooperation agreement, extension (88), September, April, and June 1964, S1679-1.

Leslie, Edward A. Basic data on the economy. International Commerce Bureau, September 1963.

Leslie, Edward A. Foreign trade regulations. International Commerce Bureau, January 1964.

Marketing quotas for Irish potatoes. *S. rp.* 962 (88-2) 12616-1.

Prohibit future trading in Irish potatoes. *H. rp.* 765 (88-1) 2543.

Senate Foreign Relations Committee. Hearings on the nomination of Raymond R. Guest, ambassador. (84-1) March 2, 1965.

89th Congress, 1965-67

Background notes. State Dept. November 1965.

Brown, Stephen C. Mineral yearbooks,

chapter 4767. Mines Bureau, Interior Dept., 1965.

Dublin, Ireland. Interparliamentary Union Dublin Conference. Report of United States delegation (89-1), 1965, SO734.

Ireland. Nomination of Raymond R. Guest as ambassador (89-1), March 2, 1965, S1657-2.

Labor conditions [note prepared in Div. of Foreign Labor conditions for inclusion in Director of Labor Organizations, Europe Labor Statistics Bureau, 1965].

Liquori, Robert E. Civil aviation survey of continental Europe and Ireland. Business and Defense Services Administration, Commerce Dept., 1965.

Woodmansee, Walter C. Mineral yearbooks, chapter 12881. Mines Bureau, Interior Dept., 1965.

90th Congress, 1967–69

Atomic energy. Agreement on the cooperation for civil uses. State Dept., June 12, 1968.

Background notes [revised]. State Dept., January 1968.

Background notes [revised]. State Dept., August 1970.

Benedict, John A. Economy, basic data. Bureau of International Commerce, January 1967.

Economic trends and their application for the U.S. International Commerce Bureau, April 1, 1969.

Economic trends and their application for the U.S. International Commerce Bureau, Commerce Dept., November 14, 1969.

House hearings on immigration [effect of 1965 law]. (91-1) December 10, 1969.

House Judiciary Committee. Hearings on making additional visas available to immigrants (90-2). Done on effect of act of October 3, 1965, July 3, September. 18, 1968.

Ireland. Immigration quotas increase and redistribution (91-1), December 10. 1969, H2569-1.

Ireland. Nuclear fuel and research agreements with foreign governments (90), March and June 1968, S1935-2.

Ireland. United States immigration policy impact on Irish immigrants (90-2), July and September 1968, H2381-5.

Ireland-United States Council for Commerce and Industry. Balance of payment deficit reduction via import restrictions and foreign travel taxes (90-2), February and March 1968, H2318-2-C.

Irish Immigration Committee of Northern Ohio. National origins quota system abolition, review (90-2), July and September 1968, H2381-5.

Mineral yearbooks, chapter 12802. Mines Bureau, Interior Dept., 1967.

Romier, A. Russell. Foreign trade regulations. Bureau of International Commerce, December 1969.

Sorenson, Roger A., and Edward A. Teshe. Selling in the Republic of Ireland. Bureau of International Commerce, April 1970.

Svedja, George J. Irish immigration in construction of the Erie Canal. National Park Service, Interior Dept., May 19, 1969.

92d Congress, 1971–73

Background notes [revised]. State Dept., Oct. 1972.

Economic trends and their implications for the U.S. International Commerce Bureau, March 26 and November 22, 1971, May 17 and November 20, 1972.

Ireland. Family assistance programs, summary (92-2), April 10, 1972, 72 S362-7.

Ireland. Immigration from Ireland and Northern Europe (91-1). December 10, 1969, 70 H521-27.

Ireland. Sugar program and quota amendments, 1971 (92-1), April and June, 71 H161-7.9, 71 S361-5.19.

Northern Ireland. Congressional study mission report (92-2), July 18, 1972, 72 H381-54.

Northern Ireland. Northern Ireland civil conflicts, causes and settlement prospects (92-2), February 28–March 1, 1972, 72 H381-45.

Northern Ireland and Ireland Assistance Act. Foreign aid to Ireland and Northern Ireland, FY86-90 authorization.

Northern Ireland Civil Rights Association. Northern Ireland civil conflict, causes and settlement prospects (92-2), February 28–March 1, 1972, 72 H381-45.17.

Northern Ireland Service Council. Northern Ireland civil conflict, causes and settlement prospects (92-2), March 1, 1972, 72 H381-45.13.

93d Congress, 1973–74

Background notes [revised]. State Dept., Oct. 1974.

Economic trends and their implications for the U.S., International Commerce Bureau, May 23 and November 23, 1973, June and December 1974.

Ireland. European Economic Community membership impact on United Sates feed grain exports (93-1), May 23, 1973, 73 H781-23.4.

Ireland. International protection of human rights (93-1), October 10, 1973, 74 H381-26.18.

Ireland. Offshore terminal Bantry Bay, tour report (93-1), June/July 1973, 74 H561-1.

Ireland. Sugar Act extension and revision (93-2), May 17, 1974, 74 H1673-6.

Ireland. Terrorism prevention and control (93-2), August 15, 1974, 75 H481-3.4.

Marketing. Domestic and International Business Administration, Commerce Dept., November 1974.

Northern Ireland. Grand jury venue, "Fort Worth Five" case (93-1), March 13, 1973, 73 H521-7.

Northern Ireland. United Nations Commission on Human rights and United States role, review (93-2), June 20, 1974, 75 H381-4.2.

94th Congress, 1975–76

Background notes. State Dept., October 1976.

Economic trends and their implications for the U.S., International Commerce Bureau, June and December 1975, December 1976.

Ireland. Congressional meeting with European Parliament, April 1976 (94-2), June 1976, 76 H462-28.

Ireland. United States tourist visa denial for suspected IRA members (94), June 11, 12, 1975, 77 H521-17.1.

Northern Ireland. Extradition treaty with Great Britain and Northern Ireland, presidential message (94-2), February 3, 1976, 76 S385-1.

Northern Ireland. Extradition treaty with Great Britain and Northern Ireland, Senate advice and consent (94-20), June 15, 1976, 76 S384-5.

Northern Ireland. Income tax convention with Great Britain and Northern Ireland, presidential message (94-2), June 24, 1976, 76 S 385-11.

Northern Ireland. Tax convention with Great Britain and Northern Ireland, presidential message (94-2), September 22, 1976, 76 S 385-17.

95th Congress, 1977–79

Background notes. State Dept., December 1978.

McGovern, George S. Ireland in 1977. Senate Foreign Relations Committee (95-1), August 1977.

Marketing in Ireland. Commerce Dept., Industry and Trade Administration, May 1978.

Northern Ireland. Congressional study mission report (95-1), August 1977, 77 S382-32.

Northern Ireland. Estate and income tax convention with United States, 1946 hearings excerpt (95-10), July 20, 1977, 78 S381-10.8.

Northern Ireland. Human rights situation, political and economic conditions, and United States visa policy implications (95-2), December 1978, H522-9.

Northern Ireland. Peace prospects, congressional study mission report (95-2), 1978, 78 H462-26.

Northern Ireland. Tax convention with Great Britain and Northern Ireland (95-2), April 25, 1978, 78 S384-2.

Northern Ireland. Tax convention with Great Britain and Northern Ireland, presidential message (95-1), June 6, 1977, 77 S3485-10.

96th Congress, 1979–80

Country, Labor Profile. Labor Dept. Bureau of International Labor Affairs. 1979.

Ireland. "Comparison of Eight Foreign Government Tourism Programs" (96-1), July 13, 1979, H502-36.

Ireland. Congressional study mission report (96-1), March 8, 1979, H202-14.

Ireland. Foreign countries small business programs (96-1), October 1979, H722-7.

Ireland. VA pension beneficiaries overseas, income and benefit characteristics study (96-2), June 24, 1980, H762-12.

Northern Ireland. Estate and gift tax convention with United States (96-1), May 3, 1979, S385-15.

Northern Ireland. Estate and gift tax convention with United States (96-1), June 15, 1979, S384-4.

Northern Ireland. Estate and gift tax convention with United States, description (96-1), July 4, 1979, S382-28.

Northern Ireland. Foreign treatment of United States banks abroad (96-2), October 1980, S242-14.

Northern Ireland. Income, estate, and gift tax conventions with United States (96-1), June 6, 1979, S381-23.

Northern Ireland. Income tax convention with United States, third protocol (96-1), April 23, 1979, S385-14.

Northern Ireland. Income tax convention with United States, third protocol (96-1), June 15, 1979, S384-3.

Northern Ireland. Income tax convention with United States, third protocol description (96-1), June 4, 1979, S382-29.

Northern Ireland. United Kingdom—United States nuclear cooperation of defense (96-2), April 2, 1980, S383-3.

Northern Ireland. United States weapons sale to Northern Ireland police (96-1), July 12, 1979, H381-8.1.

97th Congress, 1981–83

Northern Ireland. Civil conflict, congressional study mission report (97-1), July 1981, S382-17.

Pell, Clairborne. Irish Unification question. State Foreign Relations Committee (97-1), July 1981.

98th Congress, 1983–85

Ireland. Extradition treaty with U.S., presidential message (98-2), April 24, 1984, S385-7.

Ireland. Extradition treaty with U.S., Senate advice and consent (98-2), June 20, 1984, S384-12.

99th Congress, 1985–87

Ireland. Foreign aid to Ireland and Northern Ireland, FY86–FY90 authorization, presidential message (99-2), March 5, 1986, 3 H380-5.

Ireland. Foreign aid to Ireland and Northern Ireland, supplemental appropriation. FY86, presidential communication (99-2), March 5, 1986, 3 H180-17.

Ireland, Foreign aid to Ireland and Northern Ireland Fy86-Fy87 authorization (99-2), June 19, 1986, 6 S 383-4.

Ireland. Foreign aid to Ireland and Northern Ireland, supplemental appropriations, FY86, presidential communication (99-2), March 5, 1986, 3 H180-17.

Irish Republican Army. Extradition treaty with Great Britain and Northern Ireland, terrorist provisions, legal and constitutional aspects (99-1), November 5, 1985, 6 S521-40.

Northern Ireland. Extradition treaty with United States, Senate advice and consent (99-2), July 8, 1986, S 384-5.

Northern Ireland. Extradition treaty with United States, Presidential message (99-1), July 17, 1985, S385-8.

Northern Ireland. Foreign aid to Ireland and Northern Ireland, FY86–FY87 authorization (99-2), June 19, 1986, 6 S383-4.

Northern Ireland. Extradition treaty with United States, terrorist provisions, legal and constitutional aspects (99-10), November 5, 1985, 6 S521-40.

Northern Ireland. Foreign aid to Ireland and Northern Ireland, FY86–FY90 authorization, presidential message (99-2), March 5, 1986, 3 H380-5.

Section IV
Statistical Overview

All sources of statistics should be used with caution. The methods used to count immigrants differed between agencies during the same year and from year to year. For example, some agencies for some years enumerated only those whose last residence was Ireland; in other years they added Irish arrivals who had made an interim stop in another country or they considered as first-time immigrants the relatively large number of arrivals returning from a visit to Ireland. For example, Table 2 below enumerates only those newcomers arriving from Ireland for the first time, whereas for many years over the early twentieth century Table 13 presents data on all arrivals from Ireland, thus including immigrants returning to the U.S. after a visit to the homeland. Since there was no way on Table 13 to subtract the total number of Irish visitors from the total of Irish immigrants arriving for the first time, Table 13 totals for many years differ significantly from Table 2 totals for the same years. Users of these, and all other tables, should read carefully the exact techniques used by the agency that collected the data on which the table is based (listed in Sources of Tables, which follows tables). Researchers should see also articles listed in chapter 2 dealing with accuracy of data.

List of Tables

1. Immigrants from Ireland for period indicated, together with Irish-born and Irish parentage in U.S.

2. Immigrants from Ireland to the U.S., by year, 1820–1985

3. Irish-born in the U.S.: by U.S. census region and state, 1850–1920

4. Irish and Northern Irish in the U.S., by census region and state, 1930–1980

5. Regional distribution of Irish immigrants in the U.S., 1850–1980

6. Irish-born for selected years in fifteen cities of largest Irish population in 1890

7. Irish-born by area of origin in selected major U.S. cities, 1930–1980

8. Emigrants in selected occupational groups as a percentage of all emigrants over 15 years of age declaring an occupation, 1851–1855 and 1875–1880

9. Immigrants from Ireland to the U.S. by selected occupational categories, 1875–1910

10. Immigrants from Ireland to the U.S. by major occupational group, 1911–1932

11. Immigrants from Ireland to the U.S. by declared occupation, 1951–1975

12. Immigrants from Ireland to the U.S. by declared occupation, 1976–1985

13. Irish immigrants to the U.S., by gender and year, 1869–1985

14. Irish ancestry by state and census region, 1980 U.S. census.

15. Naturalization status of Irish on 1980 U.S. census.

16. Year of arrival of Irish-born on 1980 U.S. census for selected years

17. Population of Ireland, by county and province, 1821–1911

18. Population of Ireland, by county and province, 1926–1986

19. Ireland: Religion at each census of population, 1881–1971

20. Ireland: Irish speakers on each census, by province, 1861–1971

21. Population change by county and province in pre-famine Ireland, 1821–1841

22. Ireland: population change by county and province, 1841–1911

23. Emigration from Ireland by county and province, 1851–1911

24. Emigration from Ireland by province for each year, 1851–1920

25. U.S. Citizens enumerated on censuses of Ireland, 1871–1986

26. Destination of overseas emigrants from Ireland, 1841–1952

27. Distribution of emigrants from Ireland by selected age groups and percent of total, 1852–1921

28. Emigrants from Ireland by marital condition, 1883–1920

29. Ireland: Population, natural increase, emigration, and overall changes, 1881–1979

30. Population of Northern Ireland by county, 1926–1971

Table 1. *Immigrants from Ireland for Period Indicated, Together with Irish-born and Irish Parentage in U.S.*

	(1) Arriving from Ireland over census period	(2) Irish-born at end of decade	(3) Irish parentage at end of decade
1821–30	50,724	n/a	n/a
1831–40	207,381	n/a	n/a
1841–50	780,719	961,719	n/a
1851–60	914,119	1,611,304	n/a
1861–70	435,778	1,855,827	n/a
1871–80	436,871	1,854,571	3,238,580
1881–90	655,482	1,871,509	2,924,172
1891–1900	388,416	1,615,459	3,375,546
1901–10	339,065	1,352,251	3,304,015
1911–20	146,181	1,037,234	3,122,013
1921–30	210,024	744,810	2,341,712
1931–40	10,973	572,031	1,838,920
1941–50	19,789	505,285	1,891,495
1951–60	48,362	338,722	1,434,590
1961–70	32,966	251,375	1,198,845
1971–80	14,230	198,943	n/a
1981–85	5,336	n/a	n/a

Table 2. *Immigrants from Ireland to the U.S., by Year, 1820–1985*

Year	Number	Year	Number	Year	Number	Year	Number
1820	3,614	1862	23,351	1904	36,142	1946	1,816
1821	1,518	1863	55,916	1905	52,945	1947	2,574
1822	2,267	1864	63,523	1906	34,995	1948	7,534
1823	1,908	1865	29,772	1907	34,530	1949	8,678
1824	2,345	1866	36,690	1908	30,556	1940–49	22,500
1825	4,888	1867	72,879	1909	25,033	1950	5,842
1826	5,408	1868	32,068	1900–09	344,940	1951	3,144
1827	9,766	1869	40,786	1910	29,855	1952	3,526
1828	12,488	1860–69	427,419	1911	29,112	1953	4,304
1829	7,415	1870	56,996	1912	25,879	1954	4,655
1820–29	51,617	1871	57,439	1913	27,876	1955	5,222
1830	2,721	1872	68,732	1914	24,688	1956	5,607
1831	5,772	1873	77,344	1915	14,185	1957	8,227
1832	12,436	1874	53,707	1916	8,639	1958	9,134
1833	8,648	1875	37,957	1917	5,406	1959	6,595
1834	24,474	1876	19,575	1918	331	1950–59	56,256
1835	20,927	1877	14,569	1919	474	1960	6,918
1836	30,578	1878	15,932	1910–19	166,445	1961	5,738
1837	28,508	1879	20,013	1920	9,591	1962	5,118
1838	12,645	1870–79	422,264	1921	28,435	1963	5,746
1839	23,963	1880	71,603	1922	10,579	1964	6,055
1830–39	170,672	1881	72,342	1923	15,740	1965	5,187
1840	39,430	1882	76,432	1924	17,111	1966	3,267
1841	37,772	1883	81,486	1925	26,650	1967	2,765
1842	51,342	1884	63,344	1926	24,897	1968	2,995
1843	19,670	1885	51,795	1927	28,545	1969	1,981
1844	33,490	1886	49,619	1928	25,268	1960–69	45,770
1845	44,821	1887	68,370	1929	19,921	1970	1,583
1846	51,752	1888	73,513	1920–29	206,737	1971	1,614
1847	105,536	1889	65,557	1930	23,445	1972	1,780
1848	112,934	1880–89	674,061	1931	7,305	1973	2,000
1849	159,398	1890	53,024	1932	539	1974	1,572
1840–49	656,145	1891	55,706	1933	338	1975	1,285
1850	164,004	1892	51,383	1934	443	1976	1,171
1851	221,253	1893	43,578	1935	454	1977	1,238
1852	159,548	1894	30,231	1936	444	1978	1,180
1853	162,649	1895	46,304	1937	531	1979	982
1854	101,606	1896	40,262	1938	1,085	1970–79	14,405
1855	49,627	1897	28,421	1939	1,189	1980	1,006
1856	54,349	1898	25,128	1930–39	35,773	1981	902
1857	54,361	1899	31,673	1940	839	1982	949
1858	26,873	1890–99	405,710	1941	272	1983	1,101
1859	35,216	1900	35,730	1942	83	1984	1,096
1850–59	1,029,486	1901	30,561	1943	165	1985	1,288
1860	48,637	1902	29,138	1944	112	1980–85	6,342
1861	23,797	1903	35,310	1945	427		

Table 3. Irish-born in U.S.: by U.S. Census Region and State, 1850–1920

	1850	1860	1870	1880	1890	1900	1910	1920
NORTHEAST								
New England								
Connecticut	26,689	55,445	70,630	70,638	77,880	70,994	58,457	45,464
Maine	13,871	15,290	15,745	13,421	11,444	10,159	7,890	5,748
Massachusetts	115,917	185,426	216,120	226,700	259,902	249,916	222,862	183,171
New Hampshire	8,811	12,737	12,190	13,052	14,890	13,547	10,613	7,908
Rhode Island	15,944	25,285	31,534	35,281	38,920	35,501	29,715	22,253
Vermont	15,377	13,480	14,080	11,657	9,810	7,453	4,938	2,884
Subtotal	196,609	307,663	360,299	370,749	412,846	387,570	334,475	267,428
Mid-Atlantic								
New Jersey	31,092	62,006	86,784	93,079	101,059	94,844	82,749	65,971
New York	343,111	498,134	528,806	499,445	483,375	425,553	367,877	284,747
Pennsylvania	151,723	201,939	235,798	236,505	243,836	205,909	165,091	121,601
Subtotal	525,926	762,079	851,388	829,029	828,270	726,306	615,717	472,319
TOTAL	722,535	1,069,742	1,211,687	1,199,778	1,241,116	1,113,876	950,192	739,747
NORTH CENTRAL								
East North Central								
Illinois	27,786	87,573	120,162	117,343	124,498	114,563	93,451	74,274
Indiana	12,787	24,495	28,698	25,741	20,819	16,306	11,266	7,271
Ohio	51,562	76,826	82,674	78,927	70,127	55,018	40,057	29,262
Michigan	13,430	30,049	42,013	43,413	39,065	29,182	20,434	16,531
Wisconsin	21,043	49,961	48,479	41,907	33,306	23,544	14,049	7,809
Subtotal	126,608	268,904	322,026	307,331	287,815	238,613	179,257	135,147
West North Central								
Iowa	4,885	28,072	40,124	44,061	37,353	28,321	17,756	10,686
Kansas	—	3,888	10,940	14,993	15,870	11,516	8,100	4,825
Minnesota	271	12,831	21,746	25,942	28,011	22,428	15,859	10,289
Missouri	14,734	43,464	54,983	48,898	40,966	31,832	23,290	15,022
Nebraska	—	1,431	4,999	10,133	15,963	11,127	8,124	5,422

continued

Table 3. (cont'd)

	1850	1860	1870	1880	1890	1900	1910	1920
North Dakota	—	42	888	4,104	2,967	2,670	2,498	1,660
South Dakota	—	—	—	—	4,774	3,298	2,980	1,954
Subtotal	19,890	89,728	133,680	148,131	145,904	111,192	78,607	49,858
TOTAL	146,498	358,632	455,706	455,462	433,719	349,805	257,864	185,005
SOUTH								
South Atlantic								
Delaware	3,153	5,832	5,907	5,791	6,121	5,044	3,984	2,895
Florida	878	827	737	652	1,056	797	1,069	1,304
Georgia	3,202	6,586	5,093	4,148	3,374	2,293	1,655	1,112
Maryland	19,557	24,872	23,630	21,865	18,735	13,874	9,701	6,580
North Carolina	567	888	677	611	451	371	304	301
South Carolina	4,051	4,906	3,262	2,626	1,665	1,131	675	442
Virginia	—	—	5,191	4,835	4,578	3,534	2,450	1,732
West Virginia	11,643	16,501	6,832	6,459	4,799	3,342	2,290	1,459
Dist. of Columbia	2,373	7,258	8,218	7,840	7,224	6,220	5,343	4,320
Subtotal	45,784	67,670	59,547	54,827	48,003	36,606	27,471	20,145
East South Central								
Alabama	3,639	5,664	3,893	2,966	2,604	1,792	1,167	809
Kentucky	9,466	22,249	21,642	18,256	13,926	9,864	5,913	3,422
Mississippi	1,928	3,893	3,359	2,753	1,865	1,264	747	412
Tennessee	2,640	12,498	8,048	5,975	5,016	3,372	2,296	1,291
Subtotal	17,673	44,304	36,942	29,950	23,411	16,302	10,123	5,934
West South Central								
Arkansas	514	1,312	1,428	2,431	2,021	1,345	1,077	676
Louisiana	24,266	28,153	17,068	13,807	9,236	6,436	3,753	2,000
Oklahoma	—	—	—	—	329	1,384	1,800	1,321
Texas	1,403	3,480	4,031	8,103	8,201	6,173	5,355	4,333
Subtotal	26,183	32,945	22,527	24,341	19,787	15,338	11,985	8,330
TOTAL	89,640	144,919	119,016	109,118	91,201	68,246	49,579	34,409

continued

Table 3. (cont'd)

	1850	1860	1870	1880	1890	1900	1910	1920
WEST								
Mountain States								
Arizona	—	—	495	1,296	1,171	1,159	1,550	1,206
Colorado	—	624	1,685	8,263	12,352	10,132	8,710	6,191
Idaho	—	—	986	981	1,917	1,633	1,782	1,410
Montana	—	—	1,635	2,408	6,648	9,436	9,469	7,260
Nevada	—	651	5,035	5,191	2,646	1,425	1,702	970
New Mexico	292	827	543	795	966	692	644	434
Utah	106	278	502	1,321	2,045	1,516	1,656	1,207
Wyoming	—	—	1,102	1,093	1,900	1,591	1,359	956
Subtotal	398	2,380	11,983	21,348	29,645	27,584	26,872	19,634
Pacific States								
California	2,452	33,147	54,421	62,962	63,138	44,476	52,475	45,308
Oregon	196	1,267	1,967	3,659	4,891	4,210	4,995	4,203
Washington	—	1,217	1,047	2,243	7,799	7,262	10,178	8,927
Subtotal	2,648	35,631	57,435	68,864	75,828	55,948	67,648	58,438
TOTAL	3,046	38,011	69,418	90,212	105,473	83,532	94,520	78,072
UNITED STATES	961,719	1,611,304	1,855,827	1,854,570	1,871,509	1,615,459	1,352,155	1,037,233

Table 4. *Irish and Northern Irish in the U.S., by Census Region and State, 1930–1980*

	1930	1940	1950	1960	1970	1980
NORTHEAST						
New England						
Connecticut						
NI	7,090	3,717	701	2,278	1,304	671
Eire	31,328	23,837	19,865	12,262	9,456	1,784
Total	38,418	27,554	20,566	14,540	10,760	2,455
Maine						
NI	827	406	68	176	127	63
Eire	3,288	2,688	2,058	1,219	732	570
Total	4,115	3,094	2,126	1,395	859	633
Massachusetts						
NI	20,378	10,536	1,958	4,848	2,791	1,007
Eire	138,366	103,388	81,214	51,428	33,967	23,155
Total	158,744	113,924	83,172	56,276	36,758	24,162
New Hampshire						
NI	1,010	576	139	191	45	50
Eire	4,807	3,320	2,414	1,221	747	726
Total	5,817	3,896	2,553	1,412	792	776
Rhode Island						
NI	3,845	1,983	184	790	361	107
Eire	13,895	10,099	8,126	4,426	2,609	1,758
Total	17,740	12,082	8,310	5,216	2,970	1,865
Vermont						
NI	377	139	18	87	40	18
Eire	1,429	904	627	327	311	201
Total	1,806	1,043	645	414	351	219
Mid-Atlantic						
New Jersey						
NI	15,750	8,872	1,419	6,672	4,356	1,788
Eire	47,486	35,830	33,113	22,386	18,186	15,873
Total	63,236	44,702	34,532	29,058	22,542	17,661
New York						
NI	41,521	30,432	4,171	18,749	10,651	3,418
Eire	251,704	205,323	182,581	131,764	93,818	66,639
Total	293,225	235,755	186,752	150,513	104,469	70,057
Pennsylvania						
NI	35,288	19,495	1,541	9,388	5,046	1,393
Eire	62,312	46,331	44,844	22,534	14,971	11,167
Total	97,600	65,826	46,385	31,922	20,017	12,560
NORTHEAST TOTAL						
NI	126,086	76,156	10,199	43,179	24,721	8,515
Eire	554,615	431,720	374,842	247,567	174,797	121,873
Total	680,701	507,876	385,041	290,746	199,518	130,388

continued

Table 4. (*cont'd*)

	1930	1940	1950	1960	1970	1980
NORTH CENTRAL						
East North Central						
Illinois						
NI	10,054	6,559	967	3,554	1,797	857
Eire	57,208	41,947	36,075	26,880	19,579	15,449
Total	67,262	48,506	37,042	30,434	21,376	16,306
Indiana						
NI	1,045	541	58	499	328	147
Eire	3,931	2,657	2,352	1,673	1,152	825
Total	4,976	3,198	2,410	2,172	1,480	972
Ohio						
NI	5,028	2,418	399	1,835	854	526
Eire	17,879	12,816	11,146	7,184	5,086	3,856
Total	22,907	15,234	11,545	9,019	5,940	8,949
Michigan						
NI	6,138	3,601	576	3,014	1,585	852
Eire	11,390	8,905	9,958	5,582	4,362	3,715
Total	17,528	12,506	10,534	8,596	5,947	4,567
Wisconsin						
NI	1,057	508	79	414	257	162
Eire	3,473	2,236	1,808	945	977	734
Total	4,530	2,744	1,887	1,359	1,234	896
West North Central						
Iowa						
NI	1,778	747	57	395	135	135
Eire	4,179	2,671	2,066	769	534	374
Total	5,957	3,418	2,123	1,164	669	509
Kansas						
NI	780	278	26	134	75	38
Eire	1,921	1,197	963	496	388	317
Total	2,701	1,475	989	630	463	355
Minnesota						
NI	1,403	689	134	358	293	111
Eire	5,095	3,520	2,693	1,398	1,003	864
Total	6,498	4,219	2,827	1,756	1,296	975
Missouri						
NI	1,308	676	60	304	179	138
Eire	8,561	5,582	4,181	2,513	1,567	1,274
Total	9,869	6,258	4,241	2,817	1,746	1,412
Nebraska						
NI	801	337	34	119	77	42
Eire	2,502	1,514	1,058	500	343	219
Total	3,303	1,851	1,092	619	420	261
North Dakota						
NI	329	165	22	49	19	2
Eire	863	528	417	221	132	102
Total	1,192	693	439	270	151	104
South Dakota						
NI	351	147	20	72	—	7
Eire	862	573	457	161	91	96
Total	1,213	720	477	233	91	103
NORTH CENTRAL TOTAL						
NI	30,072	16,666	2,432	10,747	5,599	2,870
Eire	117,864	84,156	73,174	48,322	35,214	27,000
Total	147,936	100,822	75,606	59,069	40,813	29,870

continued

Table 4. (*cont'd*)

	1930	1940	1950	1960	1970	1980
SOUTH						
South Atlantic						
Delaware						
NI	900	372	54	242	122	57
Eire	1,364	1,274	1,103	606	522	455
Total	2,264	1,646	1,157	848	644	512
Florida						
NI	534	486	161	1,690	1,502	1,348
Eire	1,309	1,751	3,224	4,408	5,309	7,338
Total	1,843	2,237	3,385	6,098	6,811	8,686
Georgia						
NI	147	73	33	140	105	169
Eire	546	417	437	389	549	517
Total	693	490	470	529	654	686
Maryland						
NI	813	376	37	526	495	232
Eire	4,032	3,007	2,811	2,202	2,494	1,995
Total	4,845	3,383	2,848	2,728	2,989	2,227
North Carolina						
NI	63	66	24	145	121	182
Eire	253	211	311	268	380	492
Total	316	277	335	413	501	674
South Carolina						
NI	90	50	19	81	92	164
Eire	185	132	202	188	126	314
Total	275	182	221	269	218	478
Virginia						
NI	375	207	71	476	319	397
Eire	789	690	948	945	1,233	1,409
Total	1,164	897	1,019	1,421	1,552	1,806
West Virginia						
NI	222	87	19	86	57	35
Eire	659	455	393	235	198	175
Total	881	542	412	321	255	210
Dist. of Columbia						
NI	493	432	65	122	51	33
Eire	3,026	2,326	2,067	1,005	506	338
Total	3,519	2,758	2,132	1,127	557	371
East South Central						
Alabama						
NI	162	49	17	68	18	137
Eire	413	308	327	243	358	214
Total	575	357	344	311	376	351
Kentucky						
NI	191	101	17	107	49	63
Eire	1,656	892	667	437	309	332
Total	1,847	993	684	544	358	395
Mississippi						
NI	54	33	8	30	32	45
Eire	198	161	173	159	133	182
Total	252	194	181	189	165	227
Tennessee						
NI	160	72	14	63	67	93
Eire	491	326	328	176	192	286
Total	651	398	342	239	259	379

continued

Table 4. (*cont'd*)

	1930	1940	1950	1960	1970	1980
West South Central						
Arkansas						
NI	100	52	11	29	18	56
Eire	354	225	202	108	157	120
Total	434	277	213	137	175	176
Louisiana						
NI	234	120	16	111	137	118
Eire	970	691	709	563	592	471
Total	1,204	811	725	674	729	589
Oklahoma						
NI	262	107	15	94	83	44
Eire	690	371	358	203	312	285
Total	952	478	373	297	395	329
Texas						
NI	616	308	59	454	444	547
Eire	2,907	2,302	2,384	2,228	1,798	2,182
Total	3,523	2,610	2,443	2,682	2,242	2,729
SOUTH TOTAL						
NI	5,416	2,991	640	4,464	3,712	3,690
Eire	19,842	15,539	16,644	14,363	15,168	17,053
Total	25,258	18,530	17,284	18,827	18,880	20,743
WEST						
Mountain States						
Arizona						
NI	235	98	22	202	93	226
Eire	653	523	660	610	691	1,145
Total	888	621	682	812	784	1,371
Colorado						
NI	900	398	48	237	101	103
Eire	3,184	2,120	1,600	894	847	830
Total	4,084	2,518	1,648	1,131	948	933
Idaho						
NI	284	103	24	96	53	29
Eire	616	466	376	172	146	191
Total	900	569	400	268	199	220
Montana						
NI	1,095	649	55	201	47	25
Eire	3,950	2,618	2,003	938	471	239
Total	5,045	3,267	2,058	1,139	518	264
Nevada						
NI	155	74	16	71	23	56
Eire	463	324	270	202	201	474
Total	618	398	286	273	224	530
New Mexico						
NI	91	29	5	56	34	23
Eire	218	164	202	188	213	236
Total	309	193	207	244	247	259
Utah						
NI	234	93	31	95	83	36
Eire	584	362	320	139	91	152
Total	818	455	351	234	174	188
Wyoming						
NI	179	96	15	49	15	12
Eire	584	456	383	254	120	181
Total	763	552	398	303	135	193

continued

Table 4. (*cont'd*)

	1930	1940	1950	1960	1970	1980
Pacific States						
California						
NI	10,892	7,168	1,611	7,258	5,458	3,350
Eire	34,493	27,631	28,405	21,340	20,342	19,297
Total	45,385	34,799	30,016	28,598	25,800	22,647
Oregon						
NI	1,039	566	141	376	208	204
Eire	2,802	2,194	2,179	1,378	1,004	982
Total	3,841	2,760	2,320	1,754	1,212	1,186
Washington						
NI	2,154	1,329	159	1,039	626	454
Eire	4,942	3,758	3,903	2,158	1,841	1,623
Total	7,096	5,087	4,062	3,297	2,467	2,077
WEST TOTAL						
NI	17,258	10,603	2,127	9,680	6,741	4,518
Eire	52,489	40,616	40,301	28,273	25,967	23,350
Total	69,747	51,219	42,428	37,953	32,708	27,868
UNITED STATES						
NI	178,832	106,416	15,398	68,070	40,773	19,593
Eire	744,810	572,031	504,961	338,525	251,146	189,276
Total	923,642	678,447	520,359	406,595	291,919	208,869

298 Statistical Overview

Table 5. *Regional Distribution of Irish Immigrants in the U.S., 1850–1980*

	Northeast		Central		South		West		Total
	No.	%	No.	%	No.	%	No.	%	
1850	722,535	75	146,498	15	89,640	9	3,444	1	962,117
1860	1,069,742	66	358,632	22	144,919	9	40,391	3	1,613,684
1870	1,211,687	65	455,706	24	119,016	6	81,401	4	1,867,810
1880	1,199,778	64	455,462	24	109,119	6	111,560	6	1,875,919
1890	1,241,116	65	433,719	23	91,201	5	135,118	7	1,901,154
1900	1,113,876	68	349,805	21	68,246	4	111,116	7	1,643,043
1910	950,192	69	257,864	19	49,579	4	121,392	9	1,379,027
1920	739,747	70	185,005	18	34,409	3	97,706	9	1,056,867
1930	554,615	73	117,864	16	19,842	3	62,741	8	755,062
1940	431,720	75	84,520	15	15,539	3	47,649	8	579,428
1950	374,842	73	73,174	14	16,644	3	46,115	9	510,775
1960	247,567	72	48,322	14	14,363	4	31,670	9	341,922
1970	174,797	69	35,214	14	15,168	6	28,747	11	253,926
1980	127,267	64	27,825	14	17,053	9	26,798	13	198,943

Table 6. *Irish-born for Selected Years in Fifteen Cities of Largest Irish Population in 1890*

	1850	1860	1870	1880	1890	1900	1910	1920
New York	133,730	260,450	275,984	277,409	275,156	275,102	252,672	203,450
Philadelphia	72,312	95,548	96,698	101,808	110,935	98,427	83,196	64,590
Boston	35,287	45,991	56,900	64,793	71,441	70,147	66,041	57,011
Chicago	6,096	19,889	39,988	44,411	70,028	73,912	65,969	56,786
San Francisco	N/A	9,363	25,864	30,721	30,718	15,963	23,153	18,257
Pittsburg	N/A	9,297	13,119	17,110	26,643	23,690	18,873	13,989
St. Louis	9,719	29,926	23,329	29,536	24,270	19,421	14,262	9,244
Jersey City	N/A	7,380	17,665	30,390	22,159	19,314	16,124	12,451
Providence	7,635	9,534	12,085	13,939	19,040	18,686	15,801	11,900
Cleveland	N/A	5,479	9,964	11,958	13,512	13,120	11,316	9,478
Baltimore	12,057	15,536	15,223	14,238	13,389	9,690	6,806	5,074
Newark	5,564	11,167	12,481	13,451	13,234	12,792	11,225	8,840
Cincinnati	14,393	19,375	18,624	15,077	12,323	9,114	6,224	3,887
Buffalo	N/A	9,279	11,264	10,310	11,664	11,292	9,423	7,264
New Orleans	20,200	24,398	14,693	11,708	7,923	5,398	2,996	1,543
Total 15 cities	316,993	572,612	643,881	686,859	722,435	676,068	604,081	483,764
U.S. Total Irish	961,719	1,611,304	1,855,827	1,854,571	1,871,509	1,615,459	1,352,251	1,037,234
% Irish in 15 Cities	33	36	35	37	39	42	45	47

Table 7. *Irish-born by Area of Origin in Selected Major U.S. Cities, 1930–1980*

	1930	1940	1960	1970	1980
Baltimore					
NI	568	228	286	62	31
Eire	3,076	2,159	1,380	433	311
Total	3,644	2,387	1,666	495	342
Boston					
NI	6,449	2,724	3,099	532	68
Eire	43,932	34,783	38,741	12,362	6,477
Total	50,381	37,507	41,840	12,894	6,545
Buffalo					
NI	912	636	812	129	11
Eire	5,103	3,620	2,472	727	455
Total	6,015	4,256	3,284	856	466
Chicago					
NI	7,404	5,152	3,194	943	343
Eire	47,385	35,156	25,795	13,766	8,372
Total	54,789	40,308	28,989	14,709	8,715
Cincinnati					
NI	300	114	55	13	8
Eire	2,054	1,271	875	217	249
Total	2,354	1,385	930	230	257
Cleveland					
NI	1,372	825	791	178	30
Eire	6,842	5,112	4,238	1,370	679
Total	8,214	5,937	5,029	1,548	709
Detroit					
NI	3,524	2,211	2,224	447	72
Eire	6,293	4,760	4,402	1,600	680
Total	9,817	6,971	6,626	2,047	752
Jersey City					
NI	1,822	899	1,295	172	21
Eire	8,741	6,028	5,198	1,772	879
Total	10,563	6,927	6,493	1,944	900
Los Angeles					
NI	2,212	1,646	3,529	774	466
Eire	5,000	4,194	7,321	3,052	2,230
Total	7,212	5,840	10,850	3,826	2,696
Louisville					
NI	78	49	23	13	0
Eire	836	445	208	59	41
Total	914	494	231	72	41
New Orleans					
NI	184	91	44	20	35
Eire	647	420	241	164	76
Total	831	511	285	184	111
Newark					
NI	1,301	702	1,774	123	14
Eire	6,279	4,597	7,969	860	268
Total	7,580	5,299	9,743	983	282
New York					
NI	27,821	21,501	15,516	6,604	1,409
Eire	192,810	160,325	119,280	68,778	41,354
Total	220,631	181,826	134,796	75,382	42,763

continued

Table 7. (*cont'd*)

	1930	1940	1960	1970	1980
Omaha					
NI	266	101	49	34	23
Eire	993	635	342	151	53
Total	1,259	736	391	185	76
Philadelphia					
NI	20,582	11,237	7,956	2,016	393
Eire	31,359	24,826	17,745	6,060	3,314
Total	51,941	36,063	25,701	8,076	3,707
Providence					
NI	1,709	788	790	97	25
Eire	7,922	5,659	4,175	945	389
Total	9,631	6,447	4,965	1,042	414
St. Louis					
NI	555	355	188	24	8
Eire	5,057	3,217	1,900	498	253
Total	5,612	3,572	2,088	522	261
San Francisco					
NI	2,696	1,778	2,121	388	137
Eire	13,902	10,271	9,254	4,420	2,863
Total	16,598	12,049	11,375	4,808	3,000
Washington D.C.					
NI	493	432	432	51	33
Eire	3,026	2,326	2,099	506	338
Total	3,519	2,758	2,531	557	371
Selected cities total	471,505	361,273	297,813	130,360	64,579
Total Irish in U.S.	744,810	572,031	338,722	251,375	198,943
Selected cities % of total	63	63	88	52	32

Table 8. *Emigrants in Selected Occupational Groups as a Percentage of All Irish Emigrants over 15 Years of Age Declaring an Occupation, 1851–1855 and 1875–1880*

	Professional	Skilled/ Industrial Manufac.	Farmers	Laborers/ Servants
1851	2	11	8	79
1852	0	8	4	87
1853	0	7	3	90
1854	0	9	6	84
1855	0	11	1	87
1875	0	15	5	78
1876	1	19	5	72
1877	1	21	7	69
1878	1	14	7	76
1879	1	14	6	77
1880	0	9	6	85

Table 9. *Immigrants from Ireland to the U.S. by Selected Occupational Categories, 1875–1910*

	Professional		Entrepreneurs		Skilled		Farmers		Farm laborers, farm servants		Miscellaneous		
	No.	%	No.	%	No.	%	No.	%	No.	%	No.	%	Total
1875	126	1	253	1	2,586	13	992	5	15,226	78	214	1	19,407
1876	139	1	248	3	1,659	17	517	5	7,172	72	179	2	9,914
1877	90	1	240	3	1,326	18	524	7	5,162	69	142	2	7,484
1878	107	1	214	3	921	11	584	7	6,232	76	164	2	8,222
1879	128	1	224	2	1,214	11	639	6	8,240	77	202	2	10,647
1880	126	0	419	1	3,184	8	2,388	6	35,615	85	168	0	41,900
1881	118	0	392	1	2,707	7	1,648	4	34,093	87	235	1	39,193
1882	131	0	392	1	4,481	10	1,610	4	36,673	84	218	1	43,505
1883	141	0	376	1	5,080	11	1,929	4	39,043	83	235	1	46,804
1884	109	0	290	1	4,174	12	1,524	4	29,724	82	218	1	36,039
1885	122	0	274	1	2,897	10	1,464	5	25,434	83	274	1	30,465
1886	120	0	299	1	2,184	7	1,675	6	25,279	84	359	1	29,916
1887	167	0	333	1	2,959	7	1,876	5	36,053	86	292	1	41,680
1888	205	1	451	1	3,608	9	2,337	6	33,786	82	615	2	41,002
1889	200	1	401	1	3,405	9	2,163	5	33,524	84	360	1	40,053
1890	199	1	398	1	2,520	8	1,525	5	28,312	85	199	1	33,153
1891	242	1	381	1	2,389	7	1,558	5	29,809	86	242	1	34,621
1892	174	1	313	1	2,333	7	1,881	5	29,951	86	174	1	34,826
1893	150	1	301	1	2,617	9	1,985	7	24,752	82	271	1	30,076
1894	152	1	283	1	2,480	11	1,501	7	16,992	78	348	2	21,756
1895	151	1	241	1	3,527	12	1,658	6	23,995	80	573	2	30,145
1896	126	1	202	1	2,958	12	1,391	6	20,127	80	480	2	25,284
1897	109	1	218	1	2,072	10	1,222	6	17,474	80	698	3	21,793
1898	108	1	173	1	1,750	8	1,188	6	17,626	82	756	4	21,601
1899	114	0	172	1	1,802	6	286	1	25,863	90	372	1	28,609
1900	94	0	157	1	1,942	6	282	1	28,562	91	282	1	31,319
1901	121	1	169	1	1,887	8	194	1	21,579	89	242	1	24,192
1902	129	1	180	1	2,163	8	155	1	22,815	89	309	1	25,751
1903	280	1	280	1	3,263	11	466	2	26,324	85	466	2	31,079
1904	581	2	419	1	4,258	13	323	1	26,227	81	452	1	32,260
1905	617	1	617	1	6,364	13	997	2	38,329	81	570	1	47,494
1906	602	2	460	1	5,343	15	991	3	27,354	77	637	2	35,387
1907	529	2	397	1	5,392	16	893	3	25,304	77	562	2	33,077
1908	722	2	42	1	5,116	17	812	3	22,419	75	602	2	30,092
1909	501	2	326	1	3,957	16	676	3	19,236	77	351	1	25,047
1910	607	2	384	1	5,785	18	1,151	4	23,458	73	575	2	31,960

Table 10. *Immigrants from Ireland to the U.S. by Major Occupational Group, 1911–1932*

	Professional		Skilled		Misc. unskilled and others		Total declaring an occupation
	No.	%	No.	%	No.	%	
1911	712	2	6,267	18.7	26,596	79	33,575
1912	N/A		N/A		N/A		N/A
1913	794	3	5,225	17	24,756	80	30,775
1914	922	3	4,453	16	22,407	81	27,782
1915	863	5	3,584	19	14,063	76	18,510
1916	815	5	3,664	24	10,533	70	15,012
1917	693	6	3,268	28	7,779	66	11,740
1918	254	9	1,049	38	1,462	53	2,765
1919	429	9	1,814	37	2,653	54	4,896
1920	906	6	4,005	27	9,667	66	14,578
1921	1,053	3	6,307	20	23,869	76	31,229
1922	702	6	2,748	22	9,019	72	12,469
1923	1,018	5	5,848	27	14,912	68	21,778
1924	1,269	4	8,706	29	19,647	66	29,622
1925	1,264	4	6,269	19	26,069	78	33,602
1926	1,173	4	7,205	22	24,792	75	33,170
1927	1,231	4	7,676	22	26,197	75	35,104
1928	1,086	4	6,358	21	22,171	75	29,615
1929	1,021	4	4,898	21	17,839	75	23,758
1930	1,082	4	5,983	21	21,382	75	28,447
1931	429	5	1,280	16	6,184	78	7,893
1932	171	32	160	30	211	39	542

Table 11. *Immigrants from Ireland to the U.S. by Declared Occupation, 1951–1975*

	1951		1952		1953		1954		1955	
	No.	%	No.	%	No.	%	No.	%	No.	%
Prof. tech. and kindred prof.	352	12	344	12	438	12	445	11	536	12
Farmers and farm managers	97	3	85	3	138	4	181	4	174	4
Managers, officials, owners	51	2	55	2	88	2	83	2	86	2
Clerical and kindred workers	234	8	221	8	251	7	358	9	444	10
Sales workers			41	1	91	3	145	4	172	4
Craftsmen, foremen	179	6	218	8	297	8	416	10	466	11
Operatives	367	11	424	15	525	15	616	15	560	13
Private household workers	965	34	860	31	1,109	31	1,027	26	885	20
Service workers, non-household	255	9	260	9	307	8	238	6	362	8
Farm laborers and foremen	36	1	29	1	74	2	87	2	147	3
Laborers, except farm and mine	316	11	235	8	302	8	427	11	533	12
Total (declaring occups)	2,852	100	2,772	100	3,620	100	4,023	100	4,365	100
Overall total	3,739		3,796		4,655		5,232		5,975	

	1956		1957		1958		1959		1960	
	No.	%	No.	%	No.	%	No.	%	No.	%
Prof. tech. and kindred prof.	671	14	901	13	1,048	14	843	17	911	16
Farmers and farm managers	133	3	301	4	254	3	151	3	180	3
Managers, officials, owners	119	3	181	3	175	2	124	2	138	2
Clerical and kindred workers	475	10	793	12	872	12	585	12	688	12
Sales workers	163	4	286	4	289	4	156	3	199	4
Craftsmen, foremen	552	12	883	13	1,030	14	515	10	571	10
Operatives	654	14	931	14	1,032	14	740	15	814	15
Private household workers	807	17	931	14	707	10	592	12	584	11
Service workers, non-household	300	6	487	7	695	9	574	11	615	11
Farm laborers and foremen	209	4	256	4	363	5	232	5	231	4
Laborers, except farm and mine	571	12	820	12	934	13	509	10	597	11
Total (declaring occups)	4,654	100	6,770	100	7,399	100	5,021	100	5,528	100
Overall total	6,483		9,124		10,383		7,371		7,687	

continued

Table 11. (cont'd)

	1961		1962		1963		1964		1965	
	No.	%	No.	%	No.	%	No.	%	No.	%
Prof. tech. and kindred prof.	787	17	820	21	1,061	23	936	20	921	23
Farmers and farm managers	97	2	53	1	73	2	89	2	91	2
Managers, officials, owners	85	2	83	2	76	2	104	2	77	2
Clerical and kindred workers	633	14	585	15	652	14	742	16	571	14
Sales workers	207	4	132	3	154	3	196	4	107	3
Craftsmen, foremen	497	11	346	9	402	9	446	10	404	10
Operatives	638	14	477	12	510	11	550	12	430	11
Private household workers	547	12	443	11	467	10	425	9	393	10
Service workers, non-household	484	10	464	12	505	11	514	11	498	13
Farm laborers and foremen	216	5	229	6	281	6	246	5	148	4
Laborers, except farm and mine	478	10	324	8	342	8	389	8	320	8
Total (declaring occups)	4,669	100	3,956	100	4,523	100	4,637	100	3,960	100
Overall total	6,541		5,486		6,178		6,307		5,463	

	1966		1967		1968		1969		1970	
	No.	%	No.	%	No.	%	No.	%	No.	%
Prof. tech. and kindred prof.	625	28	724	40	875	40	599	44	455	43
Farmers and farm managers	39	2	19	1	22	1	21	2	23	2
Managers, officials, owners	41	2	38	2	39	2	32	2	21	2
Clerical and kindred workers	367	17	201	11	244	11	174	13	112	11
Sales workers	87	4	55	3	36	2	19	1	26	2
Craftsmen, foremen	196	9	150	8	169	8	140	10	144	14
Operatives	209	9	102	6	118	5	93	7	56	5
Private household workers	241	11	292	16	303	14	121	9	67	6
Service workers, non-household	246	11	151	8	253	12	101	7	85	8
Farm laborers and foremen	61	3	23	1	34	2	21	2	12	1
Laborers, except farm and mine	107	5	48	3	69	3	41	3	57	5
Total (declaring occups)	2,219	100	1,803	100	2,162	100	1,362	100	1,058	100
Overall total	3,241		2,624		3,004		1,989		1,562	

continued

Table 11. (cont'd)

	1971		1972		1973		1974		1975	
	No.	%	No.	%	No.	%	No.	%	No.	%
Prof. tech. and kindred prof.	410	39	471	42	550	42	345	36	315	39
Farmers and farm managers	16	2	10	1	7	1	1	0	7	1
Managers, officials, owners	35	3	47	4	51	4	58	6	39	5
Clerical and kindred workers	120	11	119	11	126	10	113	12	95	12
Sales workers	25	2	18	2	24	2	25	3	20	2
Craftsmen, foremen	142	13	121	11	167	13	125	13	114	14
Operatives	75	7	87	8	87	7	68	7	55	7
Private household workers	48	5	45	4	71	5	43	5	39	5
Service workers, non-household	88	8	100	9	112	9	93	10	79	10
Farm laborers and foremen	33	3	27	2	23	2	20	2	13	2
Laborers, except farm and mine	69	7	71	6	81	6	59	6	40	5
Total (declaring occups)	1,061	100	1,116	100	1,299	100	950	100	816	100
Overall total	1,614		1,780		2,000		1,572		1,285	

Table 12. *Immigrants from Ireland to the U.S. by Declared Occupation, 1976–1985.*

	1976		1977		1978	
	No.	%	No.	%	No.	%
Prof./technical	301	43	339	45	230	34
Admin./management	43	6	57	8	68	10
Sales	16	2	22	3	17	2
Clerical workers	81	11	105	14	81	12
Craftsmen	87	12	71	9	89	13
Operatives	45	6	41	5	43	6
Farming	5	1	5	1	0	0
Laborers	39	6	34	5	51	7
Service workers	69	10	64	9	79	12
Household workers	21	3	13	2	25	4
Total declaring occupation	707	100	751	100	683	100
No occupation declared	464		487		497	
Overall total	1,171		1,238		1,180	

	1979		1980		1982	
	No.	%	No.	%	No.	%
Prof./technical	205	35	118	26	199	40
Admin./management	72	12	46	10	74	15
Sales	15	3	16	4	20	4
Clerical workers	73	13	67	15	61	12
Craftsmen	58	10	67	15	44	9
Operatives	48	8	42	9	30	6
Farming	1	0	0	0	N/A	N/A
Laborers	33	6	29	6	25	5
Service workers	68	12	61	14	46	9
Household workers	7	1	5	1	N/A	N/A
Total declaring occupation	580	100	451	100	499	100
No occuaption declared	402		246		450	
Overall total	982		697		949	

	1983		1984		1985	
	No.	%	No.	%	No.	%
Prof./technical			231	34	263	34
Admin./management			85	13	79	10
Sales			33	5	36	5
Clerical workers	N/A		82	12	81	10
Craftsmen			93	14	105	14
Operatives			50	7	86	11
Farming			20	3	19	2
Laborers			N/A		N/A	
Service workers			85	13	108	14
Household workers			N/A		N/A	
Total declaring occupation			679	100	777	100
No occuaption declared			544		620	
Overall total			1,223		1,397	

Table 13. *Irish Immigrants to the U.S. by Gender and Year, 1869–1985*

	Male	Female	Total	Index[a]		Male	Female	Total	Index[a]
1869	22,708	18,096	40,804	125	1921	17,595	21,461	39,056	82
1870	31,414	25,582	56,996	123	1922	6,851	10,340	17,191	66
1871	30,939	26,500	57,439	117	1923	16,451	13,935	30,386	118
1872	36,548	32,184	68,732	114	1924	24,273	18,091	42,364	134
1873	40,993	36,351	77,344	113	1925	22,525	20,136	42,661	112
1874	27,047	26,660	53,707	101	1926	22,941	19,534	42,475	117
1875	18,029	19,928	37,957	90	1927	24,149	20,577	44,726	117
1876	8,938	10,637	19,575	84	1928	19,412	18,781	38,193	103
1877	6,819	7,750	14,569	88	1929	14,969	15,953	30,922	94
1878	7,203	8,729	15,932	83	1930	17,060	17,887	34,947	95
1879	9,635	10,378	20,013	93	1931	4,078	6,736	10,814	61
1880	38,151	33,452	71,603	114	1932	578	992	1,570	58
1881	37,387	34,955	72,342	107	1933–1940 No reports				
1882	40,980	35,452	76,432	116	1941	604	1,279	1,883	47
1883	41,495	39,991	81,486	104	1942–1948 No reports				
1884	31,280	32,064	63,344	98	1949	7,618	7,563	15,181	101
1885	25,187	26,608	51,795	95	1950	N/A	N/A	5,842	N/A
1886	24,425	25,194	49,619	97	1951	1,329	2,410	3,739	55
1887	35,449	32,921	68,370	108	1952	1,288	2,508	3,796	51
1888	38,459	25,054	63,513	154	1953	1,734	2,918	4,655	59
1889	33,223	32,334	65,557	103	1954	2,209	3,023	5,232	73
1890	26,344	26,680	53,024	99	1955	2,632	3,343	5,975	79
1891	27,936	27,770	55,706	101	1956	2,819	3,664	6,483	77
1892	25,699	25,684	51,383	100	1957	4,370	4,744	9,124	92
1893	N/A	N/A	45,378	N/A	1958	4,999	5,384	10,383	93
1894	N/A	N/A	30,231	N/A	1959	3,049	4,322	7,371	71
1895	N/A	N/A	46,304	N/A	1960	3,262	4,425	7,687	74
1896	17,625	22,637	40,262	78	1961	2,693	3,848	6,541	70
1897	11,549	16,872	28,421	68	1962	2,103	3,383	5,486	62
1898	9,952	15,176	25,128	66	1963	2,391	3,787	6,178	63
1899	N/A	N/A	31,673	N/A	1964	2,460	3,847	6,307	64
1900	16,672	19,058	35,730	87	1965	2,153	3,310	5,463	65
1901	12,894	17,667	30,561	73	1966	1,146	2,095	3,241	55
1902	12,936	16,202	29,138	80	1967	786	1,838	2,624	43
1903	15,966	19,344	35,310	83	1968	924	2,080	3,004	44
1904	16,127	20,015	36,142	81	1969	802	1,187	1,989	68
1905	23,841	29,104	52,945	82	1970	669	893	1,562	75
1906	18,234	16,761	34,995	109	1971	719	895	1,614	80
1907	19,027	15,503	34,530	123	1972	773	1,007	1,780	77
1908	14,021	16,535	30,556	85	1973	891	1,109	2,000	80
1909	11,962	13,071	25,033	92	1974	736	836	1,572	88
1910	15,667	14,188	29,855	110	1975	609	676	1,285	90
1911	N/A	N/A	29,112	N/A	1976	670	803	1,473	83
1912	N/A	N/A	25,879	N/A	1977	543	695	1,238	78
1913	19,072	17,951	37,023	106	1978	N/A	N/A	1,180	N/A
1914	16,793	17,105	33,898	98	1979	467	515	982	91
1915	13,015	10,488	23,503	124	1980	N/A	N/A	1,006	N/A
1916	11,258	9,378	20,636	120	1981	N/A	N/A	902	N/A
1917	7,679	9,783	17,462	78	1982	434	450	949	96
1918	2,088	2,569	4,657	81	1983	526	487	1,013	108
1919	4,518	3,392	7,910	133	1984	617	606	1,223	102
1920	10,219	10,565	20,784	97	1985	714	683	1,397	105

[a]The index was developed by dividing the males by the females and multiplying the product by 100. Thus 100 represents parity, that is, both groups in exact balance. If the index is more than 100, males predominated; if it is less than 100, females predominated.

Table 14. *Irish Ancestry by State and Census Region, 1980 U.S. Census*

	Irish single ancestry	Irish multiple ancestry	Total Irish pop.	Total population	Irish percent of total
NORTHEAST					
New England					
Connecticut	186,718	426,966	613,684	3,107,576	20%
Maine	56,335	144,964	201,299	1,124,660	18%
Massachusetts	666,567	897,533	1,564,100	5,737,037	27%
New Hampshire	52,823	139,895	192,718	920,610	21%
Rhode Island	71,816	139,134	210,950	947,154	22%
Vermont	23,353	76,624	99,977	511,456	20%
Subtotal	1,057,612	1,825,116	2,882,728	12,348,493	23%
Mid-Atlantic					
New Jersey	451,039	993,269	1,444,308	7,364,823	20%
New York	1,009,905	1,967,613	2,977,518	17,558,072	17%
Pennsylvania	621,106	1,828,004	2,449,110	11,863,895	21%
Subtotal	2,082,050	4,788,886	6,870,936	36,786,790	19%
TOTAL	3,139,662	6,614,002	9,753,664	49,135,283	20%
NORTH CENTRAL					
East North Central					
Illinois	489,307	1,538,385	2,027,692	11,426,518	18%
Indiana	228,213	789,731	1,017,944	5,490,224	19%
Ohio	422,895	1,608,856	2,031,751	10,797,630	19%
Michigan	272,749	1,249,047	1,521,796	9,262,078	16%
Wisconsin	103,228	544,425	647,653	4,705,767	14%
Subtotal	1,516,392	5,730,444	7,246,836	41,682,217	17%
West North Central					
Iowa	122,800	507,220	630,020	2,913,808	22%
Kansas	93,933	395,295	489,228	2,363,679	21%
Minnesota	96,187	510,501	606,688	4,075,970	15%
Nebraska	61,614	250,749	312,363	1,569,825	20%
North Dakota	12,752	51,795	64,547	652,717	10%
South Dakota	21,874	72,048	93,922	690,768	14%
Missouri	242,610	886,539	1,129,149	4,916,686	23%
Subtotal	651,770	2,674,147	3,325,917	17,183,453	19%
TOTAL	2,168,162	8,404,591	10,572,753	58,865,670	18%
SOUTH					
South Atlantic					
Delaware	36,446	90,408	126,854	594,338	21%
Florida	432,946	1,184,487	1,617,433	9,746,324	17%
Georgia	282,108	566,745	848,853	5,463,105	16%
Maryland	181,668	584,203	765,871	4,216,975	18%
North Carolina	246,552	625,169	871,721	5,881,766	15%
South Carolina	153,810	331,007	484,817	3,121,820	16%
Virginia	221,665	627,404	849,069	5,346,818	16%
West Virginia	106,452	275,820	382,272	1,949,644	20%
Dist. of Columbia	12,268	25,399	37,667	638,333	6%
Subtotal	1,673,915	4,310,642	5,984,557	36,959,123	16%

continued

Table 14. (*cont'd*)

	Irish single ancestry	Irish multiple ancestry	Total Irish pop.	Total population	Irish percent of total
East South Central					
Alabama	224,453	408,583	633,036	3,893,888	16%
Kentucky	230,900	441,891	672,791	3,660,777	18%
Mississippi	156,655	251,691	408,346	2,520,638	16%
Tennessee	289,258	561,691	850,949	4,591,120	19%
Subtotal	901,266	1,663,856	2,565,122	14,666,423	17%
West South Central					
Arkansas	143,495	331,666	475,161	2,286,435	21%
Louisiana	143,424	414,834	558,258	4,205,900	13%
Oklahoma	158,897	547,510	706,407	3,025,290	23%
Texas	572,732	1,847,635	2,420,367	14,229,191	17%
Subtotal	1,018,548	3,141,645	4,160,193	23,746,816	18%
TOTAL	3,593,729	9,116,143	12,709,872	75,372,362	17%
WEST					
Mountain States					
Arizona	103,312	359,465	462,777	2,718,215	17%
Colorado	108,871	465,120	573,991	2,889,964	20%
Idaho	33,420	119,484	152,904	943,935	16%
Montana	40,742	117,833	158,575	786,690	20%
Nevada	35,072	123,127	158,199	800,493	20%
New Mexico	45,328	126,800	172,128	1,302,894	13%
Utah	22,440	115,039	137,479	1,461,037	9%
Wyoming	24,097	64,617	88,714	469,557	19%
Subtotal	309,970	1,132,020	1,441,990	8,654,570	17%
Pacific States					
California	757,964	2,967,961	3,725,925	23,667,902	16%
Oregon	97,358	449,154	546,512	2,633,105	21%
Washington	137,816	687,178	824,994	4,132,156	20%
Alaska	16,535	42,639	59,174	401,851	15%
Hawaii	12,845	55,196	68,041	964,691	7%
Subtotal	1,022,518	4,202,128	5,224,646	31,799,705	16%
TOTAL	1,332,488	5,334,148	6,666,636	40,454,275	16%
UNITED STATES	10,234,041	29,468,884	38,996,518	223,827,590	17%

Table 15. *Naturalization Status of Irish on 1980 U.S. Census*

	Ireland			Northern Ireland		
	Immigrants	Citizens	% nat. cit.	Immigrants	Citizens	% nat. cit.
NORTHEAST						
New England						
Connecticut	7,184	6,080	85	671	441	66
Maine	570	466	82	63	52	84
Massachusetts	23,155	20,092	87	1,007	646	64
New Hampshire	726	587	81	50	40	80
Rhode Island	1,758	1,459	83	107	86	80
Vermont	201	152	76	18	16	89
Subtotal	33,594	28,836	86	1,916	1,281	67
Mid-Atlantic						
New Jersey	15,873	13,271	84	1,788	1,358	76
New York	66,639	55,369	83	3,418	2,453	72
Pennsylvania	11,167	9,538	85	1,393	1,097	79
Subtotal	93,673	78,178	84	6,599	4,908	74
TOTAL	160,861	135,850	84	8,515	6,189	73
NORTH CENTRAL						
East North Central						
Illinois	15,449	12,542	81	857	494	58
Indiana	825	592	72	147	88	60
Ohio	3,856	3,189	83	526	358	68
Michigan	3,715	2,945	79	852	589	69
Wisconsin	734	593	81	162	105	65
Subtotal	24,579	19,861		2,544	1,634	
West North Central						
Iowa	374	303	81	135	113	84
Kansas	317	259	82	38	16	42
Minnesota	864	663	77	111	58	52
Missouri	1,274	1,019	80	138	108	78
Nebraska	219	187	85	42	20	48
North Dakota	102	59	58	2	2	100
South Dakota	96	86	90	7	0	0
Subtotal	3,246	2,576	79	473	317	67
TOTAL	27,825	22,437	81	3,017	1,951	65
SOUTH						
South Atlantic						
Delaware	455	365	80	57	46	81
Florida	7,338	6,026	82	1,348	970	72
Georgia	517	352	68	169	84	50
Maryland	1,995	1,396	70	232	169	73
North Carolina	492	314	64	182	103	57
South Carolina	314	216	69	164	73	45
Virginia	1,409	851	60	397	178	45
West Virginia	175	125	71	35	5	14
Dist. of Columbia	338	161	48	33	17	52
Subtotal	13,033	9,806	75	2,617	1,645	63

continued

Table 15. (*cont'd*)

	Ireland			Northern Ireland		
	Immigrants	Citizens	% nat. cit.	Immigrants	Citizens	% nat. cit.
East South Central						
Alabama	214	186	87	137	105	77
Kentucky	332	192	58	63	40	64
Mississippi	182	166	91	45	20	44
Tennessee	286	205	72	93	53	57
Subtotal	1,014	749	74	338	218	65
West South Central						
Arkansas	120	60	50	56	27	48
Louisiana	471	319	68	118	69	59
Oklahoma	285	213	75	44	28	64
Texas	2,182	1,600	73	547	173	32
Subtotal	3,058	2,192	73	735	297	40
TOTAL	17,105	12,747	75	3,690	2,160	59
WEST						
Mountain States						
Arizona	1,145	935	82	226	137	61
Colorado	830	610	74	103	76	74
Indiana	191	152	80	29	22	76
Montana	239	220	92	25	25	100
Nevada	474	324	68	56	32	57
New Mexico	236	142	60	23	15	65
Utah	152	101	66	36	14	39
Wyoming	181	154	85	12	12	100
Subtotal	3,448	2,638	77	510	333	65
Pacific States						
California	19,297	13,661	71	3,350	2,082	62
Oregon	982	748	76	204	101	50
Washington	1,623	1,191	73	454	259	57
Subtotal	21,902	15,600	71	4,008	2,442	61
TOTAL	23,350	18,238	78	4,518	2,775	61
Alaska	126	86	68	30	6	20
Hawaii	138	87	63	31	15	48
TOTAL	264	173	66	61	21	34
UNITED STATES	232,853	192,083	82	20,311	13,429	66

Statistical Overview 313

Table 16. Year of Arrival of Irish-born on 1980 U.S. Census for Selected Years

	Before 1950		1950–59		1960–64		1965–69		1970–74		1975–80		Total
	No.	%	No.	%	No.	%	No.	%	No.	%	No.	%	
NORTHEAST													
New England													
Connecticut	4,514	63	1,305	18	636	9	366	5	160	2	203	3	7,184
Maine	381	67	60	11	80	14	7	1	20	4	22	4	570
Massachusetts	14,998	65	4,025	17	1,706	7	1,209	5	663	3	554	2	23,155
New Hampshire	426	59	151	21	40	6	55	8	23	3	31	4	726
Rhode Island	1,225	70	249	14	94	5	45	3	29	2	116	7	1,758
Vermont	100	50	32	16	25	12	14	7	2	1	28	14	201
Subtotal	21,644	64	5,822	17	2,581	8	1,696	5	897	3	954	3	33,594
Mid-Atlantic													
New Jersey	9,107	57	3,366	21	1,734	11	821	5	390	2	455	3	15,873
New York	40,002	60	13,534	20	6,284	9	2,933	4	2,349	4	1,537	2	66,639
Pennsylvania	7,792	70	1,690	15	768	7	388	3	284	3	245	2	11,167
Subtotal	56,901	61	18,590	20	8,786	9	4,142	4	3,023	3	2,237	2	93,679
TOTAL	78,545	62	24,412	19	11,367	9	5,838	5	3,920	3	3,191	3	127,273
North Central													
East North Central													
Illinois	7,884	51	4,135	27	1,473	9.5	635	4.1	636	4.1	686	4.4	15,449
Indiana	435	53	176	21	75	9.1	61	7.4	23	2.8	55	6.7	825
Ohio	2,276	59	819	21	259	6.7	200	5.2	80	2.1	222	5.8	3,856
Michigan	2,302	62	752	20	202	5.4	216	5.8	91	2.4	152	4.1	3,715
Wisconsin	372	51	154	21	69	9.4	42	5.7	42	5.7	55	7.5	734
Subtotal	13,269	54	6,036	25	2,078	8.4	1,154	4.6	872	3.6	1,170	4.7	24,579
West North Central													
Iowa	239	64	80	21	14	4	18	5	16	4	7	2	374
Kansas	134	42	113	36	17	5	18	6	6	2	29	9	317
Minnesota	509	59	179	21	53	6	27	3	17	2	79	9	864

continued

Table 16. *(cont'd)*

	Before 1950		1950–59		1960–64		1965–69		1970–74		1975–80		Total
	No.	%	No.	%	No.	%	No.	%	No.	%	No.	%	
Missouri	724	57	237	19	92	7	53	4	84	7	84	7	1,274
Nebraska	133	61	52	24	19	9		0	15	7		0	219
North Dakota	38	37	3	3	3	3	15	15	27	26	16	16	102
South Dakota	63	66	18	19	6	6	9	9		0		0	96
Subtotal	1,840	57	682	21	204	6	140	4	165	5	215	7	3,246
TOTAL	15,109	54	6,718	24	2,282	8	1,294	5	1,037	4	1,385	5	27,625
SOUTH													
South Atlantic													
Delaware	200	44	145	32	61	13	25	5	11	2	13	3	455
Florida	4,900	67	1,006	14	519	7	363	5	251	3	299	4	7,338
Georgia	209	40	109	21	79	15	54	10	48	9	18	3	517
Maryland	986	49	297	15	239	12	215	11	162	8	96	5	1,995
North Carolina	216	44	75	15	36	7	48	10	35	7	82	17	492
South Carolina	150	48	51	16	40	15	24	8	26	8	15	5	314
Virginia	505	36	299	21	125	9	202	14	162	11	116	8	1,409
West Virginia	81	46	28	16	14	8	18	10	21	12	13	7	175
Dist. of Columbia	131	39	38	11		0	40	12	13	4	116	34	338
Subtotal	7,378	57	2,048	16	1,121	9	989	8	729	6	768	6	13,033
East South Central													
Alabama	106	50	54	25	9	4	8	4	26	12	11	5	214
Kentucky	111	33	68	20	27	8	7	2	29	9	90	27	332
Mississippi	30	16	60	33	49	27	14	8	25	14	4	2	182
Tennessee	122	43	54	19	32	11	24	8	26	9	28	10	286
Subtotal	369	36	236	23	117	12	53	5	106	10	133	13	1,014
West South Central													
Arkansas	60	50	7	6	15	13	6	5	12	10	20	17	120
Louisiana	200	42	89	19	32	7	61	13	25	5	64	14	471

continued

Table 16. (cont'd)

	Before 1950		1950–59		1960–64		1965–69		1970–74		1975–80		Total
	No.	%	No.	%	No.	%	No.	%	No.	%	No.	%	
Oklahoma	103	36	79	28	48	17	33	12		0	22	8	285
Texas	796	36	599	27	278	13	138	6	126	6	245	11	2,182
Subtotal	1,159	38	774	25	373	12	238	8	163	5	351	11	3,058
TOTAL	8,906	52	3,058	18	1,611	9	1,280	7	998	6	1,252	7	17,105
WEST													
Mountain States													
Arizona	655	57	229	20	78	7	64	6	57	5	62	5	1,145
Colorado	255	31	318	38	98	12	59	7	53	6	47	6	830
Idaho	124	65	28	15	16	8	3	2	7	4	13	7	191
Montana	167	70	42	18	24	10	2	1		0	4	2	239
Nevada	194	41	108	23	67	14	14	3	45	9	46	10	474
New Mexico	81	34	80	34	16	7	35	15	16	7	8	3	236
Utah	71	47	19	13	30	20	18	12		0	14	9	152
Wyoming	109	60	20	11	3	2	10	6	2	1	37	20	181
Subtotal	1,656	48	844	24	332	10	205	6	180	5	231	7	3,448
Pacific States													
California	7,884	41	5,321	28	2,749	14	1,385	7	873	5	1,085	6	19,297
Oregon	544	55	245	25	69	7	40	4	11	1	73	7	982
Washington	736	45	437	27	128	8	83	5	140	9	99	6	1,623
Hawaii	47	34	28	20	24	17	4	3	12	9	23	17	138
Alaska	18	14	48	38	44	35	4	3	8	6	4	3	126
Subtotal	9,229	42	6,079	27	3,014	14	1,516	7	1,044	5	1,284	6	22,166
TOTAL	10,885	43	6,923	27	3,346	13	1,721	7	1,224	5	1,515	6	25,614
UNITED STATES	113,445	57	41,111	21	18,606	9	10,133	5	7,179	4	7,343	4	197,817

Table 17. *Population of Ireland, by County and Province, 1821–1911*

	1821	1831	1841	1851	1861	1871	1881	1891	1901	1911
LEINSTER										
Carlow	78,952	81,988	86,228	68,078	57,137	51,650	46,568	40,936	37,748	36,252
Dublin County	157,289	176,012	140,047	146,778	155,444	158,936	169,308	174,215	157,568	172,394
Dublin City	178,603	204,155	232,726	258,369	254,808	246,326	249,602	245,001	290,638	304,802
Kildare	99,065	108,424	114,488	95,723	90,946	83,614	75,804	70,206	63,566	66,627
Kilkenny	181,946	193,686	202,420	158,748	124,515	109,379	99,531	87,261	79,159	74,962
King's County	131,088	144,225	146,857	112,076	90,043	75,900	72,852	65,563	60,187	56,832
Longford	107,570	112,558	115,491	82,348	71,694	64,501	61,009	52,647	46,672	43,820
Louth	119,129	124,846	128,240	107,662	90,713	84,021	77,684	71,038	65,820	63,665
Meath	159,183	176,826	183,828	140,748	110,373	95,558	87,469	76,987	67,497	65,091
Queen's County	134,275	145,851	153,930	111,664	90,650	79,771	73,124	64,883	57,417	54,629
Westmeath	128,819	136,872	141,300	111,407	90,879	78,432	71,798	65,109	61,629	59,986
Wexford	170,806	182,713	202,033	180,158	143,954	132,666	123,854	111,778	104,104	102,273
Wicklow	110,767	121,557	126,143	98,979	86,479	78,697	70,386	62,136	60,824	60,711
TOTAL	1,757,492	1,909,713	1,973,731	1,672,738	1,457,635	1,339,451	1,278,989	1,187,760	1,152,829	1,162,044
MUNSTER										
Clare	208,089	258,322	286,394	212,440	166,305	147,864	141,457	124,483	112,334	104,232
Cork	730,444	810,732	854,118	649,308	544,818	517,076	495,607	438,432	404,611	392,104
Kerry	216,185	263,126	293,880	238,254	201,800	196,586	201,039	179,136	165,726	159,691
Limerick	277,477	315,355	330,029	262,132	217,277	191,936	180,632	158,912	146,098	143,069
Tipperary	346,896	402,563	435,553	331,567	249,106	216,713	199,612	173,188	160,232	152,433
Waterford	156,521	177,054	196,187	164,035	134,252	123,310	112,768	98,251	87,187	83,966
TOTAL	1,935,612	2,227,152	2,396,161	1,857,736	1,513,558	1,393,485	1,331,115	1,172,402	1,076,188	1,035,495
ULSTER										
Antrim	233,606	272,328	285,567	259,903	256,986	245,758	237,738	215,229	196,090	193,864
Armagh	197,427	220,134	232,393	196,084	190,086	179,260	163,177	143,289	125,392	120,291
Belfast	37,277	53,287	70,447	87,062	121,602	174,412	208,122	255,950	349,180	386,947
Cavan	195,076	227,933	243,158	174,064	153,906	140,735	129,476	111,917	97,541	91,173
Donegal	248,270	289,149	296,448	255,158	237,395	218,334	206,035	185,635	173,722	168,537

continued

Table 17. (cont'd)

	1821	1831	1841	1851	1861	1871	1881	1891	1901	1911
Down	325,410	352,012	361,446	320,817	299,302	277,294	248,190	224,008	205,889	204,303
Fermanagh	130,997	149,763	156,481	116,047	105,768	92,794	84,879	74,170	65,430	61,836
Londonderry	193,869	222,012	222,174	192,022	184,209	173,906	164,991	152,009	144,404	140,625
Monaghan	174,697	195,536	200,442	141,823	126,482	114,969	102,748	86,206	74,611	71,445
Tyrone	261,865	304,468	312,956	255,661	238,500	215,766	197,719	171,401	150,567	142,665
TOTAL	1,998,494	2,286,622	2,381,512	1,998,641	1,914,236	1,833,228	1,743,075	1,619,814	1,582,826	1,581,686
CONNACHT										
Galway	337,374	414,684	440,198	321,684	271,478	248,458	242,005	214,712	192,549	182,224
Leitrim	124,785	141,524	155,297	111,897	104,744	95,562	90,372	78,618	69,343	63,582
Mayo	293,112	366,328	388,887	274,499	254,796	246,030	245,212	219,034	199,166	192,177
Roscommon	208,729	249,613	253,591	173,436	157,272	140,670	132,490	114,397	101,791	93,956
Sligo	146,299	171,765	180,886	128,515	124,845	115,493	111,578	98,013	84,083	79,045
TOTAL	1,110,299	1,343,914	1,418,859	1,010,031	913,135	846,213	821,657	724,774	646,932	610,984
SUMMARY BY PROVINCE										
Leinster	1,757,492	1,909,713	1,973,731	1,672,738	1,457,635	1,339,451	1,278,989	1,187,760	1,152,829	1,162,044
Munster	1,935,612	2,227,152	2,396,161	1,857,736	1,513,558	1,393,485	1,331,115	1,172,402	1,076,188	1,035,495
Ulster	1,998,494	2,286,622	2,381,512	1,998,641	1,914,236	1,833,228	1,743,075	1,619,814	1,582,826	1,581,686
Connacht	1,110,229	1,343,914	1,418,859	1,010,031	913,135	846,213	821,657	724,774	646,932	610,984
Total	6,801,827	7,767,401	8,170,263	6,539,146	5,798,564	5,412,377	5,174,836	4,704,750	4,458,775	4,390,209

Table 18. *Population of Ireland, by County and Province, 1926–1986*

	1926	1936	1946	1951	1956	1961	1966	1971	1979	1986
LEINSTER										
Carlow	34,476	34,452	34,081	34,162	33,888	33,342	33,593	34,237	38,668	39,820
Dublin	505,654	586,925	636,193	693,022	705,781	718,332	795,047	852,219	983,683	1,003,164
Kildare	58,028	57,892	64,849	66,437	65,915	64,420	66,404	71,977	97,185	104,122
Kilkenny	70,990	68,614	66,712	65,235	64,089	61,668	60,463	61,473	69,156	70,806
Laoighis	51,540	50,109	49,697	48,430	47,087	45,069	44,595	45,259	49,936	51,171
Longford	39,847	37,847	36,218	34,553	32,969	30,643	28,989	28,250	30,785	31,140
Louth	62,739	64,339	66,194	68,771	69,194	67,378	69,519	74,951	86,135	88,514
Meath	62,969	61,405	66,232	66,337	66,762	65,122	67,323	71,729	90,175	95,419
Offaly	52,592	51,308	53,686	52,544	51,970	51,533	51,717	51,829	57,342	58,312
Westmeath	56,818	54,706	54,949	54,463	54,122	52,861	52,900	53,570	59,885	61,523
Wexford	95,848	94,245	91,855	90,032	87,259	83,308	83,437	86,351	96,421	99,081
Wicklow	57,591	58,569	60,451	62,590	59,906	58,473	60,428	66,295	83,950	87,449
TOTAL	1,149,092	1,220,411	1,281,117	1,336,576	1,338,942	1,332,149	1,414,415	1,498,140	1,743,321	1,790,521
MUNSTER										
Clare	95,064	89,879	85,064	81,329	77,176	73,702	73,597	75,008	84,919	87,567
Cork	365,747	355,957	343,668	341,284	336,663	330,443	339,703	352,883	396,118	402,465
Kerry	149,171	139,834	133,893	126,644	122,072	116,458	112,785	112,772	120,356	122,770
Limerick	140,343	141,153	142,559	141,239	137,881	133,339	137,357	140,459	157,407	161,661
Tipperary, N	59,645	59,551	58,103	57,009	55,697	53,696	53,843	54,337	58,476	58,984
Tipperary, S	81,370	78,284	77,911	76,304	73,718	70,126	68,969	69,228	75,265	76,277
Waterford	78,562	77,614	76,108	75,061	74,031	71,439	73,080	77,315	87,278	88,591
TOTAL	969,902	942,272	917,306	898,870	877,238	849,203	859,334	882,002	979,819	998,315
ULSTER										
Cavan	82,452	76,670	70,355	66,377	61,740	56,594	54,022	52,618	53,720	53,855
Donegal	152,508	142,310	136,317	131,530	122,059	113,842	108,549	108,344	121,941	125,112
Monaghan	65,131	61,289	57,215	55,345	52,064	47,088	45,732	46,242	50,376	51,192
TOTAL	300,091	280,269	263,887	253,252	235,863	217,524	208,303	207,204	226,037	230,159

continued

Table 18. (cont'd)

	1926	1936	1946	1951	1956	1961	1966	1971	1979	1986
CONNACHT										
Galway	169,366	168,198	165,201	160,204	155,553	149,887	148,340	149,223	167,838	172,018
Leitrim	55,907	50,908	44,591	41,209	37,056	33,470	30,572	28,360	27,844	27,609
Mayo	172,690	161,349	148,120	141,867	133,052	123,330	115,547	109,525	114,019	114,766
Roscommon	83,556	77,566	72,510	68,102	63,710	59,217	56,228	53,519	54,189	54,543
Sligo	71,388	67,447	62,375	60,513	56,850	53,561	51,263	50,275	54,610	55,474
TOTAL	552,907	525,468	492,797	471,895	446,221	419,465	401,950	390,902	418,500	424,410
SUMMARY BY PROVINCE										
Leinster	1,149,092	1,220,411	1,281,117	1,336,576	1,338,942	1,332,149	1,414,415	1,498,140	1,743,321	1,790,521
Munster	969,902	942,272	917,306	898,870	877,238	849,203	859,334	882,002	979,819	998,315
Ulster (3)	300,091	280,269	263,887	253,252	235,863	217,524	208,303	207,204	226,037	230,159
Connacht	552,907	525,468	492,797	471,895	446,221	419,465	401,950	390,902	418,500	424,410
Total	2,971,992	2,968,420	2,955,107	2,960,593	2,898,264	2,818,341	2,884,002	2,978,248	3,367,677	3,443,405

Table 19. *Ireland: Religion at Each Census of Population, 1881–1971*

	Catholic		Church of Ireland		Presbyterian	
	No.	%	No.	%	No.	%
1881	3,465,332	90	317,576	8.2	56,498	1.5
1891	3,099,003	89	286,804	8.3	51,469	1.5
1901	2,878,271	89	264,264	8.2	46,714	1.4
1911	2,812,509	90	249,535	7.9	45,486	1.4
1926	2,751,269	93	164,215	5.5	32,429	1.1
1936	2,773,920	93	145,030	4.9	28,067	0.9
1946	2,786,033	94	124,829	4.2	23,870	0.8
1961	2,673,473	95	104,016	3.7	18,953	0.7
1971	2,795,666	94	97,739	3.3	16,052	0.5

	Methodist		Jewish		Others or None	
	No.	%	No.	%	No.	%
1881	17,660	0.5	394	0.01	12,560	0.3
1891	18,513	0.5	1,506	0.04	11,399	0.3
1901	17,872	0.6	3,006	0.09	11,696	0.4
1911	16,440	0.5	3,805	0.12	11,913	0.4
1926	10,663	0.4	3,686	0.12	9,730	0.3
1936	9,649	0.3	3,749	0.13	8,005	0.3
1946	8,355	0.3	3,907	0.13	8,113	0.3
1961	6,676	0.2	3,255	0.12	11,968	0.4
1971	5,646	0.2	2,633	0.09	60,512	2.0

Table 20. *Ireland: Irish Speakers on Each Census, by Province, 1861–1971*

	1861	1871	1881	1891	1901	1911
LEINSTER						
Irish Speakers	35,704	16,247	27,452	13,677	26,436	40,225
Non-Irish speakers	1,421,931	1,323,204	1,251,537	1,174,083	1,126,393	1,121,819
Total population	1,457,635	1,339,451	1,278,989	1,187,760	1,152,829	1,162,044
% Irish speakers	2.4	1.2	2.1	1.1	2.3	3.5
MUNSTER						
Irish Speakers	545,531	386,494	445,766	307,633	276,268	228,694
Non-Irish speakers	968,027	1,006,991	885,349	864,769	799,920	806,801
Total population	1,513,558	1,393,485	1,331,115	1,172,402	1,076,188	1,035,495
% Irish speakers	36	28	33	26	26	22
CONNACHT						
Irish Speakers	409,482	330,211	366,191	274,783	245,580	217,087
Non-Irish speakers	503,653	516,002	455,466	449,991	401,352	393,897
Total population	913,135	846,213	821,657	724,774	646,932	610,984
% Irish speakers	45	39	45	38	38	36
ULSTER						
Irish Speakers	86,370	71,595	85,372	68,294	71,426	67,711
Non-Irish speakers	431,413	402,443	352,887	315,464	274,448	263,454
Total population	517,783	474,038	438,259	383,758	345,874	331,165
% Irish speakers	17	15	19	18	21	20
IRELAND						
Irish Speakers	1,077,087	804,547	924,781	664,387	619,710	553,717
Non-Irish speakers	3,325,024	3,248,640	2,945,239	2,804,307	2,602,113	2,585,971
Total population	4,402,111	4,053,187	3,870,020	3,468,694	3,221,823	3,139,688
% Irish speakers	24	20	24	19	19	18

continued

Table 20. (cont'd)

	1926	1926[a]	1936	1946	1961	1971
LEINSTER						
Irish Speakers	101,474	101,102	183,378	180,755	274,644	341,702
Non-Irish speakers	1,047,618	978,536	966,434	1,017,491	964,383	1,055,160
Total population	1,149,092	1,079,638	1,149,812	1,198,246	1,239,027	1,396,862
% Irish speakers	8.8	9.4	16	15	22	24
MUNSTER						
Irish Speakers	198,221	197,625	224,805	189,395	228,726	252,805
Non-Irish speakers	771,681	718,068	668,030	672,660	567,613	573,308
Total population	969,902	915,693	892,835	862,055	796,339	826,113
% Irish speakers	20	22	25	22	29	31
CONNACHT						
Irish Speakers	175,209	174,234	183,082	154,187	148,708	137,372
Non-Irish speakers	377,698	348,964	315,322	309,638	246,592	231,960
Total population	552,907	523,198	498,404	463,825	395,300	369,332
% Irish speakers	32	33	37	33	38	37
ULSTER						
Irish Speakers	68,607	67,841	75,336	64,388	64,342	57,550
Non-Irish speakers	231,484	216,082	190,538	183,143	140,810	137,591
Total population	300,091	283,923	265,874	247,531	205,152	195,141
% Irish speakers	23	24	28	26	31	29
IRELAND						
Irish Speakers	543,511	540,802	666,601	588,725	716,420	789,429
Non-Irish speakers	2,428,481	2,261,650	2,140,324	2,182,932	1,919,398	1,998,019
Total population	2,971,992	2,802,452	2,806,925	2,771,657	2,635,818	2,787,448
% Irish speakers	18	19	24	21	27	28

[a]These figures and those for the following years are for the population over three years of age.

Table 21. *Population Change by County and Province in Pre-Famine Ireland, 1821–1841*

	1821–1831	1831–1841	Pre-famine summary, 1821–1841	Percent all-Ireland change, 1821–1841
LEINSTER				
Carlow	3,036	4,240	7,276	0.53
Dublin County	18,723	−35,965	−17,242	−1.26
Dublin City	25,552	28,571	54,123	3.94
Kildare	9,359	6,064	15,423	1.12
Kilkenny	11,740	8,734	20,474	1.49
King's County	13,137	2,632	15,769	1.15
Longford	4,988	2,933	7,921	0.58
Louth	5,717	3,394	9,111	0.66
Meath	17,643	7,002	24,645	1.79
Queen's County	11,576	8,079	19,655	1.43
Westmeath	8,053	4,428	12,481	0.91
Wexford	11,907	19,320	31,227	2.27
Wicklow	10,790	4,586	15,376	1.12
MUNSTER				
Clare	50,233	28,072	78,305	5.70
Cork	80,288	43,386	123,674	9.01
Kerry	46,941	30,754	77,695	5.66
Limerick	37,878	14,674	52,552	3.83
Tipperary	55,667	32,990	88,657	6.46
Waterford	20,533	19,133	39,666	2.89
ULSTER				
Antrim	38,722	13,239	51,961	3.78
Armagh	22,707	12,259	34,966	2.55
Belfast	16,010	17,160	33,170	2.42
Cavan	32,857	15,225	48,082	3.50
Donegal	40,879	7,299	48,178	3.51
Down	26,602	9,434	36,036	2.62
Fermanagh	18,766	6,718	25,484	1.86
Londonderry	28,143	162	28,305	2.06
Monaghan	20,839	4,906	25,745	1.87
Tyrone	42,603	8,488	51,091	3.72
CONNACHT				
Galway	77,310	25,514	102,824	7.49
Leitrim	16,739	13,773	30,512	2.22
Mayo	73,216	22,559	95,775	6.97
Roscommon	40,884	3,978	44,862	3.27
Sligo	25,466	9,121	34,587	2.52
SUMMARY BY PROVINCE				
Leinster	152,221	64,018	216,239	15.75
Munster	291,540	169,009	460,549	33.54
Ulster	288,128	99,751	387,879	28.24
Connacht	233,685	74,945	308,630	22.47
Total change for Ireland, 1821–1841			1,373,297	100.00

Table 22. *Ireland: Population Change by County and Province, 1841–1911*

	1841–51	1851–61	1861–71	1871–81	1881–91	1891–1901	1901–11	Summary 1841–1911	Percent all-Ireland change, 1841–1911
LEINSTER									
Carlow	−18,150	−10,941	−5,487	−5,082	−5,632	−3,188	−1,496	−49,976	−1.32
Dublin County	6,731	8,666	3,492	10,372	4,907	−16,647	14,826	32,347	0.85
Dublin City	25,643	−3,561	−8,482	3,276	−4,601	45,637	14,164	72,076	1.90
Kildare	−18,765	−4,777	−7,332	−7,810	−5,598	−6,640	3,061	−47,861	−1.26
Kilkenny	−43,672	−34,233	−15,136	−9,848	−12,270	−8,102	−4,197	−127,458	−3.37
King's County	−34,781	−22,033	−14,143	−3,048	−7,289	−5,376	−3,355	−90,025	−2.38
Longford	−33,143	−10,654	−7,193	−3,492	−8,362	−5,975	−2,852	−71,671	−1.89
Louth	−20,578	−16,949	−6,692	−6,337	−6,646	−5,218	−2,155	−64,575	−1.71
Meath	−43,080	−30,375	−14,815	−8,089	−10,482	−9,490	−2,406	−118,737	−3.14
Queen's County	−42,266	−21,014	−10,879	−6,647	−8,241	−7,466	−2,788	−99,301	−2.62
Westmeath	−29,893	−20,528	−12,447	−6,634	−6,689	−3,480	−1,643	−81,314	−2.15
Wexford	−21,875	−36,204	−11,288	−8,812	−12,076	−7,674	−1,831	−99,760	−2.64
Wicklow	−27,164	−12,500	−7,782	−8,311	−8,250	−1,312	−113	−65,432	−1.73
MUNSTER									
Clare	−73,954	−46,135	−18,441	−6,407	−16,974	−12,149	−8,102	−182,162	−4.81
Cork	−204,810	−104,490	−27,742	−21,469	−57,175	−33,821	−12,507	−462,014	−12.21
Kerry	−55,626	−36,454	−5,214	4,453	−21,903	−13,410	−6,035	−134,189	−3.55
Limerick	−67,897	−44,855	−25,341	−11,304	−21,720	−12,814	−3,029	−186,960	−4.94
Tipperary	−103,986	−82,461	−32,393	−17,101	−26,424	−12,956	−7,799	−283,120	−7.48
Waterford	−32,152	−29,783	−10,942	−10,542	−14,517	−11,064	−3,221	−112,221	−2.96

continued

Table 22. (cont'd)

	1841–51	1851–61	1861–71	1871–81	1881–91	1891–1901	1901–11	Summary 1841–1911	Percent all-Ireland change, 1841–1911
ULSTER									
Antrim	−25,664	−2,917	−11,228	−8,020	−22,509	−19,139	−2,226	−91,703	−2.42
Armagh	−36,309	−5,998	−10,826	−16,083	−19,888	−17,897	−5,101	−112,102	−2.96
Belfast	16,615	34,540	52,810	33,710	47,828	93,230	37,767	316,500	8.36
Cavan	−69,094	−20,158	−13,171	−11,259	−17,559	−14,376	−6,368	−151,985	−4.02
Donegal	−41,290	−17,763	−19,061	−12,299	−20,400	−11,913	−5,185	−127,911	−3.38
Down	−40,629	−21,515	−22,008	−29,104	−24,182	−18,119	−1,586	−157,143	−4.15
Fermanagh	−40,434	−10,279	−12,974	−7,915	−10,709	−8,740	−3,594	−94,645	−2.50
Londonderry	−30,152	−7,813	−10,303	−8,915	−12,982	−7,605	−3,779	−81,549	−2.15
Monaghan	−58,619	−15,341	−11,513	−12,221	−16,542	−11,595	−3,166	−128,997	−3.41
Tyrone	−57,295	−17,161	−22,734	−18,047	−26,318	−20,834	−7,902	−170,291	−4.50
CONNACHT									
Galway	−118,514	−50,206	−23,020	−6,453	−27,293	−22,163	−10,325	−257,974	−6.82
Leitrim	−43,400	−7,153	−9,182	−5,190	−11,754	−9,275	−5,761	−91,715	−2.42
Mayo	−114,388	−19,703	−8,766	−818	−26,178	−19,868	−6,989	−196,710	−5.20
Roscommon	−80,155	−16,164	−16,602	−8,180	−18,093	−12,606	−7,835	−159,635	−4.22
Sligo	−52,371	−3,670	−9,352	−3,915	−13,565	−13,930	−5,038	−101,841	−2.69
SUMMARY BY PROVINCE									
Leinster	−300,993	−215,103	−118,184	−60,462	−91,229	−34,931	9,215	−811,687	−21.45
Munster	−538,425	−344,178	−120,073	−62,370	−158,713	−96,214	−40,693	−1,360,666	−35.95
Ulster	−374,493	−97,644	−81,008	−90,153	−123,261	−36,988	−1,130	−804,677	−21.26
Connacht	−408,828	−96,896	−66,922	−24,556	−96,883	−77,842	−35,948	−807,875	−21.34
Total change	−1,622,739	−753,821	−386,187	−237,541	−470,086	−245,975	−68,556	−3,784,905	100.00

Table 23. *Emigration from Ireland by County and Province, 1851–1911*

	1851–61	1861–71	1871–81	1881–91	1891–1901	1901–11	Total, 1851–1911
LEINSTER							
Carlow	10,713	5,405	5,440	8,064	2,610	2,428	34,660
Dublin	25,755	30,772	19,726	24,814	10,615	9,580	121,262
Kildare	12,257	7,419	5,883	8,249	2,113	2,630	38,551
Kilkenny	34,010	12,338	9,133	13,247	4,835	3,401	76,964
King's County	21,061	12,140	8,778	12,367	3,708	3,292	61,346
Longford	14,577	13,632	11,305	11,786	5,071	5,041	61,412
Louth	17,091	10,171	5,699	6,954	2,803	3,032	45,750
Meath	23,297	15,557	10,521	11,264	4,358	3,416	68,413
Queen's County	19,886	9,620	9,090	13,634	4,434	2,542	59,206
Westmeath	18,587	11,309	7,347	9,695	3,354	2,597	52,889
Wexford	27,053	16,088	13,106	11,966	3,960	2,900	75,073
Wicklow	11,173	5,387	4,591	6,242	1,691	1,779	30,863
MUNSTER							
Clare	50,033	31,667	18,796	32,421	18,031	13,597	164,545
Cork	148,009	118,669	74,209	83,533	77,072	43,593	545,085
Kerry	54,672	40,480	27,036	50,855	38,599	23,074	234,716
Limerick	62,173	46,339	22,132	33,081	14,426	11,278	189,429
Tipperary	81,068	47,269	26,465	32,762	19,050	12,307	218,921
Waterford	38,383	19,681	12,732	19,428	10,058	7,054	107,336

continued

Table 23. (cont'd)

	1851–61	1861–71	1871–81	1881–91	1891–1901	1901–11	Total, 1851–1911
ULSTER							
Antrim	77,516	54,670	59,431	45,469	14,946	32,804	284,836
Armagh	29,496	17,674	19,603	20,577	7,208	8,408	102,966
Cavan	36,502	22,348	19,376	21,679	12,033	9,535	121,291
Donegal	38,260	11,902	30,085	29,417	12,977	12,622	135,263
Down	47,906	28,270	31,132	23,638	7,837	15,709	154,492
Fermanagh	17,372	10,864	10,514	10,158	5,403	3,562	57,873
Londonderry	27,738	16,841	26,939	23,199	8,152	9,257	112,126
Monaghan	26,842	14,953	13,356	13,427	5,301	4,333	78,212
Tyrone	39,629	23,722	29,674	28,960	12,598	10,539	145,122
CONNACHT							
Galway	50,838	38,758	23,665	51,121	36,820	26,464	227,666
Leitrim	16,820	13,980	12,683	21,008	9,830	8,308	82,629
Mayo	29,317	27,496	24,705	42,368	40,703	29,961	194,550
Roscommon	27,756	21,393	13,790	23,128	16,332	11,070	113,469
Sligo	13,328	12,049	11,708	23,594	14,065	9,157	83,901
SUMMARY BY PROVINCE							
Leinster	235,460	149,838	110,619	138,282	49,552	42,638	726,389
Munster	434,338	304,105	181,370	252,080	177,236	110,903	1,460,032
Ulster	341,261	201,244	240,110	216,524	86,455	106,769	1,192,181
Connacht	138,059	113,676	86,551	161,219	117,750	84,960	702,215
Total	1,149,118	768,863	618,650	768,105	430,993	345,270	4,080,817

Table 24. Emigration from Ireland by Province for Each Year, 1851–1920

	Leinster		Munster		Ulster		Connacht		Total
	No.	%	No.	%	No.	%	No.	%	
1851	38,719	26	61,285	41	28,884	19	20,094	13	148,982
1852	46,840	25	70,484	37	42,563	23	29,205	15	189,092
1853	40,593	23	71,042	41	39,884	23	21,310	12	172,829
1854	29,599	21	59,674	43	32,213	23	17,826	13	139,312
1855	15,450	17	34,046	38	31,607	35	9,274	10	90,377
1856	13,280	15	34,505	39	31,822	36	7,952	9	87,559
1857	13,482	15	33,727	37	34,173	38	9,054	10	90,436
1858	10,161	16	18,503	29	29,179	46	5,760	9	63,603
1859	11,841	15	19,715	26	38,150	49	7,464	10	77,170
1860	13,366	17	27,428	36	27,790	36	8,172	11	76,756
1861	8,576	15	22,404	38	21,323	36	6,124	10	58,427
1862	11,368	17	33,452	51	14,115	22	6,244	10	65,179
1863	15,020	14	54,870	50	22,497	20	17,815	16	110,202
1864	19,790	19	48,397	46	19,853	19	18,121	17	106,161
1865	30,524	30	37,426	36	22,301	22	12,477	12	102,728
1866	17,379	19	36,971	40	26,259	28	12,439	13	93,048
1867	16,027	23	25,268	37	18,164	26	9,752	14	69,211
1868	10,154	20	16,857	33	14,763	29	9,692	19	51,466
1869	13,863	23	14,857	25	19,679	33	11,065	19	59,464
1870	17,093	26	15,561	24	23,030	35	10,330	16	66,014
1871	15,850	24	13,199	20	28,066	42	9,049	14	66,164
1872	18,291	23	15,308	20	34,732	45	9,660	12	77,991
1873	18,191	20	22,159	25	33,967	38	15,726	17	90,043
1874	11,710	16	24,272	33	27,734	38	9,451	13	73,167
1875	7,770	15	18,311	36	20,226	39	5,130	10	51,437
1876	4,427	12	13,275	35	16,870	45	2,973	8	37,545
1877	5,142	13	13,602	35	16,723	43	3,036	8	38,503
1878	7,371	18	12,833	31	16,240	39	4,680	11	41,124
1879	6,125	13	17,255	37	17,619	37	6,066	13	47,065
1880	16,169	17	30,654	32	28,122	29	20,519	21	95,464
1881	16,232	22	21,752	29	21,101	28	16,332	22	75,417
1882	16,057	18	28,848	32	26,081	29	18,150	20	89,136
1883	20,708	19	29,279	27	29,918	28	28,819	27	108,724
1884	14,063	19	24,363	32	21,704	29	15,733	21	75,863

continued

Table 24. (cont'd)

	Leinster		Munster		Ulster		Connacht		Total
	No.	%	No.	%	No.	%	No.	%	
1885	10,152	16	20,436	33	19,498	31	11,948	19	62,034
1886	10,350	16	21,106	33	19,637	31	12,042	19	63,135
1887	14,234	17	27,078	33	24,654	30	16,957	20	82,923
1888	13,830	18	27,719	35	21,667	28	15,468	20	78,684
1889	12,621	18	27,404	39	17,108	24	13,344	19	70,477
1890	10,415	17	23,554	38	14,277	23	13,067	21	61,313
1891	9,726	16	24,678	41	13,264	22	12,405	21	60,073
1892	7,148	14	20,050	39	11,465	23	12,204	24	50,867
1893	6,322	13	19,820	41	10,525	22	11,480	24	48,147
1894	4,916	14	16,299	45	6,242	17	8,438	24	35,895
1895	4,923	10	22,176	46	8,109	17	13,495	28	48,703
1896	3,842	10	15,485	40	7,434	19	12,234	31	38,995
1897	3,210	10	12,798	39	6,266	19	10,261	32	32,535
1898	3,340	10	13,013	40	5,577	17	10,311	32	32,241
1899	3,452	8	15,758	38	8,701	21	13,231	32	41,142
1900	3,857	9	17,933	40	9,438	21	14,060	31	45,288
1901	3,400	9	16,381	41	8,740	22	11,092	28	39,613
1902	3,694	9	15,872	39	9,091	23	11,533	29	40,190
1903	4,290	11	14,704	37	9,670	24	11,054	28	39,718
1904	4,517	12	12,606	34	10,156	28	9,623	26	36,902
1905	3,937	13	9,002	29	10,236	33	7,501	24	30,676
1906	5,079	14	10,054	28	12,331	35	7,880	22	35,344
1907	5,711	15	11,288	29	14,513	37	7,570	19	39,082
1908	3,547	15	6,423	28	8,409	36	4,916	21	23,295
1909	4,057	14	7,690	27	10,563	37	6,366	22	28,676
1910	4,258	13	8,330	26	12,271	38	7,598	23	32,457
1911	4,885	14	8,476	24	14,015	40	7,396	21	34,772
1912	3,855	13	7,167	24	11,852	40	6,470	22	29,344
1913	3,994	13	7,807	25	12,392	40	6,774	22	30,967
1914	2,860	14	5,652	28	6,612	33	5,190	26	20,314
1915	2,905	27	1,550	15	3,790	36	2,414	23	10,659
1916	1,515	21	1,056	14	2,733	37	1,998	27	7,302
1917	677	32	78	4	1,248	59	108	5	2,111
1918	567	58	55	6	329	34	29	3	980
1919	678	23	449	15	1,690	57	158	5	2,975
1920	1,706	11	4,724	30	5,300	34	3,801	24	15,531

Table 25. *U.S. Citizens Enumerated on Censuses of Ireland, 1871–1986*

Census	Number	Census	Number
1871	4,354	1946	8,509
1881	7,034	1961	6,447
1891	7,499	1971	11,145
1901	6,823	1981	16,591
1911	12,420	1986	15,350
1926	8,932		

Table 26. *Destination of Overseas Emigrants from Ireland, 1841–1952*

	United States		Canada		Australia, New Zealand[a]		Other Destinations		Total
	No.	%	No.	%	No.	%	No.	%	
1841–50	822,675	70	329,321	28	22,825	1.9	4,539	0.4	1,179,360
1851–60	989,880	81	118,118	9.7	101,541	8.3	6,726	0.6	1,216,265
1861–70	690,845	84	40,079	4.9	82,917	10	4,741	0.6	818,582
1871–80	449,549	83	25,783	4.8	61,946	11	5,425	1.0	542,703
1881–90	626,604	85	44,505	6.1	55,476	7.5	7,890	1.1	734,475
1891–1900	427,301	93	10,648	2.3	11,448	2.5	11,520	2.5	460,917
1901–10	418,995	86	38,238	7.9	11,885	2.4	16,343	3.4	485,461
1911–20	172,490	75	32,857	14	15,429	6.7	8,463	3.7	229,239
1921–25[b]	100,911	69	29,400	20	10,355	7.1	6,168	4.2	146,834
Totals									
1841–1925	4,699,250	81	668,949	12	373,822	6.4	71,815	1.3	5,813,836
1924–52[c]	168,906	80	19,195	9.1	10,682	5.1	12,152	5.8	210,935

[a] Figures for period 1924–52 are for Australia only.
[b] Five years.
[c] From the 26 counties only; after 1946 figures are for travel passports only and thus do not include children.

Table 27. Distribution of Emigrants from Ireland by Selected Age Groups and Percent of Total, 1852–1921

Age Group	0–14 No.	0–14 %	15–19 No.	15–19 %	20–24 No.	20–24 %	25–29 No.	25–29 %	30–34 No.	30–34 %	35–54 No.	35–54 %	55 and over No.	55 and over %	All ages
Males															
1852–54	56,777	22	37,104	14	70,813	27	*a*		53,328	20	39,783	15	2,803	1	260,608
1861–70	64,305	14	39,292	9	158,532	35	94,326	21	42,367	9	46,273	10	4,431	1	449,526
1871–80	46,081	13	34,904	10	108,609	32	71,644	21	35,699	10	40,547	12	4,418	1	341,902
1881–90	54,083	14	59,522	15	151,394	38	61,419	16	25,921	7	37,430	9	5,010	1	394,779
1891–1900	17,127	8	22,260	11	83,861	42	47,202	23	12,413	6	15,912	8	2,760	1	201,535
1901–10	15,607	9	19,936	12	72,479	42	36,752	21	13,368	8	12,368	7	1,756	1	172,266
1911–20	6,951	9	9,659	13	31,667	42	*a*		21,303	28	5,710	8	586	1	75,876
1921	607	11	636	12	2,113	40	*a*		1,500	28	390	7	62	1	5,308
TOTAL	261,538	14	223,313	12	679,468	36	311,343	16	205,899	11	198,413	10	21,826	1	1,901,800
Females															
1852–54	55,592	22	47,291	19	71,556	28	*a*		42,326	17	31,895	13	3,293	1	251,953
1861–70	61,105	17	49,911	14	129,193	36	50,599	14	26,209	7	41,204	11	4,581	1	362,802
1871–80	44,122	16	50,270	18	95,260	34	38,452	14	21,114	8	28,228	10	3,890	1	281,336
1881–90	51,812	14	97,651	26	133,301	36	37,576	10	18,159	5	31,842	8	4,549	1	374,890
1891–1900	16,968	7	51,265	22	102,373	44	32,724	14	10,576	5	15,536	7	2,489	1	231,931
1901–10	15,273	9	43,733	25	68,676	40	24,345	14	8,907	5	10,748	6	2,007	1	173,689
1911–20	6,614	9	19,864	27	29,353	39	*a*		13,761	18	4,594	6	690	1	74,876
1921	598	7	2,158	26	3,545	43	*a*		1,382	17	491	6	153	2	8,327
TOTAL	252,084	14	362,143	21	633,257	36	183,696	10	142,434	8	164,538	9	21,652	1	1,759,804

[a] For these years, figures for the 30–34 age group cover the 25–34 age group.

Table 28. *Emigrants from Ireland by Marital Condition, 1883–1920*

	1883–90		1891–1900		1901–10		1911–20	
	No.	%	No.	%	No.	%	No.	%
Males								
Single	270,357	87	186,410	90	159,681	91	69,474	90
Married, widowed	39,418	13	20,709	10	16,449	9	7,885	10
TOTAL	309,775		207,119		176,130		77,359	
Females								
Single	243,282	82	203,025	87	152,542	87	65,472	87
Married, widowed	52,386	18	30,727	13	22,430	13	9,917	13
TOTAL	295,668		233,752		174,972		75,389	
All emigrants	605,443		440,871		351,102		152,748	

Table 29. *Ireland: Population, Natural Increase, Emigration, and Overall Changes, 1881–1979*

Census period	Population	Natural increase (births minus deaths)	Estimated net migration	Overall change in population
1881–91	3,468,694	195,999	−597,325	−401,326
1891–1901	3,221,823	149,543	−396,414	−246,871
1901–11	3,139,688	179,404	−261,539	−82,135
1911–26	2,971,992	237,333	−405,029	−167,696
1926–36	2,968,420	163,179	−166,751	−3,572
1936–46	2,955,107	173,798	−187,111	−13,313
1951–56	2,898,264	134,434	−196,763	−62,329
1956–61	2,818,341	132,080	−212,003	−79,923
1961–66	2,884,002	146,266	−80,605	65,661
1966–71	2,978,248	148,152	−53,906	94,246
1971–79	3,368,217	281,035	108,934	389,969

Table 30. *Population of Northern Ireland by County, 1926–1971*

	1926	1937	1951	1961	1966	1971
Antrim	191,643	197,266	231,149	273,905	313,991	355,716
Armagh	110,070	108,815	114,254	117,594	125,164	133,969
Belfast	415,151	438,086	443,671	415,856	398,405	362,082
Down	209,228	210,687	241,181	266,939	286,631	311,876
Fermanagh	57,984	54,569	53,044	51,531	49,886	50,255
Londonderry	139,693	142,736	155,540	165,298	174,658	183,094
Tyrone	132,792	127,586	132,082	133,919	136,040	139,073
TOTAL	1,256,561	1,279,745	1,370,921	1,425,042	1,484,775	1,536,065

Sources of Tables

Table 1: Column 1 was computed from the *1985 Statistical Yearbook of the Immigration and Naturalization Service*. (Washington, D.C., Department of Justice: Immigration and Naturalization Service, 1985), Table Imm, pp. 2–5. It should be remembered that figures in column 1 appear to cover only those whose last residence was Ireland and thus exclude Irish arrivals who had made an interim stop in another country; columns 2 and 3 were developed from the following sources: *Historical Sources of the United States: Colonial Times to 1970*. Bureau of the Census, 1975, pt. 1, pp. 116–18, for all statistics with the following exceptions: Irish-born for 1940 from *Census of Population, 1950, Vol. 2, Characteristics of the Population* (state volumes, Table 24); U.S. native of Irish parents for 1880 was computed from Statistics of the Population at the Tenth Census, June 1, 1880 (Washington, D.C., 1883), pp. 674ff; for 1890 the figures were computed from *Report of the Population of the U.S. at the Eleventh Census, 1890, pt. 1*, (Washington, D.C., 1895), pp. 686ff.

Parentage means one or both parents born in Ireland. The drop in numbers for 1890 is probably due to a quirk in either the statistical collection or differences in defining parentage between 1890 and other years.

Totals since 1930 apply only to the twenty-six counties of Ireland.

Table 2: Computed from Immigration and

Naturalization Service, *Statistical Yearbook of the Immigration and Naturalization Service, 1985*. Washington, D.C., 1986. Table Imm 1.2, pp. 2–6. See also note on p. 287 herein.

Table 3: Computed from the following: 1850, J. D. B. DeBow, *Statistical View of the United States*, Washington, D.C.: A. O. P. Nicholson, public printer, 1854, p. 116; 1860–1920, *Census of Population, 1950*, Vol. 2, *Characteristics of the Population*, Table 24 of respective state volume. The total Irish in Dakota for 1860 was developed by comparing the *1860 Census of Population* figures, which gave a total of 5,070 Irish for all seven territories, with the 1950 *Census of Population* cited above, which gives a breakdown by territories for 1860 but leaves out "Dakota" and also leaves unexplained 42 "missing" Irish immigrants in the territories at that time. It seems reasonable to assume that for 1860 the "missing" 42 are in the "missing" Dakota territory.

Table 4: Computed from United States Census Bureau, *Census of Population, 1950, Vol. 2, Characteristics of the Population*, Table 24 of respective state volume; *Census of Population, 1960*, Table 99 of respective state volume; *Census of Population 1970, Vol. 1*, Table 141 of respective state volume; *Census of Population 1980, Vol 1, General Social and Economic Characteristics*, Table 63 of respective state volume.

Table 5: Computed from United States Census Bureau, *Census of Population, 1950, Vol. 2, Characteristics of the Population*, Table 24 of respective state volume; *Census of Population, 1960*, Table 99 of respective state volume; *Census of Population, 1970*, Vol. 1, Table 141 of respective state volume; *Census of Population 1980, Vol. 1, Characteristics of the Population*, Table 195 of respective state volume.

Table 6: Computed from data given on successive U. S. Census of Population Reports.

Table 7: Computed from data given on successive U. S. Census of Population Reports.

Table 8: Data for the years 1851 to 1855 are calculated from the *Reports of the Emigration Commissioners*, as given in Great Britain, *Sessional Papers* (HC), 1856 xxi, *Census of Ireland for the Year 1851*, xxiv, "Reports from Commissioners: 1856," pp. liii-lviii.

Although the figures for 1851 to 1855 give a clear picture of movement out of Ireland, there are certain problems involved in using them as an indicator of social position of immigrants to the New World. Brinley Thomas states that since these figures are based on enumerations of all individuals leaving Irish ports, regardless of destination, they are of little value in determining who went to the United States. Closer inspection, however, reveals that the figures for the early 1850s are based on responses from individuals not intending to return to Ireland; thus they exclude seasonal migrants (*Reports of the Emigration Commissioners, in Census of Ireland for the Year 1851*, "Reports from Commissioners: 1856," pp. liv, xci).

Moreover, during the decade from 1851 to 1861, the Irish-born population of Great Britain increased by 79,000. When we add to this figure the numbers required to replace deaths among the Irish population in Great Britain over the decade, we find that as many as 215,000 Irish migrants may have crossed the Irish Sea over the period. This would suggest that slightly over 100,000 Irish moved to Great Britain over the years from 1851 to 1855. But since the data presented above are based on responses from 747,999 departing individuals, the inclusion of 100,000 journeying to Great Britain would not significantly alter the proportions in each occupational group bound for the United States. This is particularly true in light of recent studies, which indicate that Irish migrants to English cities during the nineteenth century were distributed throughout the occupational structure to the same degree as all emigrants who departed Ireland. Similarly, although the approximately 50,000 emigrants who left home bound for Australia and New Zealand over the years from 1851 to 1855 came from all occupational levels, Irish from the middle and upper reaches of the social structure were probably overrepresented in the long-distance movement. This would strengthen our argument that the great majority who moved to the United States came from the lower levels of rural society. See Brinley Thomas, *Migration and Economic Growth*, 2d ed. (Cambridge: At the University Press, 1973), pp. 72–73; Oliver MacDonagh, "The Irish in Victoria, 1851–91: A Demographic Essay," *Historical Studies: Papers Read before the Irish Conference of Historians*, viii (Dublin, May 1969), pp. 70ff; Ireland, *Commission on Emigration and Other Population Problems, 1948–1954*

(Dublin: Stationary Office, 1955), Statistical Appendix, Table 26, p. 314.

Data for the years 1875 to 1880 are calculated from Thomas, *Migration and Economic Growth,* Table 82, p. 384; entrepreneurial group has been included with manufacturers. Numbers do not add up to 100 because of rounding. The exact percentage for professionals for the years 1852, 1853, 1854, 1855, 1875, and 1880 are respectively, 0.2, 0, 0.3, 0.3, 0.7, and 0.3.

Table 9: Computed from data given in Brinley Thomas, *Migration and Economic Growth,* 2d ed. (Cambridge: At the University Press, 1973), Table 82, pp., 384ff.

Table 10: Computed from the *Annual Reports of the Commissioner General of Emigration to the Secretary of Labor* (Washington, D.C., 1911–32).

Table 11: U.S. Department of Justice, Immigration and Naturalization Service, *Annual Report of the Immigration and Naturalization Service* (Washington, D.C.: Government Printing Office for the respective year).

Table 12: U.S. Department of Justice, Immigration and Naturalization Service, *Annual Report of the Immigration and Naturalization Service* (Washington, D.C.: Government Printing Office, 1976–77), Table 8 of respective volume; *Statistical Yearbook of the Immigration and Naturalization Service* (Washington, D.C.: Government Printing Office, 1978), Table 8; for 1979 and later years see ibid, Table Imm 6.1; data for 1981 are unavailable.

Table 13: *Reports of the Immigration Commission* (Dillingham Reports). Abstracts of the Reports of the Immigration Commission. In two volumes: volume 1, 61st Congress, 3d Session, Senate Document no. 747, Presented by Mr. Dillingham, Dec. 5, 1910. Table 9. Immigration to the United States, 1820–1910; Part 2: By country of origin and by sex, for years ending June 30, 1869 to 1910; for 1913 to 1932 see *Annual Report of the Commissioner General of Immigration to the Secretary of Labor,* (Washington, D.C.); for 1941 see *Annual Report of the Attorney General;* for 1943 to 1977 see *Annual Report of the Immigration and Naturalization Service;* for 1978 to the present see the *Statistical Yearbook of the Immigration and Naturalization Service* for the respective year. For some years, the figures include Irish arrivals returning from a visit to the homeland. See original source for details. See also note on p. 287 herein.

Table 14: Computed from the United States Bureau of the Census, *Census of Population, 1980, Vol. 1, Characteristics of the Population* (Washington, D.C.: Government Printing Office, 1981). Table 60 of respective state volume.

Table 15: Computed from the United States Bureau of the Census, *Census of Population, 1980, Vol. 1, Characteristics of the Population* (Washington, D.C.: Government Printing Office, 1981). Table 195 of respective state volume.

Table 16: Computed from the United States Bureau of the Census, *Census of Population, 1980, Vol. 1, Characteristics of the Population* (Washington, D.C.: Government Printing Office, 1981). Table 195 of respective state volume.

Table 17: Computed from successive censuses of Ireland as reported in the parliamentary papers of Great Britain.

Table 18: Successive censuses of Ireland as reported in Ireland, Central Statistics office, *Census of Population of Ireland, 1979,* Vol. 1, pp. 6–9; and Central Statistics Office, *Census of Population of Ireland, 1986,* preliminary population figures, p. 3.

Table 19: Computed from Ireland, *Statistical Abstract of Ireland, 1980* (Dublin: At the Stationary Office, 1983), Table 35, p. 48.

Table 20: Computed from Ireland, *Statistical Abstract of Ireland, 1980* (Dublin: At the Stationary Office, 1983), Table 37, p. 48. Irish speakers are defined as those who claim to speak only Irish together with those who claim to speak both Irish and English. The second set of data for 1926 and all following years are for the population over three years of age.

Table 21: Computed from data given in Table 17 above.

Table 22: Computed from data given in Table 17 above.

Table 23: Computed from successive censuses of Ireland as reported in the parliamentary papers of Great Britain.

Table 24: Computed from successive censuses of Ireland as reported in the parliamentary papers of Great Britain.

Table 25: Computed from N. H. Carrier and J. R. Jeffrey, *External Migration: A*

Study of the Available Statistics, 1815–1950 (London: Her Majesty's Stationary Office, 1953), p. 67; *Statistical Abstract of Ireland, 1938* (Dublin: At the Stationary Office, 1938), p. 33; *Statistical Abstract of Ireland, 1958* (Dublin: At the Stationary Office, 1958), p. 51; *Statistical Abstract of Ireland, 1980* (Dublin: At the Stationary Office, 1983), p. 50; preliminary reports of 1986 census of Ireland. The figures for 1926 and subsequent years apply to the Irish Free State only.

Table 26: Overseas defined as other than Great Britain. Figures are computed from Table 93 in Ireland, *Commission on Emigration and Other Population Problems, 1948–1954* (Dublin: Published at the Stationary Office, 1954). Percentages do not add up to 100 because of rounding and unknown element moving to destinations other than the above.

Table 27: Computed from Ireland, *Commission on Emigration and Other Population Problems, 1948–1954* (Dublin: Published at the Stationary Office, 1954), Statistical Appendix, Tables 27 and 29, pp. 317 and 320. Figures include the entire 32 counties. Percentages do not add up to 100 because of rounding and unknown element.

Table 28: Computed from data given in N. H. Carrier and J. R. Jeffrey, *External Migration: A Study of the Available Statistics, 1815–1950* (London: Her Majesty's Stationary Office, 1953), p. 104.

Table 29: Computed from Ireland, *Statistical Abstract of Ireland, 1980* (Dublin: At the Stationary Office, 1983), Table 6, p. 20. Figures based on census taken at end of period indicated.

Table 30. Computed from census of Ireland for respective year.

Index to Manuscript Collections and Government Manuscripts and Publications

Abbey Theatre, 213, 222, 246
Abercrombie, James, 232
Academy of Political Science, 237
Acheson, Dean, 256
Act of Union, 241
Adjutant General's Office, 268
admission laws, 267
aeronautical equipment, 278
AFL-CIO, 249
Aglionby, Francis Yates, 241
Agricultural Service, foreign, 271
agricultural statistics, 275, 276
agricultural trade agreement, 281
agriculture, 255, 271, 275, 276, 277
Air Line Pilots Association, 223
air transport services, 278, 280
airfields, 262
Alice Gold and Silver Mining Company, 229
alien contract law, 271
aliens, registration of, 265
All Hallows College, Dublin, 212
Allen, Fred (1894–1956), 216
Allen, W. Harmon van, 222
Allen, William Harvey, 237
Allgood, William C., 209
Alpine County, Nevada, 232
Althrop, Viscount, 245
American Association for the Recognition of the Irish Republic, 230
American Commission on Irish Independence, 238
American consular officers, 264
American Expeditionary Forces (1917–23), 269; tactical units, 269
American Federation of Labor, 206, 210
American Federation of State, County and Municipal Employees, 222

American Federation of Teachers, 223
American Forces in France, 269
American Friends of Irish Neutrality, 235
American Irish Historical Society, 235, 236
American Irish Historical Society, Illinois Chapter, 210
American League for an Undivided Ireland, 235, 236
American Peace Commission, 277
American products in Ireland, 276
Anaconda Company, 229
Ancient Order of Hibernians, 204, 213, 227, 230, 232
Anderson Poetry Collection, 217
Anderson, Margaret M. Casey, 231
Anderson, Mary Jane Hill, 226
Anderson, William Hamilton, 237
Angelesey, Henry William Paget: First Marquis of (1768–1854), 240
Appalachia, 242, 254
appropriations: Aid to Ireland, 284; for statue of John Barry, 279
army personnel, 268
army recruiting areas, 271
artillery units, 272
Associated Friends of Ireland in the City of Baltimore, 215
Astor Place rioters, 238
Atherton, Ray, 256
athletic clubs, Irish-American, 276
atomic energy, 280–82
automotive industry, 277
aviation, civil, 280
aviation survey, continental Europe, 282

Ballard, Mrs. Charles W., 211
banking statistics, 275
banking, during World War II, 271
Bannon, John (1829–1913), 250
Bannon, Reverend Fr. John, 208
Bantry Bay, tour report, 283
Barnard, Kate, 243
Barrus, Dr., Clara, 238
Barry family, 238
Barry, Commodore John (1745–1803), 246, 263, 265, 278
Batcheller, George Sherman (1836–1908), 233
Battle of Little Bighorn, 229, 272
Bell, Robert, 209
Bennet, William Stiles, 237
Beottiger, Anna Roosevelt, 256
Berinsky Burton Photograph Collection, 219
Bernard Road Train, 276
Berryman, John, 229
Beth El Temple, 222
Bickel, Karl A., 256
Big Creek Township, 213
Bill of Rights, 260
Billings, Warren, 202
Billmyer Family, 240
Binder, Carroll, 256
Binkerd, Robert S., 237
biologicals market, 279
Birmingham, Stephen, 217
Bissell, Thomas, 242
Blair, Mary Jane, 242
Bligh, John, Fourth Earl of Darnley (1767–1831), 241
Board of Inspection and Survey, 262
Boer War, 238
Bolivar's campaign, 277
Bonaparte, Napoleon, 210
Bond, Mary, 214
Bone, Homer T., 256
Boston Police Strike, 217

337

Index

bounty land claims, 263
Boyce, Reverend John, 222
Boyle, William M., Jr., 227
Boyton, Michael P. 275
Branford, Massachusetts, 222
Brannon, Father John, 228
Bresnahan, Mary B., 229
British Army, 246
British Board of Trade, 276
British Navy, 272
British possessions, 274
Brondel, Bishop John, 230
Brooke family, 254
Brooke, St. George Tucker, 254
Brookwood Resident Workers College, 210
Brophy, P. J., 229
Brophy, Robert S., 209
Brownigg family, 240
Brownigg, General Richard Thomas (born 1793), 240
Brownigg, John, 240
Brownigg, Priscilla Elizabeth Bailey, 240
Brownigg, Richard, 240
Brownigg, Ruth, 240
Brownigg, Thomas, 240
Brownson, Orestes, 212
Bryan, William Jennings, 238
Buhrman, Parker, 256
Burden Light, (Edward P. Keenan) 225
Burdett, Sir Francis, 245
Bureau of Census, 261
Bureau of Customs, 262
Bureau of Indian Affairs, 266
Bureau of International Labor Affairs, 283
Bureau of Labor Statistics, 272
Bureau of Land Management, 263
Bureau of Naval Personnel, 261
Bureau of Prisons, 270
Burke family, 238
Burke, Edmund, 241
business, establishment of, 280, 281
business, Irish involvement in, 261
Butler family, 221, 234
Butler, Pierce (1866–1939), 226
Butte, Montana: mining conditions and industrial relations, 276; Workingmen's Union, 229
Byrne, Donn (1889–1928), 216
Byrne, James C., 224
Byrnes, James F., 256
Byrne, John E., 219

Cahill, George, 222
Cahill, Marie, 221
Callahan family, 226
Canada, 229, 280
Canadaigua region, 235
Capston, Lieutenant J. L., 208
Carew, Sir Benjamin Hallowell, 240
Carleton, Thomas (1699–1792), 245
Carney, Jack, 238
Carroll, Bishop John, 230
Carroll, Charles, 215
Carroll, James, 217
Carson River Mills, 232
Carter, James C., 238
cartographic records, 261, 263, 271
Carvill family, 249
Casa Maria House of Hospitality, 255
Casement, Sir Roger, 204, 238, 276
Casey family, 231
Casey, Albert E., 201
Casey, Edward Francis, 224
Casey, Peter, 210
Casserly, Mr. and Mrs. Eugene, 226
Cassidy, James F., 225
Catholic Club of Greater New York, 236
Catholic Diocese records, 239, 241, 248, 254
Catholic newspapers, 19th century, 247
Catholic Telegraph, 242
Catholic-Protestant Relations, 256
cattle trade, 275
Cavanaugh, John W., 212
Cavanaugh, Michael, 242
Cavendish, Sir Henry, 207
"Celtic Library," 224
censorship, Irish newspapers, 256
census records, 205, 220, 224, 231, 242, 246, 261; California, 203; Catholic diocese of Cincinnati, 242; Colorado, 205; Iowa, 213; Ireland, 252; Kansas, 213; Massachusetts, 220; Michigan, 224; New York, 233; Rhode Island, 250; Washington Territory, 253; Wyoming, 255
Central Intelligence Agency, 228
Charillu, Paul du, 238
charitable institutions, 263
Chase, William D., 246
Chesapeake and Ohio Canal Company, 266
Chicago Federation of Labor, 209, 210
Childers, Christabel, 209
Chopin, Kate O'Flaherty, 228
Chouan rebels, 211
Chrisman and Stuarts Company, 251

Christie, James C., and Elizabeth, 226
church records, 209
Churchill, William R., 238
Churchill, Winston, 238
circuit court, 260
cities, condition of residental areas, 265
Civil Aeronautics Board, 227
civil aviation, 280
civil conflict, 283, 284
civil conflicts, causes and settlement prospects, 282
Civil War, 210, 211, 216, 217, 224, 226, 227, 228, 233, 234, 240, 244, 250, 269, 271, 272; recruitment for, 260, 264, 268, 269–70
civil works administration, 265
Clan Na Gael, 236
Clanricarde, marquis of, 207
Clapp, James, 234
Clark, Dennis, 246, 248
Clark, William H., 238
Clarke, Adam, 210
Clarke, Ambrose, 215
Clarke, General Henri Jacques, 210
Cleburne, Patrick Ronayne (1828–64), 269
Cleeve, Brian Talbot, 222
Cleveland, Grover, 238
coal industry, 254
Cobbett, William, 232
Cockran, Congressman W. Bourke (1854–1923), 235, 238
Coffey, Celia M., 231
Cohalan, Justice Daniel F., 236
Cole family, 247
College for American Council on Education, 225
College Settlement, 248
Collins, John, 216
Collins, Patrick Andrew, 222
colonial policies, 277
Colorado, 205
Colum, Mary, 224, 233
Colum, Padraic, 209, 224, 237, 238
commerce, 279
Commision of Fine Arts, 265
Committee of Public Information, 265
Committee of Vigilance of San Francisco, 202, 204
Committee on Foreign Affairs, 274
Committee on Irish Finance, 245
Committee on Pensions, 275
commodities, during World War II, 271
Conaty, Reverend Thomas J., 223
Confederate Army, 240

Index   339

confederate records, collection of war department, 269
Confederate States of America, 227, 228; army, 250
Congress of Industrial Organizations, 206
Congressional Information Service (C.I.S.), 273
congressional reports, 273
Conlan, Frank [Frank Murphy], 210
Conley, Dr. Patrick R., 250
Conley, Patrick T., 250
Connell, Evan, 217
Connelly, Matthew J., 227, 228
Connolly, Maurice, 213
conservation, promotion of, 268
Constellation, relief ship, 238, 275
Constitution, 260
consular officers, 280
consular posts, 266
Consumer Reports, 275, 276
Continental Commands, U.S. Army, 272
Conway, Katherine E., 223
Conway, Richard, 229
Conzemius, Catherine Row, 226
Cook, Nathan, 246
Cooke, Alistair, 217
Corby, Reverend William, 212
corn laws, 240, 245
Cornwall, Flora S., 209
Corrigan, Archbishop Michael, 220
Cosgrave, Liam T., 210
Cosgrave, William T., 210
cost of living, working men in cities, 276
Costello family, 246
Costello, Monico, 229
Coudert, Frederic René, 237
Coulee Dam, 254
Craig, Edward Gordon, 209
Crandall family (of Grariot County Michigan), 223
Crandall, Albert Rogers, 234
Crangle, Emily Elkus, 234
Crangle, Roland, 234
Crawford Theatre collection, 206
Crawford, John, 215
Crimean War, 216, 240
Crimmins, John D., 207
Croker, John Wilson, (1780–1857), 240
Croker, Richard, 238
Cronin, A. J.. 256
Cronin, Dr. Patrick, 211
Crosby, Harry Lillis (Bing), 254
Crowley, Thomas, 202
crude drugs, 279
Cruice, Robert Blake, 247
Cuala Press, 222, 238

Cudahy, John, 256
Cullen, Michael D. (1941–)
Cullen, Reverend Thomas, 225
Cundun, Padraig, 238
Currie, town in Minnesota, 226
Curry, Charles F., 228
Curtis family, 246
Cushing, Richard Cardinal, 221
Custer, General George Armstrong, 229, 272
customs procedures, 281
customs requirements for shipment, 278

D'Alton, John, 210
D'Arcy, Nicholas, 253
D'Arcy, William, 206
Dale, Samuel Sherman (1859–1935), 237
Dale, Thomas, 237
Daly, Charles Patrick (1816–99), 238
Daly, Maria (Lydig), 238
Dansany, Lord and Lady, 233
Davie, Preston (1881–1967), 214
Davis, Jackson (1882–1947), 239
Davis, John T., 237
Deasy, Mary, 217
Democratic National Committee, 219, 227
Department of Agriculture, 260, 268, 271
Department of Commerce, 272
Department of Commerce and Labor, 267
Department of Interior, 261, 272
Department of Justice, 267, 270; general records, 264
Department of Labor, 272
Department of State: Foreign Service Posts, 266; general records, 264
Department of Treasury, 262, 267; general records, 264
Dermody, Frank, 209
deserters, from United States military, 266, 269, 270, 272
de Valera, Prime Minister Eamon, 210, 236, 256
Devereaux family, 234
Devereus, Nicholas, 234
Devlin, Bernadette, 235
Devoy, John, 236
Dewey, Thomas B., 217
diaries: of immigration officials, 267
Dickinson, Mabel, 202
Dickstein, Samuel, 237
Dillon, John, 238
disposition of property, 275
District Courts of U.S., 260

Diversified Community Services, 248
Dixon House, 248
Dobbins family, 224
Dobbs, Arthur (1689–1764), 243
Dodd, Edith S., 209
Dolan, Joseph, 219
Dolan, Thomas F., 207
Dolphin, John F., 225
Domestic and International Business Administration, 283
Donnelly, Ignatius, 226, 246
Donoughmore, Earl of, 207
Dorman, Nora (Robinson), 209
double taxation, 279, 280
Dougherty, Marcella, 231
Dougherty, Michael J., 231
Douglas County, Nevada, 232
Dowden, Elizabeth Dickinson (West), 238
Dowling, John, 211
Dowling, Robert, 208
Downey, John G., 203
Doyle, Michael, 246
draft, military: exemption, 270; resistance, 255, 277; management of, 270
Dublin Conference, 282
Dublin Gallery of Modern Art, 237
Dublin Review (1838–1923), 204
Dugan, Ralph, 218
Dulles, John F., 256
Dun and Company (later Dun and Bradstreet), 218
Duncan, Ellen Douglas, 237
Dundas, Robert, 241
Dunfrey, William L., 219
Dungan, Ralph, 219
Dunning, William Archibald (1857–1922), 237
Dunphy, Jack, 217
Dunsany, Lord, 209, 246
duPont deNemours and company, 206
Dwyer, Anne Faussett, 211

Eakin family, genealogical material, 251
Eakin, William (1810–49), 251
Earls, Michael
Earls, Reverend Michael, 222
Early, John, 207
economic cooperation, 278
Economic Cooperation Administration, 279
Economic Cooperation Agreement, 279, 280
economic recovery programs, 279
economic review, 278, 279
Economic Survey of Irish Free State, 277
economic trends, 282, 283
Edgar, William, 238

Edgeworth, Richard, *The American Edgeworths: A Biographical Sketch of Richard Edgeworth with Letters and Documents*, 250
Education Bureau Report, 276
education, in Ireland, 276
educational data, 281
Edworth, Richard, 250
EEC membership, 281
Eggleston-Gildart-Roach family, 214
Eisenhower, Dwight D., 213
electoral records, 260
electric industry, 278
electrical markets, 278
Elliot, Richard E., 223
Elliot, Stephen, 240
Ellis County, Kansas, 213
emergency relief, federal, 265
emigration, from Ireland, 264, 275, 276
employment, 272
Erhardt, John C., 256
Erie Canal, 239, 282
Ershkowitz, Dr. Herbert, 248
Erskine, Andrew, 211
estate records, Irish, 204
estate tax, 283
Estes, George, 244
ethnic relations, Irish and Italians, 248
ethnic survey, Works Projects Association, 205
European Commission on Human Rights, 235
European Economic Community, 283
European parliament, 283
European Recovery Program, 278, 279
exclusion laws, 267
executive clemency, 271
exports and imports, Irish, 261
extradition, treaty with Great Britain and North Ireland, 273, 283; treaty with United States, 284

Faherty, Michel J., 210
Family Assistance Programs, 282
famine, in Ireland, 274
Far West, 272
Farley, James A., 256
Farmers' Cooperation Associations, 277
Farrell, James T., 248
Fay, Gerard, 209
federal laws, enforcement of, 265
federal pardons, 271
Federal Reserve System, 237

Federal Writers Project, 211, 254
feed grain exports, United States, 283
Feeney, Joseph G., 228
Feller, Daniel M., 244
Fenian Brotherhood, 206, 222, 224, 228, 235, 247, 264–66, 268, 272, 273; Canada, 271; prisoners in Ireland, 274
Fenian raids, 212, 229, 233
Fenians, commutation of sentences, 276
Field, Stanley, 256
Fine Arts, Commission of, 265
Finnegan's Wake (James Joyce), 243
First Irish Race Convention, 236
Fitch, Henry S., 210
Fitzgerald, F. Scott, 243
Fitzgerald, James, W., 242
Fitzpatrick, Bishop John, 221
Fitzpatrick, D. R., 219
Fitzpatrick, John, 209
Fleming, John, 234
Fleming, Leo, 229
Fleming, Sampson, 238
Fleming, Thomas J., 217
Flood, Daniel J., 249
Flynn, Edward J., 237, 256
Flynn, Vincent J., 225
Fogarty, John E., 250
Foley, Edward H. (1848–53)
Foley, John P., (1877–1964), 225
folklore, 249
Follet, Frederick (1804–91), 226
Forbes, Cameron, 256
Ford, Henry, 224
Ford, Patrick, 238
Foreign Affairs Committee, 274, 276, 277
Foreign Agricultural Service, 271
foreign aid, appropriation, 284
Foreign and Domestic Commerce Bureau, 279
Foreign Commerce Yearbook, 278
foreign exchange rates, 277
foreign farm products, 271
foreign labor conditions, 272
Foreign Relations Committee, 276
Foreign Service of United States of America, 278
foreign trade, 260
foreign travel taxes, 282
Forest Service, 268
Fort La Presentation, 239
"Fort Worth Fire," 283
Foster, William Zebulon, 210
Frederick, Maryland, 245
French Revolution, 240, 247

Frewen, Moreton, 238
Friendly Sons of St. Patrick, 233, 238
Friends of Irish Freedom, 216, 230, 236
Friends, Society of, 249
Fritton, J. Paul, 231
Frost, Wesley (1884–1968), 242
Fry, Miss E. M., 209
Fullerton, Robert, 250
"The Future of Political Science in America," 237

Gallaghan, James S. (1883–1950), 225
Gallagher, Hugh D., 211
Gallagher, Mary, 202
Gallatin Company, Illinois, 211
Galvin, Michael J., 227
Gardnerville, Nevada, 232
Garrett, George A., 255
Gary, Miss Nannie, 241
Gates, Bert, 229
Gates, Nelly, 229
Geary, James Aloysius, 206
Genealogical Libraries, Church of the Latter Day Saints, 202
genealogical records, 204, 205, 228, 229, 252–54
general land office, 263
geographic surveys, 262
George, Henry (1839–97), 238
Gerard, James W., 220, 237
Gerarty, Francis, 214
Gibbons family, 231
Gibbons, James, 228
Gill, Thomas P., 238
Gillen, Marrhias, 225
Gingrich, Arnold, 243
Gladstone, W. E., 235
Gladstone, William E., 275
Glashean, Mrs. Adaline, 234
Glass, James, 234
Glifford, Nathaniel T., 220
Gogarty, Oliver St. John (1878–1957)
Gold Rush, Colorado, 205
Gompers, Samuel, 210
Gonne, Maud, 209
Goodrich Social Settlement, 242
Gore-Booth, Eva (1870–1926), 249
Gorman, Arthur P., 220
Goulburn, Sir Henry, 245
government hospital for the insane, 263
Grace, John Patrick (1874–1940), 244
Graham family, 251
Graham, Hugh (1784–1865), 251
Graham, Sheila, 243
Grand Orange Lodge, 244

Index   341

grand jury venue, 283
grassland, 268
Gratz, Simon, 247
Gray, David, 234, 255, 256
Great Britain, Board of Trade, 244
Great Famine, 233
Great Northern and the Northern Pacific Railroad, 226
Greece, 280
Green, William, 210
Greeves, Ronald H., 205
Gregg, Alexander, 240
Gregory, Augusta Isabella (Persse), 209
Gregory, Lady, 209, 246
Grieve, C. M., 246
Griffin family, 240
Griffin, Martin I. J., 247
Griffin, William Joseph (1863–1959), 234
Groveland, Massachusetts, 222
Guardians of the Poor, 246
Guest, Raymond R., 281
Guignan, William H., 245
The Guild of Catholic Lawyers, 236
Guilday, Peter, 206
Guinan, Mary Louise Ceilia, 221
Guiney, Imogen, 222
Guiney, Patrick R., 223
Gunn, Bishop John Edward, 227

Hagerty, James C., 213
Hagerty, James Edward, 212
Hall, Thomas John (1883–1953), 215
Hamill, Pete, 217
Hamilton, Allen, 211
Hamlin, Chauncey J. (Jr. and Sr.), 256
handicraft, 279
Hannan, Michael J., 230
Hannigan family, 231
Harene family, 249
Harold, James, 254
Harper, Robert G., 232
Harrigan, Edward, 221
Harriman, E. H., 220
Harriman, W. A., 256
Harris, Richard Tighe, 201
Hartigan, William, 219
Harty, William, 241
Hawaii, immigration records, 208
Haynie, Hugh, 219
Healy Collection, 215
Healy, Bishop James A., 215
Healy, James O., collection on Irish History, 204
Healy, Patrick F., 207
Healy, Reverend Louis S., 223

Heffernan, John, 237
Hemingway, Ernest, 219
Henrico County, Virginia, 239
Henry, William, 223
Herbert, Victor, 216, 236
Herblock (cartoonist), 219
Herlihy, James Leo, 217
Heslin, Bishop Thomas, 227
Hessey, W. F., 209
Hester, Pat, 244
Hettrick, John T., 237
Hewitt, Joseph, 211
Hibernia Fire Company, 246
Hibernian Benevolent Society, 230
Hibernian Society, 247
Hickey, James E. (1890–1969), 232
Hickey, Thomas F., 239
Higgins, Aidan, 209
Higgins, Brian, 209
Hill, William, 250
Hinch, Benjamin P., 211
Hinch, H., 211
Historical Records Survey, 244, 265
Hoban, John (1762–1831), 262
Hobson, Bulmer, 204
Hoffman, Louisa (Gillman), 253
Hoffman, Samuel Owens, 253
Hoffman, W. Gilmore, 253
Hogan, Joseph Lloyd, 239
Hogan, Martin, 229
Holland, John P., 232
Holland, John Philip (1840–1914), 272
The Holy Door, 209
Holyoake, George Jacob, (1817–1906), 245
home rule, in Ireland, 275
Hotze, Henry, 207
House of Industry, 248
Hughes family, 240
Hughes, Archbishop John, 206, 247
Hull, Cordell, 256
human rights, 283
Humphrey, William, 250
Humphreys, Robert, 234
Huneker, James G., 246
Hurley, Monsignor, 215
Hutchinson family, 245
Hyde, Douglas, 207
Hydrographic Office, 262

Illinois Republican Council, 210
immigrant letters, 201, 240–242
Immigration and Naturalization Service, 267
immigration, 248, 273, 275, 276: effect of 1965 law, 282;

laws, violations of, 267;
records, 210, 214, 218, 244
import tariff system, 280, 281
importers, 279
income tax, 284
income tax, convention, 283
independence, Irish, 262
independent Ireland, recognition of, 264
Index (London), 207
Indian Currency Commission, 237
Industrial Commission, 276
Industrial Workers of the World, 205, 224
industrial relations, 276
industries, Irish, 276
infantry, 272
Instructive District Nursing Association, 217
internal trade, Ireland, 260
International Brotherhood of Electrical Workers, 228
international peace conference, 276
international protection of human rights, 283
International Trade Office, 279
international treaties, 260
International Workers of the World, 202
Interparliamentary Union, 282
IRA *see* Irish Republican Army
Iredell, James Jr., 245
Iredell, James Sr., 245
Ireland, Archbishop John, 226
Ireland, John, 225
Ireland, labor conditions in, 276
Ireland, Parliament, House of Commons debates (1776–89), 207
Ireland, Union to the Free State, 216
Ireland, United States citizens in, 274, 276
Irish Banking Commission, 237
Irish Bulletin, 212
Irish Catholic Benevolent Union, 247
Irish Civil War, 267
Irish College in Rome, 206
Irish Echo, 216
Irish Emancipation Society of Maryland, 215
Irish Export Board, 281
Irish Fellowship Club of Chicago, 210
Irish Forestry Act of 1928, 268
Irish Free State, 264, 271, 275, 277, 278
Irish Freedom League, 236
Irish Immigrant Aid Society of Ohio, 242

Index

Irish Immigrant Society, 275
Irish Independence Movement, 273, 277
Irish Labor movement, 239
Irish Land League, 222, 242
Irish Landlord Records, 204
Irish National Bureau, 277
Irish Parliament, 241
Irish Parliamentary Party, 242
Irish Pictorial Weekly, 216
Irish potatoes, marketing quotas, 281
Irish Progressive League of New York, 277
"Irish Question," 266
"Irish Question," hearings, 276
Irish Race Convention, 230
Irish Republican Army, 284, 271; hunger strikes, 256; suspected members, 283; veterans clubs, 236
Irish Republican Brotherhood, 236
Irish Revolution, 247
Irish Times (1859–present), 204
Irish Unification Question, 284
Irish Volunteers of America, 230
Irish War of Independence, 222, 267
Irish work condition, 272
Irish-American Athletic Club, 276
Irish-American Club Company, 242
Irish-American Colonization Company, 226
Italians, 248

Jackson, W. W., 234
Jackson, William, 232
Jay, John, 236
Jefferson, Thomas, 232
John, Augustus, 246
Johnson, Lyndon Baines, 251
Johnston family, 247
Johnston, Thomas, 245
Johnston, Zachariah, 245
Jones, Charles W., 208
Journal (of the American-Irish Historical Society), 216
Joyce, James, 213, 217, 234, 243
Judge Advocate General: Army, 270; Navy, 270
Judiciary Act of 1911, 260

Kane, Whitford, 238
Kavanagh, Patrick, 209
Kazin, Alfred, 243
Kearney, Dennis, 202
Kearney, James Edward, 239
Keating, Geoffrey, 210
Keefe, Richard, 220
Keenan, Edward P., 225
Keenan, James, 228

Keenan, Joseph G., 228
Keitinn, Seuthrum, 210
Kelly, Gene 217
Kelly, Mary, 217
Kennedy, Edward M. 219
Kennedy, John F., 218, 228, 230, 252, 256
Kennedy, Joseph P., 219, 256
Kennedy, Robert F., 217, 219
Kennedy, Rose F., 219
Kennedy, Thomas, 229
Kenny, Reverend Patrick, 206
Kenny, Sister Elizabeth, 224
Kentucky, 274
Keogh, Judge Martin J., 238
Kerens, Richard C., 268
Kernan family, 234
Kernan, Senator Francis, 234
Kerrigan, Anthony, 209
Kerwin, Michael, 228
Kickham, Charles, 206
Kilmer, Joyce, 217
Kilroe, Edwin Patrick, 237
King Family, 211
King, Campbell Denniston, 211
King, Charles Speer (born 1832), 211
King, David (1794–1877), 211
King, David Jr. (born 1838), 211
King, John Nevin (1827–1915), 211
King, John Stuart, 211
King, Joseph Rush Hays (born 1846), 211
King, Lucie Stuart (born 1842), 211
King, Sarah Ann (Denniston), 211
King, Thomas Clark (1834–66), 211
King, William Henry, 211
Kinsella, Thomas, 209
Kirkpatrick, Robert, 250
Kite, Joseph, 246
Kite, Mary, 246
Knight family, 238
Knights of Labor, 206, 207
Know Nothing party, 240, 262
Koger, J. T., 227
Korson, George, 249
Krock, Arthur, 237
Ku Klux Klan, 226
Kurtz, Charles L., 242
Kyle family, 251
Kyle, A. A., 251
KYW radio station, 248

labor, conditions, 272, 276, 282, 283
Labor party, 210
labor unions, 234, 248, 249, 254
Lacy, Ed, 217
Lake City, Minnesota, 226

Lalor, Captain J. F., 208
Lamont, Thomas W., 256
land, acquisition, 268; settlement, 263
landlord records, 204
Langton, Elizabeth, 232
Lansing, Robert, 207
Lanz, the Marquise Clara, 237
Larkin, James "Big Jim," 239, 271
Laughlin, James, 229
Lavin, Mary, 209, 217
Lawes, Lewis E., 236
Lawless, Valentine Brown, 241
Lawlor, Teresa, 204
Lawrence, David L., 228
Lawrence Mill strike, 217
Le Mintier, Monseigneur, 211
Lea, Clarence, 256
Lease, Mary Elizabeth Clyens, 214
Lee family, 231
legislation proceedings, 263
Lehman, Herbert J., 236
Levin, Mary, 233
Lewis, John Livy (1813–89), 234
licensing and exchange controls, 280
life expectancy, 277
Liverpool, Lord, 245
livestock industry, 281
living conditions, 281
living costs, 279
Loughlin, Bishop John, 233
Low (cartoonist), 219
Loyal Irish Record Book 1929–1930, 229
Lundy, Belle, 255
Lynch, Bishop P.N., 208
Lynch, Brian, 209
Lynch, Dominick, 220
Lynch, Robert B., 274
Lyster, William Narcissus, 223

MacCarthy, H. O'C., 242
MacDonald, John, 254
MacGillycuddy family, 249
MacGillycuddy, Dennis C., 249
Mackenzie, Compton, 209
Madison, James, 207
Maguire, Bernard, 207
Maher, Sister Patrick Ellen, 227
Mahon, Dr. James, 211
Mahoney, Jeremiah T., 237
Mahoney's resolution, 275
mail transportation, 274
Malet family, 241
Malone, John C., 233
Malone, William M., 228
Maloney family, 211
Manion, Ellen, 229
Manogue, Bishop Patrick, 231
Mansfield, Mike, 230

Index   343

maritime commission, 278
maritime jurisdiction, 260
marketing, 283
markets, leather products, 279
Marlborough, the Ninth Duke of, 238
Martin, John Hill (1823–1906), 247
Marty, Bishop, 250
Massachusetts League for Nursing, 217
Mather, Flora Stone, 242
Matteson, David Maydole, 207
Matthews, Francis P., 227
Maynard, Sara Casey, 207
Mayne, Rutherford (Samuel Waddell), 209
McAuley, Catherine, 215
McBreath family, 226
McBride, William, 204
McCahil, William P., 227
McCardle, James, 204
McCarran, Patrick, 231
McCarthy, Charles (1873–1921), 255
McCarthy, Charles Jr., 215
McCarthy, Eugene, 207
McCarthy, Katheryn O'Loughlin, 213
McCarthyism, 236
McCloud, Richard, 228
McConnell family, 211
McCormack, John, 256
McCormick, John and Ann, 250
McCormick, John W., 217
McCormick, John, 230
McCormick, Wilfred, 217
McCreery, Maria Maud Leonard (1883–1938), 255
McCullough family, 245
McCullough, Patrick, 220
McCullough-Hutchinson papers, 241
McDermot, Frank, 256
McDermott, Michael, 207
McDonald, Vincent, 229
McDonnell, Bishop Charles Edward, 233
McDowell, Davison (1784–1842), 250
McElroy, R. M., 238
McFadden, Bishop, 243
McGarrity, Joseph, 204
McGavock, Hugh, 240
McGohey, John F. X., 227
McGrath, Earl J., 228
McGrath, J. Howard, 227
McGuire, Charles H., 227
McHenry family, 215
McLaughlin, James, 241
McLeod, Scott, 280
McMahon, Father John, 212
McMahon, Joseph H. (1862–1939), 212

McMahon, Joseph, 223
McMahon, Rev. John, 274
McManus, Meagher, 232
McMullen and McGloin colonies, 252
McMullen family, 241, 245
McNally, Christopher, 235
McNish family, 235
McNish, Alexander, 235
McQuaid, Bernard J., 239
McSweeney, Edward (1846–1943), 225
Meagher, Thomas Francis, 238, 268, 272
meat industry, 281
medical data, Eire, 278
Meehan, Thomas F., 207
Melville, Henry Dundas, First Viscount (1742–1811), 245
Mencken, Henry Louis (1880–1956), 245
meteorological instruments, markets for, 278
Methodist Church, 210
Methodists, 227
Mexican War, 211, 272
Meyers family, 215
military: organizations, 205, 244, 268, 269, 272; history, 217; honorable discharges, 1917–37, 261
Miller, Kerby, 223
Milwaukee 14, 255
mineral yearbooks, 281
Mines Bureau, 282
mining, 205, 229, 276; organizations, 265
missionary society, 239
Mitchel and Purroy family, 237
Mitchel, Jane Verner, 238
Mitchel, John (1815–75), 237, 238
Mitchel, John Purroy, 237
mobility, social, 244
modern Irish history, 217
Molly Maguire, 244, 247
Monday, Ann, collection on the North of Ireland, 204
money, common units of, 274
Monitor, 203
Montague, John, 209
Montana Council of Defense, 229
Monthly Consumer and Trade Report, 276
Mooney, Edward, 239
Mooney, James, 242
Mooney, Tom, 202
Moore family, 241
Moore, George (1852–1933), 237, 246
Moore, Thomas, 217
Morehead City, North Carolina, 241

Mormons, 226
Morris Canal, 232
Morris, William M., 234
Morrison, Frank, 210
Morton, Levi Parsons (1824–1920), 238
"Most Favored Nation," 279
Most Holy Trinity Roman Catholic Church, 223
motion picture equipment, 278
motion picture industry, 278
Mount-Temple family, 249
Moynihan, Humphrey (1862–1943), 225
Moynihan, James H. (1882–1959), 225
Mullaly, James J., 229
Mulligan, James A., 210
Mulligan, Marian Nugent, 210
Mullin family, 231
Mullin, Helen R., 231
Murphy family, 202, 230, 231
Murphy, Charles F., 236, 238
Murphy, Charles S., 227, 228
Murphy, Richard C., 236
Murphy, Henry E., 228
Murphy, Martin, Jr., 204
Murphy, Michael, 230
Murphy, Thomas, 231
Murray County Cooperative Company, 226
Murray, James E., 230
mutual security, 280

Napoleonic Wars, 215, 240, 241
Nast, Thomas, 219
National Agricultural Organization Society, 255
National Bankruptcy Acts, 260
National Defense Act of 1920, 269
National Library of Ireland collection, 208
National Park Service, 266
National Shipping Authority, 227
National Union of Women Workers of Great Britain and Ireland, 229
Native Americans, 266
naturalization, 263, 273
naturalization laws, 201, 205, 213, 214, 215, 218, 233, 242, 246, 252, 253, 260, 265; Connecticut, 205; Hawaii, 208
Naval Academy: Ireland, 278
Naval Communication Service, 262
Naval Observatory, 262
Naval Records, 263
naval stores, 279
navigation treaty, 279
navigation: air, 278

344 Index

Navy and Marine Corps, courts martial, personnel records of, 270
Navy Department Library, 263
negotiations: United States and Britain, 260, 266, 269, 270
Neill, Edward Puffield (1823–93), 228
Nenney and Graham Company, 251
Nenney family, 251
New Creek, West Virginia, 210
New Richmond, Wisconsin, Irish settlement in, 255
New York Fire Department, 238
New York State Barge Canal, 239
New York State Election of 1949, 237
New Zealand, 280
Newspaper Guild, 223
newspapers, Irish-American, 246
Neyland, John Francis, 202
Nockels, Edward, 210
Northern Ireland and Ireland Assitance Act, 282
Northern Ireland Civil Rights Association, 282
Northern Ireland Service Council, 283
Northern Ireland, 278, 279; collection of materials, 204
Norway, 280
nuclear cooperation of defense, 284
nuclear fuel research agreements, 282
nuclear research, 281
Nugent, James, 210
Nugent, Jane White, 242
Nursing Council of the United Community Service of Boston, 217

O'Brian, John Lord, 237
O'Brien (Greeves), Ann, 205
O'Brien, Dorothy, 219
O'Brien, John, 226
O'Brien, Lawrence, 218
O'Brien, Seamus, 235
O'Callahan, Reverend Donald M., 236
O'Casey, Sean (1880–1964), 209, 238
O'Connell, Andrew, 230
O'Connell, Archbishop, 221
O'Connell, Bishop Eugene, 203
O'Connell, Cardinal, 223
O'Connell, Joseph J. Jr., 228
O'Conner family, 211
O'Connor, Edwin (1918–68), 216

O'Connor, Flannery, 208, 229
O'Connor, Frank (Michael Francis O'Donovan, 1903–66), 217, 222
O'Connor, Msgr. J. Paul, 243
O'Connor, Richard, 217
O'Connor, Thomas P., 238
O'Cork, Shannon, 217
O'Donnell, Charles Leo (1884–1934), 212
O'Donnell, Frank J. Hugh, 209
O'Donnell, George Marion, 229
O'Donnell, Joseph P. (1847–1906), 254
O'Donovan Rossa, Jeremiah, 207
O'Donovan, Michael Francis, see Frank O'Connor
O'Dwyer, Paul, 235, 237
O'Dwyer, William, 237
O'Faolain, Sean, 202, 209
O'Farrell, Jaspar, 204
O'Flaherty, Edward, 242
O'Flaherty, Father Edward, 212
O'Flaherty, Liam, 209
O'Flanagan, Dermot, 201
O'Gara, John E., 228
O'Gorman, Daniel A., 220
O'Gorman, Thomas (1843–1921), 225
O'Grady, Desmone, 209
O'Hara, John, 249
O'Hegarty, P.S., Irish History collection, 213
O'Hern, John Francis, 239
O'Kane, John, 231
O'Keefe, John, 228
O'Keefe, Timothy, (1895–1974), 225
O'Kelley, Donal, 209
O'Kelley, Sean T., 204
O'Leary, John, 207, 209
O'Mahoney, John, 242
O'Mahoney, Joseph, 237
O'Mahony, John, 206
O'Malley, Austin (1858–1932), 212
O'Malley, Francis, 212
O'Meara, Stephen, 216
O'Meara, Walter, 217
O'Neal, James, 204
O'Neil, J. J., 275
O'Neill, Eugene, 206, 217
O'Neill, Fiedhlim, 210
O'Neill, Francis, 216
O'Neill, John, 228
O'Neill, Mary Devenport, 209
O'Neill, Scannell, 207
O'Neill, Thomas P., 219
O'Reilly, John Boyle (1844–90), 216, 222
O'Reilly, Leonara, 221
O'Reilly, Mary Boyle (1875–1939), 216, 223

O'Riordan, Conal O'Connell, 209
O'Shaughnessy, I. A. (1885–1973), 225
O'Sullivan, James Edward, 254
O'Sullivan, Sean, 209
O'Toole, James, M., 221
Office of Chief of Naval Operations, 262
Office of Naval Intelligence, 262
Office of Pardon Attorney, 271
Office of Price Administration, 271
Office of Public Buildings and Grounds, 262, 265
Office of Secretary of War, 269
Office of Solicitor of Treasury, 271
Office of Superintendent of Immigration, 267
Office of the Chief Signal Officer, 269
Office of the Judge Advocate General: Army, 270; Navy, 270
Office of the Secretary of the Interior, 263
Office of War Information, 271
offshore terminal, Bantry Bay, 283
Oldden, James, 232
ophthalmic products trade, 279
oral history, 212, 226, 228, 229, 231, 232, 234, 236, 237, 248, 254, 255
Order of the Visitation of Holy Mary, 245
Orr, Margaret, 231

Palmerston, Third Viscount, 245
paper industry, 279
pardons: federal, 271
Paris, 277
parish (or diocese) records, 201, 203, 205, 208, 211, 212, 213, 214, 215, 220, 227, 231, 232, 233, 243, 244
Parsons, Geoffrey, 237
"passenger arrival records," 267
passenger lists: general, 214, 231, 232, 246, 252, 262, 267; Baltimore, 242; Boston, 220; New York, 242; Salem, Massachusetts, 222
passports, 279
Patent Office, 271
patents, 263, 280
Paulding, Mississippi 227
peace prospects, 283
Pecora, Ferdinand, 237
pedigrees, Irish, 255
Peel, Sir Robert Bart (1788–1850), 245
Peel, Viscount, 235

Peirson, Reverend Thomas, 245
Pell, Herbert Clairborne, 237, 256
penal institutions: federal, 265
Pendergast, William A., 237
pension: Army and Navy, 263
pensions, 275, 276
personnel records: Navy, 263
Peterson, Hugh, 256
petitions: Irish Immigrant Association, 274
petroleum agreement: Great Britain and United States, 279
Phelan, James D., 202
Philadelphia Society for Employment and Instruction of the Poor, 248
Phillipine National Bank, 237
Phipps, Constantine Henry, First Marquis of Normandy, 245
photographs: military men, 272; servicemen and civilians, 269
Pickering, Timothy, 232
Pickett Papers (Confederacy, State Department papers), 208
Pilot, 216
pioneers, 205
Platt, Thomas Collier (1833–1910), 205–6
Plunkett, Sir Horace Curzon, (1854–1932), 202
Plunkett, Sir Horace, 209, 238, 255
Polin, Daniel, 246
political conditions: Ireland, 279
politicians, Irish, 220
politics, Irish, 245
Poor, Alfred, 222
port arrivals, 262
post-Civil War activity, 264
Potomac Company, 266
Potts family, 241, 245
Potts, William, 245, 246
Pound, Ezra, 209
Powderly, Terence Vincent, 207
Powell family, 247
Powell, Robert, 247
Presbyterian Church, records, 250
Presbyterians, 228
Presentation Sisters, 251
presidential involvement in Irish matters, 270
presidential messages, 274, 283
press censorship, 265
prices, during World War II, 271
Primrose, Sir Henry William (1846–1923), 245
prisoners, 228, 272; convict records, 263; political, 271, 276; federal, criminal and social histories, 270; Navy and Marine Corps, personnel records, 270; U.S citizens in Ireland, 274, 276

private investments, guarantee of, 280
Progress and Poverty, 238
property disposition, 275
Proskauer, Joseph M., 237
Provost Marshal General's Bureau: Civil War, 269
Public Health Service, 267, 277
public land transactions, 263
public laws, legislative history of, 273
public opinion, 264
Purcell, Richard Joseph, 207
Purdy, Lawson, 237
Purroy, John B., 237

Quakers, *see* Society of Friends
quarantine divisions, 268
Quinlan, John, (1859–83), 201
Quinn, Robert E., 250

radio market, 278
Rafferty, Scott, 219
Rahilly, Patrick H., 226
railroad records, 210, 275
railroads, 232, 262, 263; Erie, 234; Great Northern and the Northern Pacific, 226; Panama Rail Road (1852–1951), 204; Union Pacific Railroad, 231; Winona and St. Peter Railway Company, 226
Raleigh, Sir Walter, 217
Ramage, W., report of, 241
Read, George Cambell, 261
Reardon, Timothy, 218
reciprocal trade, 278
Recorder (of the American-Irish Historical Society), 216
Red River Rebellion, 229
Redmond, John, 238
Reed, Thomas B., 238
registration of aliens, 265
Regular Army Mobile Units: United States, 272
Reilly, John, 219
Reilly, John Timon, 247
Reilly, Reverend Patrick, 247
relief for starvation, 274
religious orders, Irish, 203
Renehan, Frank, 228
rents, World War II, 271
Report on Contageous Diseases, Silver Bow County, 1908–1912, 229
Republic Miscellany, 216
Republic of Ireland, selling in, 282
Resolutions of Kentucky, 274
Revolutionary War records, 268
revolutionary activities, 265
Reynolds, Quentin, 256
Rice, Charles T., 235
Ring, Thomas, 220

Riordan, James, 202
riots, Irish, 207, 247, 248, 252, 267
road systems, 276
Robbins, Reginald C., 256
Robert Emmet Literary association, 230
Roberts, William R., 242
Robinson, Lennox, 209
Rodd family, 239
Rooney, Congressman John, 233
Roosevelt, Eleanor, 256
Roosevelt, Franklin, 256
Roosevelt, J. Hall, 256
Roosevelt, James, 256
Roosevelt, Mrs. Kermit, 256
Roosevelt, Theodore, 238
Rossa, Jeremiah O'Donovan, 206, 222
Rountree family, 252
Rowntree, Joseph Gustave, 252
rum smuggling, 261
rural cooperatative movement: United States and Ireland, 255
rural development, 260
Russell A. E. (George William), 209, 246
Russell, George, 237
Russell, John Russell, First Earl (1792–1878), 245
Russell, Martin James, 210
Rutty, John, (1698–1775), 220
Ryan, James J., 247
Ryan, Msgr. John Augustine, 212

sailors: personnel papers and muster rolls, 261
sale of merchant vessels, 278
Salisbury, Frank C., 241
Salvation Army, 239
Sampson, William, 208
San Francisco, genealogical records, 204
sanitary data: Eire, 278
Savannah, 281
Saxe, Martin, 237
Scanlon family, 202
Scattergood family, 245
Scattergood, Thomas, 245
scholarship exchange program, 280
Schuck, Victoria, 220
Schumway, R. R., 225
Scotch-Irish Congress of 1899, 251
Scotch-Irish Foundation, 247
Scotch-Irish settlement, 253
Scotch-Irish, 247
Scotch-Irish, Genealogy of, 250
Scott family, 253
Scott, Isabella (Doherty), 253
Scott, John, 253
Scott, Joseph, 235

346 Index

Scully, William, 214
Sears, David, 209
Secretary of Treasury, correspondence, 264
seed situation, 279
Selective Service System, World War I, 270
Senate Foreign Relations Committee, 280, 283
Seneca Indians, 226
Seton, Elizabeth Ann, 216
Shackleton family, 245
Shackleton, Abraham (1699–1771), 245
Shackleton, Elizabeth [Carleton] (1726–1824), 245
Shackleton, Richard (1726–92), 241, 245, 246
Shackleton, Roger (died 1766), 246
Shackleton, William (1725–70), 246
Shanahan, Thomas Joseph, 247
Shannon, James P. (1921–   ), 225
Shannon, William V., 217
Shaw Society of America, 246
Shaw, Albert, 239
Shaw, Charlotte, 209
Shaw, George Bernard (1856–1950), 209, 215, 217, 237, 239, 246
Shea, John Gilmary, 207
Sheehan, William Francis (1859–1917), 220
Sheehy, Gail, 217
Sheen, Fulton John, 239
Shenandoah Valley, settlement of, 253
Shepard, Edward M., 238
Sheppard family, 246
shipping, to Ireland, 280
Silver Bow County Board of Health, 230
Sinclair, Samuel Fleming, 202
Sinn Fein, 256
Sisters of Charity, 216
Sisters of Mercy, 215, 233
Slafter, William, 224
Smith family, 239
Smith, Alfred E., 233, 245
Smith, Dr. Matthew, 250
Smith, Goldwin (1823–1910), 235, 238
Smith, Mary and Thomas, 253
Smith, Mrs. Margaret, 238
Smith, Thomas (1783–1841), 253
Smith, William S., 238
Snoddy, Oliver, 244
social mobility, 261
social welfare organizations, Catholic, 206

Society of Friends (Quakers), 242, 244–46, 248, 253
Society of the Friendly Sons of St. Patrick, 227, 236
Society of the Friendly Sons of St. Patrick of Philadelphia, 247
Socolofsky collection, 213
Solicitor of the Treasury, 271
songs, Civil War, 241
Sorgniard, J. B., 210
South Africa, 280
Southwark House, 248
Spanish-American War, 216, 238
Spellman, Archbishop, 256
Spencer, John, 245
Spencer, William M., 210
Spooner, John C., 220
Sproul, Andrew J., 240
St. Anthony's Catholic News, 208
St. Francisville, Louisiana, 211
St. Joseph's Orphanage, 212
St. Louis Orphanage, 243
St. Vincent De Paul Society, 220
Stabler, James Pleasants (1796–1840), 215
Stanfield House, 248
State Department, 276, 277
state penitentiaries, 267
Staunton family, 241
Steele, Ephraim, 240
Stephens, James, 206–9, 242, 243
Stevenson family, 235
Stevenson, Adlai E., 220, 256
Stevenson, Samuel, 235
Stewart Robert B., 256
Stimson, Henry L., 220
Stinton family, 205
Stitt, Agnes, 250
Stockdale, Edward G., 281
A Storyteller's Holiday (George Moore), 237
Stoughton, Thomas, 220
Street, Julian, 256
Stretch, John, 229
Stuart, Francis, 209
Sugar Act, extension, 283
sugar import, quotas, 281
Sullivan's Hollow, Mississippi, 227
Sullivan, J. J., 208
Sullivan, John L. (1842–1944), 228
Sullivan, William, 242
Sulpher Springs, Mississippi, 227
Sunburst Club, 230
Superintendent of Prisons, records of, 270
surveying, 274

Sutliff, Mary Louise, 237, 238
Sweetman, John, 226
Swift, Jonathan, 248

Tammany Hall, 236, 237
Tanner, Frederick Chauncy, 237
tariff and trade regulations, 280
tax conventions, 278; Great Britain and North Ireland, 283; ratification of, 280
taxes: income, 279; deceased persons, 279; estate and gift, convention with United States, 284
Taylor family, 247
Taylor, James Wickes (1819–93), 229
Temple, Henry John, 245
tenure, 275
territorial papers on Irish, 264
terrorism, prevention of, 283
terrorists, 284
Texas, colonization of, 251, 252
textile industry, 280
Thompson, Mary, 238
Tighe family, 231
Timon, Bishop, 233
tobacco growing, 276
tobacco, market notes, 278
Tobin, Daniel J., 256
Tobin, James, 235
Tomlinson, John C., 238
Tompkins family, 253
Tone, Wolfe, 232
Toomey, Edward, 219
tourism, 284
tourist visas, 283
Townshend, George, First Marquis (1724–1807), 220, 246
trade unions, 239, 279 (*see also* specific unions)
trade: United States with Ireland, 276, 278, 279, 281
trademark regulations, 280
Treasurer of the United States, 263
treaties with Britain, 274
Truman, Harry S., 227
Tuomy, Cornelius William, 223
Turner, Dawson (1775–1859), 253
Two Essays (James Stevens), 243
Tynan, Katherine (Hinkson), 209
Tynan, Katherine, 207
typhus fever, 277

Ulster Protestant, 256
Ulster-Irish Liberty Legion, 210
Ulysses, 243
Underwood family (of Lenawee County, Michigan), 223

Index 347

Underwood, Francis Henry, 222
unemployment, 272
Unification Hearings, 279
Union Army draft, 269
Union Army, illegal recruitment information, 270
Union Pacific Railroad, 231
United Auto Workers, 223
United Communities of Southeast Philadelphia, 248
United Farm Workers, 223
United Irish Counties Association, 236
United Irish League of America, 216
United Mine Workers, 206
United Neighbors Association, 248
United Presbyterian Church in America, 247
United States Army Commands, 269
United States Army Continental Commands, 272
United States banks, foreign treatment of, 284
United States citizens imprisoned in Ireland, 274, 276
United States Coast Guard, 261
United States Congressional Committee Hearings index, 273
United States, consular correspondence from Irish ports of departure, 264
United States Irish League of America, 238
United States Marine Corps, 270
United States Navy, general records, 266; registers of officers, 261
United States policy decisions, Western Europe, 280
United States Regular Army Mobile Units, 272
United States Senate, 263
United States Shipping Board, 261
United Steel Workers, 249
unity of Ireland, 280
University House, 248
University Settlements, 248
Unself, Henry E., 240

Van Buren, Martin, 253
Vanderpoel, Halsted B., 208
venereal disease control, 268
Versailles Conference, 277
Veteran Administration pensions, 284
veterans, 260
veterinary medicine, 279
vigilantes, 202, 204
violations of alien contract law, 271
violations of immigration laws, 267
visas, 282
Visiting Nurse Association of Boston, 217
vocational rehabilitation records, 260
Vogel, Professor Morris, 248
volunteer militia movements, 268

Wadsworth, James W., 237
Walker, Frank C., 212
Walpine, William G., 274
Walsh, Edmund A., 207
Walsh, Eileen, 202
Walsh, Louis S., 215
Walsh, Reverend Louis S., 223
Walsh, Robert K., 228
Walsh, William E., 250
Walthill, Nebraska, 231
Wansborough, James, 246
War Department, 266, 272; General and Special Staffs, 271
War Information, Office of, 271
War of 1812, 211
War Shipping Administration, 278
Ward, Mary Augusta, 229
Warden, David Bailey, 215
Warren and Costello, 274
Warren, John, 274
Washington Territory, 274
Washington, George, 247
Waters family, 215
Waterson family, 251
weapons sales to North Ireland, 284
Weaver, Harriet Shaw, 243
Webster, N., 232
Welsh, Edward C., 219
Western Community House, 248

Western Federation of Miners, 205
The Western Tablet, 210
Wexford, Ireland, 280
Wheeler, Everett Pepperell (1840–1925), 239
White House, 270
White House Office of Social Correspondence, 228
Whittle, Francis M., 240
Whittle, Lewis Neale, 240
Wilbur, John (1774–1856), 246
Wilburite controversy, 246
Wilde, J. F., 235
Wilde, Lady, 209
Wilde, Oscar, 203
Wilder, Thornton, 234
Williams, Bishop John, 221
Williams, O. H., 215
Willis, Henry Parker (1864–1937), 237
Wilson, Woodrow, 236
Winant, John, 256
Wisconsin, 274
Woodward, William, 256
wool industry, 280
work conditions, immigrants, 275
work stoppages, 272
Workingman's Party, 202
Workmen Place House, 248
Works Progress Administration Historical Records Survey, 241
Works Progress Administration, 214, 226, 229, 251, 255, 265
World War I, 207, 228, 229, 261, 265, 271, 277; selective service system, 270
World War II, 238, 265, 269, 271, 272; Irish neutrality in, 255
world trade, commodities, 278
Wylie, Judge, 256

Xavier Union of New York City, 236

Yeats family, 237
Yeats, Elizabeth C., 237
Yeats, William Butler, (1865–1939) 202, 209, 213, 217, 235, 237, 246
York County Multi-Ethnic Heritage Project, 250

The Irish in America
was composed in Times Roman by World
Composition Services, Inc., Sterling, Virginia;
printed and bound by Braun-Brumfield, Inc.,
Ann Arbor, Michigan; and designed and
produced by Kachergis Book Design,
Pittsboro, North Carolina.